# Methods for Achieving Your Purpose in Writing

*The Bedford Reader* centers on common ways of thinking and writing about all kinds of subjects, from everyday experiences to complex scientific theories. Whatever your purpose in writing, one or more of these ways of thinking—or methods of development—can help you discover and shape your ideas in individual paragraphs or entire papers.

The following list connects various purposes you may have for writing and the methods for achieving those purposes. The blue boxes along the right edge of the page correspond to tabs on later pages where each method is explained.

| PURPOSE | METHOD |
| --- | --- |
| To tell a story about your subject, possibly to enlighten readers or to explain something to them | Narration |
| To help readers understand your subject through the evidence of their senses—sight, hearing, touch, smell, taste | Description |
| To explain your subject with instances that show readers its nature or character | Example |
| To explain or evaluate your subject by helping readers see the similarities and differences between it and another subject | Comparison and Contrast |
| To inform readers how to do something or how something works—how a sequence of actions leads to a particular result | Process Analysis |
| To explain a conclusion about your subject by showing readers the subject's parts or elements | Division or Analysis |
| To help readers see order in your subject by understanding the kinds or groups it can be sorted into | Classification |
| To tell readers the reasons for or consequences of your subject, explaining why or what if | Cause and Effect |
| To show readers the meaning of your subject—its boundaries and its distinctions from other subjects | Definition |
| To have readers consider your opinion about your subject or your proposal for it | Argument and Persuasion |

# THE BEDFORD READER

## READER

*Tenth Edition*

---

**X. J. Kennedy**

**Dorothy M. Kennedy**

**Jane E. Aaron**

BEDFORD/ST. MARTIN'S        BOSTON ◆ NEW YORK

FOR BEDFORD/ST. MARTIN'S

*Developmental Editor:* Christina Gerogiannis
*Production Editor:* Bernard Onken
*Production Supervisor:* Jennifer Peterson
*Senior Marketing Manager:* Karita dos Santos
*Art Director:* Donna Lee Dennison
*Text Design:* Anna Palchik, Dorothy Bungert/EriBen Graphics, and Jean Hammond
*Copy Editor:* Mary Lou Wilshaw-Watts
*Photo Research:* Katherine Mather and Candace Rose Rardon
*Cover Design:* Donna Lee Dennison
*Cover Art:* Dmitri Cavander, *Vermont*, oil on canvas
*Composition:* Stratford/TexTech
*Printing and Binding:* R.R. Donnelley & Sons Company

*President:* Joan E. Feinberg
*Editorial Director:* Denise B. Wydra
*Editor in Chief:* Karen S. Henry
*Director of Marketing:* Karen Melton Soeltz
*Director of Editing, Design, and Production:* Marcia Cohen
*Managing Editor:* Shuli Traub

Library of Congress Control Number: 2007934707

Manufactured in the United States of America.

1   2   3   4   5   6      13   12   11   10   09   08

*For information, write:* Bedford/St. Martin's, 75 Arlington Street, Boston, MA 02116
(617-399-4000)

ISBN-10: 0-312-47204-8
ISBN-13: 978-0-312-47204-7
ISBN-10: 0-312-48157-8 (high school edition)
ISBN-13: 978-0-312-48157-5

# PREFACE FOR INSTRUCTORS

"A writer" says Saul Bellow, "is a reader moved to emulate." In a nutshell, the aim of *The Bedford Reader* is to move students to be writers, through reading and emulating the good writing of others.

Like its predecessor, this tenth edition of *The Bedford Reader* works toward its aim both rhetorically and thematically. We present the rhetorical methods realistically, as we ourselves use them — as natural forms that assist invention and fruition and as flexible forms that mix easily for any purpose a writer may have. Further, we forge scores of thematic connections among selections, both in paired essays in each rhetorical chapter and in writing topics after all the selections.

Filling in this outline is a wealth of features, new and old.

## NEW FEATURES

**ENGAGING NEW READINGS BY REMARKABLE WRITERS.**   As always, we have been engrossed in freshening the book's selections. Exceptional rhetorical models that also compel students' interest, the twenty-two new selections include pieces by classic authors such as Robert Benchley, established favorites such as Gretel Ehrlich and Ian Frazier, and contemporary voices such as Yiyun Li and Edwidge Danticat. A story by James Joyce and a poem by Emily Dickinson raise the number of literary works to seven. And three new essays add to the strong collection of models by student writers.

**UNIQUE COVERAGE OF ACADEMIC WRITING.**   *The Bedford Reader* is now the only rhetorical reader to help students surmount one of their biggest hurdles in college: learning the basics of academic writing.

- **A new chapter on academic writing.** Chapter 3 now introduces the features of college writing and focuses on responding to a text as well as drawing on multiple sources. In both cases, the text and examples emphasize synthesis and integration through summary, paraphrase, and quotation. The research-writing help also includes extensive sections on evaluating sources, avoiding plagiarism, and documenting sources in MLA style.
- **Two new student essays.** Response writing and research writing are each illustrated by a student essay. Written by the same student on the same subject (media portrayals of mental illness), the papers model the way in which reading can expand and refine ideas.
- **Eight examples of documented writing.** Spread throughout the book, these readable selections give students a taste for reading and producing work that draws on and acknowledges sources.
- **An expanded introduction to argument.** The introduction to Chapter 13 more fully covers claims, thesis statements, evidence, and assumptions, and it ties these topics more clearly into inductive and deductive reasoning. A new section treats anticipating objections.

**NEW EMPHASIS ON CULTURAL LITERACY.**   The widely varied readings in the tenth edition showcase both contemporary issues and enduring concerns of US society, including perspectives on homelessness, free speech, gay rights, the environment, substance abuse, the media, immigration, and war. The essay headnotes outline the cultural and historical contexts in which the selections were written.

## TRADEMARK FEATURES

**VARIED SELECTIONS BY WELL-KNOWN AUTHORS.**   The selections in *The Bedford Reader* vary in authorship, topics, even length. We offer clear models of the methods of development by noted writers such as Annie Dillard, Amy Tan, E. B. White, and Brent Staples. Half the selections are by women, and a third touch on cultural diversity. They range in subject from family to science, from language to disability.

**EXCITING VISUAL DIMENSION.**   *The Bedford Reader* emphasizes the visual as well as the verbal. Chapter 1 on reading provides a short course in thinking critically about images, with a photograph serving as a case study. Each rhetorical chapter then opens with a striking image—an ad, a cartoon, a photograph, a painting, a chart. With accompanying text and questions, these openers incite students' own critical reading and show how the rhetorical methods work visually. Finally, several of the book's selections either take images as their starting points or use illustrations to explain or highlight key ideas.

**REALISTIC TREATMENT OF THE RHETORICAL METHODS.** *The Bedford Reader* treats the methods of development not as boxes to be stuffed full of verbiage but as tools for inventing, for shaping, and, ultimately, for accomplishing a purpose. Clear, practical chapter introductions link the methods to the range of purposes they can serve and give step-by-step guidance for writing and revising in the method. (For quick reference, the purpose–method links also appear inside the front cover, where they are keyed to the marginal page tabs in each chapter introduction.) In addition, a selection in every rhetorical chapter illustrates the method in practice: A student arrives at the method to achieve a particular writing goal, such as reporting an accident, crafting a résumé, or advertising an apartment for sublet.

Taking this realistic approach to the methods even further, we show how writers freely combine the methods to achieve their purposes: Each rhetorical introduction discusses how that method might work with others, and at least one "Other Methods" question after every selection helps students analyze how methods work together. Most significantly, Part Three provides an anthology of works by well-known writers that specifically illustrate mixed methods. The headnotes for these selections point to where each method comes into play.

**THOROUGH COVERAGE OF READING AND WRITING.** Preceding the new chapter on academic writing, two detailed chapters give concrete advice on critical reading and the writing process. Chapter 1 on critical reading includes a sample of a student's annotations on a text and practical guidelines for summarizing, analyzing, and interpreting texts and visual images. Chapter 2 on the writing process takes students from ideas through editing and includes a new student work-in-progress.

In addition, a "Focus" box in every rhetorical chapter highlights an element of writing that is especially relevant to that method—for example, verbs in narration, concrete words in description, sentence variety in example, and tone in argument and persuasion.

**EXTENSIVE THEMATIC CONNECTIONS.** *The Bedford Reader* provides substantial topics for class discussion and writing. A pair of essays in each rhetorical chapter addresses the same subject, from the ordinary (housekeeping) to the controversial (immigration), and the chapter on argument includes two essay pairs (one new) and a casebook of four essays (two new). At least one "Connections" writing topic after every selection suggests links to other selections. And an alternate thematic table of contents arranges the book's selections under more than two dozen topics.

**UNIQUE COMMENTS BY WRITERS ON WRITING.**    After their essays, poems, or stories, fifty of the book's writers offer comments on everything from grammar to revision to how they developed the reprinted piece. Besides providing rock-solid advice, these comments also prove that for the pros, too, writing is usually a challenge. Writers on Writing new to this edition include those by Yiyun Li, Gretel Ehrlich, Ian Frazier, and Emily Dickinson.

For easy access, the Writers on Writing are listed in the book's index under the topics they address. Look up *Revision*, for instance, and find that Annie Dillard, Dave Barry, Bruce Catton, and Russell Baker, among others, have something to say about this crucial stage of the writing process.

**ABUNDANT EDITORIAL APPARATUS.**    As always, we've surrounded the selections with a wealth of material designed to get students reading, thinking, and writing. To help structure students' critical approach to the selections, each one comes with two headnotes (on the author and on the selection itself), three sets of questions (on meaning, writing strategy, and language), and at least five writing topics. One writing topic encourages students to explore their responses in their journals; another suggests how to develop the journal writing into an essay; and others emphasize critical writing, research, and connections among selections.

Besides the aids with every selection, the book also includes additional writing topics for every rhetorical chapter, a glossary ("Useful Terms") that defines all terms used in the book (including all those printed in SMALL CAPITAL LETTERS), and an index that alphabetizes authors and titles and important topics (including the elements of composition and, as noted earlier, those covered in the Writers on Writing).

**EXTENSIVE INSTRUCTOR'S MANUAL.**    Available as a separate manual, bound into the instructor's edition, or through the companion Web site, *Notes and Resources for Teaching* THE BEDFORD READER suggests ways to integrate journal writing and collaboration into writing classes and ways to use the book's opening chapters on critical reading, the writing process, and academic writing. In addition, *Notes and Resources* discusses every method, every selection (with possible answers to all questions), and every Writer on Writing.

**A COMPREHENSIVE COMPANION WEB SITE.**    Web boxes in the text link to *The Bedford Reader*'s Web site (*bedfordstmartins.com/thebedfordreader*), which features a broad range of resources. For each selection, the site provides an interactive reading quiz and links to further information on the author and the author's topic. For the "Focus" boxes, the site offers *Exercise Central*, the largest online collection of grammar, usage, and writing exercises. For research writing, the site links directly to *Re:Writing*, where students can find the largest, most comprehensive collection of free resources for the writing class. And for instructors, the site provides sample syllabi, the complete text of the instructor's manual, and a reporting feature for monitoring students' progress on the reading quizzes and *Exercise Central*. The site also links to four valuable resources: the new *Teaching Central*, a rich library of bibliographies, teaching advice and blogs, classroom materials, adjunct support, and more; the new *Just-in-Time Teaching Materials*, where instructors can search and download from hundreds of teaching resources culled from Bedford/St. Martin's print and online professional resources; *The Bedford Bibliography for Teachers of Writing*; and *The St. Martin's Tutorial on Avoiding Plagiarism*.

**TWO VERSIONS.**    *The Bedford Reader* has a sibling. A shorter edition, *The Brief Bedford Reader*, features fifty selections instead of seventy-one, including five essays (rather than twelve) in Part Three.

## ACKNOWLEDGMENTS

Hundreds of the teachers and students using *The Bedford Reader* over the years have helped us shape the book. For this edition, the following teachers offered insights from their experiences that encouraged worthy changes: Avis Adams, Green River Community College; Sheila Ayers, San Joaquin Delta College; Tim Barnett, Northeastern Illinois University; Kevin J. Bessenbacher, Los Angeles Pierce College; Paula Hartman Bigham, New Glarus High School; Jennifer Black, McLennan Community College; Elizabeth Broadwell, Eastside High School; Henry James Butler, Santa Fe Community College; Sandra Cooper, Central Florida Community College; Natalie Daley, Linn Benton Community College; Jason Dew, Georgia Perimeter College; Roger Robin Ekins, Butte College; Mary Elfring, Elgin Community College; Dave Elias, Eastern Kentucky University; Kathy Ford, Lake Land College; Hank Galmish, Green River Community College; Cynthia D. Green, ADE Distance Learning Center; Darrin Grinder, Northwest Nazarene University; Tracy Heyman, Towson University; Yuri Horner, San Jacinto College South; Jeffrey Hotz, Montgomery College; Michael Hricik, Westmoreland County Community College; Mahbub Jamal, Prince George's Community College; Melissa Joarder, Delaware County Community College; Charles Johnsmeyer, Rockland Community College; Josie Kearns, University of Michigan; Dawna Kemper, Santa Monica College; Tamara Kuzmenkov,

Tacoma Community College; Jeff Larsen, Lowell High School; Lydia Lynn Lewellen, Tacoma Community College; Kimmarie Lewis, Lord Fairfax Community College; Walter Lowe, Green River Community College; Perry Wenqian Ma, Lane Community College; Paul Malanga, Pima Community College; Kimberly Manning, Chaffey College; Todd McCann, Bay de Noc Community College; Jill A. Moreno Ikari, Grossmont College; Annemarie Oldfield, Eastern New Mexico University, Roswell; Dale Peterson, Tufts University; Adam Prince, Los Angeles City College; Virginia Pruitt, Washburn University; Renee Michelle Salman, Pima Community College and Tohono O'odham Community College; John Schaffer, Blinn College; Harvey Solganick, Le Tourneau University; Adam Sonstegard, Cleveland State University; Bonita Startt, Tidewater Community College; Christian Tatu, Warren County Community College; Mary Wayne Watson, Nash Community College; A. G. "Jerry" Wemple, Bloomsburg University; Kelly Wiechart, University of the Incarnate Word; Lucette Wood, LinnBenton Community College; and Timothy Yorke, Heritage High School.

We are as ever deeply in debt to the creative people at and around Bedford/St. Martin's. Joan Feinberg, Denise Wydra, Steve Scipione, and especially Karen Henry contributed insight and support. Christina Gerogiannis, developing the book, responded to our every need with grace and skill. Her assistant, Stephanie Naudin, provided crucial back-up. Ellen Kuhl, Karin Paque, Mark Gallaher, Stefanie Wortman, and Grace Talusan helped to shape the book's apparatus and instructor's manual. Donna Dennison created the striking cover. Shuli Traub planned and oversaw the production of the book. And Bernard Onken worked under the duress of a difficult schedule to transform the raw manuscript into the book you hold.

# CONTENTS

**PREFACE FOR INSTRUCTORS**    iii

**THEMATIC CONTENTS**    xxvii

## INTRODUCTION    1

WHY READ? WHY WRITE? WHY NOT PHONE?    1
USING *THE BEDFORD READER*    2
The Selections
The Organization
The Journal Prompts, Questions, Writing Topics, and Glossary
Writers on Writing

PART ONE
## READING, WRITING, AND RESEARCH    7

1    CRITICAL READING    9

READING AN ESSAY    10
The Preliminaries
The First Reading

NANCY MAIRS   *Disability*      13

A writer with multiple sclerosis thinks she knows why the media carry so few images of people like herself with disabilities: Viewers might conclude, correctly, that "there is something ordinary about disability itself."

    Writing While Reading
    Summarizing
    Thinking Critically
    Analyzing "Disability"
    THINKING CRITICALLY ABOUT VISUAL IMAGES      25
    The Big Picture
    **Visual Image:** *A Deployed Soldier and His Daughter,* photograph by Erik S. Lesser
    Analysis
    Inference
    Synthesis
    Evaluation


2   **THE WRITING PROCESS**      **31**

    ANALYZING THE WRITING SITUATION      32
    Subject
    Audience and Purpose
    DISCOVERING IDEAS      34
    Journal Writing
    Freewriting
    The Methods of Development
    FOCUSING ON THE THESIS AND THE THESIS STATEMENT      37
    DRAFTING      38
    REVISING AND EDITING      38
    COLLABORATING      40
    AN ESSAY-IN-PROGRESS      40
    Reading and Drafting
    Revising
    Editing
    Final Draft


ROSIE ANAYA   *Mental Illness on Television*      47

Responding in part to Nancy Mairs's "Disability" (Chap. 1), a student writer argues that television should "portray psychological disability as a part of everyday life, not a crime."

**3   ACADEMIC WRITING     51**

RESPONDING TO A TEXT     52
Forming a Response
Synthesizing Your Own and Another's Views
INTEGRATING SOURCE MATERIAL     54
Summary, Paraphrase, and Quotation
Introduction of Source Material
WRITING FROM RESEARCH     56
Evaluating Sources
Working with Online Sources
Synthesizing Multiple Sources
AVOIDING PLAGIARISM     60
Examples and Revisions
Plagiarism and the Internet
Common Knowledge
SOURCE CITATION USING MLA STYLE     62
MLA Parenthetical Citations
MLA List of Works Cited
SAMPLE RESEARCH PAPER     74

ROSIE ANAYA   *The Best Kept Secret on Campus*     74

When college students suffer psychological problems—and the number who do is "staggering"—they seldom seek or receive the help they need. Drawing on sources, the student author of the response essay in Chapter 2 probes more deeply into the subject of psychological disability.

**PART TWO**
**THE METHODS     79**

**4   NARRATION: Telling a Story     81**

**Visual Image:** *How Joe's Body Brought Him Fame Instead of Shame,* advertisement for Charles Atlas

THE METHOD     82
THE PROCESS     83
Purpose and Shape
The Thesis

The Narrator in the Story
What to Emphasize
Organization
NARRATION IN PARAGRAPHS        90
Writing About Television
Writing in an Academic Discipline
NARRATION IN PRACTICE: Reporting a car accident        91


**DIFFERENCE**

MAYA ANGELOU    *Champion of the World*        93

She didn't dare ring up a sale while that epic battle was on. A noted African American writer remembers from her early childhood the night when a people's fate hung on a pair of boxing gloves.

**Maya Angelou on Writing**        97

**PAIRED SELECTIONS**

AMY TAN    *Fish Cheeks*        99

The writer remembers her teenage angst when the minister and his cute blond son attended her family's Christmas Eve dinner, an elaborate Chinese feast.

**Amy Tan on Writing**        102


ANNIE DILLARD    *The Chase*        104

Playing football, throwing snowballs, and being chased: For this writer as a child, nothing could equal the thrill of hurling herself into the game.

**Annie Dillard on Writing**        109


HAROLD TAW    *Finding Prosperity by Feeding Monkeys*        110

When he was born in Burma, the author received an assignment from a Buddhist monk. Now every year, despite plenty of obstacles, he faithfully performs an unusual ritual.


JESSICA COHEN    *Grade A: The Market for a Yale Woman's Eggs*        114

This student writer could make good money as an egg donor, but the process makes her uneasy. Is it right for parents to pay for a perfect child?

**Jessica Cohen on Writing**        121


SHIRLEY JACKSON    *The Lottery*        123

Tension builds imperceptibly in this classic short story as folks gather for their town's annual lottery. "It isn't fair, it isn't right," exclaims the winner.

**Shirley Jackson on Writing**        132


ADDITIONAL WRITING TOPICS        134

## 5   DESCRIPTION: Writing with Your Senses   137

**Visual Image:** *Doug and Mizan's House, East River,* photograph by
Margaret Morton

THE METHOD      138

THE PROCESS     139
Purpose and Audience
Dominant Impression and Thesis
Organization
Details

DESCRIPTION IN PARAGRAPHS      143
Writing About Television
Writing in an Academic Discipline

DESCRIPTION IN PRACTICE: Advertising an apartment for sublet      145

---

### FATHERS

BRAD MANNING   *Arm Wrestling with My Father*      146

In the time it takes for a strong arm to fall, a student writer discovers that becoming
an adult has changed the way he feels about his father and their physical competition.

**Brad Manning on Writing**      152

**PAIRED
SELECTIONS**

SARAH VOWELL   *Shooting Dad*      154

"All he ever cared about were guns. All I ever cared about was art." Despite their
essential difference, the writer discovers a strong resemblance between her father and
herself.

**Sarah Vowell on Writing**      162

YIYUN LI   *Orange Crush*      164

When she was growing up in China, the author and many of her compatriots desired
a powdered orange beverage. "To think that all the dreams of my youth were once
contained in this commercial drink!"

**Yiyun Li on Writing**      168

ROBERT BENCHLEY   *My Face*      170

Describing a "morbid" fascination with his reflection, a beloved humorist reveals as
much about his personality as about his appearance.

**Robert Benchley on Writing**      174

JAMES JOYCE   *Araby*   175

In this classic short story, an Irish boy who yearns for transformation seeks his first love at a fair. Instead, he finds only himself, "a creature driven and derided by vanity."

ADDITIONAL WRITING TOPICS   183


6   **EXAMPLE: Pointing to Instances**   **185**

**Visual Image:** *Low-Energy Drinks,* cartoon by Glen LeLievre

THE METHOD   186
THE PROCESS   187
The Generalization and the Thesis
The Examples
EXAMPLES IN PARAGRAPHS   190
Writing About Television
Writing in an Academic Discipline
EXAMPLES IN PRACTICE: Writing a cover letter for a job application   191


HOMELESSNESS

BARBARA LAZEAR ASCHER   *On Compassion*   193

Where do we find the compassion to help the desperate, the homeless? It's "not a character trait like a sunny disposition," says this essayist. "It must be learned, and it is learned by having adversity at our windows."
**Barbara Lazear Ascher on Writing**   197

**PAIRED
SELECTIONS**

ANNA QUINDLEN   *Homeless*   198

A journalist who confesses an aversion for "looking at the big picture, taking the global view," insists on seeing homelessness as an individual crisis.
**Anna Quindlen on Writing**   201


ANDREW KORITZ KRULL   *Celebrating the Pity of Brotherly Love*   203

When he was a boy, the older brothers of this student writer showed a special talent for torture. The brothers' "games" made an indelible, and surprising, impression on their victim.
**Andrew Koritz Krull on Writing**   206


BRENT STAPLES   *Black Men and Public Space*   208

In near-deserted streets at night, an African American writer finds that women flee from him. Relating case histories, he tells what he has discovered about "public space."
**Brent Staples on Writing**   212

ROGER ROSENBLATT   *We Are Free to Be You, Me, Stupid, and Dead*   215

How far should we go in supporting free speech? Quite far, asserts this noted essayist, even to the point of tolerating views that we find idiotic or repulsive.

**Roger Rosenblatt on Writing**      219

ADDITIONAL WRITING TOPICS      221


7    **COMPARISON AND CONTRAST:
Setting Things Side by Side      223**

**Visual Images:** *American Gothic,* painting by Grant Wood; *Rural Rehabilitation Client,* photograph by Ben Shahn

THE METHOD      224
THE PROCESS      225
Subjects for Comparison
Basis for Comparison and Thesis
Organization
Flexibility
COMPARISON AND CONTRAST IN PARAGRAPHS      229
Writing About Television
Writing in an Academic Discipline
COMPARISON AND CONTRAST IN PRACTICE: Creating a
     campaign poster      231


PERSONALITIES

SUZANNE BRITT   *Neat People vs. Sloppy People*      233

"Neat people are lazier and meaner than sloppy people," asserts the writer. As she compares and contrasts, she takes up a cudgel and chooses sides.

**Suzanne Britt on Writing**      237

PAIRED
SELECTIONS

DAVE BARRY   *Batting Clean-Up and Striking Out*      239

An expert at comedic observation takes a humorous swing at the difference between the sexes. It hinges on the importance each sex gives to dirt and baseball.

**Dave Barry on Writing**      243


BRUCE CATTON   *Grant and Lee: A Study in Contrasts*      245

The great Civil War generals Ulysses S. Grant and Robert E. Lee clearly personified their opposing traditions. But what they had in common was more vital by far.

**Bruce Catton on Writing**      250

FATEMA MERNISSI   *Size 6: The Western Women's Harem*      252

Trying to buy a skirt in a US department store leads the author, a Moroccan Muslim, to compare the relative disadvantages of women in Western and Muslim countries. Who's worse off?

GEORGE CHAUNCEY   *The Legacy of Antigay Discrimination*      260

Whatever today's prejudice against gays and lesbians, the "systematic and powerful" discrimination of fifty years ago was much worse. A historian explains the difference.

ALICE WALKER   *Everyday Use*      267

In this short story a mother weighs the interests of her two daughters, one who left home and one who didn't.

**Alice Walker on Writing**      276

ADDITIONAL WRITING TOPICS      278


8   **PROCESS ANALYSIS: Explaining Step by Step**      **281**

**Visual Image:** *Workers Making Dolls,* photograph by Wally McNamee

THE METHOD      282
THE PROCESS      283
PROCESS ANALYSIS IN PARAGRAPHS      287
Writing About Television
Writing in an Academic Discipline
PROCESS ANALYSIS IN PRACTICE: Explaining a fire-drill procedure      288


THE ENVIRONMENT

LINNEA SAUKKO   *How to Poison the Earth*      290

A prize-winning student writer sets forth the process by which we can pollute our planet. What moves her to provide such information?

**Linnea Saukko on Writing**      294

PAIRED
SELECTIONS

GRETEL EHRLICH   *Chronicles of Ice*      295

Reflecting on the formation of glaciers, an acclaimed nature writer ponders a disturbing question: What will happen to our planet if the glaciers melt away?

**Gretel Ehrlich on Writing**      300

IAN FRAZIER   *How to Operate the Shower Curtain*   302

A well-known humorist offers detailed instructions for using a seemingly simple household object.

**Ian Frazier on Writing**   306

JESSICA MITFORD   *Behind the Formaldehyde Curtain*   308

With sardonic wit, the writer, whom *Time* called "Queen of the Muckrakers," details the stages through which a sallow corpse becomes a masterwork of American mortuary art.

**Jessica Mitford on Writing**   318

DANIEL OROZCO   *Orientation*   319

You're a new employee in this short story, learning of the intricacies of the supply cabinet, the romances between coworkers, and the mysteries and dangers lurking within cubicles.

**Daniel Orozco on Writing**   325

ADDITIONAL WRITING TOPICS   327

## 9   DIVISION OR ANALYSIS: Slicing into Parts   331

**Visual Image:** *Deconstructing Lunch,* cartoon by Roz Chast

THE METHOD   332
Kinds of Division or Analysis
Analysis and Critical Thinking
THE PROCESS   334
Subjects and Theses
Evidence
DIVISION OR ANALYSIS IN PARAGRAPHS   337
Writing About Television
Writing in an Academic Discipline
DIVISION OR ANALYSIS IN PRACTICE: Writing an application essay   338

### WOMEN AND MEN

JUDY BRADY   *I Want a Wife*   340

**PAIRED
SELECTIONS**   In this feminist view of marriage, the work of a wife is divided into its roles and functions. What a wonderful boon a wife is! Shouldn't every woman have one of her own?

**PAIRED SELECTIONS**

ARMIN A. BROTT  *Not All Men Are Sly Foxes*     345

Reading bedtime stories to his daughter, a writer discovers that fictional fathers remain stuck in the old molds: sloppy, unnurturing, neglectful.

BELLA DePAULO  *The Myth of Doomed Kids*     350

Examining a study of teens with substance-abuse problems, a psychologist dispels a common myth about children of single parents.

**Bella DePaulo on Writing**     356

LAILA AYAD  *The Capricious Camera*     358

A German photograph from the time of World War II prompts a student writer to connect the subject's story to the larger narrative of Nazi racial experiments.

**Visual Image:** *Mounted Nazi Troops on the Lookout for Likely Polish Children,* photograph

JAMAICA KINCAID  *Girl*     367

In this fictional exchange, a daughter can barely insert two sentences into her mother's litany of instructions on how to become a lady, not a slut.

**Jamaica Kincaid on Writing**     370

ADDITIONAL WRITING TOPICS     372


**10   CLASSIFICATION: Sorting into Kinds     375**

**Visual Image:** *The More They Learn, the More They Earn,* graph from State Farm Bank

THE METHOD     376
Subjects and Reasons for Classification
Kinds of Classification
THE PROCESS     377
Purposes and Theses
Categories
CLASSIFICATION IN PARAGRAPHS     380
Writing About Television
Writing in an Academic Discipline
CLASSIFICATION IN PRACTICE: Crafting a résumé     381

RUSSELL BAKER  *The Plot Against People*     384

The goal of inanimate objects, declares the renowned humorist, is nothing short of the destruction of the human race.

**Russell Baker on Writing**     388

DEBORAH TANNEN   *But What Do You Mean?*   391

Sometimes an apology is not an apology, observes an expert on communication. Men and women would get along better if they understood each other's codes of speech.

**Deborah Tannen on Writing**   399

LUC SANTE   *What Secrets Tell*   401

From the "laughably trivial" to the "terrifying," secrets fulfill basic human needs. A noted writer explores what makes them so alluring.

**Luc Sante on Writing**   407

TELLING LIES

STEPHANIE ERICSSON   *The Ways We Lie*   408

Most of us couldn't get by without lying, the writer acknowledges, but even the little lies corrupt, until "moral garbage becomes as invisible to us as water is to a fish."

**Stephanie Ericsson on Writing**   417

PAIRED
SELECTIONS

WILLIAM LUTZ   *The World of Doublespeak*   418

"Pavement deficiencies" (potholes) and "a career alternative placement program" (a layoff of workers) are but two expressions that conceal unpleasant truths. An expert in such doublespeak explains the types and their effects.

**William Lutz on Writing**   426

ADDITIONAL WRITING TOPICS   428

11   CAUSE AND EFFECT: Asking Why   **431**

**Visual Image:** *Garbage In . . .*, cartoon by Mike Thompson

THE METHOD   432
THE PROCESS   433
Subjects, Purposes, and Theses
Causal Relations
Discovery of Causes
Final Word
CAUSE AND EFFECT IN PARAGRAPHS   438
Writing About Television
Writing in an Academic Discipline
CAUSE AND EFFECT IN PRACTICE: Setting the record straight in a letter
   to the editor   439

GLOBALIZATION

CHITRA DIVAKARUNI  *Live Free and Starve*  442

Forcing developing countries to put an end to child labor might not be the cure-all it seems. The children themselves, asserts this activist and fiction writer, could suffer fates much worse than working.

**Chitra Divakaruni on Writing**  446

PAIRED
SELECTIONS

MARIE JAVDANI  Plata o Plomo: *Silver or Lead*  448

Americans who use illegal drugs harm more than just themselves, argues a student writer in this carefully researched essay. Consider the plight of Miguel, a South American boy victimized by the drug trade.

**Marie Javdani on Writing**  453

SARAH ADAMS  *Be Cool to the Pizza Dude*  455

Humility, empathy, honor, and respect: A writer and teacher learns all these from kind tolerance of an annoying person.

CHRIS ANDERSON  *The Rise and Fall of the Hit*  459

What's behind the decline of megaselling albums, movies, and television shows? A technology writer says it's all about choice.

**Chris Anderson on Writing**  466

DON DeLILLO  *Videotape*  468

The narrator of this short story watches a videotaped murder over and over and over again. Why?

**Don DeLillo on Writing**  474

ADDITIONAL WRITING TOPICS  476

12  DEFINITION: Tracing a Boundary  479

**Visual Image:** *Need Is a Very Subjective Word,* advertisement for the HUMMER H2

THE METHOD  480
THE PROCESS  481
Discovery of Meanings
Methods of Development
Thesis
Evidence

DEFINITION IN PARAGRAPHS    485
Writing About Television
Writing in an Academic Discipline
DEFINITION IN PRACTICE: Explaining the mission of an
   organization    486


**HURTFUL WORDS**

GLORIA NAYLOR    *The Meanings of a Word*    488

An African American's childhood experiences with the word *nigger* taught her that the sense of a word owes everything to context.

**Gloria Naylor on Writing**    493

**PAIRED SELECTIONS**

CHRISTINE LEONG    *Being a Chink*    494

Responding to Naylor's essay, a student writer considers another word with the power to sting or unite, depending on who is using it and why.

**Christine Leong on Writing**    499


THOMAS SOWELL    *"Needs"*    501

What do we really need? The answer is important to this economist because when we adopt a broad definition of *need* "our whole economy and society suffer."


DAGOBERTO GILB    *Pride*    505

With affecting sensitivity, a fiction writer and essayist sees pride in the smallest details of a Mexican American community.

**Dagoberto Gilb on Writing**    509


EMILY DICKINSON    *"Hope" is the thing with feathers*    510

In twelve short lines, a revered American poet creates a memorable definition.

**Emily Dickinson on Writing**    513


ADDITIONAL WRITING TOPICS    514


13   **ARGUMENT AND PERSUASION:
     Stating Opinions and Proposals**    517

**Visual Image:** *Corporate America Flag,* image from Adbusters Media Foundation


THE METHOD    518
Transaction Between Reader and Writer

Elements of Argument
Reasoning
THE PROCESS     526
Finding a Subject
Organizing
ARGUMENT AND PERSUASION IN PARAGRAPHS     530
Writing About Television
Writing in an Academic Discipline
ARGUMENT AND PERSUASION IN PRACTICE: Disputing a parking
   ticket     531

COLLEEN WENKE     *Too Much Pressure*     533

Most evidence says that students cheat much more than they did fifty years ago.
This student writer argues for a certain explanation.

THE MEDIA AND THE SELF

BRIAN WILLIAMS     *But Enough About You . . .*     539

The anchor of NBC *Nightly News* contends that new media encourage a blinkered
self-celebration that just might make us "fail to meet the next great challenge."

PAIRED
SELECTIONS

ANDIE WURSTER     *Won't You Be My Friendster?*     543

At first reluctant to join in on the "time-wasting mirror gazing" of social-networking
Web sites, a young writer discovers that they can actually lower barriers of space
and culture that would otherwise divide users.

**Andie Wurster on Writing**     547

SAME-SEX MARRIAGE

KATHA POLLITT     *What's Wrong with Gay Marriage?*     548

A liberal commentator systematically refutes the arguments she hears against same-sex
marriage. Marriage, she says, is much less defined and standardized than many people
want to believe.

**Katha Pollitt on Writing**     552

PAIRED
SELECTIONS

CHARLES COLSON     *Gay "Marriage": Societal Suicide*     554

The purpose of marriage is to nurture children, says this conservative writer and prison
activist. Undermining traditional families by allowing same-sex marriage will lead to
"more criminals behind bars and more chaos in our streets."

Contents     **xxiii**

SECURITY VERSUS LIBERTY: Profiling

ADNAN R. KHAN   *Close Encounters with US Immigration*    558

Intimidated, hurt, and bemused, a Pakistani Canadian journalist questions the grueling security check he underwent at the US border.

LINDA CHAVEZ   *Everything Isn't Racial Profiling*    563

The writer didn't much like being questioned by airport security just because she doesn't "look American," but she believes the airlines are justified in singling out people who fit the profile of a terrorist.

**CASEBOOK**

SECURITY VERSUS LIBERTY: Immigration

MARK KRIKORIAN   *Safety Through Immigration Control*    567

A well-known advocate of immigration control, this writer argues that anything less than tight border security "leaves us naked in the face of the enemy."

EDWIDGE DANTICAT   *Not Your Homeland*    572

A well-known fiction writer and an immigrant from Haiti makes a deeply personal argument against what she sees as unreasonably strict immigration control.

**Edwidge Danticat on Writing**    577

ADDITIONAL WRITING TOPICS    579


PART THREE

**MIXING THE METHODS**    581


SANDRA CISNEROS   *Only Daughter*    584

The only daughter in a large Mexican American family, this respected poet and fiction writer tells how her efforts to be heard finally paid off with her father.

**Sandra Cisneros on Writing**    589

JOAN DIDION   *In Bed*    591

In sensuous detail, a leading nonfiction writer explains migraine headaches—and how her affliction has become a "friend."

**Joan Didion on Writing**    596

BARBARA EHRENREICH   *The Roots of War*    598

Making war puts human beings in a class with ants and chimpanzees among the earth's species. Abolishing war, argues this critic, requires thinking differently about it.

**Barbara Ehrenreich on Writing**    602

STEPHEN JAY GOULD   *A Biological Homage to Mickey Mouse*    604

Mickey Mouse changed over the decades, becoming softer and younger looking. A scientist with a flair for explanation proposes why and finds surprising parallels in human evolution.

**Visual Images:** *Mickey's Evolution During Fifty Years,* drawing; *The "Evolution" of Mickey Mouse,* chart; *Humans feel affection for animals with juvenile features,* drawing

**Stephen Jay Gould on Writing**    613

MARTIN LUTHER KING, JR.   *I Have a Dream*    614

With force and grace, an inspired leader champions the rights of African Americans and equality for all.

MAXINE HONG KINGSTON   *No Name Woman*    620

An adulterous woman is driven to suicide by her unforgiving family and village in China. A generation later, her American-born niece seeks to understand the story of someone whose name she has never dared to ask.

**Maxine Hong Kingston on Writing**    632

GEORGE ORWELL   *Shooting an Elephant*    634

As a young British police officer, this famous writer faced a killer elephant and the expectations of a gleeful Burmese crowd. He could not take pride in his response.

**George Orwell on Writing**    642

FRANCINE PROSE   *What Words Can Tell*    644

An acclaimed fiction writer examines the opening paragraph of a famous short story and shows that in good writing — and reading — every word counts.

**Francine Prose on Writing**    649

RICHARD RODRIGUEZ   *Aria: A Memoir of a Bilingual Childhood*    651

Recalling both the pleasures and the pains of his boyhood, a Mexican American writer reflects on his two languages, Spanish and English, and his two cultures. His argument against bilingual education may provoke debate.

**Richard Rodriguez on Writing**    663

EDWARD SAID   *Clashing Civilizations?*   665

The September 11, 2001, terrorist attacks hardened thinking about "Islam vs. the West." This well-known writer argues that such polarities are both simplistic and destructive.

JONATHAN SWIFT   *A Modest Proposal*   670

The rich devour the poor—so why not commercialize cannibalism? With scathing irony, the supreme English satirist states his views in a fit of bitter indignation.

**Jonathan Swift on Writing**   680

E. B. WHITE   *Once More to the Lake*   682

A father takes his young son on a pilgrimage to a favorite summertime scene from his own childhood, a lake in Maine. There he arrives at a startling realization.

**E. B. White on Writing**   689

**USEFUL TERMS**   691

**INDEX**   710

# THEMATIC CONTENTS

**AUTOBIOGRAPHY**

Sarah Adams, *Be Cool to the Pizza Dude*    455
Maya Angelou, *Champion of the World*    93
Robert Benchley, *My Face*    170
Armin A. Brott, *Not All Men Are Sly Foxes*    345
Sandra Cisneros, *Only Daughter*    584
Edwidge Danticat, *Not Your Homeland*    572
Joan Didion, *In Bed*    591
Annie Dillard, *The Chase*    104
Andrew Koritz Krull, *Celebrating the Pity of Brotherly Love*    203
Christine Leong, *Being a Chink*    494
Yiyun Li, *Orange Crush*    164
Brad Manning, *Arm Wrestling with My Father*    146
Fatema Mernissi, *Size 6: The Western Women's Harem*    252
Gloria Naylor, *The Meanings of a Word*    488
Richard Rodriguez, *Aria: A Memoir of a Bilingual Childhood*    651
Brent Staples, *Black Men and Public Space*    208
Amy Tan, *Fish Cheeks*    99
Harold Taw, *Finding Prosperity by Feeding Monkeys*    110
Sarah Vowell, *Shooting Dad*    154
E. B. White, *Once More to the Lake*    682
Andie Wurster, *Won't You Be My Friendster?*    543

**BIOGRAPHY**

Bruce Catton, *Grant and Lee: A Study in Contrasts*    245
Maxine Hong Kingston, *No Name Woman*    620

## CHILDHOOD AND FAMILY

Maya Angelou, *Champion of the World*     93
Judy Brady, *I Want a Wife*     340
Armin A. Brott, *Not All Men Are Sly Foxes*     345
Sandra Cisneros, *Only Daughter*     584
Charles Colson, *Gay "Marriage": Societal Suicide*     554
Bella DePaulo, *The Myth of Doomed Kids*     350
Chitra Divakaruni, *Live Free and Starve*     442
Dagoberto Gilb, *Pride*     505
Marie Javdani, *Plata o Plomo: Silver or Lead*     448
James Joyce, *Araby*     175
Jamaica Kincaid, *Girl*     367
Maxine Hong Kingston, *No Name Woman*     620
Andrew Koritz Krull, *Celebrating the Pity of Brotherly Love*     203
Christine Leong, *Being a Chink*     494
Yiyun Li, *Orange Crush*     164
Gloria Naylor, *The Meanings of a Word*     488
Katha Pollitt, *What's Wrong with Gay Marriage?*     548
Richard Rodriguez, *Aria: A Memoir of a Bilingual Childhood*     651
Amy Tan, *Fish Cheeks*     99
Harold Taw, *Finding Prosperity by Feeding Monkeys*     110
Sarah Vowell, *Shooting Dad*     154
Alice Walker, *Everyday Use*     267
E. B. White, *Once More to the Lake*     682

## CLASS

Jessica Cohen, *Grade A: The Market for a Yale Woman's Eggs*     114
Bella DePaulo, *The Myth of Doomed Kids*     350
Chitra Divakaruni, *Live Free and Starve*     442
Dagoberto Gilb, *Pride*     505
Marie Javdani, *Plata o Plomo: Silver or Lead*     448
Yiyun Li, *Orange Crush*     164
Jonathan Swift, *A Modest Proposal*     670

## COMMUNICATION

Rosie Anaya, *Mental Illness on Television*     47
Rosie Anaya, *The Best Kept Secret on Campus*     74
Chris Anderson, *The Rise and Fall of the Hit*     459
Sandra Cisneros, *Only Daughter*     584
Stephanie Ericsson, *The Ways We Lie*     408
William Lutz, *The World of Doublespeak*     418
Nancy Mairs, *Disability*     13
Gloria Naylor, *The Meanings of a Word*     488
Francine Prose, *What Words Can Tell*     644

Roger Rosenblatt, *We Are Free to Be You, Me, Stupid, and Dead*     215
Luc Sante, *What Secrets Tell*     401
Deborah Tannen, *But What Do You Mean?*     391
Brian Williams, *But Enough About You . . .*     539
Andie Wurster, *Won't You Be My Friendster?*     543

## COMMUNITY

Maya Angelou, *Champion of the World*     93
George Chauncey, *The Legacy of Antigay Discrimination*     260
Edwidge Danticat, *Not Your Homeland*     572
Barbara Ehrenreich, *The Roots of War*     598
Shirley Jackson, *The Lottery*     123
Martin Luther King, Jr., *I Have a Dream*     614
Maxine Hong Kingston, *No Name Woman*     620
Gloria Naylor, *The Meanings of a Word*     488
Richard Rodriguez, *Aria: A Memoir of a Bilingual Childhood*     651
Roger Rosenblatt, *We Are Free to Be You, Me, Stupid, and Dead*     215
Luc Sante, *What Secrets Tell*     401
Harold Taw, *Finding Prosperity by Feeding Monkeys*     110
Alice Walker, *Everyday Use*     267
Brian Williams, *But Enough About You . . .*     539
Andie Wurster, *Won't You Be My Friendster?*     543

## CULTURAL DIVERSITY

Rosie Anaya, *Mental Illness on Television*     47
Rosie Anaya, *The Best Kept Secret on Campus*     74
Maya Angelou, *Champion of the World*     93
Laila Ayad, *The Capricious Camera*     358
George Chauncey, *The Legacy of Antigay Discrimination*     260
Sandra Cisneros, *Only Daughter*     584
Charles Colson, *Gay "Marriage": Societal Suicide*     554
Edwidge Danticat, *Not Your Homeland*     572
Dagoberto Gilb, *Pride*     505
Maxine Hong Kingston, *No Name Woman*     620
Christine Leong, *Being a Chink*     494
Yiyun Li, *Orange Crush*     164
Nancy Mairs, *Disability*     13
Fatema Mernissi, *Size 6: The Western Women's Harem*     252
Gloria Naylor, *The Meanings of a Word*     488
Katha Pollitt, *What's Wrong with Gay Marriage?*     548
Richard Rodriguez, *Aria: A Memoir of a Bilingual Childhood*     651
Brent Staples, *Black Men and Public Space*     208
Amy Tan, *Fish Cheeks*     99
Harold Taw, *Finding Prosperity by Feeding Monkeys*     110

## DEATH

Edwidge Danticat, *Not Your Homeland*     572
Don DeLillo, *Videotape*     468
Shirley Jackson, *The Lottery*     123
Marie Javdani, Plata o Plomo: *Silver or Lead*     448
Maxine Hong Kingston, *No Name Woman*     620
Mark Krikorian, *Safety Through Immigration Control*     567
Jessica Mitford, *Behind the Formaldehyde Curtain*     308
Jonathan Swift, *A Modest Proposal*     670

## ENVIRONMENT

Gretel Ehrlich, *Chronicles of Ice*     295
Linnea Saukko, *How to Poison the Earth*     290

## ETHICS

Sarah Adams, *Be Cool to the Pizza Dude*     455
Barbara Lazear Ascher, *On Compassion*     193
Laila Ayad, *The Capricious Camera*     358
Jessica Cohen, *Grade A: The Market for a Yale Woman's Eggs*     114
Chitra Divakaruni, *Live Free and Starve*     442
Barbara Ehrenreich, *The Roots of War*     598
Stephanie Ericsson, *The Ways We Lie*     408
Marie Javdani, Plata o Plomo: *Silver or Lead*     448
William Lutz, *The World of Doublespeak*     418
George Orwell, *Shooting an Elephant*     634
Anna Quindlen, *Homeless*     198
Roger Rosenblatt, *We Are Free to Be You, Me, Stupid, and Dead*     215
Luc Sante, *What Secrets Tell*     401
Thomas Sowell, *"Needs"*     501
Jonathan Swift, *A Modest Proposal*     670
Colleen Wenke, *Too Much Pressure*     533

## GLOBALIZATION

Chitra Divakaruni, *Live Free and Starve*     442
Marie Javdani, Plata o Plomo: *Silver or Lead*     448

## HEALTH AND DISABILITY

Rosie Anaya, *Mental Illness on Television*     47
Rosie Anaya, *The Best Kept Secret on Campus*     74
Jessica Cohen, *Grade A: The Market for a Yale Woman's Eggs*     114
Bella DePaulo, *The Myth of Doomed Kids*     350

Joan Didion, *In Bed*     591
Nancy Mairs, *Disability*     13

## HISTORY

Laila Ayad, *The Capricious Camera*     358
Bruce Catton, *Grant and Lee: A Study in Contrasts*     245
George Chauncey, *The Legacy of Antigay Discrimination*     260
Barbara Ehrenreich, *The Roots of War*     598
Stephen Jay Gould, *A Biological Homage to Mickey Mouse*     604
Martin Luther King, Jr., *I Have a Dream*     614
Roger Rosenblatt, *We Are Free to Be You, Me, Stupid, and Dead*     215
Edward Said, *Clashing Civilizations?*     665
Jonathan Swift, *A Modest Proposal*     670

## HOMELESSNESS

Barbara Lazear Ascher, *On Compassion*     193
Anna Quindlen, *Homeless*     198

## HUMOR AND SATIRE

Sarah Adams, *Be Cool to the Pizza Dude*     455
Russell Baker, *The Plot Against People*     384
Dave Barry, *Batting Clean-Up and Striking Out*     239
Robert Benchley, *My Face*     170
Judy Brady, *I Want a Wife*     340
Suzanne Britt, *Neat People vs. Sloppy People*     233
Ian Frazier, *How to Operate a Shower Curtain*     302
Andrew Koritz Krull, *Celebrating the Pity of Brotherly Love*     203
Jessica Mitford, *Behind the Formaldehyde Curtain*     308
Daniel Orozco, *Orientation*     319
Roger Rosenblatt, *We Are Free to Be You, Me, Stupid, and Dead*     215
Linnea Saukko, *How to Poison the Earth*     290
Jonathan Swift, *A Modest Proposal*     670
Amy Tan, *Fish Cheeks*     99
Sarah Vowell, *Shooting Dad*     154

## LAW

George Chauncey, *The Legacy of Antigay Discrimination*     260
Charles Colson, *Gay "Marriage": Societal Suicide*     554
Edwidge Danticat, *Not Your Homeland*     572
Chitra Divakaruni, *Live Free and Starve*     442
Marie Javdani, *Plata o Plomo: Silver or Lead*     448
Mark Krikorian, *Safety Through Immigration Control*     567

Katha Pollitt, *What's Wrong with Gay Marriage?*     548
Roger Rosenblatt, *We Are Free to Be You, Me, Stupid, and Dead*     215
Thomas Sowell, *"Needs"*     501


## MANNERS AND MORALS

Sarah Adams, *Be Cool to the Pizza Dude*     455
Barbara Lazear Ascher, *On Compassion*     193
Jessica Cohen, *Grade A: The Market for a Yale Woman's Eggs*     114
Chitra Divakaruni, *Live Free and Starve*     442
Stephanie Ericsson, *The Ways We Lie*     408
Shirley Jackson, *The Lottery*     123
Marie Javdani, Plata o Plomo: *Silver or Lead*     448
Jamaica Kincaid, *Girl*     367
Maxine Hong Kingston, *No Name Woman*     620
Roger Rosenblatt, *We Are Free to Be You, Me, Stupid, and Dead*     215
Luc Sante, *What Secrets Tell*     401
Colleen Wenke, *Too Much Pressure*     533


## MARRIAGE

Judy Brady, *I Want a Wife*     340
Charles Colson, Gay *"Marriage": Societal Suicide*     554
Bella DePaulo, *The Myth of Doomed Kids*     350
Maxine Hong Kingston, *No Name Woman*     620
Katha Pollitt, *What's Wrong with Gay Marriage?*     548


## MEDIA

Rosie Anaya, *Mental Illness on Television*     47
Rosie Anaya, *The Best Kept Secret on Campus*     74
Chris Anderson, *The Rise and Fall of the Hit*     459
Laila Ayad, *The Capricious Camera*     358
Armin A. Brott, *Not All Men Are Sly Foxes*     345
Don DeLillo, *Videotape*     468
Stephen Jay Gould, *A Biological Homage to Mickey Mouse*     604
Nancy Mairs, *Disability*     13
Francine Prose, *What Words Can Tell*     644
Edward Said, *Clashing Civilizations?*     665
Brian Williams, *But Enough About You . . .*     539
Andie Wurster, *Won't You Be My Friendster?*     543


## MEMORY

Maya Angelou, *Champion of the World*     93
Annie Dillard, *The Chase*     104
Andrew Koritz Krull, *Celebrating the Pity of Brotherly Love*     203

Yiyun Li, *Orange Crush*     164
Brad Manning, *Arm Wrestling with My Father*     146
Gloria Naylor, *The Meanings of a Word*     488
George Orwell, *Shooting an Elephant*     634
Richard Rodriguez, *Aria: A Memoir of a Bilingual Childhood*     651
Amy Tan, *Fish Cheeks*     99
Harold Taw, *Finding Prosperity by Feeding Monkeys*     110
Sarah Vowell, *Shooting Dad*     154
E. B. White, *Once More to the Lake*     682

## MINORITY EXPERIENCE

Rosie Anaya, *Mental Illness on Television*     47
Rosie Anaya, *The Best Kept Secret on Campus*     74
Maya Angelou, *Champion of the World*     93
George Chauncey, *The Legacy of Antigay Discrimination*     260
Linda Chavez, *Everything Isn't Racial Profiling*     563
Edwidge Danticat, *Not Your Homeland*     572
Dagoberto Gilb, *Pride*     505
Adnan R. Khan, *Close Encounters with US Immigration*     558
Martin Luther King, Jr., *I Have a Dream*     614
Maxine Hong Kingston, *No Name Woman*     620
Christine Leong, *Being a Chink*     494
Nancy Mairs, *Disability*     13
Gloria Naylor, *The Meanings of a Word*     488
Richard Rodriguez, *Aria: A Memoir of a Bilingual Childhood*     651
Brent Staples, *Black Men and Public Space*     208
Amy Tan, *Fish Cheeks*     99

## THE NATURAL WORLD

Emily Dickinson, *"Hope" is the thing with feathers*     510
Gretel Ehrlich, *Chronicles of Ice*     295
Stephen Jay Gould, *A Biological Homage to Mickey Mouse*     604
Linnea Saukko, *How to Poison the Earth*     290
Harold Taw, *Finding Prosperity by Feeding Monkeys*     110
E. B. White, *Once More to the Lake*     682

## OTHER PEOPLES, OTHER CULTURES

Sandra Cisneros, *Only Daughter*     584
Edwidge Danticat, *Not Your Homeland*     572
Chitra Divakaruni, *Live Free and Starve*     442
Dagoberto Gilb, *Pride*     505
Marie Javdani, *Plata o Plomo: Silver or Lead*     448
Jamaica Kincaid, *Girl*     367
Maxine Hong Kingston, *No Name Woman*     620

Christine Leong, *Being a Chink*     494
Yiyun Li, *Orange Crush*     164
Fatema Mernissi, *Size 6: The Western Women's Harem*     252
Gloria Naylor, *The Meanings of a Word*     488
George Orwell, *Shooting an Elephant*     634
Edward Said, *Clashing Civilizations?*     665
Jonathan Swift, *A Modest Proposal*     670
Harold Taw, *Finding Prosperity by Feeding Monkeys*     110


## PLACE AND PLACES

Edwidge Danticat, *Not Your Homeland*     572
Gretel Ehrlich, *Chronicles of Ice*     295
Dagoberto Gilb, *Pride*     505
James Joyce, *Araby*     175
Edward Said, *Clashing Civilizations?*     665
E. B. White, *Once More to the Lake*     682


## POPULAR CULTURE

Rosie Anaya, *Mental Illness on Television*     47
Rosie Anaya, *The Best Kept Secret on Campus*     74
Chris Anderson, *The Rise and Fall of the Hit*     459
Armin A. Brott, *Not All Men Are Sly Foxes*     345
Don DeLillo, *Videotape*     468
Stephen Jay Gould, *A Biological Homage to Mickey Mouse*     604
Yiyun Li, *Orange Crush*     164
Nancy Mairs, *Disability*     13
Brian Williams, *But Enough About You . . .*     539
Andie Wurster, *Won't You Be My Friendster?*     543


## PSYCHOLOGY AND BEHAVIOR

Sarah Adams, *Be Cool to the Pizza Dude*     455
Rosie Anaya, *Mental Illness on Television*     47
Rosie Anaya, *The Best Kept Secret on Campus*     74
Barbara Lazear Ascher, *On Compassion*     193
Dave Barry, *Batting Clean-Up and Striking Out*     239
Robert Benchley, *My Face*     170
Suzanne Britt, *Neat People vs. Sloppy People*     233
Charles Colson, *Gay "Marriage": Societal Suicide*     554
Don DeLillo, *Videotape*     468
Bella DePaulo, *The Myth of Doomed Kids*     350
Emily Dickinson, *"Hope" is the thing with feathers*     510
Joan Didion, *In Bed*     591
Barbara Ehrenreich, *The Roots of War*     598
Stephanie Ericsson, *The Ways We Lie*     408

Stephen Jay Gould, *A Biological Homage to Mickey Mouse*    604
James Joyce, *Araby*    175
Maxine Hong Kingston, *No Name Woman*    620
Andrew Koritz Krull, *Celebrating the Pity of Brotherly Love*    203
William Lutz, *The World of Doublespeak*    418
Nancy Mairs, *Disability*    13
Katha Pollitt, *What's Wrong with Gay Marriage?*    548
Luc Sante, *What Secrets Tell*    401
Thomas Sowell, "Needs"    501
Brent Staples, *Black Men and Public Space*    208
Amy Tan, *Fish Cheeks*    99
Deborah Tannen, *But What Do You Mean?*    391
Sarah Vowell, *Shooting Dad*    154
Colleen Wenke, *Too Much Pressure*    533

## READING, WRITING, AND LANGUAGE

Armin A. Brott, *Not All Men Are Sly Foxes*    345
Sandra Cisneros, *Only Daughter*    584
Stephanie Ericsson, *The Ways We Lie*    408
Christine Leong, *Being a Chink*    494
William Lutz, *The World of Doublespeak*    418
Gloria Naylor, *The Meanings of a Word*    488
Francine Prose, *What Words Can Tell*    644
Richard Rodriguez, *Aria: A Memoir of a Bilingual Childhood*    651
Roger Rosenblatt, *We Are Free to Be You, Me, Stupid, and Dead*    215
Luc Sante, *What Secrets Tell*    401
Thomas Sowell, "Needs"    501
Deborah Tannen, *But What Do You Mean?*    391
Writers on Writing: See Index for specific writers and topics

## SCIENCE AND TECHNOLOGY

Chris Anderson, *The Rise and Fall of the Hit*    459
Russell Baker, *The Plot Against People*    384
Jessica Cohen, *Grade A: The Market for a Yale Woman's Eggs*    114
Gretel Ehrlich, *Chronicles of Ice*    295
Stephen Jay Gould, *A Biological Homage to Mickey Mouse*    604
Linnea Saukko, *How to Poison the Earth*    290
Brian Williams, *But Enough About You . . .*    539
Andie Wurster, *Won't You Be My Friendster?*    543

## SELF-DISCOVERY

Sarah Adams, *Be Cool to the Pizza Dude*    455
Robert Benchley, *My Face*    170
Sandra Cisneros, *Only Daughter*    584

Joan Didion, *In Bed*    591
Stephanie Ericsson, *The Ways We Lie*    408
James Joyce, *Araby*    175
Maxine Hong Kingston, *No Name Woman*    620
Yiyun Li, *Orange Crush*    164
Brad Manning, *Arm Wrestling with My Father*    146
George Orwell, *Shooting an Elephant*    634
Richard Rodriguez, *Aria: A Memoir of a Bilingual Childhood*    651
Brent Staples, *Black Men and Public Space*    208
Amy Tan, *Fish Cheeks*    99
Harold Taw, *Finding Prosperity by Feeding Monkeys*    110
Sarah Vowell, *Shooting Dad*    154
E. B. White, *Once More to the Lake*    682
Brian Williams, *But Enough About You . . .*    539
Andie Wurster, *Won't You Be My Friendster?*    543

## SEXUALITY

George Chauncey, *The Legacy of Antigay Discrimination*    260
Charles Colson, *Gay "Marriage": Societal Suicide*    554
James Joyce, *Araby*    175
Jamaica Kincaid, *Girl*    367
Maxine Hong Kingston, *No Name Woman*    620
Katha Pollitt, *What's Wrong with Gay Marriage?*    548

## SOCIAL CUSTOMS

Sarah Adams, *Be Cool to the Pizza Dude*    455
Chris Anderson, *The Rise and Fall of the Hit*    459
Stephanie Ericsson, *The Ways We Lie*    408
Dagoberto Gilb, *Pride*    505
Shirley Jackson, *The Lottery*    123
Maxine Hong Kingston, *No Name Woman*    620
Jessica Mitford, *Behind the Formaldehyde Curtain*    308
Daniel Orozco, *Orientation*    319
Luc Sante, *What Secrets Tell*    401
Amy Tan, *Fish Cheeks*    99
E. B. White, *Once More to the Lake*    682
Brian Williams, *But Enough About You . . .*    539
Andie Wurster, *Won't You Be My Friendster?*    543

## SPORTS AND LEISURE

Maya Angelou, *Champion of the World*    93
Dave Barry, *Batting Clean-Up and Striking Out*    239
Annie Dillard, *The Chase*    104
Andrew Koritz Krull, *Celebrating the Pity of Brotherly Love*    203

Brad Manning, *Arm Wrestling with My Father*          146
Sarah Vowell, *Shooting Dad*          154
E. B. White, *Once More to the Lake*          682


## VIOLENCE

Rosie Anaya, *Mental Illness on Television*          47
Rosie Anaya, *The Best Kept Secret on Campus*          74
Charles Colson, *Gay "Marriage": Societal Suicide*          554
Edwidge Danticat, *Not Your Homeland*          572
Barbara Ehrenreich, *The Roots of War*          598
Shirley Jackson, *The Lottery*          123
Marie Javdani, Plata o Plomo: *Silver or Lead*          448
Mark Krikorian, *Safety Through Immigration Control*          567
George Orwell, *Shooting an Elephant*          634


## WAR AND NATIONAL SECURITY

Laila Ayad, *The Capricious Camera*          358
Linda Chavez, *Everything Isn't Racial Profiling*          563
Edwidge Danticat, *Not Your Homeland*          572
Barbara Ehrenreich, *The Roots of War*          598
Adnan R. Khan, *Close Encounters with US Immigration*          558
Mark Krikorian, *Safety Through Immigration Control*          567
Edward Said, *Clashing Civilizations?*          665


## WOMEN AND MEN

Dave Barry, *Batting Clean-Up and Striking Out*          239
Judy Brady, *I Want a Wife*          340
Armin A. Brott, *Not All Men Are Sly Foxes*          345
Jessica Cohen, *Grade A: The Market for a Yale Woman's Eggs*          114
Don DeLillo, *Videotape*          468
James Joyce, *Araby*          175
Maxine Hong Kingston, *No Name Woman*          620
Andrew Koritz Krull, *Celebrating the Pity of Brotherly Love*          203
Fatema Mernissi, *Size 6: The Western Women's Harem*          252
Deborah Tannen, *But What Do You Mean?*          391


## WORK

Sarah Adams, *Be Cool to the Pizza Dude*          455
Chitra Divakaruni, *Live Free and Starve*          442
Dagoberto Gilb, *Pride*          505
Daniel Orozco, *Orientation*          319
George Orwell, *Shooting an Elephant*          634
Deborah Tannen, *But What Do You Mean?*          391

# INTRODUCTION

## WHY READ? WHY WRITE? WHY NOT PHONE?

Many prophets have predicted the doom of the word on paper, and they may yet be proved correct. We may soon be reading books and magazines mainly on pocket computers and communicating exclusively by e-mail and text message. But even if we do discard paper and pens, the basic aims and methods of writing will not fundamentally change. Whether on paper or on screen, we will need to explain our thoughts to others plainly and forcefully.

In almost any career or profession you may enter, you will be expected to read continually and also to write. This book assumes that reading and writing are a unity. Deepen your mastery of one, and you deepen your mastery of the other. The experience of carefully reading an excellent writer, noticing not only what the writer has to say but also the quality of its saying, rubs off (if you are patient and perceptive) on your own writing. "We go to college," said the poet Robert Frost, "to be given one more chance to learn to read in case we haven't learned in high school. Once we have learned to read, the rest can be trusted to add itself *unto us*."

For any writer, reading is indispensable. It turns up fresh ideas; it stocks the mind with information, understanding, examples, and illustrations; it instills critical awareness of one's surroundings. When you have a well-stocked and girded mental storehouse, you tell truths, even small and ordinary truths.

Instead of building shimmering spires of words in an attempt to make a reader think, "Wow, what a grade A writer," you write what most readers will find worth reading. Thornton Wilder, playwright and novelist, put this advice memorably: "If you write to *impress* it will always be bad, but if you write to *express* it will be good."

## USING *THE BEDFORD READER*

### The Selections

In this book, we trust, you'll find at least a few selections you will enjoy and care to remember. *The Bedford Reader* features work by many of the finest nonfiction writers and even a few sterling fiction writers and poets.

The selections deal with more than just writing and literature and such usual concerns of English courses; they cut broadly across a college curriculum. You'll find writings on science, history, business, popular culture, sociology, education, communication, the environment, technology, sports, politics, the media, and minority experience. Some writers recall their childhoods, their families, their problems and challenges. Some explore matters likely to spark debate: global warming, gay rights, sex roles, race relations, civil liberties in an age of terrorism. Some writers are intently serious; others, funny. In all, these seventy-two selections—including six stories and a poem—reveal kinds of reading you will meet in other college courses. Such reading is the usual diet of well-informed people with lively minds—who, to be sure, aren't found only on campuses.

The selections have been chosen with one main purpose in mind: to show you how good writers write. Don't feel glum if at first you find an immense gap in quality between E. B. White's writing and yours. Of course there's a gap: White is an immortal with a unique style that he perfected over half a century. You don't have to judge your efforts by comparison. The idea is to gain whatever writing techniques you can. If you're going to learn from other writers, why not go to the best of them? Do you want to know how to compare and contrast two subjects so that each becomes vividly clear? Read Bruce Catton's "Grant and Lee." Do you want to know how to tell a story about your childhood and make it stick in someone's memory? Read Maya Angelou's "Champion of the World." Incidentally, not all the selections in this book are the work of professional writers: Students, too, write essays worth studying, as proved by Rosie Anaya, Jessica Cohen, Brad Manning, Andrew Kovitz Krull, Linnea Saukko, Laila Ayad, Marie Javdani, and Colleen Wenke.

Not all the selections in this book are solely verbal, either, for much of what we "read" in the world is visual information, such as in photographs and paintings, or visual-with-verbal information, such as in advertisements, films, and Web sites. In all, we include sixteen visual works. Some of them are subjects of writing, as when a writer analyzes a photograph. Other visual works stand free, offering themselves to be understood, interpreted, and perhaps enjoyed, just as prose and poetry do.

We combine visual material with written texts to further a key aim of *The Bedford Reader:* to encourage you to think critically about what you see, hear, and read, that is, to think with an open, questioning mind. Like everyone else, you face a daily barrage of words and pictures—from the media, from your courses, from relatives and friends. Mulling over the views of the writers, artists, and others represented in this book—figuring out their motives and strategies, agreeing or disagreeing with their ideas—will help you learn to manage, digest, and use, in your own writing, what you read and hear.

## The Organization

As a glance over the table of contents will show, the selections in *The Bedford Reader* fall into two parts. In Part Two each of the ten chapters explains a familiar method of developing ideas, such as NARRATION, DESCRIPTION, EXAMPLE, CAUSE AND EFFECT, and DEFINITION. The selections in the chapter illustrate the method. Then Part Three offers an anthology of selections by well-known writers that illustrate how, most often, the methods work together.

These methods of development aren't empty jugs to pour full of any old, dull words. Neither are they straitjackets woven by fiendish English teachers to pin your writing arm to your side and keep you from expressing yourself naturally. The methods are tools for achieving your PURPOSE in writing, whatever that purpose may be. They can help you discover what you know, what you need to know, how to think critically about your subject, and how to shape your writing.

Suppose, for example, that you set out to explain what makes a certain popular singer unique. You want to discuss her voice, her music, her lyrics, her style. While putting your ideas down on paper, it strikes you that you can best illustrate the singer's distinctions by showing the differences between her and another popular singer, one she is often compared with. To achieve your purpose, then, you draw on the method of COMPARISON AND CONTRAST, and as you proceed the method prompts you to notice differences between the two singers that you hadn't dreamed of noticing. Using the methods, such little miracles of focusing and creating take place with heartening regularity. Give the methods a try. See how they help you reach your writing goals by giving you more to say, more that you think is worth saying.

Examining *The Bedford Reader*'s selections, you'll discover two important facts about the methods of development. First, they are flexible: Two people can use the same method for quite different ends, and just about any method can point a way into just about any subject in any medium. This flexibility is apparent in every method chapter:

- A photograph, advertisement, cartoon, or other image shows how the method can contribute to visual representation of an idea.
- Two sample paragraphs—one about television, one from a college text-book—illustrate the method's useful range.
- A short example shows the method in practice, as a student solves an actual writing problem such as crafting a résumé or advertising an apart-ment sublet.
- A pair of essays shows authors using the same method to focus on the same general subject but with different purposes and results.

In addition, seven works of literature show how the methods can guide authors' explorations of subjects as diverse as the experiences of a young girl or the compulsion to watch real-life crime.

The second point about the methods of development is this: A writer never sticks to just one method all the way through a piece of writing. Even when one method predominates, as in all the essays in Part Two, you'll see the writer pick up another method, let it shape a paragraph or more, and then move on to yet another method—all to achieve some overriding aim. In "Orange Crush," Yiyun Li depends heavily on description to capture the power of a new beverage for the Chinese people as they emerged from decades of deprivation and upheaval. But Li also uses narration to tell a story, examples to illustrate her points, and cause and effect to explain why the drink made such an impression.

So the methods are like oxygen, iron, and other elements that make up substances in nature: all around us, indispensable to us, but seldom found alone and isolated, in laboratory-pure states. When you read an essay in a chapter called "Description" or "Classification," don't expect it to describe or classify in every line, but do notice how the method is central to the writer's purpose. Then, when you read the selections in Part Three, notice how the "elements" of description, example, comparison, definition, and so on rise to prominence and recede as the writer's need dictates.

## The Journal Prompts, Questions, Writing Topics, and Glossary

After every selection you'll find a suggestion for responding in your jour-nal to what you've just read. (See p. 35 for more on journal writing.) Then you'll find questions on meaning, writing strategy, and language that can help you analyze the selection and learn from it. (You can see a sample of how these questions work when we analyze Nancy Mairs's "Disability," starting on p. 20.) These questions are followed by at least four suggestions for writing, including one that proposes turning your journal entry into an essay, one that links the selection with one or two others in the book, and one that asks you to read the selection and write about it with your critical faculties alert (more on this in Chap. 1). More writing topics conclude each chapter.

In this introduction and throughout the following chapters, certain terms appear in CAPITAL LETTERS. These are words helpful in discussing both the selections in this book and the reading and writing you do. If you'd like to see such a term defined and illustrated, you can find it in the glossary, Useful Terms, at the back of this book. This section offers more than just brief definitions. It is there to provide you with further information and support.

## Writers on Writing

We have tried to give this book another dimension. We want to show that the writers represented here do not produce their readable and informative text on the first try, as if by magic, leaving the rest of us to cope with writer's block, awkward sentences, and all the other difficulties of writing. Take comfort and cheer: These writers, too, struggled to make themselves interesting and clear. In proof, we visit their workshops littered with crumpled paper and forgotten coffee cups. In Chapter 2, when we discuss the writing process briefly and include an essay by a student, Rosie Anaya, we also include her drafts and her thoughts about them. Then following most of the other selections are statements by the writers, revealing how they write (or wrote), offering their tricks, setting forth things they admire about good writing.

No doubt you'll soon notice some contradictions in these statements: The writers disagree about when and how to think about their readers, about whether outlines have any value, about whether style follows subject or vice versa. The reason for the difference of opinion is, simply, that no two writers follow the same path to finished work. Even the same writer may take the left instead of the customary right fork if the writing situation demands a change. A key aim of providing Anaya's drafts and the other writers' statements on writing, then, is to suggest the sheer variety of routes open to you, the many approaches to writing and strategies for succeeding at it. At the very end of the book, an index points you toward the writers' comments on such practical matters as drafting, finding your point, and revising sentences.

# PART ONE

# READING, WRITING, AND RESEARCH

# 1

---

# CRITICAL
# READING

Whatever career you enter, much of the reading you will do—for business, not for pleasure—will probably be hasty. You'll skim: glance at words here and there, find essential facts, catch the drift of an argument. To cross oceans of print, you won't have time to paddle: You'll need to hop a jet. By skimming, you'll be able to tear through screens full of electronic mail or quickly locate the useful parts of a long report.

But other reading that you do for work, most that you do in college, and all that you do in this book call for closer attention. You may be trying to understand a new company policy, seeking the truth in a campaign ad, researching a complicated historical treaty, or (in using this book) looking for pointers to sharpen your reading and writing skills. To learn from the selections here how to write better yourself, expect to spend an hour or two in the company of each one. Does the essay assigned for today remain unread, and does class start in five minutes? "I'll just breeze through this little item," you might tell yourself. But no, give up. You're a goner.

Good writing, as every writer knows, demands toil, and so does CRITICAL READING—reading that looks beneath the surface of a work, whether written or visual, seeking to understand the creator's intentions, the strategies for achieving them, and their worthiness. Never try to gulp down a rich and potent work without chewing; all it will give you is indigestion. When you're going to read an essay or study a visual image in depth, seek out some quiet place—a library, a study cubicle, your room (provided it doesn't also hold a cranky baby or two roommates playing poker). Flick off the radio, stereo, or television. The fewer the distractions, the easier your task will be and the more you'll enjoy it.

How do you read critically? Exactly how, that is, do you see beneath the surface of a work, master its complexities, gauge its intentions and techniques, judge its value? To find out, we'll model critical-thinking processes that you can apply to the selections in this book, taking a close look at an essay, Nancy Mairs's "Disability" (p. 13), and at a photograph (p. 27).

## READING AN ESSAY

### The Preliminaries

Critical reading starts before you read the first word of a piece of writing. Like a pilot circling an airfield, you take stock of what's before you, locating clues to the work's content and the writer's biases.

#### The Title

Often the title will tell you the writer's subject, as in Suzanne Britt's "Neat People vs. Sloppy People" or Stephanie Ericsson's "The Ways We Lie." Sometimes the title immediately states the THESIS, the main point the writer will make: "I Want a Wife." Some titles spell out the method a writer proposes to follow: "Grant and Lee: A Study in Contrasts." The TONE of the title may also reveal the writer's attitude toward the material, as "The Plot Against People" or "Live Free and Starve" does.

Some titles reveal more than others. From Nancy Mairs's title, "Disability," we can infer that the author's subject is physical or mental impairment (although the inference could be wrong). Beyond that, we can't say where Mairs might take the subject. That is for us to find out as we read.

Whatever it does, a title sits atop its essay like a neon sign. It tells you what's inside or makes you want to venture in. To pick an alluring title for an essay of your own is a skill worth cultivating.

#### The Author

Whatever you know about a writer—background, special training, previous works, outlook, or ideology—often will help you guess something about the essay before you read a word of it. Is the writer on new taxes a political conservative? Expect an argument against added "revenue enhancement." Is the writer a liberal? Expect an argument that new social programs are worth the price. Is the writer a feminist? an athlete? an internationally renowned philosopher? a popular television comedian? By knowing something about a writer's background or beliefs, you may know beforehand a little of what he or she will say.

To help provide such knowledge, this book supplies biographical notes. The one on Nancy Mairs, included before "Disability" (p. 13), tells us that Mairs is a poet and nonfiction writer who has multiple sclerosis, a debilitating disease, and who strives to "speak the 'unspeakable'" about sensitive subjects. We can expect that in "Disability" Mairs writes frankly and thought provokingly from her experience as a person with disabilities.

### Where the Work Was Published

Clearly, it matters to a writer's credibility whether an article called "Creatures of the Dark Oceans" appears in *Scientific American*, a magazine for scientists and interested nonscientists, or in a popular tabloid weekly, sold at supermarket checkout counters, that is full of eye-popping sensations. But no less important, examining where a work appears can tell you for whom the writer was writing.

In this book we'll strongly urge you as a writer to think of your AUDIENCE, your readers, and to try looking at what you write as if through their eyes. To help you develop this ability, we tell you something about the sources and thus the original readers of each essay you study, in a note just before the essay. (Such a note precedes "Disability" on p. 13.) After you have read the sample essay, we'll further consider how having a sense of your readers helps you write.

### When the Work Was Published

Knowing in what year a work appeared may give you another key to understanding it. A 2002 article on ocean creatures will contain statements of fact more recent and more reliable than an essay printed in 1700—although the older essay might contain valuable information, too, and perhaps some delectable language, folklore, and poetry. In *The Bedford Reader* the introductory note on every essay tells you not only where but also when the essay was originally printed. If you're reading an essay elsewhere—say, in one of the writer's books—you can usually find this information on the copyright page.

## The First Reading

On first reading an essay, you don't want to bog down over every trouble-some particular. Mairs's "Disability" is written for an educated audience, and that means the author may use a few large words when they seem necessary. If you meet any words that look intimidating, take them in your stride. When, in reading a rich essay, you run into an unfamiliar word or name, see if you can figure it out from its surroundings. If a word stops you cold and you feel lost, circle it in pencil; you can always look it up later. (In a little while we'll come back to the helpful habit of reading with a pencil. Indeed, some readers feel more confident with pencil in hand from the start.)

The first time you read an essay, size up the forest; later, you can squint at the acorns all you like. Glimpse the essay in its entirety. When you start to read "Disability," don't even think about dissecting it. Just see what Mairs has to say.

# NANCY MAIRS

A self-described "radical feminist, pacifist, and cripple," NANCY MAIRS aims to "speak the 'unspeakable.'" Her poetry, memoirs, and essays deal with many sensitive subjects, including her struggles with the debilitating disease of multiple sclerosis. Born in Long Beach, California, in 1943, Mairs grew up in New Hampshire and Massachusetts. She received a BA from Wheaton College in Massachusetts (1964) and an MFA in creative writing (1975) and a PhD in English literature (1984) from the University of Arizona. While working on her advanced degrees, Mairs taught high school and college writing courses. Her second book of poetry, *In All the Rooms of the Yellow House* (1984), received a Western States Arts Foundation book award. Her essays are published in *Plaintext* (1986), *Remembering the Bone-House* (1988), *Carnal Acts* (1990), *Ordinary Time* (1993), *Waist High in the World: A Life Among the Nondisabled* (1996), and *A Troubled Guest* (2001). She is currently working on a book that explores how religious principles can inform social and political debates.

# *Disability*

As a writer afflicted with multiple sclerosis, Nancy Mairs is in a unique position to examine how the culture responds to people with disabilities. In this essay from *Carnal Acts*, she examines the media's depiction of disability and argues with her usual unsentimental candor that the media must treat disability as normal. The essay was first published in 1987 in the *New York Times*. To what extent is Mairs's critique of the media still valid today?

For months now I've been consciously searching for representation of 1 myself in the media, especially television. I know I'd recognize this self because of certain distinctive, though not unique, features: I am a forty-three-year-old woman crippled with multiple sclerosis; although I can still totter short distances with the aid of a brace and a cane, more and more of the time I ride in a wheelchair. Because of these appliances and my peculiar gait, I'm easy to spot even in a crowd. So when I tell you I haven't noticed any women like me on television, you can believe me.

Actually, last summer I did see a woman with multiple sclerosis portrayed 2 on one of those medical dramas that offer an illness-of-the-week like the daily special at your local diner. In fact, that was the whole point of the show: that this poor young woman had MS. She was terribly upset (understandably, I assure you) by the diagnosis, and her response was to plan a trip to Kenya while she was still physically capable of making it, against the advice of the young, fit, handsome doctor who had fallen in love with her. And she almost did it. At least, she got as far as a taxi to the airport, hotly pursued by the doctor. But at the last she succumbed to his blandishments and fled the taxi into his manly protective embrace. No escape to Kenya for this cripple.

Capitulation into the arms of a man who uses his medical powers to strip   3
one of even the urge toward independence is hardly the sort of representation I had in mind. But even if the situation had been sensitively handled, according to the woman her right to her own adventures, it wouldn't have been what I'm looking for. Such a television show, as well as films like *Duet for One* and *Children of a Lesser God*, in taking disability as its major premise, excludes the complexities that round out a character and make her whole. It's not about a woman who happens to be physically disabled; it's about physical disability as the determining factor of a woman's existence.

Take it from me, physical disability looms pretty large in one's life. But it   4
doesn't devour one wholly. I'm not, for instance, Ms. MS, a walking, talking embodiment of a chronic incurable degenerative disease. In most ways I'm just like every other woman of my age, nationality, and socioeconomic background. I menstruate, so I have to buy tampons. I worry about smoker's breath, so I buy mouthwash. I smear my wrinkling skin with lotions. I put bleach in the washer so my family's undies won't be dingy. I drive a car, talk on the telephone, get runs in my pantyhose, eat pizza. In most ways, that is, I'm the advertisers' dream: Ms. Great American Consumer. And yet the advertisers, who determine nowadays who will get represented publicly and who will not, deny the existence of me and my kind absolutely.

I once asked a local advertiser why he didn't include disabled people in his   5
spots. His response seemed direct enough: "We don't want to give people the idea that our product is just for the handicapped." But tell me truly now: If you saw me pouring out puppy biscuits, would you think these kibbles were only for the puppies of the cripples? If you saw my blind niece ordering a Coke, would you switch to Pepsi lest you be struck sightless? No, I think the advertiser's excuse masked a deeper and more anxious rationale: To depict disabled people in the ordinary activities of daily life is to admit that there is something ordinary about disability itself, that it may enter anybody's life. If it is effaced completely, or at least isolated as a separate "problem," so that it remains at a safe distance from other human issues, then the viewer won't feel threatened by her or his own physical vulnerability.

This kind of effacement or isolation has painful, even dangerous conse-   6
quences, however. For the disabled person, these include self-degradation and a subtle kind of self-alienation not unlike that experienced by other minorities. Socialized human beings love to conform, to study others and then mold themselves to the contours of those whose images, for good reasons or bad, they come to love. Imagine a life in which feasible others—others you can hope to be like—don't exist. At the least you might conclude that there is

something queer about you, something ugly or foolish or shameful. In the extreme, you might feel as though you don't exist, in any meaningful social sense, at all. Everyone else is "there," sucking breath mints and splashing cologne and swigging wine coolers. You're "not there." And if not there, nowhere.

But this denial of disability imperils even you who are able-bodied, and not just by shrinking your insight into the physically and emotionally complex world you live in. Some disabled people call you TAPs, or Temporarily Abled Persons. The fact is that ours is the only minority you can join involuntarily, without warning, at any time. And if you live long enough, as you're increasingly likely to do, you may well join it. The transition will probably be difficult from a physical point of view no matter what. But it will be a good bit easier psychologically if you are accustomed to seeing disability as a normal characteristic, one that complicates but does not ruin human existence. Achieving this integration, for disabled and able-bodied people alike, requires that we insert disability daily into our field of vision: quietly, naturally, in the small and common scenes of our ordinary lives.

———————

## Writing While Reading

In giving an essay a going-over, many readers find a pencil in hand as good as a currycomb for a horse's mane. The pencil (or pen or computer keyboard) concentrates the attention wonderfully, and, as often happens with writing, it can lead you to unexpected questions and connections. (Some readers favor markers that roll pink or yellow ink over a word or line, making the eye jump to that spot, but you can't use a highlighter to note *why* a word or an idea is important.) You can annotate your own books, underlining essential ideas, scoring key passages with vertical lines, writing questions in the margins about difficult words or concepts, venting feelings ("Bull!" "Yes!" "Says who?"). Here, as an example, are the jottings of one student, Rosie Anaya, on a paragraph of Mairs's essay:

> This kind of (effacement) or isolation has painful, even dangerous consequences, however. For the disabled person, these include (self-)degradation and a subtle kind of (self-)alienation not unlike that experienced by other minorities. Socialized human beings love to conform, to study others and then mold themselves to the contours of those whose images, for good reasons or bad, they come to love. Imagine a life in which feasible others — others you can hope to be like — don't exist. At the least you might conclude that there is something queer about you, something ugly or foolish or shameful. In the extreme, you might feel as though you don't exist, in any meaningful social sense, at all. Everyone else is "there," sucking breath mints and splashing cologne and swigging wine coolers. You're "not there." And if not there, nowhere.

*?*

*IMPORTANT*

*Why "self"?*

*True? What about individuality?*

*✔ emotions*

*examples are insignificant, but that's the point*

If a book is borrowed, you can accomplish the same thing by making notes on a separate sheet of paper or on your computer.

Whether you own the book or not, you'll need separate notes for responses that are lengthier and more substantial than the margins can contain, such as the informal responses, summaries, detailed analyses, and evaluations discussed below. For such notes, you may find a JOURNAL handy. It can be a repository of your ideas, a comfortable place to record meandering or direct thoughts about what you read. You may be surprised to find that the more you write in an unstructured way, the more you'll have to say when it's time to write a structured essay. (For more on journals, see p. 35.)

Writing while reading helps you behold the very spine of an essay, as if in an X-ray view, so that you, as much as any expert, can judge its curves and connections. You'll develop an opinion about what you read, and you'll want to express it. While reading this way, you're being a writer. Your pencil tracks or keystrokes will jog your memory, too, when you review for a test, when you take part in class discussion, or when you want to write about what you've read.

## Summarizing

It's usually good practice, especially with more difficult essays, to SUMMA-RIZE the content in writing to be sure you understand it or, as often happens, to come to understand it. (We're suggesting that you write summaries for yourself, but the technique is also useful when you discuss other people's works in your writing, as shown on p. 54.) In summarizing a work of writing, you digest, *in your own words*, what the author says: You take the essence of the author's meaning, without the supporting evidence and other details that make that gist convincing or interesting. When you are practicing reading and the work is short (the case with the reading you do in this book), you may want to make this a two-step procedure: First write a summary sentence for every paragraph or related group of paragraphs; then summarize those sentences in two or three others that capture the heart of the author's meaning.

Here is a two-step summary of "Disability." (The numbers in parentheses refer to paragraph numbers in the essay.) First, the longer version:

(1) Mairs searches the media in vain for depictions of women like herself with disabilities. (2) One TV movie showed a woman recently diagnosed with multiple sclerosis, but she chose dependence over independence. (3) Such shows oversimplify people with disabilities by making disability central to their lives. (4) People with disabilities live lives and consume goods like everyone else, but the media ignore them. (5) Showing disability as ordinary would remind nondisabled viewers that they are vulnerable. (6) The media's exclusion of others like themselves deprives people with disabilities of role models and makes them feel undesirable or invisible. (7) Nondisabled viewers lose an understanding that could enrich them and would help them adjust to disability of their own.

Now the short summary:

Mairs believes that the media, by failing to depict disability as ordinary, both marginalize viewers with disabilities and impair the outlook and coping skills of the "temporarily abled."

## Thinking Critically

Summarizing will start you toward understanding the author's meaning, but it won't take you as far as you're capable of going, or as far as you'll need to go in school or work or just to live well in our demanding Information Age. Passive, rote learning (such as memorizing the times tables in arithmetic) won't do. You require techniques for comprehending what you encounter. But more: You need tools for discovering the meaning and intentions of an essay or case study or business letter or political message. You need ways to discriminate between the trustworthy and the not so and to apply what's valid in your own work and life.

We're talking here about critical thinking—not "negative," the common conception of *critical,* but "thorough, thoughtful, question asking, judgment forming." When you approach something critically, you harness your faculties, your fund of knowledge, and your experiences to understand, appreciate, and evaluate the object. Using this book—guided by questions on meaning, writing strategy, and language—you'll read an essay and ask what the author's purpose and main idea are, how clear they are, and how well supported. You'll isolate which writing techniques the author has used to special advantage, what hits you as particularly fresh, clever, or wise—and what *doesn't* work, too. You'll discover exactly what the writer is saying, how he or she says it, and whether, in the end, it was worth saying. In class discussions and in writing, you'll tell others what you think and why.

Critical thinking is a process involving several overlapping operations: analysis, inference, synthesis, and evaluation.

### Analysis

Say you're listening to a new album by a band called Domix. Without thinking much about it, you isolate melodies, song lyrics, and instrumentals—in other words, you ANALYZE the album by separating it into its parts. Analysis is a way of thinking so basic to us that it has its own chapter (9) in this book. For reading in this book, you'll consciously analyze essays by looking at the author's main idea, support for the idea, special writing strategies, and other elements.

Analysis underlies many of the other methods of development discussed in this book, so that while you are analyzing a subject you might also (even unconsciously) begin classifying it, or comparing it with something else, or figuring out what caused it. For instance, you might compare Domix's new instrumentals with those on the band's earlier albums, or you might notice that the lyrics seem to be influenced by another band's. Similarly, in analyzing a poem you might compare several images of water, or in analyzing a journal article in psychology you might consider how the author's theories affect her interpretations of behavior.

### Inference

Say that after listening to Domix's new album, you conclude that it reveals a preoccupation with traditional blues music and themes. Now you are using INFERENCE, drawing conclusions about a work based on your store of information and experience, your knowledge of the creator's background and biases, and your analysis. When you infer, you add to the work, making explicit what was only implicit.

In critical thinking, inference is especially important in discovering a writer's ASSUMPTIONS: opinions or beliefs, often unstated, that direct the writer's choices of ideas, support, writing strategies, and language. A writer who favors gun control may assume without saying so that some individual rights (such as the right to bear arms) may be infringed for the good of the community. A writer who opposes gun control may assume the opposite—that in this case the individual's right is superior to the community's.

### Synthesis

What is Domix trying to accomplish with its new album? Is it different from the band's previous album in its understanding of the blues? Answering such questions leads you into SYNTHESIS, using your perspective to link elements into a whole or to link two or more wholes. During synthesis, you use your special aptitudes, interests, and training to reconstitute the work so that it now contains not just the original elements but also your sense of their underpinnings, relationships, and implications.

Synthesis is the core of much academic writing, as Chapter 3 shows. Sometimes you'll respond directly to a work, or you'll use it as a springboard to another subject. Sometimes you'll show how two or more works resemble each other or how they differ. Sometimes you'll draw on many works to answer a question. In all these cases, you'll be putting your critical reading to use for your own ideas.

### Evaluation

Not all critical thinking involves EVALUATION, or judging the quality of the work. You'll probably form a judgment of Domix's new album (Is the band getting better or just standing still?), but often you (and your teachers) will be satisfied with a nonjudgmental reading of a work. ("Nonjudgmental" does not mean "uncritical": You will still be expected to analyze, infer, and synthesize.) When you *do* evaluate, you determine adequacy, significance, value. You answer a question such as whether an essay moves you as it was intended to, or whether the author has proved a case, or whether the argument is even worthwhile.

## Analyzing "Disability"

The following comments on Nancy Mairs's "Disability" show how a critical reading can work. The headings "Meaning" (below), "Writing Strategy" (p. 22), and "Language" (p. 24) correspond to those organizing the questions at the end of each essay.

### Meaning

By *meaning*, we intend what the author's words say literally, of course, but also what they imply and, more generally, what the author's aims are.

**Thesis**   Every essay has—or should have—a point, a main idea the writer wants to communicate for a purpose. Some writers come right out and sum up this idea in a sentence or two, a THESIS STATEMENT. Mairs, for instance, builds her thesis over the course of the essay and then states it in paragraph 7:

> Achieving this integration [of seeing disability as normal], for disabled and able-bodied people alike, requires that we insert disability daily into our field of vision: quietly, naturally, in the small and common scenes of our ordinary lives.

Mairs holds a statement of her thesis for the end of her essay, but other authors state the thesis outright in the first or second paragraph, or they provide it in the middle, or they release it part by part, paragraph by paragraph. And some writers don't state a thesis at all, although it remains in the background controlling the essay and can be inferred by a critical reader.

You may occasionally be confused by a writer's point—"What *is* this about?"—and sometimes your confusion won't yield to repeated careful readings. That's when you'll want to toss the work aside in exasperation, but you won't always have the choice: A school or work assignment or just an urge to understand the writer's problem may keep you at it. Then it'll be up to you to figure out what the author is trying to say and why he or she fails—in essence, to clarify what's unclear—by, say, digging for buried assumptions.

**Purpose**   "No man but a blockhead," declared Samuel Johnson, "ever wrote except for money." Perhaps the eighteenth-century critic, journalist, and dictionary maker was remembering his own days as a literary drudge in London; but most people who write often do so for other reasons.

When you read an essay, you'll find it rewarding to ask, "What is this writer's PURPOSE?" By purpose, we mean the writer's apparent reason for writing: what he or she was trying to achieve with readers. A purpose is as essential to a good, pointed essay as a destination is to a trip. It affects every choice or decision the writer makes. (On vacation, of course, carefree people sometimes climb into a car without a thought and go happily rambling around. A writer may ramble like that in an early draft, with good results. But in a final draft such wandering will leave the reader pleading, "Let me out!")

In making a simple statement of a writer's purpose, we might say that the writer writes *to entertain* readers, or *to explain* something to them, or *to persuade* them. To state a purpose more fully, we might say that a writer writes not just to persuade but "to tell readers a story to illustrate the point that when you are being cheated it's a good idea to complain," or not just to entertain but "to tell a horror story to make chills shoot down readers' spines." If the essay is an argument meant to convince, a fuller statement of its writer's purpose might be "to win readers over to the writer's opinion that the school's honor code needs revision," or "to persuade readers to take action by writing their representatives and urging more federal spending for the rehabilitation of criminals."

"But," the skeptic might object, "how can I know a writer's purpose? I'm no mind reader, and even if I were, how could I tell what E. B. White was trying to do? He's dead and buried." And yet writers living and dead have revealed their purposes in their writing, just as visibly as a hiker leaves footprints.

What is Nancy Mairs's purpose in writing? If you want to be more exact, you can speak of her *main purpose* or *central purpose*, for "Disability" fulfills more than one. As a person with disabilities, Mairs clearly wants to explain her view of the media, and she is not averse to entertaining with amusing details and wry language. But Mairs's larger purpose seems to be persuading "you who are able-bodied" that by omitting or marginalizing people with disabilities, the media hurt the nondisabled as much as they do the disabled. She wants change.

We think Mairs supports her thesis well and achieves this purpose. We appreciate the twist she gives to the usual call for more representation of minorities in the media: Sure it will help the group depicted, she says, but no more than it helps the majority. If we are put off by the reminder that we may someday become disabled ourselves, that seems intentional on Mairs's part: Disability makes us uncomfortable because we are unfamiliar with it, and we shouldn't be.

Analyzing writers' purposes and their successes and failures makes you an alert and critical reader. Applied to your own writing, this analysis also gives you a decided advantage, for when you write with a clear-cut purpose in mind, aware of your assumptions, you head toward a goal. Of course, sometimes you just can't know what you are going to say until you say it, to echo the English novelist E. M. Forster. In such a situation, your purpose emerges as you write. But the earlier and more exactly you define your purpose, the easier you'll find it to fulfill.

### Writing Strategy

To the extent that Nancy Mairs holds our interest, makes us think, and convinces us to accept her thesis, it pays to ask, "How does she succeed?" (When a writer bores or angers us, we ask why he or she fails.) Conscious writers make choices intended to get their audience on their side so that they can achieve their purpose. These choices are what we mean by STRATEGY in writing.

**Audience**    Almost all writing is a *transaction* between a writer and an audience, maybe one reader, maybe millions. The success or failure of writing depends on the extent to which the writer achieves his or her purpose with the intended audience.

Mairs's original audience was the readers of the *New York Times*. She could assume educated readers with diverse interests. She could assume readers who, like the general population, are not themselves disabled or even familiar with disability, so she fills them in: "Take it from me, physical disability looms pretty large in one's life" (par. 4); "Imagine a life in which feasible others—others you can hope to be like—don't exist" (6). She could also assume readers who do not know her situation, so she takes pains to describe her disability (1) and her life (4).

For this thoughtful but somewhat blinkered audience, Mairs mixes a range of attitudes: plain talk ("I am a forty-three-year-old woman crippled with multiple sclerosis," par. 1), humor ("I put bleach in the washer so my family's undies won't be dingy," 4), and insistence ("...the advertisers, who determine nowadays who will get represented publicly and who will not, deny the existence of me and my kind absolutely," 4). The blend gives readers the facts they need, wins them over with common humanity and lightness, and conveys the gravity of the problem.

**Evidence**    A crucial part of a writer's strategy—Mairs's, too—is how he or she supports ideas, making them concrete and convincing. For this EVIDENCE, the writer may use facts, examples, reasons, expert opinions— whatever best delivers the point.

This is one place the methods of development come in — the ways of find-ing and presenting evidence around which this book is organized. Overall, Mairs's essay is an ARGUMENT, offering and defending an opinion. Within this context, Mairs uses several methods to develop her evidence:

- With COMPARISON AND CONTRAST Mairs shows the similarities and differ-ences between herself and a woman in a TV drama (pars. 2–4), between herself and nondisabled people (1, 4, 5), and between the effects on the dis-abled and on the nondisabled of not showing disability as ordinary (6–7).
- With EXAMPLES Mairs illustrates dramas she dislikes (2–3), the prod-ucts she buys (4), and the ads in which people with disabilities might appear (5).
- With DESCRIPTION Mairs shows the helplessness of the woman in the TV drama (2), the flavor of her own daily life (4), and the bad feelings expe-rienced by people with disabilities (6).
- With CAUSE AND EFFECT Mairs explains why disability is "effaced" (or rubbed out) from the media (5), how that affects people with disabili-ties (6), and how treating disability as ordinary could help the nondis-abled (7).

We have more to say about evidence when discussing argument in detail (see pp. 520–21, 527).

**Structure**   Aside from considering an audience's needs and attitudes and choosing the methods for developing ideas, probably no writing strategy is as crucial to success as finding an appropriate structure. Writing that we find interesting and clear and convincing almost always has UNITY (everything relates to the main idea) and COHERENCE (the relations between parts are clear). When we find an essay wanting, it may be because the writer got lost in digressions or couldn't make the parts fit together.

Sometimes structure almost takes care of itself. In NARRATION, for instance, events usually follow a chronological sequence, as they occurred in time. But when neither subject nor method dictates a structure, then the writer must mold and arrange ideas to pique, hold, and direct our interest.

Nancy Mairs's structure is complex for a short essay: She introduces her-self and her complaint that the media do not show people with disabilities (par. 1); dismisses a TV movie and other films centering on disability that don't satisfy her (2, 3); establishes her credentials as a consumer, someone advertisers *should* be appealing to (4); takes issue with an advertiser's view and suggests her own (5); describes the negative effects of "effacement" on people with disabilities (6); and describes the positive effects that normalizing dis-ability would have on presently nondisabled people (7).

As often occurs in arguments, Mairs's organization builds to her main idea, her thesis, which readers might find difficult to accept at the outset. For much of the essay, Mairs prepares us to accept her opinion by establishing her credentials as a disabled woman, a TV and film viewer, a normal consumer, and a humorous (not bitter), sensitive, thoughtful person.

Whether gradually unfolding the main idea or hitting us with it right away, and however the support is arranged, the decisions come out of the writer's purpose: What is the aim? What do I want readers to think or feel? What's the best way to achieve that? As you'll see in this book, there are as many options as there are writers.

## Language

To examine the element of language is often to go even more deeply into an essay and how it was made. Mairs, you'll notice, is a writer whose language is rich and varied. It isn't bookish. Many expressions from common speech lend her prose vigor and naturalness: "I can still totter" (par. 1), "the daily special at your local diner" (2), "Take it from me" (4), "sucking breath mints and splashing cologne and swigging wine coolers" (6). These and other expressions lighten the essay. At the same time, Mairs is serious about her argument, and she puts it in serious, firm words: "deny the existence of me and my kind absolutely" (4), "This kind of effacement or isolation has painful, even dangerous consequences" (6), "this denial of disability imperils even you who are able-bodied" (7).

Mairs's language not only animates and weights her meaning but also conveys her attitudes and elicits them from readers. It creates a TONE, the equivalent of tone of voice in speaking. Whether it's angry, sarcastic, or sad, joking or serious, tone carries almost as much information about a writer's purpose as the words themselves do. Mairs's tone, like her words, mixes lightness with gravity, humor with intensity. Sometimes she uses IRONY, saying one thing but meaning another, as in "If you saw my blind niece ordering a Coke, would you switch to Pepsi lest you be struck sightless?" (par. 5). She's blunt, too, revealing intimate details about her personal hygiene and her feelings. Honest and wry, she invites us to see the media's exclusion as ridiculous and then leads us to her discomfiting conclusion.

With everything you read, as with "Disability," it's instructive to study the writer's tone so that you are aware of whether and how it affects you. Pay particular attention to the CONNOTATIONS of words — their implied meanings, their associations. When one writer calls the homeless "society's downtrodden" and another calls them "human refuse," we know something of their attitudes and can use that knowledge to analyze and evaluate what they say about homelessness. In Mairs's essay, the word with the strongest connotations may be "cripple" (pars. 2, 5) because it calls up old, insensitive attitudes toward people with disabilities. Mairs's use of the word reinforces her bluntness and her frankness about her own condition. But perhaps she's also suggesting that the old attitudes are still alive, still determining what we see in the media and what we ask to see.

One other use of language is worth noting in Mairs's essay and in many others in this book: FIGURES OF SPEECH, bits of colorful language not meant to be taken literally. In one instance, Mairs says that people "study others and then mold themselves to the contours of those whose images . . . they come to love" (par. 6). That image of molding to contours is a *metaphor,* stating that one thing (behavioral change) is another (physical change). Elsewhere Mairs uses *understatement* ("Take it from me, physical disability looms pretty large in one's life," 4) and *simile*, or stating that one thing is *like* another ("medical dramas that offer an illness-of-the-week like the daily special at your local diner," 2). All the figures give Mairs's essay flavor and force. (More examples of figures of speech can be found in Useful Terms, p. 691.)

Many questions in this book point to figures of speech, to oddities of tone, or to troublesome or unfamiliar words. We don't wish to swamp you in details or make you a slave to your dictionary; we only want to get you thinking about how meaning and effect begin at the most basic level, with the word. As a writer, you can have no traits more valuable to you than a fondness and respect for words and a yen to experiment with them.

## THINKING CRITICALLY ABOUT VISUAL IMAGES

Does a particular billboard always catch your eye when you drive by it? Does a certain television commercial irritate you or make you smile? Do you look at the pictures in a magazine before you read the articles? If so, you're like everyone else in that you are subject to the visual representations coming at you continually, unbidden, from all around.

Much of the flood of visual information just washes over us, like noise to the eyes. Sometimes we do focus on an image or a whole sequence that interests us—maybe it tweaks our emotions or tells us something we want to know. But even then we aren't always thinking that an image, just as much as a sentence of words, was created by somebody for a reason. No matter what it is—Web advertisement, TV commercial, painting, music video, photograph, cartoon—a visual image originated with a creator or creators who had a purpose, an intention for how the image should look and how we, the viewers, should respond to it.

In their purposefulness, then, visual images are not much different from written texts, and they are no less open to critical thinking that will uncover their meanings and effects. To a great extent, the method for critically "reading" visuals parallels the one for essays outlined on pages 10–12 and 16–20. In short:

- *Get the big picture:* As when scoping out a written work, survey the image or sequence for a view of the whole and clues about its origins and purposes.
- *Analyze:* Discern the elements of the image or sequence.
- *Infer:* Interpret the underlying meanings of the elements and the ASSUMPTIONS and intentions of the work's creators.
- *Synthesize:* Form an idea about how the elements function together to produce a whole and to deliver a message.
- Often, *evaluate:* Judge the quality, significance, or value of the work.

One other important parallel with critical reading of written works: Always write while examining a visual image or images. Jotting down responses, questions, and other notes will not only help you remember what you were thinking but also jog further thoughts into being.

To show the critical method in action, we'll look closely at the photograph by Erik S. Lesser on the facing page, which first appeared in the magazine *US News & World Report.* Further examples of analyzing visual works appear elsewhere in *The Bedford Reader* as well: See pages 358–64 (a photograph) and 604–11 (drawings). In addition, Chapters 4–13 each open with a visual image that gives you a chance to try out the method yourself.

## The Big Picture

To examine any visual representation, it helps first to get an overview, a sense of the whole. Try making some inquiries of the work:

- What is the source of the work? Who created it—for instance, a painter, a teacher, an advertiser—and when?
- What does the work show overall? What appears to be happening?
- At a glance, why was the work created—for instance, to educate, to sell, to shock, to entertain?

The photograph on the next page was taken by Erik S. Lesser at Fort Benning, Georgia, and was used by *US News & World Report* in February 2007 to

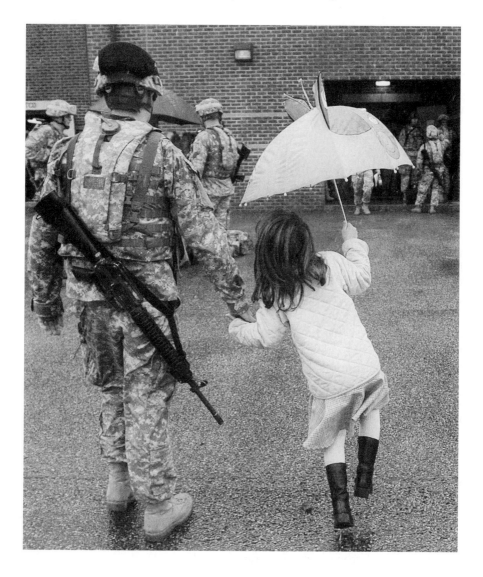

illustrate an article on the deployment of troops to Iraq. The picture shows a
young girl and a man in military uniform holding hands, with other soldiers in
the background. Evidently, the main figures are father and daughter. Given
the context, the father is probably being sent to Iraq.

## Analysis

After you've gained an overview of the visual work, begin focusing on the elements that contribute to the whole—not just the people, animals, or objects depicted but the background and what might be called the artistic elements of lighting, color, shape, and balance.

- Which elements of the image stand out? What is distinctive about each one?
- What does the composition of the image emphasize?
- If spoken or written words accompany the work, what do they say? How are they sized and placed in relation to the visual elements?

In Lesser's photograph, the dominant elements are the soldier and the girl, presumably father and daughter, holding hands and facing a brick building in the background. Other soldiers are also evident, particularly in a large rectangular door in the background building. The girl wears light-colored clothing, and she carries an umbrella, which indicates that it is raining. The father wears a camouflage uniform and helmet and carries a rifle across his back, which suggest that he is prepared to fight. He is walking (his left heel is raised), apparently headed toward the door. The daughter seems to be playfully hopping or skipping.

## Inference

Identifying the elements of the visual representation leads you to consider what they mean and how the image's creator has selected and arranged them so that viewers will respond in certain ways. As when reading a written text critically, you make explicit what may only be implicit in the work.

- What do the elements of the work say about the creator's intentions and assumptions? In particular, what does the creator seem to assume about viewers' backgrounds, needs, interests, and values?
- If the work includes written or spoken words, how do they interact with the visual components?

We can guess Erik Lesser's intentions for the photograph. He seems to assume that we viewers will instantly recognize the main figures as a soldier going off to war and his daughter coming to say good-bye. He may assume more as well: that whatever viewers think about the Iraq war, they will sympathize with this couple. The large father's steady gait, uniform, and rifle portray him as determined and courageous in going to war. The girl's brighter clothes and jaunty step show her as excited, perhaps unaware of what lies in store for her father. Lesser may see these opposites as reflecting the controversy over the war.

## Synthesis

Linking the elements and your inferences about them, you'll move into a new conception of the visual representation: your own conclusions about its overall intentions and effect.

- What general appeal does the work make to viewers? For instance, does it emphasize logical argument, emotion, or the creator's or subject's worthiness?
- What feelings, memories, moods, or ideas does the work seem intended to summon from viewers' own store of experiences? Why, given the purpose of the work, would its creator try to establish these associations?

As we see it, Lesser's photograph represents Americans' mixed feelings about the war in Iraq. The apparent rain and the yawning door are ominous, suggesting the danger facing the father and also the United States as a whole. The determination of the father despite the risk evokes our appreciation and pride; his connection with his daughter evokes our sympathy and approval as it also intensifies our anxiety for his safety. At the same time, the buoyant daughter is both sweetly supportive and sadly innocent, because she may not realize what her father's departure means. In a larger sense, these two figures could represent the joining of the armed forces and the home front in a situation that, depending on one's point of view, is noble or tragic.

When using synthesis, you may often go outside the work itself to explore its cultural context. For instance, Lesser's photograph might be compared with other photographs that depict soldiers on their way to Iraq, or it might be analyzed in the context of one or more written opinions about the war in Iraq.

## Evaluation

Often in criticizing visual works, you'll take one step beyond synthesis to evaluate success or significance or value.

- Does the work seem to fulfill its creator's intentions? Does it do what the creator wanted?
- Apart from the creator's intentions, how does the work affect you? Does it move you? amuse you? bore you? offend you?
- Was the work worth creating?

Erik Lesser's photograph seems to us masterful as concise storytelling with a big message. As Lesser seems to have intended, he distills strong and even contradictory feelings about the Iraq war into a deceptively simple image of a father and his daughter.

# 2

---

# THE WRITING
# PROCESS

The CRITICAL THINKING discussed in the previous chapter will serve you in just about every role you'll play in life—consumer, voter, friend, parent. As a student and a worker, though, you'll find critical thinking especially important as the foundation for writing. Whether to demonstrate your competence or to contribute to discussions and projects, writing will be the main way you communicate with teachers, supervisors, and peers.

Like critical thinking, writing is no snap: As this book's Writers on Writing attest, even professionals do not produce thoughtful, detailed, attention-getting prose in a single draft. Writing well demands, and rewards, a willingness to work recursively—to begin tentatively, perhaps, and then to double back, to welcome change and endure frustration, to recognize and exploit progress.

This recursive writing process is not really a single process at all, not even for an individual writer. Some people work out meticulous plans before beginning to compose sentences; others find plans stifling and prefer to just start writing; still others will work one way for one project and a different way for another. Generally, though, writers do move through four rough stages between assignment or initial idea and finished work: analysis of the writing situation, discovery, drafting, and revision.

In examining these stages, we'll have the help of a student, Rosie Anaya. Anaya wrote an essay for *The Bedford Reader* responding to Nancy Mairs's essay "Disability." Along with the final draft of her essay (pp. 47–49), Anaya also provided her notes and earlier drafts and her comments on her progress at each stage.

## ANALYZING THE WRITING SITUATION

Any writing you do will occur in a specific situation: What are you writing about? Whom are you writing to? Why are you writing about this subject to these people? Subject, audience, and purpose are the main components in the writing situation, although others may figure as well, such as length or deadline.

### Subject

Your subject may be specified or at least suggested in the writing assignment you receive. "Discuss one of the works we've read this semester in its historical and social context," reads a literature assignment; "Can you draw me up a proposal for holiday staffing?" asks your boss. If you're left to your own devices and nothing occurs to you, try the discovery techniques explained on pages 34–37 to find a subject that interests you.

In *The Bedford Reader* we've provided ideas for writing about the selections that will also give you practice in working with writing assignments. Immediately after each selection, a "Journal Writing" prompt encourages you to respond to the selection just for yourself. (See p. 35 for a discussion of journal writing.) Then, in "Suggestions for Writing," one assignment proposes turning that journal writing into an essay for others to read. Of the three or four other suggestions, one labeled "Critical Writing" asks you to take a deliberate, critical look at the selection, and another labeled "Connections" helps you relate the selection to one or two others in the book. You may not wish to take any of our suggestions as worded; they may merely urge your own thoughts toward what you want to say.

To give you an idea of the writing suggestions we provide, here are possibilities for Nancy Mairs's "Disability," the essay reprinted in the preceding chapter (p. 13):

### Journal Writing

Do you agree that many people respond with discomfort to people with disabilities? What do you feel when you see a stranger using a wheelchair: pity? sympathy? curiosity? uncertainty? admiration? fear? something else? In your journal, set down your answers to these questions as honestly as you can. What do you think causes these feelings? Consider how they are colored by your experiences with disability—whether you are disabled yourself, know someone who is disabled, or have no first-hand experience with disability.

## Suggestions for Writing

1. **FROM JOURNAL TO ESSAY**   Based on your journal reflections, write an essay that explains how your own responses to people with disabilities lead you to accept or dispute Mairs's call for depicting "disabled people in the ordinary activities of daily life."

2. Have media depictions of people with disabilities changed since Mairs wrote her essay in 1987? If so, how? If not, why? Write an essay in which you ANALYZE current media representations of disability, using specific examples to support your ideas.

3. Choose another group you think has been "effaced" in television advertising and programming—a racial, ethnic, or religious group, for instance. Write an essay detailing how and why that group is overlooked. How could representations of the group be incorporated into the media? What effects might such representation have?

4. **CRITICAL WRITING**   Reread this essay carefully. Mairs tells us about herself through details and through TONE (for example, through IRONY, intensity, and humor). Write an essay on how Mairs's self-revelations do or do not help further her THESIS.

5. **CONNECTIONS**   In "On Compassion" (p. 193), Barbara Lazear Ascher writes about the way people who are comfortable tend to respond to homeless people on the street, and she suggests that compassion must be "learned by having adversity at our window." Does what Ascher asks in relation to homeless people resemble what Mairs asks in relation to disabled people? In an essay, discuss the similarities and differences between these two writers' views of how people's attitudes could or should change.

## Audience and Purpose

We looked at AUDIENCE and PURPOSE in the previous chapter, as concerns of writers that can help us readers analyze their works. When you are *doing* the writing, considering audience and purpose moves from informative to necessary: Knowing whom you're addressing and why tells you what approach to take, what EVIDENCE to gather, how to arrange ideas, even what words to use.

You can conceive of your audience generally (your classmates? the readers of a newspaper?), but usually you'll want to think about the characteristics of readers that will affect how they respond to you:

- What do readers expect from writing like yours? A particular format or organization? Certain kinds of information? A customary level of formality?
- What do readers need to know if they are to understand you or agree with you? How much background should you provide? How thoroughly should you support your ideas? What kinds of evidence will be most effective?
- What in readers' own makeup will influence their responses? How old are they? Are they educated? Do they share your values? Are they likely to have some misconceptions about your subject?

While you are considering readers' backgrounds and inclinations, you'll also be refining your purpose. You may know early on whether you want to explain something about your subject or argue something about it — a general purpose. To be most helpful, though, your idea of purpose should include what you want readers to think or do as a result of reading your writing. For instance:

To explain two treatments for autism in young children so that readers clearly understand the similarities and differences

To defend term limits for state legislators so that readers who are now undecided on the issue will support limits

To analyze Shakespeare's *Macbeth* so that readers see the strengths as well as the flaws of the title character

To propose an online system for scheduling work shifts so that company managers decide to explore the options

We have more to say about audience and purpose in the introduction to each rhetorical method (Chaps. 4–13).


## DISCOVERING IDEAS

During the second phase of the writing process, DISCOVERY, you'll feel your way into an assignment. This is the time when you critically examine any text or image that is part of the assignment and begin to generate ideas for writing. When writing about selections in this book, you'll be reading and rereading and writing, coming to understand the work, figuring out what you think of it, figuring out what you have to *say* about it. From notes during reading to jotted phrases, lists, or half-finished paragraphs after reading, this stage should always be a writing stage. You may even produce a rough draft. The important thing is to let yourself go: Do not, above all, concern yourself with making beautiful sentences or correcting errors. Such self-consciousness at this stage will only jam the flow of thoughts. If your idea of "audience" is "teacher with sharp pencil" (not, by the way, a fair picture), then temporarily blank out your audience, too.

Several techniques can help you let go and open up during the discovery stage, among them writing in a journal, freewriting, and using the methods of development.

## Journal Writing

A JOURNAL is a notebook or tablet or computer file in which you record your thoughts *for yourself*. (Teachers sometimes assign journals and periodically collect them to see how students are doing, but even in these situations the journal is for yourself.) In keeping a journal, you don't have to worry about being understood by a reader or making mistakes: You are free to write however you want to get your thoughts down.

Kept faithfully — say, for ten or fifteen minutes a day — a journal can limber up your writing muscles, giving you more confidence and flexibility as a writer. It can also provide a place to work out personal difficulties, explore half-formed ideas, make connections between courses, or respond to reading. Here, for instance, is Rosie Anaya's initial journal entry on Nancy Mairs's "Disability":

> I think Mairs is right that disability makes a lot of people uncomfortable. I know that when I see someone in a wheelchair or on crutches I can feel pretty anxious, but that's usually because I don't know whether I should offer to help or just pretend I don't notice the disability. Honestly, I'm much more afraid of the strange woman mumbling to herself on the corner, or the man on the subway rocking back and forth in his seat. But why? It's not like they're contagious. I guess I just worry that they might lash out without warning or something.

## Freewriting

Another technique for limbering up, but more in response to specific writing assignments than as a regular habit, is *freewriting*. When freewriting, you write without stopping for ten or fifteen minutes, not halting to reread, criticize, edit, or admire. You can use partial sentences, abbreviations, question marks for uncertain words. If you can't think of anything to write about, jot "can't think" over and over until new words come (they will).

You can use this technique to find a subject for writing or to explore ideas on a subject you already have. Of course, when you've finished, you'll need to separate the promising passages from the dead ends, using those promising bits as the starting place for more freewriting or perhaps a freely written first draft.

## The Methods of Development

Since each method of development provides a different perspective on your subject, you can use the methods singly or together to discover direction, ideas, and support for the ideas. Say you already have a sense of your purpose for writing: Then you can search the methods for one or more that will help you achieve that purpose by revealing and focusing your ideas. Or say you're still in the dark about your purpose: Then you can apply each method of development systematically to throw light on your subject, as a headlight illuminates a midnight road, so that you see its possible angles.

The introductions to Chapters 4–13 suggest the purposes each method is suited for and some specific ways the method can open up your subject. For now, we've given some examples of how the methods can reveal responses, either direct or indirect, to Mairs's "Disability."

- *Narration:* Tell a story about the subject, possibly to enlighten or entertain readers or to explain something to them. Answer the journalist's questions: who, what, when, where, why, how? For instance, relate a day in the life of a person with a disability.
- *Description:* To explain or evoke the subject, focus on its look, sound, feel, smell, taste — the evidence of the senses. For instance, describe Mairs's feelings about her subject as revealed in her use of language.
- *Example:* Point to instances, or illustrations, of the subject that clarify and support your idea about it. For instance, give examples that illustrate the media's current representation of people with disabilities.
- *Comparison and contrast:* Set the subject beside something else, noting similarities or differences or both, for the purpose of either explaining or evaluating. For instance, compare and contrast characters with disabilities in two movies or TV shows.
- *Process analysis:* Explain step by step how to do something or how something works — in other words, how a sequence of actions leads to a particular result. For instance, explain a process for convincing advertisers to use people with disabilities in TV commercials.
- *Division or analysis:* Slice the subject into its parts or elements in order to show how they relate and to explain your conclusions about the subject. For instance, analyze Mairs's tone and its relation to her purpose.
- *Classification:* To show resemblances and differences among many related subjects, or the many forms of a subject, sort them into kinds or groups. For example, classify attitudes toward people with disabilities, physical and mental.
- *Cause and effect:* Explain why or what if, showing reasons for or consequences of the subject. For instance, explain how someone's life changed, and didn't change, as a result of disability.

- *Definition:* Trace a boundary around the subject to pin down its meaning. For instance, define *disability*.
- *Argument and persuasion:* Formulate an opinion or make a proposal about the subject. For instance, argue for a change in grocery or department stores to accommodate people who use wheelchairs.

## FOCUSING ON THE THESIS AND THE THESIS STATEMENT

While you're gathering ideas, begin trying to pin down your THESIS, the main idea of your writing. Without the focus of a thesis, an essay wanders and irritates and falls flat. With a focus, an essay is much more likely to click.

You may express the thesis in a sentence or two, called a THESIS STATE-MENT, like these from essays in this book:

> These were two strong men, these oddly different generals [Ulysses S. Grant and Robert E. Lee], and they represented the strengths of two conflicting currents that, through them, had come into final collision.
> —Bruce Catton, "Grant and Lee: A Study in Contrasts"

> Inanimate objects are classified into three major categories—those that don't work, those that break down and those that get lost.
> —Russell Baker, "The Plot Against People"

> A bill [to prohibit import of goods produced with children's labor] is of no use unless it goes hand in hand with programs that will offer a new life to these newly released children.
> —Chitra Divakaruni, "Live Free and Starve"

These diverse examples share a few important qualities:

- The authors assert opinions, taking positions on their subjects. They do not merely state facts, as in "Grant and Lee both signed the document ending the Civil War" or "Grant and Lee were different men."
- Each thesis statement projects a single idea. The thesis may have parts (such as Baker's three categories of objects), but the parts fit under a single umbrella idea.
- As you will see when you read the essays themselves, each thesis statement accurately forecasts the scope of its essay, neither taking on too much nor leaving out essential parts.
- Each thesis statement hints about the writer's purpose—we can tell that Catton and Baker want to explain, whereas Divakaruni wants mainly to persuade. (Explaining and persuading overlap a great deal; we're talking here about the writer's *primary* purpose.)

Every single essay in this book has a *thesis* because a central, controlling idea is a requirement of good writing. But we can give no rock-hard rules about the *thesis statement*—how long it must be or where it must appear in an essay or even whether it must appear. Indeed, the essays in this book demonstrate that writers have great flexibility in these areas, even within a given method. For your own writing, we advise stating your thesis explicitly and putting it near the beginning of your essay—at least until you've gained experience as a writer. The stated thesis will help you check that you have that necessary focus, and the early placement will tell your readers what to expect from your writing.

## DRAFTING

Sooner or later, the discovery stage yields to DRAFTING: writing out sentences and paragraphs, linking ideas, focusing them. For most writers, drafting is the occasion for exploring the relations among ideas, filling in the details to support them, beginning to work out the shape and aim of the whole. During drafting, you may clarify your purpose and your thesis, try out different arrangements of material, or experiment with tone. Sometimes, though, you may find that just spelling out thoughts into complete sentences is challenge enough for a first draft, and you'll leave issues of purpose, thesis, structure, and tone for another round.

A few suggestions for drafting:

- Give yourself time, at least a couple of hours.
- Work in a place where you won't be disturbed.
- Stay loose so that you can wander down intriguing avenues or consider changing direction altogether.
- Don't feel compelled to follow a straight path from beginning to end. If the introduction is giving you fits, skip it until later.
- Keep your eyes on what's ahead, not on the pebbles underfoot—the possible mistakes, "wrong" words, and bumpy sentences that you can attend to later. This is an important message that many inexperienced writers miss: It's okay to make mistakes. You can fix them later.

## REVISING AND EDITING

If it helps you produce writing, you may want to view your draft as a kind of dialog with readers, fulfilling their expectations, answering the questions you imagine they would ask. But some writers save this kind of thinking for the next stage, REVISION. Literally "re-seeing," revision is the price you pay for the freedom to experiment and explore. Initially the work centers on you and your material, but gradually it shifts into that transaction we spoke of earlier between you and your reader. And that means stepping outside the intense circle of you-and-the-material to see the work as a reader will, with whatever qualities you imagine that reader to have. Questions after most essays in this book ask you to analyze how the writers' ideas about their readers have influenced their writing strategies, and how you as a reader react to the writers' choices. These analyses will teach you much about responding to your own readers.

Like many writers, you will be able to concentrate better if you approach revision as at least a two-step process. First revise, focusing on fundamental, whole-essay matters such as purpose and organization; and only then edit, focusing on surface issues such as word choice and grammar. This two-step process is like inspecting a ship before it sails: First check under the water for holes to make sure the boat will stay afloat; then look above the water at what will move the boat and please the passengers, such as intact sails, sparkling hardware, and gleaming decks.

The following checklists can guide your revision and editing:

### QUESTIONS FOR REVISION

Will my purpose be clear to readers? Have I achieved it?
What is my thesis? Have I proved it?
Is the essay unified (all parts relate to the thesis)?
Is the essay coherent (the parts relate clearly)?
Will readers be able to follow the organization?
Have I given enough details, examples, and other specifics for readers to
    understand me and stay with me?
Is the tone appropriate for my purpose?
Have I used the methods of development to full advantage?

### QUESTIONS FOR EDITING

Do PARAGRAPH breaks help readers grasp related information?
Do TRANSITIONS tell readers where I am making connections, additions,
    and other changes?
Are sentences smooth and concise? Do they use PARALLELISM, EMPHASIS,
    and other techniques to clarify meaning?
Do words say what I mean, and are they as vivid as I can make them?
Are my grammar and punctuation correct?
Are any words misspelled?

## COLLABORATING

Your writing teacher may ask you to spend some time talking with your classmates, as a whole class or in small groups or pairs. You may analyze the essays in this book (perhaps answering the end-of-essay questions), read each other's journals or drafts, or plot revision strategies. Such conversation and collaboration—voicing, listening to, and arguing about ideas—can help you develop more confidence in your writing and give you a clearer sense of audience. One classmate may show you that your introduction, which you thought was lame, really worked to get her involved in your essay. Another classmate may question you in a way that helps you see how the introduction sets up expectations in the reader, expectations you're obliged to fulfill. Rosie Anaya received classmates' comments on the first draft of her paper responding to Nancy Mairs's "Disability" (see p. 43).

You may at first be anxious about collaboration: How can I judge others' writing? How can I stand others' criticism of my own writing? These are natural worries, and your teacher will try to help you with both of them—for instance, by providing a checklist to guide your critique of your classmates' writing. (The revision checklist on the previous page works for reading others' drafts as well as your own.) With practice and plentiful feedback, you'll soon appreciate how much you're learning about writing and what a good effect that knowledge has on your work. You're writing for an audience, after all, and you can't beat the immediate feedback of a live one.

## AN ESSAY-IN-PROGRESS

In the following pages, you have a chance to watch Rosie Anaya as she develops an essay through journal notes and several drafts. Her topic is the third of the writing suggestions given on page 33—about a group that has been "effaced" by the media—which she had already started exploring in her journal (p. 35). Anaya's journal notes through each stage enlighten us about her thinking as she proceeds through the writing process.

### Reading and Drafting

#### *Journal Notes on Reading*

"For months now I've been consciously searching for representation of myself in the media" (¶ 1)

- "representation of myself" = a person who just happens to have a disability (Mairs has multiple sclerosis) living a full, normal life

- Media shows disability consuming a character's life or doesn't show disability at all

Haven't the media gotten a little better about showing people with disabilities since Mairs wrote in 1987? Lots of TV shows have characters who just happen to use canes or wheelchairs.

"Effaced" (¶ 5) means to erase, or to make something disappear. I see why Mairs has a problem with this: I would be bothered, too, if I didn't see people like me represented in the media. I would feel left out, probably hurt, maybe angry.

Mairs is doing more: Invisibility is a problem for healthy people too — anybody could become disabled and wouldn't know that people with disabilities live full, normal lives (¶ 7).

Interesting that Mairs mentions emotional health more than once:

- "self-degradation and a subtle kind of self-alienation" (¶ 6)
- "you might feel as though you don't exist, in any meaningful social sense" (¶ 6)
- "the physically and emotionally complex world you live in" (¶ 7)
- "it will be a good bit easier psychologically if . . ." (¶ 7)

References to feelings and psychology raise a question about people with mental disabilities, like depression or autism or schizophrenia. How are they represented by the media?

- Definitely not as regular people with "a normal characteristic, one that complicates but does not ruin human existence" (¶ 7).
- Stories in the news about emotionally disturbed people who go over the edge and hurt or even kill people. And CSI, Law and Order, etc. always using some kind of psychological disorder to explain why someone committed a crime.

I think I have a start for an essay that answers question 3, about other minority groups that are "effaced" in the media. Except the problem with mental illness isn't just invisibility — it's also negative stereotyping. What if you're either not being represented at all, or you're represented as a danger to yourself and others? That's got to be even worse.

## *First Draft*

Nancy Mairs is upset with television and movies that don't show physical disability as a feature of normal life. She says the media shows disability consuming a character's life or it doesn't show disability at all, and she wants to see "representation of myself in the media, especially television" (p. 00).

Mairs makes a convincing argument that the media should portray physical disability as part of everyday life because "effacement" leaves the rest of us unprepared to cope in the case that we should eventually become disabled ourselves. As she explains it, anybody could become disabled, but because we rarely see people with disabilities living full, normal lives on tv, we assume that becoming disabled means life is pretty much over (p. 00). It's been more than two decades since Mairs wrote her essay, and she seems to have gotten her wish. Plenty of characters on television today who have a disability are not defined by it. But psychological disabilities are disabilities too, and they have never been shown "as a normal characteristic, one that complicates but does not ruin human existence" (p. 00).

Television routinely portrays people with mental illness as threats to themselves and to others. Think about all those stories on the evening news about a man suffering from bipolar disorder who went on a shooting spree before turning his gun on himself, or a mother who drowned her own children in the throes of postpartum depression, or a depressed teenager who commits suicide. Such events are tragic, no doubt, but although the vast majority of people with these illnesses hurt nobody, the news implies that they're all potential killers.

Fictional shows, too, are always using some kind of psychological disorder to explain why someone committed a crime. Last month on Law and Order an Iraq war veteran committed murder because he couldn't cope with his memories of the war and lashed out at a homeless person. And the last season of CSI kept coming back to a story about the "miniature killer." Over several episodes, Gil Grissom, Sara Seidel, Catherine Willows, and Nick Stokes found perfect miniature replicas of crime scenes and tried to figure out who was so obsessive/compulsive that they would go to so much trouble to re-create their crime scenes in elaborately crafted dollhouses. After chasing down a few false leads, they were surprised to discover that the serial killer was a woman whose father had rejected her because she pushed her little sister out of a treehouse and killed her when she was only six years old. She spent her childhood being shunted around between foster homes, where nobody wanted her either. She was even described by one former foster parent as "broken"! Meanwhile, the father projected his love for his dead daughter onto his ventriloquism dummy, making him seem more than a little mentally ill himself.

It is my belief that the presentation of psychological disability may do worse than the "effacement" of disability that bothered Mairs. People with mental illness are discouraged from seeking help and are sent deeper into isolation and despair. This negative stereotype hurts us all.

## Revising

### *Peer Responses to First Draft*

Your essay is fascinating. I never really thought about how mental illness is treated on tv before! But your introduction is pretty abrupt, and what is your thesis? I don't see it anywhere. Also, the essay seems to kind of fizzle out at the end.

—Liz Kingham

You do a good job showing how TV shows stereotype people with mental illness, but the CSI example goes on a bit long — it's hard to see how it all relates. Also, can you give some examples of the characters with physical disabilities you mention in paragraph 2? All the ones I can think of are from shows that have been canceled, so I wonder if the problem has really improved after all.

—Hahlil Jones

Your idea is really original, but I'm having trouble following how it connects to Mairs's argument. Could you tie the two issues together more clearly?

—Maria Child

### *Journal Notes on First Draft*

I thought I did a good job explaining myself, but Maria's right: I assume that other people interpreted Mairs the same way I did, and that's not necessarily true. Need to go through my essay and spell out what her ideas are — and then show how the problems she identified are even more important in the case of mental illness.

Hahlil's right about the CSI example — I got carried away with it. I only need to make the point that the show emphasizes the killer's mental disturbance.

The introduction and conclusion need a lot of work: a less abrupt start, a thesis statement, and a fuller conclusion that says why the media should improve the way psychological disability is portrayed — more with Mairs's point about the impact of "effacement" on "Temporarily Abled People" might help with that.

Also need to add page numbers from Mairs and work cited at end.

*Revised Draft*

Mental Illness on Television

In her essay "Disability" Nancy Mairs ~~is upset with~~ argues that television and movies ~~that don't~~ fail to show physical disability as a feature of normal life. Instead, Mairs ~~She~~ says, the media shows disability consuming a character's life or it doesn't show disability at all~~, and she wants to see "representation of myself in the media, especially television"~~ (~~p. no.~~ 13–14). But Mairs wrote her essay in 1987. Since then the situation has actually improved for physical disability. At the same time, another group — those with mental illness — have come to suffer even worse representation.

~~Mairs makes a convincing argument~~ Mairs's purpose in writing her essay was to persuade her readers that the media should portray physical disability as part of everyday life because ~~"effacement"~~ otherwise it denies or misrepresents disability, and it leaves ~~the rest of us~~ "Temporarily Abled Persons" (those without disability for now) unprepared to cope in the case that ~~we~~ they should eventually become disabled ~~ourselves~~ themselves (14–15). ~~As she explains it, anybody could become disabled, but because we rarely see people with disabilities living full, normal lives on tv, we assume that becoming disabled means life is pretty much over (p. 00). It's been more than two decades since Mairs wrote her essay, and~~ Two decades later, Mairs ~~she~~ seems to have gotten her wish. Plenty of characters on television today who have a disability are not defined by it. The title character on House walks with a cane, Heidi Petrelli of Heroes is paraplegic (so is Joe Swanson of Family Guy); Jimmy on South Park uses crutches. Even the medical examiner on CSI, Al Robbins, has prosthetic legs.

However, the media depiction of one type of disability is, if anything, worse than it was two decades ago. Although Mairs doesn't address mental illness in "Disability," mental illness falls squarely into the misrepresentation she criticizes. ~~But p~~ Psychological disabilities are disabilities too, ~~and~~ but they have never been shown "as a normal characteristic, one that complicates but does not ruin human existence" (~~p. no.~~ 15). People who cope with a disability such as depression, bipolar disorder, or obsessive-compulsive disorder as parts of their lives do not see themselves in the media; those who don't have a psychological disability now but may someday do not see that mental illness is usually a condition they can live with.

The depictions of mental illness actually go beyond Mairs's concerns, as the media actually exploits it. Television routinely portrays people with mental illness as threats to themselves and to others. Think about all those stories on the evening news about a man suffering from bipolar disorder who went on a shooting spree before turning his gun on himself, or a mother who drowned her own children in the throes of postpartum depression, or a depressed teenager who commits suicide. ~~Such events are tragic, no doubt, but although the vast majority of people with these illnesses hurt nobody, the news implies that they're all potential killers.~~ Fictional shows, too, are always using some kind of psychological disorder to explain why someone committed a crime. Last month on <u>Law and Order</u> an Iraq war veteran committed murder because he couldn't cope with his memories of the war and lashed out at a homeless person. And on the last season of <u>CSI</u> ~~kept coming back to a story about the "miniature killer." Over several episodes, Gil Grissom, Sara Seidel, Catherine Willows, and Nick Stokes found perfect miniature replicas of crime scenes and tried to figure out who was so obsessive/compulsive that they would go to so much trouble to re-create their crime scenes in elaborately crafted dollhouses. After chasing down a few false leads, they were surprised to discover that the~~ a serial killer ~~was~~ turns out to be a deranged woman ~~whose~~ who was rejected by her father and driven by delusions since childhood. ~~had rejected her because she pushed her little sister out of a treehouse and killed her when she was only six years old. She spent her childhood being shunted around between foster homes, where nobody wanted her either.~~ She was even described by one former foster parent as "broken"! ~~Meanwhile, the father projected his love for his dead daughter onto his ventriloquism dummy, making him seem more than a little mentally ill himself.~~

These programs highlight mental illness to get viewers' attention. But the media is also telling us that the proper response to people with mental illness is to be afraid of them. Mairs argues that invisibility in the media can cause people with disabilities to feel unattractive or inappropriate (14–15). It is my belief that the presentation of psychological disability may do worse. ~~than the "effacement" of disability that bothered Mairs.~~ People with mental illness are discouraged from seeking help and are sent deeper into isolation and despair. Those feelings are often cited as the fuel for violent outbursts, but ironically the media portrays such violence as inevitable with mental illness. ~~This negative stereotype hurts us all.~~

More complex and varied depictions of all kinds of impairments, both physical and mental, will weaken the negative stereotypes that are harmful to all of us. With mental illness especially, we would all be better served if psychological disability was portrayed by the media as a part of everyday life. It's not a crime.

Work Cited

Mairs, Nancy. "Disability." The Bedford Reader. Ed. X. J. Kennedy, Dorothy M.
       Kennedy, and Jane E. Aaron. 10th ed. Boston: Bedford, 2009. 13–15.

## Editing

### *Journal Notes on Revised Draft*

This is much better now that I've clarified my thesis and connected my argument better with Mairs. She adds more authority to my own point. The examples of mental illness on TV are much tighter. And the conclusion explains why this topic is important — much needed.

There's still some work to do, though. Need to fix some errors ("media" is plural) and do something about awkward sentences. Maybe give a little more explanation in a couple of places too.

### *Edited Paragraph*

Mairs's purpose in ~~writing her essay~~ "Disability" ~~was~~ is to persuade ~~her~~ readers that the media should portray physical disability as part of everyday life because otherwise ~~it~~ they ~~denies~~ deny or misrepresent~~s~~ disability~~,~~ and ~~it~~ leaves "Temporarily Abled Persons" (those without disability, for now) unprepared to cope ~~in the case that they should eventually~~ if they become disabled ~~themselves~~

(14–15). Two decades later, Mairs seems to have gotten her wish. ~~Plenty of~~ for characters ~~on television today~~ who have a disability but are not defined by it. The title character on <u>House</u>, for example, walks with a cane~~,~~. Heidi Petrelli of <u>Heroes</u> ~~is paraplegic (so is~~ and Joe Swanson of <u>Family Guy</u>~~)~~; are both paraplegic. Jimmy on <u>South Park</u> uses crutches. ~~Even~~ And ~~the~~ medical examiner Al Robbins on <u>CSI</u>~~, Al Robbins,~~ has prosthetic legs. The media still have a long way to go in representing physical disability, but they have made progress.


## Final Draft

Rosie Anaya

Professor DeBeer

English 102A

2 February 2007

Mental Illness on Television

In her essay "Disability," Nancy Mairs argues that the media, such as television and movies, fail to show physical disability as a feature of normal life. Instead, Mairs says, they show disability consuming a character's life or they don't show disability at all. Mairs wrote her essay in 1987, and since then the situation has actually improved for depiction of physical disability. At the same time, another group — those with mental illness — has come to suffer even worse representation.

Mairs's purpose in "Disability" is to persuade readers that the media should portray physical disability as part of everyday life because otherwise they deny or misrepresent disability and leave "Temporarily Abled Persons" (those without disability, for now) unprepared to cope if they become disabled (14–15). Two decades later, Mairs seems to have gotten her wish for characters who have a disability but are not defined by it. The title character on <u>House</u>, for example, walks with a cane. Heidi Petrelli of <u>Heroes</u> and Joe Swanson of <u>Family Guy</u> are both paraplegic. Jimmy on <u>South Park</u> uses crutches. And medical examiner Al Robbins on <u>CSI</u> has prosthetic legs. The media still have a long way to go in representing physical disability, but they have made progress.

*Introduction summarizes Mairs's essay and sets up Anaya's thesis.*

*Thesis statement establishes Anaya's main idea.*

*Page numbers in parentheses refer to "Work Cited" at end of paper. (See also p. 63.)*

*Examples provide support for Anaya's analysis.*

However, in depicting one type of disability, the media are, if anything, worse than they were two decades ago. Mairs doesn't address mental illness, but it falls squarely into the misrepresentation she criticizes. It has never been shown, in Mairs's words, "as a normal characteristic, one that complicates but does not ruin human existence" (15). Thus people who cope with a psychological disability such as depression, bipolar disorder, or obsessive-compulsive disorder as part of their lives do not see themselves in the media. And those who don't have a psychological disability now but may someday do not see that mental illness is usually a condition one can live with.

*Comparison and contrast extends Mairs's idea to Anaya's new subject.*

*Follow-up comments explain what quotation contributes to Anaya's thesis. (See also p. 53.)*

Unfortunately, the depictions of mental illness also go beyond Mairs's concerns, because the media actually exploit it. Television routinely portrays people with mental illness as threats to themselves and to others. TV news features stories about a man suffering from bipolar disorder who goes on a shooting spree before turning his gun on himself, a mother with postpartum depression who drowns her own children, and a teenager with depression who commits suicide. Fictional programs, especially crime dramas, regularly use mental illness to develop their plots. On Law and Order an Iraq war veteran with post-traumatic stress disorder commits murder, and on CSI a serial killer turns out to be a deranged woman — described by a former foster parent as "broken" — who was rejected by her father and has been driven by delusions since childhood.

*Topic sentence introduces new idea.*

*Examples provide evidence for Anaya's point.*

These programs and many others like them highlight mental illness to get viewers' attention, and they strongly imply that the proper response is fear. Mairs argues that the invisibility of physical disability in the media can cause people with disabilities to feel unattractive or inappropriate (14–15), but the presentation of psychological disability may do worse. It can prevent people with mental illness from seeking help and send them deeper into isolation and despair. Those feelings are often cited as the fuel for violent outbursts, but ironically the media portray such violence as inevitable with mental illness.

*Paraphrase explains one of Mairs's points in Anaya's own words. (See also p. 54.)*

*Cause and effect applies Mairs's idea to Anaya's thesis.*

Seeing more complex and varied depictions of people living with all kinds of impairments, physical and mental, can weaken the negative stereotypes that are harmful to all of us. With men-

*Conclusion reasserts thesis and explains the broader implications of the subject.*

tal illness especially, we would all be better served if the media would make an effort to portray psychological disability as a part of everyday life, not a crime.

### Work Cited

Mairs, Nancy. "Disability." The Bedford Reader. Ed. X. J. Kennedy, Dorothy M. Kennedy, and Jane E. Aaron. 10th ed. Boston: Bedford, 2009. 13–15.

"Work Cited" begins on a new page and gives complete publication information for Mairs's essay. (See also p. 65.)

# 3

---

# ACADEMIC WRITING

Reading critically (Chap. 1) and writing effectively (Chap. 2) are both key skills in academic writing, which calls on your ability to write critically about what you read. The academic disciplines—history, psychology, chemistry, and the like—have different subjects and approaches, but they share the common goal of using reading and writing to build and exchange knowledge.

For a taste of academic knowledge building, you can read some of the selections in this book, such as Rosie Anaya's "The Best Kept Secret on Campus" at the end of this chapter, George Chauncey's "The Legacy of Antigay Discrimination" (p. 260), Bella DePaulo's "The Myth of Doomed Kids" (p. 350), Laila Ayad's "The Capricious Camera" (p. 358), Marie Javdani's "*Plata o Plomo*: Silver or Lead" (p. 448), and Colleen Wenke's "Too Much Pressure" (p. 533). You may notice that these essays have in common certain features of academic writing:

- Each writer attempts to gain readers' agreement with his or her debatable idea—or THESIS—about the subject.
- To support their theses, the writers provide EVIDENCE from one or more other texts. (Ayad's subject, a photograph, is a kind of text.)

- The writers do not merely SUMMARIZE their sources; they grapple with them. They ANALYZE meaning, infer ASSUMPTIONS, and SYNTHESIZE the texts' and their own views—in short, they read and write critically.
- The writers acknowledge their use of sources with documentation that is appropriate for the discipline each is writing in—footnotes in some cases, parenthetical citations and a bibliography in other cases.
- Each writer assumes an educated audience—one that can be counted on to read critically in turn. The writers state their ideas clearly, provide information readers need to analyze those ideas, and organize ideas and evidence effectively. Further, they approach their subjects seriously and discuss evidence and opposing views fairly.

This chapter will help you achieve such academic writing yourself by responding directly to what you read (below), integrating source material into your ideas (p. 54), orchestrating multiple sources to develop and support your ideas (p. 56), avoiding plagiarism (p. 60), and documenting sources (p. 62). The chapter concludes with a sample research paper (p. 74).

## RESPONDING TO A TEXT

The essay by Rosie Anaya in the previous chapter (p. 47) illustrates one type of critical response: Anaya summarizes Nancy Mairs's essay "Disability" (p. 13), explores its implications, and uses it as a springboard to her own related subject, which she supports with personal observation and experience. Just as Anaya responds to Mairs's essay, so you can respond to any essay in this book or for that matter to anything you read or see. Using evidence from your own experiences, reading, and viewing, you can take a variety of approaches:

- Like Anaya, agree with and extend the author's ideas, providing additional examples or exploring related ideas.
- Agree with the author on some points, but disagree on others.
- Disagree with the author on one of his or her key points.
- Explain how the author achieves a particular EFFECT, such as enlisting your sympathy or sparking your anger.
- Judge the overall effectiveness of the essay—for instance, how well the writer supports the thesis, whether the argument is convincing, or whether the author succeeds in his or her stated or unstated purpose.

These suggestions and this discussion assume that you are responding to a single work, but of course you may take on two or even more works at the same time. You might, for instance, use the method of COMPARISON AND CONTRAST to show how two stories are alike or different or to find your own way between two arguments on the same issue.

## Forming a Response

Some reading you do will spark an immediate reaction, maybe because you disagree or agree strongly right from the start. Other reading may require a more gradual entry into what the author is saying and what you think about it. At the same time, you may have an assignment that narrows the scope of your response—for instance, by asking you to look at TONE or some other element of the work or by asking you to agree or disagree with the author's thesis.

Whatever your initial reaction or your assignment, you can use the tools discussed in Chapter 1 to generate and structure your response: summary, analysis, inference, synthesis, evaluation. (See pp. 17–20.) Your first goal is to understand the work thoroughly, both what it says outright and what it assumes and implies. For this step, you'll certainly need to make notes of some sort: For instance, those by Rosie Anaya on pages 40–41 include summaries of Mairs's essay, key quotations from it, interpretations of its meaning, and the beginnings of Anaya's ideas in response. Such notes may grow increasingly focused as you refine your response and return to the reading to interpret it further and gather additional passages to discuss.

## Synthesizing Your Own and Another's Views

Synthesis, as we note in Chapter 1, is the core of academic writing: Knowledge builds as writers bring their own perspectives to bear on what others have written, making their own contributions to what has come before.

When you write about a text, your perspective on it will be your thesis—the main point you have in response to the text or (if you take off in another direction) as a result of reading the text. As you develop the thesis, always keep your ideas front and center, pulling in material from the text as needed for support. In each paragraph, your idea should come first and, usually, last: State the idea, use evidence from the reading to support it, and then interpret the evidence. (As a way to encourage this final interpretation, some writing teachers ask students not to end paragraphs with source citations.)

You can see a paragraph structured like this in Rosie Anaya's essay "Mental Illness on Television" in the previous chapter:

> However, in depicting one type of disability, the media are, if anything, worse than they were two decades ago. Mairs doesn't address mental illness, but it falls squarely into the misrepresentation she criticizes. It has never been shown, in Mairs's words, "as a normal characteristic, one that complicates but does not ruin human existence" (15). Thus people who cope with a psychological disability such as depression, bipolar disorder, or obsessive-compulsive disorder as part of their lives do not see themselves in the media.

And those who don't have a psychological disability now but may someday
do not see that mental illness is usually a condition one can live with.

## INTEGRATING SOURCE MATERIAL

One key to synthesis is deciding how to present evidence from your
reading and then working the evidence into your own text smoothly and
informatively.

### Summary, Paraphrase, and Quotation

When you summarize or paraphrase a source, you express its ideas in your
own words. when you quote, you use the source's exact words, in quotation
marks. *All summaries, paraphrases, and quotations must be acknowledged in source
citations.* See pages 60–62 on avoiding plagiarism and pages 62–73 on MLA
documentation.

#### *Summary*

With SUMMARY you use your own words to condense a paragraph, an
entire article, or even a book into a few lines that convey the source's essential meaning. We discuss summary as a reading technique on page 17, and
the advice and examples there apply here as well. When responding to a text,
you may use brief summaries to catch readers up on the gist of the author's
argument or a significant point in the argument. Here, for example, is a summary of Barbara Lazear Ascher's "On Compassion," which appears on pages
193–95.

> SUMMARY    Ascher shows how contact with the homeless can be unsettling
> and depressing. Yet she also suggests that these encounters are useful because
> they can teach others to be more compassionate (193–95).

Notice how the summary identifies the source author and page numbers and
uses words that are *not* the author's. (Any of Ascher's distinctive phrasing
would have to be placed in quotation marks.)

#### *Paraphrase*

When you PARAPHRASE, you restate a specific passage in your own words.
Paraphrase adheres more closely than summary to the source author's line of
thought, so it's useful to present an author's ideas or data in detail. Generally,
use paraphrase rather than quotation for this purpose, since paraphrase shows

that you're in command of your evidence and lets your own voice come through. (See below for when to use quotations.) Here is a quotation from Ascher's essay and a paraphrase of it:

> ORIGINAL QUOTATION   "Could it be that the homeless, like [Greek drama-tists], are reminding us of our common humanity? Of course, there is a dif-ference. This play doesn't end—and the players can't go home."

> PARAPHRASE   Ascher points out an important distinction between the New York City homeless and the characters in Greek tragedies: The homeless are living real lives, not performing on a stage (195).

As with a summary, note that a paraphrase cites the original author and page number. Here is another example of paraphrase, this from an essay about immigration by David Cole:

> ORIGINAL QUOTATION   "We stand to be collectively judged by our treat-ment of immigrants, who may appear to be 'other' now but in a generation will be 'us.'"

> PARAPHRASE   Cole argues that the way the United States deals with immi-grants now will come back to haunt it when those immigrants are eventually integrated into mainstream society (110).

### Quotation

Quotations from sources can both support and enliven your own ideas— *if* you choose them well. When analyzing a primary source, such as a work of literature or a historical document, you may need to quote many passages in order to give the flavor of the author's words and evidence for your analysis. With secondary sources, however, too many quotations will clutter an essay and detract from your own voice. Select quotations that are relevant to the point you are making, that are concise and pithy, and that use lively, bold, or original language. Sentences that lack distinction—for example, a statement providing statistics on economic growth between 2000 and 2007—should be paraphrased.

Always enclose quotations in quotation marks and cite the source author and page number.

## Introduction of Source Material

With synthesis, you're always making it clear to readers what your idea is and how the evidence from your reading supports that idea. To achieve this clarity, you want to fit summaries, paraphrases, and quotations into your sen-tences and show what you make of them.

In the passage below, the writer drops a quotation awkwardly into her sentence and doesn't clarify how the quotation relates to her idea.

> NOT INTRODUCED    The problem of homelessness is not decreasing, and "It is impossible to insulate ourselves against what is at our very doorstep" (Ascher 195).

In the following revision, however, the writer indicates with "As Ascher says" that she is using the quotation to reinforce her point. This SIGNAL PHRASE also links the quotation to the writer's sentence.

> INTRODUCED    The problem of homelessness is not decreasing, nor is our awareness of it, however much we wish otherwise. As Ascher says, "It is impossible to insulate ourselves against what is at our very doorstep" (195).

You can introduce source material into your sentence by interpreting it and by mentioning the author in your text—both techniques illustrated in the previous example. The signal phrase "As Ascher says" has a number of variations:

> According to one authority . . .
>
> John Eng maintains that . . .
>
> The author of an important study, Hilda Brown, observes that . . .
>
> Ascher, the author of "On Compassion," has a different view, claiming . . .

For variety, such a phrase can also fall elsewhere in the quotation.

> "It is impossible," Ascher says, "to insulate ourselves against what is at our very doorstep" (195).

When you omit something from a quotation, signal the omission with the three spaced periods of an ellipsis mark as shown:

> "It is impossible to insulate ourselves. . . ," says Ascher (195).
>
> In Ascher's view, "Compassion . . . must be learned . . ." (195).

## WRITING FROM RESEARCH

Responding to a reading—thinking critically about it and synthesizing its ideas into your own—prepares you for the source-based writing that will occupy you for much of your academic career. In this kind of writing, you test and support your thesis by exploring and orchestrating a range of opinions and evidence found in multiple sources. The writing is source *based* but not source *dominated:* As when responding to a single work, your critical reading and your views set the direction and govern the final presentation.

## Evaluating Sources

When examining multiple works for possible use in your paper, you of course want each one to be relevant to your subject and to your thesis. But you also want it to be reliable—that is, based on good evidence, carefully reasoned. To evaluate relevance and reliability, you'll depend on your critical-reading skills of analysis, inference, and synthesis to answer a series of questions:

- What is the PURPOSE of the source, and who is the source's intended AUDIENCE?
- Is the material a primary or a secondary source?
- Is the author an expert? What are his or her credentials?
- Does the author's bias affect the reliability of his or her argument?
- Does the author support his or her argument with EVIDENCE that is complete and up to date?

### *Purpose and Audience*

The potential sources you find may have been written for a variety of reasons—for instance, to inform the public, to publish new research, to promote a product or service, to influence readers' opinions about a particular issue. While the first two of these purposes might lead to a balanced approach to the subject, the second two should raise yellow caution flags: Watch for bias that undermines the source's reliability.

A source's intended audience can suggest relevance. Was the work written for general readers? Then it may provide a helpful overview but not much detail. Was the work written for specialists? Then it will probably cover the topic in depth, but it may be difficult to understand.

### *Primary Versus Secondary Sources*

Primary sources are works by people who conducted or saw events first-hand. They include research reports, eyewitness accounts, diaries, and personal essays as well as novels, poems, and other works of literature. Secondary sources, in contrast, present and analyze the information in primary sources and include histories, reviews, and surveys of a field. Both types of source can be useful in research writing. For example, if you were writing about the debate over the assassination of President John F. Kennedy, you might seek an overview in books that discuss the evidence and propose theories about what happened—secondary sources. But you would be remiss not to read eyewitness accounts and law-enforcement documents—the primary sources.

### Author's Credentials and Bias

Before you use a source to support your ideas, investigate the author's background to be sure that he or she is trustworthy. Look for biographical information in the introduction or preface of a book or in a note at the beginning or end of an article. Is the author an expert on the topic? Do other writers cite the author of your source in their work?

Investigating the author's background and credentials will probably uncover any bias as well — that is, the author's preference for a particular view of an issue. Actually, bias itself is not a problem: Everyone has a unique outlook created by experience, training, and even research techniques. What does matter is whether the author deals frankly with his or her bias and argues reasonably despite it. (See Chap. 13 for a discussion of reasoning.)

### Evidence

Look for strong and convincing evidence to support the ideas in a source: facts, examples, reported experience, expert opinions. A source that doesn't muster convincing evidence, or much evidence at all, is not a reliable source. For very current topics, such as in medicine or technology, the source's ideas and evidence should be as up to date as possible.

## Working with Online Sources

You have two paths to online sources: the Web site of your school's library and a public search engine such as *Google* or *Yahoo!* Always start with the library path: It leads to scholarly journals, reputable newspapers, and other sources that you can trust because they have passed through filters of verification, editing, and library review. The same is not necessarily true of online sources you reach directly. Anyone can put anything on the Internet, so you're as likely to find the rantings of an extremist or an advertisement posing as science as you are to find reasonable opinions and scholarly research.

Use the criteria discussed above — gauging purpose, audience, bias, and other factors — for all online sources, including those found through the library. But broaden your evaluation when considering sources you reach directly.

### Authorship or Sponsorship

Often, you won't be able to tell easily, or at all, who put a potential source on the Internet and thus whether that author or sponsor is credible and reliable. Sometimes an abbreviation in an electronic address contains a clue to the origin of a source: *edu* for educational institution, *gov* for government body, *org* for nonprofit organization, *com* for commercial organization. More specific background on the author or sponsor may require digging. On Web sites look for pages that have information about the author or sponsor or links to such information on other sites. On blogs and in discussion groups, ask anonymous authors for information about themselves. If you can't identify an author or a sponsor at all, you probably should not use the source.

### Links or References to Sources

Most reliable sources will acknowledge borrowed evidence and ideas and tell you where you can find them. Some but not all online sources will do the same: A Web site, for instance, may provide links to its sources. Check out source citations that you find to be sure they represent a range of views. Be suspicious of any online work that doesn't acknowledge sources at all.

### Currency

Online sources tend to be more current than print sources, which can actually be a disadvantage: The most current information may not have been tested by others and so may not be reliable. Always seek to verify recent information in other online sources or in print sources.

If they aren't tended regularly by their authors or sponsors, online sources can also be deceptive—that is, they may seem current but actually be out of date. Look for a date of copyright, publication, or last revision to gauge currency. If you don't find a date (and often you won't), compare the source with others you know to be recent before using its information.

## Synthesizing Multiple Sources

In research writing as in response writing, your views should predominate over those of others. You decide which sources to use, how to treat them, and what conclusions to draw from them in order to test and support your thesis. In your writing, this thinking about sources' merits and relevance should be evident to readers. Here, for example, is a paragraph from Rosie Anaya's research paper at the end of this chapter. Notice how Anaya states her idea at the outset, guides us through the presentation of evidence from sources, and finally concludes by tying the evidence back to her idea.

Despite the prevalence of depression and related disorders on campus, however, most students avoid seeking help when they need it. The American Psychiatric Association maintains that most mental health issues—

depression especially—can be managed or overcome with treatment by therapy and/or medication. But among students with diagnosed depression, according to the American College Health Association, a mere 26 percent get therapy and only 37 percent take medication (204). One reason for such low numbers can be found in a survey conducted by mtvU, a resource network for college students, and the Jed Foundation, an organization dedicated to reducing suicide among college students: Only 22 percent of students would be willing to ask for help even if they were certain they needed it, because they perceive mental illness as embarrassing and shameful (2–3). Thus students who need help suffer additional pain—and no treatment—because they fear the stigma of mental illness.

This paragraph also illustrates other techniques of synthesis discussed in the previous section:

- In her own words, Anaya paraphrases the data and ideas of the sources, stressing her own voice and her mastery of the source material. (See p. 54.)
- Anaya integrates each paraphrase into her sentences with a signal phrase that names the source author and tells readers how the borrowed material relates to her idea. (See p. 55.)

Notice one other important feature of Anaya's paragraph as well: It clearly indicates what material Anaya has borrowed and where she borrowed it from. Such source citation is crucial to avoid plagiarism, the subject of the next section. The MLA citation style that Anaya uses is discussed on pages 62–73.

## AVOIDING PLAGIARISM

Academic knowledge building depends on the integrity and trust of its participants. When you write in college, your readers expect you to distinguish your own contributions from those of others, honestly acknowledging material that originated elsewhere. If you do otherwise—if you copy another's idea, data, or even wording without acknowledgment—then you steal that person's intellectual property. Called PLAGIARISM, this theft is a serious and often punishable offense.

### Examples and Revisions

For a blatant example of plagiarism, look at the following use of a quotation from Barbara Lazear Ascher's essay "On Compassion":

ORIGINAL QUOTATION    "Could it be that the homeless, like [Greek dramatists], are reminding us of our common humanity? Of course, there is a difference. This play doesn't end—and the players can't go home."

PLAGIARISM   The homeless are like the Greek dramatists in that they remind us of our common humanity, but of course now the players can't go home.

By not acknowledging Ascher at all, the plagiarizing writer takes claim for her idea and for much of her wording. A source citation would help—at least the idea would be credited—but still the expression of the idea would be stolen because there's no indication that it's Ascher's. Here is an acceptable revision:

CITATION AND QUOTATION MARKS   Ascher suggests that "the homeless, like [Greek dramatists], are reminding us of our common humanity," although now "the players can't go home" (195).

Plagiarism can be more subtle, too, as in the following attempt to paraphrase a quotation by David Cole:

ORIGINAL QUOTATION   "We stand to be collectively judged by our treatment of immigrants, who may appear to be 'other' now but in a generation will be 'us.'"

PLAGIARISM   Cole argues that we will be judged as a group by how we treat immigrants, who seem to be different now but eventually will be the same (110).

Even though the writer identifies Cole as the source of the information, much of the language and the sentence structure are also Cole's. In a paraphrase or summary, it's not enough to change a few words—"collectively" to "as a group," "they may appear to be 'other'" to "they may seem different," "in a generation" to "eventually." A paraphrase or summary must express the original idea in an entirely new way, both in word choice and in sentence structure, as in this acceptable paraphrase seen earlier in the chapter:

PARAPHRASE   Cole argues that the way the United States deals with immigrants now will come back to haunt it when those immigrants are eventually integrated into mainstream society (110).

## Plagiarism and the Internet

The Internet has made plagiarism both easier and riskier. Whether accidentally or deliberately, you can download source material directly into your own document with a few clicks of a mouse. And you can buy complete papers from term-paper sites. *Using downloaded material without credit, even accidentally, or turning in someone else's work as your own, even if you paid for it, is plagiarism.*

The chances of being caught plagiarizing from the Internet have also increased. Teachers can use search engines and plagiarism-detection programs to match phrases in students' papers with the same words anywhere on the Internet.

## Common Knowledge

Not all information from sources must be cited. Some falls under the category of common knowledge—facts so widely known or agreed upon that they are not attributable to a specific source. The statement "World War II ended after the United States dropped atomic bombs on Hiroshima and Nagasaki, Japan" is an obvious example: Most people recognize this statement as true. But some lesser-known information is also common knowledge. You may not know that President Dwight Eisenhower coined the term *military-industrial complex* during his 1961 farewell address; still, you could easily discover the information in encyclopedias, in books and articles about Eisenhower, and in contemporary newspaper accounts. The prevalence of the information and the fact that it is used elsewhere without source citation tell you that it's common knowledge.

In contrast, a scholar's argument that Eisenhower waited too long to criticize the defense industry, or the president's own comments on the subject in his diary, or an opinion from a Defense Department report in 1959—any of these needs to be credited. Unlike common knowledge, each of them remains the property of its author.

# SOURCE CITATION USING MLA STYLE

On the following pages we explain the documentation style of the Modern Language Association, as described in the *MLA Handbook for Writers of Research Papers*, 6th edition (2003). This style—used in English, foreign languages, and some other humanities—involves a brief parenthetical citation in the text that refers to an entry in a list of works cited at the end of the text:

PARENTHETICAL TEXT CITATION

The homeless may be to us what tragic heroes were to the ancient Greeks (Ascher 195).

ENTRY IN LIST OF WORKS CITED

Ascher, Barbara Lazear. "On Compassion." The Bedford Reader. Ed. X. J. Kennedy, Dorothy M. Kennedy, and Jane E. Aaron. 10th ed. Boston: Bedford, 2009. 193–95.

By providing the author's name and page number in your text citation, you give the reader just enough information to find the source in the list of works cited and then find the place in the source where the borrowed material appears.

## MLA Parenthetical Citations

When citing sources in your text, you have two options:

- You can identify both the author and the page number within parentheses, as in the Ascher example on the preceding page.
- You can introduce the author's name into your own sentence and use the parentheses only for the page number, as here:

Wilson points out that sharks, which have existed for 350 million years, are now more diverse than ever (301).

### A work with two or three authors

More than 90 percent of the hazardous waste produced in the United States comes from seven major industries, all energy-intensive (Romm and Curtis 70).

### A work with more than three authors

With more than three authors, name all the authors, or name only the first author followed by "et al." ("and others"). Use the same form in your list of works cited.

Gilman herself created the misconception that doctors tried to ban her story "The Yellow Wallpaper" when it appeared in 1892 (Dock, Allen, Palais, and Tracy 61).

Gilman herself created the misconception that doctors tried to ban her story "The Yellow Wallpaper" when it appeared in 1892 (Dock et al. 61).

### An entire work

Reference to an entire work does not require a page number.

Postman argues that television is destructive because of the nature of the medium itself.

### An electronic source

Most electronic sources can be cited like print sources, by author's name or, if there is no author, by title. If a source numbers screens or paragraphs instead of pages, give the reference number as in the following model, after "par." (one paragraph), "pars." (more than one paragraph), "screen," or "screens." For a source with no reference numbers at all, use the preceding model for an entire work.

One nurse questions whether doctors are adequately trained in tending patients' feelings (Van Eijk, pars. 6-7).

### A work in more than one volume

If you cite two or more volumes of the same work, identify the volume number before the page number. Separate volume number and page number with a colon.

According to Gibbon, during the reign of Gallienus "every province of the Roman world was afflicted by barbarous invaders and military tyrants" (1: 133).

### Two or more works by the same author(s)

If you cite more than one work by the same author or authors, include the work's title. If the title is long, shorten it to the first one or two main words. (The full title for the first citation below is Death at an Early Age.)

In the 1960s Kozol was reprimanded by his principal for teaching the poetry of Langston Hughes (Death 83).

Kozol believes that most people do not understand the effect that tax and revenue policies have on the quality of urban public schools (Savage Inequalities 207).

### An unsigned work

Cite an unsigned work by using a full or shortened version of the title.

In 1995 concern about Taiwan's relationship with China caused investors to transfer capital to the United States ("How the Missiles Help" 45).

### An indirect source

Use "qtd. in" ("quoted in") to indicate that you found the source you quote within another source.

Despite his tendency to view human existence as an unfulfilling struggle, Schopenhauer disparaged suicide as "a vain and foolish act" (qtd. in Durant 248).

### A literary work

Because novels, poems, and plays may be published in various editions, the page number may not be enough to lead readers to the quoted line or passage. For a novel, specify the chapter number after the page number and a semicolon.

> Among South Pacific islanders, the hero of Conrad's Lord Jim found "a totally new set of conditions for his imaginative faculty to work upon" (160; ch. 21).

For a verse play or a poem, omit the page number in favor of line numbers.

> In "Dulce et Decorum Est," Wilfred Owen undercuts the heroic image of warfare by comparing suffering soldiers to "beggars" and "hags" (lines 1-2) and describing a man dying in a poison-gas attack as "guttering, choking, drowning" (17).

If the work has parts, acts, or scenes, cite those as well (below: act 1, scene 5, lines 16–17).

> Lady Macbeth worries about her husband's ambition: "Yet I do fear thy nature; / It is too full o' the milk of human kindness" (1.5.16-17).

**More than one work**

> In the post-Watergate era, journalists have often employed aggressive reporting techniques not for the good of the public but simply to advance their careers (Gopnik 92; Fallows 64).

## MLA List of Works Cited

Your list of works cited is a complete record of your sources. Follow these guidelines for the list:

- Title the list "Works Cited." Do not enclose the title in quotation marks.
- Double-space the entire list.
- Arrange the sources alphabetically by the last name of the first author.
- Begin the first line of each entry at the left margin. Indent the subsequent lines of the entry one-half inch or five spaces.

Following are the essentials of a works-cited entry:

- Reverse the names of the author, last name first, with a comma between. If there is more than one author, give the others' names in normal order.
- Give the full title of the work, capitalizing all important words. Underline the titles of books and periodicals; use quotation marks for the titles of parts of books and articles in periodicals.

- Give publication information. For books, this information includes city of publication, publisher, date of publication. For periodicals, this information includes volume number, date of publication, and page numbers for the article you cite. For online sources such as Web sites, this information includes the date you consulted the source and the URL, or electronic address. (See pp. 69–72 for more on electronic sources.)
- Use periods between parts of each entry.

You may need to combine the models below for a given source—for instance, combine "A book with two or three authors" and "An article in an online journal" for an online article with two or three authors.

## Books

### A book with one author

Tuchman, Barbara W. The March of Folly: From Troy to Vietnam. New York: Knopf, 1984.

### A book with two or three authors

Silverstein, Olga, and Beth Rashbaum. The Courage to Raise Good Men. New York: Viking, 2004.

Trevor, Sylvia, Joan Hapgood, and William Leumi. Women Writers of the 1920s. New York: Columbia UP, 1998.

### A book with more than three authors

You may list all authors or only the first author followed by "et al." ("and others"). Use the same form in your parenthetical text citation.

Kippax, Susan, R. W. Connel, G. W. Dowsett, and June Crawford. Gay Communities Respond to Change. London: Falmer, 2004.

Kippax, Susan, et al. Gay Communities Respond to Change. London: Falmer, 2004.

### More than one work by the same author(s)

Kozol, Jonathan. Letters to a Young Teacher. New York: Crown, 2007.

---. Savage Inequalities: Children in America's Schools. New York: Crown, 1991.

### A book with an editor

Gwaltney, John Langston, ed. Drylongso: A Self-Portrait of Black America. New York: Random, 2000.

**A book with an author and an editor**

Orwell, George. The Collected Essays, Journalism and Letters of George Orwell. Ed. Sonia Orwell and Ian Angus. New York: Harcourt, 1968.

**A later edition**

Mumford, Lewis. Herman Melville: A Study of His Life and Vision. 2nd ed. New York: Harcourt, 1956.

**A work in a series**

Hall, Donald. Poetry and Ambition. Poets on Poetry. Ann Arbor: U of Michigan P, 1998.

**An anthology**

Glantz, Michael H., ed. Societal Responses to Regional Climatic Change. London: Westview, 2007.

Cite an entire anthology only when you are citing the work of the editor or you are cross-referencing it, as in the Ascher and Quindlen models below.

**A selection from an anthology**

The numbers at the end of the following entry are the page numbers on which the entire cited selection appears.

Kellog, William D. "Human Impact on Climate: The Evolution of an Awareness." Societal Responses to Regional Climatic Change. Ed. Michael H. Glantz. London: Westview, 2007. 283-96.

If you cite more than one selection from the same anthology, you may give the anthology as a separate entry and cross-reference it by the editor's or editors' last names in the selection entries.

Ascher, Barbara Lazear. "On Compassion." Kennedy, Kennedy, and Aaron 193–95.

Kennedy, X. J., Dorothy M. Kennedy, and Jane E. Aaron, eds. The Bedford Reader. 10th ed. Boston: Bedford, 2009.

Quindlen, Anna. "Homeless." Kennedy, Kennedy, and Aaron 198–200.

**A reference work**

Cheney, Ralph Holt. "Coffee." Collier's Encyclopedia. 2007 ed.

"Versailles, Treaty of." <u>The New Encyclopaedia Britannica: Macropaedia</u>. 15th
    ed. 1996.

## *Periodicals: Journals, Magazines, and Newspapers*

### An article in a journal with continuous pagination throughout the annual volume

In many journals the pages are numbered consecutively for an entire annual volume of issues, so that the year's fourth issue might run from pages 240 to 320. For this type of journal, give the volume number after the journal title, followed by the year of publication in parentheses, a colon, and the page numbers of the article.

Clayton, Richard R., and Carl G. Leukefeld. "The Prevention of Drug
    Use Among Youth: Implications of Legalization." <u>Journal of Primary
    Prevention</u> 12 (2007): 289-301.

### An article in a journal that pages issues separately

Some journals begin page numbering at 1 for each issue. For this kind of journal, give the issue number after the volume number and a period.

Vitz, Paul C. "Back to Human Dignity: From Modern to Postmodern Psychol-
    ogy." <u>Intercollegiate Review</u> 31.2 (2006): 15-23.

### An article in a monthly or bimonthly magazine

Fallows, James. "Why Americans Hate the Media." <u>Atlantic Monthly</u> Feb. 2007:
    45-64.

### An article in a weekly magazine

Gopnik, Adam. "Read All About It." <u>New Yorker</u> 12 Dec. 2006: 84-102.

### An article in a newspaper

Gorman, Peter. "It's Time to Legalize." <u>Boston Sunday Globe</u> 28 Aug. 2006,
    late ed.: 69+.

The page number "69+" means that the article begins on page 69 and continues on a later page. If the newspaper is divided into lettered sections, give both section letter and page number, as in "A7."

### An unsigned article

"How the Missiles Help California." <u>Time</u> 1 Apr. 2005: 45.

A review

Bergham, V. R. "The Road to Extermination." Rev. of Hitler's Willing
    Executioners, by Daniel Jonah Goldhagen. New York Times Book Review
    14 Apr. 2004: 6.


## Online Sources

Online sources vary greatly, and they may be and often are updated. Your aim in citing such a source should be to tell what version you used and how readers can find it for themselves. The following example includes (1) author's name, (2) the title of the work used, (3) information for the print version of the source, (4) the title of the online site, (5) the date of electronic publication, (6) the date the source was consulted, and (7) the source's complete URL (electronic address) in angle brackets (<>).

Loewenstein, Andrea Freud. "My Learning Disability: A (Digressive) Essay."
    College English 66 (2004): 585-602. National Council of Teachers
    of English. July 2004. 3 Aug. 2006 <http://www.ncte.org/portal/
    30_view.asp?id+=117302>.

The following models show various kinds of additional information to be inserted between these basic elements. If some information is unavailable, list what you can find.

### A work from a library subscription service

Library subscription services are usually available over your library's Web site and include EBSCOhost, LexisNexis, ProQuest, and InfoTrac. Provide basic information for sources you obtain from these services, as in the preceding example. In addition, provide (1) the name of the database, (2) the name of the subscription service, (3) the name of the subscribing institution (most likely your school), and (4) the name of the library. If the subscription service provides source URLs that are temporary or are unique to the subscribing library, give the URL of the service's home page (as in the example) or end with the date of your access.

Conway, Daniel W. "Reading Henry James as a Critic of Modern Moral
    Life." Inquiry 45 (2002): 319-30. Academic Search Elite. EBSCOhost.
    Santa Clara U, Orradre Lib. 20 Apr. 2007 <http://www.epnet.com>.

### An online scholarly project or professional site

Include the names, if any, of the editor and of the institution or organization that sponsors the project or site.

Shanks, Thomas, "The Case of the Cyber City Network." Markkula Network
for Applied Ethics. Ed. Kirk Hanson. 14 Aug. 2006. Santa Clara U.
12 Dec. 2006 <http://www.scu.edu/ethics/cybercity.html>.

If you are acknowledging the entire project or site rather than a short work within it, begin the entry with the project or site title.

### An online personal site

Provide the date of electronic publication if it differs from the date of your access.

McClure, Mark. "Speakers." Online Calendar of Shakespeare Conferences.
18 Apr. 2006. 23 May 2006 <http://www.mwc.edu/~mcclure/
sa_spkrs.html>.

### An online book

For a book published independently, after the title add any editor's or translator's name, either the publication information for a print version (as in the following model) or the date of electronic publication, and any sponsoring institution or organization.

Murphy, Bridget. Fictions of the Irish Emigration. Cambridge: Harvard UP,
1998. 5 Apr. 2007 <http://www.historicalfictions.unv.edu/
irel_murph.html>.

For a book published as part of a scholarly project, give any information about print publication and then follow the model above for a scholarly project.

### An article in an online journal

Base an entry for an online journal article on one of the models on page 68 for a print journal article.

Sjostrand, Odile. "Law Philosophy in Mansfield Park." Jane Austen Quarterly
33.1 (1999). 12 Oct. 2006 <http://facstaff.uww.edu/JAusten/
home.html>.

Omit page numbers (as in the example) if the journal does not provide them. If instead it provides another indication of length (sections, screens, paragraphs), give the total for the article (for instance, "15 pars.").

### An article in an online newspaper

Base an entry for an online newspaper article on the model on page 68 for a print newspaper article.

> Smith, Craig S. "A French Employee's Work Celebrates the Sloth Ethic."
>     New York Times 3 June 2006. 26 Nov. 2006 <http://www.nytimes.com/
>     2006/06/03/france.html?8hpib>.

### An article in an online magazine

Base an entry for an online magazine article on one of the models on pages 68–69 for a print magazine article.

> Brus, Michael. "Proxy War." Slate 9 July 2007. 12 July 2007 <http://
>     www.slate.com/Features/profile/profile.html>.

### Electronic mail

Give as the title the text of the e-mail's subject line, in quotation marks. "To the author" in the example means to you, the author of the paper.

> Dove, Chris. "Re: Bishop's Poems." E-mail to the author. 7 May 2007.

### A posting to a blog

> Hannon, Laura. "Wind Turbines and Birds." AccuWeather.com Global Warming
>     Blog. 16 May 2007. 18 May 2007 <http://
>     global-warming.accuweather.com>.

### A posting to an online discussion group

For a posting to a discussion group, give the posting's subject line as the title, and follow the title with "Online posting," the date of the posting, and the title of the group (without underlining or quotation marks).

> Forrester, Jane. "Embracing Mathematics." Online posting. 21 Sept. 2006.
>     Math Teaching Discussion List. 22 Sept. 2006 <http://www.acc.edu/
>     gargantuan/smart/mathteach.html>.

### An online painting, sculpture, or photograph

Matisse, Henri. La Musique. 1939. Albright-Knox Gallery, Buffalo.
    WebMuseum. 3 Mar. 2007 <http://www.ibiblio.org/wm/paint/
    matisse/matisse.musique.jpg>.

### An online television or radio program

Niebur, Gustav. "John Paul's Activist Legacy." All Things Considered.
    National Public Radio. 1 Oct. 2006. 5 Oct. 2006 <http://
    www.npr.org/programs/commentaries/2006/oct>.

### An online sound recording or clip

Roosevelt, Eleanor. Address to the United Nations. 9 Dec. 1955. Vincent
    Voice Library. Digital and Multimedia Center, U of Michigan. 16 Nov.
    2006 <http://www.lib.msu.edu/vincent/RooseveltE.xml>.

### An online film or film clip

San Francisco Earthquake and Fire. 4 Apr. 1906. American Memory. Library
    of Congress. 22 Sept. 2006 <http://memory.loc.gov/cgi-bin/D?papr:17/
    ammem_gBGh>.

## CD-ROMs and Other Portable Media

For portable databases (CD-ROMs as well as diskettes and magnetic
tapes), the content of the citation depends on whether the database is a periodical.

For a periodical, follow the models given earlier to provide full publication information. Add the title of the electronic source, the medium (for
instance, "CD-ROM"), the name of the vendor or distributor, and the date of
electronic publication:

Rausch, Janet. "So Late in the Day." Daily Sun 10 Dec. 2006, late ed.: C1.
    Daily Disk. CD-ROM. Cybernews. Jan. 2007.

Treat a portable database that is not a periodical as if it were a book, but
provide the medium and any edition or version after the title.

"China." Concise Columbia Encyclopedia. CD-ROM. 2006-07 ed. Redmond:
    Microsoft, 2006.

## *Other Sources*

### A musical composition or work of art

Dvořák, Antonín. String Quartet in E-flat, op. 97.

Hockney, David. Nichols Canyon. 1980. Private collection. David Hockney:
    A Retrospective. By Maurice Tuchman and Stephanie Barron. Los
    Angeles: Los Angeles County Museum of Art, 1988. 205.

### A television or radio program

Irving, John, guest. "Movies into Books." Talk of the Nation. PBS. KQED,
    San Francisco. 20 Nov. 2006.

### A sound recording

Mendelssohn, Felix. A Midsummer Night's Dream. Cond. Erich Leinsdorf.
    Boston Symphony Orch. RCA, 1982.

### A film, video, or DVD

Achbar, Mark, and Peter Wintonick, dirs. Manufacturing Consent: Noam
    Chomsky and the Media. Zeitgeist, 1992.

### A letter

List a published letter under the author's name, and provide full publication information.

Hemingway, Ernest. Letter to Grace Hemingway. 15 Jan. 1920. In
    Ernest Hemingway: Selected Letters. Ed. Carlos Baker. New York:
    Scribner's, 1981. 44.

For a letter that you receive, list the source under the writer's name, add "to the author," and provide the date of the correspondence.

Dove, Chris. Letter to the author. 7 May 2007.

### An interview

Kesey, Ken. Interview. "The Art of Fiction." Paris Review 130 (1994): 59-94.
Macedo, Donaldo. Personal interview. 13 May 2007.

## SAMPLE RESEARCH PAPER

In the previous chapter we saw Rosie Anaya respond to Nancy Mairs's "Disability" with her own essay on television portrayals of psychological disabilities (pp. 47–49). After completing that paper, Anaya began to wonder about some of the disturbing news stories she had seen that linked campus violence with mental illness. For a research assignment, she decided to delve further into the subject and was surprised by what she found. We reprint her research paper for three reasons: It illustrates many techniques of using and documenting sources, which are highlighted in the marginal comments; it shows a writer working with a topic that interests her in a way that arouses the readers' interest as well; and it explores a problem that affects most college students, often profoundly.

Rosie Anaya
Professor DeBeer
English 102A
5 May 2007

The Best Kept Secret on Campus

The college experience, as depicted in advertising and the movies, consists of happy scenes: students engrossed in class discussions, partying with friends, walking in small groups across campus. Such images insist that college is a great time of learning and friendship, but some students have a very different experience of emotional and psychological problems, ranging from anxiety to depression to acute bipolar disorder. These students endure social stigma and barriers to treatment that their colleges and universities must do more to help them surmount.

The numbers of college students suffering from psychological problems are staggering. A 2006 survey conducted by the American College Health Association found that 66 percent of students have experienced feelings of hopelessness, more than 75 percent have felt overwhelmed or gone through a period of severe sadness, nearly 50 percent have been so depressed that they had trouble functioning, 15 percent have been formally diagnosed with depression, and almost 10 percent have contemplated suicide (204-05). The simple fact, unknown to many, is that a college student is more likely than not to experience a

*Title arouses readers' curiosity.*

*Images establish contrast between expectations and experiences of college students. No source citation needed for Anaya's generalization.*

*Thesis statement.*

*Statistics establish the scope of the problem.*

*Citation of a paraphrase. Citation includes only page numbers because author (American College Health Association) is named in the text.*

severe psychological problem at least once. In other words, such problems are a common aspect of college life.

Despite the prevalence of depression and related disorders on campus, however, most students avoid seeking help when they need it. The American Psychiatric Association maintains that most mental-health issues — depression especially — can be managed or overcome with treatment by therapy and/or medication. But among students with diagnosed depression, according to the American College Health Association, a mere 26 percent get therapy and only 37 percent take medication (204). One reason for such low numbers can be found in a survey conducted by mtvU, a resource network for college students, and the Jed Foundation, an organization dedicated to reducing suicide among college students: Only 22 percent of students would be willing to ask for help even if they were certain they needed it, because they perceive mental illness as embarrassing and shameful (2-3). Thus students who need help suffer additional pain — and no treatment — because they fear the stigma of mental illness.

We've all heard the horror stories about what happens when a college student's mental illness goes untreated. The 2007 tragedy at Virginia Tech, where a student killed thirty-two people before turning his gun on himself, is the latest and most extreme example, but the news media have been reporting such incidents with regularity since a sniper gunned down sixteen classmates at the University of Texas in 1966. In the past few years alone, a failing student killed three professors and himself at Arizona Nursing College, a student fatally shot one classmate and wounded another at Louisiana Technical College, and a graduate student murdered a dean, a professor, and another student at the Appalachian School of Law. After repeated exposure to these kinds of stories, fear seems like a natural — and reasonable — response to mental illness on campus.

The news stories are misleading, however. In a study of fifteen years of newsmagazine coverage of bipolar disorder (a form of depression coupled with manic episodes), Carol Fletcher of Hofstra University concludes that journalists tend to link mental illness with violent crime even though most people with bipolar

---

*Side annotations:*

Follow-up comments give Anaya's interpretation of the evidence.

Students' reluctance to seek help for psychological problems.

No parenthetical citation because author (American Psychiatric Association) is named in the text and online source has no page numbers.

Introduction to study gives information about authors.

Paragraph integrates information from three sources to support Anaya's own idea.

Perceived consequences of untreated mental illness.

No source citation in this paragraph because it relies on common knowledge: facts available in several sources, not attributable to any one source.

Refutation of common perception of mental illness.

disorder are harmless. This tendency, Fletcher warns, feeds stereotypes while causing further damage to those living with mental illness:

> In a nation that generates 50 million prescriptions for antidepressants a year . . . our attitude to mental illness remains largely pornographic. The media foster a voyeuristic interest in a small minority of mentally ill who commit crimes while providing little useful information to the 20 million other sufferers of psychiatric disability.

Although there is little reason to fear people with mental disorders, we are bombarded with the message that they are dangerous. No wonder, then, that most college students hide their emotional problems from people who could help them, never guessing that half of their peers are struggling with the same issues.

As unfortunate as it is, social stigma is not the only barrier to treatment faced by students with mental illness. The uncertain availability of on-campus psychological care poses another obstacle. Creating and running a mental-health system is expensive: Some schools can afford to offer comprehensive mental-health programming that ranges from outreach to counseling to follow-up treatment, but others have minimal resources and can do little more than react to a crisis, while still others offer no counseling or treatment at all (Kadison and DiGeronimo 162-66). Struggling students who finally accept that they need help and work up the courage to ask for it may discover that they can't obtain it, at least not easily. It's not hard to imagine that most students — especially those in the grip of depression — would give up.

Even at schools that do offer mental-health services, legal restrictions can make psychiatric intervention difficult or impossible. Tamar Lewin, an education specialist with the New York Times, points out that the Americans with Disabilities Act protects people with mental illness from discrimination, so schools cannot screen for psychological disorders or force students to obtain treatment unless a court declares them to be a threat. And because nearly all college students are adults, confidentiality rules prevent schools from notifying parents or teachers of poten-

---

**Side notes:**

No parenthetical citation or block quotation for summary because author (Fletcher) is named in the text and online source has no page numbers.

Ellipsis mark indicates deletion of words from original passage.

Quotation of more than four typed lines is set off and indented ten spaces or one inch.

Long quotation is followed by Anaya's interpretation and explanation of its significance for her thesis.

Mental-health care on college campuses.

Parenthetical citation of summary includes authors' names (not given in the text) and page numbers.

Anaya's interpretation of the evidence.

Legal issues related to psychiatric care for college students.

Citations of Lewin here and in parentheses on the next page clarify boundaries of information drawn from Lewin.

tial problems without the student's written consent ("Laws" A1). This combination of social stigma and legal obstacle creates an awkward dilemma: Students suffering from mental illness are reluctant to ask for help, yet the very people who can help are prevented from reaching out. The burden of treatment rests squarely on those who are suffering.

So what should concerned colleges and universities do? Perhaps the best solution is for them to take active steps to remove the stigma associated with mental illness. Just being open about the extent of depression and related disorders among college students is a start, and it doesn't have to cost a lot of money. For example, a simple poster campaign announcing the basic statistics of mental illness and assuring students that there is no reason to be ashamed of their feelings might reduce reluctance to seek help. Even if a campus has limited mental-health facilities, prominently displaying links to good Web resources on bulletin boards and on the school's Web site is an inexpensive and easy way both to normalize mental illness and to offer help. Two excellent sites are Half of Us, which offers, among other things, a self-evaluation test for common psychological disorders and advice on where to go for help, and the American Psychiatric Association's Healthy Minds, which offers mental-health information geared to college students, video testimonials, and explanations of available treatments.

Students themselves can also take the lead in addressing mental-health issues. At the University of Pennsylvania, junior Alison Malmon started the 65-chapter student support group Active Minds after her brother's suicide jolted her into the conviction that "students [need] to talk about what they're going through, and share their experiences" (qtd. in Lewin, "From Brother's Death"). At a smaller college, a freshman who was successfully treated for depression told her story in the school paper and helped dozens of other students to recognize and seek help for their illnesses (Kadison and DiGeronimo 214-17). As these examples show, students everywhere can make an enormous difference simply by sharing their feelings.

Students are in a unique position to help each other through mental illness, but they should not be left to do this

*Citation includes shortened version of title to distinguish source from another one by the same author.*

*Anaya's interpretation of Lewin's article.*

*Anaya's own suggestions for solving the problem.*

*No parenthetical citations needed for entire Web sites named in the text.*

*Other students' efforts to solve the problem.*

*Brackets indicate word added by Anaya to clarify original quotation.*

*Citation of quotation from an indirect source. Citation includes shortened version of title to distinguish source from another one by the same author.*

*Anaya's own conclusion.*

*Conclusion summarizes Anaya's main points and restates her thesis.*

important work on their own. Colleges and universities need to
collaborate with students to erase the stigma associated with
mental illness, to encourage students to get help when they
need it, and to prevent the kinds of sensational violence that
dominate the news.

Works Cited

American College Health Association. "American College Health
    Association National College Health Assessment: Spring
    2006 Reference Group Data Report (Abridged)." Journal of
    American College Health 55.4 (2007): 195-206.

American Psychiatric Association. Healthy Minds. 2 Apr. 2007. 16
    Apr. 2007 <http://www.healthyminds.org>.

Fletcher, Carol. "Madness in Magazines: The Stigmatization of a
    Psychiatric Disability in American News Weeklies." Associ-
    ation for Education in Journalism and Mass Communication
    Conference. Toronto, Can. 5 Aug. 2004. 22 Apr. 2007
    <http://list.msu.edu/cgi-bin/wa?A2=aejmc=5349>.

Half of Us. 20 Apr. 2007. mtvU and Jed Foundation. 26 Apr.
    2007 <http://halfofus.com>.

Kadison, Richard, and Theresa Foy DiGeronimo. College of the
    Overwhelmed: The Campus Mental Health Crisis and What to
    Do About It. San Francisco: Jossey-Bass, 2004.

Lewin, Tamar. "From Brother's Death, a Crusade." New York Times
    25 Apr. 2007, late ed.: B8. Academic Search Elite.
    EBSCOhost. Rockingham Coll., Kelley Lib. 26 Apr. 2007
    <http://www.epnet.com>.

---. "Laws Limit Options When a Student Is Mentally Ill." New
    York Times 19 Apr. 2007, late ed.: A1+. Academic Search
    Elite. EBSCOhost. Rockingham Coll., Kelley Lib. 24 Apr.
    2007 <http://www.epnet.com>.

mtvU and Jed Foundation. "2006 mtvU College Mental Health
    Study: Stress, Depression, Stigma and Students." Half of Us.
    6 Mar. 2007. mtvU and Jed Foundation. 26 Apr. 2007
    <http://halfofus.com/press.aspx>.

"Works Cited" begins
on a new page.

An article from a print
journal that pages
issues separately.

An entire Web site.

A conference
presentation.

An entire Web site.

A book with two
authors.

A newspaper article
from a library sub-
scription service.

The second of two
works by the same
author.

A report from a Web
site.

# PART TWO

# THE METHODS

# 4

---

# NARRATION

## *Telling a Story*

## THE METHOD

"What happened?" you ask a friend who sports a luminous black eye. Unless he merely grunts "A golf ball," he may answer you with a narrative — a story, true or fictional.

"Okay," he sighs, "you know The Tenth Round? That nightclub down by the docks that smells of formaldehyde? Last night I heard they were giving away $500 to anybody who could stand up for three minutes against this karate expert, the Masked Samurai. And so . . ."

You lean forward. At least, you lean forward *if* you love a story. Most of us do, particularly if the story tells us of people in action or in conflict, and if it is told briskly, vividly, and with insight into the human heart. NARRATION, or storytelling, is therefore a powerful method by which to engage and hold the attention of listeners — readers as well. A little of its tremendous power flows to the public speaker who starts off with a joke, even a stale joke ("A funny thing happened to me on my way over here . . ."), and to the preacher who at the beginning of a sermon tells of some funny or touching incident.

The term *narrative* takes in abundant territory. A narrative may be short or long, factual or imagined, as artless as a tale told in a locker room or as artful as a novel by Henry James. A narrative may instruct and inform, or simply divert and regale. It may set forth some point or message, or it may be no more significant than a horror tale that aims to curdle your blood.

At least a hundred times a year, you probably resort to narration, not always for the purpose of telling an entertaining story, but often to report information or to illustrate a point. In academic writing, you will use mainly brief narratives, or ANECDOTES, that recount single incidents as a way of supporting an explanation or an ARGUMENT with the flesh and blood of real life. Early in the twentieth century, President Woodrow Wilson used an anecdote to explain why he had appointed his harshest critic to a cabinet post. He told of an acquaintance who spied a strange man urinating through her picket fence into her flower garden. She promptly invited the offender into her yard because, as she explained to him, "I'd a whole lot rather have you inside pissing out than have you outside pissing in." By telling this story, Wilson made clear his situation in regard to his political enemy more succinctly and pointedly than if he had given a more abstract explanation.

Anecdotes add color and specifics to writing, and they can be deeply revealing. In a biography of Samuel Johnson, the great eighteenth-century critic and scholar, W. Jackson Bate uses an anecdote to show that his subject was human and lovable. As Bate tells us, Dr. Johnson, a portly and imposing gentleman of fifty-five, had walked with some friends to the crest of a hill, where the great man, delighted by its steepness, said he wanted to "take a roll down." They tried to stop him. But he said he "had not had a roll for a long time," and taking out of his pockets his keys, a pencil, a purse, and other objects, lay down parallel at the edge of the hill, and rolled down its full length, "turning himself over and over till he came to the bottom."

However small the event it relates, this anecdote is memorable—partly because of its attention to detail, such as the exact list of the contents of Johnson's pockets. In such a brief story, a superhuman figure comes down to human size. In one stroke, Bate reveals an essential part of Johnson: his boisterous, hearty, and boyish sense of fun.

## THE PROCESS

### Purpose and Shape

Every good story has a purpose, and we've suggested several in the preceding section. A narrative without a purpose is bound to irritate readers, as a young child's rambling can vex an unsympathetic adult.

Whatever its length or the reason for its telling, an effective narrative holds the attention of readers. Say you're writing about therapies for autism and you want readers to see how one particular method works. In a paragraph or so, you can narrate a session you observed between an autistic child and his teacher. Your purpose will determine which of the session's events you relate—not every action and exchange but the ones that, in your eyes, convey the essence of the therapy and make it interesting for readers.

### The Thesis

In writing a news story, a reporter often begins with the conclusion, placing the main event in the opening paragraph (called the *lead*) so that readers get the essentials up front. Similarly, in using an anecdote to explain something or to argue a point, you'll want to tell readers directly what you think the story demonstrates. But in most other kinds of narration, whether fiction or nonfiction, whether to entertain or to make an idea clear, the storyteller refrains from revealing the gist of the story, its point, right at the beginning. In fact, many narratives do not contain a THESIS STATEMENT, an assertion of the idea behind the story, because such a statement can rob the reader of the very pleasure of narration, the excitement of seeing a story build. That doesn't mean the story lacks a thesis, however—far from it. The writer has every obligation to construct the narrative as if a thesis statement showed the way at the start, even when it didn't.

By the end of the story, that thesis should become obvious, as the writer builds toward a memorable CONCLUSION. In a story Mark Twain liked to tell aloud, a woman's ghost returns to claim her artificial arm made of gold, which she wore in life and which her greedy husband had unscrewed from her corpse. Carefully, Twain would build up suspense as the ghost pursued the husband upstairs to his bedroom, stood by his bed, breathed her cold breath on him, and intoned, *"Who's got my golden arm?"* Twain used to end his story by suddenly yelling at a member of the audience, *"You've got it!"*—and enjoying the victim's shriek of surprise. That final punctuating shriek may be a technique that will work only in oral storytelling, yet, like Twain, most storytellers end with a bang if they can. For another example, take specific notice in this chapter of Shirley Jackson's ending for "The Lottery" (*after* you've read the whole story, that is). The final impact need not be as dramatic as Twain's or Jackson's, either. As Maya Angelou demonstrates in her narrative in this chapter, you can achieve a lot just by leading to your point, stating your thesis at the very end. You can sometimes make your point just by saving the best incident—the most dramatic or the funniest—for last.

## The Narrator in the Story

Narratives often report personal experience, whether in reality or in fiction. The NARRATOR (or teller) of such a personal experience is the speaker, the one who was there. (Five of the selections in this chapter tell of such experiences. All use the first-PERSON *I*.) The telling is usually SUBJECTIVE, with details and language chosen to express the writer's feelings. Of course, a personal experience told in the first person can use some artful telling and some structuring. (In the course of this discussion, we'll offer advice on telling stories of different kinds.)

When a story isn't your own experience but a recital of someone else's, or of events that are public knowledge, then you proceed differently as narrator. Without expressing opinions, you step back and report, content to stay invisible. Instead of saying, "I did this; I did that," you use the third person, *he, she, it,* or *they:* "The experimenter did this; she did that." You may have been on the scene; if so, you will probably write as a spectator, from your own POINT OF VIEW (or angle of seeing). If you put together what happened from the testimony of others, you tell the story from the point of view of a nonparticipant (a witness who didn't take part). Generally, a nonparticipant is OBJECTIVE in setting forth events: unbiased, as accurate and dispassionate as possible.

When you narrate a story in the third person, you aren't a character central in the eyes of your audience. Unlike the first-person writer of a personal experience, you aren't the main actor; you are the camera operator, whose job is to focus on what transpires. Most history books and news stories are third-person narratives, and so is much fiction. (In this chapter, the story by Shirley Jackson illustrates third-person narration.) In telling of actual events, writers stick to the facts and do not invent the thoughts of participants (historical novels, though, do mingle fact and fancy in this way). And even writers of fiction and anecdote imagine the thoughts of their characters only if they want to explore psychology. Look back at the anecdote by Woodrow Wilson on page 82, and notice how much would be lost if Wilson had gone into the thoughts of his characters: "The woman was angry and embarrassed at seeing the stranger. . . ."

A final element of the narrator's place in the story is verb tense, whether present (*I stare, he stares*) or past (*I stared, he stared*). The present tense is often tempting because it gives events a sense of immediacy. Told as though everything were happening right now, Wilson's story might have begun, "Peering out her window, a woman spies a strange man. . . ." But the present tense can seem artificial because we're used to reading stories in the past tense, and it can be difficult to sustain throughout an entire narrative. (See p. 89 on consistency in tenses.) The past tense may be more removed, but it is still powerful: Just look at Maya Angelou's gripping "Champion of the World," beginning on page 93.

## What to Emphasize

### *Discovery of Details*

Whether you tell of your own experience or of someone else's, even if it is brief, you need a whole story to tell. If the story is complex, do some searching and discovering in writing. One trusty method to test your memory (or to make sure you have all the necessary elements of a story) is that of a news reporter. Ask yourself:

1. *What* happened?
2. *Who* took part?
3. *When?*
4. *Where?*
5. *Why* did this event (or these events) take place?
6. *How* did it (or they) happen?

Journalists call this handy list of questions "the five *W*'s and the *H*." The *H* — *how* — isn't merely another way of asking what happened. It means: In exactly what way or under what circumstances? If the event was a murder, how was it done — with an ax or with a bulldozer?

### Scene Versus Summary

If you have prepared well—searching your memory or doing some research—you'll have far more information on hand than you can use in your narrative. You'll need to choose carefully, to pick out just those events and details that will accomplish your purpose with your readers.

A key decision is to choose between the two main strategies of narration: to tell a story by SCENE or to tell it by SUMMARY. When you tell a story in a scene, or in scenes, you visualize each event as vividly and precisely as if you were there—as though it were a scene in a film, and your reader sat before the screen. This is the strategy of most fine novels and short stories—and of much excellent nonfiction as well. Instead of just mentioning people, you portray them. You recall dialog as best you can, or you invent some that could have been spoken. You include DESCRIPTION (a mode of writing to be dealt with fully in our next chapter).

For a lively example of a well-drawn scene, see Maya Angelou's account of a tense crowd's behavior as, jammed into a small-town store, they listen to a fight broadcast (in "Champion of the World"). Angelou prolongs one scene for almost her entire essay. Sometimes, though, a writer will draw a scene in only two or three sentences. This is the brevity we find in W. Jackson Bate's glimpse of the hill-rolling Johnson (pp. 82–83). Unlike Angelou, Bate evidently seeks not to weave a tapestry of detail but to show, in telling of one brief event, a trait of his hero's character.

When, in contrast, you tell a story by the method of summary, you relate events concisely. Instead of depicting people and their surroundings in great detail, you set down just the essentials of what happened. Most of us employ this method in most stories we tell, for it takes less time and fewer words. A summary is to a scene, then, as a simple stick figure is to a portrait in oils. This is not to dismiss simple stick figures as inferior. The economy of a story told in summary may be as effective as the lavish detail of a story told in scenes.

Again, your choice of a method depends on your answer to the questions you ask yourself: What is my purpose? Who is my audience? How fully to flesh out a scene, how much detail to include—these choices depend on what you seek to do and on how much your audience needs to know to follow you. Read the life of some famous person in an encyclopedia, and you will find the article telling its story in summary form. Its writer's purpose, evidently, is to recount the main events of a whole life in a short space. But glance through a book-length biography of the same person, and you will probably find scenes in it. A biographer writes with a different purpose: to present a detailed portrait roundly and thoroughly, bringing the subject vividly to life.

To be sure, you can use both methods in telling a single story. Often, summary will serve a writer who passes briskly from one scene to the next or hurries over events of lesser importance. Were you to write, let's say, the story of your grandfather's immigration to the United States from Cuba, you might just summarize his decision to leave Cuba and his settlement in Florida. These summaries could frame and emphasize a detailed telling of the events that you consider essential and most interesting—his nighttime escape, his harrowing voyage in a small boat, his surprising welcome by immigration authorities.

In *The Bedford Reader* we are concerned with the kind of writing you do every day in college: nonfiction writing in which you generally explain ideas, organize information you have learned, analyze other people's ideas, or argue a case. In fiction, though, we find an enormously popular and appealing use of narration and certain devices of storytelling from which all storytellers can learn. For these reasons, this chapter includes one celebrated short story by a master storyteller, Shirley Jackson. But fiction and fact barely separate Jackson's story and the equally compelling true memoirs in this chapter. All of the authors strive to make people and events come alive for us. All of them also use a tool that academic writers generally do not: dialog. Reported speech, in quotation marks, is invaluable for revealing characters' feelings.

## Organization

In any kind of narration, the simplest approach is to set down events in CHRONOLOGICAL ORDER, the way they happened. To do so is to have your story already organized for you. A chronological order is therefore an excellent sequence to follow unless you can see some special advantage in violating it. Ask: What am I trying to do? If you are trying to capture your readers' attention right away, you might begin in medias res (Latin, "in the middle of things") and open with a colorful, dramatic event, even though it took place late in the chronology. If trying for dramatic effect, you might save the most exciting or impressive event for last, even though it actually happened early. By this means, you can keep your readers in suspense for as long as possible. (You can return to earlier events by a FLASHBACK, an earlier scene recalled.) Let your purpose be your guide.

The writer Calvin Trillin has recalled why, in a narrative titled "The Tunica Treasure," he deliberately chose not to follow a chronology:

> I wrote a story on the discovery of the Tunica treasure which I couldn't begin by saying, "Here is a man who works as a prison guard in Angola State Prison, and on his weekends he sometimes looks for buried treasure that is rumored to be around the Indian village." Because the real point of the story

centered around the problems caused when an amateur wanders onto professional territory, I thought it would be much better to open with how momentous the discovery was, that it was the most important archeological
discovery about Indian contact with the European settlers to date, and *then*
to say that it was discovered by a prison guard. So I made a conscious choice
*not* to start with Leonard Charrier working as a prison guard, not to go back
to his boyhood in Bunkie, Louisiana, not to talk about how he'd always been
interested in treasure hunting—hoping that the reader would assume I was
about to say that the treasure was found by an archeologist from the Peabody
Museum at Harvard.

Trillin, by saving the fact that a prison guard made the earthshaking discovery, effectively took his reader by surprise.

No matter what order you choose, either following chronology or departing from it, make sure your audience can follow it. The sequence of events has
to be clear. This calls for TRANSITIONS of time, whether they are brief phrases
that point out exactly when each event happened ("Seven years later," "A
moment earlier"), or whole sentences that announce an event and clearly
locate it in time ("If you had known Leonard Charrier ten years earlier, you
would have found him voraciously poring over every archeology text he could
lay his hands on in the public library"). See *Transitions* in Useful Terms for a
list of possibilities.

---

### FOCUS ON VERBS

Narration depends heavily on verbs to clarify and enliven events. Strong verbs
sharpen meaning and encourage you to add other informative details:

WEAK    The wind made an awful noise.

STRONG   The wind roared around the house and rattled the trees.

Forms of *make* (as in the example above) and forms of *be* (as in the next example) can sap the life from narration:

WEAK    The noises were alarming to us.

STRONG   The noises alarmed us.

Verbs in the ACTIVE VOICE (the subject does the action) usually pack more power
into fewer words than verbs in the PASSIVE VOICE (the subject is acted upon):

WEAK PASSIVE   We were besieged in the basement by the wind, as the water at our
feet was swelled by the rain.

STRONG ACTIVE   The wind besieged us in the basement, as the rain swelled the
water at our feet.

While strengthening verbs, also ensure that they're consistent in tense. The tense you choose for relating events, present or past, should not shift unnecessarily.

INCONSISTENT TENSES   We <u>held</u> a frantic conference to consider our options. It <u>takes</u> only a minute to decide to stay put.

CONSISTENT TENSE   We <u>held</u> a frantic conference to consider our options. It <u>took</u> only a minute to decide to stay put.

**For exercises on verbs, visit Exercise Central at *bedfordstmartins.com /thebedfordreader.***

---

### CHECKLIST FOR REVISING A NARRATIVE

✔ **THESIS**   What is the point of your narrative? Will it be clear to readers by the end? Even if you don't provide a thesis statement, your story should focus on a central idea. If you can't risk readers' misunderstanding—if, for instance, you're using narration to support an argument or explain a concept—then have you stated your thesis outright?

✔ **POINT OF VIEW**   Is your narrator's position in the story appropriate for your purpose and consistent throughout? Check for awkward or confusing shifts in point of view (participant or nonparticipant; first, second, or third person) and in the tenses of verbs (present to past or vice versa).

✔ **SELECTION OF EVENTS**   Have you selected and emphasized events to suit your audience and fulfill your purpose? Tell the important parts of the story in the greatest detail. Summarize the less important, connective events.

✔ **ORGANIZATION**   If your organization is not strictly chronological (first event to last), do you have a compelling reason for altering it? If you start somewhere other than the beginning of the story or use flashbacks at any point, will your readers benefit from your creativity?

✔ **TRANSITIONS**   Have you used transitions to help clarify the order of events and their duration?

✔ **DIALOG**   If you have used dialog, quoting participants in the story, is it appropriate for your purpose? Is it concise, telling only the important, revealing lines? Does the language sound like spoken English?

✔ **VERBS**   Do strong, active verbs move your narrative from event to event? Are verb tenses consistent?

# NARRATION IN PARAGRAPHS

## Writing About Television

The following paragraph was written for *The Bedford Reader* as a kind of mini-essay. But it is easy to see how it might have worked in the context of a full essay about, say, the emotional effects of television on children. Recounting events vividly, moment by moment, the writer gives evidence for a rather dramatic effect on one little girl.

Oozing menace from beyond the stars or from the deeps, televised horror powerfully stimulates a child's already frisky imagination. As parents know, a "Creature Double Feature" has an impact that lasts long after the click of the *off* button. Recently a neighbor reported the strange case of her eight-year-old. Discovered late at night in the game room watching *The Exorcist*, the girl was promptly sent to bed. An hour later, her parents could hear her chanting something in the darkness of her bedroom. On tiptoe, they stole to her door to listen. The creak of springs told them that their daughter was swaying rhythmically to and fro, and the smell of acrid smoke warned them that something was burning. At once, they shoved open the door to find the room flickering with shadows cast by a lighted candle. Their daughter was sitting in bed, rocking back and forth as she intoned over and over, "Fiend in human form . . . Fiend in human form . . ." This case may be unique; still, it seems likely that similar events take place each night all over the screen-watching world.

> ┤ Claim to be supported by narrative
>
> Transitions (underlined) clarify sequence and pace of events
>
> Anecdote builds suspense:
>
>    Mystery
>
>    Warnings
>
>    Crisis
>
> ┤ Conclusion broadens claim

## Writing in an Academic Discipline

In this paragraph from a geology textbook, the authors use narration to illustrate a powerful geological occurrence. Following another paragraph that explains landslides more generally, the narrative places the reader at an actual event.

The news media periodically relate the terrifying and often grim details of landslides. On May 31, 1970, one such event occurred when a gigantic rock avalanche buried more than 20,000 people in Yungay and Ranrahirca, Peru. There was little warning of the impending disaster; it began and ended in just a matter of a few minutes. The avalanche started 14 kilometers from Yungay, near the summit of 6,700-meter-high Nevados Huascaran, the loftiest peak in the Peruvian Andes. Triggered by the ground motion from a strong offshore earthquake, a huge mass of rock and ice broke free from the precipitous north face of the mountain. After plunging nearly one kilometer, the material pulverized on impact and imme-

> ┤ Generalization illustrated by narrative
>
> Anecdote helps explain landslides:
>
>    Sudden beginning

diately began rushing down the mountainside, made fluid by trapped air and melted ice. The initial mass ripped loose additional millions of tons of debris <u>as it roared downhill</u>. The shock waves produced by the event created thunderlike noise and stripped nearby hillsides of vegetation. Although the material followed a previously eroded gorge, a portion of the debris jumped a 200–300-meter-high bedrock ridge that had protected Yungay from past rock avalanches and buried the entire city. <u>After inundating another town in its path</u>, Ranrahirca, the mass of debris <u>finally</u> reached the bottom of the valley where its momentum carried it across the Rio Santa and tens of meters up the opposite bank.

*Fast movement*

*Irresistible force*

*Transitions (underlined) clarify sequence and pace of events*

—Edward J. Tarbuck and Frederick K. Lutgens,
*The Earth: An Introduction to Physical Geology*

## NARRATION IN PRACTICE

Robert Guzman was on his way to class at Cañada College when his car was hit at an intersection. He reported the accident to his insurance company, and the claims adjuster asked him to supplement the standard police report with a letter explaining what happened.

"What happened?" prompted Guzman to write the following narrative. Since the accident was uncomplicated, he had little difficulty getting the events down in chronological order. In editing, though, he did add some clarifying TRANSITIONS, such as "After the light turned green" and "When I was midway through the intersection."

Robert Guzman
415 Washington St., Apt. 5
San Carlos, CA 94070
June 7, 2007

David McClure
MDN Insurance
2716 El Camino Real
San Carlos, CA 94072

Dear Mr. McClure:

Thanks for your call about my claim. Here is the report you requested about the accident I was involved in.

At about 7:30 on the morning of June 4, I was driving south on Laurel Street in San Carlos. The traffic light at the corner of Laurel and San Carlos Avenue was red and I stopped at it, the first car in the stop line.

After the light turned green, I looked to my left and right. Although I saw a car approaching from the right on San Carlos, it seemed to be slowing for the light. Since my light was green, I proceeded through the intersection.

The car, which I later found out was driven by Mr. Henry, did not stop for its red light. When I was midway through the intersection, I heard the other car's tires squeal and felt an impact. Mr. Henry's car hit the rear fender and bumper on my passenger side. My car spun clockwise and came to a stop facing north, in the northbound lane of Laurel.

Mr. Henry parked in a lot across the street, and I pulled in after him. I called the police on my cell phone, and we waited for the police to arrive. No one was injured, but my passenger-side rear fender is severely dented and my bumper is twisted like a pretzel.

As you can see, I was not at fault in this accident. I believe Mr. Henry will confirm as much. Please let me know if you have any questions or if I can help my claim in any other way.

Sincerely,

*Robert Guzman*

Robert Guzman

# MAYA ANGELOU

MAYA ANGELOU was born Marguerite Johnson in Saint Louis in 1928. After an unpleasantly eventful youth by her account ("from a broken family, raped at eight, unwed mother at sixteen"), she went on to join a dance company, star in an off-Broadway play (*The Blacks*), write six books of poetry, produce a TV series on Africa, act in the television series *Roots*, serve as a coordinator for the Southern Christian Leadership Conference, direct a feature film, win the Presidential Medal of Freedom, and secure lifetime membership in the National Women's Hall of Fame. Angelou may be best known, however, for the six books of her searching, frank, and joyful autobiography — beginning with *I Know Why the Caged Bird Sings* (1970), which she adapted for television, through *A Song Flung Up to Heaven* (2002). Her most recent books of poetry are *Celebrations: Rituals of Prayer and Peace* and *Mother: A Cradle to Hold Me*, both published in 2006. She is Reynolds Professor of American Studies at Wake Forest University.

## *Champion of the World*

"Champion of the World" is the nineteenth chapter in *I Know Why the Caged Bird Sings*; the title is a phrase taken from the chapter. Remembering her childhood, the writer tells how she and her older brother, Bailey, grew up in a town in Arkansas. The center of their lives was Grandmother and Uncle Willie's store. On the night of this story, in the late 1930s, the African American community gathers in the store to listen to a boxing match on the radio. Joe Louis, the "Brown Bomber," who was a hero to black people, is defending his heavyweight title against a white contender. (Louis successfully defended his title twenty-five times, a record that stands today.) Angelou's telling of the event both entertains us and explains what it was like to be African American in a certain time and place.

Amy Tan's "Fish Cheeks," following Angelou's essay, also explores the experience of growing up an outsider in mainly white America.

The last inch of space was filled, yet people continued to wedge themselves along the walls of the Store. Uncle Willie had turned the radio up to its last notch so that youngsters on the porch wouldn't miss a word. Women sat on kitchen chairs, dining-room chairs, stools, and upturned wooden boxes. Small children and babies perched on every lap available and men leaned on the shelves or on each other.

The apprehensive mood was shot through with shafts of gaiety, as a black    2
sky is streaked with lightning.

"I ain't worried 'bout this fight. Joe's gonna whip that cracker like it's open    3
season."

"He gone whip him till that white boy call him Momma."    4

At last the talking finished and the string-along songs about razor blades    5
were over and the fight began.

"A quick jab to the head." In the Store the crowd grunted. "A left to the    6
head and a right and another left." One of the listeners cackled like a hen and
was quieted.

"They're in a clinch, Louis is trying to fight his way out."    7

Some bitter comedian on the porch said, "That white man don't mind    8
hugging that niggah now, I betcha."

"The referee is moving in to break them up, but Louis finally pushed the    9
contender away and it's an uppercut to the chin. The contender is hanging on,
now he's backing away. Louis catches him with a short left to the jaw."

A tide of murmuring assent poured out the door and into the yard.    10

"Another left and another left. Louis is saving that mighty right . . ."    11
The mutter in the Store had grown into a baby roar and it was pierced by the
clang of a bell and the announcer's "That's the bell for round three, ladies and
gentlemen."

As I pushed my way into the Store I wondered if the announcer gave any    12
thought to the fact that he was addressing as "ladies and gentlemen" all the
Negroes around the world who sat sweating and praying, glued to their "Master's voice."[1]

There were only a few calls for RC Colas, Dr Peppers, and Hires root beer.    13
The real festivities would begin after the fight. Then even the old Christian
ladies who taught their children and tried themselves to practice turning the
other cheek would buy soft drinks, and if the Brown Bomber's victory was a
particularly bloody one they would order peanut patties and Baby Ruths also.

Bailey and I laid the coins on top of the cash register. Uncle Willie didn't    14
allow us to ring up sales during a fight. It was too noisy and might shake up the
atmosphere. When the gong rang for the next round we pushed through the
near-sacred quiet to the herd of children outside.

"He's got Louis against the ropes and now it's a left to the body and a right    15
to the ribs. Another right to the body, it looks like it was low . . . Yes, ladies
and gentlemen, the referee is signaling but the contender keeps raining the
blows on Louis. It's another to the body, and it looks like Louis is going down."

---

[1] "His master's voice," accompanied by a picture of a little dog listening to a phonograph,
was a familiar advertising slogan. (The picture still appears on some RCA recordings.) —Eds.

My race groaned. It was our people falling. It was another lynching, yet    16
another Black man hanging on a tree. One more woman ambushed and raped.
A Black boy whipped and maimed. It was hounds on the trail of a man running
through slimy swamps. It was a white woman slapping her maid for being for-
getful.

The men in the Store stood away from the walls and at attention. Women    17
greedily clutched the babes on their laps while on the porch the shufflings and
smiles, flirtings and pinching of a few minutes before were gone. This might
be the end of the world. If Joe lost we were back in slavery and beyond help.
It would all be true, the accusations that we were lower types of human
beings. Only a little higher than apes. True that we were stupid and ugly and
lazy and dirty and, unlucky and worst of all, that God Himself hated us and
ordained us to be hewers of wood and drawers of water, forever and ever, world
without end.

We didn't breathe. We didn't hope. We waited.    18

"He's off the ropes, ladies and gentlemen. He's moving towards the center    19
of the ring." There was no time to be relieved. The worst might still happen.

"And now it looks like Joe is mad. He's caught Carnera with a left hook to    20
the head and a right to the head. It's a left jab to the body and another left to
the head. There's a left cross and a right to the head. The contender's right eye
is bleeding and he can't seem to keep his block up. Louis is penetrating every
block. The referee is moving in, but Louis sends a left to the body and it's an
uppercut to the chin and the contender is dropping. He's on the canvas, ladies
and gentlemen."

Babies slid to the floor as women stood up and men leaned toward the radio.    21

"Here's the referee. He's counting. One, two, three, four, five, six,    22
seven . . . Is the contender trying to get up again?"

All the men in the store shouted, "NO."    23

"—eight, nine, ten." There were a few sounds from the audience, but they    24
seemed to be holding themselves in against tremendous pressure.

"The fight is all over, ladies and gentlemen. Let's get the microphone over    25
to the referee . . . Here he is. He's got the Brown Bomber's hand, he's holding
it up . . . Here he is . . ."

Then the voice, husky and familiar, came to wash over us—"The win-    26
nah, and still heavyweight champeen of the world . . . Joe Louis."

Champion of the world. A Black boy. Some Black mother's son. He was    27
the strongest man in the world. People drank Coca-Colas like ambrosia and
ate candy bars like Christmas. Some of the men went behind the Store and
poured white lightning in their soft-drink bottles, and a few of the bigger boys
followed them. Those who were not chased away came back blowing their
breath in front of themselves like proud smokers.

It would take an hour or more before the people would leave the Store    28
and head for home. Those who lived too far had made arrangements to stay in
town. It wouldn't do for a Black man and his family to be caught on a lonely
country road on a night when Joe Louis had proved that we were the strongest
people in the world.

---

*For a reading quiz, sources on Maya Angelou, and annotated links to further readings
on Joe Louis and on the history of segregation in the South, visit **bedfordstmartins
.com/thebedfordreader**.*

---

## Journal Writing

How do you respond to the group identification and solidarity that Angelou writes
about in this essay? What groups do you belong to, and how do you know you're a
member? Consider groups based on race, ethnic background, religion, sports, hobbies,
politics, friendship, kinship, or any other ties. (To take your journal writing further,
see "From Journal to Essay" on the next page.)

## Questions on Meaning

1. What do you take to be the author's PURPOSE in telling this story?
2. What connection does Angelou make between the outcome of the fight and the
   pride of African Americans? To what degree do you think the author's view is
   shared by the others in the store listening to the broadcast?
3. To what extent are the statements in paragraphs 16 and 17 to be taken literally?
   What function do they serve in Angelou's narrative?
4. Primo Carnera was probably *not* the Brown Bomber's opponent on the night
   Maya Angelou recalls. Louis fought Carnera only once, on June 25, 1935, and it
   was not a title match. Does the author's apparent error detract from her story?

## Questions on Writing Strategy

1. What details in the opening paragraphs indicate that an event of crucial importance is about to take place?
2. How does Angelou build up SUSPENSE in her account of the fight? At what point
   were you able to predict the winner?
3. Comment on the IRONY in Angelou's final paragraph.
4. What EFFECT does the author's use of direct quotation have on her narrative?

5. **OTHER METHODS**   Besides narration, Angelou also relies heavily on the method of DESCRIPTION. Analyze how narration depends on description in paragraph 27 alone.

## Questions on Language

1. Explain what the author means by "string-along songs about razor blades" (par. 5).
2. Point to some examples in the essay of Angelou's use of strong verbs.
3. How does Angelou's use of NONSTANDARD ENGLISH contribute to her narrative?
4. Be sure you know the meanings of these words: apprehensive (par. 2); assent (10); ambushed, maimed (16); ordained (17); ambrosia, white lightning (27).

## Suggestions for Writing

1. **FROM JOURNAL TO ESSAY**   From your journal entry, choose one of the groups you belong to and explore your sense of membership through a narrative that tells of an incident that occurred when that sense was strong. Try to make the incident come alive for your readers with vivid details, dialog, and tight sequencing of events.
2. Write an essay based on some childhood experience of your own, still vivid in your memory.
3. Do some research about the boxing career of Joe Louis. Then write an essay in which you discuss popular attitudes toward the Brown Bomber in his day.
4. **CRITICAL WRITING**   Angelou does not directly describe relations between African Americans and whites, yet her essay implies quite a lot. Write a brief essay about what you can INFER from the exaggeration of paragraphs 16–17 and the obliqueness of paragraph 28. Focus on Angelou's details and the language she uses to present them.
5. **CONNECTIONS**   Angelou's "Champion of the World" and the next essay, Amy Tan's "Fish Cheeks," both tell stories of children who felt like outsiders in predominantly white America. COMPARE AND CONTRAST the two writers' perceptions of what sets them apart from the dominant culture. How does the event each reports affect that sense of difference? Use specific examples from both essays as your EVIDENCE.

---

# *Maya Angelou on Writing*

Maya Angelou's writings have shown great variety: She has done notable work as an autobiographer, poet, short-story writer, screenwriter, journalist, and song lyricist. Asked by interviewer Sheila Weller, "Do you start each project with a specific idea?" Angelou replied:

It starts with a definite subject, but it might end with something entirely different. When I start a project, the first thing I do is write down, in longhand, everything I know about the subject, every thought I've ever had on it. This may be twelve or fourteen pages. Then I read it back through, for quite a few days, and find—given that subject—what its rhythm is. 'Cause everything in the universe has a rhythm. So if it's free form, it still has a rhythm. And once I hear the rhythm of the piece, then I try to find out what are the salient points that I must make. And then it begins to take shape.

I try to set myself up in each chapter by saying: "This is what I want to go from—from B to, say, G-sharp. Or from D to L." And then I find the hook. It's like the knitting, where, after you knit a certain amount, there's one thread that begins to pull. You know, you can see it right along the cloth. Well, in writing, I think: "Now where is that one hook, that one little thread?" It may be a sentence. If I can catch that, then I'm home free. It's the one that tells me where I'm going. It may not even turn out to be in the final chapter. I may throw it out later or change it. But if I follow it through, it leads me right out.

## For Discussion

1. How would you define the word *rhythm* as Maya Angelou uses it?
2. What response would you give a student who said, "Doesn't Angelou's approach to writing waste more time and thought than it's worth?"

# AMY TAN

AMY TAN is a gifted storyteller whose first novel, *The Joy Luck Club* (1989), met with critical acclaim and huge success. The relationships it details between immigrant Chinese mothers and their Chinese American daughters came from Tan's firsthand experience. She was born in 1952 in Oakland, California, the daughter of immigrants who had fled China's civil war in the late 1940s. She majored in English and linguistics at San Jose State University, where she received a BA in 1973 and an MA in 1974. After two more years of graduate work, Tan became a consultant in language development for disabled children and then started her own company writing reports and speeches for business corporations. Tan began writing fiction to explore her ethnic ambivalence and to find a voice for herself. Since *The Joy Luck Club*, she has published four more novels—most recently *Saving Fish from Drowning* (2005)—as well as children's books and *The Opposite of Fate* (2003), a collection of autobiographical essays. She also sings in the Rock Bottom Remainders, a rock band of writers.

## *Fish Cheeks*

In Tan's novel *The Bonesetter's Daughter* (2001), one of the characters says, "Good manners are not enough. . . . They are not the same as a good heart." Much of Tan's writing explores the tensions between keeping up appearances and having true intentions. In the brief narrative that follows, the author deftly portrays the contradictory feelings and the advantages of a girl with feet in different cultures. The essay first appeared in *Seventeen*, a magazine for teenage girls and young women, in 1987.

For a complementary view of growing up "different," read the preceding essay, Maya Angelou's "Champion of the World."

I fell in love with the minister's son the winter I turned fourteen. He was 1 not Chinese, but as white as Mary in the manger. For Christmas I prayed for this blond-haired boy, Robert, and a slim new American nose.

When I found out that my parents had invited the minister's family over 2 for Christmas Eve dinner, I cried. What would Robert think of our shabby Chinese Christmas? What would he think of our noisy Chinese relatives who lacked proper American manners? What terrible disappointment would he feel upon seeing not a roasted turkey and sweet potatoes but Chinese food?

On Christmas Eve I saw that my mother had outdone herself in creating    3
a strange menu. She was pulling black veins out of the backs of fleshy prawns.
The kitchen was littered with appalling mounds of raw food: A slimy rock cod
with bulging eyes that pleaded not to be thrown into a pan of hot oil. Tofu,
which looked like stacked wedges of rubbery white sponges. A bowl soaking
dried fungus back to life. A plate of squid, their backs crisscrossed with knife
markings so they resembled bicycle tires.

And then they arrived—the minister's family and all my relatives in a    4
clamor of doorbells and rumpled Christmas packages. Robert grunted hello,
and I pretended he was not worthy of existence.

Dinner threw me deeper into despair. My relatives licked the ends of their    5
chopsticks and reached across the table, dipping them into the dozen or so
plates of food. Robert and his family waited patiently for platters to be passed
to them. My relatives murmured with pleasure when my mother brought out
the whole steamed fish. Robert grimaced. Then my father poked his chopsticks just below the fish eye and plucked out the soft meat. "Amy, your
favorite," he said, offering me the tender fish cheek. I wanted to disappear.

At the end of the meal my father leaned back and belched loudly, thank-    6
ing my mother for her fine cooking. "It's a polite Chinese custom to show you
are satisfied," explained my father to our astonished guests. Robert was looking down at his plate with a reddened face. The minister managed to muster
up a quiet burp. I was stunned into silence for the rest of the night.

After everyone had gone, my mother said to me, "You want to be the same    7
as American girls on the outside." She handed me an early gift. It was a
miniskirt in beige tweed. "But inside you must always be Chinese. You must be
proud you are different. Your only shame is to have shame."

And even though I didn't agree with her then, I knew that she understood    8
how much I had suffered during the evening's dinner. It wasn't until many
years later—long after I had gotten over my crush on Robert—that I was able
to fully appreciate her lesson and the true purpose behind our particular menu.
For Christmas Eve that year, she had chosen all my favorite foods.

*For a reading quiz, sources on Amy Tan, and annotated links to further readings on Chinese Americans, visit **bedfordstmartins.com/thebedfordreader**.*

## Journal Writing

Do you sympathize with the shame Tan feels because of her family's differences from their non-Chinese guests? Or do you think she should have been more proud to share her family's customs? Think of an occasion when, for whatever reason, you were acutely aware of being different. How did you react? Did you try to hide your difference in order to fit in, or did you reveal or celebrate your uniqueness? (To take your journal writing further, see "From Journal to Essay" below.)

## Questions on Meaning

1. Why does Tan cry when she finds out that the boy she is in love with is coming to dinner?
2. Why does Tan's mother go out of her way to prepare a disturbingly traditional Chinese dinner for her daughter and guests? What one sentence best sums up the lesson Tan was not able to understand until years later?
3. How does the fourteen-year-old Tan feel about her Chinese background? about her mother?
4. What is Tan's PURPOSE in writing this essay? Does she just want to entertain readers, or might she have a weightier goal?

## Questions on Writing Strategy

1. How does Tan draw the reader into her story right from the beginning?
2. How does Tan use TRANSITIONS both to drive and to clarify her narrative?
3. What is the IRONY of the last sentence of the essay?
4. **OTHER METHODS**   Paragraph 3 is a passage of pure DESCRIPTION. Why does Tan linger over the food? What is the EFFECT of this paragraph?

## Questions on Language

1. The simile about Mary in the second sentence of the essay is surprising. Why? Why is it amusing? (See *Figures of speech* in Useful Terms for a definition of *simile*.)
2. How does the narrator's age affect the TONE of this essay? Give EXAMPLES of language particularly appropriate to a fourteen-year-old.
3. In which paragraph does Tan use strong verbs most effectively?
4. Make sure you know the meanings of the following words: prawns, tofu (par. 3); clamor (4); grimaced (5); muster (6).

## Suggestions for Writing

1. **FROM JOURNAL TO ESSAY**   Using Tan's essay as a model, write a brief narrative based on your journal sketch about a time when you felt different from others. Try to imitate the way Tan integrates the external events of the dinner with her own

feelings about what is going on. Your story may be humorous, like Tan's, or more serious.

2. Take a perspective like that of the minister's son, Robert: Write a narrative essay about a time when you had to adjust to participating in a culture different from your own. It could be a meal, a wedding or other rite of passage, a religious ceremony, a trip to another country. What did you learn from your experience, about yourself and others?

3. **CRITICAL WRITING**   From this essay one can INFER two very different sets of ASSUMPTIONS about the extent to which immigrants should seek to integrate themselves into the culture of their adopted country. Take either of these positions, in favor of or against assimilation (cultural integration), and make an ARGUMENT for your case.

4. **CONNECTIONS**   Both Tan and Maya Angelou, in "Champion of the World" (p. 93), write about difference from white Americans, but their POINTS OF VIEW are not the same: Tan's is a teenager's lament about not fitting in; Angelou's is an oppressed child's excitement about proving the injustice of oppression. In an essay, ANALYZE the two authors' uses of narration to convey their perspectives. What details do they focus on? What internal thoughts do they report? Is one essay more effective than the other? Why, or why not?

------

# *Amy Tan on Writing*

In 1989 Amy Tan delivered a lecture titled "Mother Tongue" at the State of the Language Symposium in San Francisco. The lecture, later published in *The Threepenny Review* in 1990, addresses Tan's own experience as a bilingual child speaking both Chinese and English. "I do think that the language spoken in the family, especially in immigrant families, which are more insular, plays a large role in shaping the language of the child. And I believe that it affected my results on achievement tests, IQ tests, and the SAT. While my English skills were never judged as poor, compared to math English could not be considered my strong suit. . . . This was understandable. Math is precise; there is only one correct answer. Whereas, for me at least, the answers on English tests were always a judgment call, a matter of opinion and personal experience."

Tan goes on to say that the necessity of adapting to different styles of expression may affect other children from bilingual households. "I've been asked, as a writer, why there are not more Asian-Americans represented in American literature. Why are there few Asian-Americans enrolled in creative-writing programs? Why do so many Chinese students go into engineering? Well, these are broad sociological questions I can't begin to answer. But I have noticed in surveys . . . that Asian students, as a whole, always do significantly better on math achievement tests than in English. And this makes me think that there are other Asian-American students whose English spoken in the home might also be described as 'broken' or 'limited.' And perhaps they also have teachers who are steering them away from writing and into math and science, which is what happened to me."

Tan admits that when she first began writing fiction, she wrote "what I thought to be wittily crafted sentences, sentences that would finally prove I had mastery over the English language." But they were awkward and self-conscious, so she changed her tactic. "I later decided I should envision a reader for the stories I would write. And the reader I decided upon was my mother, because these were stories about mothers. So with this reader in mind—and in fact, she did read my early drafts—I began to write stories using all the Englishes I grew up with: the English I spoke to my mother, . . . the English she used with me, . . . my translation of her Chinese, . . . and what I imagined to be her translation of her Chinese if she could speak in perfect English, her internal language, and for that I sought to preserve the essence, but not either an English or a Chinese structure. I wanted to capture what language ability tests can never reveal: her intent, her passion, her imagery, the rhythms of her speech and the nature of her thoughts.

"Apart from what any critic had to say about my writing, I knew I had succeeded where it counted when my mother finished reading my book and gave me her verdict: 'So easy to read.'"

## For Discussion

1. How could growing up in a household of "broken" English be a handicap for a student taking an achievement test?
2. What does the author suggest is the reason why more Asian Americans major in engineering than major in writing?
3. Why did Amy Tan's mother make a good reader?

# ANNIE DILLARD

ANNIE DILLARD is accomplished as a prose writer, poet, and literary critic. Born in 1945, she earned a BA (1967) and an MA (1968) from Hollins College in Virginia. Dillard's first published prose, *Pilgrim at Tinker Creek* (1974), attracted notice for its close, intense, and poetic descriptions of the natural world. It won her a Pulitzer Prize and comparison with Thoreau. Since then, Dillard's entranced and entrancing writing has appeared regularly in *Harper's*, *The Atlantic Monthly*, and other magazines and in her wide-ranging books, including *Holy the Firm* (1978), a prose poem; *Living by Fiction* (1982), literary criticism; *Teaching a Stone to Talk* (1982), nonfiction; *An American Childhood* (1987), autobiography; *The Writing Life* (1989), anecdotes and metaphors about writing; *For the Time Being* (1999), an exploration of how God and evil can coexist; and *The Maytrees* (2007), a novel. In 1999 Dillard was inducted into the American Academy of Arts and Letters.

# *The Chase*

Dillard's autobiography, *An American Childhood*, views experience with the sharply perceptive eyes of a child. In this chapter from the book, Dillard leads us running desperately through snow-filled backyards. Like all of her writing, this romp shows unparalleled enthusiasm for life and skill at expressing it.

Some boys taught me to play football. This was fine sport. You thought up a new strategy for every play and whispered it to the others. You went out for a pass, fooling everyone. Best, you got to throw yourself mightily at someone's running legs. Either you brought him down or you hit the ground flat on your chin, with your arms empty before you. It was all or nothing. If you hesitated in fear, you would miss and get hurt: you would take a hard fall while the kid got away, or you would get kicked in the face while the kid got away. But if you flung yourself wholeheartedly at the back of his knees—if you gathered and joined body and soul and pointed them diving fearlessly—then you likely wouldn't get hurt, and you'd stop the ball. Your fate, and your team's score, depended on your concentration and courage. Nothing girls did could compare with it. 1

Boys welcomed me at baseball, too, for I had, through enthusiastic practice, what was weirdly known as a boy's arm. In winter, in the snow, there was neither baseball nor football, so the boys and I threw snowballs at passing cars. I got in trouble throwing snowballs, and have seldom been happier since. 2

On one weekday morning after Christmas, six inches of new snow had just fallen. We were standing up to our boot tops in snow on a front yard on 3 trafficked Reynolds Street, waiting for cars. The cars traveled Reynolds Street slowly and evenly; they were targets all but wrapped in red ribbons, cream puffs. We couldn't miss.

I was seven; the boys were eight, nine, and ten. The oldest two Fahey boys     4 were there—Mikey and Peter—polite blond boys who lived near me on Lloyd Street, and who already had four brothers and sisters. My parents approved Mikey and Peter Fahey. Chickie McBride was there, a tough kid, and Billy Paul and Mackie Kean too, from across Reynolds, where the boys grew up dark and furious, grew up skinny, knowing, and skilled. We had all drifted from our houses that morning looking for action, and had found it here on Reynolds Street.

It was cloudy but cold. The cars' tires laid behind them on the snowy     5 street a complex trail of beige chunks like crenellated castle walls. I had stepped on some earlier; they squeaked. We could have wished for more traffic. When a car came, we all popped it one. In the intervals between cars we reverted to the natural solitude of children.

I started making an iceball—a perfect iceball, from perfectly white snow,     6 perfectly spherical, and squeezed perfectly translucent so no snow remained all the way through. (The Fahey boys and I considered it unfair actually to throw an iceball at somebody, but it had been known to happen.)

I had just embarked on the iceball project when we heard tire chains     7 come clanking from afar. A black Buick was moving toward us down the street. We all spread out, banged together some regular snowballs, took aim, and, when the Buick drew nigh, fired.

A soft snowball hit the driver's windshield right before the driver's face. It     8 made a smashed star with a hump in the middle.

Often, of course, we hit our target, but this time, the only time in all of     9 life, the car pulled over and stopped. Its wide black door opened; a man got out of it, running. He didn't even close the car door.

He ran after us, and we ran away from him, up the snowy Reynolds side-     10 walk. At the corner, I looked back; incredibly, he was still after us. He was in city clothes: a suit and tie, street shoes. Any normal adult would have quit, having sprung us into flight and made his point. This man was gaining on us. He was a thin man, all action. All of a sudden, we were running for our lives.

Wordless, we split up. We were on our turf; we could lose ourselves in the     11 neighborhood backyards, everyone for himself. I paused and considered. Everyone had vanished except Mikey Fahey, who was just rounding the corner of a yellow brick house. Poor Mikey, I trailed him. The driver of the Buick sensibly picked the two of us to follow. The man apparently had all day.

He chased Mikey and me around the yellow house and up a backyard path     12 we knew by heart: under a low tree, up a bank, through a hedge, down some snowy steps, and across the grocery store's delivery driveway. We smashed through a gap in another hedge, entered a scruffy backyard and ran around its back porch and tight between houses to Edgerton Avenue; we ran across Edgerton to an alley and up our own sliding woodpile to the Halls' front yard; he kept coming. We ran up Lloyd Street and wound through mazy backyards toward the steep hilltop at Willard and Lang.

He chased us silently, block after block. He chased us silently over picket       13
fences, through thorny hedges, between houses, around garbage cans, and across streets. Every time I glanced back, choking for breath, I expected he would have quit. He must have been as breathless as we were. His jacket strained over his body. It was an immense discovery, pounding into my hot head with every sliding, joyous step, that this ordinary adult evidently knew what I thought only children who trained at football knew: that you have to fling yourself at what you're doing, you have to point yourself, forget yourself, aim, dive.

Mikey and I had nowhere to go, in our own neighborhood or out of it, but       14
away from this man who was chasing us. He impelled us forward; we compelled him to follow our route. The air was cold; every breath tore my throat. We kept running, block after block; we kept improvising, backyard after backyard, running a frantic course and choosing it simultaneously, failing always to find small places or hard places to slow him down, and discovering always, exhilarated, dismayed, that only bare speed could save us—for he would never give up, this man—and we were losing speed.

He chased us through the backyard labyrinths of ten blocks before he       15
caught us by our jackets. He caught us and we all stopped.

We three stood staggering, half blinded, coughing, in an obscure hilltop       16
backyard: a man in his twenties, a boy, a girl. He had released our jackets, our pursuer, our captor, our hero: He knew we weren't going anywhere. We all played by the rules. Mikey and I unzipped our jackets. I pulled off my sopping mittens. Our tracks multiplied in the backyard's new snow. We had been breaking new snow all morning. We didn't look at each other. I was cherishing my excitement. The man's lower pants legs were wet; his cuffs were full of snow, and there was a prow of snow beneath them on his shoes and socks. Some trees bordered the little flat backyard, some messy winter trees. There was no one around: a clearing in a grove, and we the only players.

It was a long time before he could speak. I had some difficulty at first       17
recalling why we were there. My lips felt swollen; I couldn't see out of the sides of my eyes; I kept coughing.

"You stupid kids," he began perfunctorily.       18

We listened perfunctorily indeed, if we listened at all, for the chewing out       19
was redundant, a mere formality, and beside the point. The point was that he

had chased us passionately without giving up, and so he had caught us. Now he came down to earth. I wanted the glory to last forever.

But how could the glory have lasted forever? We could have run through 20 every backyard in North America until we got to Panama. But when he trapped us at the lip of the Panama Canal, what precisely could he have done to prolong the drama of the chase and cap its glory? I brooded about this for the next few years. He could only have fried Mikey Fahey and me in boiling oil, say, or dismembered us piecemeal, or staked us to anthills. None of which I really wanted, and none of which any adult was likely to do, even in the spirit of fun. He could only chew us out there in the Panamanian jungle, after months or years of exalting pursuit. He could only begin, "You stupid kids," and continue in his ordinary Pittsburgh accent with his normal righteous anger and the usual common sense.

If in that snowy backyard the driver of the black Buick had cut off our 21 heads, Mikey's and mine, I would have died happy, for nothing has required so much of me since as being chased all over Pittsburgh in the middle of winter—running terrified, exhausted—by this sainted, skinny, furious red-headed man who wished to have a word with us. I don't know how he found his way back to his car.

*For a reading quiz, sources on Annie Dillard, and annotated links to further readings on play for children and adults, visit* ***bedfordstmartins.com/thebedfordreader***.

## Journal Writing

Why do you suppose Dillard remembers in such vivid detail the rather insignificant event she describes? What incidents from your childhood seem momentous even now? List these incidents, along with some notes about their importance. (To take your journal writing further, see "From Journal to Essay" on the next page.)

## Questions on Meaning

1. What is Dillard's PURPOSE in this essay? Obviously, she wants to entertain readers, but does she have another purpose as well?
2. Does the persistence of the pursuer seem reasonable to you, given the children's prank?

3. What does the pursuer represent for the narrator? How do her feelings about him change after the chase is over, and why?
4. Why does Dillard describe the "chewing out," seemingly the object of the chase, as "redundant, a mere formality, and beside the point" (par. 19)?

## Questions on Writing Strategy

1. Why does Dillard open her story with a discussion of football? In what way does the game of football serve as a metaphor in the story? (Hint: Look at par. 13, as well as the sentence "It was all or nothing" in par. 1.) (See *Figures of speech* in Useful Terms for a definition of *metaphor*.)
2. Identify the two rapid TRANSITIONS in paragraph 2. Do they contribute to or detract from the COHERENCE of the essay?
3. Why does Dillard interrupt the story of the chase with an "immense discovery" (par. 13)? Does this interruption weaken the narrative?
4. Discuss Dillard's POINT OF VIEW. Is her perspective that of a seven-year-old girl, or that of an adult writer reflecting on her childhood experience?
5. **OTHER METHODS**   Dillard's story implicitly COMPARES AND CONTRASTS a child's and an adult's way of looking at life. What are some of the differences that Dillard implies?

## Questions on Language

1. Look up the meaning of any of the following words you don't already know: crenellated (par. 5); translucent (6); nigh (7); impelled, compelled (14); prow (16); perfunctorily (18); redundant (19); piecemeal, exalting, righteous (20).
2. Explain the contradiction in this statement: "I got in trouble throwing snowballs, and have seldom been happier since" (par. 2). Can you find other examples of paradox in what the narrator says? How is this paradox related to the narrator's apparent view of children? (See *Figures of speech* in Useful Terms for a definition of *paradox*.)
3. Why are the strong verbs Dillard uses in paragraph 20 especially appropriate?
4. What is the EFFECT of the last sentence of the essay?

## Suggestions for Writing

1. **FROM JOURNAL TO ESSAY**   Choose one significant incident from the list of childhood experiences you wrote in your journal, and narrate the incident as vividly as you can. Include the details: Where did the event take place? What did people say? How were they dressed? What was the weather like? Follow Dillard's model in putting CONCRETE IMAGES to work for an idea, in this case an idea about the significance of the incident to you then and now.
2. From what you have seen of children and adults, do you agree with Dillard's characterization of the two groups (see "Writing Strategy" question 5)? Write an essay comparing and contrasting children's and adults' attitudes toward play. (You will have to GENERALIZE, of course, but try to keep your broad statements grounded in a reality your readers will share.)

3. **CRITICAL WRITING** Dillard's narration of the chase is only six paragraphs long (pars. 10–15), but it seems longer, as if almost in real time. What techniques does Dillard use in these paragraphs to hold our attention and re-create the breathlessness of the chase? Look at concrete details, repetition, PARALLELISM, and the near absence of time-marking transitions. In ANALYZING Dillard's techniques, use plenty of quotations from the essay.
4. **CONNECTIONS** Dillard's essay and Brad Manning's "Arm Wrestling with My Father" (p. 146) both deal with childhood values and how they are transformed as one grows older. In an essay, compare and contrast the two writers' treatment of this subject. How does the TONE of each essay contribute to its effect?

---

# *Annie Dillard on Writing*

Writing for *The Bedford Reader,* Dillard has testified to her work habits. Rarely satisfied with an essay until it has gone through many drafts, she sometimes goes on correcting and improving it even after it has been published. "I always have to condense or toss openings," she affirms; "I suspect most writers do. When you begin something, you're so grateful to have begun you'll write down anything, just to prolong the sensation. Later, when you've learned what the writing is really about, you go back and throw away the beginning and start over."

Often she replaces a phrase or sentence with a shorter one. In one essay, to tell how a drop of pond water began to evaporate on a microscope slide, she first wrote, "Its contours pulled together." But that sentence seemed to suffer from "tortured abstraction." She made the sentence read instead, "Its edges shrank." Dillard observes, "I like short sentences. They're forceful, and they can get you out of big trouble."

## For Discussion

1. Why, according to Dillard, is it usually necessary for writers to revise the opening paragraphs of what they write?
2. Dillard says that short sentences "can get you out of big trouble." What kinds of "big trouble" do you suppose she means?

# HAROLD TAW

HAROLD TAW was born in Burma (now Myanmar) and immigrated to the
United States as a child with his family. He attended the University of California at Berkeley and Yale University Law School. He has practiced law in
San Francisco and Seattle and is active in Seattle philanthropies and on the
bicycle advisory board. Recently, he put his law practice on hold to concentrate full-time on writing a novel, *Adventures of the Karaoke King*.

## *Finding Prosperity by Feeding Monkeys*

In this essay Taw relates his efforts to observe an unusual tradition that he
first practiced in his native Burma. Every year, Buddhists commemorate the
birth and death of their founder, Gautama Buddha, with a symbolic watering
of the Bodhi tree, under which the philosopher is said to have achieved
enlightenment. When Taw was born, a monk urged that he perform a similar act of care for the natural world, but the ritual proved difficult when he
immigrated to the United States. Taw read this essay for the National Public
Radio series *This I Believe*, which invites people to explain the philosophies
that guide their daily lives. The essay was also published in a *This I Believe*
collection.

I could say that I believe in America because it rewarded my family's hard
work to overcome poverty. I could say that I believe in holding on to rituals
and traditions because they helped us flourish in a new country. But these concepts are more concretely expressed this way: I believe in feeding monkeys on
my birthday — something I've done without fail for thirty-five years. 1

When I was born, a blind, Buddhist monk, living alone in the Burmese
jungle, predicted that my birth would bring great prosperity to the family. To
ensure this prosperity, I was to feed monkeys on my birthday. 2

While this sounds superstitious, the practice makes karmic sense. On a
day normally given over to narcissism, I must consider my family and give
nourishment to another living creature. The monk never meant for the ritual
to be a burden. In the Burmese jungle, monkeys are as common as pigeons. He
probably had to shoo them away from his sticky rice and mangoes. It was only
in America that feeding monkeys meant violating the rules. 3

As a kid, I thought that was cool. I learned English through watching bad
television shows, and I felt like Caine from *Kung Fu*, except I was the chosen
warrior sent to defend my family. Dad and I would go to the zoo early in the
morning, just the two of us. When the coast was clear, I would throw my contraband peanuts to the monkeys. 4

I never had to explain myself until my eighteenth birthday. It was the first        5
year I didn't go with my father. I went with my friends and arrived ten minutes
after the zoo gates closed.

"*Please,*" I beseeched the zookeeper. "I feed monkeys for my family, not for        6
me. Can't you make an exception?"

"Go find a pet store," she said.        7

If only it were so easy. That time, I got lucky. I found out that a high        8
school classmate had trained the monkeys for the movie *Out of Africa,* so he
allowed me to feed his monkey. I've had other close calls. Once, a man with a
pet monkey suspected that my story was a ploy, and that I was an animal-rights
activist out to liberate his monkey. Another time, a zoo told me that outsiders
could not feed their monkeys without violating the zookeepers' collective bargaining agreement. In a pet store once, I managed to feed a marmoset being
kept in a birdcage. Another time, I was asked to wear a biohazard suit to feed
a laboratory monkey.

It's rarely easy and, yet, somehow I've found a way to feed a monkey every        9
year since I was born.

Our family has prospered in America. I believe that I have ensured this        10
prosperity by observing our family ritual and feeding monkeys on my birthday.
Do I believe that literally? Maybe. But I have faith in our family, and I believe
in honoring that faith in any way I can.

---

*For a reading quiz and annotated links to further readings on Buddhist beliefs and customs, visit* **bedfordstmartins.com/thebedfordreader**.

---

## Journal Writing

Many people have unique traditions, like Taw's tradition of feeding monkeys every
year on his birthday. List some traditions that are unique to your family, to another
group you belong to, or to you alone—for instance, a holiday celebration, a vacation
activity, a way of decompressing after a stressful week. (To take your journal writing
further, see "From Journal to Essay" on the next page.)

## Questions on Meaning

1. Why is Taw's birthday ritual so important to him? Consider not just its literal
   meaning but also its SYMBOLIC one.

2. In paragraph 3 Taw says that his ritual "makes karmic sense." What does he mean? (If necessary, look up *karma* in a dictionary.)
3. In which sentence or sentences does Taw state his THESIS most directly?
4. What would you say is Taw's PURPOSE in this essay? Is it primarily to entertain readers by explaining his odd tradition, or does he seem to have another purpose as well?

## Questions on Writing Strategy

1. What is the EFFECT of Taw's opening paragraph? Why do you think he begins the first two sentences with the phrase "I could say"?
2. Paragraph 8 contains several brief accounts of problems Taw has faced in carrying out his tradition over the years. What do these ANECDOTES contribute to the essay?
3. How would you describe Taw's use of DETAIL in this essay? Where are events compressed, and where are they expanded with a bit more detail? What events receive the most detail, and what is significant about them?
4. Identify some of the TRANSITIONS throughout the essay. How do they create COHERENCE among the different episodes that Taw narrates?
5. **OTHER METHODS**   Taw's essay uses CAUSE AND EFFECT to explain the connection between his monkey-feeding tradition and his family's success in America. What does he seem to be suggesting about the effect of traditions more generally?

## Questions on Language

1. In paragraph 6, why do you suppose Taw uses the word *beseeched* instead of a simpler, less formal verb such as *asked*?
2. What is the effect of the repetition of the word *believe* in both the opening and closing paragraphs of the essay?
3. What does Taw mean by the word *faith* in the last sentence of the essay? How does this meaning relate to the essay as a whole?
4. Be sure you know how to define the following words: flourish (par. 1); prosperity (2); narcissism (3); contraband (4); ploy (8).

## Suggestions for Writing

1. **FROM JOURNAL TO ESSAY**   Write an essay exploring one of the traditions you listed in your journal. Focus on the details of the tradition itself as well as on the significance it holds for you and for any others who participate in it with you.
2. As the headnote for this selection points out, Taw wrote his essay for *This I Believe*, a National Public Radio series in which individuals speak of the principles by which they live. Write your own brief essay about a specific value or belief that you try to live by. Like Taw, make your philosophy concrete by telling a story that shows it in action. You might consider submitting your final essay to the NPR program. Visit *thisibelieve.org* for submission guidelines and examples of other essays from the project.

3. The monk's prediction is an example of divination, the practice of foretelling the future by interpreting various types of signs. This practice plays an important role in many world religions and cultures. Do some research about a particular type of divination, such as astrology, palmistry, or tarot cards. Then report on the practice, explaining how it works and discussing its history as well as its place in modern society. Or write a similarly researched essay on a particular superstition. For example, why is the number thirteen thought to be unlucky? Why is it considered bad luck for a black cat to cross your path? Why is a four-leaf clover or a rabbit's foot believed to bring good luck?

4. **CRITICAL WRITING**   Based on what you know about the context of this piece — that it was written for a radio project calling for short submissions about people's beliefs — analyze how Taw's AUDIENCE and purpose seem to have shaped his essay. In particular, you might focus on the essay's length, tone, diction, organization, and use of scene versus summary.

5. **CONNECTIONS**   Several other essays in this book also deal with connection to one's cultural heritage — for instance, Amy Tan's "Fish Cheeks" (p. 99), Yiyun Li's "Orange Crush" (p. 164), Gloria Naylor's "The Meanings of a Word" (p. 488), Christine Leong's "Being a Chink" (p. 494), Dagoberto Gilb's "Pride" (p. 505), Maxine Hong Kingston's "No Name Woman" (p. 620), and Richard Rodriguez's "Aria: A Memoir of a Bilingual Childhood" (p. 651). Using PARA-PHRASES and quotations from Taw's essay and at least one of these others — and drawing on your own experiences, if you like — write an essay about the difficulties and value of upholding tradition.

# JESSICA COHEN

JESSICA COHEN was born in 1981 in Brussels, Belgium. The child of a journalist, she traveled extensively while growing up but now calls St. Paul, Minnesota, her hometown. Cohen graduated from Yale University in 2003 with
a degree in history. She currently works in publishing, reads "voraciously,"
and plays competitive ultimate Frisbee.

## *Grade A:*
## *The Market for a Yale Woman's Eggs*

When she was a junior in college, Cohen answered an intriguing advertisement in the school newspaper. In this essay she both narrates her unsettling
experience and reports the information she unearthed to help interpret her
experience. The essay appeared first in 2001 in *The New Journal*, a Yale
undergraduate magazine, and then in 2002 in *The Atlantic Monthly*, after
Cohen won the magazine's competition for student essayists.

Since Cohen wrote this essay, the demand for egg donors has continued
to grow. Some states, including Minnesota and California, have passed legislation to ban compensation for donated eggs, but elsewhere the practice is
lightly regulated if at all.

Early in the spring of last year a classified ad ran for two weeks in the *Yale*   1
*Daily News*: "EGG DONOR NEEDED." The couple that placed the ad was picky,
and for that reason was offering $25,000 for an egg from the right donor.

As a child I had a book called *Where Did I Come From?* It offered a full bio-   2
logical explanation, in cartoons, to answer those awkward questions that curious tots ask. But the book is now out of date. Replacing it is, for example,
*Mommy, Did I Grow in Your Tummy?: Where Some Babies Come From*, which
explains the myriad ways that children of the twenty-first century may have
entered their families, including egg donation, surrogacy, in vitro fertilization,[1] and adoption. When conception doesn't occur in the natural way, it
becomes very complicated. Once all possible parties have been accounted
for—egg donor, sperm donor, surrogate mother, paying couple—as many as
five people can be involved in conceiving and carrying a child. No wonder a
new book is necessary.

The would-be parents' decision to advertise in the *News*—and to offer a   3
five-figure compensation—immediately suggested that they were in the market for an egg of a certain rarefied type. Beyond their desire for an Ivy League

[1] Fertilization of an egg outside the body. In Latin, *in vitro* means "in glass." —EDS.

**114**

donor, they wanted a young woman over five feet five, of Jewish heritage, athletic, with a minimum combined SAT score of 1500, and attractive. I was curious—and I fit all the criteria except the SAT score. So I e-mailed Michelle and David (not their real names) and asked for more information about the process and how much the SAT minimum really meant to them. Then I waited for a reply.

Donating an egg is neither simple nor painless. Following an intensive screening and selection process the donor endures a few weeks of invasive medical procedures. First the donor and the woman who will carry the child must coordinate their menstrual cycles. Typically the donor and the recipient take birth-control pills, followed by shots of a synthetic hormone such as Lupron; the combination suppresses ovulation and puts their cycles in sync. After altering her cycle the donor must enhance her egg supply with fertility drugs in the same way an infertile woman does when trying to conceive. Shots of a fertility hormone are administered for seven to eleven days, to stimulate the production of an abnormally large number of egg-containing follicles. During this time the donor must have her blood tested every other day so that doctors can monitor her hormone levels, and she must come in for periodic ultrasounds. Thirty-six hours before retrieval day a shot of hCG, human chorionic gonadotropin, is administered to prepare the eggs for release, so that they will be ready for harvest.

The actual retrieval is done while the donor is under anesthesia. The tool is a needle, and the product, on average, is ten to twenty eggs. Doctors take that many because "not all eggs will be good," according to *Surrogate Mothers Online*, an informational Web site designed and maintained by experienced egg donors and surrogate mothers. "Some will be immature and some over-ripe."

Lisa, one of the hosts on *Surrogate Mothers Online* and an experienced egg donor, described the process as a "rewarding" experience. When she explained that once in a while something can go wrong, I braced myself for the fine print. On very rare occasions, she wrote, hyperstimulation of the ovaries can occur, and the donor must be hospitalized until the ovaries return to normal. In even rarer cases the ovaries rupture, resulting in permanent infertility or possibly even death. "I must stress that this is very rare," Lisa assured prospective donors. "I had two very wonderful experiences. . . . The second [time] I stayed awake to help the doctor count how many eggs he retrieved."

David responded to my e-mail a few hours after I'd sent it. He told me nothing about himself, and only briefly alluded to the many questions I had asked about the egg-donation process. He spent the bulk of the e-mail describing a cartoon, and then requested photos of me. The cartoon was a scene with a "couple that is just getting married, he a nerd and she a beauty," he wrote. "They are kvelling about how wonderful their offspring will be with his brains and her looks." He went on to describe the punch line: The next panel showed a nerdy-looking baby thinking empty thoughts. The following paragraph was more direct. David let me know that he and his wife were flexible on most criteria but that Michelle was "a real Nazi" about "donor looks and donor health history."

This seemed to be a commentary of some sort on the couple's situation    8
and how plans might go awry, but the message was impossible to pin down. I thanked him for the e-mail, asked where to send my pictures, and repeated my original questions about egg donation and their criteria.

In a subsequent e-mail David promised to return my photos, so I sent him    9
dorm-room pictures, the kind that every college student has lying around. Now they assumed a new level of importance. I would soon learn what this anonymous couple, somewhere in the United States, thought about my genetic material as displayed in these photographs.

Infertility is not a modern problem, but it has created a modern industry.    10
Ten percent of American couples are infertile, and many seek treatment from the $2-billion-a-year infertility industry. The approximately 370 fertility clinics across the United States help prospective parents to sift through their options. I sympathize with women who cannot use their own eggs to have children. The discovery must be a sober awakening for those who have always dreamed of raising a family. When would-be parents face this problem, however, their options depend greatly on their income. All over the world most women who can't have children must simply accept the fact and adopt, or find other roles in society. But especially here in the United States wealth can enable such couples to have a child of their own and to determine how closely that child will resemble the one they might have had—or the one they dream of having.

The Web site of Egg Donation, Inc., a program based in California, con-    11
tains a database listing approximately 300 potential donors. In order to access the list interested parties must call the company and request the user ID and the password for the month. Once I'd given the receptionist my name and address, she told me the password: *colorful*. I hung up and entered the database. Potential parents can search for a variety of features, narrowing the pool as much as they like according to ethnic origin, religion of birth, state of residence, hair color, eye color, height, and weight. I typed in the physical and religious characteristics that Michelle and David were looking for and found four potential donors. None of them had a college degree.

The standard compensation for donating an egg to Egg Donation is $3,500    12
to $5,000, and additional funds are offered to donors who have advanced
degrees or are of Asian, African-American, or Jewish descent. Couples searching for an egg at Egg Donation can be picky, but not as picky as couples advertising in the *Yale Daily News*. Should couples be able to pay a premium on
an open market for their idea of the perfect egg? Maybe a modern-day social
Darwinist would say yes.[2] Modern success is measured largely in financial
terms, so why shouldn't the most successful couples, eager to pay more, have
access to the most expensive eggs? Of course, as David illustrated in his first
e-mail, input does not always translate perfectly into output—the donor's
desirable characteristics may never actually be manifested in the child.

If couples choose not to find their eggs through an agency, they must do so    13
independently. An Internet search turned up a few sites like *Surrogate Mothers
Online*, where would-be donors and parents can post classified ads. More than
500 classifieds were posted on the site: a whole marketplace, an eBay for
genetic material.

"Hi! My name is Kimberly," one of the ads read. "I am 24 years old, 5'11"    14
with blonde hair and green eyes. I previously donated eggs and the couple was
blessed with BIG twin boys! The doctor told me I have perky ovaries!... The
doctor told me I had the most perfect eggs he had ever seen." The Web site
provided links to photographs of Kimberly and an e-mail address. Would-be
parents on the site offered "competitive" rates, generally from $5,000 to
$10,000 for donors who fit their specifications.

About a week after I sent my pictures to David and Michelle, I received a    15
third e-mail: "Got the pictures. You look perfect. I can't say this with any
authority. That is my wife's department." I thought back to the first e-mail,
where he'd written, "She's been known to disregard a young woman based on
cheekbones, hair, nose, you name it." He then shifted the focus. "My department is the SAT scores. Can you tell me more about your academic performance? What are you taking at Yale? What high school did you attend?"

The whole thing seemed like a joke. I dutifully answered his questions,    16
explaining that I was from a no-name high school in the Midwest, I couldn't do
math or science, and my academic performance was, well, average; I couldn't
help feeling a bit disconcerted by his particular interest in my SAT score.

Michelle and David now had my educational data as well as my photos.    17
They were examining my credentials and trying to imagine their child. If I was

[2] In the late nineteenth century, social Darwinism misapplied Charles Darwin's evolutionary theory of the survival of the fittest to human relations, maintaining that the wealthy are
naturally more fit than the poor for economic and social life. —EDS.

accepted, a harvest of my eggs would be fertilized by the semen of the author of the disturbing e-mails I had received. A few embryos would be implanted; the remaining, if there were any, would be frozen; and then I would be out of the picture forever.

The modern embryo has been frozen, stolen, aborted, researched, and delivered weeks early, along with five or six instant siblings. The summer of 2001 was full of embryo news, and the first big story was President Bush's deliberation on stem-cell research. The embryos available for genetic research include those frozen by fertility clinics for later use by couples attempting in vitro fertilization. [18]

Embryos took the spotlight again when Helen Beasley, a surrogate mother from Shrewsbury, England, decided to sue a San Francisco couple for parental rights to the twin fetuses she was carrying. The couple and Beasley had agreed that they would pay her $20,000 to carry one child created from a donated egg and the father's sperm. The agreement also called for selective reduction—the abortion of any additional embryos. Beasley claimed that there had been a verbal agreement that such reduction would occur by the twelfth week. The problem arose when Beasley, who had discovered she was carrying twins, was told to abort one, but the arrangements for the reduction weren't made until the thirteenth week. Fearing for her own health and objecting to the abortion of such a highly developed fetus, she refused. At that time she was suing for the right to put the babies up for adoption. She was also seeking the remainder of the financial compensation specified in the contract. The couple did not want the children, and yet had the rights to the genetic material; Beasley was simply a vessel. The case is only one of a multitude invited by modern fertility processes. On August 15, 2001, the *New York Times* reported that the New Jersey Supreme Court had upheld a woman's rights to the embryos that she and her ex-husband had created and frozen six years before. A strange case for child-custody lawyers. [19]

Nearly ten years ago, at the University of California at Irvine's Center for Reproductive Health, doctors took the leftover frozen embryos from previous clients and gave them without consent to other couples and to research centers. Discovery of the scam resulted in more than thirty prosecutions: A group of children had biological parents who hadn't consented to their existence and active parents who had been given stolen goods. Who can say whether throwing the embryos away would have been any better? [20]

Even if Michelle and David liked my data, I knew I'd have a long way to go before becoming an actual donor. The application on Egg Donation's Web site is twelve pages long—longer than Yale's entrance application. The first [21] two pages cover the basics: appearance, name, address, age, and other mundane details. After that I was asked if I'd ever filed for bankruptcy or ever had counseling, if I drank, what my goals in life were, what two of my favorite books were, what my paternal grandfather's height and weight were, what hobbies I had, what kind of relationship I would want to have with the parents and child, and so forth. A few fill-in-the-blanks were thrown in at the end: "I feel strongly about _____. I am sorry I did not _____. In ten years I want to be _____." Not even my closest friends knew all these things about me. If Egg Donation, offering about a fifth what Michelle and David were offering, wanted all this information, what might Michelle and David want?

Michelle and David were certainly trying hard. On one classified-ad site   22 I came across a request that was strangely familiar: "Loving family seeks exceptional egg donor with 1500 SAT, great looks, good family health history, Jewish heritage and athletic. Height 5'4"–5'9", Age 18–29. We will pay EXTREMELY well and will take care of all expenses. Hope to hear from you." The e-mail address was David and Michelle's familiar AOL account. Theirs was the most demanding classified on the site, but also the only one that offered to pay "EXTREMELY well."

I kept dreaming about all the things I could do with $25,000. I had gone   23 into the correspondence on a whim. But soon, despite David's casual tone and the optimistic attitude of all the classifieds and information I read, I realized that this process was something I didn't want to be a part of. I understand the desire for a child who will resemble and fit in with the family. But once a couple starts choosing a few characteristics, shooting for perfection is too easy—especially if they can afford it. The money might have changed my life for a while, but it would have led to the creation of a child encumbered with too many expectations.

After I'd brooded about these matters, I received the shortest e-mail of the   24 correspondence. The verdict on my pictures was in: "I showed the pictures to [my wife] this AM. Personally, I think you look great. She said ho-hum."

David said he might reconsider, and that he was going to keep one of my   25 pictures. That was it. No good-bye, no thanks for my willingness to be, in effect, the biological mother of their child. I guess I didn't fit their design; my genes weren't the right material for their *chef d'oeuvre*.[3] So I was rejected as a donor. I keep imagining the day when David and Michelle's child asks where he or she came from. David will describe how hard they both worked on the whole thing, how many pictures they looked at, and how much money they spent. The child will turn to them and say, "Ho-hum."

---

[3] French, "masterpiece." — EDS.

For a reading quiz and annotated links to further readings on egg and sperm donation, visit *bedfordstmartins.com/thebedfordreader*.

## Journal Writing

Would you consider offering your eggs or your sperm to a person or a couple who could
not have a biological child? Would money be important to you? Would you be more
willing to donate to an individual or to a couple? to acquaintances or relatives or to
strangers? Would you be willing to be screened and selected on the basis of your
appearance, intelligence, and personality? If a child resulted, would you want to be
involved, or not, in his or her life? In your journal, answer these questions or any others that occur to you about egg or sperm donation. (To take your journal writing further, see "From Journal to Essay" on the facing page.)

## Questions on Meaning

1. Why did Cohen respond to the ad for an egg donor? Do you think she seriously
   considered donating her eggs to the couple who placed the ad?
2. According to Cohen, conception via a donor can result in a variety of complications and difficulties. What are some of these?
3. What seems to be Cohen's primary PURPOSE in this essay?
4. Cohen states her THESIS near the end of her essay. What is this thesis?

## Questions on Writing Strategy

1. Cohen intersperses narration of her own experiences with information gleaned
   from research into egg donation. Which paragraphs focus on narration? How
   would the essay have been different if Cohen had first presented the narrative
   and then the research, or vice versa? Why do you think she mixes the two?
2. Cohen specifically lays the groundwork for her thesis at two points earlier in the
   essay. Where are these two points?
3. What is the EFFECT of Cohen's final paragraph?
4. **OTHER METHODS**   Where in the essay does Cohen rely on PROCESS ANALYSIS?
   Why is process analysis appropriate at this point?

## Questions on Language

1. Why do you think Cohen quotes the word *rewarding* in paragraph 6?
2. What is the IRONY in the husband's referring to his wife as "'a real Nazi' about
   'donor looks and donor health history'" (par. 7)?

3. Why do you think Cohen quotes so extensively from Kimberly's advertisement as an egg donor (par. 14)?
4. The term *egg donation* is not really accurate because most "donors" are in fact paid for their services. Why do you think this is the common term rather than, say, *egg marketing*?
5. Consult a dictionary if you need help defining the following: myriad, surrogacy (par. 2); rarefied (3); synthetic, ovulation, follicles (4); rupture, infertility (6); kvelling (7); embryos (17); deliberation (18); vessel (19); brooded (24).

## Suggestions for Writing

1. **FROM JOURNAL TO ESSAY**  Based on your earlier journal writing, draft an essay in which you explain your attitudes toward egg or sperm donation. You might expand your thinking to include advice you would give to a friend or relative who was considering trying to conceive a child using donated sperm or eggs.
2. Have you ever initiated a course of action but then, as events unfolded, developed second thoughts? What changed your mind? Write a narrative essay in which you relate that experience.
3. Conceiving a child by purchasing eggs or sperm raises a number of moral questions. For instance: Are there moral limits on our use of biotechnology to achieve our wishes? Is it ethical to transfer genetic material between strangers? Is it ethical to buy or sell genetic material? Should buyers be able to select "donors" for their appearance and intelligence? Research one of these questions or any other that interests you, and write an essay in which you report the various positions on the issue and defend your view.
4. **CRITICAL WRITING**  Write an essay in which you ANALYZE Cohen's TONE in this essay. You might consider how Cohen manages to suggest, without explicitly arguing, that she disapproves of egg donation as it is currently practiced.
5. **CONNECTIONS**  Both Cohen and Colleen Wenke, in "Too Much Pressure" (p. 533), explore society's quest for perfection—in grades, test scores, looks, athleticism, and so on. Using examples from both selections as well as from your own experience, write a CAUSE AND EFFECT essay on the consequences of society's obsession with perfection.

---

# *Jessica Cohen on Writing*

Jessica Cohen wrote "Grade A" because she couldn't get her experience out of her head. Putting her thoughts on paper helped confirm her decision not to pursue egg donation. "When you figure something out for yourself," Cohen says, "there is a high likelihood that someone else might like to read about it."

Cohen believes that writing "is about sitting down and doing it." "Grade A" came fairly easily to her once she put pencil to paper, probably because she cared about her topic: "It was exciting to do research on a topic I was invested in." Such topics are everywhere, Cohen points out: "Strange things happen to us all the time. We notice interesting and quirky things and wonder why they exist or how they came to exist. The kind of nonfiction writing that I like best comes from these questions."

## For Discussion

1. What are some examples of the questions Cohen refers to at the end of the second paragraph? What questions have prompted your own writing?
2. Discuss a time when writing helped you figure out something about yourself.

# SHIRLEY JACKSON

SHIRLEY JACKSON was a fiction writer best known for horror stories that probe the dark side of human nature and social behavior. But she also wrote humorously about domestic life, a subject she knew well as a wife and the mother of four children. Born in 1919 in California, Jackson moved as a teenager to Syracuse, New York, and graduated from Syracuse University in 1940. She started writing as a young girl and was highly disciplined and productive all her life. She began publishing stories in 1941, and eventually her fiction appeared in *The New Yorker, Harper's, Good Housekeeping,* and many other magazines. Her tales of family life appeared in two books, *Life among the Savages* (1953) and *Raising Demons* (1957). Her more popular (and to her more significant) suspense novels included *The Haunting of Hill House* (1959) and *We Have Always Lived in the Castle* (1962). After Jackson's death in 1965, her husband, the literary critic Stanley Edgar Hyman, published two volumes of her stories, novels, and lectures, *The Magic of Shirley Jackson* (1966) and *Come Along with Me* (1968).

## *The Lottery*

By far Jackson's best-known work and indeed one of the best-known short stories ever, "The Lottery" first appeared in *The New Yorker* in 1948 to loud applause and louder cries of outrage. The time was just after World War II, when Nazi concentration camps and the dropping of atomic bombs had revealed horrors of organized human cruelty. Jackson's husband, denying that her work purveyed "neurotic fantasies," argued instead that it was fitting "for our distressing world." Is the story still relevant today?

1 The morning of June 27th was clear and sunny, with the fresh warmth of a full-summer day; the flowers were blossoming profusely and the grass was richly green. The people of the village began to gather in the square, between the post office and the bank, around ten o'clock; in some towns there were so many people that the lottery took two days and had to be started on June 26th, but in this village, where there were only about three hundred people, the whole lottery took less than two hours, so it could begin at ten o'clock in the morning and still be through in time to allow the villagers to get home for noon dinner.

2 The children assembled first, of course. School was recently over for the summer, and the feeling of liberty sat uneasily on most of them; they tended to gather together quietly for a while before they broke into boisterous play, and their talk was still of the classroom and the teacher, of books and reprimands. Bobby Martin had already stuffed his pockets full of stones, and the

other boys soon followed his example, selecting the smoothest and roundest stones; Bobby and Harry Jones and Dickie Delacroix—the villagers pronounced this name "Dellacroy"—eventually made a great pile of stones in one corner of the square and guarded it against the raids of the other boys. The girls stood aside, talking among themselves, looking over their shoulders at the boys, and the very small children rolled in the dust or clung to the hands of their older brothers or sisters.

Soon the men began to gather, surveying their own children, speaking of 3 planting and rain, tractors and taxes. They stood together, away from the pile of stones in the corner, and their jokes were quiet and they smiled rather than laughed. The women, wearing faded house dresses and sweaters, came shortly after their menfolk. They greeted one another and exchanged bits of gossip as they went to join their husbands. Soon the women, standing by their husbands, began to call to their children, and the children came reluctantly, having to be called four or five times. Bobby Martin ducked under his mother's grasping hand and ran, laughing, back to the pile of stones. His father spoke up sharply, and Bobby came quickly and took his place between his father and his oldest brother.

The lottery was conducted—as were the square dances, the teenage club, 4 the Halloween program—by Mr. Summers, who had time and energy to devote to civic activities. He was a round-faced, jovial man and he ran the coal business, and people were sorry for him, because he had no children and his wife was a scold. When he arrived in the square, carrying the black wooden box, there was a murmur of conversation among the villagers, and he waved and called, "Little late today, folks." The postmaster, Mr. Graves, followed him, carrying a three-legged stool, and the stool was put in the center of the square and Mr. Summers set the black box down on it. The villagers kept their distance, leaving a space between themselves and the stool, and when Mr. Summers said, "Some of you fellows want to give me a hand?" there was a hesitation before two men, Mr. Martin and his oldest son, Baxter, came forward to hold the box steady on the stool while Mr. Summers stirred up the papers inside it.

The original paraphernalia for the lottery had been lost long ago, and the 5 black box now resting on the stool had been put into use even before Old Man Warner, the oldest man in town, was born. Mr. Summers spoke frequently to the villagers about making a new box, but no one liked to upset even as much tradition as was represented by the black box. There was a story that the present box had been made with some pieces of the box that had preceded it, the one that had been constructed when the first people settled down to make a village here. Every year, after the lottery, Mr. Summers began talking again about a new box, but every year the subject was allowed to fade off without anything's being done. The black box grew shabbier each year; by now it was no longer completely black but splintered badly along one side to show the original wood color, and in some places faded or stained.

Mr. Martin and his oldest son, Baxter, held the black box securely on the 6 stool until Mr. Summers had stirred the papers thoroughly with his hand. Because so much of the ritual had been forgotten or discarded, Mr. Summers had been successful in having slips of paper substituted for the chips of wood that had been used for generations. Chips of wood, Mr. Summer had argued, had been all very well when the village was tiny, but now that the population was more than three hundred and likely to keep on growing, it was necessary to use something that would fit more easily into the black box. The night before the lottery, Mr. Summers and Mr. Graves made up the slips of paper and put them in the box, and it was then taken to the safe of Mr. Summers's coal company and locked up until Mr. Summers was ready to take it to the square next morning. The rest of the year, the box was put away, sometimes one place, sometimes another; it had spent one year in Mr. Graves's barn and another year underfoot in the post office, and sometimes it was set on a shelf in the Martin grocery and left there.

There was a great deal of fussing to be done before Mr. Summers declared 7 the lottery open. There were the lists to make up — of heads of families, heads of households in each family, members of each household in each family. There was the proper swearing-in of Mr. Summers by the postmaster, as the official of the lottery; at one time, some people remembered, there had been a recital of some sort, performed by the official of the lottery, a perfunctory, tuneless chant that had been rattled off duly each year; some people believed that the official of the lottery used to stand just so when he said or sang it, others believed that he was supposed to walk among the people, but years and years ago this part of the ritual had been allowed to lapse. There had been, also, a ritual salute, which the official of the lottery had had to use in addressing each person who came up to draw from the box, but this also had changed with time, until now it was felt necessary only for the official to speak to each person approaching. Mr. Summers was very good at all this; in his clean white shirt and blue jeans, with one hand resting carelessly on the black box, he seemed very proper and important as he talked interminably to Mr. Graves and the Martins.

Just as Mr. Summers finally left off talking and turned to the assembled 8 villagers, Mrs. Hutchinson came hurriedly along the path to the square, her sweater thrown over her shoulders, and slid into place in the back of the crowd. "Clean forgot what day it was," she said to Mrs. Delacroix, who stood next to her, and they both laughed softly. "Thought my old man was out back stacking wood," Mrs. Hutchinson went on, "and then I looked out the window and the kids was gone, and then I remembered it was the twenty-seventh and came a-running." She dried her hands on her apron, and Mrs. Delacroix said, "You're in time, though. They're still talking away up there."

Mrs. Hutchinson craned her neck to see through the crowd and found her    9
husband and children standing near the front. She tapped Mrs. Delacroix
on the arm as a farewell and began to make her way through the crowd. The
people separated good-humoredly to let her through; two or three people said,
in voices just loud enough to be heard across the crowd, "Here comes your
Missus, Hutchinson," and "Bill, she made it after all." Mrs. Hutchinson
reached her husband, and Mr. Summers, who had been waiting, said cheerfully, "Thought we were going to have to get on without you, Tessie." Mrs.
Hutchinson said, grinning, "Wouldn't have me leave m'dishes in the sink,
now, would you, Joe?" and soft laughter ran through the crowd as the people
stirred back into position after Mrs. Hutchinson's arrival.

"Well now," Mr. Summers said soberly, "guess we better get started, get    10
this over with, so's we can go back to work. Anybody ain't here?"

"Dunbar," several people said. "Dunbar, Dunbar."                           11

Mr. Summers consulted his list. "Clyde Dunbar," he said. "That's right.    12
He's broke his leg, hasn't he? Who's drawing for him?"

"Me, I guess," a woman said, and Mr. Summers turned to look at her.        13
"Wife draws for her husband," Mr. Summers said. "Don't you have a grown
boy to do it for you, Janey?" Although Mr. Summers and everyone else in the
village knew the answer perfectly well, it was the business of the official of the
lottery to ask such questions formally. Mr. Summers waited with an expression
of polite interest while Mrs. Dunbar answered.

"Horace's not but sixteen yet," Mrs. Dunbar said regretfully. "Guess I gotta  14
fill in for the old man this year."

"Right," Mr. Summers said. He made a note on the list he was holding.      15
Then he asked, "Watson boy drawing this year?"

A tall boy in the crowd raised his hand. "Here," he said. "I'm drawing for  16
m'mother and me." He blinked his eyes nervously and ducked his head as several voices in the crowd said things like "Good fellow, Jack," and "Glad to see
your mother's got a man to do it."

"Well," Mr. Summers said, "guess that's everyone. Old Man Warner          17
make it?"

"Here," a voice said, and Mr. Summers nodded.                             18

A sudden hush fell on the crowd as Mr. Summers cleared his throat and      19
looked at the list. "All ready?" he called. "Now, I'll read the names — heads of
families first — and the men come up and take a paper out of the box. Keep

the paper folded in your hand without looking at it until everyone has had a turn. Everything clear?"

The people had done it so many times that they only half listened to the directions, most of them were quiet, wetting their lips, not looking around. Then Mr. Summers raised one hand high and said, "Adams." A man disengaged himself from the crowd and came forward. "Hi, Steve," Mr. Summers said, and Mr. Adams said, "Hi, Joe." They grinned at one another humorlessly and nervously. Then Mr. Adams reached into the black box and took out a folded paper. He held it firmly by one corner as he turned and went hastily back to his place in the crowd, where he stood a little apart from his family, not looking down at his hand.

"Allen," Mr. Summers said, "Anderson. . . . Bentham."

"Seems like there's no time at all between lotteries anymore," Mrs. Delacroix said to Mrs. Graves in the back row. "Seems like we got through with the last one only last week."

"Time sure goes fast," Mrs. Graves said.

"Clark. . . . Delacroix."

"There goes my old man," Mrs. Delacroix said. She held her breath while her husband went forward.

"Dunbar," Mr. Summers said, and Mrs. Dunbar went steadily to the box while one of the women said, "Go on, Janey," and another said, "There she goes."

"We're next," Mrs. Graves said. She watched while Mr. Graves came around from the side of the box, greeted Mr. Summers gravely, and selected a slip of paper from the box. By now, all through the crowd there were men holding the small folded papers in their large hands, turning them over and over nervously. Mrs. Dunbar and her two sons stood together, Mrs. Dunbar holding the slip of paper.

"Harburt. . . . Hutchinson."

"Get up there, Bill," Mrs. Hutchinson said, and the people near her laughed.

"Jones."

"They do say," Mr. Adams said to Old Man Warner, who stood next to him, "that over in the north village they're talking of giving up the lottery."

Old Man Warner snorted. "Pack of crazy fools," he said. "Listening to the young folks, nothing's good enough for *them*. Next thing you know, they'll be wanting to go back to living in caves, nobody work anymore, live *that* way for a while. Used to be a saying about 'Lottery in June, corn be heavy soon.' First thing you know, we'd all be eating stewed chickweed and acorns. There's *always* been a lottery," he added petulantly. "Bad enough to see young Joe Summers up there joking with everybody."

"Some places have already quit lotteries," Mrs. Adams said.

"Nothing but trouble in *that*," Old Man Warner said stoutly. "Pack of    34
young fools."

"Martin." And Bobby Martin watched his father go forward. "Over-    35
dyke. . . . Percy."

"I wish they'd hurry," Mrs. Dunbar said to her older son. "I wish they'd    36
hurry."

"They're almost through," her son said.    37

"You get ready to run tell Dad," Mrs. Dunbar said.    38

Mr. Summers called his own name and then stepped forward precisely and    39
selected a slip from the box. Then he called, "Warner."

"Seventy-seventh year I been in the lottery," Old Man Warner said as he    40
went through the crowd. "Seventy-seventh time."

"Watson." The tall boy came awkwardly through the crowd. Someone    41
said, "Don't be nervous, Jack," and Mr. Summers said, "Take your time, son."

"Zanini."    42

After that, there was a long pause, a breathless pause, until Mr. Summers    43
holding his slip of paper in the air, said, "All right, fellows." For a minute, no
one moved, and then all the slips of paper were opened. Suddenly, all the
women began to speak at once, saying, "Who is it?" "Who's got it?" "Is it the
Dunbars?" "Is it the Watsons?" Then the voices began to say, "It's Hutchinson.
It's Bill," "Bill Hutchinson's got it."

"Go tell your father," Mrs. Dunbar said to her older son.    44

People began to look around to see the Hutchinsons. Bill Hutchinson was    45
standing quiet, staring down at the paper in his hand. Suddenly, Tessie
Hutchinson shouted to Mr. Summers, "You didn't give him time enough to
take any paper he wanted. I saw you. It wasn't fair!"

"Be a good sport, Tessie," Mrs. Delacroix called, and Mrs. Graves said,    46
"All of us took the same chance."

"Shut up, Tessie," Bill Hutchinson said.    47

"Well, everyone," Mr. Summers said, "that was done pretty fast, and now    48
we've got to be hurrying a little more to get done in time." He consulted his
next list. "Bill," he said, "you draw for the Hutchinson family. You got any
other households in the Hutchinsons?"

"There's Don and Eva," Mrs. Hutchinson yelled. "Make *them* take their    49
chance!"

"Daughters drew with their husband's families, Tessie," Mr. Summers said    50
gently. "You know that as well as anyone else."

"It wasn't *fair*," Tessie said.    51

"I guess not, Joe," Bill Hutchinson said regretfully. "My daughter draws    52 with her husband's family, that's only fair. And I've got no other family except the kids."

"Then, as far as drawing for families is concerned, it's you," Mr. Summers said in explanation, "and as far as drawing for households is concerned, that's you, too. Right?"

"Right," Bill Hutchinson said.

"How many kids, Bill?" Mr. Summers asked formally.

"Three," Bill Hutchinson said. "There's Bill, Jr., and Nancy, and little Dave. And Tessie and me."

"All right, then," Mr. Summer said. "Harry, you got their tickets back?"

Mr. Graves nodded and held up the slips of paper. "Put them in the box, then," Mr. Summers directed. "Take Bill's and put it in."

"I think we ought to start over," Mrs. Hutchinson said, as quietly as she could. "I tell you it wasn't *fair*. You didn't give him time enough to choose. *Everybody* saw that."

Mr. Graves had selected the five slips and put them in the box, and he dropped all the papers but those onto the ground, where the breeze caught them and lifted them off.

"Listen, everybody," Mrs. Hutchinson was saying to the people around her.

"Ready, Bill?" Mr. Summers asked, and Bill Hutchinson, with one quick glance around at his wife and children, nodded.

"Remember," Mr. Summers said, "take the slips and keep them folded until each person has taken one. Harry, you help little Dave." Mr. Graves took the hand of the little boy, who came willingly with him up to the box. "Take a paper out of the box, Davy," Mr. Summers said. Davy put his hand into the box and laughed. "Take just *one* paper," Mr. Summers said. "Harry, you hold it for him." Mr. Graves took the child's hand and removed the folded paper from the tight fist and held it while little Dave stood next to him and looked up at him wonderingly.

"Nancy next," Mr. Summers said. Nancy was twelve, and her school friends breathed heavily as she went forward, switching her skirt, and took a slip daintily from the box. "Bill, Jr.," Mr. Summers said, and Billy, his face red and his feet overlarge, nearly knocked the box over as he got a paper out. "Tessie," Mr. Summers said. She hesitated for a minute, looking around defiantly, and then set her lips and went up to the box. She snatched a paper out and held it behind her.

"Bill," Mr. Summers said, and Bill Hutchinson reached into the box and felt around, bringing his hand out at last with the slip of paper in it.

The crowd was quiet. A girl whispered, "I hope it's not Nancy," and the sound of the whisper reached the edges of the crowd.

"It's not the way it used to be," Old Man Warner said clearly. "People ain't    67
the way they used to be."

"All right," Mr. Summers said. "Open the papers. Harry, you open little    68
Dave's."

Mr. Graves opened the slip of paper and there was a general sigh through    69
the crowd as he held it up and everyone could see that it was blank. Nancy
and Bill, Jr., opened theirs at the same time, and both beamed and laughed,
turning around to the crowd and holding their slips of paper above their
heads.

"Tessie," Mr. Summers said. There was a pause, and then Mr. Summers    70
looked at Bill Hutchinson, and Bill unfolded his paper and showed it. It was
blank.

"It's Tessie," Mr. Summers said, and his voice was hushed. "Show us her    71
paper, Bill."

Bill Hutchinson went over to his wife and forced the slip of paper out of    72
her hand. It had a black spot on it, the black spot Mr. Summers had made the
night before with the heavy pencil in the coal-company office. Bill Hutchinson held it up and there was a stir in the crowd.

"All right, folks," Mr. Summers said. "Let's finish quickly."    73

Although the villagers had forgotten the ritual and lost the original black    74
box, they still remembered to use stones. The pile of stones the boys had made
earlier was ready; there were stones on the ground with the blowing scraps of
paper that had come out of the box. Mrs. Delacroix selected a stone so large
she had to pick it up with both hands and turned to Mrs. Dunbar. "Come on,"
she said. "Hurry up."

Mrs. Dunbar had small stones in both hands, and she said, gasping for    75
breath, "I can't run at all. You'll have to go ahead and I'll catch up with you."

The children had stones already, and someone gave little Davy Hutchin-    76
son a few pebbles.

Tessie Hutchinson was in the center of a cleared space by now, and she    77
held her hands out desperately as the villagers moved in on her. "It isn't fair,"
she said. A stone hit her on the side of the head.

Old Man Warner was saying, "Come on, come on, everyone." Steve    78
Adams was in front of the crowd of villagers, with Mrs. Graves beside him.

"It isn't fair, it isn't right," Mrs. Hutchinson screamed and then they were    79
upon her.

*For a reading quiz, sources on Shirley Jackson, and annotated links to further read-
ings on the psychology of conformity, visit **bedfordstmartins.com/thebedfordreader**.*

_____

## Journal Writing

Think about rituals in which you participate, such as those involving holidays, meals, religious observances, family vacations, sporting events—anything that is repeated and traditional. List some of these in your journal and write about their significance to you. (To take your writing further, see "From Journal to Essay" on the next page.)

## Questions on Meaning

1. The PURPOSE of all fiction might be taken as entertainment or self-expression. Does Jackson have any other purpose in "The Lottery"?
2. When does the reader know what is actually going to occur?
3. Describe this story's community on the basis of what Jackson says of it.
4. What do the villagers' attitudes toward the black box indicate about their feelings toward the lottery?

## Questions on Writing Strategy

1. Jackson uses the third PERSON (*he, she, it, they*) to narrate the story, and she does not enter the minds of her characters. Why do you think she keeps this distant POINT OF VIEW?
2. On your first reading of the story, what did you make of the references to rocks in paragraphs 2–3? Do you think they effectively forecast the ending?
3. Jackson has a character introduce a controversial notion in paragraph 31. Why does she do this?
4. **OTHER METHODS** Jackson is exploring—or inviting us to explore—CAUSES AND EFFECTS. Why do the villagers participate in the lottery every year? What does paragraph 32 hint might have been the original reason for it?

## Questions on Language

1. Dialog provides much information not stated elsewhere in the story. Give three examples of such information about the community and its interactions.
2. Check a dictionary for definitions of the following words: profusely (par. 1); boisterous, reprimand (2); jovial, scold, paraphernalia (4); perfunctory, duly, interminably (7); petulantly (32).
3. In paragraph 64 we read that Mrs. Hutchinson "snatched" the paper out of the box. What does this verb suggest about her attitude?
4. Jackson admits to setting the story in her Vermont village in the present time (that is, 1948). Judging from the names of the villagers, where did these people's ancestors originally come from? What do you make of the names Delacroix and Zanini? What is their significance?
5. Unlike much fiction, "The Lottery" contains few FIGURES OF SPEECH. Why do you think this is?

## Suggestions for Writing

1. **FROM JOURNAL TO ESSAY**   Choose one of the rituals you wrote about in your journal, and compose a narrative about the last time you participated in this ritual. Use DESCRIPTION and dialog to convey the significance of the ritual and your own and other participants' attitudes toward it.

2. Write an imaginary narrative, perhaps set in the future, of a ritual that demonstrates something about the people who participate in it. The ritual can be, but need not be, as sinister as Jackson's lottery; yours could concern bathing, eating, dating, going to school, driving, growing older.

3. In his 1974 book *Obedience to Authority*, the psychologist Stanley Milgram reported and analyzed the results of a study he had conducted that caused a furor among psychologists and the general public. Under orders from white-coated "experimenters," many subjects administered what they believed to be life-threatening electric shocks to other people whom they could hear but not see. In fact, the "victims" were actors and received no shocks, but the subjects thought otherwise and many continued to administer stronger and stronger "shocks" when ordered to do so. Find *Obedience to Authority* in the library and compare and contrast the circumstances of Milgram's experiment with those of Jackson's lottery. For instance, who or what is the order-giving authority in the lottery? What is the significance of seeing or not seeing one's victim?

4. **CRITICAL WRITING**   In a 1960 lecture (which we quote more from in "Shirley Jackson on Writing"), Jackson said that a common response she received to "The Lottery" was "What does this story mean?" (She never answered the question.) In an essay, interpret the meaning of the story as *you* understand it. (What does it say, for instance, about social customs, conformity, guilt, obliviousness, or good and evil?) You will have to INFER meaning from such features as Jackson's own TONE as narrator, the tone of the villagers' dialog, and, of course, the events of the story. Your essay should be supported with specific EVIDENCE from the story.

5. **CONNECTIONS**   Although very different from Jackson's story, Harold Taw's "Finding Prosperity by Feeding Monkeys" (p. 110) also focuses on observing a tradition. Taken together, what do Taw's essay and Jackson's story say about both the benefits and the dangers of adhering to tradition? Write an essay in which you explore the pros and cons of maintaining rituals and traditions, giving examples from these selections and from your own experience and reading.

---

# *Shirley Jackson on Writing*

*Come Along with* Me, a posthumous collection of her work, contains a lecture by Shirley Jackson titled "Biography of a Story" — specifically, a biography of "The Lottery." Far from being born in cruelty or cynicism, the story had quite benign origins. Jackson wrote the story, she recalled, "on a bright June morning when summer seemed to have come at last, with blue skies and warm sun and no heavenly signs to warn me that my morning's work was anything but just another story. The idea had come to me while I was pushing my daughter up the hill in her stroller—it was, as I say, a warm morning, and the hill was steep, and beside my daughter the stroller held the day's groceries—and perhaps the effort of that last fifty yards up the hill put an edge on the story; at any rate, I had the idea fairly clearly in my mind when I put my daughter in her playpen and the frozen vegetables in the refrigerator, and, writing the story, I found that it went quickly and easily, moving from beginning to end without pause. As a matter of fact, when I read it over later I decided that except for one or two minor corrections, it needed no changes, and the story I finally typed up and sent off to my agent the next day was almost word for word the original draft. This, as any writer of stories can tell you, is not a usual thing. All I know is that when I came to read the story over I felt strongly that I didn't want to fuss with it. I didn't think it was perfect, but I didn't want to fuss with it. It was, I thought, a serious, straightforward story, and I was pleased and a little surprised at the ease with which it had been written; I was reasonably proud of it, and hoped that my agent would sell it to some magazine and I would have the gratification of seeing it in print."

After the story was published, however, Jackson was surprised to find both it and herself the subject of "bewilderment, speculation, and plain old-fashioned abuse." She wrote that "one of the most terrifying aspects of publishing stories and books is the realization that they are going to be read, and read by strangers. I had never fully realized this before, although I had of course in my imagination dwelt lovingly upon the thought of the millions and millions of people who were going to be uplifted and enriched and delighted by the stories I wrote. It had simply never occurred to me that these millions and millions of people might be so far from being uplifted that they would sit down and write me letters I was downright scared to open; of the three-hundred-odd letters that I received that summer I can count only thirteen that spoke kindly to me, and they were mostly from friends."

Jackson's favorite letter was one concluding, "Our brothers feel that Miss Jackson is a true prophet and disciple of the true gospel of the redeeming light. When will the next revelation be published?" Jackson's answer: "Never. I am out of the lottery business for good."

## For Discussion

1. What lesson can we draw about creative inspiration from Jackson's anecdote about the origins of "The Lottery"?
2. What seems to have alarmed Jackson about readers' reactions to her story? Do you think she was naive in expecting otherwise?

# ADDITIONAL WRITING TOPICS

## *Narration*

1. Write a narrative with one of the following as your subject. It may be (as your instructor may advise) either a first-PERSON memoir or a story written in the third person, observing the experience of someone else. Decide before you begin what your PURPOSE is and whether you are writing (1) an anecdote; (2) an essay consisting mainly of a single narrative; or (3) an essay that includes more than one story.

   A memorable experience from your early life
   A lesson you learned the hard way
   A trip into unfamiliar territory
   An embarrassing moment that taught you something
   A monumental misunderstanding
   An accident
   An unexpected encounter
   A story about a famous person or someone close to you
   A conflict or contest
   A destructive storm
   An assassination attempt
   A historical event of significance

2. Tell a true story of your early or recent school days, either humorous or serious, relating a struggle you experienced (or still experience) in school.

Note: Writing topics combining narration and description appear on page 183.

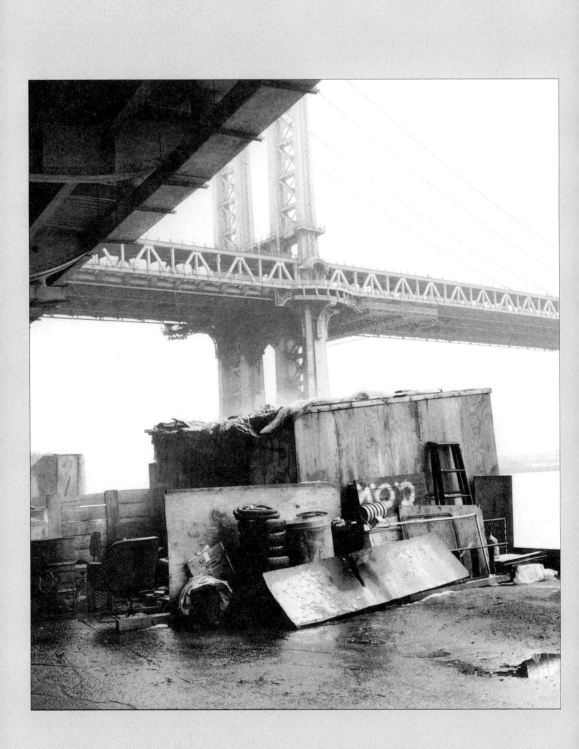

# 5

---

# DESCRIPTION

## *Writing with Your Senses*

◀ **Description in a photograph**

Margaret Morton photographs homeless communities in New York City. This photograph, titled *Doug and Mizan's House, East River*, depicts a makeshift dwelling on a Manhattan riverbank. Consider Morton's photograph as a work of description — revealing a thing through the perceptions of the senses. What do you see through her eyes? What is the house made of? What do the overhanging structure on the upper left and the bridge behind the house add to the impression of the house? If you were standing in the picture, in front of the house, what might you hear or smell? If you touched the house, what textures might you feel? What main idea do you think Morton wants this photograph to convey?

## THE METHOD

Like narration, DESCRIPTION is a familiar method of expression, already a working part of you. In any talk-fest with friends, you probably do your share of describing. You depict in words someone you've met by describing her clothes, the look on her face, the way she walks. You describe somewhere you've been, something you admire, something you just can't abide. In a diary or in e-mail to a friend, you describe your college (cast concrete buildings, crowded walks, pigeons rattling their wings); or perhaps you describe your brand-new secondhand car, from the snakelike glitter of its hubcaps to the odd antiques in its trunk, bequeathed by its previous owner. You hardly can live a day without describing (or hearing described) some person, place, or thing. Small wonder that, in written discourse, description is almost as indispensable as words.

Description reports the testimony of your senses. It invites your readers to imagine that they, too, not only see but perhaps also hear, taste, smell, and touch the subject you describe. Usually, you write a description for either of two PURPOSES: (1) to convey information without bias or emotion; or (2) to convey it with feeling.

In writing with the first purpose in mind, you write an OBJECTIVE (or *impartial*, *public*, or *functional*) description. You describe your subject so clearly and exactly that your reader will understand it or recognize it, and you leave your emotions out. The description in academic writing is usually objective: A biology report on a particular species of frog, for instance, might detail the animal's appearance (four-inch-wide body, bright orange skin with light brown spots), its sounds (hoarse clucks), and its feel (smooth, slippery). You also write this kind of description in sending a friend directions for finding your house: "Look for the green shutters on the windows and a new garbage can at the front door." Although in a personal letter describing a frog or your house you might very well become emotionally involved with it (perhaps calling one "weird" and the other a "fleabag"), in writing an objective description your purpose is not to convey your feelings. You are trying to make the frog or the house easily recognized.

The other type of descriptive writing is SUBJECTIVE (or *emotional*, *personal*, or *impressionistic*). This is the kind included in a magazine advertisement for a new car. It's what you write in your e-mail to a friend setting forth what your college is like—whether you are pleased or displeased with it. In this kind of description, you may use biases and personal feelings—in fact, they are essential. Let us consider a splendid example: a subjective description of a storm at sea. Charles Dickens, in his memoir *American Notes*, conveys his passenger's-eye view of an Atlantic steamship on a morning when the ocean is wild:

> Imagine the ship herself, with every pulse and artery of her huge body swollen and bursting . . . sworn to go on or die. Imagine the wind howling,

the sea roaring, the rain beating; all in furious array against her. Picture the sky both dark and wild, and the clouds in fearful sympathy with the waves, making another ocean in the air. Add to all this the clattering on deck and down below; the tread of hurried feet; the loud hoarse shouts of seamen; the gurgling in and out of water through the scuppers; with every now and then the striking of a heavy sea upon the planks above, with the deep, dead, heavy sound of thunder heard within a vault; and there is the head wind of that January morning.

    I say nothing of what may be called the domestic noises of the ship; such as the breaking of glass and crockery, the tumbling down of stewards, the gambols, overhead, of loose casks and truant dozens of bottled porter, and the very remarkable and far from exhilarating sounds raised in their various staterooms by the seventy passengers who were too ill to get up to breakfast.

Notice how many *sounds* are included in this primarily ear-minded description. We can infer how Dickens feels about the storm. It is a terrifying event that reduces the interior of the vessel to chaos; and yet the writer (in hearing the loose barrels and beer bottles merrily gambol, in finding humor in the sea-sick passengers' plight) apparently delights in it. Writing subjectively, he intrudes his feelings. Think of what a starkly different description of the very same storm the captain might set down—objectively—in the ship's log: "At 0600 hours, watch reported a wind from due north of 70 knots. White-caps were noticed, in height two ells above the bow. Below deck, much gear was reported adrift, and ten casks of ale were broken and their staves strewn about. Mr. Liam Jones, chief steward, suffered a compound fracture of the left leg. . . ." But Dickens, not content simply to record information, strives to ensure that the mind's eye is dazzled and the mind's ear regaled.

Description is usually found in the company of other methods of writing. Often, for instance, it will enliven NARRATION and make the people in the story and the setting unmistakably clear. Writing an ARGUMENT in her essay "Not Your Homeland" (p. 572), Edwidge Danticat begins with a description of a Florida hotel that turns out to serve as a prison for families who are trying to immigrate to the United States. Description will help a writer in examining the EFFECTS of a flood or in COMPARING AND CONTRASTING two paintings. Keep the method of description in mind when you come to try expository and argumentative writing.

## THE PROCESS

### Purpose and Audience

    Understand, first of all, why you are writing about your subject and thus what kind of description is called for. Is it appropriate to perceive and report without emotion or bias—and thus write an objective description? Or is it appropriate to express your personal feelings as well as your perceptions—and thus write a subjective description?

Give a little thought to your AUDIENCE. What do your readers need to be told, if they are to share the perceptions you would have them share, if they are clearly to behold what you want them to? If, let's say, you are describing a downtown street on a Saturday night for an audience of fellow students who live in the same city and know it well, then you need not dwell on the street's familiar geography. What must you tell? Only those details that make the place different on a Saturday night. But if you are remembering your home city, and writing for readers who don't know it, you'll need to establish a few central landmarks to sketch (in their minds) an unfamiliar street on a Saturday night.

Before you begin to write a description, go look at your subject. If that is not possible, your next best course is to spend a few minutes imagining the subject until, in your mind's eye, you can see every flyspeck on it. Then, having fixed your subject in mind, ask yourself which of its features you'll need to report to your particular audience, for your particular purpose. Ask, "What am I out to accomplish?"

## Dominant Impression and Thesis

When you consider your aim in describing, you'll begin to see what impression you intend your subject to make on readers. Let your description, as a whole, convey this one DOMINANT IMPRESSION. If you plan to write a subjective description of an old house, laying weight on its spooky atmosphere for readers you wish to make shiver, then you might mention its squeaking bats and its shadowy halls. If, however, you are describing the house in a classified ad, for an audience of possible buyers, you might focus instead on its eat-in kitchen, working fireplace, and proximity to public transportation. Details have to be carefully selected. Feel no grim duty to include every perceptible detail. To do so would only invite chaos—or perhaps, for the reader, mere tedium. Pick out the features that matter most.

Your dominant impression is like the THESIS of your description—the main idea about your subject that you want readers to take away with them. When you use description to explain or to argue, it's usually a good strategy to state that dominant impression outright, tying it to your essay's thesis or a part of it. In the biology report on a species of frog, for instance, you might preface your description with a statement like this one:

A number of unique features distinguish this frog from others in the order Anura.

Or in an argument in favor of cleaning a local toxic-waste site, you might begin with a description of the site and then state your point about it:

> This landscape is as poisonous as it looks, for underneath its barren crust are enough toxic chemicals to sicken a small village.

When you use subjective description more for its own sake—to show the reader a place or a person, to evoke feelings—you needn't always state your dominant impression as a THESIS STATEMENT, as long as the impression is there dictating the details.

## Organization

You can organize a description in several ways. In depicting the storm at sea—a subjective description—Charles Dickens sorts out the pandemonium for us. He groups the various sounds into two classes: those of sea and sailors, and the "domestic noises" of the ship's passengers—their smashing dishes, their rolling bottles, the crashing of stewards who wait on them.

Other writers of description rely on their POINT OF VIEW to help them arrange details—the physical angle from which they're perceiving and describing. In the previous chapter, on narration, we spoke of point of view: how essential it is for a story to have a narrator—one who, from a certain position, reports what takes place. A description, too, needs a consistent point of view: that of an observer who stays put and observes steadily. From this point of view, you can make a carefully planned inspection tour of your subject, moving spatially (from left to right, from near to far, from top to bottom, from center to periphery), or perhaps moving from prominent objects to tiny ones, from dull to bright, from commonplace to extraordinary—or vice versa.

The plan for you is the one that best fulfills your purpose, arranging details so that the reader firmly receives the impression you mean to convey. If you were to describe, for instance, a chapel in the middle of a desert, you might begin with the details of the lonely terrain. Then, as if approaching the chapel with the aid of a zoom lens, you might detail its exterior before going on inside. That might be a workable method to write a description *if* you wanted to create the dominant impression of the chapel as an island of beauty and feeling in the midst of desolation. Say, however, that you had a different impression in mind: to emphasize the spirituality of the chapel's interior. You might then begin your description inside the structure, perhaps with its most prominent feature, the stained glass windows. You might mention the surrounding desert later in your description, but only incidentally.

Whatever method you follow in arranging details, stick with it all the way through so that your arrangement causes no difficulty for the reader. In describing the chapel in the desert, you wouldn't necessarily proceed in the way you explored the structure, first noting its isolation, then entering and studying its windows and some of its artwork, then going outside again to see what the walls were made of, then moving back inside to finish looking at the artwork, and so on. Instead, you would lead the reader around and through (or through and around) the structure in an organized manner. Look again at Charles Dickens's description of a storm-battered ship: The scene is chaotic, but the prose is orderly.

## Details

Luckily, to write a memorable description, you don't need a storm at sea or any other awe-inspiring subject. As Sarah Vowell demonstrates in "Shooting Dad" later in this chapter, you can write about your family as effectively as you write about a tornado. The secret is in the vividness, the evocativeness of the details. Like most good describers, Vowell uses many IMAGES (language calling up concrete sensory experiences), including FIGURES OF SPEECH (expressions that do not mean literally what they say, often describing one thing in terms of another). For instance, using *metaphor* Vowell writes that "the respective work spaces governed by my father and me were jealously guarded totalitarian states in which each of us declared ourselves dictator." Using *similes*, Vowell describes shooting a pistol as a six-year-old: "The sound it made was as big as God. It kicked little me back to the ground like a bully, like a foe."

---

### FOCUS ON SPECIFIC AND CONCRETE LANGUAGE

When you write effective description, you'll convey your experience as exactly as possible. You may use figures of speech, as discussed above, and you'll definitely rely on language that is specific (tied to actual things) and concrete (tied to the senses of sight, hearing, touch, smell, and taste). Specific and concrete language enables readers to behold with the mind's eye — and to feel with the mind's fingertips.

The first sentence below shows a writer's first-draft attempt to describe something she saw. After editing, the second sentence is much more vivid.

VAGUE   Beautiful, scented wildflowers were in the field.

CONCRETE AND SPECIFIC   Backlighted by the sun and smelling faintly sweet, an acre of tiny lavender flowers spread away from me.

When editing your description, keep a sharp eye out for vague words such as *delicious, handsome, loud,* and *short* that force readers to create their own impressions or, worse, leave them with no impression at all. Using details that call on readers' sensory experiences, say why delicious or why handsome, how loud or how short. When stuck for a word, conjure up your subject and see it, hear it, touch it, smell it, taste it.

Note that *concrete* and *specific* do not mean "fancy": Good description does not demand five-dollar words when nickel equivalents are just as informative. The writer who uses *rubiginous* instead of *rusty red* actually says less because fewer readers will understand the less common word and all readers will sense a writer showing off.

**For exercises on language, visit Exercise Central at** *bedfordstmartins.com /thebedfordreader.*

---

### CHECKLIST FOR REVISING A DESCRIPTION

✔ **SUBJECTIVE OR OBJECTIVE**   Given your purpose and audience, is your description appropriately subjective (emphasizing feelings) or objective (unemotional)?

✔ **DOMINANT IMPRESSION**   What is the dominant impression of your subject? If you haven't stated it, will your readers be able to express it accurately to themselves?

✔ **POINT OF VIEW AND ORGANIZATION**   Do your point of view and organization work together to make your subject clear in readers' minds? Are they consistent?

✔ **DETAILS**   Have you provided all the details—and just those—needed to convey your dominant impression? What needs expanding? What needs condensing or cutting?

✔ **SPECIFIC AND CONCRETE LANGUAGE**   Have you used words that pin down your meaning exactly and appeal to the senses of sight, hearing, touch, taste, and smell?

## DESCRIPTION IN PARAGRAPHS

### Writing About Television

In the following paragraph written especially for *The Bedford Reader*, description works with narration to create suspense. Without even knowing the cause of the suspense, we gather tension from the details. Such a paragraph might pull us into an essay on the subject that is finally revealed only in the last sentence.

At 7:59 this Thursday night, a thick hush settles like cigarette smoke inside the sweat-scented TV room of Harris Hall. First to arrive, freshman Lee Ann squashes down into the catbird seat in front of the screen. Soon she is flanked by roommates Lisa and Kate, silent, their mouths straight lines, their upturned faces lit by the nervous flicker of a car ad. To the left and right of the couch, Pete and Anse crouch on the floor, leaning forward like runners awaiting a starting gun. Behind them, stiff standees line up at attention. Farther back still, English majors and jocks compete for an unobstructed view. Fresh from class, shirttail flapping, arm crooking a bundle of books, Dave barges into the room demanding, "Has it started? Has it started yet?" He is shushed. Somebody shushes a popped-open can of Dr Pepper whose fizz is distractingly loud. What do these students so intently look forward to? At last it starts— TV's hottest reality show.

*Dominant impression (not stated): tense expectation of something vital*

*Details (underlined) contribute to dominant impression*

*Organization proceeds from front of room (at TV) to back*

## Writing in an Academic Discipline

Description interprets a familiar painting in the following paragraph from a text on art history. The details "translate" the painting, creating a bridge between the reader and the text's reproduction of the great work.

While working on *The Battle of Anghiari*, Leonardo painted his most famous portrait, the *Mona Lisa*. The delicate *sfumato* already noted in the *Madonna of the Rocks* is here so perfected that it seemed miraculous to the artist's contemporaries. The forms are built from layers of glazes so gossamer-thin that the entire panel seems to glow with a gentle light from within. But the fame of the *Mona Lisa* comes not from this pictorial subtlety alone; even more intriguing is the psychological fascination of the sitter's personality. Why, among all the smiling faces ever painted, has this particular one been singled out as "mysterious"? Perhaps the reason is that, as a portrait, the picture does not fit our expectations. The features are too individual for Leonardo to have simply depicted an ideal type, yet the element of idealization is so strong that it blurs the sitter's character. Once again the artist has brought two opposites into harmonious balance. The smile, too, may be read in two ways: as the echo of a momentary mood, and as a timeless, symbolic expression (somewhat like the "Archaic smile" of the Greeks . . .). Clearly, the *Mona Lisa* embodies a quality of maternal tenderness which was to Leonardo the essence of womanhood. Even the landscape in the background, composed mainly of rocks and water, suggests elemental generative forces.

*(Sfumato: soft gradations of light and dark)*

*Main idea (topic sentence) of the paragraph, supported by description of "pictorial subtlety" (above) and "psychological fascination" (below)*

*Details (underlined) contribute to dominant impression*

—H. W. Janson, *History of Art*

## DESCRIPTION IN PRACTICE

Edward Johnson was leaving campus for the summer and wanted to sublet his apartment. Scouting around, he discovered that the best place to advertise his apartment was with his college's online "Housing Connection," which served as a network for students, staff, and faculty seeking short- or long-term rentals.

Johnson looked through many of the ads at "The Housing Connection," especially in his category of one-bedrooms, to see how he could make his place seem irresistible compared with the others listed. He noticed that other ads tended to be bare-bones, just the basics on rooms and rent, so he decided to use the twelve lines allotted to him to portray the special qualities of his apartment. In just a couple of drafts, he summoned the descriptive details that would attract a tenant. Here is the actual online posting:

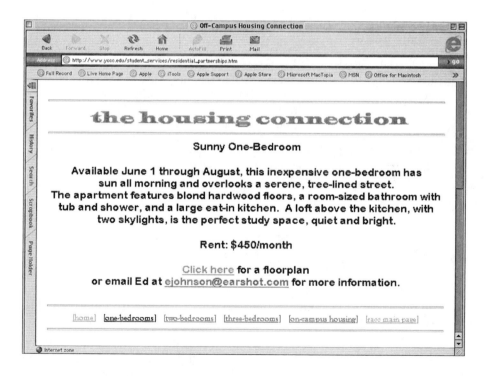

# BRAD MANNING

BRAD MANNING was born in Little Rock, Arkansas, in 1967 and grew up near Charlottesville, Virginia. He attended Harvard University, graduating in 1990 with a BA in history and religion. At Harvard he played intramural sports and wrote articles and reviews for the *Harvard Independent*. After graduation Manning wrote features and news stories for the *Charlotte Observer* and then attended law school at the University of Virginia, graduating in 1995. Now living in Charlottesville with his wife and three children, Manning is a senior resident in the University of Virginia's department of psychiatric medicine.

## *Arm Wrestling with My Father*

In this essay written for his freshman composition course, Manning explores his physical contact with his father over the years, perceiving gradual changes that are, he realizes, inevitable. For Manning, description provides a way to express his feelings about his father and to comment on relations between sons and fathers. In the essay after Manning's, Sarah Vowell uses description for similar ends, but her subject is the relationship between a daughter and her father.

Manning's essay has been published in a Harvard collection of students' writing; in *Student Writers at Work: The Bedford Prizes*; and in *Montage*, a collection of Russian and American stories published in Russian.

"Now you say when" is what he always said before an arm-wrestling match. 1
He liked to put the responsibility on me, knowing that he would always control the outcome. "When!" I'd shout, and it would start. And I would tense up, concentrating and straining and trying to push his wrist down to the carpet with all my weight and strength. But Dad would always win; I always had to lose. "Want to try it again?" he would ask, grinning. He would see my downcast eyes, my reddened, sweating face, and sense my intensity. And with squinting eyes he would laugh at me, a high laugh, through his perfect white teeth. Too bitter to smile, I would not answer or look at him, but I would just roll over on my back and frown at the ceiling. I never thought it was funny at all.

That was the way I felt for a number of years during my teens, after I had 2
lost my enjoyment of arm wrestling and before I had given up that same intense desire to beat my father. Ours had always been a physical relationship,

**146**

I suppose, one determined by athleticism and strength. We never communicated as well in speech or in writing as in a strong hug, battling to make the other gasp for breath. I could never find him at one of my orchestra concerts. But at my lacrosse games, he would be there in the stands, with an angry look, ready to coach me after the game on how I could do better. He never helped me write a paper or a poem. Instead, he would take me outside and show me a new move for my game, in the hope that I would score a couple of goals and gain confidence in my ability. Dad knew almost nothing about lacrosse and his movements were all wrong and sad to watch. But at those times I could just feel how hard he was trying to communicate, to help me, to show the love he had for me, the love I could only assume was there.

His words were physical. The truth is, I have never read a card or a letter written in his hand because he never wrote to me. Never. Mom wrote me all the cards and letters when I was away from home. The closest my father ever came, that I recall, was in a newspaper clipping Mom had sent with a letter. He had gone through and underlined all the important words about the dangers of not wearing a bicycle helmet. Our communication was physical, and that is why we did things like arm wrestle. To get down on the floor and grapple, arm against arm, was like having a conversation.

This ritual of father-son competition in fact had started early in my life, back when Dad started the matches with his arm almost horizontal, his wrist an inch from defeat, and still won. I remember in those battles how my tiny shoulders would press over our locked hands, my whole upper body pushing down in hope of winning that single inch from his calm, unmoving forearm. "Say when," he'd repeat, killing my concentration and causing me to squeal, "I did, I did!" And so he'd grin with his eyes fixed on me, not seeming to notice his own arm, which would begin to rise slowly from its starting position. My greatest efforts could not slow it down. As soon as my hopes had disappeared I'd start to cheat and use both hands. But the arm would continue to move steadily along its arc toward the carpet. My brother, if he was watching, would sometimes join in against the arm. He once even wrapped his little legs around our embattled wrists and pulled back with everything he had. But he did not have much and, regardless of the opposition, the man would win. My arm would lie at rest, pressed into the carpet beneath a solid, immovable arm. In that pinned position, I could only giggle, happy to have such a strong father.

My feelings have changed, though. I don't giggle anymore, at least not around my father. And I don't feel pressured to compete with him the way I thought necessary for years. Now my father is not really so strong as he used to be and I am getting stronger. This change in strength comes at a time when I am growing faster mentally than at any time before. I am becoming less my father and more myself. And as a result, there is less of a need to be set apart from him and his command. I am no longer a rebel in the household, wanting to stand up against the master with clenched fists and tensing jaws, trying to impress him with my education or my views on religion. I am no longer a challenger, quick to correct his verbal mistakes, determined to beat him whenever possible in physical competition.

I am not sure when it was that I began to feel less competitive with my father, but it all became clearer to me one day this past January. I was home in Virginia for a week between exams, and Dad had stayed home from work because the house was snowed in deep. It was then that I learned something I never could have guessed.

I don't recall who suggested arm wrestling that day. We hadn't done it for a long time, for months. But there we were, lying flat on the carpet, face to face, extending our right arms. Our arms were different. His still resembled a fat tree branch, one which had leveled my wrist to the ground countless times before. It was hairy and white with some pink moles scattered about. It looked strong, to be sure, though not so strong as it had in past years. I expect that back in his youth it had looked even stronger. In high school he had played halfback and had been voted "best-built body" of the senior class. Between college semesters he had worked on road crews and on Louisiana dredges. I admired him for that. I had begun to row crew in college and that accounted for some small buildup along the muscle lines, but it did not seem to be enough. The arm I extended was lanky and featureless. Even so, he insisted that he would lose the match, that he was certain I'd win. I had to ignore this, however, because it was something he always said, whether or not he believed it himself.

Our warm palms came together, much the same way we had shaken hands the day before at the airport. Fingers twisted and wrapped about once again, testing for a better grip. Elbows slid up and back making their little indentations on the itchy carpet. My eyes pinched closed in concentration as I tried to center as much of my thought as possible on the match. Arm wrestling, I knew, was a competition that depended less on talent and experience than on one's mental control and confidence. I looked up into his eyes and was ready. He looked back, smiled at me, and said softly (did he sound nervous?), "You say when."

It was not a long match. I had expected him to be stronger, faster. I was conditioned to lose and would have accepted defeat easily. However, after some struggle, his arm yielded to my efforts and began to move unsteadily toward the carpet. I worked against his arm with all the strength I could find. He was working hard as well, straining, breathing heavily. It seemed that this time was different, that I was going to win. Then something occurred to me, something unexpected. I discovered that I was feeling sorry for my father. I wanted to win but I did not want to see him lose.

It was like the thrill I had once experienced as a young boy at my grand-  10
father's lake house in Louisiana when I hooked my first big fish. There was
that sudden tug that made me leap. The red bobber was sucked down beneath
the surface and I pulled back against it, reeling it in excitedly. But when my
cousin caught sight of the fish and shouted out, "It's a keeper," I realized that
I would be happier for the fish if it were let go rather than grilled for dinner.
Arm wrestling my father was now like this, like hooking "Big Joe," the old fish
that Lake Quachita holds but you can never catch, and when you finally think
you've got him, you want to let him go, cut the line, keep the legend alive.

Perhaps at that point I could have given up, letting my father win. But it  11
was so fast and absorbing. How could I have learned so quickly how it would
feel to have overpowered the arm that had protected and provided for me all
of my life? His arms have always protected me and the family. Whenever I am
near him I am unafraid, knowing his arms are ready to catch me and keep me
safe, the way they caught my mother one time when she fainted halfway
across the room, the way he carried me, full grown, up and down the stairs
when I had mononucleosis, the way he once held my feet as I stood on his
shoulders to put up a new basketball net. My mother may have had the words
or the touch that sustained our family, but his were the arms that protected us.
And his were the arms now that I had pushed to the carpet, first the right arm,
then the left.

I might have preferred him to be always the stronger, the one who carries  12
me. But this wish is impossible now; our roles have begun to switch. I do not
know if I will ever physically carry my father as he has carried me, though I
fear that someday I may have that responsibility. More than once this year I
have hesitated before answering the phone late at night, fearing my mother's
voice calling me back to help carry his wood coffin. When I am home with
him and he mentions a sharp pain in his chest, I imagine him collapsing onto
the floor. And in that second vision I see me rushing to him, lifting him onto
my shoulders, and running.

A week after our match, we parted at the airport. The arm-wrestling  13
match was by that time mostly forgotten. My thoughts were on school. I had
been awake most of the night studying for my last exam, and by that morning
I was already back into my college-student manner of reserve and detachment. To say goodbye, I kissed and hugged my mother and I prepared to shake
my father's hand. A handshake had always seemed easier to handle than a
hug. His hugs had always been powerful ones, intended I suppose to give me
strength. They made me suck in my breath and struggle for control, and the
way he would pound his hand on my back made rumbles in my ears. So I
offered a handshake; but he offered a hug. I accepted it, bracing myself for the
impact. Once our arms were wrapped around each other, however, I sensed a

different message. His embrace was softer, longer than before. I remember how it surprised me and how I gave an embarrassed laugh as if to apologize to anyone watching.

I got on the airplane and my father and mother were gone. But as the    14
plane lifted my throat was hurting with sadness. I realized then that Dad must have learned something as well, and what he had said to me in that last hug was that he loved me. Love was a rare expression between us, so I had denied it at first. As the plane turned north, I had a sudden wish to go back to Dad and embrace his arms with all the love I felt for him. I wanted to hold him for a long time and to speak with him silently, telling him how happy I was, telling him all my feelings, in that language we shared.

In his hug, Dad had tried to tell me something he himself had discovered.    15
I hope he tries again. Maybe this spring, when he sees his first crew match, he'll advise me on how to improve my stroke. Maybe he has started doing pushups to rebuild his strength and challenge me to another match — if this were true, I know I would feel less challenged than loved. Or maybe, rather than any of this, he'll just send me a card.

*For a reading quiz and annotated links to further readings on fathers and sons, visit* **bedfordstmartins.com/thebedfordreader**.

## Journal Writing

Manning expresses conflicting feelings about his father. How do you respond to his conflict? When have you felt strongly conflicting emotions about a person or an event, such as a relative, friend, breakup, ceremony, move? Write a paragraph or two exploring your feelings. (To take your journal writing further, see "From Journal to Essay" on the facing page.)

## Questions on Meaning

1. In paragraph 3 Manning says that his father's "words were physical." What does this mean?
2. After his most recent trip home, Manning says, "I realized then that Dad must have learned something as well" (par. 14). What is it that father and son have each learned?

3. Manning says in the last paragraph that he "would feel less challenged than loved" if his father challenged him to a rematch. Does this statement suggest that he did not feel loved earlier? Why, or why not?
4. What do you think is Manning's PURPOSE in this essay? Does he want to express love for his father, or is there something more as well?

## Questions on Writing Strategy

1. Why does Manning start his essay with a match that leaves him "too bitter to smile" and then move backward to earlier bouts of arm wrestling?
2. In the last paragraph Manning suggests that his father might work harder at competing with him and pushing him to be competitive, or he might just send his son a card. Why does Manning present both of these options? Are we supposed to know which will happen?
3. Explain the fishing ANALOGY Manning uses in paragraph 10.
4. **OTHER METHODS**   Manning's essay is as much a NARRATIVE as a description: The author gives brief stories, like video clips, to show the dynamic of his relationship with his father. Look at the story in paragraph 4. How does Manning mix elements of both methods to convey his powerlessness?

## Questions on Language

1. Manning uses the word *competition* throughout this essay. Why is this a more accurate word than *conflict* to describe Manning's relationship with his father?
2. What is the EFFECT of "the arm" in this line from paragraph 4: "But the arm would continue to move steadily along its arc toward the carpet"?
3. In paragraph 9 Manning writes, "I wanted to win but I did not want to see him lose." What does this apparent contradiction mean?
4. If any of these words is unfamiliar, look it up in a dictionary: embattled (par. 4); dredges, crew (7); conditioned (9); mononucleosis (11).

## Suggestions for Writing

1. **FROM JOURNAL TO ESSAY**   Expand your journal entry into a descriptive essay that brings to life your mixed feelings about a person or an event. Focus less on the circumstances and events than on emotions, both positive and negative.
2. Write an essay that describes your relationship with a parent or another close adult. You may want to focus on just one aspect of your relationship, or one especially vivid moment, in order to give yourself the space and time to build many sensory details into your description.
3. Arm wrestling is a highly competitive sport with a long history. Research the sport in the library or on the Internet. Then write a brief essay that traces its history and explains its current standing.
4. **CRITICAL WRITING**   In paragraph 12 Manning writes, "our roles have begun to switch." Does this seem like an inevitable switch, or one that this father and son have been working to achieve? Use EVIDENCE from Manning's essay to support

your answer. Also consider whether Manning and his father would respond the same way to this question.

5. **CONNECTIONS**   Like "Arm Wrestling with My Father," the next essay, Sarah Vowell's "Shooting Dad," depicts a struggle for communication between child and parent. In an essay, COMPARE AND CONTRAST the two essays on this point. What impedes positive communication between the two authors and their fathers? In what circumstances are they able to communicate?

---

## *Brad Manning on Writing*

For *The Bedford Reader*, Brad Manning offered some valuable concrete advice on writing as a student.

You hear this a lot, but writing takes a long time. For me, this is especially true. The only difference between the "Arm Wrestling" essay and all the other essays I wrote in college (and the only reason it's in this book and not thrown away) is that I rewrote it six or seven times over a period of weeks.

If I have something to write, I need to start early. In college, I had a bad habit of putting off papers until 10 PM the night before they were due and spending a desperate night typing whatever ideas the coffee inspired. But putting off papers didn't just lower my writing quality; it robbed me of a good time.

I like starting early because I can jot down notes over a stretch of days; then I type them up fast, ignoring typos; I print the notes with narrow margins, cut them up, and divide them into piles that seem to fit together; then it helps to get away for a day and come back all fresh so I can throw away the corny ideas. Finally, I sit on the floor and make an outline with all the cutouts of paper, trying at the same time to work out some clear purpose for the essay.

When the writing starts, I often get hung up most on trying to "sound" like a good writer. If you're like me and came to college from a shy family that never discussed much over dinner, you might think your best shot is to sound like a famous writer like T. S. Eliot and you might try to sneak in words that aren't really your own like *ephemeral* or *the lilacs smelled like springtime*. But the last thing you really want a reader thinking is how good or bad a writer you are.

Also, in the essay on arm wrestling, I got hung up thinking I had to make my conflict with my father somehow "universal." So in an early draft I wrote in a classical allusion—Aeneas lifting his old father up onto his shoulders and carrying him out of the burning city of Troy.[1] I'd read that story in high school and guessed one classical allusion might make the reader think I knew a lot more. But Aeneas didn't help the essay much, and I'm glad my teacher warned me off trying to universalize. He told me to write just what was true for me.

But that was hard, too, and still is—especially in the first draft. I don't know anyone who enjoys the first draft. If you do, I envy you. But in my early drafts, I always get this sensation like I have to impress somebody and I end up overanalyzing the effects of every word I am about to write. This self-consciousness may be unavoidable (I get self-conscious calling L. L. Bean to order a shirt), but, in this respect, writing is great for shy people because you can edit all you want, all day long, until it finally sounds right. I never feel that I am being myself until the third or fourth draft, and it's only then that it gets personal and starts to be fun.

When I said that putting off papers robbed me of a good time, I really meant it. Writing the essay about my father turned out to be a high point in my life. And on top of having a good time with it, I now have a record of what happened. And my ten-month-old son, when he grows up, can read things about his grandfather and father that he'd probably not have learned any other way.

## For Discussion

1. What did Manning miss by writing his college papers at the last minute?
2. Why does Manning say that "writing is great for shy people"? Have you ever felt that you could express yourself in writing better than in speech?

---

[1] In the *Aeneid*, by the Roman poet Vergil (70–19 BC), the mythic hero Aeneas escapes from the city of Troy when it is sacked by the Greeks and goes on to found Rome.—EDS.

# SARAH VOWELL

SARAH VOWELL is best known for the smart, witty spoken essays she delivers on public radio. Born in Muskogee, Oklahoma, in 1969, Vowell grew up in Oklahoma and Montana. After graduating from Montana State University, she earned an MA in art history and criticism from the School of the Art Institute of Chicago. Radio has played a large part in Vowell's life: She worked as a DJ for her college station in Montana; she published a day-by-day diary of one year spent listening to the radio, *Radio On: A Listener's Diary* (1996); and in 1996 she became a contributing editor for *This American Life* on Public Radio International. She is a frequent guest on television talk shows as well, including David Letterman's and Jon Stewart's. Many of her essays from *This American Life* appear in her book *Take the Cannoli: Stories from the New World* (2000). Her most recent books are *Partly Cloudy Patriot* (2002), *Assassination Vacation* (2005), and *Wordy Shipmates* (2008), the last about the American Puritans. Vowell is also a regular columnist for the online magazine *Salon*, and she was the voice of the teenage superhero Violet in the animated film *The Incredibles* (2004). She lives in New York City.

# *Shooting Dad*

Vowell read "Shooting Dad," in slightly different form, on *This American Life* and then included it in *Take the Cannoli*. Like the previous essay, Brad Manning's "Arm Wrestling with My Father," this one explores the relationship between child and father. Engaged in a lifelong opposition to her father, Vowell sees their differences in terms of the Constitution: the First Amendment for her, guaranteeing freedom of religion, speech, and assembly; and the Second Amendment for her father, guaranteeing the right to bear arms. Then, with a jolt, Vowell one day realizes how much they have in common.

If you were passing by the house where I grew up during my teenage years     1
and it happened to be before Election Day, you wouldn't have needed to come inside to see that it was a house divided. You could have looked at the Democratic campaign poster in the upstairs window and the Republican one in the downstairs window and seen our home for the Civil War battleground it was. I'm not saying who was the Democrat or who was the Republican — my father or I — but I will tell you that I have never subscribed to *Guns & Ammo*, that I did not plaster the family vehicle with National Rifle Association stickers, and that hunter's orange was never my color.

About the only thing my father and I agree on is the Constitution, though       2
I'm partial to the First Amendment, while he's always favored the Second.

I am a gunsmith's daughter. I like to call my parents' house, located on a       3
quiet residential street in Bozeman, Montana, the United States of Firearms.
Guns were everywhere: the so-called pretty ones like the circa 1850 walnut
muzzleloader hanging on the wall, Dad's clients' fixer-uppers leaning into corners, an entire rack right next to the TV. I had to move revolvers out of my
way to make room for a bowl of Rice Krispies on the kitchen table.

I was eleven when we moved into that Bozeman house. We had never       4
lived in town before, and this was a college town at that. We came from Oklahoma — a dusty little Muskogee County nowhere called Braggs. My parents'
property there included an orchard, a horse pasture, and a couple of acres of
woods. I knew our lives had changed one morning not long after we moved to
Montana when, during breakfast, my father heard a noise and jumped out of
his chair. Grabbing a BB gun, he rushed out the front door. Standing in the
yard, he started shooting at crows. My mother sprinted after him screaming,
"Pat, you might ought to check, but I don't think they do that up here!" From
the look on his face, she might as well have told him that his American citizenship had been revoked. He shook his head, mumbling, "Why, shooting
crows is a national pastime, like baseball and apple pie." Personally, I preferred
baseball and apple pie. I looked up at those crows flying away and thought, I'm
going to like it here.

Dad and I started bickering in earnest when I was fourteen, after the 1984       5
Democratic National Convention. I was so excited when Walter Mondale
chose Geraldine Ferraro as his running mate that I taped the front page of the
newspaper with her picture on it to the refrigerator door. But there was some
sort of mysterious gravity surge in the kitchen. Somehow, that picture ended
up in the trash all the way across the room.

Nowadays, I giggle when Dad calls me on Election Day to cheerfully       6
inform me that he has once again canceled out my vote, but I was not always
so mature. There were times when I found the fact that he was a gunsmith
horrifying. And just *weird*. All he ever cared about were guns. All I ever cared
about was art. There were years and years when he hid out by himself in the
garage making rifle barrels and I holed up in my room reading Allen Ginsberg
poems, and we were incapable of having a conversation that didn't end in an
argument.

Our house was partitioned off into territories. While the kitchen and the       7
living room were well within the DMZ,[1] the respective work spaces governed
by my father and me were jealously guarded totalitarian states in which each

---

[1] Abbreviation for *demilitarized zone*, an area off-limits to war making. — EDS.

of us declared ourselves dictator. Dad's shop was a messy disaster area, a labyrinth of lathes. Its walls were hung with the mounted antlers of deer he'd bagged, forming a makeshift museum of death. The available flat surfaces were buried under a million scraps of paper on which he sketched his mechanical inventions in blue ballpoint pen. And the floor, carpeted with spiky metal shavings, was a tetanus shot waiting to happen. My domain was the cramped, cold space known as the music room. It was also a messy disaster area, an obstacle course of musical instruments—piano, trumpet, baritone horn, valve trombone, various percussion doodads (bells!), and recorders. A framed portrait of the French composer Claude Debussy was nailed to the wall. The available flat surfaces were buried under piles of staff paper, on which I penciled in the pompous orchestra music given titles like "Prelude to the Green Door" (named after an O. Henry short story by the way, not the watershed porn flick *Behind the Green Door*) I started writing in junior high.

8    It has been my experience that in order to impress potential suitors, skip the teen Debussy anecdotes and stick with the always attention-getting line "My dad makes guns." Though it won't cause the guy to like me any better, it will make him handle the inevitable breakup with diplomacy—just in case I happen to have any loaded family heirlooms lying around the house.

9    But the fact is, I have only shot a gun once and once was plenty. My twin sister, Amy, and I were six years old—six—when Dad decided that it was high time we learned how to shoot. Amy remembers the day he handed us the gun for the first time differently. She liked it.

10    Amy shared our father's enthusiasm for firearms and the quick-draw cowboy mythology surrounding them. I tended to daydream through Dad's activities—the car trip to Dodge City's Boot Hill, his beloved John Wayne Westerns on TV. My sister, on the other hand, turned into Rooster Cogburn Jr., devouring Duke movies with Dad. In fact, she named her teddy bear Duke, hung a colossal John Wayne portrait next to her bed, and took to wearing one of those John Wayne shirts that button on the side. So when Dad led us out to the backyard when we were six and, to Amy's delight, put the gun in her hand, she says she felt it meant that Daddy trusted us and that he thought of us as "big girls."

11    But I remember holding the pistol only made me feel small. It was so heavy in my hand. I stretched out my arm and pointed it away and winced. It was a very long time before I had the nerve to pull the trigger and I was so scared I had to close my eyes. It felt like it just went off by itself, as if I had no say in the matter, as if the gun just had this *need*. The sound it made was as big as God. It kicked little me back to the ground like a bully, like a foe. It hurt. I don't know if I dropped it or just handed it back over to my dad, but I do know that I never wanted to touch another one again. And, because I believed in the

devil, I did what my mother told me to do every time I felt an evil presence. I looked at the smoke and whispered under my breath, "Satan, I rebuke thee."

It's not like I'm saying I was traumatized. It's more like I was decided. Guns: Not For Me. Luckily, both my parents grew up in exasperating households where children were considered puppets and/or slaves. My mom and dad were hell-bent on letting my sister and me make our own choices. So if I decided that I didn't want my father's little death sticks to kick me to the ground again, that was fine with him. He would go hunting with my sister, who started calling herself "the loneliest twin in history" because of my reluctance to engage in family activities.    12

Of course, the fact that I was allowed to voice my opinions did not mean that my father would silence his own. Some things were said during the Reagan administration that cannot be taken back. Let's just say that I blamed Dad for nuclear proliferation and Contra aid. He believed that if I had my way, all the guns would be confiscated and it would take the commies about fifteen minutes to parachute in and assume control.    13

We're older now, my dad and I. The older I get, the more I'm interested in becoming a better daughter. First on my list: Figure out the whole gun thing.    14

Not long ago, my dad finished his most elaborate tool of death yet. A cannon. He built a nineteenth-century cannon. From scratch. It took two years.    15

My father's cannon is a smaller replica of a cannon called the Big Horn Gun in front of Bozeman's Pioneer Museum. The barrel of the original has been filled with concrete ever since some high school kids in the '50s pointed it at the school across the street and shot out its windows one night as a prank. According to Dad's historical source, a man known to scholars as A Guy at the Museum, the cannon was brought to Bozeman around 1870, and was used by local white merchants to fire at the Sioux and Cheyenne Indians who blocked their trade access to the East in 1874.    16

"Bozeman was founded on greed," Dad says. The courthouse cannon, he continues, "definitely killed Indians. The merchants filled it full of nuts, bolts, and chopped-up horseshoes. Sitting Bull could have been part of these engagements. They definitely ticked off the Indians, because a couple of years later, Custer wanders into them at Little Bighorn. The Bozeman merchants were out to cause trouble. They left fresh baked bread with cyanide in it on the trail to poison a few Indians."    17

Because my father's sarcastic American history yarns rarely go on for long before he trots out some nefarious ancestor of ours — I come from a long line of moonshiners, Confederate soldiers, murderers, even Democrats — he cracks that the merchants hired some "community-minded Southern soldiers from North Texas." These soldiers had, like my great-great-grandfather John    18

Vowell, fought under pro-slavery guerrilla William C. Quantrill. Quantrill is most famous for riding into Lawrence, Kansas, in 1863 flying a black flag and commanding his men pharaohlike to "kill every male and burn down every house."

"John Vowell," Dad says, "had a little rep for killing people." And since he abandoned my great-grandfather Charles, whose mother died giving birth to him in 1870, and wasn't seen again until 1912, Dad doesn't rule out the possibility that John Vowell could have been one of the hired guns on the Bozeman Trail. So the cannon isn't just another gun to my dad. It's a map of all his obsessions—firearms, certainly, but also American history and family history, subjects he's never bothered separating from each other. [19]

After tooling a million guns, after inventing and building a rifle barrel boring machine, after setting up that complicated shop filled with lathes and blueing tanks and outmoded blacksmithing tools, the cannon is his most ambitious project ever. I thought that if I was ever going to understand the ballistic bee in his bonnet, this was my chance. It was the biggest gun he ever made and I could experience it and spend time with it with the added bonus of not having to actually pull a trigger myself. [20]

I called Dad and said that I wanted to come to Montana and watch him shoot off the cannon. He was immediately suspicious. But I had never taken much interest in his work before and he would take what he could get. He loaded the cannon into the back of his truck and we drove up into the Bridger Mountains. I was a little worried that the National Forest Service would object to us lobbing fiery balls of metal onto its property. Dad laughed, assuring me that "you cannot shoot fireworks, but this is considered a fire*arm*." [21]

It is a small cannon, about as long as a baseball bat and as wide as a coffee can. But it's heavy—110 pounds. We park near the side of the hill. Dad takes his gunpowder and other tools out of this adorable wooden box on which he has stenciled "PAT G. VOWELL CANNONWORKS." Cannonworks: So that's what NRA members call a metal-strewn garage. [22]

Dad plunges his homemade bullets into the barrel, points it at an embankment just to be safe, and lights the fuse. When the fuse is lit, it resembles a cartoon. So does the sound, which warrants Ben Day dot[2] words along the lines of *ker-pow!* There's so much Fourth of July smoke everywhere I feel compelled to sing the national anthem. [23]

I've given this a lot of thought—how to convey the giddiness I felt when the cannon shot off. But there isn't a sophisticated way to say this. It's just really, really cool. My dad thought so, too. [24]

[2] Ben Day dots are colored dots in various sizes, used in comics to intensify words for actions and loud sounds. —EDS.

Sometimes, I put together stories about the more eccentric corners of the    25
American experience for public radio. So I happen to have my tape recorder
with me, and I've never seen levels like these. Every time the cannon goes off,
the delicate needles which keep track of the sound quality lurch into the bad,
red zone so fast and so hard I'm surprised they don't break.

The cannon was so loud and so painful, I had to touch my head to make    26
sure my skull hadn't cracked open. One thing that my dad and I share is
that we're both a little hard of hearing—me from Aerosmith, him from gunsmith.

He lights the fuse again. The bullet knocks over the log he was aiming at.    27
I instantly utter a sentence I never in my entire life thought I would say. I tell
him, "Good shot, Dad."

Just as I'm wondering what's coming over me, two hikers walk by. Appar-    28
ently, they have never seen a man set off a homemade cannon in the middle
of the wilderness while his daughter holds a foot-long microphone up into the
air recording its terrorist boom. One hiker gives me a puzzled look and asks,
"So you work for the radio and that's your dad?"

Dad shoots the cannon again so that they can see how it works. The other    29
hiker says, "That's quite the machine you got there." But he isn't talking about
the cannon. He's talking about my tape recorder and my microphone—which
is called a *shotgun* mike. I stare back at him, then I look over at my father's cannon, then down at my microphone, and I think, Oh. My. God. My dad and I
are the same person. We're both smart-alecky loners with goofy projects and
weird equipment. And since this whole target practice outing was my idea, I
was no longer his adversary. I was his accomplice. What's worse, I was liking it.

I haven't changed my mind about guns. I can get behind the cannon    30
because it is a completely ceremonial object. It's unwieldy and impractical,
just like everything else I care about. Try to rob a convenience store with this
110-pound Saturday night special, you'd still be dragging it in the door Sunday afternoon.

I love noise. As a music fan, I'm always waiting for that moment in a song    31
when something just flies out of it and explodes in the air. My dad is a one-
man garage band, the kind of rock 'n' roller who slaves away at his art for
no reason other than to make his own sound. My dad is an artist—a pretty
driven, idiosyncratic one, too. He's got his last *Gesamtkunstwerk*[3] all planned
out. It's a performance piece. We're all in it—my mom, the loneliest twin in
history, and me.

When my father dies, take a wild guess what he wants done with his ashes.    32
Here's a hint: It requires a cannon.

[3] German, "total work of art," specifically a work that seeks to unify all the arts. —EDS.

"You guys are going to love this," he smirks, eyeballing the cannon. "You    33
get to drag this thing up on top of the Gravellies on opening day of hunting
season. And looking off at Sphinx Mountain, you get to put me in little paper
bags. I can take my last hunting trip on opening morning."

I'll do it, too. I will have my father's body burned into ashes. I will pack    34
these ashes into paper bags. I will go to the mountains with my mother, my sister, and the cannon. I will plunge his remains into the barrel and point it into
a hill so that he doesn't take anyone with him. I will light the fuse. But I will
not cover my ears. Because when I blow what used to be my dad into the
earth, I want it to hurt.

---

*For a reading quiz, sources on Sarah Vowell, and annotated links to further readings
on fathers and daughters, visit **bedfordstmartins.com/thebedfordreader**.*

---

## Journal Writing

How do you respond to Vowell's eccentric, even obsessive, father? Do you basically
come to sympathize with him or not? Who in your life has quirky behavior that you
find charming or annoying or a little of both? Write a paragraph or two about this person, focusing on his or her particular habits or obsessions. (To take your journal writing further, see "From Journal to Essay" on the facing page.)

## Questions on Meaning

1. In her opening sentence, Vowell describes growing up in "a house divided." What
   does she mean? Where in the essay does she make the divisions in her household
   explicit?
2. Why, given Vowell's father's love of guns, was it "fine" with him that his daughter decided as a young child that she wanted nothing to do with guns (par. 12)?
   What does this attitude suggest about his character?
3. What motivated Vowell to come home to watch her father shoot off his homemade
   cannon? Why, given her aversion to guns, does she regard this cannon positively?
4. What do paragraphs 18–19, about her father's family history, contribute to Vowell's
   portrait of him?
5. What seems to be Vowell's PURPOSE in writing here? What DOMINANT IMPRESSION
   of her father does she create?

## Questions on Writing Strategy

1. Why is the anecdote Vowell relates in paragraph 4 an effective introduction both to her father and to their relationship?
2. Paragraph 8 is sort of an aside in this essay—not entirely on the main topic. What purpose does it serve?
3. What does Vowell's final sentence mean? Do you find it a satisfying conclusion to her essay? Why, or why not?
4. **OTHER METHODS**   Throughout her essay, Vowell relies on COMPARISON AND CONTRAST to express her relationship with her father (and with her twin sister in pars. 9–12). Find examples of comparison and contrast. Why is the method important to the essay? How does the method help reinforce Vowell's main point about her relationship with her father?

## Questions on Language

1. In paragraph 4 Vowell shows her father "mumbling" that "shooting crows is a national pastime, like baseball and apple pie," while she notes that she herself "preferred baseball and apple pie." How does the language here illustrate IRONY?
2. Pick out five or six concrete and specific words in paragraph 7. What do they accomplish?
3. In paragraph 9 Vowell writes, "My twin sister, Amy, and I were six years old—six—when Dad decided that it was high time we learned how to shoot. Amy remembers the day he handed us the gun for the first time differently. She liked it." What are the EFFECTS of the repetition of the word *six* in the first sentence and of the three-word final sentence?
4. Study the FIGURES OF SPEECH Vowell uses in paragraph 11 to describe the gun she shot. What is their effect?
5. Consult a dictionary if you need help in defining the following: muzzleloader (par. 3); revoked (4); bickering (5); partitioned, respective, totalitarian, labyrinth, lathes, pompous (7); colossal (10); traumatized (12); proliferation, confiscated (13); cyanide (17); nefarious, moonshiners, guerrilla, pharaohlike (18); ballistic (20); giddiness (24); adversary, accomplice (29); unwieldy (30); idiosyncratic (31).

## Suggestions for Writing

1. **FROM JOURNAL TO ESSAY**   Based on your journal writing, compose an essay that uses description to portray your subject and his or her personal quirks. Be sure to include specific incidents you've witnessed and specific details to create a vivid dominant impression of the person. You may, like Vowell, focus on the evolution of your relationship with this person—whether mainly positive or mainly negative.
2. Conflict between generations is common in many families—whether over music, clothing, hair styles, friends, or larger issues of politics, values, and religion. Write an essay about generational conflicts you have experienced in your family or that

you have witnessed in other families. Are such conflicts inevitable? How can they be resolved?

3. Gun ownership is a divisive issue in the United States. Research and explain the main arguments for and against gun control. Whatever your own position, strive for an objective presentation, neither pro nor con.

4. **CRITICAL WRITING**    Vowell's essay divides into several fairly distinct sections: paragraphs 1–4, 5–7, 8, 9–12, 13, 14–31 (which includes an aside in pars. 17–19), and 32–34. In an essay, analyze what happens in each of these sections. How do they fit together to help develop Vowell's dominant impression? How does the relative length of each section contribute to your understanding of her evolving relationship with her father?

5. **CONNECTIONS**    Both Vowell and Brad Manning, in "Arm Wrestling with My Father" (p. 146), describe their fathers. In an essay, examine words Manning and Vowell use to convey their feelings of distance from their fathers and also their feelings of closeness. Use quotations from both essays to support your analysis.

---

# Sarah Vowell on Writing

Writing for both radio and print, Sarah Vowell has discovered differences in listening and reading audiences. On *Transom.org*'s Internet discussion board, she explained how she writes differently for the two media.

[S]ometimes I feel like I'm so much more manipulative on the radio. I know how to use my voice to make you feel a certain way. And that's not writing—that's acting. I get tired of acting sometimes. Which is why it's nice to be able to go back to the cold old page. Also, real time is an unforgiving medium. I still maintain a little academic streak, and any time I read something on the air or out loud, I have to cut back on the abstract, thinky bits. I have to read a story out loud in front of an audience this week and I had to lop it off by half, to prune it of its dull information and, sometimes, its very point. Those things for you the listener, are bonuses—the listener doesn't get as much filler, the listener gets to feel more. Readers are more patient. . . .

The only real drawback I think from moving between verbal and print media is punctuation. I'm working on another book right now, and there are so many things I want to say that I have to normalize on the page because I do not think in complete, fluid sentences. I seem to think in stopgaps and asides. Which the listener doesn't notice. But the reader, I think, becomes antsy when there are too many dashes and parentheses. So that is a constant battle—(dash!) trying to retain my casual, late twentieth-century (it's where I'm from), American-girl cadences, but without driving the reader crazy with a bunch of marks all over the place. Also, I love the word *and*. And I start too many sentences with *and*. Again, no one notices out loud because that's normative speech. But do that too much on the page and it's distracting and stupid.

## For Discussion

1. What does Vowell mean by having to "normalize [her thoughts] on the page"?
2. What difficulties or rewards have you encountered trying to put ideas into written words for others to read?
3. In your experience as a speaker and a writer, what are the advantages of each form of communication? What are the disadvantages of each?

# YIYUN LI

YIYUN LI was born in Beijing, China, in 1972, the daughter of a physicist and a teacher. She attended Beijing University and moved to the United States in 1996 for graduate study in medicine at the University of Iowa. Li started writing in English when she took an adult education course, and a few years later she entered the University of Iowa's Writer's Workshop and Nonfiction Writing Program, earning master's degrees from both. Her short-story collection, *A Thousand Years of Good Prayers* (2005), won the Pushcart Prize, the Guardian First Book Award, and the Frank O'Connor International Short Story Award. Her stories and essays have appeared in *The New Yorker, The Paris Review*, and other magazines. Li teaches at Mills College in Oakland, California, and lives in Oakland with her husband and two children.

## *Orange Crush*

"Orange Crush" captures Li's teenage fascination with Fruit Treasure, which was the Chinese name for the American orange drink Tang. The powdered drink was first marketed in the United States in 1959 as an alternative to orange juice. When it arrived in China some years later, the country was just entering a period of sweeping economic change that, among other effects, allowed in Western ideas and products. To Li and many other Chinese, the fake orange beverage represented a kind of material progress and status that was new to China. "Orange Crush" was originally published in 2006 in the *New York Times Magazine* as part of a recurring food feature titled "Eat, Memory."

During the winter in Beijing, where I grew up, we always had orange and tangerine peels drying on our heater. Oranges were not cheap. My father, who believed that thrift was one of the best virtues, saved the dried peels in a jar; when we had a cough or cold, he would boil them until the water took on a bitter taste and a pale yellow cast, like the color of water drizzling out of a rusty faucet. It was the best cure for colds, he insisted.

I did not know then that I would do the same for my own children, preferring nature's provision over those orange- and pink- and purple-colored medicines. I just felt ashamed, especially when he packed it in my lunch for the annual field trip, where other children brought colorful flavored fruit drinks—made with "chemicals," my father insisted.

The year I turned sixteen, a new product caught my eye. Fruit Treasure, as Tang was named for the Chinese market, instantly won everyone's heart. Imagine real oranges condensed into a fine powder! Equally seductive was the TV commercial, which gave us a glimpse of a life that most families, including mine, could hardly afford. The kitchen was spacious and brightly lighted, whereas ours was a small cube—but at least we had one; half the people we knew cooked in the hallways of their apartment buildings, where every family's dinner was on display and their financial states assessed by the number of meals with meat they ate every week. The family on TV was beautiful, all three of them with healthy complexions and toothy, carefree smiles. (The young parents I saw on my bus ride to school were those who had to leave at six or even earlier in the morning for the two-hour commute and who had to carry their children, half-asleep and often screaming, with them because the only child care they could afford was that provided by their employers.)

The drink itself, steaming hot in an expensive-looking mug that was held 4 between the child's mittened hands, was a vivid orange. The mother talked to the audience as if she were our best friend: "During the cold winter, we need to pay more attention to the health of our family," she said. "That's why I give my husband and my child hot Fruit Treasure for extra warmth and vitamins." The drink's temperature was the only Chinese aspect of the commercial; iced drinks were considered unhealthful and believed to induce stomach disease.

As if the images were not persuasive enough, near the end of the ad an 5 authoritative voice informed us that Tang was the only fruit drink used by NASA for its astronauts—the exact information my father needed to prove his theory that all orange-flavored drinks other than our orange-peel water were made of suspicious chemicals.

Until this point, all commercials were short and boring, with catchy 6 phrases like "Our Product Is Loved by People Around the World" flashing on screen. The Tang ad was a revolution in itself: The lifestyle it represented— a more healthful and richer one, a Western luxury—was just starting to become legitimate in China as it was beginning to embrace the West and its capitalism.

Even though Tang was the most expensive fruit drink available, its sales 7 soared. A simple bottle cost seventeen yuan,[1] a month's worth of lunch money. A boxed set of two became a status hostess gift. Even the sturdy glass containers that the powder came in were coveted. People used them as tea mugs, the orange label still on, a sign that you could afford the modern American drink. Even my mother had an empty Tang bottle with a snug orange nylon net over it, a present from one of her fellow schoolteachers. She carried it from the office to the classroom and back again as if our family had also consumed a full bottle.

The truth was, our family had never tasted Tang. Just think of how many 8 oranges we could buy with the money spent on a bottle, my father reasoned. His resistance sent me into a long adolescent melancholy. I was ashamed by

---

[1] The basic unit of Chinese money, today worth about eight cents. —EDS.

our lack of style and our life, with its taste of orange-peel water. I could not wait until I grew up and could have my own Tang-filled life.

To add to my agony, our neighbor's son brought over his first girlfriend, for    9
whom he had just bought a bottle of Tang. He was five years older and a college sophomore; we had nothing in common and had not spoken more than ten sentences. But this didn't stop me from having a painful crush on him. The beautiful girlfriend opened the Tang in our flat² and insisted that we all try it. When it was my turn to scoop some into a glass of water, the fine orange powder almost choked me to tears. It was the first time I had drunk Tang, and the taste was not like real oranges but stronger, as if it were made of the essence of all the oranges I had ever eaten. This would be the love I would seek, a boy unlike my father, a boy who would not blink to buy a bottle of Tang for me. I looked at the beautiful girlfriend and wished to replace her.

My agony and jealousy did not last long, however. Two months later the    10
beautiful girlfriend left the boy for an older and richer man. Soon after, the boy's mother came to visit and was still outraged about the Tang. "What a waste of money on someone who didn't become his wife!" she said.

"That's how it goes with young people," my mother said. "Once he has a    11
wife, he'll have a better brain and won't throw his money away."

"True. He's just like his father. When he courted me, he once invited me    12
to an expensive restaurant and ordered two fish for me. After we were married, he wouldn't even allow two fish for the whole family for one meal!"

That was the end of my desire for a Tangy life. I realized that every dream    13
ended with this bland, ordinary existence, where a prince would one day become a man who boiled orange peels for his family. I had not thought about the boy much until I moved to America ten years later and discovered Tang in a grocery store. It was just how I remembered it—fine powder in a sturdy bottle—but its glamour had lost its gloss because, alas, it was neither expensive nor trendy. To think that all the dreams of my youth were once contained in this commercial drink! I picked up a bottle and then returned it to the shelf.

*For a reading quiz, sources on Yiyun Li, and annotated links to further readings on the China of Li's youth, visit **bedfordstmartins.com/thebedfordreader**.*

---

²Apartment.—Eds.

## Journal Writing

What food or drink holds a special place in your childhood memories? In your journal, write down as many sensory details about this food or drink as you can. (To take your journal writing further, see "From Journal to Essay" on the next page.)

## Questions on Meaning

1. What does Li's father's insistence on making orange-peel water instead of buying Fruit Treasure suggest about him? Clearly, it reveals his thriftiness, but what else does it say about his character?
2. In what ways does Tang/Fruit Treasure serve as a SYMBOL for Li?
3. What does Li seem to learn from her short-lived crush on the neighbor's son and from the DIALOG between their mothers? How do you interpret her realization that "every dream ended with this bland ordinary existence, where a prince would one day become a man who boiled orange peels for his family" (par. 13)?
4. What DOMINANT IMPRESSION does Li create of Tang and of her childhood longing for it? Does she state this impression in a THESIS STATEMENT or is it implied?
5. What would you say is Li's PURPOSE in this essay?

## Questions on Writing Strategy

1. Which of the five senses does Li mainly appeal to in her essay? Point to some sensory IMAGES that seem especially concrete.
2. Most of Li's essay moves in CHRONOLOGICAL ORDER. The first sentence of paragraph 2, however, jumps to the present, where Li reveals that she now makes orange-peel water for her own children. Why do you think Li placed this sentence here instead of at the end of her essay? What does it tell us about her POINT OF VIEW?
3. Comment on the IRONY in the last paragraph of the essay.
4. As the essay's headnote mentions, Li wrote this piece for a food feature titled "Eat, Memory" in the *New York Times Magazine*. What ASSUMPTIONS does she seem to make about the interests of her readers and their knowledge of Chinese culture? Where in the essay do you see EVIDENCE of these assumptions?
5. **OTHER METHODS**   How does Li use DIVISION or ANALYSIS in paragraphs 3–6 to explain Tang's appeal to Chinese consumers?

## Questions on Language

1. What is the double meaning of Li's title?
2. In paragraph 6, Li calls the Tang commercial a "revolution." Why do you think she chose this word?
3. Explain Li's play on words in the phrase "Tangy life" (par. 13).

4. Consult a dictionary if you need help in defining the following words: thrift (par. 1); provision (2); condensed, assessed (3); mittened, induce (4); capitalism (6); coveted, snug (7); melancholy (8); courted (12).

## Suggestions for Writing

1. **FROM JOURNAL TO ESSAY** In an essay, describe the food or drink you wrote about in your journal, but also do more: Like Li, focus not just on the food or beverage itself but also on its larger meaning. Why is it so special? What did it represent to you as a child? How do you feel about it now? Be sure to infuse your writing with vivid IMAGES evoking concrete sensory experiences.
2. In an essay that combines NARRATION and description, write about a material object that you longed for as a child or as a teenager, such as a toy, a pet, a car, or a pair of brand-name sneakers. Why did you want this thing so badly? Did you get what you wanted? If so, did it live up to your expectations? If you didn't get it, what was your reaction?
3. **CRITICAL WRITING** In paragraph 7, Li writes, "Even though Tang was the most expensive fruit drink available, its sales soared." Using QUOTATIONS and PARA-PHRASES from Li's essay as EVIDENCE, write an essay in which you explain the reasons for Tang's popularity in China. To further support your point, you might do some library or Internet research on China's "open door" policy, which, starting in the late 1970s, encouraged foreign investment and brought Western products into the country.
4. **CONNECTIONS** Both Li and Amy Tan, in "Fish Cheeks" (p. 99), write about how as teenagers they felt ashamed of their families because of a certain food or drink. Write an essay in which you COMPARE AND CONTRAST the ways the two writers describe food and how each writer uses food to make a larger point about the need to fit in.

---

# *Yiyun Li on Writing*

Growing up in China, Yiyun Li studied English, but she didn't learn to use the language until she arrived in the United States at age twenty-four. Now, unlike many immigrant writers, Li writes exclusively in her acquired language. She told Aida Edemariam of the *Guardian* in England that Chinese, to her, is a language of not only political repression but also emotional inversion: Her family members love one another but do not say so. "I can't write in Chinese at all," Li said. "When I write in Chinese, I censor myself." English, in con-trast, is freeing. In Li's short story "A Thousand Years of Good Prayers," a young woman, also a Chinese immigrant in the United States, explains to her father why she can't communicate with him in Chinese but can communicate with others in English:

> Baba, if you grew up in a language that you never used to express your feel-ings, it would be easier to take up another language and talk more in the new language. It makes you a new person.

Li said that she, like her character, "just feel[s] so much more comfortable in English."

## For Discussion

1. Why does Li prefer English for writing, even though it is not her native language?
2. What differences can you point out in two languages you know? The languages could be entirely different tongues, as Chinese and English are, or they could be versions of English that you use in different situations, such as among friends, among family, at work, or in school. What are the advantages and disadvantages of each language? Is one more comfortable for you than another? Why?

# ROBERT BENCHLEY

ROBERT BENCHLEY (1889–1945) was one of America's best-loved and most influential humorists, known for his witty essays about daily events and his screen portrayals of social awkwardness. Benchley was born in Worcester, Massachusetts, and attended Harvard University, where he contributed to the humor magazine the *Harvard Lampoon*. He published essays in *The New Yorker*, *Life*, and other magazines and produced fifteen books, including *Of All Things* (1921), *My Ten Years in a Quandary and How They Grew* (1936), and *Benchley Beside Himself* (1943). As an actor, he appeared in more than eighty films, many of which he also wrote. His movie work earned him a star on Hollywood's Walk of Fame.

## *My Face*

This essay was originally published in *Cosmopolitan* magazine in 1936 and then in Benchley's book *After 1903 — What?* It was recently revived in *The Art of the Personal Essay*, edited by Phillip Lopate. "My Face" is classic Benchley, a deft illumination of a human trait, amiable and self-deprecating. Benchley observes his own self-consciousness, finding complaint not only in his appearance but in his concern with his appearance. If you've ever been startled by a photograph of yourself or by your reflection in a mirror, you'll understand Benchley's position.

1    Merely as an observer of natural phenomena, I am fascinated by my own personal appearance. This does not mean that I am *pleased* with it, mind you, or that I can even tolerate it. I simply have a morbid interest in it.

2    Each day I look like someone, or some*thing*, different. I never know what it is going to be until I steal a look in the glass. (Oh, I don't suppose you really could call it stealing. It belongs to me, after all.)

3    One day I look like Wimpy, the hamburger fancier in the Popeye the Sailor saga.[1] Another day it may be Wallace Beery.[2] And a third day, if I have let my mustache get out of hand, it is Bairnsfather's Old Bill.[3] And not until I peek do I know what the show is going to be.

4    Some mornings, if I look in the mirror soon enough after getting out of bed, there is no resemblance to any character at all, either in or out of fiction,

[1] In comic strips and animated cartoons, Popeye's friend Wimpy is heavy-set with a round face, large nose, and dark mustache. — EDS.
[2] American actor Wallace Beery (1885–1949), often cast as a villain or a lovable slob, had a wide face and large nose. — EDS.
[3] Old Bill, a cartoon character by Bill Bairnsfather (1888–1959), was a grumbling soldier with a bushy, drooping mustache. — EDS.

and I turn quickly to look behind me, convinced that a stranger has spent the night with me and is peering over my shoulder in a sinister fashion, merely to frighten me. On such occasions, the shock of finding that I am actually possessor of the face in the mirror is sufficient to send me scurrying back to bed, completely unnerved.

All this is, of course, very depressing, and I often give off a low moan at     5
the sight of the new day's metamorphosis, but I can't seem to resist the temptation to learn the worst. I even go out of my way to look at myself in store-window mirrors, just to see how long it will take me to recognize myself. If I happen to have on a new hat, or am walking with a limp, I sometimes pass right by my reflection without even nodding. Then I begin to think: "You must have given off *some* visual impression into that mirror. You're not a disembodied spirit yet — I hope."

And I go back and look again, and, sure enough, the strange-looking man     6
I thought was walking just ahead of me in the reflection turns out to have been my own image all the time. It makes a fellow stop and think, I can tell you.

This almost masochistic craving to offend my own aesthetic sense by     7
looking at myself and wincing also comes out when snapshots or class photographs are being passed around. The minute someone brings the envelope containing the week's grist of vacation prints from the drug-store developing plant, I can hardly wait to get my hands on them. I try to dissemble my eagerness to examine those in which I myself figure, but there is a greedy look in my eye which must give me away.

The snapshots in which I do not appear are so much dross in my eyes, but     8
I pretend that I am equally interested in them all.

"This is very good of Joe," I say, with a hollow ring to my voice, sneaking     9
a look at the next print to see if I am in it.

Ah! Here, at last, is one in which I show up nicely. By "nicely" I mean     10
"clearly." Try as I will to pass it by casually, my eyes rivet themselves on that corner of the group in which I am standing. And then, when the others have left the room, I surreptitiously go through the envelope again, just to gaze my fill on the slightly macabre sight of Myself as others see me.

In some pictures I look even worse than I had imagined. On what I call     11
my "good days," I string along pretty close to form. But day in and day out, in mirror or in photograph, there is always that slight shock of surprise which, although unpleasant, lends a tang to the adventure of peeking. I never can quite make it seem possible that this is really Poor Little Me, the Little Me I know so well and yet who frightens me so when face to face.

My only hope is that, in this constant metamorphosis which seems to be     12
going on, a winning number may come up sometime, if only for a day. Just what the final outcome will be, it is hard to predict. I may settle down to a

constant, plodding replica of Man-Mountain Dean[4] in my old age, or change my style completely and end up as a series of Bulgarian peasant types. I may just grow old along with Wimpy.

But whatever is in store for me, I shall watch the daily modulations with 13 an impersonal fascination not unmixed with awe at Mother Nature's gift for caricature, and will take the bitter with the sweet and keep a stiff upper lip.

As a matter of fact, my upper lip is pretty fascinating by itself, in a bizarre 14 sort of way.

For a reading quiz, sources on Robert Benchley, and annotated links to further readings on self-image, visit **bedfordstmartins.com/thebedfordreader**.

---

## Journal Writing

How do you think other people see you? Consider not just your outward appearance but also your personality. In your journal, create two lists of adjectives: one for how you think other people would describe you and one for how you describe yourself. (To take your journal writing further, see "From Journal to Essay" on the facing page.)

## Questions on Meaning

1. Why is Benchley fascinated by his appearance?
2. In paragraph 11, what does Benchley mean by "good days" when he "string[s] along pretty close to form"?
3. What do you think Benchley looks like, based on his description? How well can you picture his face? Is his PURPOSE to help readers visualize his face exactly, or is it something else?
4. How does Benchley see himself? What DOMINANT IMPRESSION does he create of how he feels about his appearance? What one sentence from the essay best conveys this THESIS?

## Questions on Writing Strategy

1. In paragraph 1, Benchley says that he is fascinated by his appearance "[m]erely as an observer of natural phenomena," suggesting that he will describe his appear-

---

[4] Man-Mountain Dean was the nickname of professional wrestler Frank Simmons Leavitt (1891–1953), who weighed more than four hundred pounds and often sported a bushy beard. —EDS.

ance with the objectivity of a scientist. Is this, in fact, what he does? Would you say that his description is mainly OBJECTIVE or SUBJECTIVE? Why?

2. Point to a few sentences in the essay that make particularly effective use of CONCRETE details to convey Benchley's reactions to his face.
3. Writing in the 1930s, Benchley compares himself to people and fictional characters who may not be familiar to most readers today—Wallace Beery, for example, and Old Bill. Does Benchley seem to assume that his audience will understand these ALLUSIONS? Can readers still see Benchley's main point and enjoy the essay without being familiar with them?
4. **OTHER METHODS**  How does Benchley use CLASSIFICATION to help organize his essay?

## Questions on Language

1. How would you describe Benchley's TONE?
2. What is the effect of the word *metamorphosis* in paragraphs 5 and 12? (Check a dictionary if you don't know the meaning of the word.)
3. Find some examples of both formal and informal DICTION in the essay. What is the EFFECT of Benchley's word choice?
4. Why do you suppose Benchley chose to capitalize "Myself" (par. 10) and "Poor Little Me" (11)?
5. Consult a dictionary if you are unsure of the meaning of any of the following: morbid (par. 1); fancier, saga (3); sinister, scurrying (4); disembodied (5); masochistic, aesthetic, wincing, grist, dissemble (7); dross (8); rivet, surreptitiously, macabre (10); tang (11); plodding (12); modulations, caricature (13).

## Suggestions for Writing

1. **FROM JOURNAL TO ESSAY**  Based on the list you created in your journal, write an essay in which you COMPARE AND CONTRAST how you view yourself with how you think others view you. You might focus on a single aspect of your personality (for example, you may see yourself as assertive, while others have called you bossy) or on a number of characteristics that make up your personality as a whole.
2. Write your own essay titled "My Face." Unlike Benchley, however, focus on a single image of your face and try to create a vivid picture of your physical characteristics. Make sure that your descriptive details add up to a dominant impression. For example, if you are describing yourself as a frazzled student, you might focus on your bloodshot eyes and haywire hair.
3. **CRITICAL WRITING**  Based on this essay, ANALYZE Benchley's apparent attitude toward physical appearance. How important do you think Benchley considers looks to be? Do you see him as overly vain? How serious do you think he is in his self-criticism? How do you suppose he would react to society's current obsession with body image? Support your ideas with EVIDENCE from the essay.
4. Although Benchley seems fairly good-natured about his displeasure with his appearance, his essay raises a serious issue about society's obsession with body image. Do some research about cosmetic surgery and write a CAUSE-AND-EFFECT

essay in which you explore why more and more people are choosing to alter their appearance through such surgery.

5. **CONNECTIONS**    A number of modern humorists have been influenced by Benchley's style, including several writers in this book—Dave Barry ("Batting Clean-Up and Striking Out," p. 239), Ian Frazier ("How to Operate the Shower Curtain," p. 302), and Russell Baker, ("The Plot Against People," p. 384). Write an essay ANALYZING where you see Benchley's influence in one or more of these writers' essays. In particular, consider each writer's subject, tone, STYLE, diction, and POINT OF VIEW.

---

## *Robert Benchley on Writing*

Robert Benchley's writing is funny partly because it's polished and clear. In an essay called "Writers—Right or Wrong!" Benchley takes some writers of his day to task for being needlessly confusing. He is discussing fiction, but his point could apply to nonfiction as well.

People who begin sentences with "I may be old-fashioned but—" are usually not only old-fashioned but wrong. I never thought the time would come when I should catch myself leading off with that crack. But I feel it coming on right now. I may be old-fashioned, but I still feel that a writer has a certain obligation to his readers. If he is going to write a book (and Heaven knows there is no law making him do it) he might go at least half way toward making it understandable. That seems little enough to ask.

I am just ill-tempered enough to maintain that a writer who doesn't make his book understandable to a moderately intelligent reader is not writing that way because he is consciously adopting a diffuse style, but because he simply doesn't know how to write; that's all. It is not my fault that I can't read his book. It is his.

### For Discussion

1. Have you had times when you felt, as Benchley does, that your inability to understand a writer was the writer's fault? If so, look back at a piece of writing that you had difficulty with. What caused—and perhaps still causes—the trouble?

2. Conversely, have you had bad reading experiences when it turned out that you were at fault, maybe because you weren't concentrating while you read or because you had a preconception about the piece that interfered with the way you read it?

# JAMES JOYCE

One of the most influential writers in English, JAMES JOYCE (1882–1941) is best known for his immense and challenging novels *Ulysses* (1922) and *Finnegan's Wake* (1939), which combined wordplay and stream of consciousness into a new kind of fiction. Joyce was born near Dublin, Ireland, attended Catholic schools, and graduated in 1902 from University College in Dublin. Before *Ulysses*, Joyce published two other well-regarded works—the story collection *Dubliners* (1914) and the novel *A Portrait of the Artist as a Young Man* (1916)—both of them strongly autobiographical. All of his fiction is set in Dublin, but as a young man he left Ireland and the Catholic Church to live the rest of his life on the European continent. On June 16 each year, fans of Joyce gather in Dublin and other cities to celebrate his life and work.

## *Araby*

Originally published in *Dubliners*, "Araby" portrays a boy's awakening to romance. His fascination with a neighbor girl becomes entangled in his mind with the promise of a bazaar, or fair, called "Araby"—the nineteenth-century name for the exotic and mysterious Middle East. A similar entertainment, the Grand Oriental Fete, was actually held in 1894 in Dublin, when Joyce was living there.

You'll notice in "Araby" that the characters' speeches are marked with dashes instead of quotation marks. This style is common in some European languages, and Joyce always preferred it.

North Richmond Street, being blind,[1] was a quiet street except at the hour when the Christian Brothers' School set the boys free. An uninhabited house of two stories stood at the blind end, detached from its neighbors in a square ground. The other houses of the street, conscious of decent lives within them, gazed at one another with brown imperturbable faces.

The former tenant of our house, a priest, had died in the back drawing-room. Air, musty from having long been enclosed, hung in all the rooms, and the waste room behind the kitchen was littered with old useless papers. Among these I found a few paper-covered books, the pages of which were curled and damp: *The Abbot*, by Walter Scott, *The Devout Communicant* and *The Memoirs of Vidocq*. I liked the last best because its leaves were yellow. The wild garden behind the house contained a central apple-tree and a few straggling bushes under one of which I found the late tenant's rusty bicycle-pump.

[1] Dead-end. —EDS.

175

He had been a very charitable priest: In his will he had left all his money to institutions and the furniture of his house to his sister.

When the short days of winter came dusk fell before we had well eaten our dinners. When we met in the street the houses had grown somber. The space of sky above us was the color of ever-changing violet and towards it the lamps of the street lifted their feeble lanterns. The cold air stung us and we played till our bodies glowed. Our shouts echoed in the silent street. The career of our play brought us through the dark muddy lanes behind the houses where we ran the gantlet of the rough tribes from the cottages, to the back doors of the dark dripping gardens where odors arose from the ash-pits, to the dark odorous stables where a coachman smoothed and combed the horse or shook music from the buckled harness. When we returned to the street light from the kitchen windows had filled the areas. If my uncle was seen turning the corner we hid in the shadow until we had seen him safely housed. Or if Mangan's sister came out on the doorstep to call her brother in to his tea we watched her from our shadow peer up and down the street. We waited to see whether she would remain or go in and, if she remained, we left our shadow and walked up to Mangan's steps resignedly. She was waiting for us, her figure defined by the light from the half-opened door. Her brother always teased her before he obeyed and I stood by the railings looking at her. Her dress swung as she moved her body and the soft rope of her hair tossed from side to side.

Every morning I lay on the floor in the front parlor watching her door. The blind was pulled down within an inch of the sash so that I could not be seen. When she came out on the doorstep my heart leaped. I ran to the hall, seized my books and followed her. I kept her brown figure always in my eye and, when we came near the point at which our ways diverged, I quickened my pace and passed her. This happened morning after morning. I had never spoken to her, except for a few casual words, and yet her name was like a summons to all my foolish blood.

Her image accompanied me even in places the most hostile to romance. On Saturday evenings when my aunt went marketing I had to go to carry some of the parcels. We walked through the flaring streets, jostled by drunken men and bargaining women, amid the curses of laborers, the shrill litanies of shopboys who stood on guard by the barrels of pigs' cheeks, the nasal chanting of street singers, who sang a *come-all-you* about O'Donovan Rossa,[2] or a ballad about the troubles in our native land. These noises converged in a single sensation of life for me: I imagined that I bore my chalice safely through the

[2] Irish ballads often summoned listeners by starting "Come all you. . . ." O'Donovan Rossa was a revolutionary who encouraged violent rebellion against the British.—EDS.

throng of foes. Her name sprang to my lips at moments in strange prayers and praises which I myself did not understand. My eyes were often full of tears (I could not tell why) and at times a flood from my heart seemed to pour itself out into my bosom. I thought little of the future. I did not know whether I would ever speak to her or not or, if I spoke to her, how I could tell her of my confused adoration. But my body was like a harp and her words and gestures were like fingers running upon the wires.

One evening I went into the back drawing-room in which the priest had 6 died. It was a dark rainy evening and there was no sound in the house. Through one of the broken panes I heard the rain impinge upon the earth, the fine incessant needles of water playing in the sodden beds. Some distant lamp or lighted window gleamed below me. I was thankful that I could see so little. All my senses seemed to desire to veil themselves and, feeling that I was about to slip from them, I pressed the palms of my hands together until they trembled, murmuring: *O love! O love!* many times.

At last she spoke to me. When she addressed the first words to me I was so 7 confused that I did not know what to answer. She asked me was I going to *Araby.* I forget whether I answered yes or no. It would be a splendid bazaar, she said; she would love to go.

—And why can't you? I asked.                                           8

While she spoke she turned a silver bracelet round and round her wrist. 9 She could not go, she said, because there would be a retreat that week in her convent. Her brother and two other boys were fighting for their caps and I was alone at the railings. She held one of the spikes, bowing her head towards me. The light from the lamp opposite our door caught the white curve of her neck, lit up her hair that rested there and, falling, lit up the hand upon the railing. It fell over one side of her dress and caught the white border of a petticoat, just visible as she stood at ease.

—It's well for you, she said.                                          10

—If I go, I said, I will bring you something.                          11

What innumerable follies laid waste my waking and sleeping thoughts 12 after that evening! I wished to annihilate the tedious intervening days. I chafed against the work of school. At night in my bedroom and by day in the classroom her image came between me and the page I strove to read. The syllables of the word *Araby* were called to me through the silence in which my soul luxuriated and cast an Eastern enchantment over me. I asked for leave to go to the bazaar on Saturday night. My aunt was surprised and hoped it was not some Freemason[3] affair. I answered few questions in class. I watched my

---

[3] Freemasonry, a largely Protestant organization, was mistrusted and feared by Roman Catholics in Ireland during Joyce's time. —EDS.

master's face pass from amiability to sternness; he hoped I was not beginning to idle. I could not call my wandering thoughts together. I had hardly any patience with the serious work of life which, now that it stood between me and my desire, seemed to me child's play, ugly monotonous child's play.

On Saturday morning I reminded my uncle that I wished to go to the bazaar in the evening. He was fussing at the hall-stand, looking for the hat-brush, and answered me curtly:        13

—Yes, boy, I know.        14

As he was in the hall I could not go into the front parlor and lie at the window. I left the house in bad humor and walked slowly towards the school. The air was pitilessly raw and already my heart misgave me.        15

When I came home to dinner my uncle had not yet been home. Still it was early. I sat staring at the clock for some time and, when its ticking began to irritate me, I left the room. I mounted the staircase and gained the upper part of the house. The high cold empty gloomy rooms liberated me and I went from room to room singing. From the front window I saw my companions playing below in the street. Their cries reached me weakened and indistinct and, leaning my forehead against the cool glass, I looked over at the dark house where she lived. I may have stood there for an hour, seeing nothing but the brown-clad figure cast by my imagination, touched discreetly by the lamp-light at the curved neck, at the hand upon the railings and at the border below the dress.        16

When I came downstairs again I found Mrs. Mercer sitting at the fire. She was an old garrulous woman, a pawnbroker's widow, who collected used stamps for some pious purpose. I had to endure the gossip of the tea-table. The meal was prolonged beyond an hour and still my uncle did not come. Mrs. Mercer stood up to go: She was sorry she couldn't wait any longer, but it was after eight o'clock and she did not like to be out late, as the night air was bad for her. When she had gone I began to walk up and down the room, clenching my fists. My aunt said:        17

—I'm afraid you may put off your bazaar for this night of Our Lord.        18

At nine o'clock I heard my uncle's latchkey in the halldoor. I heard him talking to himself and heard the hall-stand rocking when it had received the weight of his overcoat. I could interpret these signs. When he was midway through his dinner I asked him to give me the money to go to the bazaar. He had forgotten.        19

—The people are in bed and after their first sleep now, he said.        20

I did not smile. My aunt said to him energetically:        21

—Can't you give him the money and let him go? You've kept him late enough as it is.        22

My uncle said he was very sorry he had forgotten. He said he believed in    23
the old saying: *All work and no play makes Jack a dull boy.* He asked me where I
was going and, when I had told him a second time he asked me did I know *The
Arab's Farewell to His Steed.*[4] When I left the kitchen he was about to recite
the opening lines of the piece to my aunt.

I held a florin[5] tightly in my hands as I strode down Buckingham Street    24
towards the station. The sight of the streets thronged with buyers and glaring
with gas recalled to me the purpose of my journey. I took my seat in a third-
class carriage of a deserted train. After an intolerable delay the train moved
out of the station slowly. It crept onward among ruinous houses and over the
twinkling river. At Westland Row Station a crowd of people pressed to the
carriage doors; but the porters moved them back, saying that it was a special
train for the bazaar. I remained alone in the bare carriage. In a few minutes the
train drew up beside an improvised wooden platform. I passed out on to the
road and saw by the lighted dial of a clock that it was ten minutes to ten. In
front of me was a large building which displayed the magical name.

I could not find any sixpenny entrance and, fearing that the bazaar would    25
be closed, I passed in quickly through a turnstile, handing a shilling to a
weary-looking man. I found myself in a big hall girdled at half its height by a
gallery. Nearly all the stalls were closed and the greater part of the hall was in
darkness. I recognized a silence like that which pervades a church after a service. I walked into the center of the bazaar timidly. A few people were gathered about the stalls which were still open. Before a curtain, over which the
words *Café Chantant* were written in colored lamps, two men were counting
money on a salver.[6] I listened to the fall of the coins.

Remembering with difficulty why I had come I went over to one of the    26
stalls and examined porcelain vases and flowered tea-sets. At the door of the
stall a young lady was talking and laughing with two young gentlemen. I
remarked their English accents and listened vaguely to their conversation.

—O, I never said such a thing!    27
—O, but you did!    28
—O, but I didn't!    29
—Didn't she say that?    30
—Yes. I heard her.    31
—O, there's a . . . fib!    32

---

[4] A popular poem relating the story of a desert nomad who sells his horse and then regrets
it.—EDS.
[5] A British coin that today would be worth about twenty cents.—EDS.
[6] A tray.—EDS.

Observing me the young lady came over and asked me did I wish to buy any-   33
thing. The tone of her voice was not encouraging; she seemed to have spoken
to me out of a sense of duty. I looked humbly at the great jars that stood like eastern guards at either side of the dark entrance to the stall and murmured:

—No, thank you.   34

The young lady changed the position of one of the vases and went back to   35
the two young men. They began to talk of the same subject. Once or twice the
young lady glanced at me over her shoulder.

I lingered before her stall, though I knew my stay was useless, to make my   36
interest in her wares seem the more real. Then I turned away slowly and
walked down the middle of the bazaar. I allowed the two pennies to fall against
the sixpence in my pocket. I heard a voice call from one end of the gallery that
the light was out. The upper part of the hall was now completely dark.

Gazing up into the darkness I saw myself as a creature driven and derided   37
by vanity; and my eyes burned with anguish and anger.

---

*For a reading quiz, sources on James Joyce, and annotated links to further readings
on the Dublin of Joyce's youth, visit **bedfordstmartins.com/thebedfordreader**.*

---

## Journal Writing

What do you remember about your first love? What was special about the person you
were attracted to? How did you act around him or her? Was your interest reciprocated?
In your journal, write about the experience. (To take your journal writing further, see
"From Journal to Essay" on the facing page.)

## Questions on Meaning

1. Throughout "Araby," we never learn the name of Mangan's sister. Why do you
   suppose Joyce left this out of the story?
2. What does Araby represent to the boy?
3. How would you characterize the adults in the story? How sympathetic are they
   toward the narrator?
4. What realization does the NARRATOR eventually come to? Where does Joyce most
   directly state this THESIS? Why do you think he places it where he does?
5. What do you think is Joyce's PURPOSE in telling this story?

## Questions on Writing Strategy

1. Throughout the story, Joyce contrasts the boy's romantic longings with the real world that surrounds him. What is the DOMINANT IMPRESSION of each? What point is Joyce making with this contrast?
2. The narrator of this story is an adult looking back on his adolescence. Identify some places in the story that reveal this POINT OF VIEW. How does the adult narrator seem to feel about his youthful desires?
3. What does the DIALOG between the adults at Araby (pars. 27–32) add to the story?
4. **OTHER METHODS**   How does Joyce use CAUSE AND EFFECT in paragraph 12? What is the point of this paragraph?

## Questions on Language

1. What is the double meaning of the word *blind* in the first paragraph? How do both meanings relate to the dominant impression of North Richmond Street?
2. How does the PERSONIFICATION in paragraph 1 help set the TONE of the passages describing the boy's environment?
3. Find some examples of religious imagery throughout the story. What point does Joyce seem to be making with these IMAGES?
4. Joyce uses a number of words that might be unfamiliar. Consult a dictionary if you need help defining any of the following: imperturbable (par. 1); musty, straggling (2); somber, gantlet, resignedly (3); diverged, summons (4); jostled, litanies, converged, chalice, throng (5); impinge, incessant, sodden (6); petticoat (9); innumerable, follies, annihilate, chafed, luxuriating, amiability, monotonous (12); curtly (13); pitilessly, misgave (15); discreetly (16); garrulous, pious (17); strode, thronged, ruinous, improvised (24); girdled (25); wares (36); derided (37).

## Suggestions for Writing

1. **FROM JOURNAL TO ESSAY**   Working from your journal entry, write an essay about your first crush. Like Joyce, you may structure your essay as a NARRATIVE, but focus on recalling striking descriptive details to convey a dominant impression of your experience and what you learned from it.
2. Joyce is known for writing about epiphanies, sudden moments of clarity or insight such as that experienced by the narrator at the end of "Araby." Write a narrative essay recounting a time when you experienced an epiphany. Whether it was triggered by something as small as a fortune cookie or as large as a car accident, try to convey as vividly as you can the events leading up to the epiphany and the moment of insight itself.
3. **CRITICAL WRITING**   ANALYZE Joyce's use of sensory IMAGES in "Araby." How does the abundant imagery help convey the story's dominant impression of the contrast between the narrator's romantic idealism and his actual surroundings? What else do the images contribute to the story? Much has been written about "Araby," so you might back up your own ideas by citing EVIDENCE from works of literary criticism.

4. **CONNECTIONS**   In "Orange Crush" (p. 164), Yiyun Li also uses description to convey an experience of adolescent longing. Write an essay comparing and contrasting Li's and Joyce's portrayals of adolescence. How are the narrators' desires and subsequent epiphanies similar and different? What do the narrators learn about themselves and about the world around them? What is each writer saying about the experience of being a teenager?

# ADDITIONAL WRITING TOPICS

## *Description*

1. This is an in-class writing experiment. Describe another person in the room so clearly and unmistakably that when you read your description aloud, your subject will be recognized. (Be OBJECTIVE. No insulting descriptions, please!)
2. Write a paragraph describing one subject from *each* of the following categories. It will be up to you to make the general subject refer to a particular person, place, or thing. Write at least one paragraph as an objective description and at least one as a SUBJECTIVE description.

**PERSON**

A friend or roommate
A typical hip-hop, jazz, or
   country musician
One of your parents
An elderly person you know
A prominent politician
A historical figure

**THING**

A car
A dentist's drill
A painting or photograph
A foggy day
A season of the year
A musical instrument

**PLACE**

An office
A classroom
A college campus
A vacation spot
A hospital emergency room
A forest

3. In a brief essay, describe your ideal place—perhaps an apartment, a dorm room, a vacation spot, a restaurant, a gym, a store, a garden, a dance club or other kind of club. With concrete details, try to make the ideal seem actual.

## *Narration and Description*

4. Use a combination of NARRATION and description to develop any one of the following topics:

Your first day on the job
Your first day at college
Returning to an old neighborhood
Getting lost
A brush with a celebrity
Delivering bad (or good) news

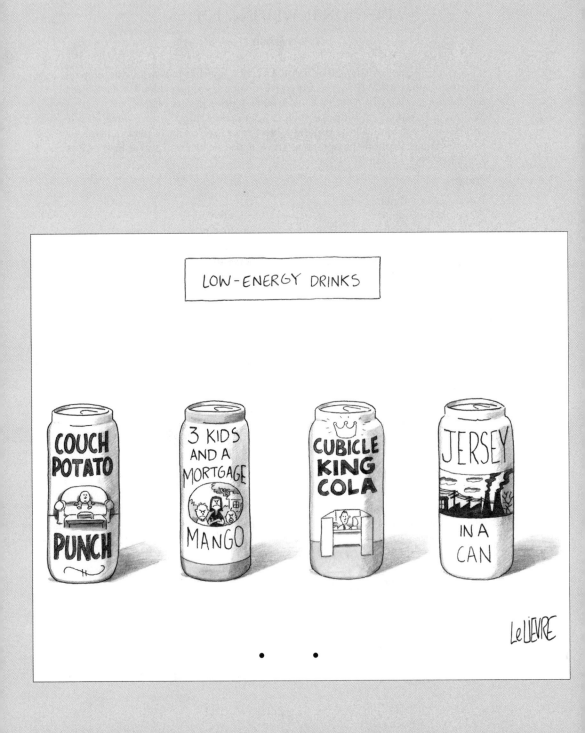

# 6

# EXAMPLE

## *Pointing to Instances*

◀ **Examples in a cartoon**

This cartoon by Greg LeLievre, from *The New Yorker* in March 2007, uses the method of example in a complex way. Most simply, the drawings propose instances of the general category stated in the title—imaginary "low-energy drinks." At the same time, the humor of the examples comes from their contrast with real caffeine-laced high-energy drinks such as Xtreme Shock Fruit Punch, Jolt Cola, Zippfizz Liquid Shot, and AMP High Energy Overdrive. Whom are these drinks marketed to? (Consider visiting a grocery store or gas station minimart to see some samples up close.) Whom does their marketing ignore? How would you express LeLievre's general idea in this cartoon?

## THE METHOD

"There have been many women runners of distinction," a writer begins, and quickly goes on, "among them Joan Benoit, Grete Waitz, Florence Griffith Joyner, and Marion Jones."

You have just seen examples at work. An EXAMPLE (from the Latin *exemplum:* "one thing selected from among many") is an instance that reveals a whole type. By selecting an example, a writer shows the nature or character of the group from which it is taken. In a written essay, examples will often serve to illustrate a general statement, or GENERALIZATION. Here, for instance, the writer Linda Wolfe makes a point about the food fetishes of Roman emperors (Domitian and Claudius ruled in the first century AD).

> The emperors used their gastronomical concerns to indicate their contempt of the country and the whole task of governing it. Domitian humiliated his cabinet by forcing them to attend him at his villa to help solve a serious problem. When they arrived he kept them waiting for hours. The problem, it finally appeared, was that the emperor had just purchased a giant fish, too large for any dish he owned, and he needed the learned brains of his ministers to decide whether the fish should be minced or whether a larger pot should be sought. The emperor Claudius one day rode hurriedly to the Senate and demanded they deliberate the importance of a life without pork. Another time he sat in his tribunal ostensibly administering justice but actually allowing the litigants to argue and orate while he grew dreamy, interrupting the discussions only to announce, "Meat pies are wonderful. We shall have them for dinner."

Wolfe might have allowed the opening sentence of her paragraph — the TOPIC SENTENCE — to remain a vague generalization. Instead, she supports it with three examples, each a brief story of an emperor's contemptuous behavior. With these examples, Wolfe not only explains and supports her generalization but also animates it.

The method of giving examples — of illustrating what you're saying with a "for instance" — is not merely helpful to all kinds of writing; it is indispensable. Writers who bore us, or lose us completely, often have an ample supply of ideas; their trouble is that they never pull their ideas down out of the clouds. A dull writer, for instance, might declare, "The emperors used food to humiliate their governments," and then, instead of giving examples, go on, "They also manipulated their families," or something — adding still another large, unillustrated idea. Specific examples are *needed* elements in effective prose. Not only do they make ideas understandable, but they also keep readers awake. (The previous paragraphs have tried — by giving examples from Linda Wolfe and from "a dull writer" — to illustrate this point.)

Example                                                       **187**

## THE PROCESS

### The Generalization and the Thesis

Examples illustrate a generalization, such as Linda Wolfe's opening statement about the Roman emperors. Any example essay is bound to have such a generalization as its THESIS, expressed in a THESIS STATEMENT. Here are two examples from the essays in this chapter:

> Sometimes I think we would be better off [in dealing with social problems] if we forgot about the broad strokes and concentrated on the details.
> —Anna Quindlen, "Homeless"

> That first encounter, and those that followed, signified that a vast, unnerving gulf lay between nighttime pedestrians—particularly women—and me.
> —Brent Staples, "Black Men and Public Space"

The thesis statement establishes the backbone, the central idea, of an essay developed by example. Then the specifics bring the idea down to earth for readers.

### The Examples

An essay developed by example will often start with an example or two. That is, you'll see something—a man pilfering a quarter for bus fare from a child's Kool-Aid stand, a friend dating another friend's fiancé (or fiancée)—and your observation will suggest a generalization (perhaps a statement about how people mishandle ethical dilemmas). But a mere example or two probably won't demonstrate your generalization for readers and thus won't achieve your PURPOSE. For that you'll need a range of instances.

Where do you find more? In anything you know—or care to learn. Start close to home. Seek examples in your own immediate knowledge and experience. Explore your conversations with others, your studies, and the storehouse of information you have gathered from books, newspapers, radio, TV, and the Internet as well as from popular hearsay: proverbs and sayings, popular songs, bits of wisdom you've heard voiced in your family.

Now and again, you may feel an irresistible temptation to make up an example out of thin air. This procedure is risky, but with imagination it can work wonderfully. When Henry David Thoreau, in *Walden*, attacked Americans' smug pride in the achievements of nineteenth-century science and industry, he wanted to illustrate that kind of invention or discovery "which distracts our attention from serious things." Two decades before the invention of the telephone, Thoreau made up the example of a transatlantic speaking tube and what it might convey: "We are eager to tunnel under the Atlantic and bring the Old World some weeks nearer to the New; but perchance the first news that will leak through into the broad, flapping American ear will be that the Princess Adelaide has the whooping cough." (Thoreau would be appalled at what we know of the British Royal Family via just the sort of communication he imagined.)

A hypothetical example can work if, like Thoreau's, it is fresh and apt; but an example from fact or experience is likely to carry more weight. Suppose you have to write about the benefits — any benefits — that recent science has conferred upon the nation. You might imagine one such benefit: the prospect of one day being able to vacation in outer space and drift about in free-fall like a soap bubble. That imagined benefit would be all right, but it is obviously a conjecture that you dreamed up without going to the library. Do a little digging on the Internet or in recent books and magazines. Your reader will feel better informed to be told that science — specifically, the NASA space program — has produced useful inventions. You add:

> Among these are the smoke detector, originally developed as Skylab equipment; the inflatable air bag to protect drivers and pilots, designed to cushion astronauts in splashdowns; a walking chair that enables paraplegics to mount stairs and travel over uneven ground, derived from the moonwalkers' surface buggy; the technique of cryosurgery, the removal of cancerous tissue by fast freezing.

By using specific examples like these, you render the idea of "benefits to society" more concrete and more definite. Such examples are not prettifications of your essay; they are necessary if you are to hold your readers' attention and convince them that you are worth listening to.

When giving examples, you'll find other methods useful. Sometimes, as in the paragraph by Linda Wolfe, an example takes the form of a NARRATIVE (Chap. 4): an ANECDOTE or a case history. Sometimes an example embodies a vivid DESCRIPTION of a person, place, or thing (Chap. 5).

Lazy writers think, "Oh well, I can't come up with any example here — I'll just leave it to the reader to find one." The flaw in this ASSUMPTION is that the reader may be as lazy as the writer. As a result, a perfectly good idea may be left suspended in the stratosphere. The linguist and writer S. I. Hayakawa tells the story of a professor who, in teaching a philosophy course, spent a whole semester on the theory of beauty. When students asked him for a few examples of beautiful paintings, symphonies, or works of nature, he refused, saying, "We are interested in principles, not in particulars." The professor himself may well have been interested in principles, but it is a safe bet that his classroom

Example                                                                 **189**

resounded with snores. In written EXPOSITION, it is undoubtedly the particulars—the pertinent examples—that keep a reader awake and having a good time, and taking in the principles besides.

---

### FOCUS ON SENTENCE VARIETY

While accumulating and detailing examples during drafting, you may find yourself writing strings of similar sentences:

UNVARIED   One example of a movie about a disease is *In the Forest.* Another example is *The Beating Heart.* Another is *Tree of Life.* These three movies treat misunderstood or little-known diseases in a way that increases the viewer's sympathy and understanding. *In the Forest* deals with a little boy who suffers from cystic fibrosis. *The Beating Heart* deals with a middle-aged woman who is weakening from multiple sclerosis. *Tree of Life* deals with a father of four who is dying from AIDS. All three movies show complex, struggling human beings caught blamelessly in desperate circumstances.

The writer of this paragraph was clearly pushing to add examples and to expand them—both essential tasks—but the resulting passage needs editing so that the writer's labor isn't so obvious. In the more readable and interesting revision, the sentences vary in structure, group similar details, and distinguish the specifics from the generalizations:

VARIED   Three movies dealing with disease are *In the Forest, The Beating Heart,* and *Tree of Life.* In these movies people with little-known or misunderstood diseases become subjects for the viewer's sympathy and understanding. A little boy suffering from cystic fibrosis, a middle-aged woman weakening from multiple sclerosis, a father of four dying from AIDS—these complex, struggling human beings are caught blamelessly in desperate circumstances.

**For exercises on sentence variety, visit Exercise Central at *bedfordstmartins
.com/thebedfordreader.***

---

### CHECKLIST FOR REVISING AN EXAMPLE ESSAY

✔ **GENERALIZATION**   What general statement do your examples illustrate? Will it be clear to readers what ties the examples together?

✔ **SUPPORT**   Do you have enough examples to establish your generalization, or will readers be left needing more?

✔ **SPECIFICS**   Are your examples detailed? Does each capture some aspects of the generalization?

> ✔ **RELEVANCE**   Do all your examples relate to your generalization? Should any be cut because they go off track?
>
> ✔ **SENTENCE VARIETY**   Have you varied sentence structures for clarity and interest?

## EXAMPLES IN PARAGRAPHS

### Writing About Television

This paragraph appears in an essay maintaining that television merely simulates, or imitates, real problems, events, activities, and institutions. The essay offers many examples of programming that only seem to represent what's real, such as morning news shows, small-claims courts, and wrestling. (Although the essay predates the recent explosion of "reality" TV, from *Survivor* to *Wife Swap*, it would apply to those shows as well.) Here the author uses specific examples of TV wrestling to show how it simulates televised football, basketball, and other sports.

To sustain the simulation, wrestling must construct and maintain a little universe of the simulated. To do this, its discourse refers in its every enunciation to the apparatus used to broadcast conventional sport. [Generalization to be illustrated] Wrestling features the same style of ringside commentary, the same interpolation of interviews, the same mystification of sporting expertise, the same freeze-frame and instant replay formats, the same faintly prurient interest in the wrestlers' private lives (not to mention parts), the same cults of personality, and so on. [Six examples] This system of understanding, however, is marshaled in the service of an event which is a parody of its originating source: "real" sport.
> —Michael Sorkin, "Faking It,"
> in *Watching Television*, ed. Todd Gitlin

### Writing in an Academic Discipline

The following paragraph from an economics textbook appears amid the author's explanation of how markets work. To dispel what might seem like clouds of theory, the author here brings an abstract principle down to earth with a concrete and detailed example.

The primary function of the market is to bring together suppliers and demanders so that they can trade with one another. Buyers and sellers do not necessarily have to be in face-to-face contact; they can signal their desires and intentions through various inter- [Generalization to be illustrated]

Example                                    **191**

mediaries. For example, the demand for green beans in California is
not expressed directly by the green bean consumers to the green
bean growers. People who want green beans buy them at a grocery
store; the store orders them from a vegetable wholesaler; the wholesaler buys them from a bean cooperative, whose manager tells local
farmers of the size of the current demand for green beans. The demanders of green beans are able to signal their demand schedule to
the original suppliers, the farmers who raise the beans, without any
personal communication between the two parties.
—Lewis C. Solmon, *Microeconomics*

Single extended example

## EXAMPLES IN PRACTICE

As a college sophomore, Kharron Reid was applying for a summer internship implementing computer networks for businesses. He put together a
résumé structured to present his previous work experience and his education
for this kind of job. (See the résumé on p. 383.)

In drafting a cover letter for the résumé, Reid at first found himself repeating all his background in a very long letter. On the advice of his school's placement office, he rewrote the letter to emphasize just what the prospective
employer would most need to know: the work, courses, and computer skills
that qualified him for the opening it had. The rewritten letter, below, focuses
on examples from the résumé to support the statement (in the second-to-last
paragraph) that "my education and my hands-on experience with networking
prepare me for the opening you have."

Kharron Reid
137 Chester St., Apt. E
Allston, MA 02134
February 23, 2007

Ms. Dolores Jackson
Human Resources Director
E-line Systems
75 Arondale Avenue
Boston, MA 02114

Dear Ms. Jackson:

I am applying for the network development internship in your information technology department, advertised in the career services office of Boston University.

I have considerable experience in network development from summer internships at NBS Systems and at Pioneer Networking. At NBS I planned and laid

the physical platforms and configured the software for seven WANs on a Windows XP server. At Pioneer, I laid the physical platforms and configured the software to connect eight workstations into a LAN. Both internships gave me experience in every stage of network development.

In the fall I will be entering my third year in Boston University's School of Management, majoring in business administration and information systems. I have completed courses in computers (including programming), information systems, and business. In addition to my experience and coursework, I am proficient in Unix, Windows XP/2000/2003, and Linux.

As the enclosed résumé indicates, my education and my hands-on experience with network development prepare me for the opening you have.

I am available for an interview at your convenience. Please call me at (617) 555-4009 or e-mail me at kreid@bu.edu.

                              Sincerely,

                              *Kharron Reid*

                              Kharron Reid

# BARBARA LAZEAR ASCHER

BARBARA LAZEAR ASCHER was born in 1946 and educated at Bennington College and Cardozo School of Law. She practiced law for two years in a private firm, where she found herself part of a power structure in which those on top resembled "the two-year-old with the biggest plastic pail and shovel on the beach. It's a life of nervous guardianship." Ascher quit the law to devote herself to writing, to explore, as she says, "what really matters." Her essays have appeared in the *New York Times*, the *Yale Review*, *Vogue*, and other periodicals and have been collected in *Playing After Dark* (1986) and *The Habit of Loving* (1989). She has also published *Landscape Without Gravity: A Memoir of Grief* (1993), about her brother's death from AIDS, and *Dancing in the Dark: Romance, Yearning, and the Search for the Sublime* (1999), about our quest for romance. Ascher has worked as an editor at several magazines and a book publisher and periodically teaches writing at Bennington.

# *On Compassion*

Ascher often writes about life in New York City, where human problems sometimes seem larger and more stubborn than in other places. In this essay Ascher uses examples from the city to address a universal need: compassion for those who require help. In New York and elsewhere in the United States, the problem of homelessness has not abated since Ascher's essay first appeared in *Elle* magazine in 1988. Using government data, the National Alliance to End Homelessness estimated in 2007 that more than 700,000 Americans were homeless. The essay following this one, Anna Quindlen's "Homeless," addresses the same issue.

The man's grin is less the result of circumstance than dreams or madness. 1 His buttonless shirt, with one sleeve missing, hangs outside the waist of his baggy trousers. Carefully plaited dreadlocks bespeak a better time, long ago. As he crosses Manhattan's Seventy-ninth Street, his gait is the shuffle of the forgotten ones held in place by gravity rather than plans. On the corner of Madison Avenue, he stops before a blond baby in an Aprica stroller. The baby's mother waits for the light to change and her hands close tighter on the stroller's handle as she sees the man approach.

The others on the corner, five men and women waiting for the crosstown 2 bus, look away. They daydream a bit and gaze into the weak rays of November light. A man with a briefcase lifts and lowers the shiny toe of his right shoe, watching the light reflect, trying to catch and balance it, as if he could hold and make it his, to ease the heavy gray of coming January, February, and March. The winter months that will send snow around the feet, calves, and knees of the grinning man as he heads for the shelter of Grand Central or Pennsylvania Station.

But for now, in this last gasp of autumn warmth, he is still. His eyes fix on     3
the baby. The mother removes her purse from her shoulder and rummages through its contents: lipstick, a lace handkerchief, an address book. She finds what she's looking for and passes a folded dollar over her child's head to the man who stands and stares even though the light has changed and traffic navigates about his hips.

His hands continue to dangle at his sides. He does not know his part. He     4
does not know that acceptance of the gift and gratitude are what make this transaction complete. The baby, weary of the unwavering stare, pulls its blanket over its head. The man does not look away. Like a bridegroom waiting at the altar, his eyes pierce the white veil.

The mother grows impatient and pushes the stroller before her, bearing     5
the dollar like a cross. Finally, a black hand rises and closes around green.

Was it fear or compassion that motivated the gift?     6

Up the avenue, at Ninety-first Street, there is a small French bread shop     7
where you can sit and eat a buttery, overpriced croissant and wash it down with rich cappuccino. Twice when I have stopped here to stave hunger or stay the cold, twice as I have sat and read and felt the warm rush of hot coffee and milk, an old man has wandered in and stood inside the entrance. He wears a stained blanket pulled up to his chin, and a woolen hood pulled down to his gray, bushy eyebrows. As he stands, the scent of stale cigarettes and urine fills the small, overheated room.

The owner of the shop, a moody French woman, emerges from the     8
kitchen with steaming coffee in a Styrofoam cup, and a small paper bag of . . . of what? Yesterday's bread? Today's croissant? He accepts the offering as silently as he came, and is gone.

Twice I have witnessed this, and twice I have wondered, what compels     9
this woman to feed this man? Pity? Care? Compassion? Or does she simply want to rid her shop of his troublesome presence? If expulsion were her motivation she would not reward his arrival with gifts of food. Most proprietors do not. They chase the homeless from their midst with expletives and threats.

As winter approaches, the mayor of New York City is moving the home-     10
less off the streets and into Bellevue Hospital. The New York Civil Liberties Union is watchful. They question whether the rights of these people who live in our parks and doorways are being violated by involuntary hospitalization.

I think the mayor's notion is humane, but I fear it is something else as    11
well. Raw humanity offends our sensibilities. We want to protect ourselves
from an awareness of rags with voices that make no sense and scream forth in
inarticulate rage. We do not wish to be reminded of the tentative state of our
own well-being and sanity. And so, the troublesome presence is removed from
the awareness of the electorate.

Like other cities, there is much about Manhattan now that resembles    12
Dickensian London. Ladies in high-heeled shoes pick their way through
poverty and madness. You hear more cocktail party complaints than usual, "I
just can't take New York anymore." Our citizens dream of the open spaces of
Wyoming, the manicured exclusivity of Hobe Sound.

And yet, it may be that these are the conditions that finally give birth to    13
empathy, the mother of compassion. We cannot deny the existence of the
helpless as their presence grows. It is impossible to insulate ourselves against
what is at our very doorstep. I don't believe that one is born compassionate.
Compassion is not a character trait like a sunny disposition. It must be
learned, and it is learned by having adversity at our windows, coming through
the gates of our yards, the walls of our towns, adversity that becomes so familiar that we begin to identify and empathize with it.

For the ancient Greeks, drama taught and reinforced compassion within    14
a society. The object of Greek tragedy was to inspire empathy in the audience so that the common response to the hero's fall was: "There, but for the
grace of God, go I." Could it be that this was the response of the mother who
offered the dollar, the French woman who gave the food? Could it be that the
homeless, like those ancients, are reminding us of our common humanity? Of
course, there is a difference. This play doesn't end—and the players can't go
home.

---

*For a reading quiz, sources on Barbara Lazear Ascher, and annotated links to further
readings on homelessness, visit **bedfordstmartins.com/thebedfordreader**.*

---

## Journal Writing

Using Ascher's essay as a springboard, consider a personal experience that involved
misfortune. Have you ever needed to beg on the street, been evicted from an apartment, or had to scrounge for food? Have you ever been asked for money by beggars,

worked in a soup kitchen, or volunteered at a shelter or public hospital? Write about such an experience in your journal. (To take your journal writing further, see "From Journal to Essay" below.)

## Questions on Meaning

1. What do the two men in Ascher's essay exemplify?
2. What is Ascher's THESIS? What is her PURPOSE?
3. What solution to homelessness is introduced in paragraph 10? What does Ascher think of this possibility?
4. How do you interpret Ascher's last sentence? Is she optimistic or pessimistic about whether people will learn compassion?

## Questions on Writing Strategy

1. Which comes first, the GENERALIZATIONS or the supporting examples? Why has Ascher chosen this order?
2. What assumptions does the author make about her AUDIENCE?
3. Why do the other people at the bus stop look away (par. 2)? What does Ascher's DESCRIPTION of their activities say about them?
4. Look at the sentences in paragraph 13. How does the variety in their structure reinforce Ascher's meaning?
5. **OTHER METHODS**   Ascher explores CAUSES AND EFFECTS. Do you agree with her that exposure to others' helplessness increases our compassion? Why, or why not?

## Questions on Language

1. What is the difference between empathy and compassion? Why does Ascher say that "empathy [is] the mother of compassion" (par. 13)?
2. Find definitions for the following words: plaited, dreadlocks, bespeak (par. 1); stave, stay (7); expletives (9); inarticulate, electorate (11).
3. What are the implications of Ascher's ALLUSION to "Dickensian London" (par. 12)?
4. Examine the language Ascher uses to describe the two homeless men. Is it OBJECTIVE? sympathetic? negative?

## Suggestions for Writing

1. **FROM JOURNAL TO ESSAY**   Write an essay on the experience you explored in your journal, using examples to convey the effect the experience had on you.
2. Write an essay on the problem of homelessness in your town or city. Use examples to support your view of the problem and a possible solution.
3. In paragraph 10 Ascher refers to the involuntary hospitalization of homeless people and the concerns such government action raises among supporters of individual rights, such as the American Civil Liberties Union. What is your opinion of the rights of homeless people to live on the streets? How do you distinguish among the individual's rights, the community's responsibilities to the individual,

and the community's rights? (For instance, what if a homeless person seems sick? What if he or she seems unstable, if not violent?) You may work solo on this assignment—stating your ideas and supporting them with EVIDENCE from your own observations and experience—or you may conduct research to discover legal and other arguments and data to support your ideas.

4. **CRITICAL WRITING**    In her last paragraph, Ascher mentions but does not address another key difference between the characters in Greek tragedy and the homeless on today's streets: The former were "heroes"—gods and goddesses, kings and queens—whereas the latter are placeless, poor, anonymous, even reviled. Does this difference negate Ascher's comparison between Greek theatergoers and ourselves or her larger point about how compassion is learned? Answer in a brief essay, saying why or why not.

5. **CONNECTIONS**    The next essay, Anna Quindlen's "Homeless," also uses examples to make a point about homelessness. What are some of the differences in the examples each writer uses? In a brief essay, explore whether and how these differences create different TONES in the two works.

---

## Barbara Lazear Ascher on Writing

A lawyer before she was a full-time writer, Barbara Lazear Ascher thinks that her legal training helped her become a stronger writer.

"I believe there is a kind of legal thinking that becomes part of your own thinking," she told Jean W. Ross of *Contemporary Authors*. "What it did for me was help me to become quite a tight writer. My pieces are very short, and I think a lot of that has to do with the training in law, which is to tell the facts and the theories, and then put it all together and close it up. I might have been a more excessive writer if I hadn't had the legal training."

For Ascher, the essay is the ideal form of expression. "I'm quite impatient, so it's very satisfying to have a small space in which to tell what it was you wanted to tell. You get to the point right away instead of having to drag it out and slowly reveal it."

### For Discussion

1. How did her legal training help Ascher when she became a writer? How does a "tight writer" help readers as well?

2. How might an "excessive writer" have trouble with the essay form? What, in your view, is "excessive" writing?

# ANNA QUINDLEN

ANNA QUINDLEN was born in 1952 and graduated from Barnard College in 1974. She worked as a reporter for the *New York Post* and the *New York Times* before taking over the *Times*'s "About New York" column, serving as the paper's deputy metropolitan editor, and in 1986 creating her own weekly column, "Life in the Thirties." Between 1989 and 1994 Quindlen wrote a twice-weekly op-ed column for the *Times* on social and political issues, earning a Pulitzer Prize in 1992. In 1999 she began writing "The Last Word," a biweekly column for *Newsweek* magazine. Her essays and columns are collected in *Living Out Loud* (1988), *Thinking Out Loud* (1993), and *Loud and Clear* (2004). Her latest nonfiction book is *London: A Tour of the World's Greatest Fictional City* (2006). Quindlen has also published two books for children and five successful novels: *Object Lessons* (1991), *One True Thing* (1994), *Black and Blue: A Novel* (1998), *Blessings* (2002), and *Rise and Shine* (2006).

# *Homeless*

In this essay from *Living Out Loud*, Quindlen mingles a reporter's respect for details with a passionate regard for life. She uses examples to explore the same topic as Barbara Lazear Ascher (p. 193) from a different slant. Both essays date from the late 1980s, but both also remain fresh because of the persistence of homelessness as a social problem.

Her name was Ann, and we met in the Port Authority Bus Terminal several Januarys ago. I was doing a story on homeless people. She said I was wasting my time talking to her; she was just passing through, although she'd been passing through for more than two weeks. To prove to me that this was true, she rummaged through a tote bag and a manila envelope and finally unfolded a sheet of typing paper and brought out her photographs.

They were not pictures of family, or friends, or even a dog or cat, its eyes brown-red in the flashbulb's light. They were pictures of a house. It was like a thousand houses in a hundred towns, not suburb, not city, but somewhere in between, with aluminum siding and a chain-link fence, a narrow driveway running up to a one-car garage and a patch of backyard. The house was yellow. I looked on the back for a date or a name, but neither was there. There was no need for discussion. I knew what she was trying to tell me, for it was something I had often felt. She was not adrift, alone, anonymous, although her bags and her raincoat with the grime shadowing its creases had made me believe she was. She had a house, or at least once upon a time had had one. Inside were curtains, a couch, a stove, potholders. You are where you live. She was somebody.

I've never been very good at looking at the big picture, taking the global view, and I've always been a person with an overactive sense of place, the legacy of an Irish grandfather. So it is natural that the thing that seems most wrong with the world to me right now is that there are so many people with no homes. I'm not simply talking about shelter from the elements, or three square meals a day or a mailing address to which the welfare people can send the check—although I know that all these are important for survival. I'm talking about a home, about precisely those kinds of feelings that have wound up in cross-stitch and French knots on samplers over the years.

Home is where the heart is. There's no place like it. I love my home with a ferocity totally out of proportion to its appearance or location. I love dumb things about it: the hot-water heater, the plastic rack you drain dishes in, the roof over my head, which occasionally leaks. And yet it is precisely those dumb things that make it what it is—a place of certainty, stability, predictability, privacy, for me and for my family. It is where I live. What more can you say about a place than that? That is everything.

Yet it is something that we have been edging away from gradually during my lifetime and the lifetimes of my parents and grandparents. There was a time when where you lived often was where you worked and where you grew the food you ate and even where you were buried. When that era passed, where you lived at least was where your parents had lived and where you would live with your children when you became enfeebled. Then, suddenly where you lived was where you lived for three years, until you could move on to something else and something else again.

And so we have come to something else again, to children who do not understand what it means to go to their rooms because they have never had a room, to men and women whose fantasy is a wall they can paint a color of their own choosing, to old people reduced to sitting on molded plastic chairs, their skin blue-white in the lights of a bus station, who pull pictures of houses out of their bags. Homes have stopped being homes. Now they are real estate.

People find it curious that those without homes would rather sleep sitting up on benches or huddled in doorways than go to shelters. Certainly some prefer to do so because they are emotionally ill, because they have been locked in before and they are damned if they will be locked in again. Others are afraid of the violence and trouble they may find there. But some seem to want something that is not available in shelters, and they will not compromise, not for a cot, or oatmeal, or a shower with special soap that kills the bugs. "One room," a woman with a baby who was sleeping on her sister's floor, once told me, "painted blue." That was the crux of it; not size or location, but pride of ownership. Painted blue.

This is a difficult problem, and some wise and compassionate people are        8
working hard at it. But in the main I think we work around it, just as we walk around it when it is lying on the sidewalk or sitting in the bus terminal—the problem, that is. It has been customary to take people's pain and lessen our own participation in it by turning it into an issue, not a collection of human beings. We turn an adjective into a noun: the poor, not poor people; the homeless, not Ann or the man who lives in the box or the woman who sleeps on the subway grate.

Sometimes I think we would be better off if we forgot about the broad        9
strokes and concentrated on the details. Here is a woman without a bureau. There is a man with no mirror, no wall to hang it on. They are not the homeless. They are people who have no homes. No drawer that holds the spoons. No window to look out upon the world. My God. That is everything.

*For a reading quiz, sources on Anna Quindlen, and annotated links to further readings on homelessness, visit **bedfordstmartins.com/thebedfordreader**.*

---

## Journal Writing

What does the word *home* mean to you? Does it involve material things, privacy, family, a sense of permanence? In your journal, explore your ideas about this word. (To take your journal writing further, see "From Journal to Essay" on the facing page.)

## Questions on Meaning

1. What is Quindlen's THESIS?
2. What distinction is Quindlen making in her CONCLUSION with the sentences "They are not the homeless. They are people who have no homes"?
3. Why does Quindlen believe that having a home is important?

## Questions on Writing Strategy

1. Why do you think Quindlen begins with the story of Ann? How else might Quindlen have begun her essay?

2. What is the EFFECT of Quindlen's examples of her own home?
3. What key ASSUMPTIONS does the author make about her AUDIENCE? Are the assumptions reasonable? Where does she specifically address an assumption that might undermine her view?
4. How does Quindlen vary the sentences in paragraph 7 that give examples of why homeless people avoid shelters?
5. **OTHER METHODS**   Quindlen uses examples to support an ARGUMENT. What position does she want readers to recognize and accept?

## Questions on Language

1. What is the effect of "My God" in the last paragraph?
2. How might Quindlen be said to give new meaning to the old CLICHÉ "Home is where the heart is" (par. 4)?
3. What is meant by "crux" (par. 7)? Where does the word come from?

## Suggestions for Writing

1. **FROM JOURNAL TO ESSAY**   Write an essay that gives a detailed DEFINITION of *home* by using your own home(s), hometown(s), or experiences with home(s) as supporting examples. (See Chap. 12 if you need help with definition.)
2. Have you ever moved from one place to another? What sort of experience was it? Write an essay about leaving an old home and moving to a new one. Was there an activity or a piece of furniture that helped ease the transition?
3. Estimates of the number of homeless people in the United States vary widely. Research the numbers, and then write an essay in which you present your findings and propose reasons for the variations.
4. **CRITICAL WRITING**   Write a brief essay in which you agree or disagree with Quindlen's assertion that a home is "everything." Can one, for instance, be a fulfilled person without a home? In your answer, take account of the values that might underlie an attachment to home; Quindlen mentions "certainty, stability, predictability, privacy" (par. 4), but there are others, including some (such as fear) that are less positive.
5. **CONNECTIONS**   COMPARE AND CONTRAST the views of homelessness and its solution in Quindlen's "Homeless" and Barbara Lazear Ascher's "On Compassion" (p. 193). Use specific passages from each essay to support your comparison.

---

# *Anna Quindlen on Writing*

Anna Quindlen started her writing career as a newspaper reporter. "I had wanted to be a writer for most of my life," she recalls in the introduction to her book *Living Out Loud*, "and in the service of the writing I became a reporter.

For many years I was able to observe, even to feel, life vividly, but at second-hand. I was able to stand over the chalk outline of a body on a sidewalk dappled with black blood; to stand behind the glass and look down into an operating theater where one man was placing a heart in the yawning chest of another; to sit in the park on the first day of summer and find myself profes-sionally obligated to record all the glories of it. Every day I found answers: who, what, when, where, and why."

Quindlen was a good reporter, but the business of finding answers did not satisfy her personally. "In my own life," she continues, "I had only questions." Then she switched from reporter to columnist at the *New York Times*. It was "exhilarating," she says, that "my work became a reflection of my life. After years of being a professional observer of other people's lives, I was given the opportunity to be a professional observer of my own. I was permitted—and permitted myself—to write a column, not about my answers, but about my questions. Never did I make so much sense of my life as I did then, for it was inevitable that as a writer I would find out most clearly what I thought, and what I only thought I thought, when I saw it written down. . . . After years of feeling secondhand, of feeling the pain of the widow, the joy of the winner, I was able to allow myself to feel those emotions for myself."

## For Discussion

1. What were the advantages and disadvantages of news reporting, according to Quindlen?
2. What did Quindlen feel she could accomplish in a column that she could not accomplish in a news report? What evidence of this difference do you see in her essay "Homeless"?

# ANDREW KORITZ KRULL

ANDREW KORITZ KRULL is a chemistry major at Iowa State University with plans to pursue a doctor of pharmacy degree. He was born in Mankato, Minnesota, in 1986 and grew up in Nebraska and Iowa. At Iowa State, Krull works at the limnology laboratory, which tests for contaminants in lakes.

## *Celebrating the Pity of Brotherly Love*

Krull wrote this essay for a composition class and then published it in 2006 in the "My Turn" feature of *Newsweek* magazine. Using examples, he explains how as a child he was both beaten down and lifted up by his brothers. Krull's essay will seem familiar to almost anyone who has siblings.

Everyone has seen the sitcoms where the older brother gives the younger brother a friendly punch in the arm once in a while, or a "noogie" here and there. I envy that younger brother; I never had the luxury of a mere noogie. Older brothers are vicious creatures who feed off the vulnerability and gullibility of younger brothers. We must eliminate the possibility of having older brothers. Yes, I encourage parents to stop at one boy. The results of brotherhood can be disastrous.

I have two older brothers. There is Scott, who is five years older, and Brett, who is two years older. Around the age of one, I began to walk. I obviously can't remember this far back, but my memory was jogged by my sibling tormentors. As I learned to walk, I'm told I would hobble around like a drunk on a Saturday night. Meanwhile, my brothers would perch behind the sofa and throw pillows at me. Oblivious, I kept up with my routine until — thwack! — a pillow would hit the back of my head and down I would go. As Scott now puts it, "We'd have to get the right spin on the pillow, or else it wouldn't work. You didn't seem to mind: Once we hit you, you'd just get back up and keep walking." This "game" could go on for hours.

Another favorite activity of theirs was to make me into a "Polish sausage." This consisted of forcing me to lie down on top of a blanket on the floor, sometimes by physical force, other times by promising to play my favorite board game, Stratego, when we were finished.

First, assorted pillows and plastic toys were placed inside the blanket with me to simulate cheese, pickles and condiments. After this, I was wrapped in the first blanket, then rolled through a second, third and sometimes fourth blanket. Two massive rubber bands, usually used to hold Scott's broken trumpet case together, were then fastened on each end of the "sausage" to prevent my escape.

If I started crying at this point, the game would come to an end. However, if I decided to keep my mouth shut and think hopefully of Stratego, I would then be placed between two beanbags. I was now a "hamburger." This is where the game got slightly painful. My brothers knew it was impossible for me to get out of the blankets on my own. Knowing this, they would then proceed to jump off the couch and onto me. I had plenty of padding, so there were no serious physical injuries, but there were lasting emotional scars. I still flinch whenever I see a beanbag. And I wonder why my mother never figured out why the pillows always got holes.

Brotherhood is depicted as something that will strengthen your personality and mature you. I doubt that when Brett persuaded me to ride my tricycle off the front steps, it did anything for my character. A commonly advocated position is that we should treat everyone as if they were our brothers. This is a preposterous notion. I don't think many people would appreciate it if I called them "elf guy," as my brothers commonly refer to me because of my short stature and relatively pointy ears. Treating everyone as a brother would make the world a terrible place. Can you imagine a place where a couple of guys are there your whole life to make sure you're doing fine — so they can tease you?

I tease them, too, of course. I tell them I'll never forgive them for what they made me into. I loathe Brett for protecting me from the bullies at school who viewed me as an easy target. I despise Scott for staying up extra late to help me with all my schoolwork. It wrenches my gut to think of all the camping trips we have gone on, and the times we would sit for hours doing nothing but laughing and making fun of each other.

Imitating my brothers was my purpose in life as a child, and even now I follow their examples. They treat women respectfully and don't abuse alcohol or drugs? Darn it, I'll act that way too! After all, whenever I would do something incredibly foolish, my brothers were always there to beat the stupidity out of me.

If you think my case is an isolated one, you are gravely mistaken. There are probably millions of young men around the world who would not be the same men they are today had it not been for their older brothers.

Parents, consider yourself warned about the effects of brotherhood. And don't even get me started on what having a younger sister can do to you.

---

*For a reading quiz and annotated links to further readings on sibling relationships, visit **bedfordstmartins.com/thebedfordreader**.*

## Journal Writing

Do you have any brothers or sisters? If so, describe what life with your sibling(s) was like. Did you get along for the most part, or did you fight a lot? What did you learn from each other? If you have no brothers or sisters, reflect on your feelings about growing up an only child. (To take your journal writing further, see "From Journal to Essay" below.)

## Questions on Meaning

1. What solution to the problems of brotherhood does Krull propose in paragraph 1? Does he mean it? How do you know?
2. Is Krull's PURPOSE solely to amuse and entertain readers, or does he also have a more serious point to make?
3. On the surface, Krull seems to state his THESIS in paragraph 1. His real thesis, however, emerges near the end of the essay. What sentence best sums up Krull's central idea? How could this sentence be understood in more than one way?

## Questions on Writing Strategy

1. What GENERALIZATION do the examples in paragraphs 2–6 illustrate? Where in the essay does Krull explicitly state this generalization?
2. How do the examples in paragraphs 7 and 8 differ from the examples in paragraphs 2–6?
3. Give some examples of HYPERBOLE and IRONY in Krull's essay.
4. To whom does Krull directly address his essay? Considering his purpose, do you think that this is his real AUDIENCE?
5. **OTHER METHODS**   Where does Krull use PROCESS ANALYSIS? What do these passages contribute to the essay?

## Questions on Language

1. In paragraph 2, why does Krull put quotation marks around the word *game?*
2. What is the EFFECT of the strong verbs Krull uses in paragraph 7?
3. Consult a dictionary if you are unsure of the meanings of any of the following: vulnerability, gullibility (par. 1); hobble, oblivious (2); flinch (5); advocated, preposterous, stature (6); wrenches (7).

## Suggestions for Writing

1. **FROM JOURNAL TO ESSAY**   Using your journal entry as a springboard, write an essay in which you COMPARE AND CONTRAST the experience of being a sibling with the experience of being an only child. (To portray the situation you didn't grow up in—as an only child or as a sibling—draw on your imagination or the

experiences of people you know.) What are the benefits and drawbacks of each situation? Overall, which do you think is better for a child?

2. Using Krull's selection as a model, try your hand at writing a humorous essay about a love-hate relationship. You might write about a relationship with a family member, a friend, a pet, or even an inanimate object like a car. Like Krull, use concrete examples to illustrate the ups and downs of the relationship.

3. Krull refers to his older brothers as his "sibling tormenters" (par. 2). Teasing, bickering, competing, and even tormenting are part of many sibling relationships. Do some research on sibling rivalry and SYNTHESIZE your findings in a report that focuses on the following questions: What is sibling rivalry? What are its possible CAUSES? What are its possible EFFECTS, both positive and negative? What role can parents play in moderating conflict?

4. **CRITICAL WRITING**    ANALYZE Krull's use of humor in this essay. What is it that makes his essay funny? In particular, consider his use of irony, hyperbole, and humorous IMAGES. You might also do some library or Internet research on humor writing to further support your analysis.

5. **CONNECTIONS**    Krull's relationship with his siblings is complex. The brothers clearly love each other despite their conflicts; however, they don't seem to express this love directly. In "Arm Wrestling with My Father" (p. 146), Brad Manning describes a similarly complex relationship with a parent. Using examples from both selections to support your point, write an essay exploring what these two writers suggest about male communication styles. Consider doing some outside research to further support your essay.

---

# *Andrew Koritz Krull on Writing*

For *The Bedford Reader*, Andrew Koritz Krull described how "Celebrating the Pity of Brotherly Love" came to be published in *Newsweek* magazine.

One assignment in my introductory English class in college was to write a narrative. This narrative was to use your personal experience to convince the reader to switch sides on a topic. I couldn't think of anything serious to say, so my rough draft consisted of a mishmash of stories about the antics of my brothers and me. During this process I thought to myself, "Wow, life would have been a lot more boring without brothers." This spawned the idea of sarcastically suggesting that we should have no brothers in society. I reworked this idea into a couple of the stories where I was the victim and handed in a paper I was very pleased with.

Several weeks later, I found that I had received a B+ for my essay. I was very frustrated, and I remembered how my teacher had mentioned *Newsweek's*

"My Turn" column as an example for narratives. I mailed my essay to *Newsweek* and received a call from one of their editors a few months later. I guess the point of this entire story is to take into account suggestions your teachers have to say, but take them with a grain of salt. Have confidence in your writing.

## For Discussion

1. Why do you think Krull was "frustrated" by the grade he received on his essay?
2. Have you had a writing experience in which you disagreed with your teacher's or someone else's suggestions for how you could improve your work? What was the outcome?

# BRENT STAPLES

BRENT STAPLES is a member of the editorial board of the *New York Times*. Born in 1951 in Chester, Pennsylvania, Staples has a BA in behavioral science from Widener University in Chester and a PhD in psychology from the University of Chicago. Before joining the *New York Times* in 1985, he worked for the *Chicago Sun-Times*, the *Chicago Reader*, *Chicago* magazine, and *Down Beat* magazine. At the *Times*, Staples writes on culture, politics, reading, and special education, championing the cause of children with learning disabilities. He has also contributed to the *New York Times Magazine*, *New York Woman*, *Ms.*, *Harper's*, and other magazines. His memoir, *Parallel Time: Growing Up in Black and White*, appeared in 1994.

# *Black Men and Public Space*

"Black Men and Public Space" appeared in the December 1986 issue of *Harper's* magazine and was then published, in a slightly different version, in Staples's memoir, *Parallel Time*. To explain a recurring experience of African American men, Staples relates incidents when he has been "a night walker in the urban landscape." Sometimes his only defense against others' stereotypes is to whistle.

My first victim was a woman—white, well dressed, probably in her late 1 twenties. I came upon her late one evening on a deserted street in Hyde Park, a relatively affluent neighborhood in an otherwise mean, impoverished section of Chicago. As I swung onto the avenue behind her, there seemed to be a discreet, uninflammatory distance between us. Not so. She cast back a worried glance. To her, the youngish black man—a broad six feet two inches with a beard and billowing hair, both hands shoved into the pockets of a bulky military jacket—seemed menacingly close. After a few more quick glimpses, she picked up her pace and was soon running in earnest. Within seconds she disappeared into a cross street.

That was more than a decade ago. I was twenty-two years old, a graduate 2 student newly arrived at the University of Chicago. It was in the echo of that terrified woman's footfalls that I first began to know the unwieldy inheritance I'd come into—the ability to alter public space in ugly ways. It was clear that she thought herself the quarry of a mugger, a rapist, or worse. Suffering a bout of insomnia, however, I was stalking sleep, not defenseless wayfarers. As a softy who is scarcely able to take a knife to a raw chicken—let alone hold one to a person's throat—I was surprised, embarrassed, and dismayed all at once. Her flight made me feel like an accomplice in tyranny. It also made it clear that I was indistinguishable from the muggers who occasionally seeped into the area from the surrounding ghetto. That first encounter, and those that followed, signified that a vast, unnerving gulf lay between nighttime pedestrians — particularly women — and me. And I soon gathered that being perceived as dangerous is a hazard in itself. I only needed to turn a corner into a dicey situation, or crowd some frightened, armed person in a foyer somewhere, or make an errant move after being pulled over by a policeman. Where fear and weapons meet — and they often do in urban America — there is always the possibility of death.

In that first year, my first away from my hometown, I was to become thoroughly familiar with the language of fear. At dark, shadowy intersections, I could cross in front of a car stopped at a traffic light and elicit the *thunk, thunk, thunk, thunk* of the driver — black, white, male, or female — hammering down the door locks. On less traveled streets after dark, I grew accustomed to but never comfortable with people crossing to the other side of the street rather than pass me. Then there were the standard unpleasantries with policemen, doormen, bouncers, cabdrivers, and others whose business it is to screen out troublesome individuals *before* there is any nastiness. 3

I moved to New York nearly two years ago and I have remained an avid night walker. In central Manhattan, the near-constant crowd cover minimizes tense one-on-one street encounters. Elsewhere — in SoHo, for example, where sidewalks are narrow and tightly spaced buildings shut out the sky — things can get very taut indeed. 4

After dark, on the warrenlike streets of Brooklyn where I live, I often see women who fear the worst from me. They seem to have set their faces on neutral, and with their purse straps strung across their chests bandolier-style, they forge ahead as though bracing themselves against being tackled. I understand, of course, that the danger they perceive is not a hallucination. Women are particularly vulnerable to street violence, and young black males are drastically overrepresented among the perpetrators of that violence. Yet these truths are no solace against the kind of alienation that comes of being ever the suspect, a fearsome entity with whom pedestrians avoid making eye contact. 5

It is not altogether clear to me how I reached the ripe old age of twenty-two without being conscious of the lethality nighttime pedestrians attributed to me. Perhaps it was because in Chester, Pennsylvania, the small, angry industrial town where I came of age in the 1960s, I was scarcely noticeable against a backdrop of gang warfare, street knifings, and murders. I grew up one of the good boys, had perhaps a half-dozen fistfights. In retrospect, my shyness of combat has clear sources. 6

As a boy, I saw countless tough guys locked away; I have since buried several, too. They were babies, really — a teenage cousin, a brother of twenty-two, 7 a childhood friend in his mid-twenties — all gone down in episodes of bravado played out in the streets. I came to doubt the virtues of intimidation early on. I chose, perhaps unconsciously, to remain a shadow — timid, but a survivor.

The fearsomeness mistakenly attributed to me in public places often has a    8
perilous flavor. The most frightening of these confusions occurred in the late 1970s and early 1980s, when I worked as a journalist in Chicago. One day, rushing into the office of a magazine I was writing for with a deadline story in hand, I was mistaken for a burglar. The office manager called security and, with an ad hoc posse, pursued me through the labyrinthine halls, nearly to my editor's door. I had no way of proving who I was. I could only move briskly toward the company of someone who knew me.

Another time I was on assignment for a local paper and killing time before    9
an interview. I entered a jewelry store on the city's affluent Near North Side. The proprietor excused herself and returned with an enormous red Doberman pinscher straining at the end of a leash. She stood, the dog extended toward me, silent to my questions, her eyes bulging nearly out of her head. I took a cursory look around, nodded, and bade her good night.

Relatively speaking, however, I never fared as badly as another black male    10
journalist. He went to nearby Waukegan, Illinois, a couple of summers ago to work on a story about a murderer who was born there. Mistaking the reporter for the killer, police officers hauled him from his car at gunpoint and but for his press credentials would probably have tried to book him. Such episodes are not uncommon. Black men trade tales like this all the time.

Over the years, I learned to smother the rage I felt at so often being taken    11
for a criminal. Not to do so would surely have led to madness. I now take precautions to make myself less threatening. I move about with care, particularly late in the evening. I give a wide berth to nervous people on subway platforms during the wee hours, particularly when I have exchanged business clothes for jeans. If I happen to be entering a building behind some people who appear skittish, I may walk by, letting them clear the lobby before I return, so as not to seem to be following them. I have been calm and extremely congenial on those rare occasions when I've been pulled over by the police.

And on late-evening constitutionals I employ what has proved to be an    12
excellent tension-reducing measure: I whistle melodies from Beethoven and Vivaldi and the more popular classical composers. Even steely New Yorkers hunching toward nighttime destinations seem to relax, and occasionally they even join in the tune. Virtually everybody seems to sense that a mugger wouldn't be warbling bright, sunny selections from Vivaldi's *Four Seasons*. It is my equivalent of the cowbell that hikers wear when they know they are in bear country.

*For a reading quiz, sources on Brent Staples, and annotated links to further readings on racial stereotyping, visit **bedfordstmartins.com/thebedfordreader**.*

## Journal Writing

Staples explains how he perceives himself altering public space. Write in your journal about a time when you felt as if *you* altered public space — in other words, you changed people's attitudes or behavior just by being in a place or entering a situation. If you haven't had this experience, write about a time when you saw someone else alter public space in this way. (To take your journal writing further, see "From Journal to Essay" on the following page.)

## Questions on Meaning

1. What is the PURPOSE of this essay? Do you think Staples believes that he (or other African American men) will cease "to alter public space in ugly ways" in the near future? Does he suggest any long-term solution for "the kind of alienation that comes of being ever the suspect" (par. 5)?
2. In paragraph 5 Staples says he understands that the danger women fear when they see him "is not a hallucination." Do you take this to mean that Staples perceives himself to be dangerous? Explain.
3. Staples says, "I chose, perhaps unconsciously, to remain a shadow — timid, but a survivor" (par. 7). What are the usual CONNOTATIONS of the word *survivor*? Is "timid" one of them? How can you explain this apparent discrepancy?

## Questions on Writing Strategy

1. The concept of altering public space is relatively abstract. How does Staples convince you that this phenomenon really takes place?
2. Staples employs a large number of examples in a fairly small space. How does he avoid having the piece sound like a list? How does he establish COHERENCE among all these examples? (Look, for example, at details and TRANSITIONS.)
3. **OTHER METHODS**   Many of Staples's examples are actually ANECDOTES — brief NARRATIVES. The opening paragraph is especially notable. Why is it so effective?

## Questions on Language

1. What does the author accomplish by using the word *victim* in the essay's first paragraph? Is the word used literally? What TONE does it set for the essay?

2. Be sure you know how to define the following words, as used in this essay: afflu-ent, uninflammatory (par. 1); unwieldy, tyranny, pedestrians (2); intimidation (7); congenial (11); constitutionals (12).

3. The word *dicey* (par. 2) comes from British slang. Without looking it up in your dictionary, can you figure out its meaning from the context in which it appears?

## Suggestions for Writing

1. **FROM JOURNAL TO ESSAY**    Write an essay narrating your experience of either altering public space yourself or being a witness when someone else altered pub-lic space. What changes did you observe in people's behavior? Was your behavior similarly affected? In retrospect, do you think your reactions were justified?

2. Write an essay using examples to show how a trait of your own or of someone you know well always seems to affect people, whether positively or negatively.

3. The ironic term *DWB* (driving while black) expresses the common perception that African American drivers are more likely than white drivers to be pulled over by authorities for minor infractions—or no infraction at all. Research and write an essay about the accuracy of this perception in one state or municipality: Is there truth to it? If African Americans have been discriminated against, what if anything have the appropriate governments done to address the problem?

4. **CRITICAL WRITING**    Consider, more broadly than Staples does, what it means to alter public space. Staples would rather not have the power to do so, but it *is* a power, and it could perhaps be positive in some circumstances (wielded by a street performer, for instance, or the architect of a beautiful new building on cam-pus). Write an essay expanding on Staples's essay in which you examine the pros and cons of altering public space. Use specific examples as your EVIDENCE.

5. **CONNECTIONS**    Like Staples, Barbara Lazear Ascher, in "On Compassion" (p. 193), considers how people regard and respond to "the Other," the one who is viewed as different. In an essay, COMPARE AND CONTRAST the POINTS OF VIEW of these two authors. How does point of view affect each author's selection of details and tone?

---

# *Brent Staples on Writing*

In comments written especially for *The Bedford Reader*, Brent Staples talks about the writing of "Black Men and Public Space": "I was only partly aware of how I felt when I began this essay. I knew only that I had this collection of experiences (facts) and that I felt uneasy with them. I sketched out the expe-riences one by one and strung them together. The bridge to the essay—what I wanted to say, but did not know when I started—sprang into life quite unex-pectedly as I sat looking over these experiences. The crucial sentence comes right after the opening anecdote, in which my first 'victim' runs away from me: 'It was in the echo of that terrified woman's footfalls that I first began to know the unwieldy inheritance I'd come into—the ability to alter public space in ugly ways.' 'Aha!' I said. 'This is why I feel bothered and hurt and frustrated when this happens. I don't want people to think I'm stalking them. I want some fresh air. I want to stretch my legs. I want to be as anonymous as any other person out for a walk in the night.'"

A news reporter and editor by training and trade, Staples sees much similarity between the writing of a personal essay like "Black Men and Public Space" and the writing of, say, a murder story for a daily newspaper. "The newspaper murder," he says, "begins with standard newspaper information: the fact that the man was found dead in an alley in such-and-such a section of the city; his name, occupation, and where he lived; that he died of gunshot wounds to such-and-such a part of his body; that arrests were or were not made; that such-and-such a weapon was found at the scene; that the police have established no motive; etc.

"Personal essays take a different tack, but they, too, begin as assemblies of facts. In 'Black Men and Public Space,' I start out with an anecdote that crystallizes the issue I want to discuss—what it is like to be viewed as a criminal all the time. I devise a sentence that serves this purpose and also catches the reader's attention: 'My first victim was a woman—white, well dressed, probably in her late twenties.' The piece gives examples that are meant to illustrate the same point and discusses what those examples mean.

"The newspaper story stacks its details in a specified way, with each piece taking a prescribed place in a prescribed order. The personal essay begins often with a flourish, an anecdote, or the recounting of a crucial experience, then goes off to consider related experiences and their meanings. But both pieces rely on reporting. Both are built of facts. Reporting is the act of finding and analyzing facts.

"A fact can be a state of the world—a date, the color of someone's eyes, the arc of a body that flies through the air after having been struck by a car. A fact can also be a feeling—sorrow, grief, confusion, the sense of being pleased, offended, or frustrated. 'Black Men and Public Space' explores the relationship between two sets of facts: (1) the way people cast worried glances at me and sometimes run away from me on the streets after dark, and (2) the frustration and anger I feel at being made an object of fear as I try to go about my business in the city."

Personal essays and news stories share one other quality as well, Staples thinks: They affect the writer even when the writing is finished. "The discoveries I made in 'Black Men and Public Space' continued long after the essay was published. Writing about the experiences gave me access to a whole range of internal concerns and ideas, much the way a well-reported news story opens the door onto a given neighborhood, situation, or set of issues."

## For Discussion

1. In recounting how his essay developed, what does Staples reveal about his writing process?
2. How, according to Staples, are essay writing and news writing similar? How are they different?
3. What does Staples mean when he says that "writing about the experiences gave me access to a whole range of internal concerns and ideas"?

# ROGER ROSENBLATT

ROGER ROSENBLATT is a columnist for *Time* magazine and appears regularly on PBS's *Newshour with Jim Lehrer*. He was born in 1940 in New York City and received a PhD from Harvard University. He has been a journalist and commentator most of his career, winning a Peabody, an Emmy, and two George Polk awards for his reflections on culture and politics. *Children of War* (1983), about children growing up in war zones around the world, won the Robert F. Kennedy prize. Rosenblatt's other nonfiction works include *Witness: The World Since Hiroshima* (1985), *Life Itself: Abortion in the American Mind* (1992), and *Anything Can Happen: Notes on My Inadequate Life and Yours* (2003). His most recent book is a novel, *Lapham Rising* (2006).

# *We Are Free to Be*
# *You, Me, Stupid, and Dead*

This essay is the second chapter and the second reason in *Where We Stand: Thirty Reasons for Loving Our Country* (2002). (Some of the other reasons are "We Don't Stop the Presses" and "We Shame Monsters.") Here Rosenblatt champions the freedom of speech guaranteed by the First Amendment to the US Constitution. To show the courage of the Founding Fathers—the men who drafted the Constitution—he gives examples of both outrageous expression and outrageous attempts to stifle expression.

Everyone loves free expression as long as it isn't exercised. Several years ago, Mahmoud Abdul-Rauf, a basketball player for the Denver Nuggets, refused to stand up for the playing of the national anthem because of personal religious convictions. The National Basketball Association greeted his decision by suspending him from the league until someone suggested that the Founding Fathers had actually meant it when they allowed someone to do something that would outrage the rest of us. 1

Similarly, major league baseball suspended John Rocker, the famous nutcase relief pitcher for the Atlanta Braves, when Rocker said that he did not want to ride New York City's Number 7 subway with all those single moms, queers, and illegal aliens. The court did not interfere, perhaps because the Constitution only states that government has no right to prevent free expression; it grants no affirmative licenses. I don't really get the difference between the two cases, but I know that Rocker had a perfect, or rather imperfect, right to sound like a jackass. 2

The rights of jackasses are more than a national staple. The strange beauty of American freedom is that it is ungovernable, that it always runs 3

slightly ahead of human temperament. You think you know what you will tolerate. A man on a soapbox speaks out for China. Fine. An editorial calls for
sympathy with the Taliban. (Gulp) okay. But then a bunch of Nazis want to
march around Skokie, Illinois, or Harlem, and, hold on a minute! And what
the hell is this? An art exhibit called "African-American Flag" in New Jersey.
Or this? An exhibit in the Phoenix Art Museum called "What Is the Proper
Way to Display the US Flag?"

Now that one was a doozie. The exhibit required observers to walk across     4
an American flag on the floor to get to what was displayed on a wall. "That's
my flag, and I'm going to defend it," said a visitor to the museum as he tried to
take the flag from the floor. "No son of a bitch is going to do that."

The thing that I like best about sons of bitches doing that and worse, as     5
long as they do not cry "fire" in a crowded flag, is (a) it enhances my appreciation of the wild courage of the Founders, and (b) it expands my mind, which
could use some expanding. Freedom is like a legal drug. *How far will we go?* is
not a rhetorical question here. Another exhibit in Chicago showed a flag with
the word "think" where the stars should have been. Think. I hate it when that
happens.

You think you know how far freedom will go in America, and then you     6
meet another jackass. In the 1990s, I wrote a story for the *New York Times
Magazine* about the Philip Morris company[1] called "How Do They Live with
Themselves?" The answer to that question, which came from the company
executives I interviewed, turned out to be "Quite comfortably, thanks." The
reason that their consciences did not seem to bother them about manufacturing an addictive lethal product was that their customers were engaging in the
blessed American activity of freedom of choice. They were right—at least
until new laws or lawsuits would prove them wrong. People technically had
the choice of becoming addicted to cigarettes or not. I doubt that any of the
Philip Morris people would ever step on the flag.

Since free is the way people's minds were made to be, it has been instruc-     7
tive for me to spend time in places where freedom was limited. In the Soviet
Union,[2] it was fascinating to see how many ways the workers of the world
managed to squeeze free thought through the cracks of their utopian cells:
the secret publication of books, the pirated music, the tricky subversive lines
of poetry read at vast gatherings of tens of thousands. And the below-the-
surface comedy. I was checking out of a hotel in Tbilisi. Checking out of Russian hotels was always a feat—they didn't have dollars, they didn't have

---

[1] The largest manufacturer of tobacco products. —EDS.
[2] The former Communist federation of Russia and fourteen other republics. —EDS.

rubles, no one had ever checked out before. The clerk at the desk spoke little English, and she wanted to tell me that another, more fluent, clerk would be along shortly. "Mr. Rosenblatt," she said. "Would you mind coming back in fifteen years?" We both exploded in laughter because we knew it was remotely possible.

The mind expands, the mind settles, then is shaken up, resists, and expands again. One of the great ongoing stupidities of the country are school boards and library committees that ban certain books they deem dangerous. On the positive side, though, the folks who do the banning offer some delightful defenses for their decisions. The three literary works most frequently banned in our country are *Macbeth*, *King Lear*, and *The Great Gatsby*.[3] The reason school boards offer for banning *Macbeth* is that the play promotes witchcraft. Perhaps it does. One doesn't think of *Macbeth* as promoting things, but if it did, witchcraft would be it. They don't say why they want to ban *King Lear*. Promotes ingratitude, I suppose. I assume that *The Great Gatsby* promotes Long Island.

Sometimes the reasons offered for censoring certain works are obscure, thus intriguing. In Georgia, the Harry Potter books were recently burned because they were said to encourage kids to want to be sorcerers. In Spokane, Washington, they wanted to remove the children's picture book *Where's Waldo?* from the elementary school library. People objected to *Where's Waldo?*, they said, because it contains "explicit subject matter." A plea for surrealism, I imagine. In Springfield, Virginia, they banned a book called *Hitler's Hang-Ups* because it offered "explicit sexual details about Hitler's life." Given the *other* tendencies of Hitler's life, I should think the sexual details would be relatively acceptable. And, in the town of Astoria, Oregon, a book called *Wait Till Helen Comes* was challenged in an elementary school for giving "a morbid portrayal of death." Now they've gone too far.

---

*For a reading quiz, sources on Roger Rosenblatt, and annotated links to further readings on freedom of speech, visit **bedfordstmartins.com/thebedfordreader**.*

---

[3] *Macbeth* and *King Lear* are tragedies by William Shakespeare (1564–1616). *The Great Gatsby* is a novel by F. Scott Fitzgerald (1896–1940), set on Long Island, New York. —EDS.

---

## Journal Writing

Rosenblatt draws on some particularly controversial examples to illustrate his point about free speech. Which of these examples do you react to most strongly? Why? In your journal, explore your response to that example, explaining whether you basically agree or disagree with a person's right to free speech in that situation. (To take your journal writing further, see "From Journal to Essay" on the facing page.)

## Questions on Meaning

1. What GENERALIZATION, or THESIS, governs Rosenblatt's choice of examples? Where does he state it most directly?
2. How do the examples of censorship in paragraphs 8–9 relate to Rosenblatt's thesis?
3. Is Rosenblatt suggesting that he agrees with the views of people such as John Rocker (par. 2) or the executives at Philip Morris (6)? How do these examples relate to Rosenblatt's PURPOSE in this essay?
4. Rosenblatt says that he likes the free expression of people "as long as they do not cry 'fire' in a crowded flag" (par. 5). What does he mean by this strange phrase?

## Questions on Writing Strategy

1. Based on the content of this essay, how would you describe Rosenblatt's intended AUDIENCE?
2. In most of his essay Rosenblatt writes in the first PERSON (*I*). However, in paragraphs 3 and 6, he briefly switches to the second person (*you*). What is the EFFECT of this tactic?
3. How are the examples in paragraph 3 organized? What point is Rosenblatt making here?
4. In paragraph 9 Rosenblatt offers four examples of books that have caused controversy around the country. How does he use sentence variety to make the paragraph interesting to read?
5. **OTHER METHODS**  How does Rosenblatt use COMPARISON AND CONTRAST in paragraphs 1 and 2? What point is he making with this comparison?

## Questions on Language

1. Find three instances of Rosenblatt's SARCASM. What is the effect of this sarcasm?
2. Rosenblatt calls people "jackasses" several times throughout the essay. What is his point in using this derogatory term?
3. Look up any of the following words you don't already know: temperament, soapbox (par. 3); doozie (4); rhetorical question (5); utopian, subversive, feat, rubles (7); deem (8); explicit, surrealism, morbid (9).

## Suggestions for Writing

1. **FROM JOURNAL TO ESSAY**   Expand your journal entry into an essay arguing either for or against the right to free speech in one of the situations that Rosenblatt describes. You may need to do some library or Internet research to back up your argument.

2. Do some research on an issue related to free speech on campus. For example: Should schools adopt codes banning speech that might offend any group based on race, gender, ethnicity, religion, or sexual orientation? Should administrators have control over what students publish in school newspapers? What is the proposed Academic Bill of Rights, and how would its enactment affect the exchange of ideas on campuses? Write an essay in which you give background information on the issue and support your own view in a well-reasoned ARGUMENT.

3. In paragraph 5 Rosenblatt explains that he supports freedom of speech because "it expands my mind, which could use some expanding." When has your mind been expanded by opening yourself up to a new experience or to a view that was different from your own? Perhaps you attended a religious service with a friend, visited another country, took a course with an instructor whose political views you disagreed with, or learned something interesting from a book you thought you would hate. What did you gain from the experience? Write an essay about the importance of expanding your mind, using concrete examples (or a single extended example) to support your point.

4. **CRITICAL WRITING**   Free speech made international headlines in 2006 when a Danish newspaper published twelve editorial cartoons depicting the Islamic prophet Muhammad. The cartoons, which many people viewed as offensive, sparked protests and even violent riots around world. Research the controversy so that you understand the views for and against publication of the cartoons. In an essay, briefly SUMMARIZE the controversy, and then ANALYZE how you think Rosenblatt might have responded to it. How could he have used the incident as an additional example in his essay? Use PARAPHRASES and QUOTATIONS from the essay to support your point.

5. **CONNECTIONS**   In "The Meanings of a Word" (p. 488), Gloria Naylor explains how African Americans redefined a demeaning term and gained power by confronting racist language head-on. Drawing on both Naylor's and Rosenblatt's essays as EVIDENCE, argue against a hypothetical law banning people from using derogatory labels. What benefits come from allowing people to speak their minds, even when their words might be hurtful?

---

# *Roger Rosenblatt on Writing*

Visiting the University of Nebraska at Lincoln, Rosenblatt made a speech titled "Why Write About the World? The Moral Function of Storytelling." In an interview before the speech, Jim Ballard asked Rosenblatt to summarize what he'd be talking about.

As a reporter you see so much of the destruction of the world and so many difficult things to write about. In recent years I've been in Sudan, in Rwanda, and before that in Cambodia, Northern Ireland, Israel, Beirut, and so forth. And after a while you ask yourself, "Why write about it? What good does it do to communicate?" If you don't learn to justify that, then I think you're in trouble professionally, maybe even personally.

Why write? Why tell a story? If you see cyclical patterns of really terrible and self-destructive things in the world, and you know writing about them isn't going to change the pattern, why do it? I came to the conclusion that it's almost a biological instinct. We do it because we're born to tell each other stories. That's the way we make a connection not just with one another in the present, but among generations. We're born storytellers, and we want to get one another's attention. We have something to say. I suppose ultimately the story we have to tell is the story of ourselves, of our lives.

## For Discussion

1. What does Rosenblatt say is the purpose of writing if it isn't to change things? Do you agree with him?
2. When have you experienced the urge to write? Consider any situation from texting a friend to writing an essay about an event in your life to writing a research paper. What motivated you? What did you accomplish?

# ADDITIONAL WRITING TOPICS

## *Example*

1. Select one of the following general statements, or set forth a general statement of your own that one of these inspires. Making it your central idea (or THESIS), support it in an essay full of examples. Draw your examples from your reading, your studies, your conversation, or your own experience.

   Compared to voice phone, text messaging has many advantages (or many disadvantages).
   Individual consumers can help slow down global warming.
   People one comes to admire don't always at first seem likable.
   Good (or bad) habits are necessary to the nation's economy.
   Each family has its distinctive lifestyle.
   Certain song lyrics, closely inspected, promote violence.
   Comic books are going to the dogs.
   At some point in life, most people triumph over crushing difficulties.
   Churchgoers aren't perfect.
   TV commercials suggest that buying the advertised product will improve your love life.
   Home cooking can't win over fast food (or vice versa).
   Ordinary lives sometimes give rise to legends.
   Some people I know are born winners (or losers).
   Books can change our lives.
   Certain machines *do* have personalities.
   Some road signs lead drivers astray.

2. In a brief essay, make a GENERALIZATION about the fears, joys, or contradictions that members of minority groups seem to share. To illustrate your generalization, draw examples from personal experience, from outside reading, or from two or three of the essays in this book by the following authors: Nancy Mairs (p. 13), Maya Angelou (p. 93), Amy Tan (p. 99), Harold Taw (p. 110), Brent Staples (p. 208), Gloria Naylor (p. 488), Christine Leong (p. 494), Dagoberto Gilb (p. 505), Sandra Cisneros (p. 584), Martin Luther King, Jr. (p. 614), and Richard Rodriguez (p. 651).

# 7

## COMPARISON AND CONTRAST

*Setting Things Side by Side*

◀ **Comparison and contrast in a painting and a photograph**

Created just five years apart, these works relate in time as well as subject. On the top, the painting *American Gothic,* by the Iowan Grant Wood (1892–1942), depicts farmers in 1930, before the Great Depression was fully under way. On the bottom, the photograph *Rural Rehabilitation Client,* by the Lithuanian-born New Jerseyan Ben Shahn (1899–1969), depicts recipients of a federal aid program in Arkansas in 1935, at the Depression's low point. Closely examine the people in each image (clothes, postures, expressions) and their settings. What striking and not-so-striking similarities do you notice? What is the most obvious difference? What are some more subtle differences? What does the medium of each work (painting versus photography) contribute to the differences? How would you summarize the visions of rural folk conveyed by Wood and Shahn?

## THE METHOD

Should we pass laws to regulate pornography or just let pornography run wild? Which team do you place your money on, the Cowboys or the Forty-Niners? To go to school full-time or part-time: What are the rewards and drawbacks of each way of life? How do the Republican and the Democratic platforms stack up against each other? How is the work of Picasso like or unlike that of Matisse? These are questions that may be addressed by the dual method of COMPARISON AND CONTRAST. In comparing, you point to similar features of the subjects; in contrasting, to different features. (The features themselves you identify by the method of DIVISION or ANALYSIS; see Chap. 9.)

With the aid of comparison and contrast, you can show why you prefer one thing to another, one course of action to another, one idea to another. In an argument in which you support one of two possible choices, a careful and detailed comparison and contrast of the choices may be extremely convincing. In an expository essay, it can demonstrate that you understand your subjects thoroughly. That is why, on exams that call for essay answers, often you will be asked to compare and contrast. Sometimes the examiner will come right out and say, "Compare and contrast nineteenth-century methods of treating drug addiction with those of the present day." Sometimes, however, comparison and contrast won't even be mentioned by name; instead, the examiner will ask, "What resemblances and differences do you find between John Updike's short story 'A & P' and the Grimm fairy tale 'Godfather Death'?" Or, "Explain the relative desirability of holding a franchise as against going into business as an independent proprietor." But those—as you realize when you begin to plan your reply—are just other ways of asking you to compare and contrast.

In practice, the two methods are usually inseparable because two subjects are generally neither entirely alike nor entirely unlike. When Bruce Catton sets out to portray the Civil War generals Ulysses S. Grant and Robert E. Lee (p. 245), he considers both their similarities and their differences. Often, as in this case, the similarities make the subjects comparable at all and the differences make comparison worthwhile.

A good essay in comparing and contrasting serves a PURPOSE. Most of the time, the writer of such an essay has one of two purposes in mind:

1. *The purpose of showing each of two subjects distinctly by considering both, side by side.* Writing with such a purpose, the writer doesn't necessarily find one of the subjects better than the other. In his essay on Grant and Lee, Bruce Catton does not favor either general but concludes that each reflected strong currents of American history.

2. *The purpose of choosing between two things.* To EVALUATE subjects, a writer shows how one is better than the other on the basis of some standard: Which of two short stories more convincingly captures the experience of being a teenager? Which of two chemical processes works better to clean waste water? To answer either question, the writer has to consider the features of both subjects—both positive and negative—and then choose the subject whose positive features more clearly predominate.

## THE PROCESS

### Subjects for Comparison

When you find yourself considering two subjects side by side or preferring one subject over another, you have already embarked on comparison and contrast. Just be sure that your two subjects display a clear basis for comparison. In other words, they should have something significant in common. Comparison usually works best with two of a kind: two means of reading for the visually impaired, two Civil War generals, two short stories on the same subject, two processes for cleaning waste water, two mystery writers, two schools of political thought.

It can sometimes be effective to find similarities between evidently unlike subjects—a city and a country town, say—and a special form of comparison, ANALOGY, always equates two very unlike things, explaining one in terms of the other. (In an analogy you might explain how the human eye works by comparing it to a simple camera, or you might explain the forces in a thunderstorm by comparing them to armies in battle.) In any comparison of unlike things, you must have a valid reason for bringing the two together—that is, the similarities must be significant. In a comparision of a city and a country town, for instance, the likenesses must extend beyond the obvious ones that people live in both places, both have streets and shops, and so on.

### Basis for Comparison and Thesis

Beginning to identify the shared and dissimilar features of your subjects will get you started, but the comparison won't be manageable for you or interesting to your readers unless you also limit it. You would be overly ambitious to try to compare and contrast the Russian way of life with the American way of life in five hundred words; you couldn't include all the important similarities and differences. In a brief paper, you would be wise to select a single basis for comparison: to show, for instance, how day-care centers in Russia and the United States are both like and unlike each other.

This basis for comparison will eventually underpin the THESIS of your essay—the claim you have to make about the similarities and dissimilarities of two things or about one thing's superiority over another. Here, from essays in this chapter, are THESIS STATEMENTS that clearly lay out what's being compared and why:

> Neat people are lazier and meaner than sloppy people.
> —Suzanne Britt, "Neat People vs. Sloppy People"

> These were two strong men, these oddly different generals, and they represented the strengths of two conflicting currents that, through them, had come into collision.
> —Bruce Catton, "Grant and Lee: A Study in Contrasts"

Notice that each author not only identifies his or her subjects (neat and sloppy people, two generals) but also previews the purpose of the comparison, whether to evaluate (Britt) or to explain (Catton).

## Organization

Even with a limited basis for comparison, the method of comparison and contrast can be tricky without some planning. We suggest that you make an outline (preferably in writing), using one of two organizations described below. Say you're writing an essay on two banjo-pickers, Jed and Jake. Your purpose is to explain the distinctive identities of the two players, and your thesis statement might be the following:

> Jed and Jake are both excellent banjo-pickers whose differences reflect their training.

Here are the two ways you might arrange your comparison:

1. *Subject by subject.* Set forth all your facts about Jed, then do the same for Jake. Next, sum up their similarities and differences. In your conclusion, state what you think you have shown.

   1. *Jed*
      Training
      Choice of material
      Technical dexterity
      Playing style
   2. *Jake*
      Training
      Choice of material
      Technical dexterity
      Playing style

SUMMARY
CONCLUSION

This procedure works for a paper of a few paragraphs, but for a longer one, it has a built-in disadvantage: Readers need to remember all the facts about subject 1 while they read about subject 2. If the essay is long and lists many facts, this procedure may be burdensome.

2. *Point by point.* Usually more workable in writing a long paper than the first method, the second scheme is to compare and contrast as you go. You consider one point at a time, taking up your two subjects alternately. In this way, you continually bring the subjects together, perhaps in every paragraph. Notice the differences in the outline:

1. *Training*
   *Jed:* studied under Earl Scruggs
   *Jake:* studied under Bela Fleck

2. *Choice of material*
   *Jed:* bluegrass
   *Jake:* jazz-oriented

3. *Technical dexterity*
   *Jed:* highly skilled
   *Jake:* highly skilled

4. *Playing style*
   *Jed:* rapid-fire
   *Jake:* impressionistic
   SUMMARY
   CONCLUSION

For either the subject-by-subject or the point-by-point scheme, your conclusion might be: Although similar in skills, the two differ greatly in aims and in personalities. Jed is better suited to the Grand Ol' Opry and Jake to a concert hall.

No matter how you group your points, they have to balance; you can't discuss Jed's on-stage manner without discussing Jake's, too. If you have nothing to say about Jake's on-stage manner, then you might as well omit the point. A surefire loser is the paper that proposes to compare and contrast two subjects but then proceeds to discuss quite different elements in each: Jed's playing style and Jake's choice of material, Jed's fondness for Italian food and Jake's hobby of antique-car collecting. The writer of such a paper doesn't compare and contrast the two musicians at all, but provides two quite separate discussions.

By the way, a subject-by-subject organization works most efficiently for a *pair* of subjects. If you want to write about *three* banjo-pickers, you might first consider Jed and Jake, then Jake and Josh, then Josh and Jed—but it would probably be easiest to compare and contrast all three point by point.

## Flexibility

As you write, an outline will help you see the shape of your paper and keep your procedure in mind. But don't be the simple tool of your outline. Few essays are more boring to read than the long comparison and contrast written mechanically. The reader comes to feel like a weary tennis spectator whose head has to swivel from side to side: now Jed, now Jake; now Jed again, now back to Jake. You need to mention the same features of both subjects, it is true, but no law decrees *how* you must mention them. You need not follow your outline in lockstep order, or cover similarities and differences at precisely the same length, or spend a hundred words on Jed's banjo-picking skill just because you spend a hundred words on Jake's. Your essay, remember, doesn't need to be as symmetrical as a pair of salt and pepper shakers. What is your outline but a simple means to organize your account of a complicated reality? As you write, keep casting your thoughts upon a living, particular world—not twisting and squeezing that world into a rigid scheme, but moving through it with open senses, being patient and faithful and exact in your telling of it.

### FOCUS ON PARAGRAPH COHERENCE

With several points of comparison and alternating subjects, a comparison will be easy for your readers to follow only if you frequently clarify what subject and what point you are discussing. Two techniques, especially, can help you guide readers through your comparison: transitions and repetition or restatement.

- Use TRANSITIONS as signposts to tell readers where you, and they, are headed. Some transitions indicate that you are shifting between subjects, either finding resemblances between them (*also, like, likewise, similarly*) or finding differences (*but, however, in contrast, instead, unlike, whereas, yet*). Other transitions indicate that you are moving on to a new point (*in addition, also, furthermore, moreover*).

  Traditional public schools depend for financing, of course, on tax receipts and on other public money like bonds, and as a result they generally open enrollment to all students without regard to background, skills, or special needs. Magnet schools are similarly funded by public money. But they often require prospective students to pass a test or other hurdle for admission. In addition, whereas traditional public schools usually offer a general curriculum, magnet schools often focus on a specialized program emphasizing an area of knowledge or competence, such as science and technology or performing arts.

- Use repetition or restatement of subjects and points of comparison to clarify and link sentences. Here is the same passage on schools with its repetitions and restatements underlined:

  Traditional public schools depend for financing, of course, on tax receipts and on other public money like bonds, and as a result they generally open enrollment to all students without regard to background, skills, or special needs. Magnet schools are similarly funded by public money. But they often require prospective students to pass a test or other hurdle for admission. In addition, whereas traditional public schools usually offer a general curriculum, magnet schools often focus on a specialized program emphasizing an area of knowledge or competence, such as science and technology or performing arts.

**For exercises on transitions, visit Exercise Central at *bedfordstmartins.com /thebedfordreader*.**

Comparison and Contrast

---

### CHECKLIST FOR REVISING A COMPARISON AND CONTRAST

✔ **PURPOSE**   What is the aim of your comparison: to explain two subjects or to evaluate them? Will the purpose be clear to readers from the start?

✔ **SUBJECTS**   Are the subjects enough alike, sharing enough features, to make comparison worthwhile?

✔ **THESIS**   Does your thesis establish a limited basis for comparison so that you have room and time to cover all the relevant similarities and differences?

✔ **ORGANIZATION**   Does your arrangement of material, whether subject by subject or point by point, do justice to your subjects and help readers follow the comparison?

✔ **BALANCE AND FLEXIBILITY**   Have you covered the same features of both subjects? At the same time, have you avoided a rigid back-and-forth movement that could bore or exhaust a reader?

✔ **COHERENCE**   Have you used transitions and repetition or restatement to clarify which subjects and which points you are discussing?

---

## COMPARISON AND CONTRAST IN PARAGRAPHS

### Writing About Television

The following example, written especially for *The Bedford Reader*, uses point-by-point comparison for a clear purpose: to evaluate television drama, then and now, and to express a preference for one over the other. Notice that the writer is fair—acknowledging (toward the end) that today's dramas also have fine actors and have none of the primitiveness of yesterday's dramas.

Though written to be freestanding, this paragraph on drama might do good work in a full essay about, say, the chief differences between TV programming in the medium's early days and programming now.

Seen on aged 16-millimeter film, the original production of Paddy Chayevsky's *Marty* makes clear the differences between television drama of 1953 and that of today. <u>Today</u> there's no weekly Goodyear Playhouse to showcase original one-hour plays by important authors; most scriptwriters collaborate, all but anonymously, on serials about familiar characters. *Marty* features no bodice ripping, no drug busts, no deadly illness, no laugh track. <u>Instead</u>, it simply shows the awakening of love between a heavyset butcher and a mousy high-school teacher: both single, lonely, and shy, never twice dating the same person. <u>Unlike the writer of today</u>, Chayevsky couldn't set scenes outdoors or on location. In one small studio, in slow lingering takes (some five minutes long—not eight to twelve seconds, <u>as we now expect</u>), the camera probes the faces of two seated characters as Marty and his pal Angie plan Saturday night ("What do you want to do?"—"I dunno. What do *you* want to do?"). Oddly, the effect is spellbinding. To bring such scenes to life, the actors must project with vigor; and <u>like the finer actors of today</u>, Rod Steiger as Marty exploits each moment. <u>In 1953</u>, plays were telecast live. <u>Today</u>, well-edited videotape may eliminate blown lines, but a chill slickness prevails. Technically, *Marty* is primitive, yet it probes souls. Most televised drama <u>today</u> displays a physically larger world—only to nail a box around it.

*Point-by-point comparison supporting this topic sentence*

1. Original plays vs. serials

2. Simple love story vs. violence and sex

3. Studio sets with long takes vs. locations with short takes

4. Good acting vs. good acting

5. Live vs. videotaped

6. Primitive and probing vs. big and limited

*Transitions (underlined) clarify the comparison*

## Writing in an Academic Discipline

Taken from a textbook on architectural history, the following subject-by-subject comparison explains the differences between two competing theories of architecture in Russia in the 1920s and 1930s. The paragraph is one of several in which the author demonstrates how modernist architects divided into those concerned mainly with form and those concerned mainly with social progress.

In Russia, too, modernists fell into two camps. They squared off against each other in public debate and in Vkhutemas, a school of architecture organized in 1920 along lines parallel to the Bauhaus. "The measure of architecture is architecture," went the motto of one camp. They believed in an unfettered experimentalism of form.

*Subject-by-subject comparison supporting this topic sentence*

1. First camp: experimental

The rival camp had a problem-solving orientation. The architect's main mission, in their view, was to share in the common task of achieving the transformation of society promised by the October Revolution [of 1917]. They were keen on standardization, user interviews, and ideological prompting. They worked on new building programs that would consolidate the social order of communism. These they referred to as "social condensers."

—Spiro Kostof, *A History of Architecture*

2. Second camp: problem solving (receives more attention because it eventually prevailed)

## COMPARISON AND CONTRAST IN PRACTICE

In her sophomore year in college, Susan Wheeler was running for president of her dormitory. She prepared a campaign statement for the student newspaper's coverage of the election, and she also created the flier on the next page for posting throughout the dorm.

Wheeler believed that her campaign platform was much stronger than her opponent's, and she decided to highlight the differences by showing her ideas alongside her opponent's (in a point-by-point arrangement). But her draft needed work to make the points more concise and to give them PARALLEL wording that would clarify and stress the contrasts. Originally, the first three points read as follows:

*Susan Wheeler*
- A supporter of all extra-curricular activities
- Actively participates in student government association
- The food plans should be more flexible for all students

*Matt Parker*
- Supports mainly sports and cheerleading
- He is not in the student government association
- Does not mention the food plans

In Wheeler's final draft (next page), the parallel wording (each point beginning with a verb) is both easier to read and more emphatic.

# Susan Wheeler
## for
# Dorm President

### Here are the reasons why:

**Susan Wheeler**

- Supports all extracurricular activities
- Participates actively in student government association
- Wants to make food plans more flexible for all students
- Wants to extend bookstore hours
- Wants to increase quantity and accessibility of copiers
- Wants a 24-hour computer lab in the dorm
- Has made Dean's List every semester

**Matt Parker**

- Supports mainly sports and cheerleading
- Does not participate in student government association
- Does not mention the food plans
- Does not mention extending bookstore hours
- Does not mention copier problems
- Does not mention a computer lab
- Has not made Dean's List

# Vote May 2

## SUSAN WHEELER FOR PRESIDENT...
## WE'LL DO IT TOGETHER!

# SUZANNE BRITT

SUZANNE BRITT was born in Winston-Salem, North Carolina, and studied at Salem College and Washington University, where she earned an MA in English. Britt has written for *Sky Magazine*, the *New York Times*, *Newsweek*, the *Boston Globe*, and many other publications. She teaches English at Meredith College in North Carolina and has published a history of the college and two English textbooks. Her other books are collections of her essays: *Skinny People Are Dull and Crunchy like Carrots* (1982) and *Show and Tell* (1983).

# *Neat People*
# *vs.*
# *Sloppy People*

"Neat People vs. Sloppy People" appears in Britt's collection *Show and Tell*. Mingling humor with seriousness (as she often does), Britt has called the book a report on her journey into "the awful cave of self: You shout your name and voices come back in exultant response, telling you their names." In this essay, Britt uses comparison mainly to entertain by showing us aspects of our own selves, awful or not. For another approach to a similar subject, see the next essay, by Dave Barry.

I've finally figured out the difference between neat people and sloppy people. The distinction is, as always, moral. Neat people are lazier and meaner than sloppy people.

Sloppy people, you see, are not really sloppy. Their sloppiness is merely the unfortunate consequence of their extreme moral rectitude. Sloppy people carry in their mind's eye a heavenly vision, a precise plan, that is so stupendous, so perfect, it can't be achieved in this world or the next.

Sloppy people live in Never-Never Land. Someday is their métier. Someday they are planning to alphabetize all their books and set up home catalogs. Someday they will go through their wardrobes and mark certain items for tentative mending and certain items for passing on to relatives of similar shape and size. Someday sloppy people will make family scrapbooks into which they will put newspaper clippings, postcards, locks of hair, and the dried corsage from their senior prom. Someday they will file everything on the surface of their desks, including the cash receipts from coffee purchases at the snack shop. Someday they will sit down and read all the back issues of *The New Yorker*.

For all these noble reasons and more, sloppy people never get neat. They 4 aim too high and wide. They save everything, planning someday to file, order, and straighten out the world. But while these ambitious plans take clearer and clearer shape in their heads, the books spill from the shelves onto the floor, the clothes pile up in the hamper and closet, the family mementos accumulate in every drawer, the surface of the desk is buried under mounds of paper, and the unread magazines threaten to reach the ceiling.

Sloppy people can't bear to part with anything. They give loving atten- 5 tion to every detail. When sloppy people say they're going to tackle the surface of a desk, they really mean it. Not a paper will go unturned; not a rubber band will go unboxed. Four hours or two weeks into the excavation, the desk looks exactly the same, primarily because the sloppy person is meticulously creating new piles of papers with new headings and scrupulously stopping to read all the old book catalogs before he throws them away. A neat person would just bulldoze the desk.

Neat people are bums and clods at heart. They have cavalier attitudes 6 toward possessions, including family heirlooms. Everything is just another dust-catcher to them. If anything collects dust, it's got to go and that's that. Neat people will toy with the idea of throwing the children out of the house just to cut down on the clutter.

Neat people don't care about process. They like results. What they want 7 to do is get the whole thing over with so they can sit down and watch the rasslin' on TV. Neat people operate on two unvarying principles: Never handle any item twice, and throw everything away.

The only thing messy in a neat person's house is the trash can. The 8 minute something comes to a neat person's hand, he will look at it, try to decide if it has immediate use and, finding none, throw it in the trash.

Neat people are especially vicious with mail. They never go through their 9 mail unless they are standing directly over a trash can. If the trash can is beside the mailbox, even better. All ads, catalogs, pleas for charitable contributions, church bulletins, and money-saving coupons go straight into the trash can without being opened. All letters from home, postcards from Europe, bills, and paychecks are opened, immediately responded to, then dropped in the trash can. Neat people keep their receipts only for tax purposes. That's it. No sentimental salvaging of birthday cards or the last letter a dying relative ever wrote. Into the trash it goes.

Neat people place neatness above everything, even economics. They are 10 incredibly wasteful. Neat people throw away several toys every time they walk through the den. I knew a neat person once who threw away a perfectly good dish drainer because it had mold on it. The drainer was too much trouble to wash. And neat people sell their furniture when they move. They will sell a La-Z-Boy recliner while you are reclining in it.

Neat people are no good to borrow from. Neat people buy everything in    11
expensive little single portions. They get their flour and sugar in two-pound bags. They wouldn't consider clipping a coupon, saving a leftover, reusing plastic nondairy whipped cream containers, or rinsing off tin foil and draping it over the unmoldy dish drainer. You can never borrow a neat person's newspaper to see what's playing at the movies. Neat people have the paper all wadded up and in the trash by 7:05 AM.

Neat people cut a clean swath through the organic as well as the inorganic    12
world. People, animals, and things are all one to them. They are so insensitive. After they've finished with the pantry, the medicine cabinet, and the attic, they will throw out the red geranium (too many leaves), sell the dog (too many fleas), and send the children off to boarding school (too many scuff-marks on the hardwood floors).

---

*For a reading quiz, sources on Suzanne Britt, and annotated links to further readings on personality traits, visit* ***bedfordstmartins.com/thebedfordreader.***

---

## Journal Writing

Britt suggests that grouping people according to oppositions, such as neat versus sloppy, reveals other things about them. Write about the oppositions you use to evaluate people. Smart versus dumb? Fit versus out of shape? Hip versus clueless? Rich versus poor? Outgoing versus shy? Open-minded versus narrow-minded? (To take your journal writing further, see "From Journal to Essay" on the next page.)

## Questions on Meaning

1. "Suzanne Britt believes that neat people are lazy, mean, petty, callous, wasteful, and insensitive." How would you respond to this statement?
2. Is the author's main PURPOSE to make fun of neat people, to assess the habits of neat and sloppy people, to help neat and sloppy people get along better, to defend sloppy people, to amuse and entertain, or to prove that neat people are morally inferior to sloppy people? Discuss.

3. What is meant by "as always" in the sentence "The distinction is, as always, moral" (par. 1)? Does the author seem to be suggesting that any and all distinctions between people are moral?

## Questions on Writing Strategy

1. What is the general TONE of this essay? What words and phrases help you determine that tone?
2. Britt mentions no similarities between neat and sloppy people. Does that mean this is not a good comparison and contrast essay? Why might a writer deliberately focus on differences and give very little or no time to similarities?
3. Consider the following GENERALIZATIONS: "For all these noble reasons and more, sloppy people never get neat" (par. 4) and "The only thing messy in a neat person's house is the trash can" (8). How can you tell that these statements are generalizations? Look for other generalizations in the essay. What is the EFFECT of using so many?
4. How does Britt use repetition to clarify her comparison?
5. **OTHER METHODS** Although filled with generalizations, Britt's essay does not lack for EXAMPLES. Study the examples in paragraph 11, and explain how they do and don't work the way examples should: to bring the generalizations about people down to earth.

## Questions on Language

1. Consult your dictionary for definitions of these words: rectitude (par. 2); métier, tentative (3); accumulate (4); excavation, meticulously, scrupulously (5); salvaging (9).
2. How do you understand the use of the word *noble* in the first sentence of paragraph 4? Is it meant literally? Are there other words in the essay that appear to be written in a similar tone?

## Suggestions for Writing

1. **FROM JOURNAL TO ESSAY** From your journal entry, choose your favorite opposition for evaluating people, and write an essay in which you compare and contrast those who pass your "test" with those who fail it. You may choose to write a tongue-in-cheek essay, as Britt does, or a serious one.
2. Write an essay in which you compare and contrast two apparently dissimilar groups of people: for example, blue-collar workers and white-collar workers, people who write a lot of e-mail and people who don't bother with it, runners and football players, readers and TV watchers, or any other variation you choose. Your approach may be either lighthearted or serious, but make sure you come to some conclusion about your subjects. Which group do you favor? Why?
3. ANALYZE the similarities and differences between two characters in your favorite novel, story, film, or television show. Which aspects of their personalities make them work well together, within the context in which they appear? Which char-

acteristics work against each other, and therefore provide the necessary conflict to hold the reader's or viewer's attention?

4. **CRITICAL WRITING**   Britt's essay is remarkable for its exaggeration of the two types. Write a brief essay analyzing and contrasting the ways Britt characterizes sloppy people and neat people. Be sure to consider the CONNOTATIONS of the words, such as "moral rectitude" for sloppy people (par. 2) and "cavalier" for neat people (6).

5. **CONNECTIONS**   Neither Suzanne Britt nor the author of the next essay, Dave Barry, seems to have much sympathy for neat people. Write a brief essay in which you explain why neatness matters. Or if you haven't a clue why, then write a brief essay in which you explain the benefits of dirt and disorder.

---

## *Suzanne Britt on Writing*

Asked to tell how she writes, Suzanne Britt contributed the following comment to *The Bedford Reader*.

The question "How do you write?" gets a snappy, snappish response from me. The first commandment is "Live!" And the second is like unto it: "Pay attention!" I don't mean that you have to live high or fast or deep or wise or broad. And I certainly don't mean you have to live true and upright. I just mean that you have to suck out all the marrow of whatever you do, whether it's picking the lint off the navy-blue suit you'll be wearing to Cousin Ione's funeral or popping an Aunt Jemimah frozen waffle into the toaster oven or lying between sand dunes, watching the way the sea oats slice the azure sky. The ominous question put to me by students on all occasions of possible accountability is "Will this count?" My answer is rock bottom and hard: "Everything counts," I say, and silence falls like prayers across the room.

The same is true of writing. Everything counts. Despair is good. Numbness can be excellent. Misery is fine. Ecstasy will work — or pain or sorrow or passion. The only thing that won't work is indifference. A writer refuses to be shocked and appalled by anything going or coming, rising or falling, singing or soundless. The only thing that shocks me, truth to tell, is indifference. How dare you not fight for the right to the crispy end piece on the standing-rib roast? How dare you let the fragrance of Joy go by without taking a whiff of it? How dare you not see the old woman in the snap-front housedress and the rolled-down socks, carrying her Polident and Charmin in a canvas tote that says, simply, elegantly, Le Bag?

After you have lived, paid attention, seen connections, felt the harmony, writhed under the dissonance, fixed a Diet Coke, popped a big stick of Juicy

Fruit in your mouth, gathered your life around you as a mother hen gathers her brood, as a queen settles the folds in her purple robes, you are ready to write. And what you will write about, even if you have one of those teachers who makes you write about, say, Guatemala, will be something very exclusive and intimate — something just between you and Guatemala. All you have to find out is what that small intimacy might be. It is there. And having found it, you have to make it count.

There is no rest for a writer. But there is no boredom either. A Sunday morning with a bottle of extra-strength aspirin within easy reach and an ice bag on your head can serve you very well in writing. So can a fly buzzing at your ear or a heart-stopping siren in the night or an interminable afternoon in a biology lab in front of a frog's innards.

All you need, really, is the audacity to believe, with your whole being, that if you tell it right, tell it truly, tell it so we can all see it, the "it" will play in Peoria, Poughkeepsie, Pompeii, or Podunk. In the South we call that conviction, that audacity, an act of faith. But you can call it writing.

## For Discussion

1. What advice does Britt offer a student assigned to write a paper about, say, Guatemala? If you were that student, how would you go about taking her advice?
2. Where in her comment does the author use colorful and effective FIGURES OF SPEECH?
3. What is the TONE of Britt's remarks? Sum up her attitude toward her subject, writing.

# DAVE BARRY

DAVE BARRY is a humorist whom the *New York Times* has called "the funniest man in America." Barry was born in 1947 in Armonk, New York, and graduated from Haverford College in 1969. He worked as a journalist for five years and lectured businesspeople on writing for eight years while he began to establish himself as a columnist. As a syndicated columnist for two decades, Barry published humor writing in several hundred newspapers. He retired from his weekly column in 2005 but still writes occasional essays as well as a blog. He also has published thirty books, including *Bad Habits: A 100% Fact Free Book* (1985), *The World According to Dave Barry* (1994), *Dave Barry in Cyberspace* (1996), and *Dave Barry's Money Secrets* (2006), the last offering funny advice on everything from buying a new car to filing taxes to talking to children about money. In 1988 Barry received the Pulitzer Prize for "distinguished commentary," although, he says, "nothing I've ever written fits the definition." (He thinks he won because his columns stood out from the "earthshakingly important" competition.) Barry lives in Miami.

## *Batting Clean-Up and Striking Out*

This essay from *Dave Barry's Greatest Hits* (1988) illustrates Barry's gift, in the words of critic Alison Teal, "for taking things at face value and rendering them funny on those grounds alone, for rendering every ounce of humor out of a perfectly ordinary experience." Like Suzanne Britt in the previous essay, Barry contrasts two styles of dealing with a mess.

The primary difference between men and women is that women can see extremely small quantities of dirt. Not when they're babies, of course. Babies of both sexes have a very low awareness of dirt, other than to think it tastes better than food.

But somewhere during the growth process, a hormonal secretion takes place in women that enables them to see dirt that men cannot see, dirt at the level of *molecules*, whereas men don't generally notice it until it forms clumps large enough to support agriculture. This can lead to tragedy, as it did in the ill-fated ancient city of Pompeii, where the residents all got killed when the local volcano erupted and covered them with a layer of ash twenty feet deep.[1]

---

[1] Pompeii, in what is now southern Italy, was buried in the eruption of Mount Vesuvius in AD 79. — EDS.

**239**

Modern people often ask, "How come, when the ashes started falling, the Pompeii people didn't just *leave?*" The answer is that in Pompeii, it was the custom for the men to do the housework. They never even *noticed* the ash until it had for the most part covered the children. "Hey!" the men said (in Latin). "It's mighty quiet around here!" This is one major historical reason why, to this very day, men tend to do extremely little in the way of useful housework.

What often happens in my specific family unit is that my wife will say to me: "Could you clean Robert's bathroom? It's filthy." So I'll gather up the Standard Male Cleaning Implements, namely a spray bottle of Windex and a wad of paper towels, and I'll go into Robert's bathroom, and it *always looks perfectly fine*. I mean, when I hear the word "filthy" used to describe a bathroom, I think about this bar where I used to hang out called Joe's Sportsman's Lounge, where the men's room had bacteria you could enter in a rodeo. 3

Nevertheless, because I am a sensitive and caring kind of guy, I "clean" the bathroom, spraying Windex all over everything including the six hundred action figures each sold separately that God forbid Robert should ever take a bath without, and then I wipe it back off with the paper towels, and I go back to whatever activity I had been engaged in, such as doing an important project on the Etch-a-Sketch, and a little while later my wife will say: "I hate to rush you, but could you do Robert's bathroom? It's really *filthy*." She is in there looking at the very walls I *just Windexed*, and she is seeing *dirt! Everywhere!* And if I tell her I already *cleaned* the bathroom, she gives me this look that she has perfected, the same look she used on me the time I selected Robert's outfit for school and part of it turned out to be pajamas. 4

The opposite side of the dirt coin, of course, is sports. This is an area where men tend to feel very sensitive and women tend to be extremely callous. I have written about this before and I always get irate letters from women who say they are the heavyweight racquetball champion of someplace like Iowa and are sensitive to sports to the point where they could crush my skull like a ripe grape, but I feel these women are the exception. 5

A more representative woman is my friend Maddy, who once invited some people, including my wife and me, over to her house for an evening of stimulating conversation and jovial companionship, which sounds fine except that this particular evening occurred *during a World Series game*. If you can imagine such a social gaffe. 6

We sat around the living room and Maddy tried to stimulate a conversation, but we males could not focus our attention on the various suggested topics because we could actually *feel* the World Series television and radio broadcast rays zinging through the air, penetrating right into our bodies, causing our dental fillings to vibrate, and all the while the women were behaving 7 *as though nothing were wrong.* It was exactly like that story by Edgar Allan Poe where the murderer can hear the victim's heart beating louder and louder even though he (the murder victim) is dead, until finally he (the murderer) can't stand it anymore, and he just *has* to watch the World Series on television.[2] That was how we felt.

Maddy's husband made the first move, coming up with an absolutely bril-  8 liant means of escape: *He used their baby.* He picked up Justine, their seven-month-old daughter, who was fussing a little, and announced: "What this child needs is to have her bottle and watch the World Series." And just like that he was off to the family room, moving very quickly for a big man holding a baby. A second male escaped by pretending to clear the dessert plates. Soon all four of us were in there, watching the Annual Fall Classic, while the women prattled away about human relationships or something. It turned out to be an extremely pivotal game.

For a reading quiz, sources on Dave Barry, and annotated links to further readings on gender differences, visit **bedfordstmartins.com/thebedfordreader**.

---

## Journal Writing

Are you ever baffled by the behavior of members of the opposite sex — or members of your own sex, if you often find yourself behaving differently from most of them? List traits of men or women that you find foreign or bewildering, such as that they do or do not want to talk about their feelings or that they can spend countless hours watching sports on television or shopping. (To take your journal writing further, see "From Journal to Essay" on the next page.)

## Questions on Meaning

1. What is the PURPOSE of Barry's essay? How do you know?
2. How OBJECTIVE is Barry's portrayal of men and women? Does he seem to understand one sex better than the other? Does he seek to justify and excuse male sloppiness and antisocial behavior?

---

[2]Except for the World Series ending, Barry refers to Poe's story "The Tell-Tale Heart" (1843). —EDS.

3. What can you INFER about Barry's attitude toward the differences between the sexes? Does he see a way out?

## Questions on Writing Strategy

1. Barry's comparison is organized point by point—differences in sensitivity to dirt, then differences in sensitivity to sports. What is the EFFECT of this organization? Or, from another angle, what would have been the effect of a subject-by-subject organization—just men, then just women (or vice versa)?
2. How does Barry set the TONE of this piece from the very first paragraph?
3. The first sentence looks like a THESIS STATEMENT but turns out not to be complete. Where does Barry finish his statement of the essay's thesis? Does it hurt or help the essay that the thesis is divided? Why?
4. How does Barry's ALLUSION to Poe's "The Tell-Tale Heart" (par. 7) enhance Barry's own story?
5. In paragraph 5, how does Barry indicate that he's changing points of comparison?
6. **OTHER METHODS**   How persuasive is the historical EXAMPLE cited in paragraph 2 as EVIDENCE for Barry's claims about men's and women's differing abilities to perceive dirt? Must examples always be persuasive?

## Questions on Language

1. Define these words: hormonal (par. 2); implements (3); callous, irate (5); jovial, gaffe (6); prattled, pivotal (8).
2. Paragraph 4 begins with a textbook example of a run-on sentence. Does Barry need a better copy editor, or is he going for an effect here? If so, what is it?
3. What effect does Barry achieve with frequent italics (for example, *just Windexed,* par. 4) and capital letters ("Standard Male Cleaning Implements," 3)?
4. Why does Barry use the word *males* instead of *men* in paragraphs 7 and 8?

## Suggestions for Writing

1. **FROM JOURNAL TO ESSAY**   From the list you compiled in your journal, choose the trait of men or women that seems to have the most potential for humor. Write an essay similar to Barry's, exaggerating the difference to the point where it becomes the defining distinction between men and women.
2. How well do you conform to Barry's GENERALIZATIONS about your gender? In what ways are you stereotypically male or female? Do such generalizations amuse or merely annoy you? Why?
3. Considerable research has examined whether the differences between women and men are caused by heredity or by the environment. Explore some of this research, and write an essay ANALYZING what you discover. Based on your reading, do you think gender differences result primarily from biology or from social conditioning?
4. **CRITICAL WRITING**   Barry is obviously not afraid of offending women: He claims to have already done so (par. 5), and yet he persists. Do you take offense at any of

this essay's stereotypes of women and men? If so, explain the nature of the offense as coolly as you can. Whether you take offense or not, can you see any virtue in using such stereotypes for humor? For instance, does the humor help undermine the stereotypes or merely strengthen them? Write an essay in which you address these questions, using quotations from Barry as examples and evidence.

5. **CONNECTIONS**   Write an essay about the humor gained from exaggeration, relying on Barry's essay and Suzanne Britt's "Neat People vs. Sloppy People" (p. 233). Why is exaggeration often funny? What qualities does humorous exaggeration have? Quote and PARAPHRASE from Barry's and Britt's essays for your support.

---

# *Dave Barry on Writing*

For Dave Barry, coming up with ideas for humorous writing is no problem. "Just about anything's a topic for a humor column," he told an interviewer for *Contemporary Authors* in 1990, "any event that occurs in the news, anything that happens in daily life—driving, shopping, reading, eating. You can look at just about anything and see humor in it somewhere."

Writing challenges, for Barry, occur after he has his idea. "Writing has always been hard for me," he says. "The hard part is getting the jokes to come, and it never happens all at once for me. I very rarely have any idea where a column is going to go when it starts. It's a matter of piling a little piece here and a little piece there, fitting them together, going on to the next part, then going back and gradually shaping the whole piece into something. I know what I want in terms of reaction, and I want it to have a certain feel. I know when it does and when it doesn't. But I'm never sure when it's going to get there. That's what writing is. That's why it's so painful and slow. But that's more technique than anything else. You don't rely on inspiration—I don't, anyway, and I don't think most writers do. The creative process is just not an inspirational one for most people. There's a little bit of that and a whole lot of polishing."

A humor writer must be sensitive to readers, trying to make them smile, but Barry warns against catering to an audience. "I think it's a big mistake to write humor for anybody but yourself, to try to adopt any persona other than your own. If I don't at some point think something is funny, then I'm not going to write it." Not that his own sense of humor will always make a piece fly. "Thinking of it in rough form is one thing," Barry confesses, "and shaping and polishing it so that you like the way it reads is so agonizingly slow that by the time you're done, you don't think anything is funny. You think this is something you might use to console a widow."

More often, though, the shaping and polishing—the constant revision—do work. "Since I know how to do that," Barry says, "since I do it every day of the week and have for years and years, I'm confident that if I keep at it I'll get something."

## For Discussion

1. Do you agree with Barry that "[y]ou can look at just about anything and see humor in it somewhere"? What topics might be off-limits for humor?
2. What does successful writing depend on, according to Barry? What role does inspiration play?
3. How might Barry's views on writing be relevant to your own experiences as a writer? What can a humor writer teach a college writer?

# BRUCE CATTON

BRUCE CATTON (1899–1978) was one of America's best-known historians of the American Civil War. As a boy in Benzonia, Michigan, Catton acted out historical battles on local playing fields. In his memoir *Waiting for the Morning Train* (1972), he recalls how he would listen by the hour to the memories of Union army veterans. His studies at Oberlin College interrupted by service in World War I, Catton never finished his bachelor's degree. Instead, he worked as a reporter, columnist, and editorial writer for the *Cleveland Plain Dealer* and other newspapers, then became a speechwriter and information director for government agencies. Of Catton's eighteen books, seventeen were written after his fiftieth year. *A Stillness at Appomattox* (1953) won him both a Pulitzer Prize for History and a National Book Award; other notable works include *This Hallowed Ground* (1956) and *Gettysburg: The Final Fury* (1974). From 1954 until his death, Catton edited *American Heritage*, a magazine of history. President Gerald Ford awarded him a Medal of Freedom for his life's accomplishment.

# *Grant and Lee:*
# *A Study in Contrasts*

"Grant and Lee: A Study in Contrasts" first appeared in *The American Story*, a book of essays written by eminent historians for interested general readers. Ulysses S. Grant and Robert E. Lee were opposing generals of the Civil War, Grant commanding forces of the North and Lee commanding forces of the South (called the Confederacy). The war lasted from 1861 to 1865, ending with Lee's surrender to Grant at the meeting Catton describes. Contrasting the two great generals allows Catton to portray not only two very different men but also the conflicting traditions they represented. Catton's essay builds toward the conclusion that, in one outstanding way, the two leaders were more than a little alike.

When Ulysses S. Grant and Robert E. Lee met in the parlor of a modest house at Appomattox Court House, Virginia, on April 9, 1865, to work out the terms for the surrender of Lee's Army of Northern Virginia, a great chapter in American life came to a close, and a great new chapter began.

These men were bringing the Civil War to its virtual finish. To be sure, other armies had yet to surrender, and for a few days the fugitive confederate government would struggle desperately and vainly, trying to find some way to go on living now that its chief support was gone. But in effect it was all over when Grant and Lee signed the papers. And the little room where they wrote out the terms was the scene of one of the poignant, dramatic contrasts in American history.

They were two strong men, these oddly different generals, and they repre-   3
sented the strengths of two conflicting currents that, through them, had come
into final collision.

Back of Robert E. Lee was the notion that the old aristocratic concept   4
might somehow survive and be dominant in American life.

Lee was tidewater Virginia, and in his background were family, culture,   5
and tradition . . . the age of chivalry transplanted to a New World which was
making its own legends and its own myths. He embodied a way of life that had
come down through the age of knighthood and the English country squire.
America was a land that was beginning all over again, dedicated to nothing
much more complicated than the rather hazy belief that all men had equal
rights, and should have an equal chance in the world. In such a land Lee stood
for the feeling that it was somehow of advantage to human society to have a
pronounced inequality in the social structure. There should be a leisure class,
backed by ownership of land; in turn, society itself should be keyed to the land
as the chief source of wealth and influence. It would bring forth (according to
this ideal) a class of men with a strong sense of obligation to the community;
men who lived not to gain advantage for themselves, but to meet the solemn
obligations which had been laid on them by the very fact that they were privileged. From them the country would get its leadership; to them it could look
for the higher values—of thought, of conduct, of personal deportment—to
give it strength and virtue.

Lee embodied the noblest elements of this aristocratic ideal. Through   6
him, the landed nobility justified itself. For four years, the Southern states had
fought a desperate war to uphold the ideals for which Lee stood. In the end, it
almost seemed as if the Confederacy fought for Lee; as if he himself was the
Confederacy . . . the best thing that the way of life for which the Confederacy
stood could ever have to offer. He had passed into legend before Appomattox.
Thousands of tired, underfed, poorly clothed Confederate soldiers, long since
past the simple enthusiasm of the early days of the struggle, somehow considered Lee the symbol of everything for which they had been willing to die. But
they could not quite put this feeling into words. If the Lost Cause, sanctified
by so much heroism and so many deaths, had a living justification, its justification was General Lee.

Grant, the son of a tanner on the Western frontier, was everything Lee   7
was not. He had come up the hard way, and embodied nothing in particular
except the eternal toughness and sinewy fiber of the men who grew up beyond
the mountains. He was one of a body of men who owed reverence and obeisance to no one, who were self-reliant to a fault, who cared hardly anything
for the past but who had a sharp eye for the future.

These frontier men were the precise opposites of the tidewater aristocrats.    8
Back of them, in the great surge that had taken people over the Alleghenies
and into the opening Western country, there was a deep, implicit dissatisfac-
tion with a past that had settled into grooves. They stood for democracy, not
from any reasoned conclusion about the proper ordering of human society, but
simply because they had grown up in the middle of democracy and knew how
it worked. Their society might have privileges, but they would be privileges
each man had won for himself. Forms and patterns meant nothing. No man
was born to anything, except perhaps to a chance to show how far he could
rise. Life was competition.

Yet along with this feeling had come a deep sense of belonging to a    9
national community. The Westerner who developed a farm, opened a shop, or
set up in business as a trader could hope to prosper only as his own community
prospered—and his community ran from the Atlantic to the Pacific and from
Canada down to Mexico. If the land was settled, with towns and highways and
accessible markets, he could better himself. He saw his fate in terms of the
nation's own destiny. As its horizons expanded, so did his. He had, in other
words, an acute dollars-and-cents stake in the continued growth and development of his country.

And that, perhaps, is where the contrast between Grant and Lee becomes    10
most striking. The Virginia aristocrat, inevitably, saw himself in relation to his
own region. He lived in a static society which could endure almost anything
except change. Instinctively, his first loyalty would go to the locality in which
that society existed. He would fight to the limit of endurance to defend it,
because in defending it he was defending everything that gave his own life its
deepest meaning.

The Westerner, on the other hand, would fight with an equal tenacity for    11
the broader concept of society. He fought so because everything he lived by
was tied to growth, expansion, and a constantly widening horizon. What he
lived by would survive or fall with the nation itself. He could not possibly
stand by unmoved in the face of an attempt to destroy the Union. He would
combat it with everything he had, because he could only see it as an effort to
cut the ground out from under his feet.

So Grant and Lee were in complete contrast, representing two diametri-    12
cally opposed elements in American life. Grant was the modern man emerging; beyond him, ready to come on the stage, was the great age of steel and
machinery, of crowded cities and a restless, burgeoning vitality. Lee might
have ridden down from the old age of chivalry, lance in hand, silken banner
fluttering over his head. Each man was the perfect champion of his cause,
drawing both his strengths and his weaknesses from the people he led.

Yet it was not all contrast, after all. Different as they were—in background, in personality, in underlying aspiration—these two great soldiers had much in common. Under everything else, they were marvelous fighters. Furthermore, their fighting qualities were really very much alike.    13

Each man had, to begin with, the great virtue of utter tenacity and fidelity. Grant fought his way down the Mississippi Valley in spite of acute personal discouragement and profound military handicaps. Lee hung on in the trenches at Petersburg after hope itself had died. In each man there was an indomitable quality . . . the born fighter's refusal to give up as long as he can still remain on his feet and lift his two fists.    14

Daring and resourcefulness they had, too; the ability to think faster and move faster than the enemy. These were the qualities which gave Lee the dazzling campaigns of Second Manassas and Chancellorsville and won Vicksburg for Grant.    15

Lastly, and perhaps greatest of all, there was the ability, at the end, to turn quickly from war to peace once the fighting was over. Out of the way these two men behaved at Appomattox came the possibility of a peace of reconciliation. It was a possibility not wholly realized, in the years to come, but which did, in the end, help the two sections to become one nation again . . . after a war whose bitterness might have seemed to make such a reunion wholly impossible. No part of either man's life became him more than the part he played in their brief meeting in the McLean house at Appomattox. Their behavior there put all succeeding generations of Americans in their debt. Two great Americans, Grant and Lee—very different, yet under everything very much alike. Their encounter at Appomattox was one of the great moments of American history.    16

*For a reading quiz, sources on Bruce Catton, and annotated links to further readings on the American Civil War, Ulysses S. Grant, and Robert E. Lee, visit **bedfordstmartins .com/thebedfordreader**.*

---

## Journal Writing

How do you respond to the opposing political beliefs represented by Grant and Lee? During the American Civil War, nearly every citizen had an opinion and chose sides. Do you think Americans today commit themselves as strongly to political and social causes? In your journal, explain why, or why not. (To take your journal writing further, see "From Journal to Essay" on the next page.)

## Questions on Meaning

1. What is Bruce Catton's PURPOSE in writing: to describe the meeting of two generals at a famous moment in history; to explain how the two men stood for opposing social forces in America; or to show how the two differed in personality?
2. SUMMARIZE the background and the way of life that produced Robert E. Lee; then do the same for Ulysses S. Grant. According to Catton, what ideals did each man represent?
3. In the historian's view, what essential traits did the two men have in common? Which trait does Catton think most important of all? For what reason?
4. How does this essay help you understand why Grant and Lee were such determined fighters?

## Questions on Writing Strategy

1. From the content of this essay, and from knowing where it first appeared, what can you infer about Catton's original AUDIENCE? At what places in "Grant and Lee: A Study in Contrasts" does the writer expect of his readers a familiarity with US history?
2. What EFFECT does the writer achieve by setting both his INTRODUCTION and his CONCLUSION in Appomattox?
3. For what reasons does Catton contrast the two generals *before* he compares them? Suppose he had reversed his outline, and had dealt first with Grant's and Lee's mutual resemblances. Why would his essay have been less effective?
4. Closely read the first sentence of every paragraph and underline each word or phrase in it that serves as a TRANSITION. Then review your underlinings. How much COHERENCE has Catton given his essay?
5. What is the TONE of this essay—that is, what is the writer's attitude toward his two subjects? Is Catton poking fun at Lee by imagining the Confederate general as a knight of the Middle Ages, "lance in hand, silken banner fluttering over his head" (par. 12)?
6. **OTHER METHODS** In identifying "two conflicting currents," Catton uses CLASSIFICATION to sort Civil War–era Americans into two groups represented by Lee and Grant. Catton then uses ANALYSIS to tease out the characteristics of each current, each type. How do classification and analysis serve Catton's comparison and contrast?

## Questions on Language

1. In his opening paragraph, Catton uses a metaphor: American life is a book containing chapters. Find other FIGURES OF SPEECH in his essay (consulting Useful Terms if you need help). What do the figures of speech contribute?
2. Look up *poignant* in the dictionary. Why is it such a fitting word in paragraph 2? Why wouldn't *touching, sad,* or *teary* have been as good?

3. What information do you glean from the sentence "Lee was tidewater Virginia" (par. 5)?
4. Define *aristocratic* as Catton uses it in paragraphs 4 and 6.
5. Define *obeisance* (par. 7) and *indomitable* (14).

## Suggestions for Writing

1. **FROM JOURNAL TO ESSAY**   Using your journal entry as a starting point, write an essay that offers an explanation for public participation in or commitment to political and social causes today. What fires people up or turns them off? To help focus your essay, zero in on a specific issue, such as education, government spending, health insurance, or gun control.
2. In a brief essay full of specific examples, discuss: Do the "two diametrically opposed elements in American life" (as Catton calls them) still exist in the country today? Are there still any "landed nobility"?
3. In your thinking and your attitudes, whom do you more closely resemble—Grant or Lee? Compare and contrast your outlook with that of one famous American or the other. (A serious tone for this topic isn't required.)
4. **CRITICAL WRITING**   Although slavery, along with other issues, helped precipitate the Civil War, Catton in this particular essay does not deal with it. Perhaps he assumes that his readers will supply the missing context themselves. Is this a fair ASSUMPTION? If Catton had recalled the facts of slavery, would he have undermined any of his assertions about Lee? (Though the general of the pro-slavery Confederacy, Lee was personally opposed to slavery.) In a brief essay, judge whether or not the omission of slavery weakens the essay, and explain why.
5. **CONNECTIONS**   In paragraph 3 Catton writes that Grant and Lee signified "two conflicting currents" in American society. In "Safety Through Immigration Control" (p. 567) and "Not Your Homeland" (p. 572), Mark Krikorian and Edwidge Danticat present opposing viewpoints on an issue currently causing a divide in American society: immigration. Do some research into pro-immigration and anti-immigration opinions, and write an essay in which you compare and contrast the ideals and beliefs that underlie each side's position. Like Catton, make your purpose explanation, not evaluation: Treat the two positions impartially.

---

# *Bruce Catton on Writing*

Most of Bruce Catton's comments on writing, those that have been preserved, refer to the work of others. As editor of *American Heritage*, he was known for his blunt, succinct comments on unsuccessful manuscripts: "This article can't be repaired and wouldn't be much good if it were." Or: "The high-water mark of this piece comes at the bottom of page one, where the naked Indian nymph offers the hero strawberries. Unfortunately, this level is not maintained."

In a memoir published in *Bruce Catton's America* (1979), Catton's associate Oliver Jensen marvels that, besides editing *American Heritage* for twenty-four years (and contributing to nearly every issue), Catton managed to produce so many substantial books. "Concentration was no doubt the secret, that and getting an early start. For many years Catton was always the first person in the office, so early that most of the staff never knew when he did arrive. On his desk the little piles of yellow sheets grew slowly, with much larger piles in the wastebasket. A neat and orderly man, he preferred to type a new page than correct very much in pencil."

His whole purpose as a writer, Catton once said, was "to reexamine [our] debt to the past."

## For Discussion

1. To which of Catton's traits does Oliver Jensen attribute the historian's impressive output?
2. Which characteristics of Catton the editor would you expect to have served him well as a writer?

# FATEMA MERNISSI

A teacher, a writer, and an activist, FATEMA MERNISSI was born in 1940 in Fez, Morocco, and was educated at the University of Rabat in Morocco, the Sorbonne in Paris, and Brandeis University in Massachusetts, from which she earned a PhD in sociology. Mernissi soon established herself as both a scholar and a lively writer on subjects ranging from feminism to religion. Her books, originally written in either French or English, include *Beyond the Veil: Male-Female Dynamics in Modern Muslim Society* (1975, revised in 1987), *Islam and Democracy: Fear of the Modern World* (1992), *Dreams of Trespass: Tales of a Harem Girlhood* (1994), and *Women's Rebellion and Islamic Memory* (1996). Mernissi is a professor and research scholar at the University of Mohammed V in Morocco, and she is currently studying the effects of globalization on children's identities. In 2004 she received the Erasmus Prize for having made an "exceptionally important contribution to European culture, society, or social science."

# Size 6: The Western Women's Harem

Mernissi was raised in a harem, an enclave of women and children within a traditional Muslim household, off-limits to men. Traveling outside the Middle East, she encounters common Western misconceptions of a harem as either a "peaceful pleasure-garden" or an "orgiastic feast" in which "men reign supreme over obedient women"—when in fact Muslim men and women both acknowledge the inequality of the harem and women resist men in any way they can. In *Scheherazade Goes West: Different Cultures, Different Harems* (2001), Mernissi explores the "mystery of the Western harem," trying to understand why outsiders imagine harem women as totally compliant and unthreatening to men. In this last chapter from the book, Mernissi finds her answer.

Note that Mernissi provides source citations for the book she quotes in paragraph 20. The citations are in the format of *The Chicago Manual of Style* (2003).

It was during my unsuccessful attempt to buy a cotton skirt in an American department store that I was told my hips were too large to fit into a size 6. That distressing experience made me realize how the image of beauty in the West can hurt and humiliate a woman as much as the veil does when enforced by the state police in extremist nations such as Iran, Afghanistan, or Saudi Arabia. Yes, that day I stumbled onto one of the keys to the enigma of passive beauty in Western harem fantasies. The elegant saleslady in the American store looked at me without moving from her desk and said that she had no skirt my size. "In this whole big store, there is no skirt for me?" I said. "You are joking." I felt very suspicious and thought that she just might be too tired to help me. I could understand that. But then the saleswoman added a condescending judgment, which sounded to me like an imam's fatwa.[1] It left no room for discussion:

"You are too big!" she said.          2

"I am too big compared to what?" I asked, looking at her intently, because          3
I realized that I was facing a critical cultural gap here.

"Compared to a size 6," came the saleslady's reply.          4

Her voice had a clear-cut edge to it that is typical of those who enforce          5
religious laws. "Size 4 and 6 are the norm," she went on, encouraged by my bewildered look. "Deviant sizes such as the one you need can be bought in special stores."

That was the first time that I had ever heard such nonsense about my size.          6
In the Moroccan streets, men's flattering comments regarding my particularly generous hips have for decades led me to believe that the entire planet shared their convictions. It is true that with advancing age, I have been hearing fewer and fewer flattering comments when walking in the medina, and sometimes the silence around me in the bazaars is deafening. But since my face has never met with the local beauty standards, and I have often had to defend myself against remarks such as *zirafa* (giraffe), because of my long neck, I learned long ago not to rely too much on the outside world for my sense of self-worth. In fact, paradoxically, as I discovered when I went to Rabat as a student, it was the self-reliance that I had developed to protect myself against "beauty blackmail" that made me attractive to others. My male fellow students could not believe that I did not give a damn about what they thought about my body. "You know, my dear," I would say in response to one of them, "all I need to survive is bread, olives, and sardines. That you think my neck is too long is your problem, not mine."

In any case, when it comes to beauty and compliments, nothing is too          7
serious or definite in the medina, where everything can be negotiated. But things seemed to be different in that American department store. In fact, I have to confess that I lost my usual self-confidence in that New York environment. Not that I am always sure of myself, but I don't walk around the Moroccan streets or down the university corridors wondering what people are thinking about me. Of course, when I hear a compliment, my ego expands like a cheese soufflé, but on the whole, I don't expect to hear much from others. Some mornings, I feel ugly because I am sick or tired; others, I feel wonderful because it is sunny out or I have written a good paragraph. But suddenly, in that peaceful American store that I had entered so triumphantly, as

[1] An *imam* is a Muslim leader. A *fatwa* is a Muslim legal opinion or ruling. —EDS.

a sovereign consumer ready to spend money, I felt savagely attacked. My hips, until then the sign of a relaxed and uninhibited maturity, were suddenly being condemned as a deformity. . . .

"And who says that everyone must be a size 6?" I joked to the saleslady         8
that day, deliberately neglecting to mention size 4, which is the size of my skinny twelve-year-old niece.

At that point, the saleslady suddenly gave me an anxious look. "The norm         9
is everywhere, my dear," she said. "It's all over, in the magazines, on television, in the ads. You can't escape it. There is Calvin Klein, Ralph Lauren, Gianni Versace, Giorgio Armani, Mario Valentino, Salvatore Ferragamo, Christian Dior, Yves Saint-Laurent, Christian Lacroix, and Jean-Paul Gaultier. Big department stores go by the norm." She paused and then concluded, "If they sold size 14 or 16, which is probably what you need, they would go bankrupt."

She stopped for a minute and then stared at me, intrigued. "Where on       10
earth do you come from? I am sorry I can't help you. Really, I am." And she looked it too. She seemed, all of a sudden, interested, and brushed off another woman who was seeking her attention with a cutting, "Get someone else to help you, I'm busy." Only then did I notice that she was probably my age, in her late fifties. But unlike me, she had the thin body of an adolescent girl. Her knee-length, navy blue, Chanel dress had a white silk collar reminiscent of the subdued elegance of aristocratic French Catholic schoolgirls at the turn of the century. A pearl-studded belt emphasized the slimness of her waist. With her meticulously styled short hair and sophisticated makeup, she looked half my age at first glance.

"I come from a country where there is no size for women's clothes," I told      11
her. "I buy my own material and the neighborhood seamstress or craftsman makes me the silk or leather skirt I want. They just take my measurements each time I see them. Neither the seamstress nor I know exactly what size my new skirt is. We discover it together in the making. No one cares about my size in Morocco as long as I pay taxes on time. Actually, I don't know what my size is, to tell you the truth."

The saleswoman laughed merrily and said that I should advertise my       12
country as a paradise for stressed working women. "You mean you don't watch your weight?" she inquired, with a tinge of disbelief in her voice. And then, after a brief moment of silence, she added in a lower register, as if talking to herself: "Many women working in highly paid fashion-related jobs could lose their positions if they didn't keep to a strict diet."

Her words sounded so simple, but the threat they implied was so cruel that      13
I realized for the first time that maybe "size 6" is a more violent restriction imposed on women than is the Muslim veil. Quickly I said good-bye so as not to make any more demands on the saleslady's time or involve her in any more

unwelcome, confidential exchanges about age-discriminating salary cuts. A surveillance camera was probably watching us both.

Yes, I thought as I wandered off, I have finally found the answer to my harem enigma. Unlike the Muslim man, who uses space to establish male domination by excluding women from the public arena, the Western man manipulates time and light. He declares that in order to be beautiful, a woman must look fourteen years old. If she dares to look fifty, or worse, sixty, she is beyond the pale. By putting the spotlight on the female child and framing her as the ideal of beauty, he condemns the mature woman to invisibility. In fact, the modern Western man enforces Immanuel Kant's nineteenth-century theories:[2] To be beautiful, women have to appear childish and brainless. When a woman looks mature and self-assertive, or allows her hips to expand, she is condemned as ugly. Thus, the walls of the European harem separate youthful beauty from ugly maturity.          14

These Western attitudes, I thought, are even more dangerous and cunning than the Muslim ones because the weapon used against women is time. Time is less visible, more fluid than space. The Western man uses images and spotlights to freeze female beauty within an idealized childhood, and forces women to perceive aging — that normal unfolding of the years — as a shameful devaluation. "Here I am, transformed into a dinosaur," I caught myself saying aloud as I went up and down the rows of skirts in the store, hoping to prove the saleslady wrong — to no avail. This Western time-defined veil is even crazier than the space-defined one enforced by the ayatollahs.[3]          15

The violence embodied in the Western harem is less visible than in the Eastern harem because aging is not attacked directly, but rather masked as an aesthetic choice. Yes, I suddenly felt not only very ugly but also quite useless in that store, where, if you had big hips, you were simply out of the picture. You drifted into the fringes of nothingness. By putting the spotlight on the prepubescent female, the Western man veils the older, more mature woman, wrapping her in shrouds of ugliness. This idea gives me the chills because it tattoos the invisible harem directly onto a woman's skin. Chinese foot-binding worked the same way: Men declared beautiful only those women who had small, childlike feet. Chinese men did not force women to bandage their feet to keep them from developing normally — all they did was to define the beauty ideal. In feudal China, a beautiful woman was the one who voluntarily sacrificed her right to unhindered physical movement by mutilating her own feet, and thereby proving that her main goal in life was to please men. Similarly, in the Western world, I was expected to shrink my hips into a size 6 if I          16

[2] Kant (1724–1804) was a German philosopher. — EDS.
[3] Among Shiite Muslims, the authorities who interpret religious law. — EDS.

wanted to find a decent skirt tailored for a beautiful woman. We Muslim women have only one month of fasting, Ramadan, but the poor Western woman who diets has to fast twelve months out of the year. "*Quelle horreur*,"[4] I kept repeating to myself, while looking around at the American women shopping. All those my age looked like youthful teenagers. . . .

Now, at last, the mystery of my Western harem made sense. Framing youth as beauty and condemning maturity is the weapon used against women in the West just as limiting access to public space is the weapon used in the East. The objective remains identical in both cultures: to make women feel unwelcome, inadequate, and ugly.                                                17

The power of the Western man resides in dictating what women should wear and how they should look. He controls the whole fashion industry, from cosmetics to underwear. The West, I realized, was the only part of the world where women's fashion is a man's business. In places like Morocco, where you design your own clothes and discuss them with craftsmen and -women, fashion is your own business. Not so in the West. . . .                                        18

But how does the system function? I wondered. Why do women accept it?      19

Of all the possible explanations, I like that of the French sociologist Pierre Bourdieu the best. In his latest book, *La Domination Masculine*, he proposes something he calls "*la violence symbolique*": "Symbolic violence is a form of power which is hammered directly on the body, and as if by magic, without any apparent physical constraint. But this magic operates only because it activates the codes pounded in the deepest layers of the body."[5] Reading Bourdieu, I had the impression that I finally understood Western man's psyche better. The cosmetic and fashion industries are only the tip of the iceberg, he states, which is why women are so ready to adhere to their dictates. Something else is going on on a far deeper level. Otherwise, why would women belittle themselves spontaneously? Why, argues Bourdieu, would women make their lives more difficult, for example, by preferring men who are taller or older than they are? "The majority of French women wish to have a husband who is older and also, which seems consistent, bigger as far as size is concerned," writes Bourdieu.[6] Caught in the enchanted submission characteristic of the symbolic violence inscribed in the mysterious layers of the flesh, women relinquish what he calls "les signes ordinaires de la hiérarchie sexuelle," the ordinary signs of sexual hierarchy, such as old age and a larger body. By so      20

---

[4] French, "What a horror."—EDS.
[5] Pierre Bourdieu, *La Domination Masculine* (Paris: Editions du Seuil, 1998), p. 44.
[6] Ibid., p. 41.

doing, explains Bourdieu, women spontaneously accept the subservient position. It is this spontaneity Bourdieu describes as magic enchantment.[7]

Once I understood how this magic submission worked, I became very happy that the conservative ayatollahs do not know about it yet. If they did, they would readily switch to its sophisticated methods, because they are so much more effective. To deprive me of food is definitely the best way to paralyze my thinking capabilities. . . .                                                                                                21

"I thank you, Allah, for sparing me the tyranny of the 'size 6 harem,'" I repeatedly said to myself while seated on the Paris-Casablanca flight, on my way back home at last. "I am so happy that the conservative male elite does not know about it. Imagine the fundamentalists switching from the veil to forcing women to fit size 6."                                                                                                                                                      22

How can you stage a credible political demonstration and shout in the streets that your human rights have been violated when you cannot find the right skirt?                                                                                                                                                                                                                                                    23

---

For a reading quiz, sources on Fatema Mernissi, and annotated links to further readings on harems and on cultural ideals of attractiveness, visit **bedfordstmartins.com /thebedfordreader.**

---

## Journal Writing

Within your peer group, what constitutes the norm of physical attractiveness for women and for men? (Don't focus on the ideal here, but on what is expected for a person not to be considered *un*attractive.) Are the norms similar for women and for men? (To take your journal writing further, see "From Journal to Essay" on the next page.)

## Questions on Meaning

1. What two subjects does Mernissi compare? Where does she state her THESIS initially, and where later does she restate and expand on it? What does Mernissi conclude is the same about the two subjects?
2. What is the saleswoman's initial attitude toward Mernissi? How does her attitude seem to change, and how does this change contribute to Mernissi's point?

[7] Ibid., p. 42.

3. Why does Mernissi believe Western attitudes toward women are "more danger-ous and cunning" than Muslim attitudes (par. 15)?

## Questions on Writing Strategy

1. What is the PURPOSE of paragraphs 6–7? What do these paragraphs contribute to Mernissi's larger point?
2. What two further comparisons does Mernissi make in paragraph 16? What TRAN-SITIONS does she use to signal the shift of subject within these comparisons?
3. **OTHER METHODS**   Mernissi devotes considerable attention to a NARRATIVE of her adventure in the department store. Why does she tell this story in such detail? What does it contribute to the essay?

## Questions on Language

1. What are the CONNOTATIONS of the saleswoman's word *deviant* (par. 5)?
2. Why is the metaphor of the veil in paragraph 16 especially appropriate? (See *Fig-ures of speech* in Useful Terms if you need a definition of *metaphor*.)
3. Consult a dictionary if you are unsure of the meaning of any of the following: enigma (par. 1); generous, medina, bazaars, paradoxically (6); soufflé, sovereign (7); subdued (10); cunning, devaluation (15); aesthetic, prepubescent, unhin-dered, mutilating (16).

## Suggestions for Writing

1. **FROM JOURNAL TO ESSAY**   Based on your journal entry, draft an essay in which you compare and contrast standards of attractiveness for women and men within your peer group. Be sure to consider how strictly the standards are applied to each gender.
2. Write an essay about a time when your self-confidence was shaken because of how someone else treated or spoke to you. Like Mernissi, explain why you had been confident of yourself before this encounter and what effect it had on you.
3. Mernissi comes from the country of Morocco. Put her essay in context by researching the history and culture of Morocco. Then write an essay in which you discuss what you have learned about the country. How is Morocco different from the more "extremist nations" Mernissi refers to in her first paragraph?
4. **CRITICAL WRITING**   Respond to Mernissi's essay. Do you agree with her views about "the tyranny of the 'size 6 harem'"? Does Mernissi provide enough EVI-DENCE to convince you of her views? Even if you agree with her take on her department-store experience, do you think her conclusions apply across the board, as she implies: For instance, do they apply among the poor and working class as well as among the affluent? Write an essay that ANALYZES and EVALUATES Mernissi's thesis and the support for it.
5. **CONNECTIONS**   When Mernissi asks who declared size 6 to be the norm in the United States, the sales clerk implicates the media: "The norm is everywhere, my dear. . . . It's all over, in the magazines, on television, in the ads. You can't escape

it" (par. 9).  In "Orange Crush" (p. 164), Yiyun Li also touches on the power of advertising, describing how a beverage ad captivated Chinese consumers. Using examples from both essays as well as from your own experience and observations, write an essay exploring a positive or a negative EFFECT of advertising on consumers. You might do some library or Internet research to further support your point.

# GEORGE CHAUNCEY

GEORGE CHAUNCEY is a professor of history at Yale University, specializing in twentieth-century gay and lesbian history. He was born in 1954 in Tennessee and grew up there and in Arkansas, Kentucky, Georgia, and Virginia. He received a BA, an MA, and a PhD from Yale, where he became active in groups championing gay and lesbian rights. His PhD dissertation received an award from Yale's history department for being "a pioneering work of scholarship." It became his first book, also an award winner: *Gay New York: Gender, Urban Culture, and the Making of the Gay Male World, 1890–1940* (1994). As an expert in the history of gay rights, Chauncey has testified in several landmark court cases. He is currently working on *The Strange Career of the Closet*, which examines issues of class and race among homosexuals after World War II.

# *The Legacy of Antigay Discrimination*

As a history student and a gay-rights activist in college, Chauncey discovered that history "is important politically: Historical analysis is important to understand present social arrangements and how they can be changed." This essay is the opening chapter in Chauncey's second book, *Why Marriage? The History Shaping Today's Debate over Gay Equality* (2004). The essay makes a historical contrast: In nine sentences beginning "Fifty years ago," Chauncey sets out aspects of current gay life or gay rights that did not exist half a century ago, and he then details the situation of discrimination that did exist. In the rest of his book, Chauncey shows how this contrast explains and strengthens the case for equal rights for homosexuals, including marriage rights.

As a scholarly work, Chauncey's essay includes acknowledgments of the author's sources. The footnotes follow the format of *The Chicago Manual of Style*, generally used in history.

1. The place of lesbians and gay men in American society has dramatically changed in the last half century. The change has been so profound that the harsh discrimination once faced by gay people has virtually disappeared from popular memory. That history bears repeating, since its legacy shapes today's debate over marriage.

2. Although most people recognize that gay life was difficult before the growth of the gay movement in the 1970s, they often have only the vaguest sense of why: that gay people were scorned and ridiculed, made to feel ashamed, afraid, and alone. But antigay discrimination was much more systematic and powerful than this.

3. Fifty years ago, there was no *Will & Grace* or *Ellen*, no *Queer Eye for the Straight Guy*, no *Philadelphia* or *The Hours*, no annual Lesbian, Gay, Bisexual,

and Transgender (LGBT) film festival. In fact, Hollywood films were *prohibited* from including lesbian or gay characters, discussing gay themes, or even inferring the existence of homosexuality. The Hollywood studios established these rules (popularly known as the Hays Code) in the 1930s under pressure from a censorship movement led by Catholic and other religious leaders, who threatened them with mass boycotts and restrictive federal legislation. The absolute ban on gay representation, vigorously enforced by Hollywood's own censorship board, remained in effect for some thirty years and effectively prohibited the discussion of homosexuality in the most important medium of the mid-twentieth century, even though some film makers found subtle ways to subvert it.

Censorship extended to the stage as well. In 1927, after a serious lesbian drama opened on Broadway to critical acclaim—and after Mae West announced that she planned to open a play called *The Drag*—New York State passed a "padlock law" that threatened to shut down for a year any theater that dared to stage a play with lesbian or gay characters. Given Broadway's national importance as a staging ground for new plays, this law had dramatic effects on American theater for a generation.[1]

Fifty years ago, no openly gay people worked for the federal government. In fact, shortly after he became president in 1953, Dwight Eisenhower issued an executive order that banned homosexuals from government employment, civilian as well as military, and required companies with government contracts to ferret out and fire their gay employees. At the height of the McCarthy witch-hunt,[2] the US State Department fired more homosexuals than Communists. In the 1950s and 1960s literally thousands of men and women were discharged or forced to resign from civilian positions in the federal government because they were suspected of being gay or lesbian.[3] It was only in 1975 that the ban on gay federal employees was lifted, and it took until the late 1990s before such discrimination in federal hiring was prohibited.

Fifty years ago, countless teachers, hospital workers, and other state and municipal employees also lost their jobs as a result of official policy. Beginning in 1958, for instance, the Florida Legislative Investigation Committee, which

---

[1] Kaier Curtin, *"We Can Always Call Them Bulgarians": The Emergency of Lesbians and Gay Men on the American Stage* (Boston: Alyson, 1987). George Chauncey, *Gay New York: Gender, Urban Culture, and the Making of the Gay Male World, 1890–1940* (New York: Basic Books, 1994), 311–13.

[2] US Senator Joseph McCarthy (1908–1957) spearheaded aggressive investigations of suspected Communists in the 1940s and 1950s.—Eds.

[3] David K. Johnson, *The Lavender Scare: The Cold War Persecution of Gays and Lesbians in the Federal Government* (Chicago: University of Chicago Press, 2004), 166 and passim; Robert D. Dean, *Imperial Brotherhood: Gender and the Making of Cold War Foreign Policy* (Amherst: University of Massachusetts Press, 2001).

had been established by the legislature in 1956 to investigate and discredit civil rights activists, turned its attention to homosexuals working in the state's universities and public schools. Its initial investigation of the University of Florida resulted in the dismissal of fourteen faculty and staff members, and in the next five years it interrogated some 320 suspected gay men and lesbians. Under pressure from the committee, numerous teachers gave up their jobs and countless students were forced to drop out of college.[4]

Fifty years ago, there were no gay business associations or gay bars adver-  7 tising in newspapers. In fact, many gay-oriented businesses were illegal and gay people had no right to public assembly. In many states, following the repeal of Prohibition in 1933, it even became illegal for restaurants and bars to serve lesbians or gay men. The New York State Liquor Authority, for instance, issued regulations prohibiting bars, restaurants, cabarets, and other establishments with liquor licenses from employing or serving homosexuals or allowing homosexuals to congregate on their premises.[5] The authority's ratio-nale was that the mere presence of homosexuals made an establishment "dis-orderly," and when the courts rejected that argument the authority began using evidence gathered by plainclothes investigators of one man trying to pick up another or of patrons' unconventional gender behavior to provide proof of a bar's disorderly character.[6] . . .

Fifty years ago, elected officials did not court the gay vote and the nation's  8 mayors did not proclaim LGBT Pride Week. Instead, many mayors periodi-cally declared war on homosexuals—or sex deviates, as they were usually called. In many cities, gay residents knew that if the mayor needed to show he was tough on crime and vice just before an election, he would order a crack-down on gay bars. Hundreds of people would be arrested. Their names put in the paper. Their meeting places closed. This did not just happen once or twice, or just in smaller cities. Rather, it happened regularly in every major city, from New York and Miami to Chicago, San Francisco, and LA. After his administration's commitment to suppressing gay life became an issue in his 1959 re-election campaign, San Francisco's mayor launched a two-year-long crackdown on the city's gay bars and other meeting places. Forty to sixty men and women were arrested every week in bar sweeps, and within two years almost a third of the city's gay bars had been closed.[7] Miami's gay scene was

[4] Stacy Braukman, " 'Nothing Else Matters But Sex': Cold War Narratives of Deviance and the Search for Lesbian Teachers in Florida, 1959–1963," *Feminist Studies* 27 (2001): 553, 555; See also 553–57, 573, and n.3.

[5] Chauncey, *Gay New York*, 173, 337.

[6] Chauncey, *Gay New York*, 377.

[7] John D'Emilio, *Sexual Politics, Sexual Communities: The Making of a Homosexual Minority, 1940–1970* (Chicago: University of Chicago Press, 1981), 182–84.

relentlessly attacked by the police and press in 1954. New York launched major crackdowns on gay bars as part of its campaign to "clean up the city" before both the 1939 and 1964 World's Fairs. During the course of a 1955 investigation of the gay scene in Boise, Idaho, 1,400 people were interrogated and coerced into identifying the names of other gay residents.[8] Across America, homosexuals were an easy target, with few allies.

Fifty years ago, there was no mass LGBT movement. In fact, the handful of early gay activists risked everything to speak up for their rights. When the police learned of the country's earliest known gay political group, which had been established by a postal worker in Chicago in 1924, they raided his home and seized his group's files and membership list. A quarter century later, when the first national gay rights group, the Mattachine Society, was founded, it repeatedly had to reassure its anxious members that the police would not seize its membership list. The US Post Office banned its newspaper from the mails in 1954, and in some cities the police shut down newsstands that dared to carry it. In 1959, a few weeks after Mattachine held its first press conference during a national convention in Denver, the police raided the homes of three of its Denver organizers; one lost his job and spent sixty days in jail. Such harassment and censorship of free speech made it difficult for people to organize or speak on their own behalf and for all Americans to debate and learn about gay issues.[9]

Fifty years ago, no state had a gay rights law. Rather, every state had a sodomy law and other laws penalizing homosexual conduct. Beginning in the late nineteenth century, municipal police forces began using misdemeanor charges such as disorderly conduct, vagrancy, lewdness, and loitering to harass gay men.[10] In 1923, the New York State legislature tailored its statutes to specify for the first time that a man's "frequent[ing] or loiter[ing] about any public place soliciting men for the purpose of committing a crime against nature or other lewdness" was punishable as a form of disorderly conduct.[11] Many more

[8] D'Emilio, *Sexual Politics*, 51; Chauncey, *Gay New York*, 340; Chauncey, *The Strange Career of the Closet: Gay Culture, Consciousness, and Politics from the Second World War to the Gay Liberation Era* (New York, Basic Books, forthcoming); John Gerassi, *The Boys of Boise: Furor, Vice, and Folly in an American City* (New York: Macmillan, 1966); Fred Fejes, "Murder, Perversion, and Moral Panic: The 1954 Media Campaign Against Miami's Homosexuals and the Discourse of Civic Betterment," *Journal of the History of Sexuality* 9 (2000): 305–47.

[9] On the Chicago group, see Jonathan Ned Katz, *Gay American History: Lesbians and Gay Men in the U.S.A.* (New York: Crowell, 1976), 385–89; Katz, *The Gay/Lesbian Almanac* (New York: Morrow, 1983), 554–61; on Mattachine, see D'Emilio, *Sexual Politics*, 115, 120–21.

[10] See John D'Emilio and Estelle B. Freedman, *Intimate Matters: A History of Sexuality in America* (San Francisco/New York: Harper and Row, 1988), 150–56, 202–15; Chauncey, *Gay New York*, 137–41, 183–86, 197–98, 249–50; Paul Boyer, *Urban Masses and Moral Order in America, 1820–1920* (Cambridge: Harvard University Press, 1978), 191–219.

[11] Chauncey, *Gay New York*, 172.

men were arrested and prosecuted under this misdemeanor charge than for the felony charge of sodomy, since misdemeanor laws carried fewer procedural protections for defendants. Between 1923 and 1966, when Mayor John Lindsay ordered the police to stop using entrapment by plainclothes officers to secure arrests of gay men, more than 50,000 men had been arrested on this charge in New York City alone.[12] The number of arrests escalated dramatically after the Second World War. More than 3,000 New Yorkers were arrested every year on this charge in the late 1940s. By 1950, Philadelphia's six-man "morals squad" was arresting more gay men than the courts knew how to handle, some 200 a month. In the District of Columbia, there were more than a thousand arrests every year.[13]

Fifty years ago, more than half of the nation's states, including New York,    11 Michigan, and California, enacted laws authorizing the police to force persons who were convicted of certain sexual offenses, including sodomy — or, in some states, merely suspected of being "sexual deviants" — to undergo psychiatric examinations. Many of these laws authorized the indefinite confinement of homosexuals in mental institutions, from which they were to be released only if they were cured of their homosexuality, something prison doctors soon began to complain was impossible. The medical director of a state hospital in California argued, "Whenever a doubt arises in the judge's mind" that a suspect "might be a sexual deviate, maybe by his mannerisms or his dress, something to attract the attention, I think he should immediately call for a psychiatric examination." Detroit's prosecuting attorney demanded the authority to arrest, examine, and possibly confine indefinitely "anyone who exhibited abnormal sexual behavior, whether or not dangerous."[14]

Fifty years ago, in other words, homosexuals were not just ridiculed and    12 scorned. They were systematically denied their civil rights: their right to free assembly, to patronize public accommodations, to free speech, to a free press, to a form of intimacy of their own choosing. And they confronted a degree of policing and harassment that is almost unimaginable to us today.

---

[12] Chauncey, "A Gay World, Vibrant and Forgotten," *New York Times*, 26 June 1994, E17.
    [13] John D'Emilio, "The Homosexual Menace: The Politics of Sexuality in Cold War America," in *Passion and Power: Sexuality in History*, eds. Kathy Peiss and Christina Simmons, with Robert A. Padgug (Philadelphia: Temple University Press, 1989), 231; Chauncey, "The Postwar Sex Crime Panic," in *True Stories from the American Past*, ed. William Graebner (New York: McGraw-Hill, 1993), 160–78.
    [14] Estelle B. Freedman, "'Uncontrolled Desires': The Response to the Sexual Psychopath, 1920–1960," *Journal of American History* 74 (1987): 83–106; Chauncey, "Postwar Sex Crime Panic."

*For a reading quiz, sources on George Chauncey, and annotated links to further readings on lesbian and gay rights, visit **bedfordstmartins.com/thebedfordreader**.*

## Journal Writing

When have you either witnessed or been the object of unfair treatment based on race, ethnicity, language, religion, gender, age, sexual preference, economic background, or some other factor? What happened, and what was your reaction? (To take your journal writing further, see "From Journal to Essay" on the next page.)

## Questions on Meaning

1. What is Chauncey's THESIS? Where does he state it?
2. What seems to be Chauncey's PURPOSE in this essay?
3. In paragraph 2, Chauncey says that antigay discrimination fifty years ago was "much more systematic" than most people realize. What does he mean by this?

## Questions on Writing Strategy

1. Chauncey organizes his essay point by point. What are the main points of comparison?
2. Why does Chauncey spend more time discussing the treatment of gays and lesbians fifty years ago than discussing their treatment today? What ASSUMPTIONS does he make about his reader's knowledge of gay rights?
3. Discuss Chauncey's use of TRANSITIONS and REPETITION. What is the EFFECT of these devices?
4. Throughout his essay, Chauncey cites a number of statistics, or facts expressed numerically (see, for example, par. 10). What do these statistics accomplish?
5. **OTHER METHODS**   Discuss how Chauncey uses EXAMPLE to develop his comparison and contrast. What is the effect of his use of numerous examples?

## Questions on Language

1. How would you describe the overall TONE of this essay: serious? detached? passionate? angry? astonished? Point to some words and phrases that support your answer.
2. In paragraph 5, Chauncey says that companies with government contracts were required to "ferret out and fire their gay employees." What is the CONNOTATION of the verb *ferret*? (If necessary, look up *ferret* in a dictionary.) Given Chauncey's purpose, why is this a better verb than *search out* or *find*?

3. Why does Chauncey use quotation marks around the phrases *morals squad* (par. 10) and *sexual deviants* (11)?
4. Consult a dictionary if necessary to learn the meanings of the following words: profound (par. 1); scorned (2); boycotts, subtle, subvert (3); discredit (6); repeal, cabarets (7); deviates, vice, coerced, allies (8); sodomy, vagrancy, lewdness, statutes, soliciting, procedural, entrapment, escalated (10); enacted (11); patronize (12).

## Suggestions for Writing

1. **FROM JOURNAL TO ESSAY**    Write a narrative essay about the unfair treatment you recorded in your journal. Use vivid detail to re-create the incident and your reaction to it, but also reflect on its larger significance. Do you view the incident as fairly unusual, or do you think it is symptomatic of widespread prejudice? What are the causes of this prejudice, and how does it affect the people it is directed against?
2. Choose a subject that has seen significant change in the past fifty years or so—for example, gender roles, fashion, manners, a particular sport, ideals of beauty, or the rights of another group such as women, African Americans, or immigrants. Do some research on the topic and then write an essay in which you compare and contrast the situation then and now. Support your essay with specific EVIDENCE from your experience, observation, and research.
3. Although the entertainment media have clearly come a long way in the portrayal of gay and lesbian characters in the past fifty years, some critics complain that there is still much progress to be made. Write an essay in which you EVALUATE the representation of gays and lesbians in the media, considering examples of your own choosing or those mentioned by Chauncey (par. 3). Overall, do you find the portrayals to be negative or positive? What messages do these portrayals send to audiences? How might the portrayals be improved?
4. **CRITICAL WRITING**    Evaluate the effectiveness of Chauncey's essay. What do you think of the use of evidence? How successful is the author's attempt to convince readers that gays and lesbians "confronted a degree of policing and harassment that is almost unimaginable to us today" (par. 12)? Is the essay weakened by the fact that Chauncey doesn't mention prejudice and discrimination that gays and lesbians still face today? Why, or why not?
5. **CONNECTIONS**    Both Chauncey and Martin Luther King, Jr., in "I Have a Dream" (p. 614), defend the rights of a group that has faced harsh discrimination in American society, but their techniques are very different. Write an essay in which you compare and contrast Chauncey's essay with King's speech, focusing on the two writers' purposes, tones, points of view, persuasive appeals, and use of repetition and parallelism. What gives each selection its power? What makes each writer's piece particularly effective for his writing situation?

# ALICE WALKER

ALICE WALKER is best known for her novel *The Color Purple* (1982), which won both a Pulitzer Prize and an American Book Award, was made into a movie by Steven Spielberg, and was adapted to the stage. Born into a share-cropping family in Eatonton, Georgia, in 1944, Walker is the youngest of eight children. She spent two years at Spelman College in Atlanta before transferring to Sarah Lawrence College. Upon graduation in 1965, Walker became active in the civil rights movement, helping to register voters in Georgia by day and pursuing her writing by night. She has won fellowships from the Radcliffe Institute, the Guggenheim Foundation, and the National Endowment for the Arts. In addition to *The Color Purple*, Walker's novels include *The Third Life of Grange Copeland* (1970), *The Temple of My Familiar* (1989), and *Now Is the Time to Open Up Your Heart* (2004). She has also writ-ten many volumes of poetry and short stories; several children's books; a biography of Langston Hughes; an anthology of the work of Zora Neale Hurston; and five other books of nonfiction, including *In Search of Our Moth-ers' Gardens* (1983) and, most recently, *We Are the Ones We Have Been Wait-ing For: Light in a Time of Darkness* (2006). Walker has taught at numerous colleges and universities, including Jackson State College, Wellesley, Yale, and the University of California at Berkeley.

# *Everyday Use*

In this short story about family, Walker reveals two sisters through the eyes of their mother. Published in 1973, the story reflects differences then emerg-ing in the perspectives of African Americans, too. The city sister, Dee, look-ing toward her African roots, has changed her name and her style along with her attitudes. The country sister, Maggie, clings to more recent traditions. "Everyday Use" first appeared in *Harper's* magazine and then in Walker's col-lection *In Love and Trouble: Stories of Black Women* (1973).

I will wait for her in the yard that Maggie and I made so clean and wavy  1
yesterday afternoon. A yard like this is more comfortable than most people know. It is not just a yard. It is like an extended living room. When the hard clay is swept clean as a floor and the fine sand around the edges lined with tiny, irregular grooves, anyone can come and sit and look up into the elm tree and wait for the breezes that never come inside the house.

Maggie will be nervous until after her sister goes: She will stand hopelessly  2
in corners, homely and ashamed of the burn scars down her arms and legs, eye-ing her sister with a mixture of envy and awe. She thinks her sister has held

life always in the palm of one hand, that "no" is a word the world never learned to say to her.

You've no doubt seen those TV shows where the child who has "made it" is confronted, as a surprise, by her own mother and father, tottering in weakly from backstage. (A pleasant surprise, of course: What would they do if parent and child came on the show only to curse out and insult each other?) On TV mother and child embrace and smile into each other's faces. Sometimes the mother and father weep, the child wraps them in her arms and leans across the table to tell how she would not have made it without their help. I have seen these programs. 3

Sometimes I dream a dream in which Dee and I are suddenly brought together on a TV program of this sort. Out of a dark and soft-seated limousine I am ushered into a bright room filled with many people. There I meet a smiling, gray, sporty man like Johnny Carson who shakes my hand and tells me what a fine girl I have. Then we are on the stage and Dee is embracing me with tears in her eyes. She pins on my dress a large orchid, even though she has told me once that she thinks orchids are tacky flowers. 4

In real life I am a large, big-boned woman with rough, man-working hands. In the winter I wear flannel nightgowns to bed and overalls during the day. I can kill and clean a hog as mercilessly as a man. My fat keeps me hot in zero weather. I can work outside all day, breaking ice to get water for washing; I can eat pork liver cooked over the open fire minutes after it comes steaming from the hog. One winter I knocked a bull calf straight in the brain between the eyes with a sledge hammer and had the meat hung up to chill before nightfall. But of course all this does not show on television. I am the way my daughter would want me to be: a hundred pounds lighter, my skin like an uncooked barley pancake. My hair glistens in the hot bright lights. Johnny Carson has much to do to keep up with my quick and witty tongue. 5

But that is a mistake. I know even before I wake up. Who ever knew a Johnson with a quick tongue? Who can even imagine me looking a strange white man in the eye? It seems to me I have talked to them always with one foot raised in flight, with my head turned in whichever way is farthest from them. Dee, though. She would always look anyone in the eye. Hesitation was no part of her nature. 6

"How do I look, Mama?" Maggie says, showing just enough of her thin body enveloped in pink skirt and red blouse for me to know she's there, almost hidden by the door. 7

"Come out into the yard," I say. 8

Have you ever seen a lame animal, perhaps a dog run over by some care-    9
less person rich enough to own a car, sidle up to someone who is ignorant
enough to be kind to him? That is the way my Maggie walks. She has been like
this, chin on chest, eyes on ground, feet in shuffle, ever since the fire that
burned the other house to the ground.

Dee is lighter than Maggie, with nicer hair and a fuller figure. She's a    10
woman now, though sometimes I forget. How long ago was it that the other
house burned? Ten, twelve years? Sometimes I can still hear the flames and
feel Maggie's arms sticking to me, her hair smoking and her dress falling off her
in little black papery flakes. Her eyes seemed stretched open, blazed open by
the flames reflected in them. And Dee. I see her standing off under the sweet
gum tree she used to dig gum out of; a look of concentration on her face as she
watched the last dingy gray board of the house fall in toward the red-hot brick
chimney. Why don't you do a dance around the ashes? I'd wanted to ask her.
She had hated the house that much.

I used to think she hated Maggie, too. But that was before we raised the    11
money, the church and me, to send her to Augusta to school. She used to read
to us without pity; forcing words, lies, other folks' habits, whole lives upon us
two, sitting trapped and ignorant underneath her voice. She washed us in a
river of make-believe, burned us with a lot of knowledge we didn't necessarily
need to know. Pressed us to her with the serious way she read, to shove us away
at just the moment, like dimwits, we seemed about to understand.

Dee wanted nice things. A yellow organdy dress to wear to her graduation    12
from high school; black pumps to match a green suit she'd made from an old
suit somebody gave me. She was determined to stare down any disaster in her
efforts. Her eyelids would not flicker for minutes at a time. Often I fought off
the temptation to shake her. At sixteen she had a style of her own: and knew
what style was.

I never had an education myself. After second grade the school was closed    13
down. Don't ask me why: In 1927 colored asked fewer questions than they do
now. Sometimes Maggie reads to me. She stumbles along good-naturedly but
can't see well. She knows she is not bright. Like good looks and money, quick-
ness passed her by. She will marry John Thomas (who has mossy teeth in an
earnest face) and then I'll be free to sit here and I guess just sing church songs
to myself. Although I never was a good singer. Never could carry a tune. I was
always better at a man's job. I used to love to milk till I was hooked in the side
in '49. Cows are soothing and slow and don't bother you, unless you try to
milk them the wrong way.

I have deliberately turned my back on the house. It is three rooms, just    14 like the one that burned, except the roof is tin; they don't make shingle roofs anymore. There are no real windows, just some holes cut in the sides, like the portholes in a ship, but not round and not square, with rawhide holding the shutters up on the outside. This house is in a pasture, too, like the other one. No doubt when Dee sees it she will want to tear it down. She wrote me once that no matter where we "choose" to live, she will manage to come see us. But she will never bring her friends. Maggie and I thought about this and Maggie asked me, "Mama, when did Dee ever *have* any friends?"

She had a few. Furtive boys in pink shirts hanging about on washday after     15
school. Nervous girls who never laughed. Impressed with her they worshiped the well-turned phrase, the cute shape, the scalding humor that erupted like bubbles in lye. She read to them.

When she was courting Jimmy T she didn't have much time to pay to us,     16
but turned all her faultfinding power on him. He *flew* to marry a cheap city gal from a family of ignorant flashy people. She hardly had time to recompose herself.

When she comes I will meet—but there they are!     17

Maggie attempts to make a dash for the house, in her shuffling way, but I     18
stay her with my hand. "Come back here," I say. And she stops and tries to dig a well in the sand with her toe.

It is hard to see them clearly through the strong sun. But even the first     19
glimpse of leg out of the car tells me it is Dee. Her feet were always neat-looking, as if God himself had shaped them with a certain style. From the other side of the car comes a short, stocky man. Hair is all over his head a foot long and hanging from his chin like a kinky mule tail. I hear Maggie suck in her breath. "Uhnnnh," is what it sounds like. Like when you see the wriggling end of a snake just in front of your foot on the road. "Uhnnnh."

Dee next. A dress down to the ground, in this hot weather. A dress so loud     20
it hurts my eyes. There are yellows and oranges enough to throw back the light of the sun. I feel my whole face warming from the heat waves it throws out. Earrings gold, too, and hanging down to her shoulders. Bracelets dangling and making noises when she moves her arm up to shake the folds of the dress out of her armpits. The dress is loose and flows, and as she walks closer, I like it. I hear Maggie go "Uhnnnh" again. It is her sister's hair. It stands straight up like the wool on a sheep. It is black as night and around the edges are two long pigtails that rope about like small lizards disappearing behind her ears.

"Wa-su-zo-Tean-o!"[1] she says, coming on in that gliding way the dress     21

---

[1] "Wa-su-zo-Tean-o" and "Asalamalakim" (next sentence) are greetings spelled as the mother hears them.—EDS.

makes her move. The short stocky fellow with the hair to his navel is all grinning and he follows up with "Asalamalakim, my mother and sister!" He moves to hug Maggie but she falls back, right up against the back of my chair. I feel her trembling there and when I look up I see the perspiration falling off her chin.

"Don't get up," says Dee. Since I am stout it takes something of a push.     22
You can see me trying to move a second or two before I make it. She turns, showing white heels through her sandals, and goes back to the car. Out she peeks next with a Polaroid. She stoops down quickly and lines up picture after picture of me sitting there in front of the house with Maggie cowering behind me. She never takes a shot without making sure the house is included. When a cow comes nibbling around the edge of the yard she snaps it and me *and* the house. Then she puts the Polaroid in the back seat of the car, and comes up and kisses me on the forehead.

Meanwhile Asalamalakim is going through the motions with Maggie's     23
hand. Maggie's hand is as limp as a fish, and probably as cold, despite the sweat, and she keeps trying to pull it back. It looks like Asalamalakim wants to shake hands but wants to do it fancy. Or maybe he don't know how people shake hands. Anyhow, he soon gives up on Maggie.

"Well," I say. "Dee."                                                         24

"No, Mama," she says. "Not 'Dee,' Wangero Leewanika Kemanjo!"                 25

"What happened to 'Dee'?" I wanted to know.                                   26

"She's dead," Wangero said. "I couldn't bear it any longer being named       27
after the people who oppress me."

"You know as well as me you was named after your aunt Dicie," I said.        28
Dicie is my sister. She named Dee. We called her "Big Dee" after Dee was born.

"But who was *she* named after?" asked Wangero.                              29

"I guess after Grandma Dee," I said.                                         30

"And who was she named after?" asked Wangero.                                31

"Her mother," I said, and saw Wangero was getting tired. "That's about as    32
far back as I can trace it," I said. Though, in fact, I probably could have carried it back beyond the Civil War through the branches.

"Well," said Asalamalakim, "there you are."                                  33

"Uhnnnh," I heard Maggie say.                                                34

"There I was not," I said, "before 'Dicie' cropped up in our family, so why   35
should I try to trace it that far back?"

He just stood there grinning, looking down on me like somebody inspect-      36
ing a Model A car. Every once in a while he and Wangero sent eye signals over my head.

"How do you pronounce this name?" I asked.                                   37

"You don't have to call me by it if you don't want to," said Wangero.        38

"Why shouldn't I?" I asked. "If that's what you want us to call you, we'll    39
call you."

"I know it might sound awkward at first," said Wangero.    40

"I'll get used to it," I said. "Ream it out again."    41

Well, soon we got the name out of the way. Asalamalakim had a name    42
twice as long and three times as hard. After I tripped over it two or three times
he told me to just call him Hakim-a-barber. I wanted to ask him was he a barber, but I didn't really think he was, so I didn't ask.

"You must belong to those beef-cattle peoples down the road," I said.    43
They said "Asalamalakim" when they met you, too, but they didn't shake
hands. Always too busy: feeding the cattle, fixing the fences, putting up salt-
lick shelters, throwing down hay. When the white folks poisoned some of the
herd the men stayed up all night with rifles in their hands. I walked a mile and
a half just to see the sight.

Hakim-a-barber said, "I accept some of their doctrines, but farming and    44
raising cattle is not my style." (They didn't tell me, and I didn't ask, whether
Wangero [Dee] had really gone and married him.)

We sat down to eat and right away he said he didn't eat collards and pork    45
was unclean. Wangero, though, went on through the chitlins and corn bread,
the greens and everything else. She talked a blue streak over the sweet potatoes. Everything delighted her. Even the fact that we still used the benches her
daddy made for the table when we couldn't afford to buy chairs.

"Oh, Mama!" she cried. Then turned to Hakim-a-barber. "I never knew    46
how lovely these benches are. You can feel the rump prints," she said, running
her hands underneath her and along the bench. Then she gave a sigh and her
hand closed over Grandma Dee's butter dish. "That's it!" she said. "I knew
there was something I wanted to ask you if I could have." She jumped up from
the table and went over in the corner where the churn stood, the milk in it
clabber by now. She looked at the churn and looked at it.

"This churn top is what I need," she said. "Didn't Uncle Buddy whittle it    47
out of a tree you all used to have?"

"Yes," I said.    48

"Uh-huh," she said happily. "And I want the dasher,[2] too."    49

"Uncle Buddy whittle that, too?" asked the barber.    50

Dee (Wangero) looked up at me.    51

"Aunt Dee's first husband whittled the dash," said Maggie so low you    52
almost couldn't hear her. "His name was Henry, but they called him Stash."

"Maggie's brain is like an elephant's," Wangero said, laughing. "I can use    53
the churn top as a centerpiece for the alcove table," she said, sliding a

---

[2] The plunger of the butter churn. — EDS.

plate over the churn, "and I'll think of something artistic to do with the dasher."

When she finished wrapping the dasher the handle stuck out. I took it for a moment in my hands. You didn't even have to look close to see where hands pushing the dasher up and down to make butter had left a kind of sink in the wood. In fact, there were a lot of small sinks; you could see where thumbs and fingers had sunk into the wood. It was beautiful light yellow wood, from a tree that grew in the yard where Big Dee and Stash had lived.                                     54

After dinner Dee (Wangero) went to the trunk at the foot of my bed and started rifling through it. Maggie hung back in the kitchen over the dishpan. Out came Wangero with two quilts. They had been pieced by Grandma Dee and then Big Dee and me had hung them on the quilt frames on the front porch and quilted them. One was in the Lone Star pattern. The other was Walk Around the Mountain. In both of them were scraps of dresses Grandma Dee had worn fifty and more years ago. Bits and pieces of Grandpa Jarrell's Paisley shirts. And one teeny faded blue piece, about the size of a penny match-box, that was from Great Grandpa Ezra's uniform that he wore in the Civil War.                                     55

"Mama," Wangero said sweet as a bird. "Can I have these old quilts?"                                     56

I heard something fall in the kitchen, and a minute later the kitchen door slammed.                                     57

"Why don't you take one or two of the others?" I asked. "These old things was just done by me and Big Dee from some tops your grandma pieced before she died."                                     58

"No," said Wangero. "I don't want those. They are stitched around the borders by machine."                                     59

"That'll make them last better," I said.                                     60

"That's not the point," said Wangero. "These are all pieces of dresses Grandma used to wear. She did all this stitching by hand. Imagine!" She held the quilts securely in her arms, stroking them.                                     61

"Some of the pieces, like those lavender ones, come from old clothes her mother handed down to her," I said, moving up to touch the quilts. Dee (Wangero) moved back just enough so that I couldn't reach the quilts. They already belonged to her.                                     62

"Imagine!" she breathed again, clutching them closely to her bosom.                                     63

"The truth is," I said, "I promised to give them quilts to Maggie, for when she marries John Thomas."                                     64

She gasped like a bee had stung her.                                     65

"Maggie can't appreciate these quilts!" she said. "She'd probably be back-ward enough to put them to everyday use."                                     66

"I reckon she would," I said. "God knows I been saving 'em for long enough with nobody using 'em. I hope she will!" I didn't want to bring up how                                     67

I had offered Dee (Wangero) a quilt when she went away to college. Then she had told me they were old-fashioned, out of style.

"But they're *priceless!*" she was saying now, furiously; for she has a temper. 68 "Maggie would put them on the bed and in five years they'd be in rags. Less than that!"

"She can always make some more," I said. "Maggie knows how to quilt." 69

Dee (Wangero) looked at me with hatred. "You just will not understand. 70 The point is these quilts, *these* quilts!"

"Well," I said, stumped. "What would *you* do with them?" 71

"Hang them," she said. As if that was the only thing you *could* do with 72 quilts.

Maggie by now was standing in the door. I could almost hear the sound 73 her feet made as they scraped over each other.

"She can have them, Mama," she said, like somebody used to never win- 74 ning anything, or having anything reserved for her. "I can 'member Grandma Dee without the quilts."

I looked at her hard. She had filled her bottom lip with checkerberry snuff 75 and it gave her face a kind of dopey, hangdog look. It was Grandma Dee and Big Dee who taught her how to quilt herself. She stood there with her scarred hands hidden in the folds of her skirt. She looked at her sister with something like fear but she wasn't mad at her. This was Maggie's portion. This was the way she knew God to work.

When I looked at her like that something hit me in the top of my head 76 and ran down to the soles of my feet. Just like when I'm in church and the spirit of God touches me and I get happy and shout. I did something I never had done before: hugged Maggie to me, then dragged her on into the room, snatched the quilts out of Miss Wangero's hands and dumped them into Mag- gie's lap. Maggie just sat there on my bed with her mouth open.

"Take one or two of the others," I said to Dee. 77

But she turned without a word and went out to Hakim-a-barber. 78

"You just don't understand," she said, as Maggie and I came out to the car. 79

"What don't I understand?" I wanted to know. 80

"Your heritage," she said. And then she turned to Maggie, kissed her, and 81 said, "You ought to try to make something of yourself, too, Maggie. It's really a new day for us. But from the way you and Mama still live you'd never know it."

She put on some sunglasses that hid everything above the tip of her nose 82 and her chin.

Maggie smiled; maybe at the sunglasses. But a real smile, not scared. After 83 we watched the car dust settle I asked Maggie to bring me a dip of snuff. And then the two of us sat there just enjoying, until it was time to go in the house and go to bed.

For a reading quiz, sources on Alice Walker, and annotated links to further readings on African American heritage, visit **bedfordstmartins.com/thebedfordreader**.

## Journal Writing

Do you think the quilts stitched by the narrator's mother should be put to "everyday use," or should they be preserved as a reminder of family and cultural heritage? Write about something owned by you or your family that has been passed down from earlier generations. Is it still in everyday use? Why, or why not? (To take your journal writing further, see "From Journal to Essay" on the next page.)

## Questions on Meaning

1. Walker's short story is based on two sets of contrasts, a direct one between people and a more indirect one between attitudes. What are these contrasts?
2. Why has Dee taken on a new name? What is the point of the conversation in which she and her mother discuss the origin of her given name (pars. 24–35)?
3. Why do you think Dee makes sure to include the house when taking photographs of her mother and sister (par. 22)? Why does she want the quilts stitched by her grandmother? What IRONY can you find in her behavior?
4. Why do you think Walker titled this story "Everyday Use"?

## Questions on Writing Strategy

1. What might Walker's PURPOSE have been in creating the contrasting sisters? What might the characters represent?
2. In what way does the conclusion of the story echo the beginning? What is the EFFECT of the story's opening and closing in this way?
3. **OTHER METHODS**   Walker's story is, of course, a NARRATIVE. Where does Walker use DESCRIPTION to enhance her narration?

## Questions on Language

1. The mother states in paragraph 13 that she is uneducated and earlier says that she doesn't have a "quick tongue" (par. 6). Does the mother's language seem consistent with and appropriate for her educational background? Why, or why not?
2. What is the effect of the mother's referring to her daughter repeatedly as "Dee (Wangero)" and finally, in paragraph 76, as "Miss Wangero"?
3. Be sure you know the meanings of the following words, checking a dictionary if necessary: awe (par. 2); tottering (3); rawhide (14); scalding, lye (15); churn, clabber (46); snuff (75).

## Suggestions for Writing

1. **FROM JOURNAL TO ESSAY**   Develop an essay about the family object or objects that you wrote about in your journal entry. Carefully describe the object, and explain its history, significance, and current use.
2. Think of siblings you know who are quite different from each other in looks, interests, behavior, or other attributes. (Your subjects could be you and your own sibling.) In an essay, compare and contrast the two people.
3. Beginning in the late 1960s and early 1970s, many African Americans resembled Walker's character Dee in embracing their heritage—particularly their roots in Africa—to claim a history beyond slavery and segregation. Research the specifics of this movement, and write an essay on how it influenced literature, education, fashion, and other aspects of American life.
4. **CRITICAL WRITING**   ANALYZE the character of Dee/Wangero, in relation to her mother and sister as well as in her own right. How do you think Walker wants readers to respond to this character? How do you respond to her? Be sure to support your analysis with appropriate quotations from the text.
5. **CONNECTIONS**   "Everyday Use" was published ten years after Martin Luther King, Jr., delivered his famous "I Have a Dream" speech (p. 614). How does the story reflect the themes of "I Have a Dream"? How is Walker commenting on the civil rights movement and its aftermath?

---

# *Alice Walker on Writing*

In an interview with David Bradley in the *New York Times Magazine*, Alice Walker described her method of writing as waiting for friendly spirits to visit her. Usually, she doesn't outline or devote much time to preliminary organization. She plunges in with a passion, and she sees a definite purpose in most of her work: to correct injustices. "I was brought up to try to see what was wrong, and right it. Since I am a writer, writing is how I right it. I was brought up to look at things that are out of joint, out of balance, and to try to bring them into balance. And as a writer that's what I do."

An articulate feminist, Walker has written in support of greater rights for women, including African American women. If most of her works are short—stories, essays, and poems—there is a reason: She sees thick, long-winded volumes as alien to a female sensibility. "The books women write can be more like us—much thinner, much leaner, much cleaner."

Much of Alice Walker's writing has emerged from painful experience: She has written of her impoverished early days on a Georgia sharecropper's farm, a childhood accident with a BB gun that cost her the sight of one eye, a traumatic abortion, years as a civil rights worker in Mississippi. "I think," she says, "writing really helps you heal yourself. I think if you write long enough, you will be a healthy person. That is, if you write what you need to write, as opposed to what will make money or what will make fame."

## For Discussion

1. What does the author mean when she speaks of the importance of writing "what you need to write"?
2. What writers can you think of whose work has helped to right the world's wrongs?
3. Can you cite any exceptions to Walker's generalization that long books are alien to women's sensibilities?

# ADDITIONAL WRITING TOPICS

## *Comparison and Contrast*

1. In an essay replete with EXAMPLES, compare and contrast the two subjects in any one of the following pairs:

   The main characters of two films, stories, or novels
   Women and men as consumers
   The styles of two runners
   Liberals and conservatives: their opposing views of the role of government
   How city dwellers and country dwellers spend their leisure time
   The presentation styles of two television news commentators

2. Approach a comparison and contrast essay on one of the following general subjects by explaining why you prefer one thing to the other:

   Vehicles: hybrids and conventional engines; sedans and SUVs; American and Asian; Asian and European
   Computers: Macs and PCs
   Two buildings on campus or in town
   Two football teams
   Two horror movies
   Television when you were a child and television today
   City life and small-town or rural life
   Malls and main streets
   Two neighborhoods
   Two sports

3. Write an essay in which you compare a reality (what actually exists) with an ideal (what should exist). Some possible topics:

   The affordable car
   Available living quarters
   A job
   The college curriculum
   Public transportation
   Financial aid for college students

# 8

# PROCESS ANALYSIS

*Explaining Step by Step*

◀ **Process analysis in a photograph**

In a factory in Shenzhen, China, workers create dolls for export to the United States. The single image catches several steps in the doll-making process. At the very back of the assembly line, flat, unstuffed dolls begin the journey past the ranks of workers who stuff the body parts, using material prepared by other workers on the sides. A supervisor, hands behind his or her back, oversees the process. What do you think the photographer, Wally McNamee, wants viewers to understand about this process? What do you imagine the workers themselves think about it?

## THE METHOD

A chemist working for a soft-drink firm is asked to improve on a competitor's product, Green Tea Tonic. First, she chemically tests a sample to figure out what's in the drink. This is the method of DIVISION or ANALYSIS, the separation of something into its parts in order to understand it (see the following chapter). Then the chemist writes a report telling her boss how to make a drink like Green Tea Tonic, but better. This recipe is a special kind of analysis, called PROCESS ANALYSIS: explaining step by step how to do something or how something is done.

Like any type of analysis, process analysis divides a subject into its components: It divides a continuous action into stages. Processes much larger and more involved than the making of a green tea drink also may be analyzed. When geologists explain how a formation such as the Grand Canyon occurred—a process taking several hundred million years—they describe the successive layers of sediment deposited by oceans, floods, and wind; then the great uplift of the entire region by underground forces; and then the erosion, visible to us today, by the Colorado River and its tributaries, by little streams and flash floods, by crumbling and falling rock, and by wind. Exactly what are the geologists doing in this explanation? They are taking a complicated event (or process) and dividing it into parts. They are telling us what happened first, second, and third, and what is still happening today.

Because it is useful in explaining what is complicated, process analysis is a favorite method of scientists such as geologists. The method, however, may be useful to anybody. Two PURPOSES of process analysis are very familiar to you:

- A *directive process analysis* explains how to do something or make something. You meet it when you read a set of instructions for taking an exam or for conducting a chemistry experiment ("From a 5-milliliter burette, add hydrochloride to a 20-milliliter beaker of water . . .").
- An *informative process analysis* explains how something is done or how it takes place. You see it in textbook descriptions of how atoms behave when they split, how lions hunt, and how a fertilized egg develops into a child.

In this chapter, you will find examples of both kinds of process analysis—both the "how to" and the "how." For instance, Linnea Saukko offers a directive for destroying the environment (not to be taken literally), while Jessica Mitford spellbindingly informs us of how corpses are embalmed.

Sometimes process analysis is used very imaginatively. Foreseeing that eventually the sun will burn out and all life on Earth will perish, an astronomer who cannot possibly behold the end of the world nevertheless can write a process analysis of it. An exercise in learned guesswork, such an essay divides a vast and almost inconceivable event into stages that, taken one at a time, become clearer and more readily imaginable.

Whether it is useful or useless (but fun or scary to imagine), an effective process analysis can grip readers and even hold them fascinated. Say you were proposing a change in the procedures for course registration at your school. You could argue your point until you were out of words, but you would get nowhere if you failed to tell your readers exactly how the new process would work: That's what makes your proposal sing. Leaf through a current issue of a newsstand magazine, and you will find that process analysis abounds. You may meet, for instance, articles telling you how to tenderize cuts of meat, sew homemade designer jeans, lose fat, cut hair, arouse a bored mate, and score at Internet stock trading. Less practical, but not necessarily less interesting, are the informative articles: how brain surgeons work, how diamonds are formed, how cities fight crime. Readers, it seems, have an unslakable thirst for process analysis. In every issue of the *New York Times Book Review*, we find an entire best-seller list devoted to "Advice, How-to, and Miscellaneous," including books on how to make money in real estate, how to lose weight, how to find a good mate, and how to lose a bad one. Evidently, if anything will still make an American crack open a book, it is a step-by-step explanation of how he or she, too, can be a success at living.

## THE PROCESS

Here are suggestions for writing an effective process analysis of your own. (In fact, what you are about to read is itself a process analysis.)

1. *Understand clearly the process you are about to analyze.* Think it through. This preliminary survey will make the task of writing far easier for you.
2. *Consider your thesis.* What is the point of your process analysis: Why are you bothering to tell readers about it? The THESIS STATEMENT for a process analysis need do no more than say what the subject is and maybe outline its essential stages. For instance:

   The main stages in writing a process analysis are listing the steps in the process, drafting to explain the steps, and revising to clarify the steps.

   But your readers will surely appreciate something livelier and more pointed, something that says "You can use this" or "This may surprise you" or "Listen up." Here are two thesis statements from essays in this chapter:

   [In a mortuary the body] is in short order sprayed, sliced, pierced, pickled, trussed, trimmed, creamed, waxed, painted, rouged, and neatly dressed— transformed from a common corpse into a Beautiful Memory Picture.
   —Jessica Mitford, "Behind the Formaldehyde Curtain"

Poisoning the earth can be difficult because the earth is always trying to cleanse and renew itself.          —Linnea Saukko, "How to Poison the Earth"

3. *Think about preparatory steps.* If the reader should do something before beginning the process, list these steps. For instance, you might begin, "Assemble the needed equipment: a 20-milliliter beaker, a 5-milliliter burette, safety gloves, and safety goggles."

4. *List the steps or stages in the process.* Try setting them down in chronological order, one at a time—if this is possible. Some processes, however, do not happen in an orderly sequence, but occur all at once. If, for instance, you are writing an account of a typical earthquake, what do you mention first? The shifting of underground rock strata? Cracks in the earth? Falling houses? Bursting water mains? Toppling trees? Mangled cars? Casualties? Here is a subject for which the method of CLASSIFICATION (Chap. 10) may come to your aid. You might sort out apparently simultaneous events into categories: injury to people; damage to homes, to land, to public property.

5. *Check the completeness and order of the steps.* Make sure your list includes *all* the steps in the right order. Sometimes a stage of a process may contain a number of smaller stages. Make sure none has been left out. If any seems particularly tricky or complicated, underline it on your list to remind yourself when you write your essay to slow down and detail it with extra care.

6. *Define your terms.* Ask yourself, "Do I need any specialized or technical terms?" If so, be sure to define them. You'll sympathize with your reader if you have ever tried to assemble a bicycle according to a directive that begins, "Position sleeve casing on wheel center in fork with shaft in tong groove, and gently but forcibly tap in medium pal nut head."

7. *Use time-markers or* TRANSITIONS. These words or phrases indicate *when* one stage of a process stops and the next begins, and they greatly aid your reader in following you. Here, for example, is a paragraph of plain medical prose that makes good use of helpful time-markers (underlined). (The paragraph is adapted from Alan Frank Guttmacher's *Pregnancy and Birth: A Book for Expectant Parents.*)

In the human, thirty-six hours after the egg is fertilized, a two-cell egg appears. A twelve-cell development takes place in seventy-two hours. The egg is still round and has increased little in diameter. In this respect it is like a real estate development. At first a road bisects the whole area, then a cross road divides it into quarters, and later other roads divide it into eighths and twelfths. This happens without the taking of any more land, simply by subdivision of the original tract. On the third or fourth day, the egg passes from the Fallopian tube into the uterus. By the fifth day the original single large cell has subdivided into sixty small cells and floats about the slitlike uterine cavity a day or two longer, then adheres to the cavity's inner lining. By the twelfth day the human egg is already firmly implanted. Impregnation is now completed, as yet unbeknown to the woman. At present, she has not even had time to miss her first menstrual period, and other symptoms of pregnancy are still several days distant.

Brief as these time-markers are, they define each stage of the human egg's journey. Note how the writer, after declaring in the second sentence that the egg forms twelve cells, backtracks for a moment and retraces the process by which the egg has subdivided, comparing it (by a brief ANALOGY) to a piece of real estate. When using time-markers, vary them so that they won't seem mechanical. If you can, avoid the monotonous repetition of a fixed phrase (*In the fourteenth stage . . . , In the fifteenth stage . . .*). Even boring time-markers, though, are better than none at all. As in any chronological NARRATIVE, words and phrases such as *in the beginning, first, second, next, then, after that, three seconds later, at the same time*, and *finally* can help a process to move smoothly in the telling and lodge firmly in the reader's mind.

8. *Be specific.* When you write a first draft, state your analysis in generous detail, even at the risk of being wordy. When you revise, it will be easier to delete than to amplify.

9. *Revise.* When your essay is finished, reread it carefully against the checklist on the next page. You might also enlist a friend's help. If your process analysis is a directive ("How to Eat an Ice-Cream Cone Without Dribbling"), see if the friend can follow your instructions without difficulty. If your process analysis is informative ("How a New Word Enters the Dictionary"), ask the friend whether the process unfolds as clearly in his or her mind as it does in yours.

---

### FOCUS ON CONSISTENCY

While drafting a process analysis, you may start off with subjects or verbs in one form and then shift to another form because the original choice feels awkward. In directive analyses, shifts occur most often with the subjects *a person* and *one*:

> INCONSISTENT   To keep the car from rolling while changing the tire, one should first set the car's emergency brake. Then you should block the three other tires with objects like rocks or chunks of wood.

In informative analyses, shifts usually occur from singular to plural as a way to get around *he* when the meaning includes males and females:

INCONSISTENT   The poll <u>worker</u> first checks each voter against the registration list. Then <u>they</u> ask the voter to sign another list.

To repair inconsistencies, start with a subject that is both comfortable and sustainable:

CONSISTENT   To keep the car from rolling while changing the tire, <u>you</u> should set the car's emergency brake. Then <u>you</u> should block the three other tires with objects like rocks or chunks of wood.

CONSISTENT   Poll <u>workers</u> first check each voter against the registration list. Then <u>they</u> ask the voter to sign another list.

Sometimes, writers try to avoid naming or shifting subjects by using PASSIVE verbs that don't require actors:

INCONSISTENT   To keep the car from rolling while changing the tire, <u>one</u> should first set the car's emergency brake. Then the three other tires <u>should be blocked</u> with objects like rocks or chunks of wood.

INCONSISTENT   First each voter <u>is checked</u> against the registration list. Then the voter <u>is asked</u> to sign another list.

In directive analyses, avoid passive verbs by using *you,* as shown in the consistent example above, or use the commanding form of verbs, in which *you* is understood as the subject:

CONSISTENT   To keep the car from rolling while changing the tire, first <u>set</u> the car's emergency brake. Then <u>block</u> the three other tires with objects like rocks or chunks of wood.

In informative analyses, passive verbs may be necessary if you don't know who the actor is or want to emphasize the action over the actor. But identifying the actor is generally clearer and more concise:

CONSISTENT   Poll <u>workers</u> first check each voter against the registration list. Then <u>they</u> ask the voter to sign another list.

**For exercises on consistency and passive verbs, visit Exercise Central at** *bedfordstmartins.com/thebedfordreader.*

---

## CHECKLIST FOR REVISING A PROCESS ANALYSIS

✔ **THESIS**   Does your process analysis have a point? Have you made sure readers know what it is?

✔ **ORGANIZATION**   Have you arranged the steps of your process in a clear chronological order? If steps occur simultaneously, have you grouped them so that readers perceive some order?

---

✔ **COMPLETENESS**   Have you included all the necessary steps and explained each one fully? Is it clear how each one contributes to the result?

✔ **DEFINITIONS**   Have you explained the meanings of any terms your readers may not know?

✔ **TRANSITIONS**   Do time-markers distinguish the steps of your process and clarify their sequence?

✔ **CONSISTENCY**   Have you maintained comfortable, consistent, and clear subjects and verb forms?

---

# PROCESS ANALYSIS IN PARAGRAPHS

## Writing About Television

The following paragraph, written especially for *The Bedford Reader*, explains the process of setting a digital video recorder to record a television program. Though composed to be freestanding, the paragraph (ideally with an accompanying illustration) could easily be dropped into a complete set of instructions on how to operate the DVR.

Your DVR allows you to schedule recording of any television programming up to two weeks in advance. Start at the on-screen command center (CMND on the DVR remote) and use the remote's arrow and "Select" keys to move around on screens and to make choices. At the command center, select "Record" and then, at the next screen, "Choose title." Using the alphabet that appears, spell out the program title. When the title is complete, select "Done." At the program screen following, select "Choose episodes." A list of available episodes then appears, and you can select the particular ones you want to record. When you're finished, press "TV" on the remote to view live television.

> Process to be explained with directive analysis
> General instruction for all steps
> Step 1, Step 2
> Step 3
> Step 4
> Step 5
> Step 6
> Step 7
> Transitions (underlined) clarify steps

## Writing in an Academic Discipline

This paragraph on our descent into sleep comes from a psychology textbook's section on "the most perplexing of our biological rhythms." Before this paragraph the authors review the history of sleep research; after it they continue to analyze the night-long process that follows this initial descent.

When you first climb into bed, close your eyes, and relax, your brain emits bursts of *alpha waves* in a regular, high-amplitude, low-frequency rhythm of 8–12 cycles per second. Alpha is associated

> Steps preceding process

with relaxing or not concentrating on anything in particular. Gradually these waves slow down even further and you drift into the
Land of Nod, passing through four stages, each deeper than the previous one.

Process to be explained with informative analysis

1. *Stage 1.* Your brain waves become small and irregular, indicating activity with low voltage and mixed frequencies. You feel
   yourself drifting on the edge of consciousness, in a state of light
   sleep. If awakened, you may recall fantasies or a few visual
   images.

   *Step 1*

2. *Stage 2.* Your brain emits occasional short bursts of rapid, high-
   peaking waves called *sleep spindles*. Light sounds or minor noises
   probably won't disturb you.

   *Step 2*

3. *Stage 3.* In addition to the waves characteristic of stage 2, your
   brain occasionally emits very slow waves of about 1–3 cycles
   per second, with very high peaks. These *delta waves* are a sure
   sign that you will be hard to arouse. Your breathing and pulse
   have slowed down, your temperature has dropped, and your
   muscles are relaxed.

   *Step 3*

4. *Stage 4.* Delta waves have now largely taken over, and you are
   in deep sleep. It will take vigorous shaking or a loud noise to
   awaken you, and you won't be very happy about it. Oddly
   enough, though, if you talk or walk in your sleep, this is when
   you are likely to do so.

   *Step 4*

—Carole Wade and Carol Tavris, Psychology

## PROCESS ANALYSIS IN PRACTICE

As a sophomore at Mary Washington College in Virginia, Jennifer Meska
was a resident assistant in a freshman dormitory, responsible for students' welfare and, when necessary, for establishing dormitory rules.

In the following memo to the dorm's residents, Meska explained what students must do in the three-times-yearly fire drills. Meska's aim in drafting the
memo was to outline the drill procedure so that students could remember and
follow it—in other words (though she didn't think of the task this way), to
write a clear directive process analysis.

In her first draft, Meska ran the steps of the process together in a paragraph, and for some steps she omitted explanations that might motivate
residents to follow them. The bulleted list in her revision and the added
explanations make the steps more distinct and memorable.

TO: Residents of Russell Hall
FROM: Jennifer Meska
DATE: September 6, 2006
SUBJECT: Fire-drill procedure

To prepare for the possibility of a fire in our residence hall, we will run three unannounced fire drills throughout the year. These drills will familiarize you with the potentially lifesaving procedures to be used during a real fire.

**A loud buzzing noise and flashing lights will signal the start of a fire drill.** Each resident has three minutes to complete the following tasks and exit the building:

- Close all bedroom and bathroom windows to prevent additional oxygen from feeding the fire.

- Turn off all electrical appliances, including computers, televisions, fans, radios, and lights. Turning off appliances will prevent electrical surges from starting additional fires.

- Grab a towel to cover your mouth in case you come across any smoke-filled passages, and wear shoes to protect your feet from any dangerous debris.

- Don't take anything else with you. In a real fire, delay could cost you your life.

- Close your door behind you to retard the spread of the fire.

- Go immediately to the nearest exit.

The fire drills are mandated by the state, and all residence halls must pass them in the required three minutes. If you have any questions, please let me know.

Process Analysis

## LINNEA SAUKKO

LINNEA SAUKKO was born in Warren, Ohio, in 1956. After receiving a degree in environmental quality control from Muskingum Area Technical College, she spent three years as an environmental technician, developing hazardous waste programs and acting as adviser on chemical safety at a large corporation. Concerned about the lack of safe methods for disposing of hazardous waste, Saukko went back to school to earn a BA in geology (Ohio State University, 1985) so that she could help address this issue. She currently lives in Hilliard, Ohio, and works as a groundwater manager at the Ohio Environmental Protection Agency, evaluating various sites for possible contamination of the groundwater.

# *How to Poison the Earth*

"How to Poison the Earth" was written in response to an assignment given in a freshman composition class and was awarded a Bedford Prize in Student Writing. It was subsequently published in *Student Writers at Work: The Bedford Prizes*. Saukko's essay is largely a directive process analysis, but it is also a SATIRE: By outwardly showing us one way to guarantee the fate of the earth, the author implicitly urges us not to do it.

Saukko focuses in this essay on the toxins, or poisons, that make earth, air, and water dangerous for life. The actions and risks she addresses have not abated, but in recent years they have been eclipsed by public concern about global warming. The next essay, Gretel Ehrlich's "Chronicles of Ice," takes on that environmental problem.

Poisoning the earth can be difficult because the earth is always trying to cleanse and renew itself. Keeping this in mind, we should generate as much waste as possible from substances such as uranium-238, which has a half-life (the time it takes for half of the substance to decay) of one million years, or plutonium, which has a half-life of only 0.5 million years but is so toxic that if distributed evenly, ten pounds of it could kill every person on the earth. Because the United States generates about eighteen tons of plutonium per year, it is about the best substance for long-term poisoning of the earth. It would help if we would build more nuclear power plants because each one generates only 500 pounds of plutonium each year. Of course, we must include persistent toxic chemicals such as polychlorinated biphenyl (PCB) and di-

1

290

chlorodiphenyl trichloroethane (DDT) to make sure we have enough toxins to poison the earth from the core to the outer atmosphere. First, we must develop many different ways of putting the waste from these nuclear and chemical substances in, on, and around the earth.

Putting these substances in the earth is a most important step in the poisoning process. With deep-well injection we can ensure that the earth is poisoned all the way to the core. Deep-well injection involves drilling a hole that is a few thousand feet deep and injecting toxic substances at extremely high pressures so they will penetrate deep into the earth. According to the Environmental Protection Agency (EPA), there are about 360 such deep injection wells in the United States. We cannot forget the groundwater aquifers that are closer to the surface. These must also be contaminated. This is easily done by shallow-well injection, which operates on the same principle as deep-well injection, only closer to the surface. The groundwater that has been injected with toxins will spread contamination beneath the earth. The EPA estimates that there are approximately 500,000 shallow injection wells in the United States.

Burying the toxins in the earth is the next best method. The toxins from landfills, dumps, and lagoons slowly seep into the earth, guaranteeing that contamination will last a long time. Because the EPA estimates there are only about 50,000 of these dumps in the United States, they should be located in areas where they will leak to the surrounding ground and surface water.

Applying pesticides and other poisons on the earth is another part of the poisoning process. This is good for coating the earth's surface so that the poisons will be absorbed by plants, will seep into the ground, and will run off into surface water.

Surface water is very important to contaminate because it will transport the poisons to places that cannot be contaminated directly. Lakes are good for long-term storage of pollutants while they release some of their contamination to rivers. The only trouble with rivers is that they act as a natural cleansing system for the earth. No matter how much poison is dumped into them, they will try to transport it away to reach the ocean eventually.

The ocean is very hard to contaminate because it has such a large volume and a natural buffering capacity that tends to neutralize some of the contamination. So in addition to the pollution from rivers, we must use the ocean as a dumping place for as many toxins as possible. The ocean currents will help transport the pollution to places that cannot otherwise be reached.

Now make sure that the air around the earth is very polluted. Combustion and evaporation are major mechanisms for doing this. We must continuously pollute because the wind will disperse the toxins while rain washes them from the air. But this is good because a few lakes are stripped of all living animals each year from acid rain. Because the lower atmosphere can cleanse itself fairly easily, we must explode nuclear test bombs that shoot radioactive particles high into the upper atmosphere where they will circle the earth for years. Gravity must pull some of the particles to earth, so we must continue exploding these bombs.

So it is that easy. Just be sure to generate as many poisonous substances as      8
possible and be sure they are distributed in, on, and around the entire earth at a greater rate than it can cleanse itself. By following these easy steps we can guarantee the poisoning of the earth.

---

*For a reading quiz and annotated links to further readings on pollution, visit* **bedfordstmartins.com/thebedfordreader**.

---

## Journal Writing

Saukko's essay is SATIRE—that is, an indirect attack on human follies or flaws, using IRONY to urge behavior exactly opposite what is really desired. In your journal, explore when you have proposed satirical solutions to problems that seem ridiculous or overwhelming—for example, suggesting breaking all the dishes so that they don't have to be washed again or barring pedestrians from city streets so that they don't interfere with cars. What kinds of situations might lead you to make suggestions like these? (To take your journal writing further, see "From Journal to Essay" on the facing page.)

## Questions on Meaning

1. Is the author's main PURPOSE to amuse and entertain, to inform readers of ways they can make better use of natural resources, to warn readers about threats to the future of our planet, or to make fun of scientists? Support your answer with EVIDENCE from the essay.
2. Describe at least three of the earth's mechanisms for cleansing its land, water, and atmosphere, as presented in this essay.
3. According to Saukko, many of our actions are detrimental, if not outright destructive, to our environment. Identify these practices and discuss them. If these activities are harmful to the earth, why are they permitted? Do they serve some other important goal or purpose? If so, what? Are there other ways that these goals might be reached?

## Questions on Writing Strategy

1. How detailed and specific are Saukko's instructions for poisoning the earth? Which steps in this process would you be able to carry out, once you finished reading the essay? In what instances might an author choose not to provide concrete, comprehensive instructions for a procedure? Relate your answer to the TONE and purpose of this essay.
2. How is Saukko's essay organized? Follow the process carefully to determine whether it happens chronologically, with each step depending on the one before it, or whether it follows another order. How effective is this method of organization and presentation?
3. For what AUDIENCE is this essay intended? How can you tell?
4. What is the tone of this essay? Consider especially the title and the last paragraph as well as examples from the body of the essay. How does the tone contribute to Saukko's satire?
5. What consistent sentence subject does Saukko use in explaining "how to poison the earth"? Who is to perform the process?
6. **OTHER METHODS**    Saukko doesn't mention every possible pollutant but instead focuses on certain EXAMPLES. Why do you think she chooses these particular examples? What serious pollutants can you think of that Saukko doesn't mention specifically?

## Questions on Language

1. How do the phrases "next best method" (par. 3), "another part of the poisoning process" (4), and "[l]akes are good for long-term storage of pollutants" (5) signal the tone of this essay? Should they be read literally, ironically, metaphorically, or some other way?
2. Be sure you know how to define the following words: generate, nuclear, toxins (par. 1); lagoons, contamination (3); buffering, neutralize (6); combustion (7).

## Suggestions for Writing

1. **FROM JOURNAL TO ESSAY**    Choose one of the solutions you wrote about in your journal, or propose a solution to a problem that your journal entry has suggested. Write an essay detailing this satirical solution, paying careful attention to explaining each step of the process and to maintaining your satiric tone throughout.
2. Write an essay defending and justifying the use of nuclear power plants, pesticides, or another pollutant Saukko mentions. This essay will require some research because you will need to argue that the benefits of these methods outweigh their hazardous and destructive effects. Be sure to support your claims with factual information and statistics. Or approach the issue from the same point of view that Saukko did and argue against the use of nuclear power plants or pesticides. Substantiate your argument with data and facts, and be sure to propose alternative sources of power or alternative methods of insect control.
3. **CRITICAL WRITING**    What does Saukko gain or lose by using satire and irony to make her point? What would be the comparative strengths and weaknesses of an

essay that approached the same pollution problems straightforwardly and sincerely, perhaps urging or pleading with readers to stop polluting?

4. **CONNECTIONS**   In the next essay, "Chronicles of Ice," Gretel Ehrlich explores an environmental problem that Saukko doesn't address: global warming. Using evidence from Ehrlich's piece and from research, write a satirical essay loosely based on Saukko's entitled "How to Warm Up the Earth." Like Saukko, use irony to persuade readers to do the opposite of what you suggest. Your purpose should be to warn readers about the dangers of global warming.

---

## *Linnea Saukko on Writing*

"After I have chosen a topic," says Linnea Saukko, "the easiest thing for me to do is to write about how I really feel about it. The goal of 'How to Poison the Earth' was to inform people, or, more specifically, to open their eyes.

"As soon as I decided on my topic, I made a list of all the types of pollution and I sat down and basically wrote the paper in less than two hours. The information seemed to pour from me onto the page. Of course I did a lot of editing afterward, but I never changed the idea and the tone that I started with."

### For Discussion

When have you had the experience of writing on a subject that compelled your words to pour forth with little effort? What was the subject? What did you learn from this experience?

## GRETEL EHRLICH

GRETEL EHRLICH is a writer known for her affinity with nature at its loneliest and chilliest. She was born in Santa Barbara, California, in 1946 and attended Bennington College and the film school at the University of California, Los Angeles. She worked as a documentary filmmaker for ten years and then settled in Wyoming to learn sheepherding and to write. Her first book, *The Solace of Open Spaces* (1985), tells of life on the plains of Wyoming. It won an award from the American Academy and Institute of Arts and Letters. Since then Ehrlich has published two books of poetry; several books of fiction, including the novel *Heart Mountain* (1988) and the story collection *Drinking Dry Clouds* (reissued 2005); and half a dozen nonfiction works, ranging from memoir (*A Match to the Heart*, 1994) to travel (*This Cold Heaven: Seven Seasons in Greenland*, 2001) to biography (*John Muir: Nature's Visionary*, 2000).

# *Chronicles of Ice*

"Chronicles of Ice" was excerpted in *Orion* magazine from Ehrlich's book *The Future of Ice: A Journey into Cold* (2004), which recounts the author's travels to some of the world's most remote places. Like Linnea Saukko in the previous essay, Ehrlich is worried about the effects that human activity—what Ehrlich elsewhere calls "the democracy of gratification"—is having on the environment. In this essay she visits the Perito Moreno glacier in southern Argentina, part of an ice field that is second only to Antarctica in size. Using process analysis, she explains both how glaciers form and how, with human help, they decline.

A trapped turbulence—as if wind had solidified. Then noise: timpani    1
and a hard crack, the glacier's internal heat spilling out as an ice stream far below. I've come on a bus from El Calafate, Argentina, to visit the World Heritage glacier Perito Moreno, to see its bowls, lips, wombs, fenders, gravelly elbows, ponds, and ice streams, and to learn whatever lessons a glacier has to teach.

Some glaciers retreat, some surge, some do both, advancing and retreating    2
even as the climate warms. Perito Moreno is 257 square kilometers[1] across. It advances two meters a day at the center. From where I'm standing, I can look

[1] About ninety-nine square miles. —EDS.

directly down on the glacier's snout. Two spires tilt forward, their lips touching. They meet head to head, but their bodies are hollow. Sun scours them as they twist toward light.

I walk down stairs to a platform that gives me a more intimate view. A row   3
of ice teeth is bent sideways, indicating basal movement. Out of the corner of my eye I see something fall. A spectator gasps. An icy cheekbone crumbles. People come here to see only the falling and failings, not the power it takes for the glacier to stay unified.

A glacier is not static. Snow falls, accretes, and settles until finally its own   4
weight presses it down. The flakes become deformed. They lose coherence and pattern, become something crystalline called *firn* which then turns to ice. As an ice mountain grows, its weight displaces its bulk and it spreads outward, filling whole valleys, hanging off mountains, running toward seas.

There are warm glaciers and cold glaciers, depending on latitude and   5
altitude. Cold glaciers don't slide easily; they're fixed and frozen to rock. They move like men on stilts—all awkwardness, broken bones of sheared rock. Internal deformation affects flow patterns; melting occurs faster at the margins than in the center. Warm glaciers have internal melt-streams at every level and torrents of water flow out from under the ice at the glacier's foot. The "sole" of the glacier is close to the melting point and slides easily over rock. Friction creates heat, heat increases sole-melt, slipperiness, and speed. The quasi-liquid surface that results is a disordered layer, a complicated boundary where heat and cold, melting and freezing, play off each other and are inextricably bound, the way madness and sanity, cacophony and stillness, are.

Because ice melts as it moves and moves as it melts, a glacier is always   6
undermining itself. It lives by giving itself away.

A glacier balances its gains and losses like a banker. Accumulation has to   7
exceed ablation[2] for a glacier to grow. At the top, snow stacks up and does not melt. Midway down, the area of "mass balance" is where the profits and losses of snow can go either way. Surface melting can mean that water percolates down, refreezes, melts, and freezes again, creating a lens of ice. Below this region of equilibrium, ablation occurs. Profits are lost when the rate of melting exceeds the rate of accumulation. But a glacier will still advance if enough snow falls at the top and stays. . . .

A glacier is an archivist and historian. It registers every fluctuation of   8
weather. It saves everything no matter how small or big, including pollen, dust, heavy metals, bugs, and minerals. As snow becomes firn and then ice,

[2] Reduction by melting, erosion, and other means. —EDS.

oxygen bubbles are trapped in the glacier, providing samples of ancient atmosphere: carbon dioxide and methane. Records of temperatures and levels of atmospheric gases from before industrialization can be compared with those after—a mere 150 years. We can now see that the steady gains in greenhouse gases and air and water temperatures have occurred only since the rise of our smokestack and tailpipe society.

A glacier is time incarnate. When we lose a glacier—and we are losing    9
most of them—we lose history, an eye into the past; we lose stories of how living beings evolved, how weather vacillated, why plants and animals died. The retreat and disappearance of glaciers—there are only 160,000 left—means we're burning libraries and damaging the planet, possibly beyond repair. Bit by bit, glacier by glacier, rib by rib, we're living the Fall. . . .

Twenty thousand years ago temperatures plummeted and ice grew from    10
the top of the world like vines and ground covers. Glaciers sprouted and surged, covering 10 million square miles—more than thirteen times what they cover now. As a result of their worldwide retreat and a global decrease in winter snow cover, the albedo effect—the ability of ice and snow to deflect heat back into space—is quickly diminishing. Snow and ice are the Earth's built-in air conditioner—crucial to the health of the planet. Without winter's white mantle, Earth will become a heat sponge. As heat escalates, all our sources of fresh water will disappear.

Already, warmer temperatures are causing meltwater to stream into oceans,    11
changing temperature and salinity; sea ice and permafrost are thawing, pulsing methane into the air; seawater is expanding, causing floods and intrusions. Islands are disappearing, and vast human populations in places like Bangladesh are in grave danger. The high-mountain peoples of Peru, Chile, and Bolivia who depend on meltwater from snowpack are at risk; the Inuit cultures in Alaska, Arctic Canada, Siberia, and Greenland that depend on ice for transportation, and live on a diet of marine mammals, could disappear.

In temperate climates everywhere, the early onset of spring and the late    12
arrival of winter are creating ecosystem pandemonium. It is not unreasonable to think that a whole season can become extinct, at least for a time. Winter might last only one day—minor punctuation in a long sentence of heat. Mirages rising from shimmering heat waves would be the only storms. . . .

The bus takes me back to town. I get out near a grove of trees where loose    13
horses wander. It's good to be in a place where there are such freedoms. All over the world the life of rocks, ice, mountains, snow, oceans, islands, albatross, sooty gulls, whales, crabs, limpets, and guanaco once flowed up into the

bodies of the people who lived in small hunting groups and villages, and out came killer-whale prayers, condor chants, crab feasts, and guanaco songs. Life went where there was food. Food occurred in places of great beauty, and the act of living directly fueled people's movements, thoughts, and lives.

Everything spoke. Everything made a sound—birds, ghosts, animals, oceans, bogs, rocks, humans, trees, flowers, and rivers—and when they passed each other a third sound occurred. That's why weather, mountains, and each passing season were so noisy. Song and dance, sex and gratitude, were the season-sensitive ceremonies linking the human psyche to the larger, wild, weather-ridden world. 14

Now, the enterprise we human beings in the "developed world" have engaged in is almost too darkly insane to contemplate. Our bent has been to "improve" on nature and local culture, which has meant that we've reduced the parallel worlds of spirit, imagination, and daily life to a single secularized pile. The process of empire-building is a kind of denigration. Nothing that's not nuts and bolts and money-making is allowed in. Our can-do optimism and our head-in-the-sand approach to economics—one that takes only profit, and not the biological health of our planet, into account—has left us one-sided. 15

When did we begin thinking that weather was something to be rescued from? Why did we trade in our ceremonial lives for the workplace? Is this a natural progression or a hiccup in human civilization that we'll soon renounce? 16

I eat at a rustic bar with other travelers. It's late when night comes, maybe 10:30. In the darkness, Perito Moreno is still calving and moving, grabbing snowflakes, stirring weather, spitting out ice water, and it makes me smile. 17

*For a reading quiz, sources on Gretel Ehrlich, and annotated links to further readings on glaciers and global warming, visit **bedfordstmartins.com/thebedfordreader**.*

---

## Journal Writing

In your journal, write about a powerful natural phenomenon that you have witnessed—for example, a thunderstorm, a blizzard, an earthquake, a hurricane, a tornado, or a fire. What was your emotional response to the experience? (To take your journal writing further, see "From Journal to Essay" on the facing page.)

# Questions on Meaning

1. What does Ehrlich mean by "our smokestack and tailpipe society" (par. 8)? What point is she making here?
2. How is destroying glaciers similar to "burning libraries" (par. 9)?
3. According to Ehrlich's last paragraphs, what does the disappearance of glaciers suggest about humans' changing relationship to nature?
4. What do you think is Ehrlich's PURPOSE in explaining the life cycle of a glacier? What does she seem to want readers to take away from the essay? Where do you first see evidence of this purpose in the essay?
5. What would you say is Ehrlich's implied THESIS?

# Questions on Writing Strategy

1. Examine the organization of the essay. What major sections does it fall into? Why do you think Ehrlich chose to order the essay as she did?
2. Where in the essay does Ehrlich use process analysis? What does this method contribute to her overall purpose in the essay?
3. This essay originally appeared in the nature magazine *Orion*. How can you tell that the magazine is intended for general readers, not for a specialized AUDIENCE of professional geologists or ecologists? What else can you assume about the magazine's audience?
4. **OTHER METHODS**   Examine Ehrlich's use of CAUSE AND EFFECT in paragraphs 10–11. How does she organize the effects here?

# Questions on Language

1. Identify some places in the essay where Ehrlich gives human qualities to the glacier. What is the effect of these uses of PERSONIFICATION?
2. What does Ehrlich ALLUDE to with the sentence, "Bit by bit, glacier by glacier, rib by rib, we're living the Fall" (par. 9)?
3. Consult a dictionary if any of the following words are unfamiliar: turbulence, timpani, gravelly (par. 1); scours (2); basal (3); static, accretes, crystalline (4); torrents, inextricably, cacophony (5); percolates, equilibrium (7); archivist, fluctuation (8); incarnate, vacillated (9); mantle (10); meltwater, salinity, permafrost (11); temperate, pandemonium (12); albatross, limpets, guanaco (13); psyche (14); enterprise, bent, secularized, denigration (15); rustic, calving (17).

# Suggestions for Writing

1. **FROM JOURNAL TO ESSAY**   Write an essay exploring the natural phenomenon that you wrote about in your journal. Like Ehrlich, you might begin and end your essay by grounding the phenomenon in your personal experience of it, but focus on analyzing the general process by which it occurs and reflecting on its significance. What makes this force of nature so impressive? What impact does it have on people and on the environment? Use vivid IMAGES that will make the process come to life for your readers.

2. Scientists believe that glaciers are shrinking because of rising temperatures caused in large part by carbon dioxide emissions. Use a carbon calculator on the Internet, such as the one provided by the Nature Conservancy at *nature.org/initiatives/climatechange/calculator*, to measure your impact on climate change. What can you do in your daily life to reduce carbon emissions? Do further research, if necessary, and then write a process analysis laying out the steps by which you personally will help to stem global warming.

3. **CRITICAL WRITING**   EVALUATE Ehrlich's success in making a complicated geologic process clear and engaging for a nonspecialist audience. Consider, in particular, her use of concrete images, personification, and ANALOGY. What do these techniques contribute to the essay?

4. **CONNECTIONS**   In the previous essay, "How to Poison the Earth" (p. 290), Linnea Saukko also attempts to inspire readers to care more about the future of the earth. The two writers use very different techniques to achieve this purpose, however. COMPARE AND CONTRAST Saukko's approach with Ehrlich's. Do you find one essay more effective than the other? Why?

---

## *Gretel Ehrlich on Writing*

In a wide-ranging interview with Jonathan White, Gretel Ehrlich answered the question "Does writing serve as a tool to bring you closer to nature?"

I wouldn't say my writing brings me closer to nature — maybe it brings the people who read what I write closer to nature. It's tough to bring yourself to the truths that result from experience. I take all my cues about writing from the images around me. In writing, you work to find a language that actually embodies the life of what you are writing about. Wallace Stevens[1] calls this "the palm at the end of the mind." I'm not saying I have succeeded, but as with any form of expression, whether it's writing, painting, or dance, you try to go directly from the gut.

The Navajo talk about the land as if it were parts of the body and soul. I sometimes think of landscape that way. It's a matter of transposing identities and seeing how that makes you feel and think. You can easily spend a day noticing the human aspects of a tree or the treeness inside you. I don't mean to trivialize it; allowing the life of other beings to enter yours is an important and valuable skill for a writer and for all humans. When you surrender like that, you can't write from the ego, which is so dominant in our culture. I like the word *inter-living*, because in order to express something well you need to

---

[1] American poet (1879–1955). —EDS.

have observed the details of it so closely that the boundary between its life and yours becomes blurred. . . .

When our cows were pregnant in the spring, they would lie down in the snow and groan in the late afternoon sun. I'd go out and sit with them for hours — just hang out with them. I learned a lot from doing that. The more I gave myself over to being with them, the more equality I felt between us. They have a kingdom of their own consciousness, and you can enter into as much of that as you want. I think that's what writers have to do. When you write fiction, you give yourself over to the characters; when you write nonfiction, it's the same. Emerson[2] said, "You must treat the days respectfully, you must be a day yourself. And not interrogate life like a college professor. Everything in the universe goes by indirection. There are no straight lines."

## For Discussion

1. What do you make of the Wallace Stevens line "the palm at the end of the mind"? How might this line relate to Ehrlich's goal of finding "a language that actually embodies the life of what you are writing about"?
2. Ehrlich says that writing comes "from the gut," from having "observed the details of [the subject] so closely that the boundary between its life and yours becomes blurred." To what extent does this view apply to writing as you've experienced it? Are there stages of the writing process or types of writing in which letting go works well and other stages or types in which it doesn't?

---

[2] Ralph Waldo Emerson (1803–1882), American philosopher, poet, and essayist. — Eds.

# IAN FRAZIER

Born in 1951 in Cleveland, Ohio, IAN FRAZIER writes both humor and more serious nonfiction in which close observation reveals unnoticed qualities of his subjects. He grew up in Ohio and graduated in 1973 from Harvard University, where he worked on the humor magazine the *Harvard Lampoon*. Shortly after college, Frazier moved to New York City and became a staff writer for *The New Yorker*. While continuing to write for the magazine, he has also written books such as *Great Plains* (1989) and *On the Rez* (2000). His essays have been collected in *Dating Your Mom* (1986), *Coyote v. Acme* (1996), *The Fish's Eye* (2002), and, most recently, *Gone to New York* (2005). Frazier lives with his family in Montclair, New Jersey.

## *How to Operate the Shower Curtain*

In this 2007 essay from *The New Yorker*, Frazier targets a daily annoyance that may never before have been addressed in writing. Does your shower curtain sometimes stick to your body? Does the curtain tear off its rod? Providing an admirably clear if complicated process analysis, Frazier tells you what to do.

Dear Guest: The shower curtain in this bathroom has been purchased 1 with care at a reputable "big box" store in order to provide maximum convenience in showering. After you have read these instructions, you will find with a little practice that our shower curtain is as easy to use as the one you have at home.

You'll note that the shower curtain consists of several parts. The top hem, 2 closest to the ceiling, contains a series of regularly spaced holes designed for the insertion of shower-curtain rings. As this part receives much of the everyday strain of usage, it must be handled correctly. Grasp the shower curtain by its leading edge and gently pull until it is flush with the wall. Step into the tub, if you have not already done so. Then take the other edge of shower curtain and cautiously pull it in opposite direction until it, too, adjoins the wall. A little moisture between shower curtain and wall tiles will help curtain to stick.

Keep in mind that normal bathing will cause you unavoidably to bump 3 against shower curtain, which may cling to you for a moment owing to the natural adhesiveness of water. Some guests find the sensation of wet plastic on their naked flesh upsetting, and overreact to it. Instead, pinch the shower curtain between your thumb and forefinger near where it is adhering to you and simply move away from it until it is disengaged. Then, with the ends of your fingers, push it back to where it is supposed to be.

If shower curtain reattaches itself to you, repeat process above. Under certain atmospheric conditions, a convection effect creates air currents outside shower curtain which will press it against you on all sides no matter what you do. If this happens, stand directly under showerhead until bathroom microclimate stabilizes.

Many guests are surprised to learn that all water pipes in our system run off a single riser. This means that the opening of any hot or cold tap, or the flushing of a toilet, interrupts flow to shower. If you find water becoming extremely hot (or cold), exit tub promptly while using a sweeping motion with one arm to push shower curtain aside.

REMEMBER TO KEEP SHOWER CURTAIN *INSIDE* TUB AT ALL TIMES! Failure to do this may result in baseboard rot, wallpaper mildew, destruction of living-room ceiling below, and possible dripping onto catered refreshments at social event in your honor that you are about to attend. So be careful!

This shower curtain comes equipped with small magnets in shape of disks which have been sewn into the bottom hem at intervals. These serve no purpose whatsoever and may be ignored. Please do not tamper with them. The vertical lines, or pleats, which you may have wondered about, are there for a simple reason: user safety. If you have to move from the tub fast, as outlined above, the easy accordion-type folding motion of the pleats makes that possible. The gray substance in some of the inner pleat folds is a kind of insignificant mildew, less toxic than what is found on some foreign cheeses.

When detaching shower curtain from clinging to you or when exiting tub during a change in water temperature, bear in mind that there are seventeen mostly empty plastic bottles of shampoo on tub edge next to wall. These bottles have accumulated in this area over time. Many have been set upside down in order to concentrate the last amounts of fluid in their cap mechanisms, and are balanced lightly. Inadvertent contact with a thigh or knee can cause all the bottles to be knocked over and to tumble into the tub or behind it. If this should somehow happen, we ask that you kindly pick the bottles up and put them back in the same order in which you found them. Thank you.

While picking up the bottles, a guest occasionally will lose his or her balance temporarily, and, in even rarer cases, fall. If you find this occurring, remember that panic is the enemy here. Let your body go limp, while reminding yourself that the shower curtain is not designed to bear your weight. Grabbing onto it will only complicate the situation.

If, in a "worst case" scenario, you do take hold of the shower curtain, and the curtain rings tear through the holes in the upper hem as you were warned they might, remain motionless and relaxed in the position in which you come to rest. If subsequently you hear a knock on the bathroom door, respond to any questions by saying either "Fine" or "No, I'm fine." When the questioner goes away, stand up, turn off shower, and lay shower curtain flat on floor and up against tub so you can see the extent of the damage. With a sharp object—a nail file, a pen, or your teeth—make new holes in top hem next to the ones that tore through.

Now lift shower curtain with both hands and reattach it to shower-curtain 11 rings by unclipping, inserting, and reclipping them. If during this process the shower curtain slides down and again goes onto you, reach behind you to shelf under medicine cabinet, take nail file or curved fingernail scissors, and perform short, brisk slashing jabs on shower curtain to cut it back. It can always be repaired later with safety pins or adhesive tape from your toiletries kit.

At this point, you may prefer to get the shower curtain out of your way 12 entirely by gathering it up with both arms and ripping it down with a sharp yank. Now place it in the waste receptacle next to the john. In order that anyone who might be overhearing you will know that you are still all right, sing "Fat Bottomed Girls," by Queen, as loudly as necessary. While waiting for tub to fill, wedge shower curtain into waste receptacle more firmly by treading it underfoot with a regular high-knee action as if marching in place.

We are happy to have you as our guest. There are many choices you could 13 have made, but you are here, and we appreciate that. Operating the shower curtain is kind of tricky. Nobody is denying that. If you do not wish to deal with it, or if you would rather skip the whole subject for reasons you do not care to reveal, we accept your decision. You did not ask to be born. There is no need ever to touch the shower curtain again. If you would like to receive assistance, pound on the door, weep inconsolably, and someone will be along.

*For a reading quiz, sources on Ian Frazier, and annotated links to further readings on American humor writing, visit **bedfordstmartins.com/thebedfordreader**.*

---

## Journal Writing

Do Frazier's humorously complex directions remind you of any real instructions you've seen—perhaps for assembling a piece of furniture or using a tool? Or does the essay bring to mind a product or process that is as annoying as shower curtains or showering can be, such as using an umbrella on a windy day or flossing your teeth? In your journal, write about why the instructions are ridiculous or why the product or process is annoying. (To take your journal writing further, see "From Journal to Essay" below.)

## Questions on Meaning

1. According to the essay, what problems are users likely to encounter in using the shower curtain?
2. What is the THESIS of the host, Frazier's NARRATOR? What is Frazier's own implied thesis?
3. What is Frazier's PURPOSE in this essay?

## Questions on Writing Strategy

1. Instructions sometimes include headings to help guide readers through the various stages of the process being described. If Frazier had used headings for each stage of operating the shower curtain, what might they have been? (For example, par. 2 could be headed "Entering the Tub.")
2. Frazier uses *you* or imperative sentences that imply *you* ("Now lift shower curtain . . .") almost everywhere in the essay, but occasionally he shifts to "a guest" or "some guests" (for example, in par. 9). Why is this shift appropriate?
3. In paragraph 1, Frazier writes, "After you have read these instructions, you will find with a little practice that our shower curtain is as easy to use as the one you have at home." In the concluding paragraph, however, he writes, "Operating the shower curtain is kind of tricky. Nobody is denying that." Explain this contradiction.
4. **OTHER METHODS**   What role does CAUSE AND EFFECT play in paragraphs 7–12?

## Questions on Language

1. Identify a few instances of JARGON — inflated, wordy language and unnecessarily complicated word order — that Frazier uses for humorous effect in the essay.
2. Throughout the essay, Frazier often omits the article *the* before a noun. For example, *shower curtain* and *process* would normally be proceeded by *the* in the following: "If shower curtain reattaches itself to you, repeat process above" (par. 4). Why do you think Frazier chose to omit *the*?
3. Be sure you know the meanings of the following words: reputable (par. 1); adjoins (2); disengaged (3); convection, microclimate (4); riser (5); inadvertent (8); subsequently (10); treading (12); inconsolably (13).

## Suggestions for Writing

1. **FROM JOURNAL TO ESSAY**   Try your hand at writing a humorous process analysis for a product that should be easy to use or for a procedure that should be simple. You might imitate overly complicated instructions or write your own. Make your analysis detailed and clear.

2. Research some lawsuits that have caused companies to be overly cautious in the warning labels and instructions that they include with their products. Write a report in which you SUMMARIZE several cases and comment on what you think these examples reveal about our society.

3. Examine the directions for a product that you own. (If you don't have any handy, you can find directions for many products posted on the Web.) Pretending that you have no idea how to use the product at hand, EVALUATE the effectiveness of the instructions. Are all the necessary steps covered fully? Are unfamiliar terms defined clearly? Overall, would you be able to follow the instructions without difficulty?

4. **CRITICAL WRITING**  ANALYZE Frazier's TONE in this essay, focusing on how his DICTION, use of jargon, and sentence structures contribute to the essay's humor. Support your ideas with specific EVIDENCE from the essay.

5. **CONNECTIONS**  In "The World of Doublespeak" (p. 418), William Lutz defines doublespeak as "language that pretends to communicate but really doesn't" (par. 2). Write an essay explaining how the type of instructions that Frazier parodies are an example of doublespeak. What category or categories of doublespeak do such instructions illustrate? Use PARAPHRASES and QUOTATIONS from both essays to support your ideas.

---

## *Ian Frazier on Writing*

Both Ian Frazier's humor writing and his more serious nonfiction rely on his ability to see familiar subjects with a fresh eye. In a conversation with Jason Roberts for *The Believer*, Frazier explains why not knowing everything actually benefits a writer.

I'm opposed to expertise. For some reason, when I feel I am becoming an expert, I sabotage the whole thing. I mean, I've written about the West but I would never want to think of myself as somebody who writes about the West, as an expert on that subject. . . . In any subject, there will be the received wisdom about it, and you already know what that is. When I wrote *Great Plains*, as I was reading about the Great Plains I read a number of times that "the Plains Indians were the finest light cavalry the world had ever known." Now about the fourth time I read that sentence I realized it's just . . . something that you stamp on a book about the West. And it means zero. It's just a sound, as opposed to something. If you tell somebody you're writing a book about a subject—it doesn't really matter about the subject—you will immediately get the received wisdom back.

## For Discussion

1. What benefit does Frazier get from not being an expert on the subjects he writes about?
2. What is the difference between *received wisdom*, as Frazier uses the term, and *common knowledge*, or widely known facts? The latter is indispensable in writing (see p. 62). Why does Frazier view the former as undesirable?

# JESSICA MITFORD

Born in Batsford Mansion, England, in 1917, the daughter of Lord and Lady Redesdale, JESSICA MITFORD devoted much of her early life to defying her aristocratic upbringing. In her autobiography *Daughters and Rebels* (1960), she tells how she received a genteel schooling at home, then as a young woman moved to Loyalist Spain during the violent Spanish Civil War. Later, she immigrated to the United States, where for a time she worked in Miami as a bartender. She became one of her adopted country's most noted reporters: *Time* called her "Queen of the Muckrakers." Exposing with her typewriter what she regarded as corruption, abuse, and absurdity, Mitford wrote *The American Way of Death* (1963, revised as *The American Way of Death Revisited* in 1998), *Kind and Unusual Punishment: The Prison Business* (1973), and *The American Way of Birth* (1992). *Poison Penmanship* (1979) collects articles from *The Atlantic Monthly*, *Harper's*, and other magazines. *A Fine Old Conflict* (1976) is the second volume of Mitford's autobiography. And a novel, *Grace Had an English Heart* (1989), examines how the media transform ordinary people into celebrities. Jessica Mitford died in 1996.

# *Behind the Formaldehyde Curtain*

The most famous (or infamous) thing Jessica Mitford wrote is *The American Way of Death*, a critique of the funeral industry. In this selection from the book, Mitford analyzes the twin processes of embalming and restoring a corpse, the practices she finds most objectionable. You may need a stable stomach to enjoy the selection, but in it you'll find a clear, painstaking process analysis, written with masterly style and outrageous wit. (For those who want to know, Mitford herself was cremated after her death.)

The drama begins to unfold with the arrival of the corpse at the mortuary.   1

Alas, poor Yorick! How surprised he would be to see how his counterpart   2
of today is whisked off to a funeral parlor and is in short order sprayed, sliced, pierced, pickled, trussed, trimmed, creamed, waxed, painted, rouged, and neatly dressed — transformed from a common corpse into a Beautiful Memory Picture. This process is known in the trade as embalming and restorative art, and is so universally employed in the United States and Canada that the funeral director does it routinely, without consulting corpse or kin. He regards as eccentric those few who are hardy enough to suggest that it might be dispensed with. Yet no law requires embalming, no religious doctrine commends it, nor is it dictated by considerations of health, sanitation, or even of personal daintiness. In no part of the world but in Northern America is it widely used.

The purpose of embalming is to make the corpse presentable for viewing in a suitably costly container; and here too the funeral director routinely, without first consulting the family, prepares the body for public display.

Is all this legal? The processes to which a dead body may be subjected are     3 after all to some extent circumscribed by law. In most states, for instance, the signature of next of kin must be obtained before an autopsy may be performed, before the deceased may be cremated, before the body may be turned over to a medical school for research purposes; or such provision must be made in the decedent's will. In the case of embalming, no such permission is required nor is it ever sought.[1] A textbook, *The Principles and Practices of Embalming,* comments on this: "There is some question regarding the legality of much that is done within the preparation room." The author points out that it would be most unusual for a responsible member of a bereaved family to instruct the mortician, in so many words, to "embalm" the body of a deceased relative. The very term *embalming* is so seldom used that the mortician must rely upon custom in the matter. The author concludes that unless the family specifies otherwise, the act of entrusting the body to the care of a funeral establishment carries with it an implied permission to go ahead and embalm.

Embalming is indeed a most extraordinary procedure, and one must won-     4 der at the docility of Americans who each year pay hundreds of millions of dollars for its perpetuation, blissfully ignorant of what it is all about, what is done, how it is done. Not one in ten thousand has any idea of what actually takes place. Books on the subject are extremely hard to come by. They are not to be found in most libraries or bookshops.

In an era when huge television audiences watch surgical operations in     5 the comfort of their living rooms, when, thanks to the animated cartoon, the geography of the digestive system has become familiar territory even to the nursery school set, in a land where the satisfaction of curiosity about almost all matters is a national pastime, the secrecy surrounding embalming can, surely, hardly be attributed to the inherent gruesomeness of the subject. Custom in this regard has within this century suffered a complete reversal. In the early days of American embalming, when it was performed in the home of the deceased, it was almost mandatory for some relative to stay by the embalmer's side and witness the procedure. Today, family members who might wish to be

---

[1] Partly because of Mitford's attack, the Federal Trade Commission now requires the funeral industry to provide families with itemized price lists, including the price of embalming, to state that embalming is not required, and to obtain the family's consent to embalming before charging for it. Shortly before her death, however, Mitford observed that the FTC had "watered down" the regulations and "routinely ignored" consumer complaints about the funeral industry. — EDS.

in attendance would certainly be dissuaded by the funeral director. All others, except apprentices, are excluded by law from the preparation room.

A close look at what does actually take place may explain in large measure    6
the undertaker's intractable reticence concerning a procedure that has become his major *raison d'être*. Is it possible he fears that public information about embalming might lead patrons to wonder if they really want this service? If the funeral men are loath to discuss the subject outside the trade, the reader may, understandably, be equally loath to go on reading at this point. For those who have the stomach for it, let us part the formaldehyde curtain. . . .

The body is first laid out in the undertaker's morgue — or rather, Mr. Jones    7
is reposing in the preparation room — to be readied to bid the world farewell.

The preparation room in any of the better funeral establishments has the    8
tiled and sterile look of a surgery, and indeed the embalmer–restorative artist who does his chores there is beginning to adopt the term *dermasurgeon* (appropriately corrupted by some mortician-writers as "demi-surgeon") to describe his calling. His equipment, consisting of scalpels, scissors, augers, forceps, clamps, needles, pumps, tubes, bowls, and basins, is crudely imitative of the surgeon's, as is his technique, acquired in a nine- or twelve-month post-high-school course in an embalming school. He is supplied by an advanced chemical industry with a bewildering array of fluids, sprays, pastes, oils, powders, creams, to fix or soften tissue, shrink or distend it as needed, dry it here, restore the moisture there. There are cosmetics, waxes, and paints to fill and cover features, even plaster of Paris to replace entire limbs. There are ingenious aids to prop and stabilize the cadaver: a Vari-Pose Head Rest, the Edwards Arm and Hand Positioner, the Repose Block (to support the shoulders during the embalming), and the Throop Foot Positioner, which resembles an old-fashioned stocks.

Mr. John H. Eckels, president of the Eckels College of Mortuary Science,    9
thus describes the first part of the embalming procedure: "In the hands of a skilled practitioner, this work may be done in a comparatively short time and without mutilating the body other than by slight incision — so slight that it scarcely would cause serious inconvenience if made upon a living person. It is necessary to remove the blood, and doing this not only helps in the disinfecting, but removes the principal cause of disfigurements due to discoloration."

Another textbook discusses the all-important time element: "The ear-    10
lier this is done, the better, for every hour that elapses between death and embalming will add to the problems and complications encountered. . . ." Just how soon should one get going on the embalming? The author tells us, "On the basis of such scanty information made available to this profession through its rudimentary and haphazard system of technical research, we must conclude

that the best results are to be obtained if the subject is embalmed before life is completely extinct — that is, before cellular death has occurred. In the average case, this would mean within an hour after somatic death." For those who feel that there is something a little rudimentary, not to say haphazard, about this advice, a comforting thought is offered by another writer. Speaking of fears entertained in early days of premature burial, he points out, "One of the effects of embalming by chemical injection, however, has been to dispel fears of live burial." How true; once the blood is removed, chances of live burial are indeed remote.

To return to Mr. Jones, the blood is drained out through the veins and replaced by embalming fluid pumped in through the arteries. As noted in *The Principles and Practices of Embalming,* "every operator has a favorite injection and drainage point — a fact which becomes a handicap only if he fails or refuses to forsake his favorites when conditions demand it." Typical favorites are the carotid artery, femoral artery, jugular vein, subclavian vein. There are various choices of embalming fluid. If Flextone is used, it will produce a "mild, flexible rigidity. The skin retains a velvety softness, the tissues are rubbery and pliable. Ideal for women and children." It may be blended with B. and G. Products Company's Lyf-Lyk tint, which is guaranteed to reproduce "nature's own skin texture . . . the velvety appearance of living tissue." Suntone comes in three separate tints: Suntan; Special Cosmetic Tint, a pink shade "especially indicated for female subjects"; and Regular Cosmetic Tint, moderately pink. 11

About three to six gallons of a dyed and perfumed solution of formaldehyde, glycerin, borax, phenol, alcohol, and water is soon circulating through Mr. Jones, whose mouth has been sewn together with a "needle directed upward between the upper lip and gum and brought out through the left nostril," with the corners raised slightly "for a more pleasant expression." If he should be bucktoothed, his teeth are cleaned with Bon Ami and coated with colorless nail polish. His eyes, meanwhile, are closed with flesh-tinted eye caps and eye cement. 12

The next step is to have at Mr. Jones with a thing called a trocar. This is a long, hollow needle attached to a tube. It is jabbed into the abdomen, poked around the entrails and chest cavity, the contents of which are pumped out and replaced with "cavity fluid." This done, and the hole in the abdomen sewn up, Mr. Jones's face is heavily creamed (to protect the skin from burns which may be caused by leakage of the chemicals), and he is covered with a sheet and left unmolested for a while. But not for long — there is more, much more, in store for him. He has been embalmed, but not yet restored, and the best time to start the restorative work is eight to ten hours after embalming, when the tissues have become firm and dry. 13

The object of all this attention to the corpse, it must be remembered, is to     14
make it presentable for viewing in an attitude of healthy repose. "Our customs
require the presentation of our dead in the semblance of normality . . . un-
marred by the ravages of illness, disease, or mutilation," says Mr. J. Sheridan
Mayer in his *Restorative Art*. This is rather a large order since few people die
in the full bloom of health, unravaged by illness and unmarked by some dis-
figurement. The funeral industry is equal to the challenge: "In some cases the
gruesome appearance of a mutilated or disease-ridden subject may be quite
discouraging. The task of restoration may seem impossible and shake the confidence of the embalmer. This is the time for intestinal fortitude and determination. Once the formative work is begun and affected tissues are cleaned or
removed, all doubts of success vanish. It is surprising and gratifying to discover
the results which may be obtained."

The embalmer, having allowed an appropriate interval to elapse, returns     15
to the attack, but now he brings into play the skill and equipment of sculptor
and cosmetician. Is a hand missing? Casting one in plaster of Paris is a simple
matter. "For replacement purposes, only a cast of the back of the hand is necessary; this is within the ability of the average operator and is quite adequate."
If a lip or two, a nose, or an ear should be missing, the embalmer has at hand
a variety of restorative waxes with which to model replacements. Pores and
skin texture are simulated by stippling with a little brush, and over this cosmetics are laid on. Head off? Decapitation cases are rather routinely handled.
Ragged edges are trimmed, and head joined to torso with a series of splints,
wires, and sutures. It is a good idea to have a little something at the neck — a
scarf or a high collar — when time for viewing comes. Swollen mouth? Cut
out tissue as needed from inside the lips. If too much is removed, the surface
contour can easily be restored by padding with cotton. Swollen necks and
cheeks are reduced by removing tissue through vertical incisions made down
each side of the neck. "When the deceased is casketed, the pillow will hide
the suture incisions . . . as an extra precaution against leakage, the suture may
be painted with liquid sealer."

The opposite condition is more likely to present itself — that of emaciation.     16
His hypodermic syringe now loaded with massage cream, the embalmer seeks
out and fills the hollowed and sunken areas by injection. In this procedure the
backs of the hands and fingers and the under-chin area should not be neglected.

Positioning the lips is a problem that recurrently challenges the ingenuity     17
of the embalmer. Closed too tightly, they tend to give a stern, even disapproving
expression. Ideally, embalmers feel, the lips should give the impression of
being ever so slightly parted, the upper lip protruding slightly for a more
youthful appearance. This takes some engineering, however, as the lips tend
to drift apart. Lip drift can sometimes be remedied by pushing one or two

straight pins through the inner margin of the lower lip and then inserting them between the two front upper teeth. If Mr. Jones happens to have no teeth, the pins can just as easily be anchored in his Armstrong Face Former and Denture Replacer. Another method to maintain lip closure is to dislocate the lower jaw, which is then held in its new position by a wire run through holes which have been drilled through the upper and lower jaws at the midline. As the French are fond of saying, *il faut souffrir pour être belle*.[2]

If Mr. Jones has died of jaundice, the embalming fluid will very likely turn him green. Does this deter the embalmer? Not if he has intestinal fortitude. Masking pastes and cosmetics are heavily laid on, burial garments and casket interiors are color-correlated with particular care, and Jones is displayed beneath rose-colored lights. Friends will say "How *well* he looks." Death by carbon monoxide, on the other hand, can be rather a good thing from the embalmer's viewpoint: "One advantage is the fact that this type of discoloration is an exaggerated form of a natural pink coloration." This is nice because the healthy glow is already present and needs but little attention. [18]

The patching and filling completed, Mr. Jones is now shaved, washed, and dressed. Cream-based cosmetic, available in pink, flesh, suntan, brunette, and blond, is applied to his hands and face, his hair is shampooed and combed (and, in the case of Mrs. Jones, set), his hands manicured. For the horny-handed son of toil special care must be taken; cream should be applied to remove ingrained grime, and the nails cleaned. "If he were not in the habit of having them manicured in life, trimming and shaping is advised for better appearance—never questioned by kin." [19]

Jones is now ready for casketing (this is the present participle of the verb "to casket"). In this operation his right shoulder should be depressed slightly "to turn the body a bit to the right and soften the appearance of lying flat on the back." Positioning the hands is a matter of importance, and special rubber positioning blocks may be used. The hands should be cupped slightly for a more lifelike, relaxed appearance. Proper placement of the body requires a delicate sense of balance. It should lie as high as possible in the casket, yet not so high that the lid, when lowered, will hit the nose. On the other hand, we are cautioned, placing the body too low "creates the impression that the body is in a box." [20]

Jones is next wheeled into the appointed slumber room where a few last touches may be added—his favorite pipe placed in his hand or, if he was a great reader, a book propped into position. (In the case of little Master Jones a Teddy bear may be clutched.) Here he will hold open house for a few days, visiting hours 10 AM to 9 PM. [21]

[2] You have to suffer to be beautiful. —EDS.

All now being in readiness, the funeral director calls a staff conference to          22
make sure that each assistant knows his precise duties. Mr. Wilber Kriege
writes: "This makes your staff feel that they are a part of the team, with a definite assignment that must be properly carried out if the whole plan is to succeed. You never heard of a football coach who failed to talk to his entire team
before they go on the field. They have drilled on the plays they are to execute
for hours and days, and yet the successful coach knows the importance of making even the benchwarming third-string substitute feel that he is important if
the game is to be won." The winning of *this* game is predicated upon glass-
smooth handling of the logistics. The funeral director has notified the pall-
bearers whose names were furnished by the family, has arranged for the
presence of clergyman, organist, and soloist, has provided transportation for
everybody, has organized and listed the flowers sent by friends. In *Psychology of
Funeral Service* Mr. Edward A. Martin points out, "He may not always do as
much as the family thinks he is doing, but it is his helpful guidance that they
appreciate in knowing they are proceeding as they should. . . . The important
thing is how well his services can be used to make the family believe they are
giving unlimited expression to their own sentiment."

The religious service may be held in a church or in the chapel of the          23
funeral home; the funeral director vastly prefers the latter arrangement, for
not only is it more convenient for him but it affords him the opportunity to
show off his beautiful facilities to the gathered mourners. After the clergyman
has had his say, the mourners queue up to file past the casket for a last look at
the deceased. The family is *never* asked whether they want an open-casket ceremony; in the absence of their instruction to the contrary, this is taken for
granted. Consequently well over 90 percent of all American funerals feature
the open casket—a custom unknown in other parts of the world. Foreigners
are astonished by it. An English woman living in San Francisco described her
reaction in a letter to the writer:

> I myself have attended only one funeral here—that of an elderly fel-
> low worker of mine. After the service I could not understand why everyone
> was walking towards the coffin (sorry, I mean casket), but thought I had
> better follow the crowd. It shook me rigid to get there and find the casket
> open and poor old Oscar lying there in his brown tweed suit, wearing a sun-
> tan makeup and just the wrong shade of lipstick. If I had not been extremely
> fond of the old boy, I have a horrible feeling that I might have giggled. Then
> and there I decided that I could never face another American funeral—
> even dead.

The casket (which has been resting throughout the service on a Classic          24
Beauty Ultra Metal Casket Bier) is now transferred by a hydraulically operated
device called Porto-Lift to a balloon-tired, Glide Easy casket carriage which

will wheel it to yet another conveyance, the Cadillac Funeral Coach. This may be lavender, cream, light green—anything but black. Interiors, of course, are color-correlated, "for the man who cannot stop short of perfection."

At graveside, the casket is lowered into the earth. This office, once the prerogative of friends of the deceased, is now performed by a patented mechanical lowering device. A "Lifetime Green" artificial grass mat is at the ready to conceal the sere earth, and overhead, to conceal the sky, is a portable Steril Chapel Tent ("resists the intense heat and humidity of summer and the terrific storms of winter . . . available in Silver Gray, Rose, or Evergreen"). Now is the time for the ritual scattering of earth over the coffin, as the solemn words "earth to earth, ashes to ashes, dust to dust" are pronounced by the officiating cleric. This can today be accomplished "with a mere flick of the wrist with the Gordon Leak-Proof Earth Dispenser. No grasping of a handful of dirt, no soiled fingers. Simple, dignified, beautiful, reverent! The modern way!" The Gordon Earth Dispenser (at $5) is of nickel-plated brass construction. It is not only "attractive to the eye and long wearing"; it is also "one of the 'tools' for building better public relations" if presented as "an appropriate non-commercial gift" to the clergyman. It is shaped something like a saltshaker. 25

Untouched by human hand, the coffin and the earth are now united. 26

It is in the function of directing the participants through this maze of gadgetry that the funeral director has assigned to himself his relatively new role of "grief therapist." He has relieved the family of every detail, he has revamped the corpse to look like a living doll, he has arranged for it to nap for a few days in a slumber room, he has put on a well-oiled performance in which the concept of *death* has played no part whatsoever—unless it was inconsiderately mentioned by the clergyman who conducted the religious service. He has done everything in his power to make the funeral a real pleasure for everybody concerned. He and his team have given their all to score an upset victory over death. 27

*For a reading quiz, sources on Jessica Mitford, and annotated links to further readings on customs related to death, visit* **bedfordstmartins.com/thebedfordreader.**

## Journal Writing

Presumably, morticians embalm and restore corpses, and survivors support the work, because the practices are thought to ease the shock of death. Now that you know what goes on behind the scenes, how do you feel about a loved one's undergoing these procedures? (To take your journal writing further, see "From Journal to Essay" on the facing page.)

## Questions on Meaning

1.  What was your emotional response to this essay? Can you analyze your feelings?
2.  To what does the author attribute the secrecy surrounding the embalming process?
3.  What, according to Mitford, is the mortician's intent? What common obstacles to fulfilling it must be surmounted?
4.  What do you understand from Mitford's remark in paragraph 10, on dispelling fears of live burial: "How true; once the blood is removed, chances of live burial are indeed remote"?
5.  Do you find any implied PURPOSE in this essay? Does Mitford seem primarily out to rake muck, or does she offer any positive suggestions to Americans?

## Questions on Writing Strategy

1.  What is Mitford's TONE? In her opening two paragraphs, exactly what shows her attitude toward her subject?
2.  Why do you think Mitford goes into so much grisly detail in analyzing the processes of embalming and restoration? How does the detail serve her purpose?
3.  What is the EFFECT of calling the body Mr. Jones (or Master Jones)?
4.  Paragraph by paragraph, what TRANSITIONS does the author employ? (If you need a refresher on this point, see the discussion of transitions on p. 704.)
5.  To whom does Mitford address her process analysis? How do you know she isn't writing for an AUDIENCE of professional morticians?
6.  Consider one of the quotations from the journals and textbooks of professionals and explain how it serves the author's general purpose.
7.  Why do you think Mitford often uses PASSIVE verbs to describe the actions of embalmers—for instance, "the blood is drained," "If Flextone is used," and "It may be blended" in paragraph 11? Are the passive verbs effective or ineffective? Why?
8.  **OTHER METHODS**   In paragraph 8, Mitford uses CLASSIFICATION in listing the embalmer's equipment and supplies. What groups does she identify, and why does she bother sorting the items at all?

## Questions on Language

1.  Explain the ALLUSION to Yorick in paragraph 2.
2.  What IRONY do you find in this statement in paragraph 7: "The body is first laid out in the undertaker's morgue—or rather, Mr. Jones is reposing in the

preparation room"? Pick out any other words or phrases in the essay that seem ironic. Comment especially on those you find in the essay's last two sentences.

3. Why is it useful to Mitford's purpose that she cites the brand names of morticians' equipment and supplies (the Edwards Arm and Hand Positioner, Lyf-Lyk tint)? List all the brand names in the essay that are memorable.

4. Define the following words or terms: counterpart (par. 2); circumscribed, autopsy, cremated, decedent, bereaved (3); docility, perpetuation (4); inherent, mandatory (5); intractable, reticence, *raison d'être*, formaldehyde (6); "derma-" (in *dermasurgeon*), augers, forceps, distend, stocks (8); somatic (10); carotid artery, femoral artery, jugular vein, subclavian vein, pliable (11); glycerin, borax, phenol, bucktoothed (12); trocar, entrails (13); stippling, sutures (15); emaciation (16); jaundice (18); predicated (22); queue (23); hydraulically (24); cleric, sere (25); therapist (27).

## Suggestions for Writing

1. **FROM JOURNAL TO ESSAY**    Drawing on your personal response to Mitford's essay in your journal, write a brief essay that ARGUES either for or against embalming and restoration. Consider the purposes served by these practices, both for the mortician and for the dead person's relatives and friends, as well as their costs and effects.

2. Search the Web or consult a periodical index for sources of information about the phenomenon of quick-freezing the dead. Set forth this process, including its hoped-for result of being able to revive the corpses in the far future.

3. ANALYZE some other process whose operations may not be familiar to everyone. (Have you ever held a job, or helped out in a family business, that has taken you behind the scenes? How is fast food prepared? How are cars serviced? How is a baby sat? How is a house constructed?) Detail it step by step, including transitions to clarify the steps.

4. **CRITICAL WRITING**    In attacking the funeral industry, Mitford also, implicitly, attacks the people who pay for and comply with the industry's attitudes and practices. What ASSUMPTIONS does Mitford seem to make about how we ought to deal with death and the dead? (Consider, for instance, her statements about the "docility of Americans, . . . blissfully ignorant" [par. 4] and the funeral director's making "the funeral a real pleasure for everybody concerned" [27].) Write an essay in which you interpret Mitford's assumptions and agree or disagree with them, based on your own reading and experience. If you like, defend the ritual of the funeral, or the mortician's profession, against Mitford's attack.

5. **CONNECTIONS**    In "Size 6: The Western Women's Harem" (p. 252), Fatema Mernissi also comments on Americans' obsession with physical appearance. Taken together, what do Mitford's and Mernissi's essays say about the importance of the body in our culture? Write an essay either defending or criticizing Americans' preoccupation with the way they look.

---

## *Jessica Mitford on Writing*

"Choice of subject is of cardinal importance," declared Jessica Mitford in *Poison Penmanship*. "One does by far one's best work when besotted by and absorbed in the matter at hand." After *The American Way of Death* was pub-lished, Mitford received hundreds of letters suggesting alleged rackets that ought to be exposed, and to her surprise, an overwhelming majority of these letters complained about defective and overpriced hearing aids. But Mitford never wrote a book blasting the hearing aid industry. "Somehow, although there may well be need for such an exposé, I could not warm up to hearing aids as a subject for the kind of thorough, intensive, long-range research that would be needed to do an effective job." She once taught a course at Yale on muckraking, with each student choosing a subject to investigate. "Those who tackled hot issues on campus, such as violations of academic freedom or fail-ure to implement affirmative-action hiring policies, turned in some excellent work; but the lad who decided to investigate 'waste in the Yale dining halls' was predictably unable to make much of this trivial topic." (The editors inter-ject: We aren't sure that the topic is necessarily trivial, but obviously not everyone would burn to write about it!)

The hardest problem Mitford faced in writing *The American Way of Death*, she recalled, was doing her factual, step-by-step account of the embalming process. She felt "determined to describe it in all its revolting details, but how to make this subject palatable to the reader?" Her solution was to cast the whole process analysis in the official JARGON of the mortuary industry, draw-ing on lists of taboo words and their EUPHEMISMS (or acceptable synonyms), as published in the trade journal *Casket & Sunnyside*: "Mr., Mrs., Miss Blank, not corpse or body; preparation room, not morgue; reposing room, not laying-out room. . . ." The story of Mr. Jones thus took shape, and Mitford's use of jargon, she found, added macabre humor to the proceedings.

### For Discussion

1. What seem to be Mitford's criteria for an effective essay or book?
2. What is muckraking? Why do you suppose anyone would want to do it?

# DANIEL OROZCO

DANIEL OROZCO was born in 1957 and grew up in San Francisco. After graduating from Stanford University in 1979, he held temporary positions doing clerical work while studying writing at San Francisco State University and rediscovering a passion for literature. He received an MFA in writing from the University of Washington, was a creative-writing fellow at Stanford, and currently teaches at the University of Idaho. In 2006 he won a writing fellowship from the National Endowment for the Arts and his story "Samoza's Dream" was a finalist for a National Magazine Award in fiction. Orozco's stories have appeared in *Harper's*, *Story*, and other magazines and have been chosen for *The Best American Short Stories*, the *Pushcart Prize Anthology*, and *The Best American Mystery Stories*. Orozco also writes a regular column for the *San Francisco Chronicle Book Review*.

## *Orientation*

Drawing on his experience as an office temp, Orozco created this story in which an employee introduces a newcomer to a company's procedures and people. Like the comic strip *Dilbert* and the TV show *The Office*, the story is a critique of cubicle culture, this one with its own humorously sinister undercurrents. First published in *Seattle Review* in 1994, "Orientation" appeared in *The Best American Short Stories 1995*. It has also been read on public radio's *This American Life* and even adapted as a dance piece.

Those are the offices and these are the cubicles. That's my cubicle there, 1 and this is your cubicle. This is your phone. Never answer your phone. Let the Voicemail System answer it. This is your Voicemail System Manual. There are no personal phone calls allowed. We do, however, allow for emergencies. If you must make an emergency phone call, ask your supervisor first. If you can't find your supervisor, ask Phillip Spiers, who sits over there. He'll check with Clarissa Nicks, who sits over there. If you make an emergency phone call without asking, you may be let go.

These are your IN and OUT boxes. All the forms in your IN box must be 2 logged in by the date shown in the upper left-hand corner, initialed by you in the upper right-hand corner, and distributed to the Processing Analyst whose name is numerically coded in the lower left-hand corner. The lower right-hand corner is left blank. Here's your Processing Analyst Numerical Code Index. And here's your Forms Processing Procedures Manual.

You must pace your work. What do I mean? I'm glad you asked that. We 3 pace our work according to the eight-hour workday. If you have twelve hours of work in your IN box, for example, you must compress that work into the eight-hour day. If you have one hour of work in your IN box, you must expand that work to fill the eight-hour day. That was a good question. Feel free to ask questions. Ask too many questions, however, and you may be let go.

That is our receptionist. She is a temp. We go through receptionists here. They quit with alarming frequency. Be polite and civil to the temps. Learn their names, and invite them to lunch occasionally. But don't get close to them, as it only makes it more difficult when they leave. And they always leave. You can be sure of that.

The men's room is over there. The women's room is over there. John LaFountaine, who sits over there, uses the women's room occasionally. He says it is accidental. We know better, but we let it pass. John LaFountaine is harmless, his forays into the forbidden territory of the women's room simply a benign thrill, a faint blip on the dull flat line of his life.

Russell Nash, who sits in the cubicle to your left, is in love with Amanda Pierce, who sits in the cubicle to your right. They ride the same bus together after work. For Amanda Pierce, it is just a tedious bus ride made less tedious by the idle nattering of Russell Nash. But for Russell Nash, it is the highlight of his day. It is the highlight of his life. Russell Nash has put on forty pounds, and grows fatter with each passing month, nibbling on chips and cookies while peeking glumly over the partitions at Amanda Pierce, and gorging himself at home on cold pizza and ice cream while watching adult videos on TV.

Amanda Pierce, in the cubicle to your right, has a six-year-old son named Jamie, who is autistic. Her cubicle is plastered from top to bottom with the boy's crayon artwork—sheet after sheet of precisely drawn concentric circles and ellipses, in black and yellow. She rotates them every other Friday. Be sure to comment on them. Amanda Pierce also has a husband, who is a lawyer. He subjects her to an escalating array of painful and humiliating sex games, to which Amanda Pierce reluctantly submits. She comes to work exhausted and freshly wounded each morning, wincing from the abrasions on her breasts, or the bruises on her abdomen, or the second-degree burns on the backs of her thighs.

But we're not supposed to know any of this. Do not let on. If you let on, you may be let go.

Amanda Pierce, who tolerates Russell Nash, is in love with Albert Bosch, whose office is over there. Albert Bosch, who only dimly registers Amanda Pierce's existence, has eyes only for Ellie Tapper, who sits over there. Ellie Tapper, who hates Albert Bosch, would walk through fire for Curtis Lance. But Curtis Lance hates Ellie Tapper. Isn't the world a funny place? Not in the ha-ha sense, of course.

Anika Bloom sits in that cubicle. Last year, while reviewing quarterly reports in a meeting with Barry Hacker, Anika Bloom's left palm began to bleed. She fell into a trance, stared into her hand, and told Barry Hacker when and how his wife would die. We laughed it off. She was, after all, a new employee. But Barry Hacker's wife is dead. So unless you want to know exactly when and how you'll die, never talk to Anika Bloom.

Colin Heavey sits in that cubicle over there. He was new once, just like  11 you. We warned him about Anika Bloom. But at last year's Christmas Potluck, he felt sorry for her when he saw that no one was talking to her. Colin Heavey brought her a drink. He hasn't been himself since. Colin Heavey is doomed. There's nothing he can do about it, and we are powerless to help him. Stay away from Colin Heavey. Never give any of your work to him. If he asks to do something, tell him you have to check with me. If he asks again, tell him I haven't gotten back to you.

This is the Fire Exit. There are several on this floor, and they are marked  12 accordingly. We have a Floor Evacuation Review every three months, and an Escape Route Quiz once a month. We have our Biannual Fire Drill twice a year, and our Annual Earthquake Drill once a year. These are precautions only. These things never happen.

For your information, we have a comprehensive health plan. Any cata-  13 strophic illness, any unforeseen tragedy is completely covered. All dependents are completely covered. Larry Bagdikian, who sits over there, has six daughters. If anything were to happen to any of his girls, or to all of them, if all six were to simultaneously fall victim to illness or injury—stricken with a hideous degenerative muscle disease or some rare toxic blood disorder, sprayed with semiautomatic gunfire while on a class field trip, or attacked in their bunk beds by some prowling nocturnal lunatic—if any of this were to pass, Larry's girls would all be taken care of. Larry Bagdikian would not have to pay one dime. He would have nothing to worry about.

We also have a generous vacation and sick leave policy. We have an  14 excellent disability insurance plan. We have a stable and profitable pension fund. We get group discounts for the symphony, and block seating at the ballpark. We get commuter ticket books for the bridge. We have Direct Deposit. We are all members of Costco.

This is our kitchenette. And this, this is our Mr. Coffee. We have a coffee  15 pool, into which we each pay two dollars a week for coffee, filters, sugar, and CoffeeMate. If you prefer Cremora or half-and-half to CoffeeMate, there is a special pool for three dollars a week. If you prefer Sweet 'n Low to sugar, there is a special pool for two-fifty a week. We do not do decaf. You are allowed to join the coffee pool of your choice, but you are not allowed to touch the Mr. Coffee.

This is the microwave oven. You are allowed to *heat* food in the micro-  16 wave oven. You are not, however, allowed to *cook* food in the microwave oven.

We get one hour for lunch. We also get one fifteen-minute break in the          17
morning, and one fifteen-minute break in the afternoon. Always take your
breaks. If you skip a break, it is gone forever. For your information, your break
is a privilege, not a right. If you abuse the break policy, we are authorized to
rescind your breaks. Lunch, however, is a right, not a privilege. If you abuse
the lunch policy, our hands will be tied, and we will be forced to look the
other way. We will not enjoy that.

This is the refrigerator. You may put your lunch in it. Barry Hacker, who          18
sits over there, steals food from this refrigerator. His petty theft is an outlet for
his grief. Last New Year's Eve, while kissing his wife, a blood vessel burst in her
brain. Barry Hacker's wife was two months pregnant at the time, and lingered
in a coma for half a year before dying. It was a tragic loss for Barry Hacker. He
hasn't been himself since. Barry Hacker's wife was a beautiful woman. She was
also completely covered. Barry Hacker did not have to pay one dime. But his
dead wife haunts him. She haunts all of us. We have seen her, reflected in the
monitors of our computers, moving past our cubicles. We have seen the dim
shadow of her face in our photocopies. She pencils herself in in the receptionist's appointment book, with the notation: To see Barry Hacker. She has
left messages in the receptionist's Voicemail box, messages garbled by the electronic chirrups and buzzes in the phone line, her voice echoing from an
immense distance within the ambient hum. But the voice is hers. And
beneath her voice, beneath the tidal *whoosh* of static and hiss, the gurgling
and crying of a baby can be heard.

In any case, if you bring a lunch, put a little something extra in the bag for          19
Barry Hacker. We have four Barrys in this office. Isn't that a coincidence?

This is Matthew Payne's office. He is our Unit Manager, and his door is          20
always closed. We have never seen him, and you will never see him. But he is
here. You can be sure of that. He is all around us.

This is the Custodian's Closet. You have no business in the Custodian's          21
Closet.

And this, this is our Supplies Cabinet. If you need supplies, see Curtis          22
Lance. He will log you in on the Supplies Cabinet Authorization Log, then
give you a Supplies Authorization Slip. Present your pink copy of the Supplies
Authorization Slip to Ellie Tapper. She will log you in on the Supplies Cabinet Key Log, then give you the key. Because the Supplies Cabinet is located
outside the Unit Manager's office, you must be very quiet. Gather your supplies quietly. The Supplies Cabinet is divided into four sections. Section One
contains letterhead stationery, blank paper and envelopes, memo and note
pads, and so on. Section Two contains pens and pencils and typewriter and
printer ribbons, and the like. In Section Three we have erasers, correction fluids, transparent tapes, glue sticks, et cetera. And in Section Four we have

paper clips and push pins and scissors and razor blades. And here are the spare blades for the shredder. Do not touch the shredder, which is located over there. The shredder is of no concern to you.

Gwendolyn Stich sits in that office there. She is crazy about penguins, and collects penguin knickknacks: penguin posters and coffee mugs and stationery, penguin stuffed animals, penguin jewelry, penguin sweaters and T-shirts and socks. She has a pair of penguin fuzzy slippers she wears when working late at the office. She has a tape cassette of penguin sounds which she listens to for relaxation. Her favorite colors are black and white. She has personalized license plates that read PEN GWEN. Every morning, she passes through all the cubicles to wish each of us a *good* morning. She brings Danish on Wednesdays for Hump Day morning break, and doughnuts on Fridays for TGIF afternoon break. She organizes the Annual Christmas Potluck, and is in charge of the Birthday List. Gwendolyn Stich's door is always open to all of us. She will always lend an ear, and put in a good word for you; she will always give you a hand, or the shirt off her back, or a shoulder to cry on. Because her door is always open, she hides and cries in a stall in the women's room. And John LaFountaine—who, enthralled when a woman enters, sits quietly in his stall with his knees to his chest—John LaFountaine has heard her vomiting in there. We have come upon Gwendolyn Stich huddled in the stairwell, shivering in the updraft, sipping a Diet Mr. Pibb and hugging her knees. She does not let any of this interfere with her work. If it interfered with her work, she might have to be let go.

Kevin Howard sits in that cubicle over there. He is a serial killer, the one they call the Carpet Cutter, responsible for the mutilations across town. We're not supposed to know that, so do not let on. Don't worry. His compulsion inflicts itself on strangers only, and the routine established is elaborate and unwavering. The victim must be a white male, a young adult no older than thirty, heavyset, with dark hair and eyes, and the like. The victim must be chosen at random, before sunset, from a public place; the victim is followed home, and must put up a struggle; et cetera. The carnage inflicted is precise: the angle and direction of the incisions; the layering of skin and muscle tissue; the rearrangement of the visceral organs; and so on. Kevin Howard does not let any of this interfere with his work. He is, in fact, our fastest typist. He types as if he were on fire. He has a secret crush on Gwendolyn Stich, and leaves a red-foil-wrapped Hershey's Kiss on her desk every afternoon. But he hates Anika Bloom, and keeps well away from her. In his presence, she has uncontrollable fits of shaking and trembling. Her left palm does not stop bleeding.

In any case, when Kevin Howard gets caught, act surprised. Say that he seemed like a nice person, a bit of a loner, perhaps, but always quiet and polite.

This is the photocopier room. And this, this is our view. It faces south-    26
west. West is down there, toward the water. North is back there. Because we
are on the seventeenth floor, we are afforded a magnificent view. Isn't it beautiful? It overlooks the park, where the tops of those trees are. You can see a segment of the bay between those two buildings there. You can see the sun set in
the gap between those two buildings over there. You can see this building
reflected in the glass panels of that building across the way. There. See? That's
you, waving. And look there. There's Anika Bloom in the kitchenette, waving back.

Enjoy this view while photocopying. If you have problems with the pho-    27
tocopier, see Russell Nash. If you have any questions, ask your supervisor. If
you can't find your supervisor, ask Phillip Spiers. He sits over there. He'll
check with Clarissa Nicks. She sits over there. If you can't find them, feel free
to ask me. That's my cubicle. I sit in there.

*For a reading quiz, sources on Daniel Orozco, and annotated links to further read-
ings on office culture, visit* **bedfordstmartins.com/thebedfordreader***.*

---

## Journal Writing

Think of a situation in which you had to learn new procedures, customs, or people.
You may have had a lot of help, as in a training program, or you may have had to go it
alone. In your journal write down what you recall most vividly about the process of
your orientation. (To take your journal writing further, see "From Journal to Essay" on
the facing page.)

## Questions on Meaning

1. This story seems to be a SATIRE, but what exactly is being satirized?
2. Where does the story's speaker provide information like that in a true job orientation? information that seems appropriate but exaggerated? information that is
   inappropriate for an orientation, even outrageous? What does this mix of information add to the story?
3. What view of the human condition does Orozco seem to offer in this story?

## Questions on Writing Strategy

1. What is the EFFECT of the last paragraph's echo of the first paragraph?
2. What other repetition do you notice in paragraphs 1, 3, 8, and 23? What is its effect?
3. What parts of this story illustrate process analysis?
4. **OTHER METHODS**   What do the EXAMPLES in paragraph 13 suggest about the speaker's interests and attitudes?

## Questions on Language

1. How would you describe the speaker's overall TONE? What does this tone contribute to the effect of the story?
2. In paragraph 18 the speaker's tone shifts rather dramatically. What is the shift? How do you account for it?
3. Where does Orozco satirize the language of bureaucracy most obviously?
4. Consult a dictionary if you are uncertain of the meaning of any of the following: cubicles (par. 1); forays, benign (5); autistic, abrasions (7); degenerative, nocturnal (13); rescind (17); TGIF, enthralled (23).

## Suggestions for Writing

1. **FROM JOURNAL TO ESSAY**   Compose an essay that explains the process of orientation you wrote about in your journal. Depending on your experience, you may present the process in formal stages or relate what happened in a NARRATIVE.
2. Expand your knowledge about working in an office by interviewing friends and family members who have done so. (If you have worked in an office, add your information to the others'.) Ask about experiences with supervisors, coworkers, procedures, and equipment. In an essay SYNTHESIZE what you discover. What do offices seem to have in common, and how do they differ?
3. **CRITICAL WRITING**   Analyze how Orozco structures his story. How does the speaker move from one stop on the tour to the next? Does the story seem to build in a particular way? What does the organization contribute to the story's effect?
4. **CONNECTIONS**   Both Orozco in this story and Don DeLillo in the story "Videotape" (p. 468) create speakers who address a *you* directly. In an essay consider the similarities and differences between the two authors' speakers and how they seem to conceive of their listeners.

---

# *Daniel Orozco on Writing*

In an interview with Will Allison for *Novel and Short Story Writer's Market*, Orozco talks about taking his time while writing. "My slowness as a writer seems to be part of a deliberate composition process," he says. "Before I actually begin writing a story, it goes through what I call Gestation and Frustration. Gestation: A story for me begins as an image or situation knocking around in my head, followed by months of notes jotted on scraps of paper, or entered into a file on my PC. This is followed finally by attempts at writing a first draft. Then, Frustration: I can set an unfinished draft aside for anywhere from days to months, during which time I do some reading or research on the story—a great way to avoid actually writing it—or I research or write another story. Eventually, I get back to finishing the first draft, and then I get to revising."

Most of Orozco's process is dedicated to revision, a stage he enjoys more than the initial drafting even though it can be more difficult. In 2001 Orozco published a story that he had worked on intermittently since 1978. "Orientation," which took eleven months, was, Orozco says, "the fastest I'd ever written anything." Asked whether his slow writing process bothers him, Orozco admits, "I used to bitch and moan about . . . how long it would take me to squeeze out a story." But he's learned to accept his writing process as something he can't—and wouldn't—change: "Now I embrace it as simply the way I write stories, stories that I am happy with. I used to wish I wrote faster, but I don't anymore. It's like wishing I were taller—it just ain't gonna happen."

## For Discussion

1. Why won't Orozco change his writing process? What does it do for him that another process might not?
2. Do you consider yourself a particularly slow or fast writer? Do you have trouble getting down the first draft, or do you find it more difficult to revise?

# ADDITIONAL WRITING TOPICS
## *Process Analysis*

1. Write a *directive* process analysis (a "how-to" essay) in which, drawing on your own knowledge, you instruct someone in doing or making something. Divide the process into steps, and be sure to detail each step thoroughly. Some possible subjects (any of which may be modified or narrowed):

   How to create a Web site or a blog
   How to post a video on *YouTube*
   How to enlist people's confidence
   How to bake bread
   How to meditate
   How to teach a child to swim
   How to select a science fiction novel
   How to drive a car in snow or rain
   How to prepare yourself to take an intelligence test
   How to compose a photograph
   How to judge cattle
   How to buy a used motorcycle
   How to enjoy an opera
   How to organize your own rock group
   How to eat an artichoke
   How to groom a horse
   How to belly dance
   How to build (or fly) a kite
   How to start weight training
   How to aid a person who is choking
   How to behave on a first date
   How to get your own way
   How to kick a habit
   How to lose weight
   How to win at poker
   How to make an effective protest or complaint

   Or, if you don't like any of those topics, what else do you know that others might care to learn from you?

2. Step by step, working in chronological order, write a careful *informative* analysis of any one of the following processes. (This is not to be a "how-to" essay, but an essay that explains how something works or happens.) Make use of DESCRIPTION wherever necessary, and be sure to include frequent TRANSITIONS. If one of these topics gives you a better idea for a paper, go with your own subject.

   How a student is processed during orientation or registration
   How the student newspaper gets published
   How a particular Web search engine works
   How a stereo amplifier or an MP3 player works

How a professional umpire (or an acupuncturist, or some other professional) does his or her job

How an air conditioner (or other household appliance) works

How birds teach their young (or some other process in the natural world: how sharks feed, how a snake swallows an egg, how the human liver works)

How police control crowds

How people usually make up their minds when shopping for new cars (or new clothes)

3. Write a directive process analysis in which you use a light TONE. Although you need not take your subject in deadly earnest, your humor will probably be effective only if you take the method of process analysis seriously. Make clear each stage of the process and explain it in sufficient detail. Possible topics:

How to get through the month of November (or March)

How to flunk out of college swiftly and efficiently

How to outwit a pinball machine

How to choose a mate

How to go broke

How to sell something that nobody wants

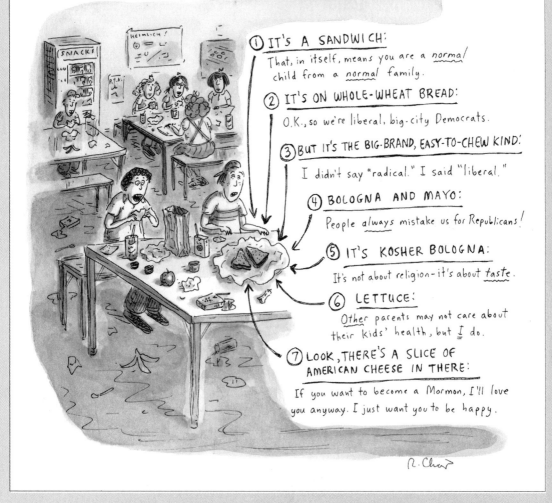

# 9

---

# DIVISION OR ANALYSIS

*Slicing into Parts*

◄ **Division or analysis in a cartoon**

The cartoonist Roz Chast is well known for witty and perceptive comments on the everyday, made through words and simple,
almost childlike drawings. Dividing or analyzing, this cartoon
identifies the elements of a boy's sandwich to discover what the
elements can tell about the values and politics of the parent who
made the sandwich. The title, "Deconstructing Lunch," refers to a
type of analysis that focuses on the multiple meanings of the subject and especially its internal contradictions. Summarize what
the sandwich reveals about the boy's parent. What contradictions
do you spot in his or her values or politics? What might Chast be
saying more generally about food choices?

## THE METHOD

A chemist working for a soft-drink company is asked to improve on a competitor's product, Green Tea Tonic. (In Chap. 8, the same chemist was working on a different part of the same problem.) To do the job, the chemist first
has to figure out what's in the drink. She smells the stuff and tastes it. Then
she tests a sample chemically to discover the actual ingredients: water, green
tea, corn syrup, citric acid, sodium benzoate, coloring. Methodically, the chemist has performed DIVISION or ANALYSIS: She has separated the beverage into
its components. Green Tea Tonic stands revealed, understood, ready to be
bettered.

Division or analysis (the terms are interchangeable) is a key skill in learning and in life. It is an instrument allowing you to slice a large and complicated subject into smaller parts that you can grasp and relate to one another.
With analysis you comprehend — and communicate — the structure of things.
And when it works, you find in the parts an idea or conclusion about the subject that makes it clearer, truer, more comprehensive, or more vivid than
before you started.

If you have worked with the previous two chapters, you have already used
division or analysis in explaining a process (Chap. 8) and in comparing and
contrasting (Chap. 7). To make a better Green Tea Tonic (a process), the
chemist might prepare a recipe that divides the process into separate steps or
actions ("First, boil a gallon of water . . ."). When the batch is done, she might
taste-test the two drinks, analyzing and then comparing their green tea flavor,
sweetness, and acidity. As you'll see in following chapters, too, division or
analysis figures in all the other methods of developing ideas, for it is basic to
any concerted thought, explanation, or evaluation.

### Kinds of Division or Analysis

Although division or analysis always works the same way — separating a
whole, singular subject into its elements, slicing it into parts — the method
can be more or less difficult depending on how unfamiliar, complex, and
abstract the subject is. Obviously, it's going to be much easier to analyze a
chicken (wings, legs, thighs . . .) than a poem by T. S. Eliot (this image, that
allusion . . .), easier to analyze the structure of a small business than that of a
multinational conglomerate. Just about any subject *can* be analyzed and will
be the clearer for it. In "I Want a Wife," an essay in this chapter, Judy Brady
divides the role of a wife into its various functions or services. In an essay
called "Teacher" from his book *Pot Shots at Poetry* (1980), Robert Francis

divides the knowledge of poetry he imparted to his class into six pie sections. The first slice is what he told his students that they knew already.

> The second slice is what I told them that they could have found out just as well or better from books. What, for instance, is a sestina?
> The third slice is what I told them that they refused to accept. I could see it on their faces, and later I saw the evidence in their writing.
> The fourth slice is what I told them that they were willing to accept and may have thought they accepted but couldn't accept since they couldn't fully understand. This also I saw in their faces and in their work. Here, no doubt, I was mostly to blame.
> The fifth slice is what I told them that they discounted as whimsy or something simply to fill up time. After all, I was being paid to talk.
> The sixth slice is what I didn't tell them, for I didn't try to tell them all I knew. Deliberately I kept back something—a few professional secrets, a magic formula or two.

There are always multiple ways to divide or analyze a subject, just as there are many ways to slice a pie. Francis could have divided his knowledge of poetry into knowledge of rhyme, knowledge of meter, knowledge of imagery, and so forth—basically following the components of a poem. In other words, the outcome of an analysis depends on the rule or principle used to do the slicing. This fact accounts for some of the differences among academic disciplines: A psychologist, say, may look at the individual person primarily as a bundle of drives and needs, whereas a sociologist may emphasize the individual's roles in society. Even within disciplines, different factions analyze differently, using different principles of division or analysis. Some psychologists are interested mainly in thought, others mainly in behavior; some psychologists focus mainly on emotional development, others mainly on moral development.

## Analysis and Critical Thinking

Analysis plays a fundamental role in CRITICAL THINKING, READING, and WRITING, topics discussed in Chapters 1 and 3. In fact, *analysis* and *criticism* are deeply related: The first comes from a Greek word meaning "to undo," the second from a Greek word meaning "to separate."

Critical thinking, reading, and writing go beneath the surface of the object, word, image, or whatever the subject is. When you work critically, you divide the subject into its elements, INFER the buried meanings and ASSUMPTIONS that define its essence, and SYNTHESIZE the parts into a new whole that is now informed by your perspective. Say a campaign brochure quotes a candidate as favoring "reasonable government expenditures on reasonable highway projects." The candidate will support new roads, right? Wrong. As a critical reader of the brochure, you quickly sense something fishy in the use (twice) of *reasonable*. As an informed reader, you know (or find out) that the candidate has consistently opposed new roads, so the chances of her finding a highway project "reasonable" are slim. At the same time, her stand has been unpopular, so of course she wants to seem "reasonable" on the issue. Read critically, then, a campaign statement that seems to offer mild support for highways is actually a slippery evasion of any such commitment.

Analysis (a convenient term for the overlapping operations of analysis, inference, and synthesis) is very useful for exposing such evasiveness, but that isn't its only function. If you've read this far in this book, you've already done quite a bit of analytical/critical thinking as you read and analyzed the selections. The method will also help you understand a sculpture, perceive the importance of a case study in sociology, or form a response to an environmental impact report. And the method can be invaluable for straight thinking about popular culture, from TV to toys, as two selections in this chapter demonstrate.

## THE PROCESS

### Subjects and Theses

Keep an eye out for writing assignments requiring division or analysis — in college and work, they won't be few or hard to find. They will probably include the word *analyze* or a word implying analysis such as *evaluate, examine, explore, interpret, discuss,* or *criticize.* Any time you spot such a term, you know your job is to separate the subject into its elements, to infer their meanings, to explore the relations among them, and to draw a conclusion about the subject.

Almost any coherent entity — object, person, place, concept — is a fit subject for analysis *if* the analysis will add to the subject's meaning or significance. Little is deadlier than the rote analytical exercise that leaves the parts neatly dissected and the subject comatose on the page. As a writer, you have to animate the subject, and that means finding your interest. What about your subject seems curious? What's appealing? or mysterious? or awful? And what will be your PURPOSE in writing about the subject: Do you simply want to explain it, or do you want to argue for or against it?

Such questions can help you find the principle or framework you will use to divide the subject into parts. (As we mentioned before, there's more than one way to slice most subjects.) Say you've got an assignment to write about a sculpture in a nearby park. Why do you like the sculpture, or why don't you? What elements of its creation and physical form make it art? What is the point of such public art? What does this sculpture do to this park, or vice versa? Any of these questions could suggest a slant on the subject, a framework for analysis, and a purpose for writing, getting your analysis moving.

Finding your principle of analysis will lead you to your essay's THESIS as well — the main point you want to make about your subject. Expressed in a THESIS STATEMENT, this idea will help keep you focused and help your readers see your subject as a whole rather than a bundle of parts. Here is the thesis statement in one of this chapter's selections:

> [Children's books that ignore] men who share equally in raising their children and show nothing but part-time or no-time fathers are only going to create yet another generation of men who have been told since boyhood — albeit subtly — that mothers are the truer parents and that fathers play, at best, a secondary role in the home.
>                        — Armin A. Brott, "Not All Men Are Sly Foxes"

See the next page for more on the thesis statement in analysis.

In developing an essay by analysis, having an outline at your elbow can be a help. You don't want to overlook any parts or elements that should be included in your framework. (You needn't mention every feature in your final essay or give them all equal treatment, but any omissions or variations should be conscious.) And you want to use your framework consistently, not switching carelessly (and confusingly) from, say, the form of the sculpture to the cost of public art. In writing her brief essay "I Want a Wife," Judy Brady must have needed an outline to work out carefully the different activities of a wife, so that she covered them all and clearly distinguished them.

## Evidence

Making a valid analysis is chiefly a matter of giving your subject thought, but for the result to seem useful and convincing to your readers, it will have to refer to the concrete world. The method requires not only cogitation, but open eyes and a willingness to provide EVIDENCE. The nature of the evidence will depend entirely on what you are analyzing — physical details for a sculpture, quotations for a poem, financial data for a business case study, statistics for a psychology case study, and so forth. The idea is to supply enough evidence to justify and support your particular slant on the subject.

A final caution: It's possible to get carried away with one's own analysis, to become so enamored of the details that the subject itself becomes dim or distorted. You can avoid this danger by keeping the subject literally in front of you as you work (or at least imagining it vividly) and by maintaining an outline. It often helps to reassemble your subject at the end of the essay, placing it in a larger context, speculating on its influence, or affirming its significance. By the end of the essay, your subject must be a coherent whole truly represented by your analysis, not twisted, inflated, or obliterated. The reader should be intrigued by your subject, yes, but also able to recognize it on the street.

---

### FOCUS ON THE THESIS STATEMENT

Readers will have an easier time following your analysis—and will more likely appreciate it—if they have a hook on which to hang the details. Your thesis statement can be that hook if you use it to establish your framework, your principle of analysis.

In each of the following pairs, the first statement is too vague to work as a hook: It conveys the writer's general opinion but not its basis. Each revised statement clarifies the point.

VAGUE    The sculpture is a beautiful piece of work.

REVISED    Although it may not be obvious at first, this smooth bronze sculpture represents the city dweller's relationship with nature.

VAGUE    The sculpture is a waste of money.

REVISED    The huge bronze sculpture in the middle of McBean Park demonstrates that so-called public art may actually undermine the public interest.

A well-focused thesis statement can help you as well, because it gives you a yardstick to judge how complete, consistent, and supportive your analysis is. Don't be discouraged, though, if your thesis statement doesn't come to you until *after* you've written a first draft and had a chance to discover your interest. Writing about your subject may be the best way for you to find its meaning and significance.

---

### CHECKLIST FOR REVISING A DIVISION OR ANALYSIS ESSAY

✔ **PRINCIPLE OF ANALYSIS AND THESIS**    What is your particular slant on your subject, the rule or principle you have used to divide your subject into its elements? Do you specify it in your thesis statement?

✔ **COMPLETENESS**    Have you considered all the subject's elements required by your principle of analysis?

✔ **CONSISTENCY**    Have you applied your principle of analysis consistently, viewing your subject from a definite slant?

✔ **EVIDENCE** Is your division or analysis well supported with concrete details, quotations, data, or statistics, as appropriate?

✔ **SIGNIFICANCE** Why should readers care about your analysis? Have you told them something about your subject that wasn't obvious on its surface?

✔ **TRUTH TO SUBJECT** Is your analysis faithful to the subject, not distorted, exaggerated, deflated?

## DIVISION OR ANALYSIS IN PARAGRAPHS

### Writing About Television

The following paragraph analyzes the components of a television laugh track, the recorded chorus that tells us when a comedy is funny. Though written especially for *The Bedford Reader*, not as part of an essay, this brief analysis could itself be one component in an examination of TV comedy. Or, with the related paragraph on pages 380–81, illustrating CLASSIFICATION, it could contribute to an essay on, say, how the producers of TV comedies manipulate viewers.

Most television comedies, even some that boast live audiences, rely on the laugh machine to fill too-quiet moments on the soundtrack. The effect of a canned laugh comes from its four overlapping elements. The first is style, from titter to belly laugh. The second is intensity, the volume, ranging from mild to medium to earsplitting. The third ingredient is duration, the length of the laugh, whether quick, medium, or extended. And finally, there's the number of laughers, from a lone giggler to a roaring throng. According to rumor (for its exact workings are a secret), the machine contains a bank of thirty-two tapes. Furiously working keys and tromping pedals, the operator plays the tapes singly or in combination to blend the four ingredients, as a maestro weaves a symphony out of brass, woodwinds, percussion, and strings.

*Principle of analysis: elements creating the effect of a canned laugh*

1. Style
2. Intensity
3. Duration
4. Number

*Details and examples clarify elements*

### Writing in an Academic Discipline

The next paragraph appeared first in a scholarly journal and then in a textbook on medical ethics. The author discusses four possible models for the doctor-patient relationship, ending with the one detailed in this paragraph. The careful analysis supports his preference for this model over the others.

*Division or Analysis*

The model of social relationship which fits these conditions [of realistic equality between patient and doctor] is that of the contract or covenant. The notion of contract should not be loaded with legalistic implications, but taken in its more symbolic form as in the traditional religious or marriage "contract" or "covenant." Here two individuals or groups are interacting in a way where there are obligations and expected benefits for both parties. The obligations and benefits are limited in scope, though, even if they are expressed in somewhat vague terms. The basic norms of freedom, dignity, truth-telling, promise-keeping, and justice are essential to a contractual relationship. The premise is trust and confidence even though it is recognized that there is not a full mutuality of interests. Social sanctions institutionalize and stand behind the relationship, in case there is a violation of the contract, but for the most part the assumption is that there will be a faithful fulfillment of the obligations.

—Robert M. Veatch,
"Models for Medicine in a Revolutionary Age"

Principle of analysis: elements of a contract between doctor and patient

1. Obligations and benefits for both parties

2. Obligations and benefits limited

3. Freedom, dignity, and other norms

4. Trust and confidence

5. Support of social sanctions (meaning that society upholds the relationship)

## DIVISION OR ANALYSIS IN PRACTICE

During her sophomore year at Boston University, Cortney Keim applied for transfer to Pomona College in California. As part of its application, Pomona requested a statement about Keim, her academic goals, and her reasons for wanting to transfer.

Keim tried several approaches to her statement, struggling to present herself as serious and unique. In one draft, she followed the cue of Pomona's request — providing a brief autobiography, a list of goals, and an explanation for choosing Pomona — but that version seemed obvious and dull. In the end, Keim settled on the fresher approach you see here. She first divides herself into parts and then details each one, showing its relevance to Pomona.

### Application Statement of Cortney Keim

In applying for transfer to Pomona, I seek to develop the three main components of myself: actor, student, and explorer.

Pomona's strong theater curriculum will give me the background I need to embark on a career in acting. As unstable a career as it may prove to be, acting is my fire. I have always liked entertaining others (in high school, I was voted class clown), even if it involves making a display of myself. As I have had the chance to act in varied plays over the last few years, I have also found that interpreting an author's text allows me paradoxically to express myself and to lose myself. And, yes, I have loved the appreciation of an audience, the sighs or laughs in the right places, the applause at the end.

Yet acting is not all. In high school and for two years at Boston University, I have also relished the liberal arts courses I've taken and the writing I've done in those courses. The courses have introduced me to worlds of information and ideas I wouldn't have known otherwise, and the writing has let me make up my own text, my own version of reality. Liberal arts courses are hard work, harder in many ways than acting, but the work pays off. Pomona's respected liberal arts curriculum will help me become the rounded, thoughtful, disciplined student I hope to be for the rest of my life.

It's also significant to me that Pomona is a small school in California, so different from the huge university I attend now and so far from the East Coast city where I have lived all my life. The explorer in me needs a new horizon. At Pomona I anticipate the opportunity to be more involved in the activities of the college and to get to know a wider variety of people. In southern California, I expect to become familiar with a new climate, geography, and ecosystem.

Pomona promises to help me fulfill my needs to act, learn, and explore. In return, I promise to contribute whatever I can to the college and the larger community.

# JUDY BRADY

JUDY BRADY, born in 1937 in San Francisco, where she now lives, earned a BFA in painting from the University of Iowa in 1962. Drawn into political action by her work in the feminist movement, she went to Cuba in 1973, where she studied class relationships as a way of understanding change in a society. When she was diagnosed with cancer in 1980, Brady became an activist against what she calls "the cancer establishment." ("Cancer is, after all, a multibillion dollar business," she says.) In 1991 she published *1 in 3: Women with Cancer Confront an Epidemic,* an anthology of writings by women. She is a board member of Greenaction, an environmental justice organization, and a founding member of the Toxic Links Coalition. She writes articles for Breast Cancer Action in San Francisco and recently provided a chapter for a Canadian book, *Sweeping the Earth: Women Taking Action for a Healthy Planet.*

# *I Want a Wife*

"I Want a Wife" first appeared in the Spring 1972 issue of Ms. magazine, which had started the year before as a vehicle for the modern feminist movement, then in its first decade. "I Want a Wife" became one of the best-known manifestos in popular feminist writing. In the essay, Brady trenchantly divides the work of a wife into its multiple duties and functions, leading to an inescapable conclusion. If you find that Brady stereotypes men, read the essay after hers, Armin A. Brott's "Not All Men Are Sly Foxes," for a different view.

I belong to that classification of people known as wives. I am A Wife. 1
And, not altogether incidentally, I am a mother.

Not too long ago a male friend of mine appeared on the scene fresh from 2
a recent divorce. He had one child, who is, of course, with his ex-wife. He is looking for another wife. As I thought about him while I was ironing one evening, it suddenly occurred to me that I, too, would like to have a wife. Why do I want a wife?

I would like to go back to school so that I can become economically inde- 3
pendent, support myself, and, if need be, support those dependent upon me. I want a wife who will work and send me to school. And while I am going to school I want a wife to take care of my children. I want a wife to keep track of

the children's doctor and dentist appointments. And to keep track of mine, too. I want a wife to make sure my children eat properly and are kept clean. I want a wife who will wash the children's clothes and keep them mended. I want a wife who is a good nurturant attendant to my children, who arranges for their schooling, makes sure that they have an adequate social life with their peers, takes them to the park, the zoo, etc. I want a wife who takes care of the children when they are sick, a wife who arranges to be around when the children need special care, because, of course, I cannot miss classes at school. My wife must arrange to lose time at work and not lose the job. It may mean a small cut in my wife's income from time to time, but I guess I can tolerate that. Needless to say, my wife will arrange and pay for the care of the children while my wife is working.

I want a wife who will take care of *my* physical needs. I want a wife who   4
will keep my house clean. A wife who will pick up after my children, a wife who will pick up after me. I want a wife who will keep my clothes clean, ironed, mended, replaced when need be, and who will see to it that my personal things are kept in their proper place so that I can find what I need the minute I need it. I want a wife who cooks the meals, a wife who is a *good* cook. I want a wife who will plan the menus, do the necessary grocery shopping, prepare the meals, serve them pleasantly, and then do the cleaning up while I do my studying. I want a wife who will care for me when I am sick and sympathize with my pain and loss of time from school. I want a wife to go along when our family takes vacation so that someone can continue to care for me and my children when I need a rest and change of scene.

I want a wife who will not bother me with rambling complaints about a   5
wife's duties. But I want a wife who will listen to me when I feel the need to explain a rather difficult point I have come across in my course of studies. And I want a wife who will type my papers for me when I have written them.

I want a wife who will take care of the details of my social life. When my   6
wife and I are invited out by my friends, I want a wife who will take care of the babysitting arrangements. When I meet people at school that I like and want to entertain, I want a wife who will have the house clean, will prepare a special meal, serve it to me and my friends, and not interrupt when I talk about things that interest me and my friends. I want a wife who will have arranged that the children are fed and ready for bed before my guests arrive so that the children do not bother us. I want a wife who takes care of the needs of my guests so that they feel comfortable, who makes sure that they have an ashtray, that they are passed the hors d'oeuvres, that they are offered a second helping of the food, that their wine glasses are replenished when necessary, that their coffee is served to them as they like it. And I want a wife who knows that sometimes I need a night out by myself.

I want a wife who is sensitive to my sexual needs, a wife who makes love    7
passionately and eagerly when I feel like it, a wife who makes sure that I am
satisfied. And, of course, I want a wife who will not demand sexual attention
when I am not in the mood for it. I want a wife who assumes the complete
responsibility for birth control, because I do not want more children. I want a
wife who will remain sexually faithful to me so that I do not have to clutter up
my intellectual life with jealousies. And I want a wife who understands that
*my* sexual needs may entail more than strict adherence to monogamy. I must,
after all, be able to relate to people as fully as possible.

If, by chance, I find another person more suitable as a wife than the wife I    8
already have, I want the liberty to replace my present wife with another one.
Naturally, I will expect a fresh, new life; my wife will take the children and be
solely responsible for them so that I am left free.

When I am through with school and have a job, I want my wife to quit    9
working and remain at home so that my wife can more fully and completely
take care of a wife's duties.

My God, who *wouldn't* want a wife?    10

---

*For a reading quiz, sources on Judy Brady, and annotated links to further readings
on feminism and on gender roles, visit **bedfordstmartins.com/thebedfordreader**.*

---

## Journal Writing

Brady addresses the traditional obligations of a wife and mother. In your journal, jot
down parallel obligations of a husband and father. (To take your journal writing further, see "From Journal to Essay" on the facing page.)

## Questions on Meaning

1. Sum up the duties of a wife as Brady sees them.
2. To what inequities in the roles traditionally assigned to men and to women does
   "I Want a Wife" call attention?
3. What is the THESIS of this essay? Is it stated or implied?
4. Is Brady unfair to men?

# Questions on Writing Strategy

1. What EFFECT does Brady obtain with the title "I Want a Wife"?
2. What do the first two paragraphs accomplish?
3. What is the TONE of this essay?
4. How do you explain the fact that Brady never uses the pronoun *she* to refer to a wife? Does this make her prose unnecessarily awkward?
5. What principle does Brady use to analyze the role of wife? Can you think of some other principle for analyzing the job?
6. Knowing that this essay was first published in *Ms.* magazine in 1972, what can you guess about its intended readers? Does "I Want a Wife" strike a college AUDIENCE today as revolutionary?
7. **OTHER METHODS**   Although she mainly divides or analyzes the role of wife, Brady also uses CLASSIFICATION to sort the many duties and responsibilities into manageable groups. What are the groups?

# Questions on Language

1. What is achieved by the author's frequent repetition of the phrase "I want a wife"?
2. Be sure you know how to define the following words as Brady uses them: nurturant (par. 3); replenished (6); adherence, monogamy (7).
3. In general, how would you describe the DICTION of this essay? How well does it suit the essay's intended audience?

# Suggestions for Writing

1. **FROM JOURNAL TO ESSAY**   Working from your journal entry, write an essay titled "I Want a Husband" in which, using examples as Brady does, you enumerate the roles traditionally assigned to men in our society.
2. Imagining that you want to employ someone to do a specific job, divide the task into its duties and functions. Then, guided by your analysis, write an accurate job description in essay form.
3. **CRITICAL WRITING**   As indicated in the note introducing it, Brady's essay was first published in 1972 in *Ms.*, a feminist magazine. Do some research about the evolving role of women between, say, 1970 and today. How have women's expectations, opportunities, and positions changed? One approach is to locate statistics for then and now about women in higher education (studying and teaching), in medicine and other professions, in the workforce, as wives and mothers, as homemakers, and so on. Based on your research, write an essay in which you SUMMARIZE Brady's view as you understand it and then EVALUATE her essay. Consider: Is Brady fair? If not, is unfairness justified? Is the essay relevant today? If not, what has changed? Provide specific EVIDENCE from your experience, observation, and research.
4. **CONNECTIONS**   Both "I Want a Wife" and the next essay, Armin A. Brott's "Not All Men Are Sly Foxes," challenge traditional ideas about how men and women are supposed to divide the labor in a marriage. However, Brady's STYLE is fast

paced and her tone is sarcastic, while Brott is more methodical and earnest. Which method of addressing these issues do you find more effective? Why? Write an essay that COMPARES AND CONTRASTS the essays' tones, styles, POINTS OF VIEW, and OBJECTIVE versus SUBJECTIVE language. What conclusions can you draw about the connection between the writers' strategies and their messages?

# ARMIN A. BROTT

ARMIN A. BROTT is a writer and parenting expert who lives in Oakland, California. Born in 1958, he received a BA in Russian from San Francisco State University and an MBA that he calls "less useful than the degree in Russian" before embarking on a career in marketing. He turned to writing when his first child was born because he "wanted to be an active, involved father." Since that time, he has contributed to the *New York Times Magazine*, the *Washington Post, Reader's Digest, Family Circle, Parenting, Playboy*, and other magazines. He treats issues that affect men: education, health, and especially fatherhood. His seven books on fatherhood include *The Expectant Father* (1995, with Jennifer Ash), *The Single Father* (1999), *Throwaway Dads* (1999), and *Father for Life: A Journey of Joy, Challenge, and Change* (2003). Brott also does a twice-weekly podcast called *DaddyCast* and hosts a weekly national radio show called *Positive Parenting*.

## *Not All Men Are Sly Foxes*

The view of men taken by Judy Brady in the previous essay is of course not shared by everyone. In one defense of men, the National Fatherhood Initiative has pointed out that fathers in television shows and commercials fall into three categories: "dumb, dangerous, or disaffected." And in this 1992 essay from *Newsweek* magazine, Brott claims that while women and men are not yet equal in child care, children's books are hardly helping. He uses analysis to show that the Sly Fox remains much more common than the Caring Dad.

If you thought your child's bookshelves were finally free of openly (and 1 not so openly) discriminatory materials, you'd better check again. In recent years groups of concerned parents have persuaded textbook publishers to portray more accurately the roles that women and minorities play in shaping our country's history and culture. *Little Black Sambo* has all but disappeared from library and bookstore shelves; feminist fairy tales by such authors as Jack Zipes have, in many homes, replaced the more traditional (and obviously sexist) fairy tales. Richard Scarry, one of the most popular children's writers, has reissued new versions of some of his classics; now female animals are pictured doing the same jobs as male animals. Even the terminology has changed: Males and females are referred to as mail "carriers" or "firefighters."

**345**

There is, however, one very large group whose portrayal continues to fol-  2
low the same stereotypical lines as always: fathers. The evolution of children's
literature didn't end with *Goodnight Moon* and *Charlotte's Web*. My local public library, for example, previews 203 new children's picture books (for the
under-five set) each *month*. Many of these books make a very conscious effort
to take women characters out of the kitchen and the nursery and give them
professional jobs and responsibilities.

Despite this shift, mothers are by and large still shown as the primary care-  3
givers and, more important, as the primary nurturers of their children. Men in
these books — if they're shown at all — still come home late after work and
participate in the child rearing by bouncing baby around for five minutes
before putting the child to bed.

In one of my two-year-old daughter's favorite books, *Mother Goose and the*  4
*Sly Fox,* "retold" by Chris Conover, a single mother (Mother Goose) of seven
tiny goslings is pitted against (and naturally outwits) the sly Fox. Fox, a
neglectful and presumably unemployed single father, lives with his filthy, hungry pups in a grimy hovel littered with the bones of their previous meals.
Mother Goose, a successful entrepreneur with a thriving lace business, still
finds time to serve her goslings homemade soup in pretty porcelain cups. The
story is funny and the illustrations marvelous, but the unwritten message is
that women take better care of their kids and men have nothing else to do but
hunt down and kill innocent, law-abiding geese.

The majority of other children's classics perpetuate the same negative  5
stereotypes of fathers. Once in a great while, people complain about *Babar*'s
colonialist slant (little jungle-dweller finds happiness in the big city and
brings civilization — and fine clothes — to his backward village). But I've
never heard anyone ask why, after his mother is killed by the evil hunter,
Babar is automatically an "orphan." Why can he find comfort only in the arms
of another female? Why do Arthur's and Celeste's mothers come alone to the
city to fetch their children? Don't the fathers care? Do they even have fathers?
I need my answers ready for when my daughter asks.

I recently spent an entire day on the children's floor of the local library  6
trying to find out whether these same negative stereotypes are found in the
more recent classics-to-be. The librarian gave me a list of the twenty most
popular contemporary picture books and I read every one of them. Of the
twenty, seven don't mention a parent at all. Of the remaining thirteen, four
portray fathers as much less loving and caring than mothers. In *Little Gorilla,*
we are told that the little gorilla's "mother loves him" and we see Mama gorilla
giving her little one a warm hug. On the next page we're also told that his
"father loves him," but in the illustration, father and son aren't even touching. Six of the remaining nine books mention or portray mothers as the only

parent, and only three of the twenty have what could be considered "equal" treatment of mothers and fathers.

The same negative stereotypes also show up in literature aimed at the *parents* of small children. In *What to Expect the First Year,* the authors answer almost every question the parents of a newborn or toddler could have in the first year of their child's life. They are meticulous in alternating between references to boys and girls. At the same time, they refer almost exclusively to "mother" or "mommy." Men, and their feelings about parenting, are relegated to a nine-page chapter just before the recipe section.

Unfortunately, it's still true that, in our society, women do the bulk of the child care, and that thanks to men abandoning their families, there are too many single mothers out there. Nevertheless, to say that portraying fathers as unnurturing or completely absent is simply "a reflection of reality" is unacceptable. If children's literature only reflected reality, it would be like prime-time TV and we'd have books filled with child abusers, wife beaters and criminals.

Young children believe what they hear — especially from a parent figure. And since, for the first few years of a child's life, adults select the reading material, children's literature should be held to a high standard. Ignoring men who share equally in raising their children and continuing to show nothing but part-time or no-time fathers is only going to create yet another generation of men who have been told since boyhood — albeit subtly — that mothers are the truer parents and that fathers play, at best, a secondary role in the home. We've taken major steps to root out discrimination in what our children read. Let's finish the job.

*For a reading quiz, sources on Armin A. Brott, and annotated links to further readings on gender roles and on children's books, visit **bedfordstmartins.com /thebedfordreader.***

## Journal Writing

Do you agree with Brott that young children are strongly influenced by the books parents or teachers read to them? In your journal, list particular books from your childhood that stand out in your memory. What made these books come alive so that you still remember them today — the story, the illustrations, the language? (To take your journal writing further, see "From Journal to Essay" on the following page.)

## Questions on Meaning

1. What is the THESIS of Brott's essay? Where is it stated succinctly?
2. What does Brott ASSUME about his AUDIENCE in this essay? To what extent do you fit his assumptions?
3. Brott points out a difference between the illustration of the little gorilla with his mother and the one of him with his father (par. 6). Why is this difference significant?
4. What is the EFFECT of Brott's concluding sentences: "We've taken major steps to root out discrimination in what our children read. Let's finish the job"?

## Questions on Writing Strategy

1. What principle of analysis does Brott use in examining the children's books? What elements does he perceive in these books?
2. What purpose does paragraph 7, with its reference to books for parents, serve in this essay about children's books?
3. **OTHER METHODS**   In paragraph 4, Brott provides vivid DESCRIPTION of Mother Goose's and Sly Fox's homes to show the differences between the two parents. What CONCRETE details help explain these differences?

## Questions on Language

1. What is the difference between "caregivers" and "nurturers" as Brott uses the words in paragraph 3?
2. How would you analyze Brott's TONE? Give specific words and sentences that you think contribute to the tone.
3. If some of the following words are unfamiliar, look them up in a dictionary: discriminatory (par. 1); stereotypical, evolution (2); goslings, neglectful, hovel, entrepreneur, porcelain (4); perpetuate, colonialist (5); meticulous, exclusively, relegated (7); albeit, subtly (9).

## Suggestions for Writing

1. **FROM JOURNAL TO ESSAY**   Working from your journal entry, write a brief essay that explores the messages sent by one of your childhood books. Did the book contain positive role models? negative ones? moral messages? values that you now embrace or reject? Did you learn anything in particular from this book? Based on your recollections, come to your own conclusions about what's appropriate or not in children's books.
2. Write an essay that analyzes another type of writing by examining its elements. You may choose any kind of writing that's familiar to you: news article, sports article, mystery, romance, science fiction, biography, and so on. Be sure to make your principle of analysis clear to your readers.
3. Brott's essay was written some years ago. Have images of fathers in children's books changed since then, or have they remained essentially the same? Read through a sampling of children's books published in the past five years — either in

a library or in the children's section of a bookstore. Then write an essay in which you report your findings, being sure to analyze several specific books.

4. **CRITICAL WRITING**   "If children's literature only reflected reality," Brott claims, "it would be like prime-time TV and we'd have books filled with child abusers, wife beaters and criminals" (par. 8). However, Brott also suggests that "reality" contains a significant number of responsible, loving fathers. Does the claim about "reality" being "like prime-time TV" detract from Brott's argument on behalf of good fathers? Write an essay in which you explain how (or whether) Brott resolves this contradiction in his essay. It will probably be helpful to provide a clear DEFINITION of *reality* in this context.

5. **CONNECTIONS**   Look over Judy Brady's "I Want a Wife" (p. 340) and make a list of her implied complaints about the traditional roles of a wife. Now make a list of the responsibilities that Brott implies a good father is happy to take on. How could Brott's essay be viewed as a sort of response or solution to some of the problems Brady raises? Write an essay explaining the changes in traditional gender roles suggested by "I Want a Wife" and "Not All Men Are Sly Foxes" together.

# BELLA DePAULO

BELLA DePAULO is a psychologist who specializes in lying and lie detection and in the ways single people are perceived in US society. She was born in 1953 in Scranton, Pennsylvania, earned a BA from Vassar College in 1975, and received a PhD in psychology from Harvard University in 1979. She has published over a hundred articles in scholarly journals, and her research has been supported by the National Science Foundation, the National Institute of Mental Health, and the National Academy of Education. She has also published articles for general audiences in the *Wall Street Journal*, *Time*, *Psychology Today*, and other periodicals, and she has appeared on *The Today Show* and other television and radio shows. DePaulo is currently a visiting professor at the University of California, Santa Barbara.

# *The Myth of Doomed Kids*

In her recent book *Singled Out: How Singles Are Stereotyped, Stigmatized, and Ignored, and Still Live Happily Ever After* (2006), DePaulo challenges myths about unmarried people. "The Myth of Doomed Kids" (editors' title) is an excerpt from the book. The opening paragraph refers to the early 1980s, when debates over public-assistance programs sometimes reduced single mothers to the stereotype of the welfare recipient who neglects her children and scams the system for her own benefit. Recent discussion may have become less blatantly hostile to single parents, but the idea persists that their children are at great risk for psychological problems.

Parents who are single get pummeled in the public discourse — especially    1
if they are poor. President Ronald Reagan seared a scathing image onto the national psyche when he described the Welfare Queen in her welfare Cadillac, who only pretended to have an array of dead husbands so she could bilk the public assistance system for even more ill-gotten gains. The queen had a short life — not because she was single but because she never existed. She was fabricated.[1] Her legacy, though, has been enduring.

As insulting as single parents must find such apocryphal morality tales,    2

---

[1] Reporters tried to find the Welfare Queen to interview her, but they never did find anyone who met Reagan's description. The closest they came was a woman from Chicago who was in fact charged with welfare fraud. Reagan claimed that the Welfare Queen used eighty names; the Chicago woman used four. Reagan also claimed that the queen had bilked the system for more than $150,000; the fraud alleged to have been committed by the Chicago woman amounted to $8,000. See "'Welfare Queen' Becomes Issue in Reagan Campaign," *New York Times*, February 15, 1980, and David Zucchino, *The Myth of the Welfare Queen* (New York: Simon & Schuster, 1999), 65.

they seethe even more, I think, when it is their children who are chided. True, their kids are rarely branded as bastards anymore, but often they are still described as illegitimate or as products of "broken" homes. Then there are those ominous prognostications of lives filled with delinquency, failure, and despair, emanating like black smoke from the labs of evil scientists. . . .

I want some numbers. Don't worry, I'm not going to plow through every   3
study linking the fate of children to whether they live with one or both parents. I'm just going to choose one. And since I'm going to present just one, it had better be good, and it is. First, it documents drug use, one of the most widely heralded "risks" of growing up with just one parent. Second, the results are drawn from "the principal source of data about drug use in the United States." I'll call it the National Drug Abuse Survey.[2] The people who were sampled for the research represent the population of the United States, ages twelve and older. The report focused on the subgroup often believed to be the most worrisome — adolescents ages twelve to seventeen. More than 22,000 participated.

The fear for the children of single parents is not just that they will try   4
drugs or alcohol but that the use will become a problem. The substance abuse might result in symptoms such as anxiety, irritability, or depression. The abusers might be unable to use less often, even if they try, and may need more and more of the substance to achieve the same high. Abusers might also get less work done than they had before they became so taken with the alcohol or the drug. To be classified as having a problem with drugs or alcohol, the adolescent had to report at least two such troublesome experiences in the past year.

The numbers in the table show the percentage of adolescents in each fam-   5
ily type who had a substance-abuse problem. The family types included single-mother and single-father families, mother-and-father families, and two other two-parent families: mother and stepfather, and father and stepmother.

| | Substance-Abuse Problems Among Twelve- to Seventeen-Year-Olds | |
| --- | --- |
| **%** | **Family Type** |
| 4.5 | Mother plus father |
| 5.3 | Mother plus stepfather |
| 5.7 | Mother only |
| 11.0 | Father only |
| 11.8 | Father plus stepmother |

[2] John P. Hoffman and Robert A. Johnson, "A National Portrait of Family Structure and Adolescent Drug Use," *Journal of Marriage and Family* 60 (1998): 633–45.

The first thing to notice is the overall rates of substance abuse. In every   6
type of family, at least 88 percent of the adolescents do *not* have a problem
with drugs or alcohol. Second, what the pro-marriage advocates have claimed
all along is that kids raised by their own mom and dad should do better than
all the others. They do. And not because two is a magic number. Adolescents
living with a father and stepmother had more drug-abuse problems than all
the rest.

The most important comparison, I think, is the one the culture has   7
obsessed about the most: How do the kids raised by a single mom compare
with the kids raised by their mother and father? Again, the adolescents living
with their own two parents do better: 4.5 percent of them have substance-
abuse problems, compared with 5.7 percent of the adolescents living with only
their mom. It is a difference, but not much of one.

In the preceding table, I list only some of the family types included in the   8
National Drug Abuse Survey. I wanted to highlight the single-parent and two-
parent homes, since those are the ones that have most often been subject to
debate. . . . Here now is the full list of family types described in the report, and
the corresponding rates of substance-abuse problems.

| | Substance-Abuse Problems<br>Among Twelve- to Seventeen-Year-Olds |
|---|---|
| % | Family Type |
| 3.4 | Mother plus father plus other relative |
| 4.5 | Mother plus father |
| 5.3 | Mother plus stepfather |
| 5.7 | Mother only |
| 6.0 | Mother plus other relative |
| 7.2 | Other relative only |
| 8.1 | Other family type |
| 11.0 | Father only |
| 11.8 | Father plus stepmother |

"Other relative" included relatives other than a mother or father. Typically, they were grandparents, aunts, or uncles.
"Other family types" included miscellaneous combinations of adults, including adults to whom the children were not related.

The mom-plus-dad family has been knocked off its perch. Kids are even   9
less likely to have substance-abuse problems if they live with Mom, Dad, and
another relative—typically a grandparent, aunt, or uncle. Notice also that

there are two new family types that do not include Mom or Dad: other relatives only, and other family types. (In the latter, the kids live with miscellaneous combinations of people, including adults to whom they are not related.) The rate of substance abuse is only a few percentage points higher in the families in which neither a mother nor a father is present than in the families that include both Mom and Dad. . . .

I want to return now to the two family types that set off so much of the sound and fury about mothers who need to be stigmatized, children who need to have their suffering acknowledged, and monsters in the making. They are the single-mother families, in which 5.7 percent of the kids had substance-abuse problems, and the mom-plus-dad families, in which 4.5 percent did. Here's the question that bothers me: Why is this difference so small? 10

Think about it this way. If you had a town with a hundred adolescents living with their mother and father, and another hundred living just with their mothers, there would be four or five substance-abusing kids in the former group, and maybe six in the latter. Think about all the advantages that adolescents supposedly have when they live with Mom and Dad rather than just Mom. There are two adults in the home to help them, care about them, and spend time with them. The adults can also support each other, and that, too, can redound to the benefit of the kids. There are two sources of income. And there is no source of stigma or shame attached to growing up in a home with your own mother and father. 11

For double the money, time, love, and attention, the kids of mom-plus-dad families did not seem to be doing all that much better than the kids of single moms. There must be something wrong with my blather about all that emotional goodness that kids in nuclear families get that children living with just their moms do not. 12

If it really were true that the children of single mothers had only one adult in their lives to care for them, love them, spend time with them, and contribute to their well-being and that their moms had no adults in their lives to help them, and if it were also true that the children in nuclear families had two fully devoted adults in their lives, loving them and each other—well, then it would be astounding that there could be so little difference in the problem behaviors of the two sets of adolescents. 13

I think there are several ways around this dilemma. The first is to let go of the fantasy that all children living in nuclear families have two totally engaged parents who lavish their love and attention on all their children, and on each other, in a home free of anger, conflict, or recriminations. The second is to grab onto a different sort of possibility—that many children living with single mothers have other important adults in their lives, too. . . . 14

I also mean all the kids who have grandparents, aunts, uncles, neighbors, teachers, family friends, and others who care about them and make sure they know it.

It is true that the other important adults in the lives of the children of    15 single parents do not always live in the same home as the children. That means that they are not always on the scene to help with homework or cover for Mom while she runs to the store. Again, though, it is important to remember that two-parent homes are not always homes with two continually available parents. And something else is important: Although mutual love and support is what adults hope to enjoy when they live together and raise children, sometimes what they get instead is chaos, strife, and even abuse.

*For a reading quiz, sources on Bella DePaulo, and annotated links to further readings on children in single-parent families and substance abuse, visit **bedfordstmartins .com/thebedfordreader**.*

## Journal Writing

In what kind of family did you grow up? Did you live with both of your parents in one household? with a parent and a stepparent? with a single mother? with a single father? with a large extended family? How do you respond to DePaulo's characterization of your particular family structure? Based on your experience, is she fair? (To take your journal writing further, see "From Journal to Essay" on the facing page.)

## Questions on Meaning

1. Is Ronald Reagan's "Welfare Queen" real or imaginary? Why does DePaulo open her discussion with a description of this person?
2. What do you think is the THESIS of this selection? Where, if at all, does DePaulo state it?
3. What ASSUMPTIONS does DePaulo make about the love and support provided by a traditional two-parent family versus that provided by nontraditional families?
4. How do the rates of drug abuse among teenagers living with both parents compare with those among teenagers living with a single mother?
5. What does the author think of "those ominous prognostications of lives filled with delinquency, failure, and despair, emanating like black smoke from the labs of evil scientists" (par. 2)?

## Questions on Writing Strategy

1. This excerpt from DePaulo's book *Singled Out* started the chapter titled "Myth #7: Attention, Single Parents: Your Kids Are Doomed." Based on this information, what can you INFER about the author's intended AUDIENCE and her PURPOSE in writing?
2. What is DePaulo analyzing in this selection? What principle does she use to dissect her subject, and how does she reassemble the parts into a new whole?
3. What do the two tables contribute to DePaulo's analysis? Why does she use two tables? How do they differ?
4. **OTHER METHODS**   DePaulo disputes one claim of CAUSE AND EFFECT and makes another. What are the two claims?

## Questions on Language

1. Locate several examples of COLLOQUIAL language in this selection, and explain how such language sets DePaulo's TONE. Why is—or isn't—this tone appropriate for her subject and her audience?
2. What are the CONNOTATIONS of the words *mom* and *dad*? Why do you think the author chose these words over the more formal *mother* and *father* in some spots?
3. The phrase "sound and fury" in paragraph 10 is an ALLUSION to a famous line in Shakespeare's *Macbeth*, act 5, scene 5:

> Life's but a walking shadow; a poor player,
> That struts and frets his hour upon the stage,
> And then is heard no more. It is a tale
> Told by an idiot, full of sound and fury,
> Signifying nothing.

How does this allusion serve DePaulo?
4. Consult your dictionary if any of the following words are unfamiliar: scathing, bilk, fabricated (par. 1); apocryphal, seethe, chided, ominous, prognostications (2); heralded (3); stigmatized (10); redound (11); blather (12); recriminations (14); strife (15).

## Suggestions for Writing

1. **FROM JOURNAL TO ESSAY**   Drawing on your journal entry, write an essay that analyzes DePaulo's characterization of one of the types of families she describes in her essay. Explain why her assumptions about that family structure are or are not accurate, and offer your own characterizations as appropriate. Alternatively, you may want to describe a type of family that DePaulo leaves out of her discussion, explaining why she should have considered it in her analysis.
2. Despite significant changes in the 1990s, welfare reform is an ongoing battle in the United States. Research the main arguments for and against requiring single mothers to find work outside the home after a limited time on public assistance. Then write an essay in which you SUMMARIZE your findings. If your research—or your own experience—leads you to form an opinion favoring one side of the issue, present and support that as well.

3. **CRITICAL WRITING**   Using the information in footnote 2, locate the research study by Hoffman and Johnson and read it critically yourself. In an essay, weigh DePaulo's use of the study: Does she represent it accurately and fairly? Why, or why not?

4. **CONNECTIONS**   In his essay "Needs" (p. 501), Thomas Sowell argues that most of what we think is necessary for a happy life is not really necessary at all. In an essay, apply Sowell's evaluation of *need* to DePaulo's examination of social concerns for children raised in nontraditional families. Do children need two parents to become well-adjusted adults? Why or why not?

---

## *Bella DePaulo on Writing*

Bella DePaulo spent more than two decades studying deception and then switched topics to explore the misperceptions of singlehood. On her Web site (*belladepaulo.com*), she discusses how the change—and the sometimes negative responses to it—affected her.

It has been an absolutely exhilarating experience. I am passionate about the topic. Even though I had lived as a singleton my entire life, the study of singlehood was entirely new to me. I read voraciously, on topics I knew nothing about previously. I constantly examined the claims that were made about singles in the media, and even in scientific journals, and again and again found them misleading or totally inaccurate. I thought about why this was happening, talked to lots of people, and read some more. Before I began writing about singles, I had an area of academic expertise, on deception. I had written more than one hundred scholarly papers on the topic. None of that writing was anything like the experiences I have had writing about singles.

I was interested in deception; I'm passionate about singles. When I sat down to write about deception, I already knew what I was going to say; when I sat down to write about singles, I learned something new almost every time. I still do. The cultural discourse on singlehood is stuck in a rut, and has been for decades. In writing *Singled Out*, I was blasting my way outside of that narrow box, and loving every step of the way.

OK, not every step. There were times when people read what I had written and did not exactly bubble over with enthusiasm. Those were difficult times. But now, even some of the very negative reactions are heartening. For example, when people totally disagree with my point of view, and are angered by my position, I know I have struck a nerve. I do not enjoy their ire—effusive praise is much more fun—but I love it when they are engaged by my arguments and examples. More than just about anything else, I want people to think—no, to *re*think what they thought they already knew. Even if they cycle back to their original position, it will be a more informed position.

## For Discussion

1. What does DePaulo appreciate about negative reactions to her work?
2. When have you learned something by writing? Was the experience unexpected, or did you seek discovery?

# LAILA AYAD

Born in 1981, LAILA AYAD grew up in Columbia, Maryland, a planned community based on ideals of racial, social, and economic diversity and balance. "Being exposed at an early age to such a diverse community and coming from a multiethnic family have given me great insight into different cultures and perspectives," says Ayad. After graduating from New York University in 2003 with a degree in theater and English literature, Ayad embarked on an acting career that has included a ten-month tour with a musical theater company in cities across the United States. When not on stage, Ayad paints and draws and continues to write.

## *The Capricious Camera*

Ayad began college as an art major and produced this essay for a writing class in her sophomore year. The essay first appeared in 2001 in Mercer Street, a journal of writing by New York University students. With an artist's eye for detail, Ayad explores the elements of a photograph to find its meaning. The analysis takes her to Nazi Germany before and during World War II.

In the years between 1933 and 1945, Germany was engulfed by the rise of a powerful new regime and the eventual spoils of war. During this period, Hitler's quest for racial purification turned Germany not only at odds with itself, but with the rest of the world. Photography as an art and as a business became a regulated and potent force in the fight for Aryan domination, Nazi influence, and anti-Semitism. Whether such images were used to promote Nazi ideology, document the Holocaust, or scare Germany's citizens into accepting their own changing country, the effect of this photography provides enormous insight into the true stories and lives of the people most affected by Hitler's racism. In fact, this photography has become so widespread in our understanding and teaching of the Holocaust that often other factors involved in the Nazis' racial policy have been undervalued in our history textbooks — especially the attempt by Nazi Germany to establish the Nordic Aryans as a master race through the Lebensborn experiment, a breeding and adoption program designed to eliminate racial imperfections. It is not merely people of other persecuted races who can become victims in a racial war, but also those we would least expect — the persecuting race itself.

To understand the importance of this often shrouded side of Nazi Germany we might look at the photograph captioned "Mounted Nazi troops on the lookout for likely Polish children." Archived by Catrine Clay and Michael Leapman, this black-and-white photo depicts a young girl in the foreground,

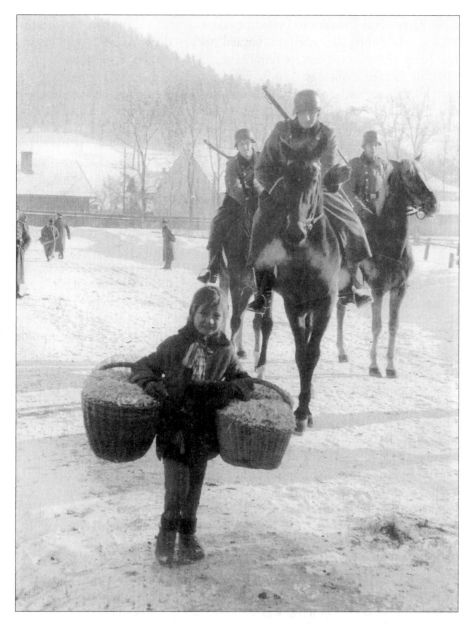

Mounted Nazi troops on the lookout for likely Polish children.

carrying two large baskets and treading across a rural and snow-covered coun-
tryside, while three mounted and armed Nazi soldiers follow closely behind
her. In the distance, we can see farmhouses and a wooden fence, as well as four
other uniformed soldiers or guards. Though the photograph accompanies the
text without the name of the photographer, year, or information as to where it
was found, Clay and Leapman suggest that the photo was taken in Poland
between 1943 and 1945.

Who is this young white girl surrounded by armed soldiers? Is she being    3
protected, watched, persecuted? It would be easy enough to assume that she is
Jewish, but unlike photos documenting the Holocaust, with *this* image the
intent is uncertain. In our general ignorance of the events surrounding this
photo, the picture can be deceiving, and yet it is the picture that can also be
used to shed light on the story.

Looking just at the photo, and ignoring the descriptive caption, there are    4
some interesting visual and artistic effects that help a viewer better understand the circumstances surrounding the image. One of its most prominent
features is the way the photographer decides to focus on only one young child
in the foreground, while including seven Nazi soldiers behind her. The effect
is overwhelming, and in gazing at the image, one is struck by the magnitude
and force of the oppressing men in sharp contrast to the innocence and helplessness of the lone girl. By juxtaposing one child with seven men, the image
comes across strongly as both cruel and terribly frightening. In addition, the
child in the foreground is a young girl, which only adds to the potency of the
image. The photographer makes the soldiers appear far more menacing and
unjust, in that there appears to be no physical way in which a young girl could
possibly defend herself against these men.

What is additionally interesting about this particular aspect of the photo    5
is that the seven men are not grouped together, or in any way concentrated
right next to the child. There are three directly behind the girl, one a little
farther behind and to the left, one even slightly farther behind and to the
right, and two very far off in the distance, walking in the opposite direction.
This placement of the soldiers not only gives the photo an excellent sense of
depth, but also conveys to the viewer a sense that the entire surroundings, not
just the little girl, are being controlled and surveyed. It allows the viewer to
imagine and wonder in what way other children, or perhaps just the other
parts of the village, are being similarly restricted. For the young girl, and the
viewer, it allows no way out; all angles and directions of the photo are covered
by symbols of oppression, producing an eerily suffocating effect.

The child is the only person in the photo looking directly at the photog-    6
rapher. Whether this technique was manipulated on purpose remains to be
seen, but it goes without saying that the effect is dramatic. Her gaze is wistful

and innocent. In contrast, the men occupying the rest of the photo, and most prominently the three mounted ones in the foreground, are gazing either away or down. While it is uncertain what the soldiers behind the child are staring at, their downward stare causes their heads to hang in almost shameful disgrace. They do not look at the child, and yet they do not look at the photographer, who is quite obviously standing in front of them. Is this because they do not see that there is a picture being taken, or perhaps the photographer is another soldier, and this picture is simply routine in recording the progress of their work?

If not a Nazi soldier, the photographer could be a Polish citizen; if this were the case, it might change our interpretation of the photo. Suddenly, the girl's facial expression and direct gaze seem pleading, while, for fear of being caught, the photographer snaps the picture quickly, in the exact moment the soldiers are looking away. Perhaps the soldiers did not mind having their picture taken. Many Polish were considered, after all, their racial equals, and maybe they would have respected and appreciated an amateur photographer's interest in their work.

While all of these scenarios are seemingly plausible, the purpose of the photograph is still uncertain. There are also several possibilities. One is that the Nazis commissioned the photograph, as they did others at the time, to properly record the events surrounding the development of their plan. In an article entitled "The Camera as Weapon: Documentary Photography and the Holocaust," Sybil Milton describes the ways in which Nazi photographers worked:

> Nazi professional photographers produced in excess of one-quarter million images. Their work was officially regulated and licensed. . . . All photos were screened by military censors subservient to official directives of the Propaganda Ministry. . . . Press photographers of World War II rarely showed atrocities and seldom published prints unfavorable to their own side. (1)

However, while the evidence is compelling, Milton recognizes another possibility that significantly changes the motive for the photo: "Portable cameras, and other technical innovations like interchangeable lenses and multiple exposure film, meant that nonprofessionals owned and used cameras with ease. Many soldiers carried small Leica or Ermanox cameras in their rucksacks or pillaged optical equipment from the towns they occupied" (2). While it is possible that the photograph was taken by a soldier seeking to document the work in Poland for his own interests, this probability, against the numerous commissioned photographs and the nature of the subject matter being documented, is unlikely. The photo alone, while intriguing in its image, tells only half of the story, and without a definitive context can become akin to a "choose your own adventure" novel. In other words, the possibilities for a photographic purpose are all laid out, but the true meaning or end remains undetermined. Unlike hand-made art, which in its very purpose begs to be viewed through various interpretations, photography, and particularly photojournalism, captures a certain moment in time, featuring specific subject matter, under a genuine set of circumstances. The picture is not invented, it is real life, and in being so demands to be viewed alongside its agenda, for without this context, it may never be fully understood.

When we turn to the caption describing the photograph, "Mounted Nazi   9 troops on the lookout for likely Polish children," the book *Master Race* and its accompanying story can now properly be discussed. Instead of typically dealing with the issues of a racist Nazi Germany as it relates to the Holocaust, and the other forms of racial extermination and discrimination that were subsequently involved, Clay and Leapman's book looks at the other side of the coin. It is important in dealing with and understanding the concept of racism to realize that racists are not simply those who dislike others; they are also those who worship themselves. In *Mein Kampf* Hitler outlined the inspiration for his racial tyranny by saying, "The products of human culture, the achievements in art, science and technology . . . are almost exclusively the creative product of the Aryan." He was heavily influenced by the work of racially charged popular science writers, such as H. F. K. Gunther, who in his *Ethnology of the German Nation* wrote: "The man of Nordic race is not only the most gifted but also the most beautiful. . . . The man's face is hard and chiseled, the woman's tender, with rose-pink skin and bright triumphant eyes" (qtd. in Clay and Leapman 17). Through the course of the book, the topic of racism in Nazi Germany focuses intently on the concept of racial purification. By following the work of the carefully selected (meaning those of impeccable Aryan ancestry) members of Himmler's elite SS corps, Clay and Leapman introduce the history of Germany's failed *Lebensborn* experiment and the homes that were created by the Third Reich to breed and raise "perfect Aryans" (ix).

In a disturbing segment on Hitler's racial utopia, Clay and Leapman   10 describe the practice of eugenics, improving humankind by eliminating undesirable genetic traits and breeding those that were considered superior. The SS soldiers who are commonly known for forcing the Jews into concentration camps are mentioned, but this time they are discussed as the same men who were ordered to father white babies with volunteer German and Norwegian mothers. However, it is the final fact, the story of the SS soldiers who occupied surrounding countries and then stole children "who looked as if they might further improve the breed," that becomes the focus and ultimate subject matter of the photograph (ix).

Looking at the photograph in this context, the soldier no longer appears   11 to be protecting the Polish children, but hunting them. The word "likely" in the caption denotes this. Children who possessed strong Nordic or Aryan qualities were systematically taken from their native countries, adopted by German parents (who were paid by the Nazi regime), taught to forget their families and former lives, and raised to breed not only many children of their own but, above all, families that would uphold Nazi ideology. For Hitler and Heinrich Himmler, who was appointed Commissar for Consolidating German Nationhood, exterminating the racially impure was merely preparation. It was the process of breeding and stealing children that Himmler considered central and key in the ultimate goal for racial purification:

> Obviously in such a mixture of peoples there will always be some racially good types. Therefore I think that it is our duty to take their children with us, to remove them from their environment, if necessary by robbing or stealing them. . . . My aim has always been the same, to attract all the Nordic blood in the world and take it for ourselves. (qtd. in Clay and Leapman 91)

Additionally, Himmler's objective in targeting children, rather than adults, was a planned and strategic tool. Through teachings at school, children were used to control their parents by being encouraged to report what they did and said. Himmler realized that older people would be less enthusiastic about his ideas, so he made every effort to win the minds of the next generation.

What is perhaps most compelling about the *Lebensborn* experiment and 12 thus most poignant when viewing the photograph is the reminder that for every child that was stolen from nations like Poland, his or her family was being equally betrayed. One Polish girl recounted the events of her kidnapping years later, describing both her and her father's reaction to the incident:

> Three SS men came into the room and put us up against a wall. . . . They immediately picked out the fair children with blue eyes — seven altogether, including me. . . . My father, who tried to stop my being taken away, was threatened by the soldiers. They even said he would be taken to a concentration camp. But I have no idea what happened to him later. (qtd. in Clay and Leapman 95)

The girl who spoke above just as easily could have been the young girl being followed by soldiers in the photograph, only moments after she was taken. Such incidents force us to broaden our sense of whom the Nazis victimized. While there is no mistaking the victimization of the Jewish population and other races in Germany, amidst these better-known hate crimes the Nazis were also perpetrating a horrific exploitation of the so-called "white" race.

The complexities surrounding this photograph remind us that the story of 13 any photograph is liable to contain ambiguity. As an art, photography relies on the imagination of the viewer; not *knowing* provides the viewer with a realm of interesting possibilities. Context matters even with art, and playing with possible contexts gives a photograph diverse meanings. It is in these various viewpoints that we find pleasure, amusement, fear, or wonder. It is perhaps in the shift to photojournalism that determining a particular context becomes even more important. In fact, even if the original photographer saw the image as artistic, subsequent events compel us to try to see the image of the Polish girl with Nazis as journalism. In this endeavor, we must uncover as much as possible about the surrounding context. As much as we can, we need to know this girl's particular story. Without a name, date, place, or relevant data, this girl would fall even further backwards into the chapters of unrecorded history.

## Works Cited

"Mounted Nazi Troops on the Lookout for Likely Polish Children." Clay and Leapman, 87.

Clay, Catrine, and Michael Leapman. *Master Race: The* Lebensborn *Experiment in Nazi Germany.* London: Hodder, 1995.

Hitler, Adolf. *Mein Kampf.* Vol. 2, chap. 3. *Hitler Historical Museum.* 1996–2000. 1 Dec. 2000 <http://www.hitler.org/writings/Mein_Kampf>.

Milton, Sybil. "The Camera as Weapon: Documentary Photography and the Holocaust." 1970. *Museum of Tolerance Online.* Simon Wiesenthal Center. 6 Dec. 2000 <http://motlc.wiesenthal.com/resources/books/annual1/chap03.html>.

*For a reading quiz and annotated links to further readings on the Holocaust and on the* Lebensborn *experiment, visit **bedfordstmartins.com/thebedfordreader**.*

## Journal Writing

Ayad uncovers an aspect of Nazi history that is not well known and may seem startling. Think of a time when you learned something that surprised you about history, science, or culture — either in a class or through independent research. In your journal, write about your discovery and how it affected you. (To take your journal writing further, see "From Journal to Essay" on the next page.)

## Questions on Meaning

1. Ayad's essay pursues two threads: certain events in German history and certain characteristics of photography, especially photojournalism. Each thread in essence has its own THESIS, stated in paragraphs 1 and 8. What are these theses? Where in the essay does Ayad bring them together?
2. Ayad writes about events in history that she thinks some readers do not know about. What are these events?
3. What do you see as Ayad's PURPOSE in this essay?

## Questions on Writing Strategy

1. Why does Ayad devote so much of her essay to discussing the photograph? What is the EFFECT of her speculations about the content and the creation of the photograph?
2. Ayad's AUDIENCE was originally the teacher and students in her writing class. What does she ASSUME readers already know about Nazi Germany? What does she assume they may not know?
3. What is the effect of Ayad's last two sentences? Why does Ayad end this way?
4. **OTHER METHODS**   Where in the essay does Ayad draw on DESCRIPTION? Why is description crucial to Ayad's analysis?

## Questions on Language

1. What words and phrases does Ayad use in paragraphs 4–6 to communicate her own feelings about the photograph? What are those feelings?
2. Why does Ayad quote Adolf Hitler and H. F. K. Gunther (par. 9), Heinrich Himmler (11), and the Polish woman who was kidnapped as a child (12)? What does Ayad achieve with these quotations?
3. What is the effect of the word *targeting* in paragraph 11?
4. Consult a dictionary if you are unsure of the meaning of any of the following: capricious (title); Aryan, anti-Semitism, ideology, Nordic (par. 1); shrouded, elucidate (2); juxtaposing (4); suffocating (5); scenarios, plausible, commissioned, pillaged, definitive (8); extermination, tyranny, impeccable (9); poignant (12); ambiguity, subsequent (13).

## Suggestions for Writing

1. **FROM JOURNAL TO ESSAY**   Using your journal writing as a starting point, draft an essay about a surprising discovery you made in a class or on your own. If it will be helpful, do some research to extend your knowledge of the subject. Involve your readers in the essay by distinguishing general knowledge—that is, what they probably know already—from the new information.
2. Locate a photograph that you find especially striking, perhaps in a library book or through an online photo collection such as Corbis (*pro.corbis.com*). Write an essay that describes and analyzes the image, using a thesis statement and vivid language to make your interpretation clear.

3. **CRITICAL WRITING**    Some of Ayad's paragraphs are long, especially 1, 8, 9, and 11. How COHERENT are these long paragraphs? Write a brief essay in which you analyze two of them in terms of their organization, the TRANSITIONS or other devices that connect sentences, and any problems with coherence that you see.

4. **CONNECTIONS**    In "Shooting an Elephant" (p. 634), George Orwell writes about the actions of an occupying government from the perspective of an official uncomfortable with his role and reluctant to perform his duties. Write an essay in which you imagine how one of the mounted soldiers in Ayad's photograph may have felt about his role in Germany's *Lebensborn* experiment, whether enthusiastic or, like Orwell, doubtful.

# JAMAICA KINCAID

JAMAICA KINCAID was born Elaine Potter Richardson in 1949 on the Caribbean island of Antigua. She attended school in Antigua and struggled to become independent of her mother and her place. "I was supposed to be full of good manners and good speech," she has recalled. "Where the hell I was going to go with it I don't know." Kincaid took it to New York, where she went at age seventeen to work as a family helper. She briefly attended Franconia College on a photography scholarship and did odd jobs in New York. In the early 1970s, she became friends with George Trow, a writer for *The New Yorker*. Soon she was contributing to the magazine, and in 1976 she became a staff writer. Soon after, she began writing fiction, producing a collection of stories, *At the Bottom of the River* (1983), and four novels, *Annie John* (1985), *Lucy* (1990), *The Autobiography of My Mother* (1996), and *Mr. Potter* (2002) — all based on her own life on Antigua and as an immigrant. Her nonfiction books include *A Small Place* (1988), also about Antigua; *My Brother* (1997), a National Book Award finalist; and *Talk Stories* (2000), a collection of her "Talk of the Town" pieces from *The New Yorker*. An avid gardener, Kincaid has also written *My Garden (Book)* (1999) and *Among Flowers: A Walk in the Himalayas* (2004). She is a visiting professor at Harvard University and lives in Vermont.

## *Girl*

This very short story was collected in *At the Bottom of the River*. Much as Judy Brady does in "I Want a Wife" (p. 340), Kincaid analyzes the domain of the title female, both the roles she is expected to fill and the relationship with her mother, whose commanding, hectoring voice fills the story. The writer Stephanie Vaughn has said that Kincaid's story "spills out in a single breath. . . . Its exhilarating motion gives me the sense of a writer carried over the precipice by the energy of her own vision."

Wash the white clothes on Monday and put them on the stone heap; wash the color clothes on Tuesday and put them on the clothesline to dry; don't walk barehead in the hot sun; cook pumpkin fritters in very hot sweet oil; soak your little cloths right after you take them off; when buying cotton to make yourself a nice blouse, be sure that it doesn't have gum on it, because that way it won't hold up well after a wash; soak salt fish overnight before you cook it; is it true that you sing benna[1] in Sunday school?; always eat your food in such a way that it won't turn someone else's stomach; on Sundays try to walk like a

---

[1] Calypso music. — EDS.

lady and not like the slut you are so bent on becoming; don't sing benna in
Sunday school; you mustn't speak to wharf-rat boys, not even to give directions; don't eat fruits on the street—flies will follow you; *but I don't sing benna
on Sundays at all and never in Sunday school;* this is how to sew on a button; this
is how to make a buttonhole for the button you have just sewed on; this is how
to hem a dress when you see the hem coming down and so to prevent yourself from looking like the slut I know you are so bent on becoming; this is
how you iron your father's khaki shirt so that it doesn't have a crease; this
is how you iron your father's khaki pants so that they don't have a crease;
this is how you grow okra—far from the house, because okra tree harbors red
ants; when you are growing dasheen,[2] make sure it gets plenty of water or else
it makes your throat itch when you are eating it; this is how you sweep a corner; this is how you sweep a whole house; this is how you sweep a yard; this is
how you smile to someone you don't like too much; this is how you smile to
someone you don't like at all; this is how you smile to someone you like completely; this is how you set a table for tea; this is how you set a table for dinner; this is how you set a table for dinner with an important guest; this is how
you set a table for lunch; this is how you set a table for breakfast; this is how
to behave in the presence of men who don't know you very well, and this way
they won't recognize immediately the slut I have warned you against becoming; be sure to wash every day, even if it is with your own spit; don't squat
down to play marbles—you are not a boy, you know; don't pick people's flowers—you might catch something; don't throw stones at blackbirds, because it
might not be a blackbird at all; this is how to make a bread pudding; this is
how to make doukona;[3] this is how to make pepper pot; this is how to make a
good medicine for a cold; this is how to make a good medicine to throw away
a child before it even becomes a child; this is how to catch a fish; this is how
to throw back a fish you don't like, and that way something bad won't fall on
you; this is how to bully a man; this is how a man bullies you; this is how to
love a man, and if this doesn't work there are other ways, and if they don't
work don't feel too bad about giving up; this is how to spit up in the air if
you feel like it, and this is how to move quick so that it doesn't fall on you; this
is how to make ends meet; always squeeze bread to make sure it's fresh; *but
what if the baker won't let me feel the bread?;* you mean to say that after all you
are really going to be the kind of woman who the baker won't let near the
bread?

---

[2] Taro, a tropical plant with an edible tuber. —EDS.
[3] A pudding made of plantains, fruit similar to bananas. —EDS.

For a reading quiz, sources on Jamaica Kincaid, and annotated links to further readings on Kincaid's native Antigua, visit **bedfordstmartins.com/thebedfordreader**.

## Journal Writing

Are the motherly warnings received by the girl of this story anything like the warnings or instructions that were drilled into you when you were a young adolescent? In
your journal, explore the advice you remember receiving while growing up. Who took
responsibility for instructing you in "proper" behavior? (To take your journal writing
further, see "From Journal to Essay" on the following page.)

## Questions on Meaning

1. What are the CONNOTATIONS of the phrase "wharf-rat boys"? Why is the girl of
   the title supposed to avoid them?
2. What does it mean to "be the kind of woman who the baker won't let near the
   bread" (last line)?
3. What do the elements of the mother's advice add up to? What kind of life does
   she depict for her daughter?

## Questions on Writing Strategy

1. Why do you think Kincaid wrote her story as one long sentence? What does she
   achieve?
2. What does Kincaid convey through the one comment and one question in
   italics?
3. Toward the end of this story, the mother says, "this is how to spit up in the air if
   you feel like it, and this is how to move quick so that it doesn't fall on you." What
   is the EFFECT of this particular piece of advice? What effect would it have if it were
   the last line of the story?
4. **OTHER METHODS** The many obligations of a girl/woman can be CLASSIFIED into
   groups of skills and behaviors. What categories do you see? How do they help
   organize the story?

## Questions on Language

1. What do the repeated directions about how to "sweep," "smile," and "set a table"
   suggest?
2. What can you conclude about the girl from the mother's scolding, "don't squat
   down to play marbles—you are not a boy, you know"?

3. Make sure you know the meanings of the following words: fritters, khaki, okra.
4. The fiction writer Stephanie Vaughn advises reading "Girl" aloud. She says, "I find that it is best to stand up when you read this story aloud, and to take a breath from the deepest region of your belly. When your lungs are full, when your shoulders are back, you begin to speak the story, and then you find that you are singing." Try it yourself. How is reading the story aloud different from reading it to yourself?

### Suggestions for Writing

1. **FROM JOURNAL TO ESSAY**   "Adolescents' heads are stuffed with advice intended to make them conform to rigid cultural roles and values." Based on your own experience, do you agree or disagree with this statement? Write an essay explaining your position, using EXAMPLES from your journal entry as support.
2. It's fair to assume that "Girl" is at least partly autobiographical because Kincaid has often written or spoken about the influence of her mother. In "Jamaica Kincaid on Writing" (following), the author mentions rebelling against her mother's "magic." Elsewhere, she has said that her mother's close attention made Kincaid's past "a kind of museum. . . . Clearly, the way I became a writer is that my mother wrote my life for me and told it to me." What adult has had a large influence on you? How are you different today because of him or her? Write an essay identifying the parts of yourself that you can attribute to this person — in other words, analyzing yourself as the product of this person's interest (or lack of interest) in you.
3. **CRITICAL WRITING**   The story's speaker repeatedly and gloomily connects her daughter and a "slut." Write an essay analyzing Kincaid's use of *slut*. How does the mother seem to be defining this word? Why does she repeat it so often? Should we ASSUME that the daughter actually is a "slut"? What might be the effect of this repetition on the daughter? What is the effect on you, the reader?
4. **CONNECTIONS**   Judy Brady, in "I Want a Wife" (p. 340), and Kincaid both analyze women's traditional roles, although they have different perspectives on those roles. How are the roles they describe similar? What do the speakers' TONES convey about their attitudes toward their roles? Write an essay explaining how Brady and Kincaid use word choice, sentence structures, repetition, and other elements of tone to clarify their speakers' values and feelings.

---

## *Jamaica Kincaid on Writing*

In a 1990 interview with Louise Kennedy in the *Boston Globe*, Jamaica Kincaid says that making sense of life is what motivates her writing. "I started out feeling alone," she remarks. "I grew up in a place where I was very alone. I didn't know then that I wanted to write; I didn't have that thought. But even if I had, I would have had no one to tell it to. They would have laughed before they threw me in a pond or something." With this beginning, Kincaid came to believe that the point of writing is not to please the reader. "Sometimes I feel—'I've pushed too far, I don't care, I don't care if you don't like this. I know it and it makes sense to me.'" The point, then, is to understand the world through the self. "I'm trying to discover the secret of myself. . . . For me everything passes through the self."

Kincaid's writing helps her come to terms with the conflicts in her life. "I could be dead or in jail. If you don't know how to make sense of what's happened to you, if you see things but can't express them—it's so painful." Part of Kincaid's pain growing up was the "magic" her mother held over her, a power that fueled Kincaid's rebellion. "That feeling of rebellion is doomed," she says. "You can't succeed. But it's worth trying because you find out that you can't. You have to try, or you die."

Although her native Antigua figures strongly in her writing, Kincaid cannot write there. "When I'm in the place where I'm from, I can't really think. I just absorb it; I take it all in. Then I come back and take it out and unpack it and walk through it." Her need for distance has led her to live in Vermont, "the opposite of where I come from. It changes. It's mountainous. It has seasons." As for Antigua, Kincaid says, "I don't know how to live there, but I don't know how to live without there."

## For Discussion

1. How can not caring about the reader's response liberate a writer?
2. What does Kincaid mean by "everything passes through the self"? Do you experience this process from time to time?
3. How does the author view her place of birth? Do you find her last statement contradictory?

# ADDITIONAL WRITING TOPICS

## *Division or Analysis*

Write an essay by the method of division or analysis using one of the following subjects (or choose your own subject). In your essay, make sure your purpose and your
principle of division or analysis are clear to your readers. Explain the parts of your subject so that readers know how each relates to the others and contributes to the whole.

1. The slang or technical terminology of a group such as stand-up comedians or
   computer hackers
2. An especially bad movie, television show, or book
3. A doll, game, or other toy from childhood
4. A typical TV commercial for a product such as laundry soap, deodorant, beer, or
   a luxury or an economy car
5. An appliance or a machine, such as a stereo speaker, a motorcycle, a microwave
   oven, or a camera
6. An organization or association, such as a social club, a sports league, or a support
   group
7. The characteristic appearance of a rock singer or a classical violinist
8. A year in the life of a student
9. Your favorite poem
10. A short story, an essay, or another work that made you think
11. The government of your community
12. The most popular restaurant (or other place of business) in town
13. The Bible
14. A band or an orchestra
15. A painting or statue

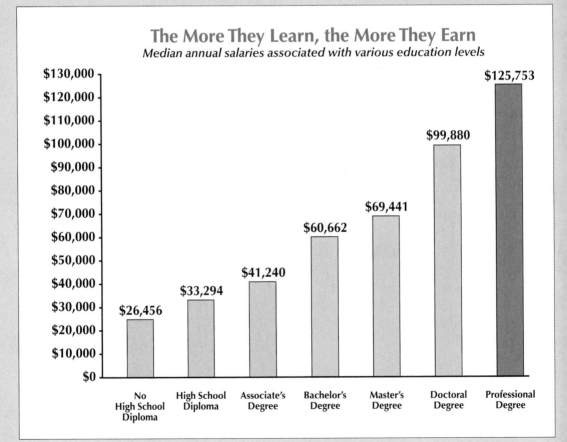

## The More They Learn, the More They Earn
*Median annual salaries associated with various education levels*

| | |
|---|---|
| No High School Diploma | $26,456 |
| High School Diploma | $33,294 |
| Associate's Degree | $41,240 |
| Bachelor's Degree | $60,662 |
| Master's Degree | $69,441 |
| Doctoral Degree | $99,880 |
| Professional Degree | $125,753 |

# 10

---

# CLASSIFICATION

*Sorting into Kinds*

◀ **Classification in a chart**

Posted on the Web site of State Farm Bank, this bar chart uses data from the US Census Bureau to show the earning potential of seven levels of education, from no high school diploma through professional degree, such as law or medicine. (Notice that the use of color further classifies the seven education levels into three groups.) This chart and another one titled "College Costs Continue to Rise" support State Farm's offer to help its customers "make education more affordable" through various savings and investment plans. How might the charts help persuade customers to turn to State Farm for help?

## THE METHOD

To CLASSIFY is to make sense of the world by arranging many units — trucks, chemical elements, wasps, students — into more manageable groups. Zoologists classify animals, botanists classify plants — and their classifications help us to understand a vast and complex subject: life on earth. To help us find books in a library, librarians classify books into categories: fiction, biography, history, psychology, and so forth. For the convenience of readers, newspapers run classified advertising, grouping many small ads into categories such as Help Wanted and Cars for Sale.

### Subjects and Reasons for Classification

The subject of a classification is always a number of things, such as peaches or political systems. (In contrast, DIVISION or ANALYSIS, the topic of the preceding chapter, usually deals with a solitary subject, a coherent whole, such as *a* peach or *a* political system.) The job of classification is to sort the things into groups or classes based on their similarities and differences. Say, for instance, you're going to write an essay about how people write. After interviewing a lot of writers, you determine that writers' processes differ widely, mainly in the amount of planning and rewriting they entail. (Notice that this determination involves analyzing the process of writing, separating it into steps. See Chap. 8.) On the basis of your findings, you create groups for planners, one-drafters, and rewriters. Once your groups are defined (and assuming they are valid), your subjects (the writers) almost sort themselves out.

Classification is done for a PURPOSE. In a New York City guidebook, Joan Hamburg and Norma Ketay discuss low-priced hotels. (Notice that already they are examining the members of a group: low-priced as opposed to medium- and high-priced hotels.) They cast the low-priced hotels into categories: Rooms for Singles and Students, Rooms for Families, Rooms for Servicepeople, and Rooms for General Occupancy. Always their purpose is evident: to match up the visitor with a suitable kind of room. When a classification has no purpose, it seems a silly and hollow exercise.

Just as you can ANALYZE a subject (or divide a pie) in many ways, you can classify a subject according to many principles. A different New York guidebook might classify all hotels according to price: grand luxury, luxury, moderate, low-priced (Hamburg and Ketay's category), fleabag, and flophouse. The purpose of this classification would be to match visitors to hotels fitting their pocketbooks. The principle you use in classifying things depends on your purpose. A linguist might explain the languages of the world by classifying them according to their origins (Romance languages, Germanic languages, Coptic languages . . .), but a student battling with a college language requirement might try to entertain fellow students by classifying languages into three groups: hard to learn, harder to learn, and unlearnable.

## Kinds of Classification

The simplest classification is binary (or two-part), in which you sort things out into (1) those with a certain distinguishing feature and (2) those without it. You might classify a number of persons, let's say, into smokers and nonsmokers, heavy metal fans and nonfans, runners and nonrunners, believers and nonbelievers. Binary classification is most useful when your subject is easily divisible into positive and negative categories.

Classification can be complex as well. As we are reminded by the English writer Jonathan Swift (1667–1745),

> So, naturalists observe, a flea
> Hath smaller fleas that on him prey,
> And these have smaller yet to bite 'em.
> And so proceed *ad infinitum*.

In being faithful to reality, you will sometimes find that you have to sort out the members of categories into subcategories. Hamburg and Ketay did something of the kind when they subclassified the class of low-priced New York hotels. Writing about the varieties of one Germanic language, such as English, a writer could identify the subclasses of British English, North American English, Australian English, and so on.

As readers, we all enjoy watching a clever writer sort things into categories. We like to meet classifications that strike us as true and familiar. This pleasure may account for the appeal of magazine articles that classify things ("The Seven Common Garden Varieties of Moocher," "Five Embarrassing Types of Social Blunder"). Usefulness as well as pleasure may explain the popularity of classifications that EVALUATE things. The magazine *Consumer Reports* sorts products as varied as computer monitors and canned tuna into groups based on quality (excellent, good, fair, poor, and not acceptable), and then, using DESCRIPTION, discusses each product. (Of a frozen pot pie: "Bottom crust gummy, meat spongy when chewed, with nondescript old-poultry and stale-flour flavor.")

# THE PROCESS

## Purposes and Theses

Classification will usually come into play when you want to impose order on a complex subject that includes many items. In one essay in this chapter, for instance, Stephanie Ericsson tackles the lies people tell one another.

Sometimes you may use classification humorously, as Russell Baker does in another essay in this chapter, to give a charge to familiar experiences. Whichever use you make of classification, though, do it for a reason. The files of composition instructors are littered with student essays in which nothing was ventured and nothing gained by classification.

Things can be classified into categories that reveal truth or into categories that don't tell us a thing. To sort out ten US cities according to their relative freedom from air pollution or their cost of living or the degree of progress they have made in civil rights might prove highly informative and useful. Such a classification might even tell us where we'd want to live. But to sort out the cities according to a superficial feature such as the relative size of their cat and dog populations wouldn't interest anyone, probably, except a veterinarian looking for a job.

Your purpose, your THESIS, and your principle of classification will all overlap at the point where you find your interest in your subject. Say you're curious about how other students write. Is your interest primarily in the materials they use (computer, felt-tip pen, pencil), in where and when they write, or in how much planning and rewriting they do? Any of these could lead to a principle for sorting the students into groups. And that principle should be revealed in your THESIS STATEMENT, letting readers know why you are classifying. Here, from the essays in this chapter, are two examples of classification thesis statements:

> Inanimate objects are classified into three major categories—those that don't work, those that break down and those that get lost.
> —Russell Baker, "The Plot Against People"

> [I]t's not easy to entirely eliminate lies from our lives. No matter how pious we may try to be, we will still embellish, hedge, and omit to lubricate the daily machinery of living. But . . . acceptance of lies becomes a cultural cancer that eventually shrouds and reorders reality until moral garbage becomes as invisible to us as water is to a fish.
> —Stephanie Ericsson, "The Ways We Lie"

## Categories

For a workable classification, make sure that the categories you choose don't overlap. If you were writing a survey of popular magazines for adults and you were sorting your subject into categories that included women's magazines and sports magazines, you might soon run into trouble. Into which category would you place *Women's Sports*? The trouble is that both categories take in the same item. To avoid this problem, you'll need to reorganize your classification on a different principle. You might sort out the magazines by their audiences: magazines mainly for women, magazines mainly for men, magazines for both women and men. Or you might group them according to subject matter: sports magazines, literary magazines, astrology magazines, fashion magazines, celebrity magazines, trade journals, and so on. *Women's Sports* would fit into either of those classification schemes, but into only *one* category in each scheme.

When you draw up a scheme of classification, be sure also that you include all essential categories. Omitting an important category can weaken the effect of your essay, no matter how well written it is. It would be a major oversight, for example, if you were to classify the residents of a dormitory according to their religious affiliations and not include a category for the numerous non-affiliated. Your reader might wonder if your carelessness in forgetting a category extended to your thinking about the topic as well.

Some form of outline can be helpful to keep the classes and their members straight as you develop and draft ideas. You might experiment with a diagram in which you jot down headings for the groups, with plenty of space around them, and then let each heading accumulate members as you think of them, the way a magnet attracts paper clips. This kind of diagram offers more flexibility than a vertical list or an outline, and it may be a better aid for keeping categories from overlapping or disappearing.

### FOCUS ON PARAGRAPH DEVELOPMENT

A crucial aim of classification is to make sure each group is clear: what's counted in, what's counted out, and why. You'll provide the examples and other details that make the groups clear as you develop the paragraph(s) devoted to each group.

The following paragraph barely outlines one group in a four-part classification of ex-smokers into zealots, evangelists, the elect, and the serene:

> The second group, evangelists, does not condemn smokers but encourages them to quit. Evangelists think quitting is easy, and they preach this message, often earning the resentment of potential converts.

Contrast this bare-bones adaptation with the actual paragraphs written by Franklin E. Zimring in his essay "Confessions of a Former Smoker":

> By contrast, the antismoking evangelist does not condemn smokers. Unlike the zealot, he regards smoking as an easily curable condition, as a social disease, and not a sin. The evangelist spends an enormous amount of time seeking and preaching to the unconverted. He argues that kicking the habit is not *that* difficult. After all, *he* did it; moreover, as he describes it, the benefits of quitting are beyond measure and the disadvantages are nil.

> The hallmark of the evangelist is his insistence that he never misses tobacco. Though he is less hostile to smokers than the zealot, he is resented more. Friends and loved ones who have been the targets of his preachments frequently greet the resumption of smoking by the evangelist as an occasion for unmitigated glee.

In the second sentence of each paragraph, Zimring explicitly contrasts evangelists with zealots, the group he previously defined. And he does more as well: He provides specific examples of the evangelist's message (first paragraph) and of others' reactions to him (second paragraph). These details pin down the group, making it distinct from other groups and clear in itself.

---

## CHECKLIST FOR REVISING A CLASSIFICATION

✔ **PURPOSE**   Have you classified for a reason? Will readers see why you bothered?

✔ **PRINCIPLE OF CLASSIFICATION**   Will readers also see what rule or principle you have used for sorting individuals into groups? Is this principle apparent in your thesis sentence?

✔ **CONSISTENCY**   Does each representative of your subject fall into one category only, so that categories don't overlap?

✔ **COMPLETENESS**   Have you mentioned all the essential categories suggested by your principle of classification?

✔ **PARAGRAPH DEVELOPMENT**   Have you provided enough examples and other details so that readers can easily distinguish each category from the others?

---

## CLASSIFICATION IN PARAGRAPHS

### Writing About Television

Written for *The Bedford Reader*, the following paragraph uses classification to explain how a TV comedy's taped laugh track combines various laughs to sound like an actual rib-tickled audience. With the related paragraph on page 337, which ANALYZES the elements of any particular kind of laugh, this paragraph could be part of a full behind-the-scenes essay on how TV comedies make us laugh, even despite ourselves.

Most canned laughs produced by laugh machines fall into one of five reliable sounds. There are *titters*, light vocal laughs with which an imaginary audience responds to a comedian's least wriggle or grimace. Some producers rely heavily on *chuckles*, deeper, more chesty

*Topic sentence names principle of classification*

*Categories:*
*1. Titters*
*2. Chuckles*

responses. Most profound of all, *belly laughs* are summoned to acclaim broader jokes and sexual innuendos. When provided at full
level of sound and in longest duration, the belly laugh becomes the
Big Boffola. There are also *wild howls* or *screamers,* extreme responses
used not more than three times per show, lest they seem fake. These
are crowd laughs, and yet the machine also offers *freaky laughs,* the
piercing, eccentric screeches of solitary kooks. With them, a producer affirms that even a canned audience may include one thorny
individualist.

*Right margin notes:*
3. Belly laughs

4. Wild howls or screamers

5. Freaky laughs

Examples clearly distinguish categories

## Writing in an Academic Discipline

This paragraph comes from a textbook on human physical and cultural
evolution. The author offers a standard classification of hand grips in order to
explain one of several important differences between human beings and their
nearest relatives, apes and monkeys.

There are two distinct ways of holding and using tools: the
*power grip* and the *precision grip,* as John Napier termed them.
Human infants and children begin with the power grip and progress
to the precision grip. Think of how a child holds a spoon: first in the
power grip, in its fist or between its fingers and palm, and later
between the tips of the thumb and first two fingers, in the precision
grip. Many primates have the power grip also. It is the way they get
firm hold of a tree branch. But neither a monkey nor an ape has a
thumb long enough or flexible enough to be completely *opposable*
through rotation at the wrist, able to reach comfortably to the tips
of all the other fingers, as is required for our delicate yet strong precision grip. It is the opposability of our thumb and the independent
control of our fingers that make possible nearly all the movements
necessary to handle tools, to make clothing, to write with a pencil,
to play a flute.            —Bernard Campbell, *Humankind Emerging*

*Right margin notes:*
Topic sentence names principle of classification

Two categories explained side by side

Second category explained in greater detail

*Right vertical text:* Classification

## CLASSIFICATION IN PRACTICE

The summer between his sophomore and junior years of college, Kharron
Reid was seeking an internship in computer networking. After seeing several
likely openings posted at his school's placement office, he began compiling a
résumé that would make him appealing to potential employers.

Part of Reid's challenge in drafting his résumé was to bring order to what
seemed a complex and unwieldy subject, his life. The main solution was to
classify his activities and interests into clearly defined groups, such as work
experience, education, and special skills. Classification wasn't a conscious
choice for Reid: He didn't think, "I must classify." Instead, he recognized from
advice he'd seen on résumé writing that some sorting was required.

In his first draft, Reid worked to emphasize his qualifications for the internship he sought. The group that gave him the most trouble was work experience: Should he list his jobs with the specifics of each one? Or should he further sort his work experience into skills (such as computer skills, administrative skills, and communication skills) and then list the specifics of his jobs under each subcategory? He tried the résumé both ways and finally opted for the former arrangement, which seemed more straightforward, potentially less confusing to readers.

Before he could prepare his final draft, Reid also needed to decide which to put first, the category of education or the category of work experience. Here, he decided on work experience first because it was directly related to the internships he now sought; his education was more broad based.

Reid's final résumé appears on the facing page. For the cover letter he wrote to go with the résumé, see pages 191–92.

**Kharron Reid**
137 Chester Street, Apt. E
Allston, MA 02134
(617) 555-4009
kreid@bu.edu

OBJECTIVE

An internship that offers experience in information systems

EXPERIENCE

*Pioneer Networking,* Damani, MI, May–September 2006

As an intern, worked as a LAN specialist using a Unix-based server
- Connected eight workstations onto a LAN by laying physical platform and configuring software
- Assisted network engineer in monitoring operations of LAN

*NBS Systems Corp.,* Denniston, MI, June–September 2005

As an intern, helped install seven WANs using Windows XP
- Planned layout for WANs
- Installed physical platform and configured servers

SPECIAL SKILLS

Computer proficiency:

| | | |
|---|---|---|
| Windows 98/XP, | QuarkXPress | HTML |
| Windows NT/2000/2003 | Adobe Photoshop | XML |
| Unix | and InDesign | JavaScript |
| Linux 2.4 and 2.6 | | |

Internet research

INTERESTS

Building computers, designing Web sites, wrestling

EDUCATION

*Boston University, School of Management,* 2005 to present

Current standing: sophomore
Double major: business administration and information systems
Courses: introductory and advanced programming, information systems 1 and 2, basic business courses

*Lahser High School,* Bloomfield Hills, MI, 2001–2005

Graduated with academic, college-preparatory degree

REFERENCES

Available on request from Office of Career Services, Boston University, 19 Deerfield Street, Boston, MA 02215

Classification

# RUSSELL BAKER

RUSSELL BAKER is one of America's notable humorists and political satirists. Born in 1925 in Virginia, Baker was raised in New Jersey and Maryland by his widowed mother. After serving in the navy during World War II, he earned a BA from Johns Hopkins University in 1947. He became a reporter for the *Baltimore Sun* that year and then joined the *New York Times* in 1954, covering the State Department, the White House, and Congress. From 1962 until his retirement from the *Times* in 1998, he wrote a popular column that ranged over the merely bothersome (unreadable menus) and the serious (the Cold War). Baker has twice received the Pulitzer Prize, once for distinguished commentary and again for the first volume of his autobiography, *Growing Up* (1982). The most recent addition to the autobiography is *Looking Back* (2002). Many of Baker's columns have been collected in books, such as *There's a Country in My Cellar* (1990). Baker has also written fiction and children's books, edited *Russell Baker's Book of American Humor* (1993), and served as host of *Masterpiece Theatre* on public television.

# *The Plot Against People*

The critic R. Z. Sheppard has commented that Baker can "best be appreciated for doing what a good humorist has always done: writing to preserve his sanity for at least one more day." In this piece from the *New York Times* in 1968, Baker uses classification for that purpose, taking aim, as he has often done, at things. In the decades since this piece was written, the proliferation of electronic gadgets has, if anything, intensified the plot Baker imagines.

1    Inanimate objects are classified into three major categories — those that don't work, those that break down and those that get lost.

2    The goal of all inanimate objects is to resist man and ultimately to defeat him, and the three major classifications are based on the method each object uses to achieve its purpose. As a general rule, any object capable of breaking down at the moment when it is most needed will do so. The automobile is typical of the category.

3    With the cunning typical of its breed, the automobile never breaks down while entering a filling station with a large staff of idle mechanics. It waits until it reaches a downtown intersection in the middle of the rush hour, or until it is fully loaded with family and luggage on the Ohio Turnpike.

4    Thus it creates maximum misery, inconvenience, frustration and irritability among its human cargo, thereby reducing its owner's life span.

5    Washing machines, garbage disposals, lawn mowers, light bulbs, auto-

matic laundry dryers, water pipes, furnaces, electrical fuses, television tubes, hose nozzles, tape recorders, slide projectors—all are in league with the automobile to take their turn at breaking down whenever life threatens to flow smoothly for their human enemies.

Many inanimate objects, of course, find it extremely difficult to break down. Pliers, for example, and gloves and keys are almost totally incapable of breaking down. Therefore, they have had to evolve a different technique for resisting man. 6

They get lost. Science has still not solved the mystery of how they do it, and no man has ever caught one of them in the act of getting lost. The most plausible theory is that they have developed a secret method of locomotion which they are able to conceal the instant a human eye falls upon them. 7

It is not uncommon for a pair of pliers to climb all the way from the cellar to the attic in its single-minded determination to raise its owner's blood pressure. Keys have been known to burrow three feet under mattresses. Women's purses, despite their great weight, frequently travel through six or seven rooms to find hiding space under a couch. 8

Scientists have been struck by the fact that things that break down virtually never get lost, while things that get lost hardly ever break down. 9

A furnace, for example, will invariably break down at the depth of the first winter cold wave, but it will never get lost. A woman's purse, which after all does have some inherent capacity for breaking down, hardly ever does; it almost invariably chooses to get lost. 10

Some persons believe this constitutes evidence that inanimate objects are not entirely hostile to man, and that a negotiated peace is possible. After all, they point out, a furnace could infuriate a man even more thoroughly by getting lost than by breaking down, just as a glove could upset him far more by breaking down than by getting lost. 11

Not everyone agrees, however, that this indicates a conciliatory attitude among inanimate objects. Many say it merely proves that furnaces, gloves and pliers are incredibly stupid. 12

The third class of objects—those that don't work—is the most curious of all. These include such objects as barometers, car clocks, cigarette lighters, flashlights and toy-train locomotives. It is inaccurate, of course, to say that they never work. They work once, usually for the first few hours after being brought home, and then quit. Thereafter, they never work again. 13

In fact, it is widely assumed that they are built for the purpose of not working. Some people have reached advanced ages without ever seeing some of these objects—barometers, for example—in working order. 14

Science is utterly baffled by the entire category. There are many theories about it. The most interesting holds that the things that don't work have 15 attained the highest state possible for an inanimate object, the state to which things that break down and things that get lost can still only aspire.

They have truly defeated man by conditioning him never to expect any-   16
thing of them, and in return they have given man the only peace he receives from inanimate society. He does not expect his barometer to work, his electric locomotive to run, his cigarette lighter to light or his flashlight to illuminate, and when they don't it does not raise his blood pressure.

He cannot attain that peace with furnaces and keys and cars and women's   17
purses as long as he demands that they work for their keep.

---

*For a reading quiz, sources on Russell Baker, and annotated links to additional humor writing, visit **bedfordstmartins.com/thebedfordreader**.*

## Journal Writing

What other ways can you think of to classify inanimate objects? In your journal, try expanding on Baker's categories, or create new categories of your own based on a different principle — for example, objects no student can live without or objects no student would want to be caught dead with. (To take your journal writing further, see "From Journal to Essay" on the facing page.)

## Questions on Meaning

1. What is Baker's THESIS?
2. Why don't things that break down get lost, and vice versa?
3. Does Baker have any PURPOSE other than to make his readers smile?
4. How have inanimate objects "defeated man"?

## Questions on Writing Strategy

1. What is the EFFECT of Baker's principle of classification? What categories are omitted here, and why?
2. In paragraphs 6–10, how does Baker develop the category of things that get lost? Itemize the strategies he uses to make the category clear.
3. Find three places where Baker uses hyperbole. (See *Figures of speech* in Useful Terms if you need a definition.) What is the effect of the hyperbole?
4. How does the essay's INTRODUCTION help set its TONE? How does the CONCLUSION reinforce the tone?

5. **OTHER METHODS**   How does Baker use NARRATION to portray inanimate objects in the act of "resisting" people? Discuss how these mini-narratives make his classification more persuasive.

## Questions on Language

1. Look up any of these words that are unfamiliar: plausible, locomotion (par. 7); invariably, inherent (10); conciliatory (12).
2. What are the CONNOTATIONS of the word "cunning" (par. 3)? What is its effect in this context?
3. Why does Baker use such expressions as "man," "some people," and "their human enemies" rather than *I* to describe those who come into conflict with inanimate objects? How might the essay have been different if Baker had relied on *I*?

## Suggestions for Writing

1. **FROM JOURNAL TO ESSAY**   Write a brief, humorous essay based on one classification system from your journal entry. It may be helpful to use narration or DESCRIPTION in your classification. FIGURES OF SPEECH, especially hyperbole and understatement, can help you to establish a comic tone.
2. Think of a topic that would not generally be considered appropriate for a serious classification (some examples: game-show winners, body odors, stupid pet tricks, knock-knock jokes). Select a principle of classification and write a brief essay sorting the subject into categories. You may want to use a humorous tone; then again, you may want to approach the topic "seriously," counting on the contrast between subject and treatment to make your IRONY clear.
3. **CRITICAL WRITING**   In a short essay, discuss the likely AUDIENCE for "The Plot Against People." (Recall that it was first published in the *New York Times*.) What can you INFER from his EXAMPLES about Baker's own age and economic status? Does he ASSUME his audience is similar? How do the connections between author and audience help establish the essay's humor? Could this humor be seen as excluding some readers?
4. **CONNECTIONS**   Baker's essay bears comparison with "My Face" by another great humorist, Robert Benchley (p. 170). Each man writes about himself with a self-deprecating, mock-serious tone. Read both works closely, and write an essay in which you COMPARE AND CONTRAST the words the authors use to present themselves and their situations.

## *Russell Baker on Writing*

In "Computer Fallout," an essay from the October 11, 1987, *New York Times Magazine*, Baker sets out to prove that computers make a writer's life easier, but he ends up somewhere else entirely. Although Baker wrote this piece when word processors were still fairly new on the writing scene, those who share his affliction will recognize the experience even today.

The wonderful thing about writing with a computer instead of a typewriter or a lead pencil is that it's so easy to rewrite that you can make each sentence almost perfect before moving on to the next sentence.

An impressive aspect of using a computer to write with

One of the plusses about a computer on which to write

Happily, the computer is a marked improvement over both the typewriter and the lead pencil for purposes of literary composition, due to the ease with which rewriting can be effectuated, thus enabling

What a marked improvement the computer is for the writer over the typewriter and lead pencil

The typewriter and lead pencil were good enough in their day, but if Shakespeare had been able to access a computer with a good writing program

If writing friends scoff when you sit down at the computer and say, "The lead pencil was good enough for Shakespeare

One of the drawbacks of having a computer on which to write is the ease and rapidity with which the writing can be done, thus leading to the inclusion of many superfluous terms like "lead pencil," when the single word "pencil" would be completely, entirely and utterly adequate.

The ease with which one can rewrite on a computer gives it an advantage over such writing instruments as the pencil and typewriter by enabling the writer to turn an awkward and graceless sentence into one that is practically perfect, although it

The writer's eternal quest for the practically perfect sentence may be ending at last, thanks to the computer's gift of editing ease and swiftness to those confronting awkward, formless, nasty, illiterate sentences such as

Man's quest is eternal, but what specifically is it that he quests, and why does he

Mankind's quest is

Man's and woman's quest

Mankind's and womankind's quest

Humanity's quest for the perfect writing device

Eternal has been humanity's quest

Eternal have been many of humanity's quests

From the earliest cave writing, eternal has been the quest for a device that will forever prevent writers from using the word "quest," particularly when modified by such adjectives as "eternal," "endless," "tireless" and

Many people are amazed at the ease

Many persons are amazed by the ease

Lots of people are astounded when they see the nearly perfect sentences I write since upgrading my writing instrumentation from pencil and typewriter to

Listen, folks, there's nothing to writing almost perfect sentences with ease and rapidity provided you've given up the old horse-and-buggy writing mentality that says Shakespeare couldn't have written those great plays if he had enjoyed the convenience of electronic compositional instrumentation.

Folks, have you ever realized that there's nothing to writing almost

Have you ever stopped to think, folks, that maybe Shakespeare could have written even better if

To be or not to be, that is the central focus of the inquiry.

In the intrapersonal relationships played out within the mind as to the relative merits of continuing to exist as opposed to not continuing to exist

Live or die, a choice as ancient as humanities' eternal quest, is a tough choice which has confounded mankind as well as womankind ever since the option of dreaming was first perceived as a potentially negating effect of the quiescence assumed to be obtainable through the latter course of action.

I'm sick and tired of Luddites saying pencils and typewriters are just as good as computers for writing nearly perfect sentences when they — the Luddites, that is — have never experienced the swiftness and ease of computer writing which makes it possible to compose almost perfect sentences in practically no time at

Folks, are you sick and tired of

Are you, dear reader

Good reader, are you

A lot of you nice folks out there are probably just as sick and tired as I am of hearing people say they are sick and tired of this and that and

Listen, people, I'm just as sick and tired as you are of having writers and TV commercial performers who oil me in cornpone politician prose addressed to "you nice folks out

A curious feature of computers, as opposed to pencils and typewriters, is that when you ought to be writing something more interesting than a nearly perfect sentence

Since it is easier to revise and edit with a computer than with a typewriter or pencil, this amazing machine makes it very hard to stop editing and revising long enough to write a readable sentence, much less an entire newspaper column.

## For Discussion

1. What is Baker's unstated THESIS? Does he convince you?
2. Do you find yourself ever having the problem Baker finally admits to in the last paragraph?

# DEBORAH TANNEN

DEBORAH TANNEN is a linguist who is best known for her popular studies of communication between men and women. Born and raised in New York City, Tannen earned a BA from Harpur College (now the State University of New York at Binghamton); MAs from Wayne State University and the University of California at Berkeley; and a PhD in linguistics from Berkeley. She is University Professor at Georgetown University, has published many scholarly articles and books, and has lectured on linguistics all over the world. But her renown is more than academic: With television talk-show appearances, speeches to businesspeople and senators, and best-selling books, Tannen has become, in the words of one reviewer, "America's conversational therapist." The books include *You Just Don't Understand* (1990), *The Argument Culture* (1998), *I Only Say This Because I Love You* (2001), and *You're Wearing That?* (2006), the last about communication between mothers and daughters.

# *But What Do You Mean?*

Why do men and women so often communicate badly, if at all? This question has motivated much of Tannen's research and writing, including the essay here. Excerpted in *Redbook* magazine from Tannen's book *Talking from 9 to 5* (1994), "But What Do You Mean?" classifies the conversational areas where men and women have the most difficulty communicating at work.

Conversation is a ritual. We say things that seem obviously the thing to say, without thinking of the literal meaning of our words, any more than we expect the question "How are you?" to call forth a detailed account of aches and pains. 1

Unfortunately, women and men often have different ideas about what's appropriate, different ways of speaking. Many of the conversational rituals common among women are designed to take the other person's feelings into account, while many of the conversational rituals common among men are designed to maintain the one-up position, or at least avoid appearing one-down. As a result, when men and women interact — especially at work — it's often women who are at the disadvantage. Because women are not trying to avoid the one-down position, that is unfortunately where they may end up. 2

Here, the biggest areas of miscommunication. 3

## 1. Apologies

Women are often told they apologize too much. The reason they're told to stop doing it is that, to many men, apologizing seems synonymous with putting oneself down. But there are many times when "I'm sorry" isn't self-deprecating, 4 or even an apology; it's an automatic way of keeping both speakers on an equal footing. For example, a well-known columnist once interviewed me and gave me her phone number in case I needed to call her back. I misplaced the number and had to go through the newspaper's main switchboard. When our conversation was winding down and we'd both made ending-type remarks, I added, "Oh, I almost forgot—I lost your direct number, can I get it again?" "Oh, I'm sorry," she came back instantly, even though she had done nothing wrong and *I* was the one who'd lost the number. But I understood she wasn't really apologizing; she was just automatically reassuring me she had no intention of denying me her number.

Even when "I'm sorry" *is* an apology, women often assume it will be the    5
first step in a two-step ritual: I say "I'm sorry" and take half the blame, then you take the other half. At work, it might go something like this:

A: When you typed this letter, you missed this phrase I inserted.

B: Oh, I'm sorry. I'll fix it.

A: Well, I wrote it so small it was easy to miss.

When both parties share blame, it's a mutual face-saving device. But if one    6
person, usually the woman, utters frequent apologies and the other doesn't, she ends up looking as if she's taking the blame for mishaps that aren't her fault. When she's only partially to blame, she looks entirely in the wrong.

I recently sat in on a meeting at an insurance company where the sole    7
woman, Helen, said "I'm sorry" or "I apologize" repeatedly. At one point she said, "I'm thinking out loud. I apologize." Yet the meeting was intended to be an informal brainstorming session, and *everyone* was thinking out loud.

The reason Helen's apologies stood out was that she was the only person    8
in the room making so many. And the reason I was concerned was that Helen felt the annual bonus she had received was unfair. When I interviewed her colleagues, they said that Helen was one of the best and most productive workers—yet she got one of the smallest bonuses. Although the problem might have been outright sexism, I suspect her speech style, which differs from that of her male colleagues, masks her competence.

Unfortunately, not apologizing can have its price too. Since so many    9
women use ritual apologies, those who don't may be seen as hard-edged. What's important is to be aware of how often you say you're sorry (and why), and to monitor your speech based on the reaction you get.

## 2. Criticism

A woman who cowrote a report with a male colleague was hurt when she    10
read a rough draft to him and he leapt into a critical response—"Oh, that's

too dry! You have to make it snappier!" She herself would have been more likely to say, "That's a really good start. Of course, you'll want to make it a little snappier when you revise."

Whether criticism is given straight or softened is often a matter of convention. In general, women use more softeners. I noticed this difference when talking to an editor about an essay I'd written. While going over changes she wanted to make, she said, "There's one more thing. I know you may not agree with me. The reason I noticed the problem is that your other points are so lucid and elegant." She went on hedging for several more sentences until I put her out of her misery: "Do you want to cut that part?" I asked—and of course she did. But I appreciated her tentativeness. In contrast, another editor (a man) I once called summarily rejected my idea for an article by barking, "Call me when you have something new to say." 11

Those who are used to ways of talking that soften the impact of criticism may find it hard to deal with the right-between-the-eyes style. It has its own logic, however, and neither style is intrinsically better. People who prefer criticism given straight are operating on an assumption that feelings aren't involved: "Here's the dope. I know you're good; you can take it." 12

## 3. Thank-Yous

A woman manager I know starts meetings by thanking everyone for coming, even though it's clearly their job to do so. Her "thank-you" is simply a ritual. 13

A novelist received a fax from an assistant in her publisher's office; it contained suggested catalog copy for her book. She immediately faxed him her suggested changes and said, "Thanks for running this by me," even though her contract gave her the right to approve all copy. When she thanked the assistant, she fully expected him to reciprocate: "Thanks for giving me such a quick response." Instead, he said, "You're welcome." Suddenly, rather than an equal exchange of pleasantries, she found herself positioned as the recipient of a favor. This made her feel like responding, "Thanks for nothing!" 14

Many women use "thanks" as an automatic conversation starter and closer; there's nothing literally to say thank you for. Like many rituals typical of women's conversation, it depends on the goodwill of the other to restore the balance. When the other speaker doesn't reciprocate, a woman may feel like someone on a seesaw whose partner abandoned his end. Instead of balancing in the air, she has plopped to the ground, wondering how she got there. 15

## 4. Fighting

Many men expect the discussion of ideas to be a ritual fight—explored    16
through verbal opposition. They state their ideas in the strongest possible
terms, thinking that if there are weaknesses someone will point them out, and
by trying to argue against those objections, they will see how well their ideas
hold up.

Those who expect their own ideas to be challenged will respond to    17
another's ideas by trying to poke holes and find weak links—as a way of *helping*. The logic is that when you are challenged you will rise to the occasion:
Adrenaline makes your mind sharper; you get ideas and insights you would
not have thought of without the spur of battle.

But many women take this approach as a personal attack. Worse, they find    18
it impossible to do their best work in such a contentious environment. If
you're not used to ritual fighting, you begin to hear criticism of your ideas as
soon as they are formed. Rather than making you think more clearly, it makes
you doubt what you know. When you state your ideas, you hedge in order to
fend off potential attacks. Ironically, this is more likely to *invite* attack because
it makes you look weak.

Although you may never enjoy verbal sparring, some women find it help-    19
ful to learn how to do it. An engineer who was the only woman among four
men in a small company found that as soon as she learned to argue she was
accepted and taken seriously. A doctor attending a hospital staff meeting
made a similar discovery. She was becoming more and more angry with a male
colleague who'd loudly disagreed with a point she'd made. Her better judgment told her to hold her tongue, to avoid making an enemy of this powerful
senior colleague. But finally she couldn't hold it in any longer, and she rose to
her feet and delivered an impassioned attack on his position. She sat down in
a panic, certain she had permanently damaged her relationship with him. To
her amazement, he came up to her afterward and said, "That was a great rebuttal. I'm really impressed. Let's go out for a beer after work and hash out our
approaches to this problem."

## 5. Praise

A manager I'll call Lester had been on his new job six months when he    20
heard that the women reporting to him were deeply dissatisfied. When he
talked to them about it, their feelings erupted; two said they were on the verge
of quitting because he didn't appreciate their work, and they didn't want to
wait to be fired. Lester was dumbfounded: He believed they were doing a fine
job. Surely, he thought, he had said nothing to give them the impression he
didn't like their work. And indeed he hadn't. That was the problem. He had

said *nothing*—and the women assumed he was following the adage "If you can't say something nice, don't say anything." He thought he was showing confidence in them by leaving them alone.

Men and women have different habits in regard to giving praise. For ex-  21
ample, Deirdre and her colleague William both gave presentations at a conference. Afterward, Deirdre told William, "That was a great talk!" He thanked
her. Then she asked, "What did you think of mine?" and he gave her a lengthy
and detailed critique. She found it uncomfortable to listen to his comments.
But she assured herself that he meant well, and that his honesty was a signal
that she, too, should be honest when he asked for a critique of his performance.
As a matter of fact, she had noticed quite a few ways in which he could have
improved his presentation. But she never got a chance to tell him because he
never asked—and she felt put down. The worst part was that it seemed she had
only herself to blame, since she *had* asked what he thought of her talk.

But had she really asked for his critique? The truth is, when she asked for  22
his opinion, she was expecting a compliment, which she felt was more or less
required following anyone's talk. When he responded with criticism, she figured, "Oh, he's playing 'Let's critique each other'"—not a game she'd initiated, but one which she was willing to play. Had she realized he was going to
criticize her and not ask her to reciprocate, she would never have asked in the
first place.

It would be easy to assume that Deirdre was insecure, whether she was  23
fishing for a compliment or soliciting a critique. But she was simply talking
automatically, performing one of the many conversational rituals that allow us
to get through the day. William may have sincerely misunderstood Deirdre's
intention—or may have been unable to pass up a chance to one-up her when
given the opportunity.

## 6. Complaints

"Troubles talk" can be a way to establish rapport with a colleague. You  24
complain about a problem (which shows that you are just folks) and the other
person responds with a similar problem (which puts you on equal footing). But
while such commiserating is common among women, men are likely to hear it
as a request to *solve* the problem.

One woman told me she would frequently initiate what she thought  25
would be pleasant complaint-airing sessions at work. She'd talk about situations that bothered her just to talk about them, maybe to understand them
better. But her male office mate would quickly tell her how she could improve
the situation. This left her feeling condescended to and frustrated. She was
delighted to see this very impasse in a section in my book *You Just Don't*

*Understand,* and showed it to him. "Oh," he said, "I see the problem. How can we solve it?" Then they both laughed, because it had happened again: He short-circuited the detailed discussion she'd hoped for and cut to the chase of finding a solution.

Sometimes the consequences of complaining are more serious: A man might take a woman's lighthearted griping literally, and she can get a reputation as a chronic malcontent. Furthermore, she may be seen as not up to solving the problems that arise on the job. 26

## 7. Jokes

I heard a man call in to a talk show and say, "I've worked for two women and neither one had a sense of humor. You know, when you work with men, there's a lot of joking and teasing." The show's host and the guest (both women) took his comment at face value and assumed the women this man worked for were humorless. The guest said, "Isn't it sad that women don't feel comfortable enough with authority to see the humor?" The host said, "Maybe when more women are in authority roles, they'll be more comfortable with power." But although the women this man worked for *may* have taken themselves too seriously, it's just as likely that they each had a terrific sense of humor, but maybe the humor wasn't the type he was used to. They may have been like the woman who wrote to me: "When I'm with men, my wit or cleverness seems inappropriate (or lost!) so I don't bother. When I'm with my women friends, however, there's no hold on puns or cracks and my humor is fully appreciated." 27

The types of humor women and men tend to prefer differ. Research has shown that the most common form of humor among men is razzing, teasing, and mock-hostile attacks, while among women it's self-mocking. Women often mistake men's teasing as genuinely hostile. Men often mistake women's mock self-deprecation as truly putting themselves down. 28

Women have told me they were taken more seriously when they learned to joke the way the guys did. For example, a teacher who went to a national conference with seven other teachers (mostly women) and a group of administrators (mostly men) was annoyed that the administrators always found reasons to leave boring seminars, while the teachers felt they had to stay and take notes. One evening, when the group met at a bar in the hotel, the principal asked her how one such seminar had turned out. She retorted, "As soon as you left, it got much better." He laughed out loud at her response. The playful insult appealed to the men — but there was a trade-off. The women seemed to back off from her after this. (Perhaps they were put off by her using joking to align herself with the bosses.) 29

Tannen / But What Do You Mean? **397**

There is no "right" way to talk. When problems arise, the culprit may be  30
style differences — and *all* styles will at times fail with others who don't share
or understand them, just as English won't do you much good if you try to speak
to someone who knows only French. If you want to get your message across,
it's not a question of being "right"; it's a question of using language that's
shared — or at least understood.

*For a reading quiz, sources on Deborah Tannen, and annotated links to further
readings on gender differences in communication, visit **bedfordstmartins.com
/thebedfordreader**.*

## Journal Writing

Tannen's ANECDOTE about the newspaper columnist (par. 4) illustrates that much of
what we say is purely automatic. Do you excuse yourself when you bump into inanimate objects? When someone says, "Have a good trip," do you answer, "You too," even
if the other person isn't going anywhere? Do you find yourself overusing certain words
or phrases such as "like" or "you know"? Pay close attention to these kinds of verbal
tics in your own and others' speech. Over the course of a few days, note as many of
them as you can in your journal. (To take your journal writing further, see "From Journal to Essay" on the following page.)

## Questions on Meaning

1. What is Tannen's PURPOSE in writing this essay? What does she hope it will
   accomplish?
2. What does Tannen mean when she writes, "Conversation is a ritual" (par. 1)?
3. What does Tannen see as the fundamental difference between men's and
   women's conversational strategies?
4. Why is "You're welcome" not always an appropriate response to "Thank you"?

## Questions on Writing Strategy

1. This essay has a large cast of characters: twenty-three to be exact. What function
   do these characters serve? How does Tannen introduce them to the reader? Does
   she describe them in sufficient detail?

2. Whom does Tannen see as her primary AUDIENCE? ANALYZE her use of the pronoun *you* in paragraphs 9 and 19. Whom does she seem to be addressing here? Why?

3. Analyze how Tannen develops the category of apologies in paragraphs 4–9. Where does she use EXAMPLE, DEFINITION, and COMPARISON AND CONTRAST?

4. How does Tannen's DESCRIPTION of a columnist as "well-known" (par. 4) contribute to the effectiveness of her example?

5. **OTHER METHODS**   For each of her seven areas of miscommunication, Tannen compares and contrasts male and female communication styles and strategies. SUMMARIZE the main source of misunderstanding in each area.

## Questions on Language

1. What is the EFFECT of "I put her out of her misery" (par. 11)? What does this phrase usually mean?

2. What does Tannen mean by a "right-between-the-eyes style" (par. 12)? What is the FIGURE OF SPEECH involved here?

3. What is the effect of Tannen's use of figurative verbs, such as "barking" (par. 11) and "erupted" (20)? Find at least one other example of the use of a verb in a non-literal sense.

4. Look up any of the following words whose meanings you are unsure of: synonymous, self-deprecating (par. 4); lucid, tentativeness (11); intrinsically (12); reciprocate (14); adrenaline, spur (17); contentious, hedge (18); sparring, rebuttal (19); adage (20); soliciting (23); commiserating (24); initiate, condescended, impasse (25); chronic, malcontent (26); razzing (28); retorted (29).

## Suggestions for Writing

1. **FROM JOURNAL TO ESSAY**   Write an essay classifying the examples from your journal entry into categories of your own devising. You might sort out the examples by context ("phone blunders," "faulty farewells"), by purpose ("nervous tics," "space fillers"), or by some other principle of classification. Given your subject matter, you might want to adopt a humorous TONE.

2. How well does your style of communication conform to that of your gender as described by Tannen? Write a short essay about a specific communication problem or misunderstanding you have had with someone of the opposite sex (sibling, friend, parent, significant other). How well does Tannen's differentiation of male and female communication styles account for your particular problem?

3. How true do you find Tannen's assessment of miscommunication between the sexes? Consider the conflicts you have observed between your parents, among fellow students or coworkers, in fictional portrayals in books and movies. You could also go beyond your personal experiences and observations by researching the opinions of other experts (linguists, psychologists, sociologists, and so on). Write an essay confirming or questioning Tannen's GENERALIZATIONS, backing up your (and perhaps others') views with your own examples.

4. **CRITICAL WRITING**   Tannen insists that "neither [communication] style is intrinsically better" (par. 12), that "There is no 'right' way to talk" (30). What do you

make of this refusal to take sides in the battle of the sexes? Is Tannen always successful? Is absolute neutrality possible, or even desirable, when it comes to such divisive issues?

5. **CONNECTIONS**    What pictures of men and women emerge from Tannen's essay and from Dave Barry's "Batting Clean-Up and Striking Out" (p. 239)? In an essay, DEFINE each sex as portrayed by these two authors, and then agree or disagree with the definitions. Support your opinions with examples from your own observations and experience.

---

## *Deborah Tannen on Writing*

Though Deborah Tannen's "But What Do You Mean?" is written for a general audience, Tannen is a linguistics scholar who does considerable academic writing. One debate among scholarly writers is whether it is appropriate to incorporate one's experiences and biases into academic writing, especially given the goal of objectivity in conducting and reporting research. The October 1996 *PMLA* (*Publications of the Modern Language Association*) printed a discussion of the academic uses of the personal, with contributions from more than two dozen scholars. Tannen's comments, excerpted here, focused on the first-person *I*.

When I write academic prose, I use the first person, and I instruct my students to do the same. The principle that researchers should acknowledge their participation in their work is an outgrowth of a humanistic approach to linguistic analysis. . . . Understanding discourse is not a passive act of decoding but a creative act of imagining a scene (composed of people engaged in culturally recognizable activities) within which the ideas being talked about have meaning. The listener's active participation in sense making both results from and creates interpersonal involvement. For researchers to deny their involvement in their interpreting of discourse would be a logical and ethical violation of this framework. . . .

[O]bjectivity in the analysis of interactions is impossible anyway. Whether they took part in the interaction or not, researchers identify with one or another speaker, are put off or charmed by the styles of participants. This one reminds you of a cousin you adore; that one sounds like a neighbor you despise. Researchers are human beings, not atomic particles or chemical elements. . . .

Another danger of claiming objectivity rather than acknowledging and correcting for subjectivity is that scholars who don't reveal their participation in interactions they analyze risk the appearance of hiding it. "Following is an exchange that occurred between a professor and a student," I have read in articles in my field. The speakers are identified as "A" and "B." The reader is not told that the professor, A (of course the professor is A and the student B), is the author. Yet that knowledge is crucial to contextualizing the author's interpretation. Furthermore, the impersonal designations A and B are another means of constructing a false objectivity. They obscure the fact that human interaction is being analyzed, and they interfere with the reader's understanding. The letters replace what in the author's mind are names and voices and personas that are the basis for understanding the discourse. Readers, given only initials, are left to scramble for understanding by imagining people in place of letters.

Avoiding self-reference by using the third person also results in the depersonalization of knowledge. Knowledge and understanding do not occur in abstract isolation. They always and only occur among people. . . . Denying that scholarship is a personal endeavor entails a failure to understand and correct for the inevitable bias that human beings bring to all their enterprises.

## For Discussion

1. In arguing for the use of the first-person *I* in academic prose, Tannen is speaking primarily about its use in her own field, linguistics. From your experience with academic writing, is Tannen's argument applicable to other disciplines as well, such as history, biology, psychology, or government? Why, or why not? What have your teachers in various courses advised you about writing in the first person?

2. Try this experiment on the effects of the first person and third person (*he, she, they*): Write a passage of academic prose in one person or the other. (Tannen's example of professor A and student B can perhaps suggest a direction for your passage, or you may have one already written in a paper you've submitted.) Rewrite the passage in the other person, and ANALYZE the two versions. Does one sound more academic than the other? What are the advantages and disadvantages of each one?

# LUC SANTE

LUC SANTE was born in 1954 in Belgium, a background that he explores in his memoir *The Factory of Facts* (1998). His family immigrated to the United States when he was five years old, settling in New Jersey. From that vantage, Sante became enamored of nearby New York City, where he attended Columbia University and about which he eventually wrote *Low Life: Lures and Snares of Old New York* (1991). Sante's reviews and essays have been published in *The New York Review of Books, Slate*, and the *New Republic*, and he has received a Whiting Writer's Award, a Guggenheim Fellowship, and a literature award from the American Academy of Arts and Letters. His most recent books, both published in 2007, are a collection of his magazine pieces entitled *Kill All Your Darlings* and a translation of a French novel, Felix Feneon's *Novels in Three Lines*. Sante teaches writing and the history of photography at Bard College.

# *What Secrets Tell*

In this selection Sante explores the kinds of secrets people keep, some age-old, some more recent. As Sante sees it, secrets are paradoxical, or self-contradictory: They are hidden, of course, but at the same time they enlarge our sense of the world. This second function makes secrets indispensable, a "motor of life." "What Secrets Tell" is excerpted from a longer essay that first appeared in 2000 in the *New York Times Magazine*.

Secrets are a permanent feature of the human condition. We need secrets the way we need black holes, for their mystery; the way we need landspeed records, for their enlargement of scale; the way we need sexy models in advertisements, for their seductively false promises; the way we need lotteries, for their vague possibility. We also need them the way we need bank vaults and sock drawers and glove compartments. Anybody who doesn't carry around one or two secrets probably has all the depth of a place mat.

But then the word *secret* conceals under its mantle a teeming and motley population of types. Secrets cater to the entire range of human susceptibilities, from the laughably trivial to the terrifyingly fundamental. Principal landmarks along the way include:

**Personal Secrets** In other words, those secrets that are chiefly of interest to the persons who carry them around. You know the sort: You pick your nose when no one's looking; your real first name is Eustace; you wear a truss for non-medical reasons. If such things were revealed, your ego might take a beating and your intimates could gain a weapon for use in squabbles or extortions, but the foundations of your house would not be shaken.

**Romantic Secrets**   They run the gamut. That interval of passion you      4
once shared with your dentist when the two of you were stuck in an elevator with a bottle of Cherry Kijafa may remain swathed in gauze for all eternity, although your partner might eventually demand to know the identity of this "Shirley" whose name you utter in your sleep. That you enjoy above all the erotic sensation of being pinched with tweezers until you bleed might not matter a whole lot to anyone, unless you decide to run for office, and then you will find yourself sending discreet sums of money to people you haven't thought of in years. Couples often tacitly erect a whole edifice of secrets, based on real or imagined causes for jealousy. This can be relatively harmless, or it can be a symptom of the relationship's becoming a regime.

**Secrets in Gossip**   That is, the wheat left over when gossip's chaff is sifted      5
out. Secrets that surface as gossip are usually of the mildest sort, personal eccentricities and romantic peccadilloes not of much interest outside a closed circle. (It is understood that there is a direct correlation between the degree of triviality of the secret transmitted as gossip and the rank of the gossip's subject within that circle.) Gossip, though, demonstrates how secrets can become currency, as the teller invests the hearer with power in exchange for esteem. The possession of a secret concerning another is, like all forms of power, something of a burden, a weight pressing one's lips together, which can be relieved only by telling someone else. This, added to a hunger for knowledge on the part of all within the gossip circle, keeps the wheel of the secret-fueled gossip economy turning.

**Trade Secrets**   The monetary economy, meanwhile, revolves around a      6
wide and diverse range of secrets. A business strategy is a secret until it becomes a fait accompli.[1] The details of the financial health of a company are kept as secret as the law allows. Anyone with a degree of power in the market is continually keeping secrets—from competitors, from the press, from anyone who is an outsider, including friends and family, but sometimes from colleagues and office mates. The reasons are obvious: Everyone is naked in a cutthroat world, and secrets are clothing. It goes without saying that secrets protect innovations and that they also hide various extralegal undertakings— the ostensibly respectable bank that takes in laundry[2] on the side, for example.

---

[1] From French, "a completed act."—EDS.
[2] Money being channeled illegally. —EDS.

Business also employs secrets strategically, as secrets qua[3] secrets, usually painting the word *secret* in letters ten stories tall. Naturally the new car model will differ little from the previous year's, but a bit of cloak-and-dagger about it will increase public interest. The "secret recipe" is on a par with "new and improved" as a carny barker's hook. The cake mix or soft drink or laundry soap may, of course, actually include a secret ingredient, known only to staff chemists and highly placed executives, but very often a "secret ingredient" is rumored or bruited about primarily as a lure to the gulls of the public.

**Secret Formulas**   The public hunger for secrets is primordial. It is first and foremost a matter of curiosity, but it also springs from a painful awareness of rank and a belief that things are different upstairs, with a more or less fanciful idea of the specifics. These days, with fortune-building running at a pitch not seen since the 1920s, there is widespread demand for financial folklore. You can make a lot of money catering to the suspicion that there exist shortcuts known only to a few. That some people are richer, thinner, more charismatic or whiter of teeth may be a result of a variety of imponderable factors, but for everyone who in moments of desperation has imagined that there must be some simple trick, some formula or high sign or investment routine or hidden spa, there is an author with a book aimed at the exact combination of vulnerability and prurient imagination. Such publications run along the entire span of implied legitimacy based upon demographics, from the crudities aimed at the supermarket-tabloid constituency (diets centered on junk food named in the Bible, for instance) to the overpriced hardcover pamphlets catering to the anxieties of the managerial class by dressing up received ideas with slogans and numbered lists. For centuries, the secret has been a sure-fire sales gimmick. All you have to do is combine the banal and the esoteric. 7

**Secret Societies**   There are probably a lot fewer than there once were, but somewhere in America, no doubt, insurance adjusters and trophy engravers still gather once a month in acrylic gowns and button-flap underwear to exchange phrases in pseudobiblical double Dutch and then get down to the business of drinking beer. It helps them feel special to be the only ones in town who know the three-finger handshake. The setup descends from the heresies of the Middle Ages by the way of the pecking order of the playground. We can laugh at them, now that they are so enfeebled, but there was a time not long ago when they dominated the social life of male middle-class America, and in many ways their pretensions are not so far removed from those of the Mafia or the CIA. 8

[3] From Latin, "as" or "in the character of." — EDS.

**Mystical Secrets**   The secret is bait. The secret leads votaries by the nose      9
through a maze of connected chambers, in each of which they must ante up.
Only when they have finally tumbled to there being no secret (and they have
run through the better part of their inheritances) can they truly be counted as
initiates. But few have the stamina to get that far, and most instead spend
their spare afternoons consuming one tome after another promoting the
secrets of, variously, the pyramids, the Templars, the ascended masters, the
elders of Mu, the Essene scrolls, and so on through greater and lesser degrees
of perceived legitimacy, all of which flutter around the edges of the secret,
none of which make so bold as to suggest what it might consist of.

**State Secrets**   "Our laws are not generally known; they are kept secret by      10
the small group of nobles who rule us," wrote Kafka[4] in one of his miniature
stories. "We are convinced that these ancient laws are scrupulously administered; nevertheless it is an extremely painful thing to be ruled by laws that one
does not know." This is the essence of state secrets. A government does not
have to be totalitarian, particularly, to possess a stratum of laws whose existence cannot be generally known because they describe the limits of the
knowable. It is forbidden for unauthorized persons to possess certain kinds of
information. What kinds of information? Well, that's the trouble; if you knew
that, you would already know too much. State secrets range all the way from
banal prohibitions on photographing customs booths and power plants to the
highest levels of technical esoterica.

**Atomic Secrets**   "Stop me if you've heard this atomic secret," cracked      11
William Burroughs in *Naked Lunch*.[5] Atomic secrets may be the world's most
famous class of secret, an oxymoron, surely, but for the fact that few enough
people would recognize or understand an atomic secret if it landed in their
mailboxes. The workaday state secret may be a matter of mere protocol or protection of resources, not unlike industries safeguarding the peculiarities of
their production methods. The atomic secret, however, ascends to the level of
the sacred because it manifests in concrete form the terror that mystics can
only suggest: the end of the world. The secret of life may be an empty proposition, but the secret of death is actually legible to those who possess the language and the tools. . . .

People need secrets because they need the assurance that there is some-      12
thing left to discover, that they have not exhausted the limits of their envi-

---

[4] Franz Kafka (1883–1924) was a Czech poet and fiction writer. —EDS.
[5] Burroughs (1914–1997), an American writer, published the controversial novel *Naked Lunch* in 1962. —EDS.

ronment, that a prize might lie in wait like money in the pocket of an old jacket, that the existence of things beyond their ken might propose as a corollary that their own minds contain unsuspected corridors. People need uncertainty and destabilization the way they need comfort and security. It's not that secrets make them feel small but that they make the world seem bigger—a major necessity these days, when sensations need to be extreme to register at all. Secrets reawaken that feeling from childhood that the ways of the world were infinitely mysterious, unpredictable and densely packed, and that someday you might come to know and master them. Secrets purvey affordable glamour, suggest danger without presenting an actual threat. If there were no more secrets, an important motor of life would be stopped, and the days would merge into a continuous blur. Secrets hold out the promise, false but necessary, that death will be deferred until their unveiling.

*For a reading quiz, sources on Luc Sante, and annotated links to further readings on secrets, visit **bedfordstmartins.com/thebedfordreader**.*

## Journal Writing

In paragraph 5 Sante focuses on gossip as the sharing of secrets. Write about how, in your experience, people participate in "gossip circles," as Sante calls them. What do people gossip about in different contexts? To what extent can the concept of "gossip circles" be applied, as well, to the popularity of gossip columns, celebrity magazines, and entertainment news programs? What other kinds of gossip can you think of? (To take your journal writing further, see "From Journal to Essay" on the following page.)

## Questions on Meaning

1. How would you summarize Sante's THESIS? Where in the essay does he state it most directly?
2. Why, according to Sante, do we "need secrets" (pars. 1 and 12)? What benefits do they provide for individuals and for groups?
3. What is your response to the categories of secrets that Sante establishes? What strikes you as most interesting in his discussion of each type? How do you suppose Sante expected readers to respond?
4. Which of the secrets that Sante writes about does he suggest are not true secrets at all? What is his point in including these?

# Questions on Writing Strategy

1. What scheme does Sante use to arrange his categories? How is this order reflected in his thesis?
2. Look closely at Sante's final paragraph. How effective is it as a conclusion to the essay? Why?
3. For each category of secret, Sante names the type in a heading. What is the EFFECT of the sentence that immediately follows each heading? Why do you think Sante opened the paragraphs in these ways?
4. **OTHER METHODS**   How does Sante use EXAMPLE? What would his essay be like without illustrations? (To find out, remove all the examples from paragraph 4. What's left?)

# Questions on Language

1. This essay was originally published in the *New York Times Magazine*, a publication aimed at a general AUDIENCE of educated readers. Choose one paragraph, and point to specific examples of vocabulary that seems aimed at such readers. What is the effect of such vocabulary on you as a reader?
2. At the end of paragraph 7, Sante says that secret formulas succeed in attracting buyers because they "combine the banal and the esoteric." What do *banal* and *esoteric* mean? What is Sante's point here?
3. In paragraph 11 Sante says, "Atomic secrets may be the world's most famous class of secret," which he refers to as an "oxymoron." What is an *oxymoron*, and how is Sante's statement an example of it? Can any sense be made of the sentence?
4. Look up any of the following words whose meanings you are unsure of: mantle, motley, susceptibilities (par. 2); gamut, tacitly, edifice, regime (4); chaff, peccadilloes, esteem (5); ostensibly, bruited, gulls (6); primordial, imponderable, prurient, demographics (7); heresies, enfeebled (8); votaries, ante, tome (9); scrupulously, totalitarian, stratum (10); protocol (11); ken, corollary, purvey, deferred (12).

# Suggestions for Writing

1. **FROM JOURNAL TO ESSAY**   Based on your journal entry, write an essay in which you classify different instances of gossip into several categories. You might sort the examples according to intention (idle gossip, malicious gossip, etc.), context (gossip among friends, office gossip, etc.), or another principle that you discover. Be sure to explain each category clearly, using specific examples. In your conclusion, try to go further and make a GENERALIZATION about the role or function of gossip in human relationships.
2. Write about a time when a secret affected your life in some important way—either a secret you felt the need to keep or a secret that was kept from you. You might develop your essay as NARRATION or explore the secret in terms of CAUSE AND EFFECT. You might also consider the secret in terms of Sante's observations about secrets generally. As you plan and draft your essay, think carefully about your intended audience. What do they need to know to understand the full importance of the secret?

3. The plots of novels, films, and plays often center on secrets: A spy goes under-cover to discover a clandestine plan; a crusader seeks to expose harmful business practices; a long-kept secret comes back to haunt the main character. Brainstorm a list of novels, films, and plays whose plots involve secrets. Then write an essay in which you classify these fictional examples of secrets into categories.
4. **CRITICAL WRITING**   Sante makes strong claims for the importance of secrets to our fundamental humanity. Focusing particularly on paragraphs 1 and 12, write an essay in which you SUMMARIZE some of these claims in your own words and then EVALUATE their truth based on your own experiences, observations, and reading.
5. **CONNECTIONS**   In the next selection, Stephanie Ericsson presents categories of lies people tell. In an essay, explore the connection between lies and secrets. In what ways are they similar and different? Which of Sante's secrets could be con-sidered lies, and which of Ericsson's lies could be considered secrets?

---

## *Luc Sante on Writing*

As a teacher of writing, Luc Sante has the opportunity to preach what he practices. In an interview with Peter Doyle of *Scan*, Sante explains one of the points he stresses to writing students.

I try with fluctuating success to convey the need to treat language as a physical substance, with each word having a weight and a shape and a color and an odor. For most people of all ages, language is merely a means to an end. As a result they can convey ideas, but do it lifelessly.

### For Discussion

What do you think Sante means when he says that words should have "weight . . . shape . . . color . . . odor"? Select a paragraph in Sante's essay "What Secrets Tell" and examine the words for these qualities. Would you say that Sante achieves his goal of lively writing?

## STEPHANIE ERICSSON

STEPHANIE ERICSSON is an insightful and frank writer who composes out of her own life. Her book on loss, *Companion Through the Darkness: Inner Dialogues on Grief* (1993), grew out of journal entries and extensive research into the grieving process following the sudden death of her husband while she was pregnant. Ericsson was born in 1953, grew up in San Francisco, and began writing at the age of fifteen. After studying filmmaking in college, she became a screenwriter's assistant and later a writer of situation comedies and advertising. During these years she struggled with substance abuse; after her recovery in 1980 she published *Shamefaced* and *Women of AA: Recovering Together* (both 1985). *Companion into the Dawn: Inner Dialogues on Loving* (1994) is Ericsson's most recent book. She lives in Minneapolis with her two children.

## *The Ways We Lie*

Psychologists have claimed that most people lie at least once a day, and one recent study found that college students lied in half of their conversations with their mothers. In this essay from the *Utne Reader* in 1992, Ericsson classifies the kinds of lies we all tell at one time or another. Lying, she finds, may be unavoidable and even sometimes beneficial. But then how do we know when to stop?

William Lutz's "The World of Doublespeak," the essay following Ericsson's, also uses classification to examine types of lies, specifically the verbal substitutions that make "the bad seem good, the negative appear positive."

The bank called today and I told them my deposit was in the mail, even though I hadn't written a check yet. It'd been a rough day. The baby I'm pregnant with decided to do aerobics on my lungs for two hours, our three-year-old daughter painted the living-room couch with lipstick, the IRS put me on hold for an hour, and I was late to a business meeting because I was tired. 1

I told my client that traffic had been bad. When my partner came home, his haggard face told me his day hadn't gone any better than mine, so when he asked, "How was your day?" I said, "Oh, fine," knowing that one more straw might break his back. A friend called and wanted to take me to lunch. I said I was busy. Four lies in the course of a day, none of which I felt the least bit guilty about. 2

We lie. We all do. We exaggerate, we minimize, we avoid confrontation, 3 we spare people's feelings, we conveniently forget, we keep secrets, we justify lying to the big-guy institutions. Like most people, I indulge in small falsehoods and still think of myself as an honest person. Sure I lie, but it doesn't hurt anything. Or does it?

I once tried going a whole week without telling a lie, and it was paralyzing. 4 I discovered that telling the truth all the time is nearly impossible. It means living with some serious consequences: The bank charges me $60 in overdraft fees, my partner keels over when I tell him about my travails, my client fires me for telling her I didn't feel like being on time, and my friend takes it personally when I say I'm not hungry. There must be some merit to lying.

But if I justify lying, what makes me any different from slick politicians or 5 the corporate robbers who raided the S&L industry? Saying it's okay to lie one way and not another is hedging. I cannot seem to escape the voice deep inside me that tells me: When someone lies, someone loses.

What far-reaching consequences will I, or others, pay as a result of my lie? 6 Will someone's trust be destroyed? Will someone else pay *my* penance because I ducked out? We must consider the *meaning of our actions*. Deception, lies, capital crimes, and misdemeanors all carry meanings. *Webster's* definition of *lie* is specific:

> 1: a false statement or action especially made with the intent to deceive;
> 2: anything that gives or is meant to give a false impression.

A definition like this implies that there are many, many ways to tell a lie. 7 Here are just a few.

## The White Lie

*A man who won't lie to a woman has very little consideration for her feelings.*
—Bergen Evans

The white lie assumes that the truth will cause more damage than a 8 simple, harmless untruth. Telling a friend he looks great when he looks like hell can be based on a decision that the friend needs a compliment more than a frank opinion. But, in effect, it is the liar deciding what is best for the lied to. Ultimately, it is a vote of no confidence. It is an act of subtle arrogance for anyone to decide what is best for someone else.

Yet not all circumstances are quite so cut-and-dried. Take, for instance, 9 the sergeant in Vietnam who knew one of his men was killed in action but listed him as missing so that the man's family would receive indefinite compensation instead of the lump-sum pittance the military gives widows and children. His intent was honorable. Yet for twenty years this family kept their hopes alive, unable to move on to a new life.

## Façades

*Et tu, Brute?*
—Caesar

We all put up façades to one degree or another. When I put on a suit to go    10
to see a client, I feel as though I am putting on another face, obeying the
expectation that serious businesspeople wear suits rather than sweatpants. But
I'm a writer. Normally, I get up, get the kid off to school, and sit at my computer in my pajamas until four in the afternoon. When I answer the phone,
the caller thinks I'm wearing a suit (though the UPS man knows better).

But façades can be destructive because they are used to seduce others into    11
an illusion. For instance, I recently realized that a former friend was a liar.
He presented himself with all the right looks and the right words and offered
lots of new consciousness theories, fabulous books to read, and fascinating
insights. Then I did some business with him, and the time came for him to pay
me. He turned out to be all talk and no walk. I heard a plethora of reasonable
excuses, including in-depth descriptions of the big break around the corner. In
six months of work, I saw less than a hundred bucks. When I confronted him,
he raised both eyebrows and tried to convince me that I'd heard him wrong,
that he'd made no commitment to me. A simple investigation into his past
revealed a crowded graveyard of disenchanted former friends.

## Ignoring the Plain Facts

*Well, you must understand that Father Porter is only human.*
—A Massachusetts priest

In the '60s, the Catholic Church in Massachusetts began hearing com-    12
plaints that Father James Porter was sexually molesting children. Rather
than relieving him of his duties, the ecclesiastical authorities simply moved
him from one parish to another between 1960 and 1967, actually providing
him with a fresh supply of unsuspecting families and innocent children to
abuse. After treatment in 1967 for pedophilia, he went back to work, this
time in Minnesota. The new diocese was aware of Father Porter's obsession
with children, but they needed priests and recklessly believed treatment had
cured him. More children were abused until he was relieved of his duties a year
later. By his own admission, Porter may have abused as many as a hundred
children.

Ignoring the facts may not in and of itself be a form of lying, but con-    13
sider the context of this situation. If a lie is *a false action done with the intent
to deceive*, then the Catholic Church's conscious covering for Porter created
irreparable consequences. The church became a co-perpetrator with Porter.

## Deflecting

*When you have no basis for an argument, abuse the plaintiff.*
          —Cicero

I've discovered that I can keep anyone from seeing the true me by being   14
selectively blatant. I set a precedent of being up-front about intimate issues,
but I never bring up the things I truly want to hide; I just let people assume I'm
revealing everything. It's an effective way of hiding.

Any good liar knows that the way to perpetuate an untruth is to deflect   15
attention from it. When Clarence Thomas exploded with accusations that
the Senate hearings were a "high-tech lynching," he simply switched the
focus from a highly charged subject to a radioactive subject.[1] Rather than
defending himself, he took the offensive and accused the country of racism.
It was a brilliant maneuver. Racism is now politically incorrect in official
circles—unlike sexual harassment, which still rewards those who can get
away with it.

Some of the most skilled deflectors are passive-aggressive people who,   16
when accused of inappropriate behavior, refuse to respond to the accusations.
This you-don't-exist stance infuriates the accuser, who, understandably, screams
something obscene out of frustration. The trap is sprung and the act of de-
flection successful, because now the passive-aggressive person can indignantly
say, "Who can talk to someone as unreasonable as you?" The real issue is forgotten and the sins of the original victim become the focus. Feeling guilty of
name-calling, the victim is fully tamed and crawls into a hole, ashamed. I
have watched this fighting technique work thousands of times in disputes
between men and women, and what I've learned is that the real culprit is not
necessarily the one who swears the loudest.

## Omission

*The cruelest lies are often told in silence.*
          —R. L. Stevenson

Omission involves telling most of the truth minus one or two key facts   17
whose absence changes the story completely. You break a pair of glasses that
are guaranteed under normal use and get a new pair, without mentioning that
the first pair broke during a rowdy game of basketball. Who hasn't tried something like that? But what about omission of information that could make a difference in how a person lives his or her life?

---

[1] Ericsson refers to the 1991 hearings to confirm Thomas for the Supreme Court, at which
Thomas was accused by Anita Hill of sexual harassment.—EDS.

For instance, one day I found out that rabbinical legends tell of another 18 woman in the Garden of Eden before Eve. I was stunned. The omission of the Sumerian goddess Lilith from Genesis—as well as her demonization by ancient misogynists as an embodiment of female evil—felt like spiritual robbery. I felt like I'd just found out my mother was really my stepmother. To take seriously the tradition that Adam was created out of the same mud as his equal counterpart, Lilith, redefines all of Judeo-Christian history.

Some renegade Catholic feminists introduced me to a view of Lilith that 19 had been suppressed during the many centuries when this strong goddess was seen only as a spirit of evil. Lilith was a proud goddess who defied Adam's need to control her, attempted negotiations, and when this failed, said adios and left the Garden of Eden.

This omission of Lilith from the Bible was a patriarchal strategy to keep 20 women weak. Omitting the strong-woman archetype of Lilith from Western religions and starting the story with Eve the Rib has helped keep Christian and Jewish women believing they were the lesser sex for thousands of years.

## Stereotypes and Clichés

*Where opinion does not exist, the status quo becomes stereotyped and all originality is discouraged.* —Bertrand Russell

Stereotype and cliché serve a purpose as a form of shorthand. Our need for 21 vast amounts of information in nanoseconds has made the stereotype vital to modern communication. Unfortunately, it often shuts down original thinking, giving those hungry for the truth a candy bar of misinformation instead of a balanced meal. The stereotype explains a situation with just enough truth to seem unquestionable.

All the "isms"—racism, sexism, ageism, et al.—are founded on and 22 fueled by the stereotype and the cliché, which are lies of exaggeration, omission, and ignorance. They are always dangerous. They take a single tree and make it a landscape. They destroy curiosity. They close minds and separate people. The single mother on welfare is assumed to be cheating. Any black male could tell you how much of his identity is obliterated daily by stereotypes. Fat people, ugly people, beautiful people, old people, large-breasted women, short men, the mentally ill, and the homeless all could tell you how much more they are like us than we want to think. I once admitted to a group of people that I had a mouth like a truck driver. Much to my surprise, a man stood up and said, "I'm a truck driver, and I never cuss." Needless to say, I was humbled.

## Groupthink

*Who is more foolish, the child afraid of the dark, or the man afraid
of the light?*                                            —Maurice Freehill

Irving Janis, in *Victims of Group Think*, defines this sort of lie as a psycho-     23
logical phenomenon within decision-making groups in which loyalty to the
group has become more important than any other value, with the result that
dissent and the appraisal of alternatives are suppressed. If you've ever worked
on a committee or in a corporation, you've encountered groupthink. It
requires a combination of other forms of lying—ignoring facts, selective
memory, omission, and denial, to name a few.

The textbook example of groupthink came on December 7, 1941. From as     24
early as the fall of 1941, the warnings came in, one after another, that Japan
was preparing for a massive military operation. The navy command in Hawaii
assumed Pearl Harbor was invulnerable—the Japanese weren't stupid enough
to attack the United States' most important base. On the other hand, racist
stereotypes said the Japanese weren't smart enough to invent a torpedo effective in less than 60 feet of water (the fleet was docked in 30 feet); after all, US
technology hadn't been able to do it.

On Friday, December 5, normal weekend leave was granted to all the     25
commanders at Pearl Harbor, even though the Japanese consulate in Hawaii
was busy burning papers. Within the tight, good-ole-boy cohesiveness of the
US command in Hawaii, the myth of invulnerability stayed well entrenched.
No one in the group considered the alternatives. The rest is history.

## Out-and-Out Lies

*The only form of lying that is beyond reproach is lying for its
own sake.*                                            —Oscar Wilde

Of all the ways to lie, I like this one the best, probably because I get tired     26
of trying to figure out the real meanings behind things. At least I can trust the
bald-faced lie. I once asked my five-year-old nephew, "Who broke the fence?"
(I had seen him do it.) He answered, "The murderers." Who could argue?

At least when this sort of lie is told it can be easily confronted. As the per-     27
son who is lied to, I know where I stand. The bald-faced lie doesn't toy with
my perceptions—it argues with them. It doesn't try to refashion reality, it tries
to refute it. *Read my lips. . . .* No sleight of hand. No guessing. If this were the
only form of lying, there would be no such things as floating anxiety or the
adult-children-of-alcoholics movement.

## Dismissal

*Pay no attention to that man behind the curtain!*
*I am the Great Oz!*        —The Wizard of Oz

Dismissal is perhaps the slipperiest of all lies. Dismissing feelings, percep-    28
tions, or even the raw facts of a situation ranks as a kind of lie that can do as
much damage to a person as any other kind of lie.

The roots of many mental disorders can be traced back to the dismissal of    29
reality. Imagine that a person is told from the time she is a tot that her perceptions are inaccurate. *"Mommy, I'm scared."* "No you're not, darling." *"I
don't like that man next door, he makes me feel icky."* "Johnny, that's a terrible
thing to say, of course you like him. You go over there right now and be nice
to him."

I've often mused over the idea that madness is actually a sane reaction to    30
an insane world. Psychologist R. D. Laing supports this hypothesis in *Sanity,
Madness and the Family,* an account of his investigation into the families of
schizophrenics. The common thread that ran through all of the families he
studied was a deliberate, staunch dismissal of the patient's perceptions from a
very early age. Each of the patients started out with an accurate grasp of reality, which, through meticulous and methodical dismissal, was demolished
until the only reality the patient could trust was catatonia.

Dismissal runs the gamut. Mild dismissal can be quite handy for forgiving    31
the foibles of others in our day-to-day lives. Toddlers who have just learned to
manipulate their parents' attention sometimes are dismissed out of necessity.
Absolute attention from the parents would require so much energy that no
one would get to eat dinner. But we must be careful and attentive about how
far we take our "necessary" dismissals. Dismissal is a dangerous tool, because
it's nothing less than a lie.

## Delusion

*We lie loudest when we lie to ourselves.*
                            —Eric Hoffer

I could write the book on this one. Delusion, a cousin of dismissal, is the    32
tendency to see excuses as facts. It's a powerful lying tool because it filters out
information that contradicts what we want to believe. Alcoholics who believe
that the problems in their lives are legitimate reasons for drinking rather than
results of the drinking offer the classic example of deluded thinking. Delusion
uses the mind's ability to see things in myriad ways to support what it wants to
be the truth.

But delusion is also a survival mechanism we all use. If we were to fully    33
contemplate the consequences of our stockpiles of nuclear weapons or global

warming, we could hardly function on a day-to-day level. We don't want to incorporate that much reality into our lives because to do so would be paralyzing.

Delusion acts as an adhesive to keep the status quo intact. It shamelessly    34
employs dismissal, omission, and amnesia, among other sorts of lies. Its most cunning defense is that it cannot see itself.

•   •   •

*The liar's punishment . . . is that he cannot believe anyone else.*
—George Bernard Shaw

These are only a few of the ways we lie. Or are lied to. As I said earlier, it's    35
not easy to entirely eliminate lies from our lives. No matter how pious we may try to be, we will still embellish, hedge, and omit to lubricate the daily machinery of living. But there is a world of difference between telling functional lies and living a lie. Martin Buber once said, "The lie is the spirit committing treason against itself." Our acceptance of lies becomes a cultural cancer that eventually shrouds and reorders reality until moral garbage becomes as invisible to us as water is to a fish.

How much do we tolerate before we become sick and tired of being sick    36
and tired? When will we stand up and declare our *right* to trust? When do we stop accepting that the real truth is in the fine print? Whose lips do we read this year when we vote for president? When will we stop being so reticent about making judgments? When do we stop turning over our personal power and responsibility to liars?

Maybe if I don't tell the bank the check's in the mail I'll be less tolerant of    37
the lies told me every day. A country song I once heard said it all for me: "You've got to stand for something or you'll fall for anything."

*For a reading quiz, sources on Stephanie Ericsson, and annotated links to further readings on lying, visit **bedfordstmartins.com/thebedfordreader**.*

---

### Journal Writing

Ericsson says, "We lie. We all do" (par. 3)—and that must mean you, too. In your journal, write about lies you have told. When is the last time you remember lying? What was the most significant lie you ever told? What circumstances have justified lying? Have you ever been ashamed of a lie or faced consequences for lying? (To take your journal writing further, see "From Journal to Essay" below.)

## Questions on Meaning

1. What is Ericsson's THESIS?
2. Does Ericsson think it's possible to eliminate lies from our lives? What EVIDENCE does she offer?
3. If it were possible to eliminate lies from our lives, why would that be desirable?
4. What is this essay's PURPOSE?

## Questions on Writing Strategy

1. Ericsson starts out by recounting her own four-lie day (pars. 1–2). What is the EFFECT of this INTRODUCTION?
2. At the beginning of each kind of lie, Ericsson provides an epigraph, a short quotation that forecasts a theme. Which of these epigraphs work best, do you think? What are your criteria for judgment?
3. How does Ericsson develop her discussion of delusion in paragraphs 32–34?
4. What is the message of Ericsson's CONCLUSION? Does the conclusion work well? Why, or why not?
5. **OTHER METHODS**   Examine the way Ericsson uses DEFINITION and EXAMPLE to support her classification. Which definitions are clearest? Which examples are the most effective? Why?

## Questions on Language

1. In paragraph 35 Ericsson writes, "Our acceptance of lies becomes a cultural cancer that eventually shrouds and reorders reality until moral garbage becomes as invisible to us as water is to a fish." How do the two FIGURES OF SPEECH in this sentence—cancer and garbage—relate to each other?
2. Occasionally Ericsson's anger shows through, as in paragraphs 12–13 and 18–20. Is the TONE appropriate in these cases? Why, or why not?
3. Look up any of these words you do not know: haggard (par. 2); travails (4); façades (10); plethora (11); ecclesiastical, pedophilia (12); irreparable, co-perpetrator (13); patriarchal, archetype (20); gamut (31); myriad (32); reticent (36).
4. Ericsson uses several words and phrases from the fields of psychology and sociology. Define: passive-aggressive (par. 16); floating anxiety, adult-children-of-alcoholics movement (27); schizophrenics, catatonia (30).

## Suggestions for Writing

1. **FROM JOURNAL TO ESSAY**   Develop one or more of the lies you recalled in your journal into an essay. You may choose to elaborate on your lies by classifying according to some principle or by NARRATING the story of a particular lie and its outcome. Give your reader a sense of your motivation for lying in the first place.

2. Ericsson writes, "All the 'isms'—racism, sexism, ageism, et al.—are founded on and fueled by the stereotype and the cliché, which are lies of exaggeration, omission, and ignorance. They are always dangerous. They take a single tree and make it a landscape" (par. 22). Write an essay discussing stereotypes and how they work to encourage prejudice. Use Ericsson's definition as a base, and expand it to include stereotypes you find particularly injurious. How do these stereotypes oversimplify? How are they "dangerous"?

3. Research pathological liars—that is, people who because of a psychological disorder are compelled to tell lies. In an essay, develop an extended definition of the pathological liar.

4. **CRITICAL WRITING**   EVALUATE the success of Ericsson's essay, considering especially how well her evidence supports her GENERALIZATIONS. Are there important categories she overlooks, exceptions she does not account for, gaps in definitions? Offer specific evidence for your own view, whether positive or negative.

5. **CONNECTIONS**   Ericsson begins her essay by acknowledging her own lies, and she often uses the first-person *I* or *we* in explaining her categories. In contrast, the author of the following essay, William Lutz, takes a more distant approach in classifying the dishonest language called *doublespeak*. Which of these two approaches, confessional or more distant, do you find more effective, and why? When, in your view, is it appropriate to inject yourself into your writing, and when is it not?

---

## *Stephanie Ericsson on Writing*

In an interview on the *Amazon.com* Web site, Stephanie Ericsson discussed when and why she began writing. At first, she said, she did not write to communicate but to find and express herself.

I was fifteen in the year 1968, in the heart of hippie-saturated San Francisco, and like the world, I, too, underwent a major transformation. These spiritual awakenings tend to sound lofty, but the truth is that they are always messy. I began writing regularly then, when I lost my family. There was no one to tell my feelings to, so I turned to the blank white page. The page will never contradict you, never ignore you, and never judge you. I could put the chaos outside of me, and move on. It was a survival tool that I became attached to.

### For Discussion

1. Do you agree with Ericsson's assessment of the "blank white page" as benevolent and nonjudgmental?

2. In the passage above, Ericsson is talking about writing for oneself. Is it merely the absence of an audience that makes such writing potentially therapeutic? Why does articulating her thoughts—if only for herself—help Ericsson "move on"?

# WILLIAM LUTZ

WILLIAM LUTZ was born in 1940 in Racine, Wisconsin. He received a BA from Dominican College, an MA from Marquette University, a PhD from the University of Nevada at Reno, and a JD from Rutgers School of Law. Since 1971 Lutz has taught at Rutgers University in Camden, New Jersey. For much of his career, Lutz's interest in words and composition has made him an active campaigner against misleading and irresponsible language. For fourteen years he edited the *Quarterly Journal of Doublespeak*, and he has written three popular books on such language: *Doublespeak: From Revenue Enhancement to Terminal Living* (1989), *The New Doublespeak: Why No One Knows What Anyone's Saying Anymore* (1996), and *Doublespeak Defined: Cut Through the Bull\*\*\*\* and Get to the Point!* (1999). In 1996 Lutz received the George Orwell Award for Distinguished Contribution to Honesty and Clarity in Public Language.

# *The World of Doublespeak*

In the previous essay, Stephanie Ericsson examines the damage caused by the outright lies we tell each other every day. But what if our language doesn't lie, exactly, and instead just obscures meanings we'd rather not admit to? Such intentional fudging, or *doublespeak*, is the sort of language Lutz specializes in, and here he uses classification to expose its many guises. "The World of Doublespeak" abridges the first chapter in Lutz's book *Doublespeak;* the essay's title is the chapter's subtitle.

There are no potholes in the streets of Tucson, Arizona, just "pavement 1 deficiencies." The Reagan Administration didn't propose any new taxes, just "revenue enhancement" through new "user's fees." Those aren't bums on the street, just "non-goal oriented members of society." There are no more poor people, just "fiscal underachievers." There was no robbery of an automatic teller machine, just an "unauthorized withdrawal." The patient didn't die because of medical malpractice, it was just a "diagnostic misadventure of a high magnitude." The US Army doesn't kill the enemy anymore, it just "services the target." And the doublespeak goes on.

Doublespeak is language that pretends to communicate but really doesn't. 2 It is language that makes the bad seem good, the negative appear positive, the unpleasant appear attractive or at least tolerable. Doublespeak is language that avoids or shifts responsibility, language that is at variance with its real or purported meaning. It is language that conceals or prevents thought; rather than extending thought, doublespeak limits it.

Doublespeak is not a matter of subjects and verbs agreeing; it is a matter of words and facts agreeing. Basic to doublespeak is incongruity, the incongruity between what is said or left unsaid, and what really is. It is the incongruity between the word and the referent, between seem and be, between the essential function of language—communication—and what doublespeak does—mislead, distort, deceive, inflate, circumvent, obfuscate.

## How to Spot Doublespeak

How can you spot doublespeak? Most of the time you will recognize doublespeak when you see or hear it. But, if you have any doubts, you can identify doublespeak just by answering these questions: Who is saying what to whom, under what conditions and circumstances, with what intent, and with what results? Answering these questions will usually help you identify as doublespeak language that appears to be legitimate or that at first glance doesn't even appear to be doublespeak.

### First Kind of Doublespeak

There are at least four kinds of doublespeak. The first is the euphemism, an inoffensive or positive word or phrase used to avoid a harsh, unpleasant, or distasteful reality. But a euphemism can also be a tactful word or phrase which avoids directly mentioning a painful reality, or it can be an expression used out of concern for the feelings of someone else, or to avoid directly discussing a topic subject to a social or cultural taboo.

When you use a euphemism because of your sensitivity for someone's feelings or out of concern for a recognized social or cultural taboo, it is not doublespeak. For example, you express your condolences that someone has "passed away" because you do not want to say to a grieving person, "I'm sorry your father is dead." When you use the euphemism "passed away," no one is misled. Moreover, the euphemism functions here not just to protect the feelings of another person, but to communicate also your concern for that person's feelings during a period of mourning. When you excuse yourself to go to the "restroom," or you mention that someone is "sleeping with" or "involved with" someone else, you do not mislead anyone about your meaning, but you do respect the social taboos about discussing bodily functions and sex in direct terms. You also indicate your sensitivity to the feelings of your audience, which is usually considered a mark of courtesy and good manners.

However, when a euphemism is used to mislead or deceive, it becomes    7
doublespeak. For example, in 1984 the US State Department announced that
it would no longer use the word "killing" in its annual report on the status of
human rights in countries around the world. Instead, it would use the phrase
"unlawful or arbitrary deprivation of life," which the department claimed was
more accurate. Its real purpose for using this phrase was simply to avoid discussing the embarrassing situation of government-sanctioned killings in countries that are supported by the United States and have been certified by the
United States as respecting the human rights of their citizens. This use of a
euphemism constitutes doublespeak, since it is designed to mislead, to cover
up the unpleasant. Its real intent is at variance with its apparent intent. It is
language designed to alter our perception of reality.

The Pentagon, too, avoids discussing unpleasant realities when it refers to    8
bombs and artillery shells that fall on civilian targets as "incontinent ord-
nance." And in 1977 the Pentagon tried to slip funding for the neutron bomb
unnoticed into an appropriations bill by calling it a "radiation enhancement
device."

### Second Kind of Doublespeak

A second kind of doublespeak is jargon, the specialized language of a    9
trade, profession, or similar group, such as that used by doctors, lawyers, engi-
neers, educators, or car mechanics. Jargon can serve an important and useful
function. Within a group, jargon functions as a kind of verbal shorthand that
allows members of the group to communicate with each other clearly, efficiently, and quickly. Indeed, it is a mark of membership in the group to be able
to use and understand the group's jargon.

But jargon, like the euphemism, can also be doublespeak. It can be — and    10
often is — pretentious, obscure, and esoteric terminology used to give an air of
profundity, authority, and prestige to speakers and their subject matter. Jargon
as doublespeak often makes the simple appear complex, the ordinary profound, the obvious insightful. In this sense it is used not to express but
impress. With such doublespeak, the act of smelling something becomes
"organoleptic analysis," glass becomes "fused silicate," a crack in a metal support beam becomes a "discontinuity," conservative economic policies become
"distributionally conservative notions."

Lawyers, for example, speak of an "involuntary conversion" of property    11
when discussing the loss or destruction of property through theft, accident,
or condemnation. If your house burns down or if your car is stolen, you have
suffered an involuntary conversion of your property. When used by lawyers in

a legal situation, such jargon is a legitimate use of language, since lawyers can be expected to understand the term.

However, when a member of a specialized group uses its jargon to commu-    12
nicate with a person outside the group, and uses it knowing that the non-member does not understand such language, then there is doublespeak. For example, on May 9, 1978, a National Airlines 727 airplane crashed while attempting to land at the Pensacola, Florida, airport. Three of the fifty-two passengers aboard the airplane were killed. As a result of the crash, National made an after-tax insurance benefit of $1.7 million, or an extra 18¢ a share dividend for its stockholders. Now National Airlines had two problems: It did not want to talk about one of its airplanes crashing, and it had to account for the $1.7 million when it issued its annual report to its stockholders. National solved the problem by inserting a footnote in its annual report which explained that the $1.7 million income was due to "the involuntary conversion of a 727." National thus acknowledged the crash of its airplane and the subsequent profit it made from the crash, without once mentioning the accident or the deaths. However, because airline officials knew that most stockholders in the company, and indeed most of the general public, were not familiar with legal jargon, the use of such jargon constituted doublespeak.

### Third Kind of Doublespeak

A third kind of doublespeak is gobbledygook or bureaucratese. Basically,    13
such doublespeak is simply a matter of piling on words, of overwhelming the audience with words, the bigger the words and the longer the sentences the better. Alan Greenspan, then chair of President Nixon's Council of Economic Advisors, was quoted in *The Philadelphia Inquirer* in 1974 as having testified before a Senate committee that "It is a tricky problem to find the particular calibration in timing that would be appropriate to stem the acceleration in risk premiums created by falling incomes without prematurely aborting the decline in the inflation-generated risk premiums."

Nor has Mr. Greenspan's language changed since then. Speaking to the    14
meeting of the Economic Club of New York in 1988, Mr. Greenspan, now Federal Reserve chair, said, "I guess I should warn you, if I turn out to be particularly clear, you've probably misunderstood what I've said." Mr. Greenspan's doublespeak doesn't seem to have held back his career.

Sometimes gobbledygook may sound impressive, but when the quote is    15
later examined in print it doesn't even make sense. During the 1988 presidential campaign, vice-presidential candidate Senator Dan Quayle explained

the need for a strategic-defense initiative by saying, "Why wouldn't an en- hanced deterrent, a more stable peace, a better prospect to denying the ones who enter conflict in the first place to have a reduction of offensive systems and an introduction to defense capability? I believe this is the route the coun- try will eventually go."

The investigation into the *Challenger* disaster in 1986 revealed the double-   16 speak of gobbledygook and bureaucratese used by too many involved in the shuttle program. When Jesse Moore, NASA's associate administrator, was asked if the performance of the shuttle program had improved with each launch or if it had remained the same, he answered, "I think our performance in terms of the liftoff performance and in terms of the orbital performance, we knew more about the envelope we were operating under, and we have been pretty accurately staying in that. And so I would say the performance has not by design drastically improved. I think we have been able to characterize the performance more as a function of our launch experience as opposed to it improving as a function of time." While this language may appear to be jar- gon, a close look will reveal that it is really just gobbledygook laced with jar- gon. But you really have to wonder if Mr. Moore had any idea what he was saying.

### Fourth Kind of Doublespeak

The fourth kind of doublespeak is inflated language that is designed to   17 make the ordinary seem extraordinary; to make everyday things seem impres- sive; to give an air of importance to people, situations, or things that would not normally be considered important; to make the simple seem complex. Often this kind of doublespeak isn't hard to spot, and it is usually pretty funny. While car mechanics may be called "automotive internists," elevator opera- tors members of the "vertical transportation corps," used cars "pre-owned" or "experienced cars," and black-and-white television sets described as having "non-multicolor capability," you really aren't misled all that much by such language.

However, you may have trouble figuring out that, when Chrysler "initiates   18 a career alternative enhancement program," it is really laying off five thou- sand workers; or that "negative patient-care outcome" means the patient died; or that "rapid oxidation" means a fire in a nuclear power plant.

The doublespeak of inflated language can have serious consequences. In   19 Pentagon doublespeak, "pre-emptive counterattack" means that American forces attacked first; "engaged the enemy on all sides" means American troops were ambushed; "backloading of augmentation personnel" means a retreat by American troops. In the doublespeak of the military, the 1983 invasion of

Grenada was conducted not by the US Army, Navy, Air Force, and Marines, but by the "Caribbean Peace Keeping Forces." But then, according to the Pentagon, it wasn't an invasion, it was a "predawn vertical insertion." . . .

## The Dangers of Doublespeak

Doublespeak is not the product of carelessness or sloppy thinking. Indeed,    20
most doublespeak is the product of clear thinking and is carefully designed and constructed to appear to communicate when in fact it doesn't. It is language designed not to lead but mislead. It is language designed to distort reality and corrupt thought. . . . In the world created by doublespeak, if it's not a tax increase, but rather "revenue enhancement" or "tax base broadening," how can you complain about higher taxes? If it's not acid rain, but rather "poorly buffered precipitation," how can you worry about all those dead trees? If that isn't the Mafia in Atlantic City, but just "members of a career-offender cartel," why worry about the influence of organized crime in the city? If Supreme Court Justice William Rehnquist wasn't addicted to the pain-killing drug his doctor prescribed, but instead it was just that the drug had "established an interrelationship with the body, such that if the drug is removed precipitously, there is a reaction," you needn't question that his decisions might have been influenced by his drug addiction. If it's not a Titan II nuclear-armed intercontinental ballistic missile with a warhead 630 times more powerful than the atomic bomb dropped on Hiroshima, but instead, according to air force colonel Frank Horton, it's just a "very large, potentially disruptive re-entry system," why be concerned about the threat of nuclear destruction? Why worry about the neutron bomb escalating the arms race if it's just a "radiation enhancement weapon"? If it's not an invasion, but a "rescue mission" or a "predawn vertical insertion," you won't need to think about any violations of US or international law.

Doublespeak has become so common in everyday living that many people    21
fail to notice it. Even worse, when they do notice doublespeak being used on them, they don't react, they don't protest. Do you protest when you are asked to check your packages at the desk "for your convenience," when it's not for your convenience at all but for someone else's? You see advertisements for "genuine imitation leather," "virgin vinyl," or "real counterfeit diamonds," but do you question the language or the supposed quality of the product? Do you question politicians who don't speak of slums or ghettos but of the "inner city" or "substandard housing" where the "disadvantaged" live and thus avoid talking about the poor who have to live in filthy, poorly heated, ramshackle apartments or houses? Aren't you amazed that patients don't die in the hospital anymore, it's just "negative patient-care outcome"?

Doublespeak such as that noted earlier that defines cab drivers as "urban   22
transportation specialists," elevator operators as members of the "vertical
transportation corps," and automobile mechanics as "automotive internists"
can be considered humorous and relatively harmless. However, when a fire in
a nuclear reactor building is called "rapid oxidation," an explosion in a nuclear
power plant is called an "energetic disassembly," the illegal overthrow of a
legitimate government is termed "destabilizing a government," and lies are
seen as "inoperative statements," we are hearing doublespeak that attempts to
avoid responsibility and make the bad seem good, the negative appear positive, something unpleasant appear attractive; and which seems to communicate but doesn't. It is language designed to alter our perception of reality and
corrupt our thinking. Such language does not provide us with the tools we
need to develop, advance, and preserve our culture and our civilization. Such
language breeds suspicion, cynicism, distrust, and, ultimately, hostility.

Doublespeak is insidious because it can infect and eventually destroy the   23
function of language, which is communication between people and social
groups. This corruption of the function of language can have serious and far-
reaching consequences. We live in a country that depends upon an informed
electorate to make decisions in selecting candidates for office and deciding
issues of public policy. The use of doublespeak can become so pervasive that it
becomes the coin of the political realm, with speakers and listeners convinced
that they really understand such language. After a while we may really believe
that politicians don't lie but only "misspeak," that illegal acts are merely
"inappropriate actions," that fraud and criminal conspiracy are just "miscerti-
fication." President Jimmy Carter in April of 1980 could call the aborted raid
to free the American hostages in Teheran an "incomplete success" and really
believe that he had made a statement that clearly communicated with the
American public. So, too, could President Ronald Reagan say in 1985 that
"ultimately our security and our hopes for success at the arms reduction talks
hinge on the determination that we show here to continue our program to
rebuild and refortify our defenses" and really believe that greatly increasing
the amount of money spent building new weapons would lead to a reduction
in the number of weapons in the world. If we really believe that we understand such language and that such language communicates and promotes
clear thought, then the world of *1984*,[1] with its control of reality through language, is upon us.

[1] In a section omitted from this abridgement of his chapter, Lutz discusses *Nineteen Eighty-Four*, the 1949 novel by George Orwell in which a frightening totalitarian state devises a language, called *newspeak*, to shape and control thought in politically acceptable forms. (For an example of Orwell's writing, see p. 634.) —EDS.

For a reading quiz, sources on William Lutz, and annotated links to further readings on doublespeak, visit **bedfordstmartins.com/thebedfordreader**.

## Journal Writing

Now that you know the name for it, when have you read or heard examples of doublespeak? Over the next few days, jot down examples of doublespeak that you recall or that you read and hear — from politicians or news commentators; in the lease for your dwelling or your car; in advertising and catalogs; from bosses, teachers, or other figures of authority; in overheard conversations. (To take your journal writing further, see "From Journal to Essay" on the following page.)

## Questions on Meaning

1. What is Lutz's THESIS? Where does he state it?
2. According to Lutz, four questions can help us identify doublespeak. What are they? How can they help us distinguish between truthful language and doublespeak?
3. What, according to Lutz, are "the dangers of doublespeak"?
4. What ASSUMPTIONS does the author make about his readers' educational backgrounds and familiarity with his subject?

## Questions on Writing Strategy

1. What principle does Lutz use for creating his four kinds of doublespeak — that is, what mainly distinguishes the groups?
2. How does Lutz develop the discussion of euphemism in paragraphs 5–8?
3. Lutz quotes Alan Greenspan twice in paragraphs 13–14. What is surprising about the comment in paragraph 14? Why does Lutz include this second quotation?
4. Lutz uses many quotations that were quite current when he first published this piece in 1989 but that now may seem dated — for instance, references to Presidents Carter and Reagan or to the nuclear arms race. Do these EXAMPLES undermine Lutz's essay in any way? Is his discussion of doublespeak still valid today? Explain your answers.
5. **OTHER METHODS** Lutz's essay is not only a classification but also a DEFINITION of *doublespeak* and an examination of CAUSE AND EFFECT. Where are these other methods used most prominently? What do they contribute to the essay?

## Questions on Language

1. How does Lutz's own language compare with the language he quotes as doublespeak? Do you find his language clear and easy to understand?

2. ANALYZE Lutz's language in paragraphs 22 and 23. How do the CONNOTATIONS of words such as "corrupt," "hostility," "insidious," and "control" strengthen the author's message?

3. The following list of possibly unfamiliar words includes only those found in Lutz's own sentences, not those in the doublespeak he quotes. Be sure you can define variance (par. 2); incongruity, referent (3); taboo (5); condolences (6); esoteric, profundity (10); condemnation (11); ramshackle (21); cynicism (22); insidious (23).

## Suggestions for Writing

1. **FROM JOURNAL TO ESSAY**   Choose at least one of the examples of doublespeak noted in your journal, and write an essay explaining why it qualifies as doublespeak. Which of Lutz's categories does it fit under? How did you recognize it? Can you understand what it means?

2. Just about all of us have resorted to doublespeak at one time or another—when making an excuse, when trying to conceal the fact that we're unprepared for an exam, when trying to impress a supervisor or potential employer. Write a NARRATIVE about a time you used deliberately unclear language, perhaps language that you yourself didn't understand. What were the circumstances? Did you consciously decide to use unclear language, or did it just leak out? How did others react to your use of this language?

3. The National Council of Teachers of English has posted a number of articles from the *Quarterly Review of Doublespeak*, which Lutz once edited, on its Web site at *www.ncte.org/about/press/116444.htm.* (Your library may also subscribe to the journal.) Read a few related articles from the journal, and based on them write an essay in which you challenge, expand, or add more examples to Lutz's categories.

4. **CRITICAL WRITING**   Can you determine from his essay who Lutz believes is responsible for the proliferation of doublespeak? Whose responsibility is it to curtail the use of doublespeak: just those who use it? the schools? the government? the media? we who hear it? Write an essay that considers these questions, citing specific passages from the essay and incorporating your own ideas.

5. **CONNECTIONS**   Read Stephanie Ericsson's "The Ways We Lie" (p. 408), which classifies the lies we tell in our daily lives. In what way, if any, do doublespeakers also lie? How, if at all, do the intentions of Ericsson's liars and Lutz's doublespeakers differ? How, if at all, are their intentions the same? Are the results of lying and doublespeak, according to each author, different or the same? Write an essay that answers these questions and that points out any other similarities or differences you notice between liars and doublespeakers. Use EVIDENCE from the two essays or from your own experience to support your thesis.

---

## *William Lutz on Writing*

In 1989 C-SPAN aired an interview between Brian Lamb and William Lutz. Lamb asked Lutz about his writing process. "I have a rule about writing,"

Lutz answered, "which I discovered when I wrote my dissertation: You never write a book, you write three pages, or you write five pages. I put off writing my dissertation for a year, because I could not think of writing this whole thing. . . . I had put off doing this book [*Doublespeak*] for quite a while, and my wife said, 'You've got to do the book.' And I said, 'Yes, I am going to, just as soon as I . . . ,' and, of course, I did every other thing I could possibly think of before that, and then I realized one day that she was right, I had to start writing. . . . So one day, I sit down and say, 'I am going to write five pages—that's all—and when I am done with five pages, I'll reward myself.' So I do the five pages, or the next time I will do ten pages or whatever number of pages, but I set a number of pages."

Perhaps wondering just how high Lutz's daily page count might go, Lamb asked Lutz how much he wrote at one time. "It depends," Lutz admitted. "I always begin a writing session by sitting down and rewriting what I wrote the previous day—and that is the first thing, and it does two things. First of all, it makes your writing a little bit better, because rewriting is the essential part of writing. And the second thing is to get you flowing again, get back into the mainstream. Truman Capote[1] once gave the best piece of advice for writers ever given. He said, 'Never pump the well dry; always leave a bucket there.' So, I never stop writing when I run out of ideas. I always stop when I have something more to write about, and write a note to myself, 'This is what I am going to do next,' and then I stop. The worst feeling in the world is to have written yourself dry and have to come back the next day, knowing that you are dry and not knowing where you are going to pick up at this point."

## For Discussion

1. Though his work is devoted to words and writing, William Lutz once spent a great deal of time avoiding writing. What finally got him to stop procrastinating? When you are avoiding a writing assignment, is it the length of the project or something else that prevents you from getting to work?
2. Lutz always rewrites before he starts writing about the idea that he didn't develop on the previous day. How come? Do you think Lutz's strategy is a good one?

[1] Truman Capote (1924–84) was an American journalist and fiction writer. —EDS.

---

# ADDITIONAL WRITING TOPICS
## *Classification*

Write an essay by the method of classification, in which you sort one of the following subjects into categories of your own. Make clear your PURPOSE in classifying and the basis of your classification. Explain each class with DEFINITIONS and EXAMPLES (you may find it helpful to make up a name for each group). Check your classes to be sure they neither gap nor overlap.

1. Commuters, or people who use public transportation
2. Environmental problems or environmental solutions
3. Web sites
4. Vegetarians
5. Talk shows
6. The ills or benefits of city life
7. The recordings you own
8. Families
9. Stand-up comedians
10. Present-day styles of marriage
11. Vacations
12. College students today
13. Movies for teenagers or men or women
14. Waiters you'd never tip
15. Comic strips
16. Movie monsters
17. Sports announcers
18. Inconsiderate people
19. Radio stations
20. Mall millers (people who mill around malls)

GARBAGE IN...

# 11

---

# CAUSE AND EFFECT

*Asking Why*

◀ **Cause and effect in a cartoon**

With simple drawings and perhaps a few words, editorial car-
toonists often make striking comments on events. This cartoon by
Mike Thompson, published in the *Detroit Free Press*, proposes a
cause to explain a disturbing effect. What is the effect? What,
according to Thompson, is the cause? How does the caption
"Garbage in . . ." reinforce Thompson's explanation? What other
causes might explain the effect depicted here? Do you agree or
disagree with Thompson's view? Why?

## THE METHOD

Press the button of a doorbell and, inside the house or apartment, chimes sound. Why? Because the touch of your finger on the button closed an electrical circuit. But why did you ring the doorbell? Because you were sent by your dispatcher: You are a bill collector calling on a customer whose payments are three months overdue.

The touch of your finger on the button is the *immediate cause* of the chimes: the event that precipitates another. That you were ordered by your dispatcher to go ring the doorbell is a *remote cause*: an underlying, more basic reason for the event, not apparent to an observer. Probably, ringing the doorbell will lead to some results: The door will open, and you may be given a check—or have the door slammed in your face.

To figure out reasons and results is to use the method of CAUSE AND EFFECT. Either to explain events or to argue for one version of them, you try to answer the question "Why did something happen?" or "What were the consequences?" or "What might be the consequences?" As part of answering such a question, you use DIVISION or ANALYSIS (Chap. 9) to separate the flow of events into causes.

Seeking causes, you can ask, for example, "Why do birds migrate?" "What has caused sales of Detroit-made cars to pick up (or decline) lately?" "What were the principal causes of America's involvement in the war in Vietnam?" Looking for effects, you can ask, "What have been the effects of the birth-control pill on the typical American family?" "What impact have handheld computers had on the nursing profession?" You can look to a possible future and ask, "Of what use might a course in psychology be to me if I become an office manager?" "Suppose an asteroid the size of a sofa were to strike Philadelphia—what would be the probable consequences?"

Don't, by the way, confuse cause and effect with the method of PROCESS ANALYSIS (Chap. 8). Some process analysis essays, too, deal with happenings; but they focus more on repeatable events (rather than unique ones) and they explain *how* (rather than why) something happened. If you were explaining the process by which the doorbell rings, you might break the happening into stages—(1) the finger presses the button; (2) the circuit closes; (3) the current travels the wire; (4) the chimes make music—and you'd set forth the process in detail. But why did the finger press the button? What happened because the doorbell rang? To answer those questions, you need cause and effect.

In trying to explain why things happen, you can expect to find a whole array of causes—interconnected, perhaps, like the strands of a spiderweb. You'll want to do an honest job of unraveling, and this may take time. For a jury to acquit or convict an accused slayer, weeks of testimony from witnesses, detectives, and psychiatrists may be required, then days of deliberation. It took a great historian, Jakob Burckhardt, most of his lifetime to set forth a few reasons for the dawn of the Italian Renaissance. To be sure, juries must take great care when a life hangs in the balance; and Burckhardt, after all, was writing an immense book. To produce a college essay, you don't have forty years; but before you start to write, you will need to devote extra time and thought to seeing which facts are the causes, and which matter most.

To answer the questions "Why?" and "What followed as a result?" may sometimes be hard, but it can be satisfying—even illuminating. Indeed, to seek causes and effects is one way for the mind to discover order in a reality that otherwise might seem random and pointless.

## THE PROCESS

### Subjects, Purposes, and Theses

The method of cause and effect tends to suggest itself: If you have a subject and soon start thinking "Why?" or "What results?" or "What if?" then you are on the way to analyzing causation. Your subject may be impersonal—like a change in voting patterns or the failure or success of a business—or it may be quite personal. Indeed, an excellent cause-and-effect paper may be written on a subject very near to you. You can ask yourself why you behaved in a certain way at a certain moment. You can examine the reasons for your current beliefs and attitudes. Writing such a paper, you might happen upon a truth you hadn't realized before.

Whether your subject is personal or impersonal, make sure it is manageable: You should be able to get to the bottom of it, given the time and information available. For a 500-word essay due Thursday, the causes of teenage rebellion would be a less feasible topic than why a certain thirteen-year-old you know ran away from home.

Before rushing to list causes or effects, stop a moment to consider what your PURPOSE might be in writing. Much of the time you'll seek simply to explain what did or might occur, discovering and laying out the connections as clearly and accurately as you can. But when reasonable people could disagree over causes or effects, you will want to go further, arguing for one interpretation over others. You'll still need to be clear and accurate in presenting your interpretation, but you'll also need to treat the others fairly. (See Chap. 13 on argument and persuasion.)

When you have a grip on your subject and your purpose, you can draft a tentative THESIS STATEMENT to express the main point of your analysis. The

statement may be hypothetical at this stage, before you have gathered EVI-
DENCE and sorted out the complexity of causes and effects. Still, a statement
framed early can help direct your later thinking and research.

The essays in this chapter provide good examples of thesis statements that
put across, concisely, the author's central finding about causes and effects.
Here are a few examples:

> A bill like the one we've just passed [to ban imports from factories that use
> child labor] is of no use unless it goes hand in hand with programs that will
> offer a new life to these newly released children.
> —Chitra Divakaruni, "Live Free and Starve"

> To begin to solve the problem [of the illegal drug trade], we need to under-
> stand what's happening in drug-source countries, how the United States can
> and can't help there, and what, instead, can be done at home.
> —Marie Javdani, "*Plata o Plomo:* Silver or Lead"

> [Because of the Internet,] we are abandoning the tyranny of the top [media
> producers] and becoming a niche nation again, defined not by our geography
> but by our interests.         —Chris Anderson, "The Rise and Fall of the Hit"

## Causal Relations

Your toughest job in writing a cause-and-effect essay may be figuring out
what caused what. Sometimes one event will appear to trigger another, and it
in turn will trigger yet another, and another still, in an order we call a *causal
chain*. A classic example of such a chain is set forth in a Mother Goose rhyme:

> For want of a nail the shoe was lost,
> For want of a shoe the horse was lost,
> For want of a horse the rider was lost,
> For want of a rider the battle was lost,
> For want of a battle the kingdom was lost—
> And all for the want of a nail.

In reality, causes are seldom so easy to find as that missing nail: They tend to
be many and complicated. A battle may be lost for more than one reason. Perhaps the losing general had fewer soldiers and had a blinding hangover the
morning he mapped out his battle strategy. Perhaps winter set in, expected
reinforcements failed to arrive, and a Joan of Arc inspired the winning army.
The downfall of a kingdom is not to be explained as though it were the toppling of the last domino in a file. Still, one event precedes another in time,
and in discerning causes you don't ignore chronological order; you pay attention to it.

When you can see a number of apparent causes, weigh them and assign each a relative importance. Which do you find matter most? Often, you will see that causes are more important or less so: major or minor. If you seek to explain why your small town has fallen on hard times, you might note that two businesses shut down: a factory employing three hundred and a drugstore employing six. The factory's closing is a *major cause*, leading to significant unemployment in the town, while the drugstore's closing is perhaps a *minor cause*—or not a cause at all but an effect. In writing about the causes, you would emphasize the factory and mention the drugstore only briefly if at all.

When seeking remote causes, look only as far back as necessary. Explaining your town's misfortunes, you might see the factory's closing as the immediate cause. You could show what caused the shutdown: a dispute between union and management. You might even go back to the cause of the dispute (announced firings) and the cause of the firings (loss of sales to a competitor). A paper showing effects might work in the other direction, moving from the factory closing to its impact on the town: unemployment, the closing of stores (including the drugstore), people packing up and moving away.

Two cautions about causal relations are in order here. One is to beware of confusing coincidence with cause. In the logical FALLACY called *post hoc* (short for the Latin *post hoc, ergo propter hoc*, "after this, therefore because of this"), one assumes, erroneously, that because A happened before B, A must have caused B. This is the error of the superstitious man who decides that he lost his job because a black cat walked in front of him. Another error is to oversimplify causes by failing to recognize their full number and complexity— claiming, say, that violent crime is simply a result of "all those gangster shows on TV." Avoid such wrong turns in reasoning by patiently looking for evidence before you write, and by giving it careful thought. (For a fuller list of such fallacies, or errors in reasoning, see pp. 524–26.)

## Discovery of Causes

To help find causes of actions and events, you can ask yourself a few searching questions. These have been suggested by the work of the literary critic Kenneth Burke:

1. *What act am I trying to explain?*
2. *What is the character, personality, or mental state of whoever acted?*
3. *In what scene or location did the act take place, and in what circumstances?*
4. *What instruments or means did the person use?*
5. *For what purpose did the person act?*

Burke calls these elements a *pentad* (or set of five): the *act*, the *actor*, the *scene*, the *agency*, and the *purpose*. If you were a detective trying to explain why a liquor store burned down, you might ask these questions:

1. *Act:* Was the fire deliberately set by someone, or was there an accident?
2. *Actors:* If the fire was arson, who set it: the store's worried, debt-ridden owner? a mentally disturbed anti-alcohol crusader? a drunk who had been denied a purchase?
3. *Scene:* Was the shop near a church? a mental hospital? a fireworks factory?
4. *Agency, or means of the act:* Was the fire caused by faulty electrical wiring? a carelessly tossed cigarette butt? a flaming torch? rags soaked in kerosene?
5. *Purpose:* If the fire wasn't accidental, was it set to collect insurance? to punish drinkers? to get revenge?

You can further deepen your inquiry by seeing relationships between the terms of the pentad. Ask, for instance, what does the actor have to do with this scene? (Is he or she the neighbor across the street, who has been staring at the liquor shop resentfully for years?)

Don't worry if not all the questions apply, if not all the answers are immediately forthcoming. Burke's pentad isn't meant to be a grim rigmarole; it is a means of discovery, to generate a lot of possible material for you—insights, observations, hunches to pursue. It won't solve each and every human mystery, but sometimes it will helpfully deepen your thought.

### Final Word

In stating what you believe to be causes and effects, don't be afraid to voice a well-considered hunch. Your instructor doesn't expect you to write, in a short time, a definitive account of the causes of an event or a belief or a phenomenon—only to write a coherent and reasonable one. To discern all causes—including remote ones—and all effects is beyond the power of any one human mind. Still, admirable and well-informed writers on matters such as politics, economics, and world and national affairs are often canny guessers and brave drawers of inferences. At times, even the most cautious and responsible writer has to leap boldly over a void to strike firm ground on the far side. Consider your evidence. Focus your thinking. Look well before leaping. Then take off.

## FOCUS ON CLARITY AND CONCISENESS

While drafting a cause-and-effect analysis, you may need to grope a bit to discover just what you think about the sequence and relative importance of reasons and consequences. Your sentences may grope a bit, too, reflecting your initial confusion or your need to circle around your ideas in order to find them. The following draft passage reveals such difficulties:

> WORDY AND UNCLEAR   Employees often worry about suggestive comments from others. The employee may not only worry but feel the need to discuss the situation with coworkers. One thing that is an effect of sexual harassment, even verbal harassment, in the workplace is that productivity is lost. Plans also need to be made to figure out how to deal with future comments. Engaging in these activities is sure to take time and concentration from work.

Drafting this passage, the writer seems to have built up to the idea about lost productivity (third sentence) after providing support for it in the first two sentences. The fourth sentence then adds more support. And sentences 2–4 all show a writer working out his ideas: Sentence subjects and verbs do not focus on the main actors and actions of the sentences, words repeat unnecessarily, and word groups run longer than needed for clarity.

These problems disappear from the edited version below, which moves the idea of the passage up front, uses subjects and verbs to state what the sentences are about (underlined), and cuts unneeded words.

> CONCISE AND CLEAR   Even verbal sexual <u>harassment</u> in the workplace <u>causes</u> a loss of productivity. Worrying about suggestive comments from others, discussing those comments with coworkers, planning how to deal with future comments — these <u>activities</u> <u>consume</u> time and concentration that a harassed employee could spend on work.

**For exercises on clarity and conciseness, visit Exercise Central at**
*bedfordstmartins.com/thebedfordreader.*

## CHECKLIST FOR REVISING A CAUSE-AND-EFFECT ESSAY

✔ **SUBJECT**  Have you been able to cover your subject adequately in the time and space available? Should you perhaps narrow the subject so that you can fairly address the important causes and/or effects?

✔ **THESIS**  For your readers' benefit, have you focused your analysis by stating your main idea succinctly in a thesis statement?

✔ **COMPLETENESS**  Have you included all relevant causes or effects? Does your analysis reach back to locate remote causes or forward to locate remote effects?

Cause and Effect

> ✔ **CAUSAL RELATIONS**   Have you presented a clear pattern of causes or effects? Have you distinguished the remote from the immediate, the major from the minor?
>
> ✔ **ACCURACY AND FAIRNESS**   Have you avoided the *post hoc* fallacy, assuming that A caused B just because it preceded B? Have you also avoided oversimplifying and instead covered causes or effects in all their complexity?
>
> ✔ **CLARITY AND CONCISENESS**   Have you edited your draft to foreground your main points and tighten your sentences?

## CAUSE AND EFFECT IN PARAGRAPHS

### Writing About Television

In the following paragraph, the writer poses and concisely answers a question about the near-absence of soccer from mainstream American TV. The paragraph was written especially for *The Bedford Reader*, but it could serve as a component of a full essay, perhaps one analyzing how television affects sports in general.

Why is it that, despite a growing interest in soccer among American athletes, and despite its ranking as the most popular sport in the world, the major US television networks all but ignore it? Granted, soccer sometimes makes it to the all-sports channels, but mostly it's shut out. The reason stems partly from the basic nature of commercial television, which exists not to inform and entertain but to sell. During most major sporting events on television—football, baseball, basketball, boxing—producers can take advantage of natural interruptions in the action to broadcast sales pitches; or, if the natural breaks occur too infrequently, the producers can contrive time-outs for the sole purpose of airing lucrative commercials. But soccer is played in two solid halves of forty-five minutes each; not even injury to a player is cause for a time-out. How, then, to insert the requisite number of commercial breaks without resorting to false fouls or other questionable tactics? After CBS aired a soccer match in 1967, players reported, according to Stanley Frank, that before the game the referee had instructed them "to stay down every nine minutes." The resulting hue and cry rose all the way to the House Communications Subcommittee. From that day to this, no one has been able to figure out how to screen advertising jingles during a televised soccer game. The result is that most commercial television has treated soccer as if it didn't exist.

*Margin notes:* Topic sentence: question to be answered. Analysis of causes. Commercial TV requires commercial breaks. Soccer is played with only one break. Example of failed attempt to adapt soccer to TV. Result: little soccer on TV

Cause and Effect **439**

## Writing in an Academic Discipline

This paragraph from a textbook on American history explains the causes of a "fateful decision" in the 1960s—fateful because, as the authors' text goes on to explain, the decision had grave and far-reaching consequences for the United States.

Many factors played a role in [President Lyndon] Johnson's fateful decision [to escalate the Vietnam War]. But the most obvious explanation is that the new president faced many pressures to expand the American involvement and only a very few to limit it. As the untested successor to a revered and martyred president, he felt obliged to prove his worthiness for the office by continuing the policies of his predecessor. Aid to South Vietnam had been one of the most prominent of those policies. Johnson also felt it necessary to retain in his administration many of the important figures of the Kennedy years. In doing so, he surrounded himself with a group of foreign-policy advisers—Secretary of State Dean Rusk, Secretary of Defense Robert McNamara, National Security Adviser McGeorge Bundy—who strongly believed not only that the United States had an important obligation to resist communism in Vietnam, but that it possessed the ability and resources to make that resistance successful. As a result, Johnson seldom had access to information making clear how difficult the new commitment might become. A compliant Congress raised little protest to, and indeed at one point openly endorsed, Johnson's use of executive powers to lead the nation into war. And for several years at least, public opinion remained firmly behind him—in part because Barry Goldwater's bellicose remarks about the war during the 1964 campaign made Johnson seem by comparison to be a moderate on the issue. Above all, intervention in South Vietnam was fully consistent with nearly twenty years of American foreign policy. An anti-Communist ally was appealing to the United States for assistance; all the assumptions of the containment doctrine seemed to require the nation to oblige. Johnson seemed unconcerned that the government of South Vietnam existed only because the United States had put it there, and that the regime had never succeeded in acquiring the loyalty of its people. Vietnam, he believed, provided a test of American willingness to fight Communist aggression, a test he was determined not to fail.
—Richard N. Current et al., *American History: A Survey*

Topic sentence: summary of causes to be discussed

Causes:
Need to prove worthiness

Advisers urging involvement and shutting off alternative views

Congressional cooperation

Support of public opinion

Consistency with American foreign policy against Communism

## CAUSE AND EFFECT IN PRACTICE

An ardent supporter of her school's track team, Kate Krueger was a sophomore during the team's first winning season in many years. At the end of the season, the student newspaper published a letter to the editor saying that the successes were due to a new coach. Krueger found this explanation inadequate and decided to say so in her own letter. The cause-and-effect analysis below appeared in the newspaper the following week.

Between the first draft and the final version of her letter, Krueger made one significant addition. At first, she ignored any contributions of the new coach, thinking that the original letter writer had more than covered them. But since Krueger actually agreed that the coach had helped the team, her first draft did what she accused the letter of doing: It oversimplified. In her revision, Krueger acknowledged the coach's contributions while also detailing the other causes she saw at work.

May 2, 2007

To the Editor:

I take issue with Tom Boatz's letter that was printed in the April 30 *Weekly*. Boatz attributes the success of this year's track team solely to the new coach, John Barak. I have several close friends who are athletes on the track team, so as an interested observer and fan I believe that Boatz oversimplified the causes of the team's recent success.

To be sure, Coach Barak did improve the training regimen and overall morale, and these have certainly contributed to the winning season. Both Coach Barak and the team members themselves can share credit for an impressive work ethic and a sense of camaraderie unequaled in previous years. However, several factors outside Coach Barak's control may have been even more influential.

This year's team gained several phenomenal freshman athletes, such as Kristin Hall, who anchored the 4x400 and 4x800 relays and played an integral part in setting several school records, and Eric Asper, who was undefeated in the shot put.

Even more important, and also unmentioned by Tom Boatz, is the college's increased funding for the track program. Last year the school allotted 50 percent more for equipment, and the results have been dramatic. For example, the new vaulting poles are now the correct length and correspond to the weights of the individual athletes, giving them more power and height. Some vaulters have been able to vault as much as a foot higher than their previous records. Similarly, new starting blocks have allowed the team's sprinters to drop valuable seconds off their times.

I agree with Tom Boatz that Coach Barak deserves much credit for the track team's successes. But the athletes do, too, and so does the college for at last supporting its track program.

—KATE KRUEGER '09

# CHITRA DIVAKARUNI

Born in 1956 in Calcutta, India, CHITRA BANERJEE DIVAKARUNI spent nineteen years in her homeland before immigrating to the United States. She holds an MA from Wright State University and a PhD from the University of California at Berkeley. Her books, often addressing the immigrant experience in America, include the novels *The Mistress of Spice* (1997), *Sister of My Heart* (1999), *The Vine of Desire* (2002), *Queen of Dreams* (2004), and *The Palace of Illusions* (2008); the story collections *Arranged Marriage* (1995) and *The Unknown Errors of Our Lives* (2001); and the poetry collections *Leaving Yuba City* (1997) and *Black Candle* (2000). Divakaruni has received a number of awards for her work, including the Before Columbus Foundation's 1996 American Book Award. She teaches creative writing at the University of Houston and serves on the boards of several organizations that help women and children.

# *Live Free and Starve*

Many of the consumer goods sold in the United States—shoes, clothing, toys, rugs—are made in countries whose labor practices do not meet US standards for safety and fairness. Americans have been horrified at tales of children put to work by force or under contracts (called *indentures*) with the children's parents. Some in the United States government have tried to stop or at least discourage such practices: For instance, the bill Divakaruni cites in her first paragraph, which was signed into law, requires the US Customs Service to issue a detention order on goods that are suspected of having been produced by forced or indentured child labor; and a bill to ban goods made with any kind of child labor has been introduced in Congress every year since 1993. In this essay from *Salon* magazine in 1997, Divakaruni argues that these efforts, however well intentioned they are, mean dreadful consequences for the very people they are designed to protect.

For a different perspective on the effects of globalization, see the next essay, Marie Javdani's "*Plata o Plomo*: Silver or Lead."

Some days back, the House passed a bill that stated that the United States 1 would no longer permit the import of goods from factories where forced or indentured child labor was used. My liberal friends applauded the bill. It was a triumphant advance in the field of human rights. Now children in Third World countries wouldn't have to spend their days chained to their posts in

factories manufacturing goods for other people to enjoy while their childhoods slipped by them. They could be free and happy, like American children.

I am not so sure.                                                                       2

It is true that child labor is a terrible thing, especially for those children          3
who are sold to employers by their parents at the age of five or six and have
no way to protect themselves from abuse. In many cases it will be decades—
perhaps a lifetime, due to the fines heaped upon them whenever they make
mistakes—before they can buy back their freedom. Meanwhile these children, mostly employed by rug-makers, spend their days in dark, ill-ventilated
rooms doing work that damages their eyes and lungs. They aren't even
allowed to stand up and stretch. Each time they go to the bathroom, they suffer a pay cut.

But is this bill, which, if it passes the Senate and is signed by President          4
Clinton, will lead to the unemployment of almost a million children, the
answer? If the children themselves were asked whether they would rather
work under such harsh conditions or enjoy a leisure that comes without the
benefit of food or clothing or shelter, I wonder what their response would be.

It is easy for us in America to make the error of evaluating situations in          5
the rest of the world as though they were happening in this country and propose solutions that make excellent sense—in the context of our society. Even
we immigrants, who should know better, have wiped from our minds the
memory of what it is to live under the kind of desperate conditions that force
a parent to sell his or her child. Looking down from the heights of Maslow's
pyramid,[1] it seems inconceivable to us that someone could actually prefer
bread to freedom.

When I was growing up in Calcutta, there was a boy who used to work in          6
our house. His name was Nimai, and when he came to us, he must have been
about ten or so, just a little older than my brother and I. He'd been brought to
our home by his uncle, who lived in our ancestral village and was a field
laborer for my grandfather. The uncle explained to my mother that Nimai's
parents were too poor to feed their several children, and while his older brothers were already working in the fields and earning their keep, Nimai was too
frail to do so. My mother was reluctant to take on a sickly child who might
prove more of a burden than a help, but finally she agreed, and Nimai lived
and worked in our home for six or seven years. My mother was a good
employer—Nimai ate the same food that we children did and was given new

---

[1] The psychologist Abraham Maslow (1908–70) proposed a "hierarchy of needs" in the
shape of a five-level pyramid with survival needs at the bottom and "self-actualization" and
"self-transcendence" at the top. According to Maslow, one must satisfy the needs at each level
before moving up to the next. —EDS.

clothes during Indian New Year, just as we were. In the time between his chores—dusting and sweeping and pumping water from the tube-well and running to the market—my mother encouraged him to learn to read and write. Still, I would not disagree with anyone who says that it was hardly a desirable existence for a child.

But what would life have been like for Nimai if an anti–child-labor law    7
had prohibited my mother from hiring him? Every year, when we went to visit our grandfather in the village, we were struck by the many children we saw by the mud roads, their ribs sticking out through the rags they wore. They trailed after us, begging for a few paise.[2] When the hunger was too much to bear, they stole into the neighbors' fields and ate whatever they could find—raw potatoes, cauliflower, green sugar cane and corn torn from the stalk—even though they knew they'd be beaten for it. Whenever Nimai passed these children, he always walked a little taller. And when he handed the bulk of his earnings over to his father, there was a certain pride in his eye. Exploitation, you might be thinking. But he thought he was a responsible member of his family.

A bill like the one we've just passed is of no use unless it goes hand in    8
hand with programs that will offer a new life to these newly released children. But where are the schools in which they are to be educated? Where is the money to buy them food and clothing and medication, so that they don't return home to become the extra weight that capsizes the already shaky raft of their family's finances? Their own governments, mired in countless other problems, seem incapable of bringing these services to them. Are we in America who, with one blithe stroke of our congressional pen, rendered these children jobless, willing to shoulder that burden? And when many of these children turn to the streets, to survival through thievery and violence and begging and prostitution—as surely in the absence of other options they must—are we willing to shoulder that responsibility?

*For a reading quiz, sources on Chitra Divakaruni, and annotated links to further readings on globalization and its effects on workers, visit* **bedfordstmartins.com** **/thebedfordreader.**

---

[2] *Paise* are the smallest unit of Indian currency, worth a fraction of an American penny.— EDS.

## Journal Writing

Write a journal response to Divakaruni's argument against legislation that bans goods produced by forced or indentured child laborers. Do you basically agree or disagree with the author? Why? (To take your journal writing further, see "From Journal to Essay" below.)

## Questions on Meaning

1. What do you take to be Divakaruni's PURPOSE in this essay? At what point did it become clear?
2. What is Divakaruni's THESIS? Where is it stated?
3. What are "Third World countries" (par. 1)?
4. From the further information given in the footnote on page 443, what does it mean to be "[l]ooking down from the heights of Maslow's pyramid" (par. 5)? What point is Divakaruni making here?
5. In paragraph 8 Divakaruni suggests some of the reasons that children in other countries may be forced or sold into labor. What are they?

## Questions on Writing Strategy

1. In her last paragraph, Divakaruni asks a series of RHETORICAL QUESTIONS. What is the EFFECT of this strategy?
2. How does the structure of paragraph 3 clarify causes and effects?
3. **OTHER METHODS**   What does the extended EXAMPLE of Nimai (pars. 6–7) contribute to Divakaruni's argument? What, if anything, does it add to Divakaruni's authority? What does it tell us about child labor abroad?

## Questions on Language

1. Divakaruni says that laboring children could otherwise be "the extra weight that capsizes the already shaky raft of their family's finances" (par. 8). How does this metaphor capture the problem of children in poor families? (See *Figures of speech* in Useful Terms for a definition of *metaphor*.)
2. What do the words in paragraph 7 tell you about Divakaruni's attitude toward the village children? Is it disdain? pity? compassion? horror?
3. Consult a dictionary if you need help in defining the following: indentured (par. 1); inconceivable (5); exploitation (7); mired, blithe (8).

## Suggestions for Writing

1. **FROM JOURNAL TO ESSAY**   Starting from your journal entry, write a letter to your congressional representative or one of your senators who takes a position for or against laws such as that opposed by Divakaruni. You can use quotations from

Divakaruni's essay if they serve your purpose, but the letter should center on your own views of the issue. When you've finished your letter, send it. (You can find your representative's and your senators' names and addresses on the Web at *house.gov/writerep* and *senate.gov.*)

2. David Parker, a photographer and doctor, has documented child laborers in a series of powerful photographs (*www.hsph.harvard.edu/gallery/intro.html*). He asks viewers, "Under what circumstances and conditions should children work?" Look at Parker's photographs, and answer his question in an essay. What kind of paid work, for how many hours a week, is appropriate for, say, a ten- or twelve-year-old child? Consider: What about children working in their family's business? Where do you draw the line between occasional babysitting or lawn mowing and full-time factory work?

3. Research the history of child labor in the United States, including the development of child-labor laws. Then write an essay in which you explain how and why the laws evolved and what the current laws are.

4. **CRITICAL WRITING**    Divakaruni's essay depends significantly on appeals to readers' emotions (see p. 521). Locate one emotional appeal that either helps to convince you of the author's point or, in your mind, weakens the argument. What does the appeal ASSUME about the reader's (your) feelings or values? Why are the assumptions correct or incorrect in your case? How, specifically, does the appeal strengthen or undermine Divakaruni's argument?

5. **CONNECTIONS**    In the next essay, "*Plata o Plomo:* Silver or Lead" (p. 448), Marie Javdani examines another global relationship that can harm children: the international traffic in cocaine, heroin, and other drugs. To what extent do you think the people in one country are responsible for what happens in other countries as a result of their actions? Write a brief essay that answers this question, explaining clearly the beliefs and values that guide your answer.

---

## *Chitra Divakaruni on Writing*

Chitra Divakaruni is both a writer and a community worker, reaching out to immigrants and other groups through organizations such as Maitri, a refuge for abused women that Divakaruni helped to found. In a 1998 interview in *Atlantic Unbound* (the online version of *The Atlantic Monthly*), Katie Bolick asked Divakaruni how her activism and writing affected each other. Here is Divakaruni's response.

Being helpful where I can has always been an important value for me. I did community work in India, and I continue to do it in America, because being involved in my community is something I feel I need to do. Activism has given me enormous satisfaction—not just as a person, but also as a writer. The lives of people I would have only known from the outside, or had stereotyped notions of, have been opened up to me. My hotline work with Maitri has certainly influenced both my life and my writing immensely. Overall, I have a great deal of sensitivity that I did not have before, and a lot of my preconceptions have changed. I hope that translates into my writing and reaches my readers.

## For Discussion

1. What evidence does "Live Free and Starve" give to support Divakaruni's statement about how her activist work has affected her writing?
2. What does Divakaruni mean when she speaks of lives that she "would have only known from the outside"? Of what use is "insider's" knowledge to an activist? to a writer?
3. Do you have a project or activity—comparable to Divakaruni's activism—that you believe positively affects your writing? What is it? How does it help you as you write?

# MARIE JAVDANI

MARIE JAVDANI was born in Albuquerque, New Mexico, and attended the University of Oregon, where she earned a BA in geography and was published in *Harvest*, the university's annual writing publication. In school she became interested in international development, and afterward she worked as a research assistant for Harvard's Center for International Development. She is now studying for a master's degree in geography at the University of Oregon, with plans to pursue a PhD in African studies. Always an avid reader, Javdani cites her father and the children's authors Shel Silverstein and Roald Dahl as her early inspirations to write. She is also a musician, currently playing the marimba, an African percussion instrument similar to the xylophone.

# Plata o Plomo: *Silver or Lead*

Like Chitra Divakaruni in the previous selection, Javdani is concerned in this essay with how actions taken in the United States can affect people in foreign lands, often without our realizing it. To make her argument concrete, Javdani tells the stories of two boys, Eric, an American, and Miguel, a Colombian. (Colombia is a country in South America.) Reminding us that global problems start and end with people, the boys represent cause and effect at their most specific. Javdani wrote this paper for her freshman writing course and revised it for *The Bedford Reader* in 2004. It is documented in MLA style, described on pages 62–73, except that italic type replaces underlining.

At 8:00 on a Friday night, Eric walks down the street in his American hometown whistling. Tonight, for the first time in almost a week, Eric does not have to do homework or chores. Tonight Eric is a free spirit. Best of all, tonight Eric has scored some drugs. He and his friends will trade their bland, controlled existence for some action and a little bit of fun.

At 8:00 on a Friday night, Miguel creeps down the road in his Colombian village praying. Tonight, for the last time in his life, Miguel will have to watch where he is going and listen anxiously for distant gunshots. Tonight Miguel will die. The guerillas who have been threatening him and his father will end his life for some coca and a lot of money.

Eric and Miguel represent opposite poles in what the United States government refers to as the "war on drugs." Miguel's home is where it starts. In his little village, drug production is the only possible way of life. Eric's home is where it ends. In his suburban paradise, the stress of homework and ex-girlfriends requires weekend breaks for drugs. All but ignoring both youths, congresspeople, governors, and presidents talk about how their actions will combat the flow of drugs into our homeland. In an attempt to find the quickest route around a complicated problem, the United States sends billions in aid dollars every year to the governments of Latin American "drug-source" countries such as Colombia, Ecuador, Bolivia, and Peru (Carpenter 205). But the solution isn't working: Political turmoil and violence continue to plague the countries to which we are sending aid, and illegal drug use in the United States remains fairly constant (Vásquez 571–75). To begin to solve the problem, we need to understand what's happening in drug-source countries, how the United States can and can't help there, and what, instead, can be done at home.

Miguel's country, Colombia, is one of the top recipients of US money and military weaponry and equipment. According to the US Department of State, Colombia produces nearly 80 percent of the world's cocaine as well as a significant amount of the US heroin supply. Drug production has become a way of life for Colombians. Some call it the *plata o plomo* mentality. As Gonzalo Sanchez explains it, *plata o plomo* is literally translated as "silver or lead" and means that one can either take the money—drug money, bribe money, and so on—or take a bullet (7). Since 1964, the country has been essentially run by drug lords and leftist extremists, mainly the FARC (the military wing of the Colombian Communist Party), whose guerilla presence is much stronger and more threatening than that of the actual government. In response, extreme right-wing paramilitary forces act in an equally deadly manner. Both of these groups raid villages continually, looking to root out "traitors" and executing whomever they please (Sanchez 12–15).

According to the humanitarian organization Human Rights Watch, US aid money has helped fund, supply, and train Colombian military units that maintain close alliances with paramilitary groups. Although Colombia has recently taken a tougher stance toward the paramilitaries and peace negotiations are in progress, the US State Department, major human rights organizations, and the United Nations claim that the Colombian government is still linked to illicit paramilitary activities. For example, government forces have often invaded, emptied, and then left a guerilla-held area, clearing the way for paramilitary fighters to take control (Carpenter 162). Human rights groups also criticize what Adam Isacson calls a "forgive and forget" government policy toward paramilitary leaders accused of crimes, including promises of amnesty in return for gradual demobilization (251–52). Although the US has threatened to suspend aid if Colombia does not break such ties with paramilitary groups, the full amount of promised aid continues to be granted (Human Rights Watch).

For the past forty years, the people of Colombia have found themselves between a rock and a hard place over the production of coca, the plant used for making cocaine and heroin. Under threats from the rebel drug lords, who now control many areas, civilians must either allow their land to be cultivated for the growth of coca or put themselves and their families at deadly risk. At the same time, however, the consequence of "cooperation" with the rebels is execution by paramilitary groups or even by the Colombian government. Some coca farmers, fearful of the government, willingly form alliances with rebels who offer to protect their farms for a fee (Vásquez 572).

Entire villages get caught in the crossfire between paramilitaries and rebels. In the past ten years, over 35,000 civilians have lost their lives in the conflict and hundreds of thousands have been forced from their homes (Carpenter 215). A terrible incident in the town of Bellavista was reported in the *New York Times* in 2002 (Forero, "Colombian War"). Paramilitary forces took over the town in an attempt to gain control of jungle smuggling routes. When leftist rebels arrived ready to fight a battle, the paramilitaries fled, leaving the civilians trapped and defenseless. Most of the villagers huddled together in their church, and 117 were killed when a stray rocket destroyed the church.

What is to be done to prevent such atrocities? The United States rushes aid to Colombia, hoping to stop the violence and the drugs. Unfortunately, the solutions attempted so far have had their own bad results. For instance, eradicating coca fields has alienated peasants, who then turn to the rebels for support, and it has also escalated violence over the reduced coca supply (Vásquez 575). Money intended to help peasants establish alternative crops has ended up buying weapons for branches of the military that support paramilitary operations (Human Rights Watch). Not long ago $2 million intended for the Colombian police just disappeared (Forero, "Two Million").

Obviously, the United States needs to monitor how its dollars are used in Colombia. It can continue to discourage the Colombian government from supporting the paramilitaries and encourage it to seek peace among the warring factions. But ultimately the United States is limited in what it can do by international law and by the tolerance of the US people for foreign intervention.

Instead, the United States should be looking to its homefront and should focus on cutting the demand for drugs. Any economist will affirm that where there is demand, there will be supply. A report by the United Nations Office on Drugs and Crime connects this basic economic principle to illegal drugs:

> Production of illicit drugs is market driven. In the United States alone, illicit drugs are an $80 billion market. More than $70 billion of that amount goes to traffickers, those who bring the drugs to market. Stopping the demand would stop their business. (26)

The United States should reduce demand by dramatically increasing both treatment and education. The first will help people stop using drugs. The second will make users aware of the consequences of their choices.

The war on drugs is not fought just in the jungles of some distant country.   11
It takes place daily at our schools, in our homes, and on our streets. People my
age who justify their use of illegal drugs by saying "It's my life, and I can do
with it what I please" should be made aware that they are funding drug lords
and contributing to the suffering of people across the globe, including in
Colombia. Eric's "little bit of fun" is costing Miguel his life.

## Works Cited

Carpenter, Ted Galen. *Peace and Freedom: Foreign Policy for a Constitutional Republic.* Washington: Cato, 2002.

Forero, Juan. "Colombian War Brings Carnage to Village Altar." *New York Times* 9 May 2002. *LexisNexis Academic.* LexisNexis. U Oregon, Knight Lib. 18 Mar. 2004 <http:// www.lexisnexis.com>.

---. "Two Million in US Aid to Colombia Missing from Colombian Police Fund." *New York Times* 11 May 2002. *LexisNexis Academic.* LexisNexis. U Oregon, Knight Lib. 18 Mar. 2004 <http://www.lexisnexis.com>.

Human Rights Watch. *World Report 2003.* 2004. *Human Rights Watch.* 9 Mar. 2004 <http://www.hrw.org/wr2k3.html>.

Isacson, Adam. "Optimism, Pessimism, and Terrorism: The United States and Colombia in 2003." *Brown Journal of World Affairs* 10.2 (2004): 245–55.

Sanchez, Gonzalo. *Violence in Colombia.* Wilmington: Scholarly Resources, 1992.

United Nations. Office on Drugs and Crime. *Drug Consumption Stimulates Cultivation and Trade.* 3 Dec. 2003. 18 Mar. 2004 <http://www.unodc.org /unodc/report2003-12-3.html>.

United States. Dept. of State. *International Narcotics Control Strategy Report, 2003.* Jan. 2004. 12 Mar. 2004 <http://www.state.gov/g/inl/rls/nrcrpt /2003/>.

Vásquez, Ian. "The International War on Drugs." *Cato Handbook for Congress: Policy Recommendations for the 108th Congress.* Ed. Edward H. Crane and David Boaz. Washington: Cato, 2003. 567–76. *Cato Institute.* 2003. 18 Mar. 2004 <http://www.cato.org/pubs/handbook/hb108/hb108-56.pdf>.

*For a reading quiz and annotated links to further readings on the causes and effects of the illegal drug trade, visit **bedfordstmartins.com/thebedfordreader**.*

## Journal Writing

What do you think about Javdani's solution to the twin problems of violence in drug-producing countries and drug use in the United States (pars. 10–11)? Do you think her solution would work? Why, or why not? (To take your journal writing further, see "From Journal to Essay" below.)

## Questions on Meaning

1. Where does Javdani state her THESIS? How does she develop the thesis?
2. Why do the Colombian peasants often support the Communist rebels rather than the government?
3. What, according to Javdani, are the problems caused by the US government's sending "billions in aid dollars every year to the governments of Latin American 'drug-source' countries" (par. 3)? What does Javdani offer as a solution?

## Questions on Writing Strategy

1. Who seems to be Javdani's intended AUDIENCE for this essay? How does she appeal to this audience?
2. With whom do Javdani's sympathies lie? What EVIDENCE in the essay supports your answer?
3. Javdani cites a variety of outside sources throughout the essay. What is the EFFECT of her use of these sources?
4. **OTHER METHODS**   Why does Javdani use COMPARISON AND CONTRAST in her opening paragraphs? What is the effect of her returning to this comparison in her conclusion?

## Questions on Language

1. In paragraph 6 Javdani describes the people of Colombia as "between a rock and a hard place over the production of coca." What does she mean?
2. How and why does Javdani use IRONY to describe Eric in paragraph 3?
3. Why does Javdani use quotation marks around *traitors* (par. 4) and *cooperation* (6)?
4. Consult a dictionary if you are unsure of the meanings of any of the following words: guerillas (par. 2); turmoil, plague (3); paramilitary (4); humanitarian, amnesty, demobilization (5); atrocities, eradicating, alienated (8).

## Suggestions for Writing

1. **FROM JOURNAL TO ESSAY**   Working from your journal writing and, like Javdani, drawing on research, develop an essay that lays out your view of the most effective ways to curtail either the production or the consumption of illegal drugs.

Which current US government efforts are successful, and which fall short? What more could be done?

2. Write a report on the use of illegal drugs by US adolescents, focusing on an aspect of the problem that interests you, such as how widespread it is, what groups it affects most and least, or what drugs are involved. An excellent starting place for your research is Monitoring the Future, a long-term study of "the behavior, attitudes, and values" of students and young adults. Its 2006 report, *National Results on Adolescent Drug Use*, is available at *monitoringthefuture.org/pubs/monographs/overview2006.pdf.*

3. **CRITICAL WRITING**   Is Javdani's essay an effective ARGUMENT? Consider the development of the thesis, the organization, the evidence, and the clarity of the presentation. What would you say are the strengths and weaknesses of this argument?

4. **CONNECTIONS**   Javdani's essay and Chitra Divakaruni's "Live Free and Starve" (p. 442) both look at effects of globalization, the increasing economic, cultural, and political connections among nations and their people. Write a brief essay discussing what you see as the main advantages and the main disadvantages of globalization. For instance, advantages might include the availability in this country of varied ethnic foods or of relatively inexpensive consumer goods that were produced elsewhere, while disadvantages might include the loss of American manufacturing jobs to foreign factories or the strong international drug trade.

---

## *Marie Javdani on Writing*

In an interview for *The Bedford Reader*, we asked Marie Javdani to describe her writing process.

Depending on my writing topic, it can often take a while to get a good start. If it's a topic I chose myself and am interested in or am at least somewhat knowledgeable about, the first steps are usually much easier. I usually start by brainstorming an outline by just writing things as I think of them. What questions do I want to answer? How does this topic actually affect people? Once I get a start, the writing process usually goes fairly quickly. I try to write in a way that I would speak if I were, for instance, teaching on the subject. That tends to make my work more readable. As for the introduction, I try to stay away from prescribed formats. I try to think of what would make me want to read more about a topic or to put a spin on it that makes it stand out. Also, I tend to write my introduction last. I've found that if I write it first it typically doesn't match what I write once I get "on a roll." If I plan ahead properly, I don't usually have to do more than two drafts unless I come upon new research that makes me need to rearrange my arguments. I try to write early enough to leave it alone for a few days before I go back and proofread it.

> Javdani also offered suggestions for college writers based on her own experiences as a student.

From a student's perspective, the best thing you can do to improve your writing is to be interested in your topic. On the same note, however, don't soapbox. Just say what you want to say, support it, and move on. If you're writing for an assignment for which you weren't able to choose the topic, try to take an angle that you think no one else will take. . . . Do take the time to spell-check and edit your writing. The spelling checker on the computer is not sufficient. You're (not *your*) in college and you know (not *no*) better. Try reading your writing out loud to yourself. If it doesn't sound good when you say it, it doesn't sound good on paper either.

## For Discussion

1. Do you share Javdani's experience that it's usually easier to write when you're interested in your topic? How does your writing process differ when you're interested beforehand from when you're not?
2. Why do you think Javdani advises "don't soapbox"? (If you aren't sure what *soapbox* means, look it up in a dictionary.)

# SARAH ADAMS

SARAH ADAMS was born in 1968 in New London, Connecticut, and grew up in Milwaukee, Wisconsin. She earned a BA in English from the University of Wisconsin at Madison (1994) and an MA in literature from the University of Wisconsin at Eau Claire (2002). Adams currently lives in Port Orchard, Washington, and teaches composition at Olympic College and Pierce College.

# Be Cool to the Pizza Dude

According to the Bureau of Labor Statistics, pizza deliverers have the fifth most dangerous job in the United States, plagued as they are by frequent robberies and traffic accidents. They may drive carelessly, as Adams observes in this essay, but extending tolerance and courtesy their way can have profound consequences. Adams read this essay on the NPR radio series *This I Believe*, which invites people of all sorts to explain the philosophies and values that guide them. The essay was printed in a 2006 book named after the series.

If I have one operating philosophy about life, it is this: "Be cool to the pizza delivery dude; it's good luck." Four principles guide the pizza dude philosophy. 1

*Principle 1:* Coolness to the pizza delivery dude is a practice in humility and forgiveness. I let him cut me off in traffic, let him safely hit the exit ramp from the left lane, let him forget to use his blinker without extending any of my digits out the window or toward my horn because there should be one moment in my harried life when a car may encroach or cut off or pass and I let it go. Sometimes when I have become so certain of my ownership of my lane, daring anyone to challenge me, the pizza dude speeds by in his rusted Chevette. His pizza light atop his car glowing like a beacon reminds me to check myself as I flow through the world. After all, the dude is delivering pizza to young and old, families and singletons, gays and straights, blacks, whites, and browns, rich and poor, and vegetarians and meat lovers alike. As he journeys, I give safe passage, practice restraint, show courtesy, and contain my anger. 2

*Principle 2:* Coolness to the pizza delivery dude is a practice in empathy. Let's face it: We've all taken jobs just to have a job because some money is better than none. I've held an assortment of these jobs and was grateful for the paycheck that meant I didn't have to share my Cheerios with my cats. In the big pizza wheel of life, sometimes you're the hot bubbly cheese and sometimes you're the burnt crust. It's good to remember the fickle spinning of that wheel. 3

*Principle 3:* Coolness to the pizza delivery dude is a practice in honor, and   4
it reminds me to honor honest work. Let me tell you something about these
dudes: They never took over a company and, as CEO,[1] artificially inflated the
value of the stock and cashed out their own shares, bringing the company to
the brink of bankruptcy, resulting in twenty thousand people losing their jobs
while the CEO builds a home the size of a luxury hotel. Rather, the dudes
sleep the sleep of the just.

*Principle 4:* Coolness to the pizza delivery dude is a practice in equality. My   5
measurement as a human being, my worth, is the pride I take in performing
my job—any job—and the respect with which I treat others. I am the equal
of the world not because of the car I drive, the size of the TV I own, the weight
I can bench-press, or the calculus equations I can solve. I am the equal to all I
meet because of the kindness in my heart. And it all starts here—with the
pizza delivery dude.

Tip him well, friends and brethren, for that which you bestow freely and   6
willingly will bring you all the happy luck that a grateful universe knows how
to return.

*For a reading quiz and annotated links to further readings on values, visit*
**bedfordstmartins.com/thebedfordreader**.

---

## Journal Writing

How would you express your primary "operating philosophy about life"? Like Adams,
try to express it using concrete EXAMPLES. For instance, you might illustrate "Don't
sweat the small stuff" with an example such as "When the grocery store checkout line
is long, take refuge in the tabloids." (To take your journal writing further, see "From
Journal to Essay" on the facing page.)

## Questions on Meaning

1. What does "the pizza delivery dude" represent to Adams? What in her description
   of him leads you to your response? Why does she feel it is important to be "cool"
   to him and his kind?
2. In your own words, what four virtues does Adams gain by being cool to the pizza
   dude? What do these suggest about Adams's values?

[1] Chief executive officer, a company's highest-ranking executive. —EDS.

3. How do you interpret the final paragraph of the essay? How does this paragraph relate to Adams's PURPOSE? What larger point do you suppose Adams might be making here?

## Questions on Writing Strategy

1. What is notable about the opening sentences in paragraphs 2 through 5? What EFFECT do they have on the essay?
2. How does Adams develop paragraph 2? How does this development help clarify her point?
3. Why do you suppose Adams presents her four principles in the order that she does?
4. **OTHER METHODS**  Where in the essay does Adams use COMPARISON AND CONTRAST? What purpose does it serve?

## Questions on Language

1. How does Adams seem to define *cool* as it's used in her title? What other meanings can the word have?
2. Adams's essay was written to be read aloud on the radio. Read a couple of paragraphs aloud yourself. How would you characterize the TONE?
3. In paragraph 5 Adams lists four things that do *not* make her "the equal of the world." What does each of these things represent to her more generally?
4. Consult a dictionary if you are unsure of the meanings of any of the following words: harried (par. 2); empathy, fickle (3); bestow (6).

## Suggestions for Writing

1. **FROM JOURNAL TO ESSAY**  Develop your journal writing about your central philosophy of life into an essay that explains to your AUDIENCE the benefits of this philosophy both to you personally and, if appropriate, to others. Be sure to express yourself in concrete terms. You might consider submitting your final essay to the NPR series *This I Believe*. Visit *thisibelieve.org* for submission guidelines and examples of other essays from the project.
2. In paragraph 3, Adams writes, "In the big pizza wheel of life, sometimes you're the hot bubbly cheese and sometimes you're the burnt crust." Write an essay in which you explore this idea from your own experience and your observations of others. Do you agree that fortune is fickle, or do you feel that people are essentially in charge of their own fates? Develop your ideas using specific examples.
3. Think about the values Adams cites in this essay: *humility, forgiveness, empathy, honor,* and *equality.* Choose one of these words, and write a DEFINITION essay that explains its meaning for you. Use examples from your own experiences, observations, and reading to make your definition concrete.
4. **CRITICAL WRITING**  What impression of herself does Adams create in this essay? What adjectives would you use to describe the writer as she reveals herself on the page? Cite specific language from the essay to support your ANALYSIS.

5. **CONNECTIONS**  In "On Compassion" (p. 193), Barbara Lazear Ascher examines how people respond to the homeless and asks, "Could it be that the homeless . . . are reminding us of our common humanity?" How might this idea of a "common humanity" relate to Adams's injunction to "be cool to the pizza dude"? Write an essay in which you propose ways to acknowledge and/or benefit the "common humanity" of "young and old, families and singletons, gays and straights, blacks, whites, and browns, rich and poor, and vegetarians and meat lovers alike" (par. 2)?

# CHRIS ANDERSON

CHRIS ANDERSON was born in England in 1961 and moved with his family to Washington, DC, where he attended high school and obtained a BS degree from George Washington University. Anderson did research at Los Alamos National Laboratory and then held editorial positions at *Nature*, *Science*, and *The Economist* magazines. Anderson is now editor-in-chief of *Wired* magazine, which has received five National Magazine awards under his editorship. In 2005 he was named editor of the year by *Advertising Age*. Anderson's book *The Long Tail: Why the Future of Business Is Selling Less of More* (2006) has attracted wide notice for proposing a significant shift in the way business works in the Internet age. He lives in Berkeley, California, with his wife and their four children.

## *The Rise and Fall of the Hit*

In *The Long Tail* Anderson argues that the Internet allows businesses to target small groups of customers that previously could not be reached because of limited shelves in stores, movie screens in cineplexes, pages in newspapers, and air time on the radio. Now, instead of aiming for blockbusters — selling vast quantities of a few items — businesses can do even better by selling small quantities of a vast number of items. The result, Anderson says, is maximum choice for consumers. In "The Rise and Fall of the Hit," which Anderson adapted from his book for *Wired* magazine, he applies this new model to the music landscape.

On March 21, 2000, Jive Records released *No Strings Attached*, the much-anticipated second album from NSync. The album debuted strong. It sold 1.1 million copies its first day and 2.4 million in the first week, making it the fastest-selling album ever. It went on to top the charts for eight weeks, moving 10 million copies by the end of the year. The music industry had cracked the commercial code. With NSync, a pop-idol boy band fronted by the charismatic Justin Timberlake, Jive had perfected the elusive formula for making a hit. In retrospect it was so obvious: What worked for the Monkees could now be replicated on an industrial scale. It was all about looks and scripted personalities. The music itself, which was outsourced to a small army of professionals (there are sixty people credited with creating *No Strings Attached*), hardly mattered.

Labels were on a roll. Between 1990 and 2000, album sales had doubled, the fastest growth rate in the history of the industry. Half of the top-grossing 100 albums ever were sold during that decade.

But even as NSync was celebrating its huge launch, the ground was shift-    3
ing. Total music sales fell during 2000, for only the second time in a decade.
Over the next few years, even after the economy recovered, the music industry continued to suffer. Something fundamental had changed. Sales fell 2.5
percent in 2001, 6.8 percent in 2002, and just kept dropping. By the end of
2005 (down another 8.3 percent), album sales in the United States had
declined 20 percent from their 1999 peak. Twenty-one of the all-time top 100
albums were released in the five-year period between 1996 and 2000. The
next five years produced only two—Norah Jones's *Come Away With Me* and
OutKast's *Speakerboxxx/The Love Below*—ranking 79 and 91, respectively.

It's altogether possible that NSync's first-week record may never be bro-    4
ken. The band could go down in history not just for launching Timberlake but
also for marking the peak of the hit bubble—the last bit of manufactured pop
to use the twentieth century's fine-tuned marketing machine to its fullest
before the gears were stripped and the wheels fell off.

Music itself hasn't gone out of favor—just the opposite. There has never    5
been a better time to be an artist or a fan, and there has never been more
music made or listened to. But the traditional model of marketing and selling
music no longer works. The big players in the distribution system—major
record labels, retail giants—depend on huge, platinum hits. These days,
though, there are not nearly enough of those to support the industry in the
style to which it has become accustomed. We are witnessing the end of an era.

What caused a generation of the industry's best customers—fans in their    6
teens and twenties—to abandon the record store? The labels cried piracy:
*Napster* and other online file-sharing networks, along with CD burning and
trading, had given rise to an underground economy of stolen music. Of course,
there's something to that. Despite countless record-industry lawsuits, traffic
on the peer-to-peer file-trading networks has continued to grow, and about 10
million users now share music files each day.

But technology didn't just allow fans to sidestep the cash register. It also    7
offered massive, unprecedented choice in terms of what they could hear. The
average file-trading network has more songs than any music store—by a factor of more than 100. Music fans had the opportunity for limitless choice, and
they took it. Today, listeners have not only stopped buying as many CDs,
they're also losing their taste for the blockbuster hits that used to bring throngs
into record stores on release days. If they have to choose between a packaged
act and something new, more and more people are opting for exploration.

Technology also gave consumers a new way to buy music. Rather than    8
having to purchase an entire album to get a couple of good tracks, they can
buy songs à la carte for 99 cents each. The online music industry is primarily

a singles business, which depresses album sales further. Meanwhile, the music marketing machine has lost its power. When consumers were buying mainly from record stores, prominent in-store displays could drive tremendous demand, which is why the labels paid so much for them. But now most of the largest record store chains, from Tower Records to Sam Goody, are either in bankruptcy or emerging from it with greatly diminished clout.[1] MTV doesn't play much music anymore, and money-losing *Spin* magazine was just, well, spun off for a fire-sale sum.

When it comes to lost marketing power, nothing compares to the decline    9
of rock radio. In 1993, Americans spent an average of 23 hours and 15 minutes per week tuned to a local station. As of summer 2005, that figure had dropped to 19 hours and 15 minutes. Time spent listening to the radio is now at a twelve-year low, and rock music is among the formats suffering the most. Since 1998, the rock radio audience has dropped 26 percent. What's killing rock radio? A perfect storm of competition. Start with the 1996 Telecommunications Act, which added more than 700 FM stations to the dial. This fragmented the market and depressed the economics of the incumbents. At the same time, the limits of ownership in each market were relaxed, which led to a nationwide roll up by Clear Channel and Infinity, whose operating efficiencies included bringing cookie-cutter playlists to once-distinctive local stations.

Then came the cell phone, which gave people something else to do dur-    10
ing their commutes. And finally, the iPod, the ultimate personal radio. With 10,000 of your favorite songs on tap, who needs FM? . . .

Before you shed too many tears for the declining hit, remember that the    11
era of the blockbuster was an anomaly. Before the Industrial Revolution,[2] culture was mostly local — niches were geographic. The economy was agrarian, which distributed populations as broadly as the land. Distance divided people, giving rise to such diversity as regional accents and folk music, and the lack of rapid transportation and communications limited the mixing of cultures and the propagation of ideas and trends.

Influences varied from town to town, because the vehicles for carrying    12
common culture were so limited. There was a reason the church was the main

---

[1] In 2006 and 2007 Tower Records and Sam Goody stores all but disappeared. Tower is now only a music-download Web site, and most of the remaining Sam Goody stores were renamed FYE. — EDS.

[2] *Industrial Revolution* refers to the sweeping social, economic, and technological changes during the late eighteenth and early nineteenth centuries, caused by the use of machines rather than manual labor for production. — EDS.

**TV's no. 1 show is attracting a dwindling share of the audience.**

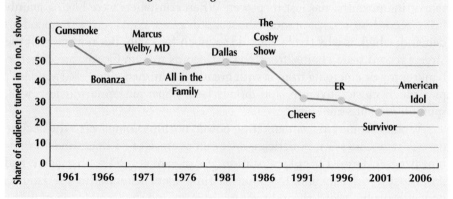

**The number of albums going gold or platinum has dropped since 2001.**

**Mainstream rock is losing listeners; talk radio is growing.**

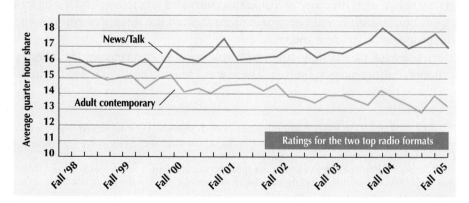

cultural unifier in Western Europe: It had the best distribution infrastructure and, thanks to Gutenberg's press, the most mass-produced item (the Bible).

But in the early nineteenth century, modern industry and the growth of    13
the railroad system led to a wave of urbanization and the rise of Europe's great cities. These new hives of commerce and hubs of transportation mixed people like never before, creating a powerful engine of new culture. All it needed was mass media to give it flight.

In the mid- to late nineteenth century, several technologies emerged to    14
do just that. First commercial printing technology improved and went mainstream. Then the new "wet plate" technique made photography popular. Finally, in 1877, Edison invented the phonograph. These developments led to the first great wave of pop culture, carried by such media as newspapers and magazines, novels, printed sheet music, records, and children's books.

Along with news, newspapers spread word of the latest fashions from the    15
urban style centers of New York, London, and Paris. Then, at the end of the nineteenth century, the moving picture gave the stars of stage a way to play many towns simultaneously and reach a much wider audience. Such potent carriers of culture had the effect of linking people across time and space, effectively synchronizing society. For the first time, it was a safe bet that not only did your neighbors read the same news you read in the morning and know the same music and movies, people across the country did too.

We are a gregarious species, highly influenced by what others do. And film    16
was a medium that could not only show us what other people were doing but could endow it with such an intoxicating glamour that it was hard to resist. It was the dawn of the celebrity age.

The arrival of broadcast media—first radio, then TV—homogenized our    17
adulation even more. The power of electromagnetic waves is that they spread in all directions essentially for *free*, a trait that made them as mind-blowing when they were introduced as the Internet would be some sixty years later. Broadcast emerged as the best vehicle for stardom ever.

From 1935 through the 1950s, the golden age of radio led to the rise of    18
national broadcast celebrities like Edward R. Murrow. Then television took over. By 1953, an astounding 72 percent of TV households watched *I Love Lucy* on Monday night.

This marked the peak of the so-called water-cooler effect, the buzz in the    19
office around a shared cultural event. In the 1950s and 1960s, nearly everyone you worked with had seen Walter Cronkite read the news the previous night and then tuned into whatever top program followed: *The Beverly Hillbillies*, *Gunsmoke*, *The Andy Griffith Show*.

Throughout the '70s, '80s, and '90s, even as more channels arrived, tele-    20
vision continued to be the great American unifier. Nearly every year, TV

advertising set a new record as companies paid more and more for prime time. And why not? Prime-time TV defined the mainstream.

Then came the great unraveling. A new medium arose, one even more  21
powerful than broadcast, and its distribution economics favored infinite niches, not one-size-fits-all fare. The Internet's peer-to-peer architecture is optimized for a symmetrical traffic load, with as many senders as receivers and data transmissions spread out over geography and time. In other words, it's the opposite of broadcast. . . . We are abandoning the tyranny of the top and becoming a niche nation again, defined not by our geography but by our interests. Instead of the weak connections of the office water cooler, we're increasingly forming our own tribes, groups bound together more by affinity and shared interests than by broadcast schedules. These days our water coolers are increasingly virtual—there are many different ones, and the people who gather around them are self-selected.

The mass market is yielding to a million minimarkets. Hits will always be  22
with us, but they have lost their monopoly. Blockbusters must now compete with an infinite number of niche offerings, which can be distributed just as easily. Justin Timberlake still makes albums, but today he has thousands of bands on *MySpace* as rivals. The hierarchy of attention has inverted—credibility now rises from below. MTV and Tower Records no longer decide who will win. You do.

---

*For a reading quiz, sources on Chris Anderson, and annotated links to further readings on the effects of the Internet on popular culture, visit* **bedfordstmartins.com /thebedfordreader**.

---

## Journal Writing

How are you likely to access various kinds of popular culture? Make a list of what you've seen or heard over the past six months and what the medium was—whether the Internet or more traditional channels such as TV, radio, movie theaters, magazines, and books. (To take your journal writing further, see "From Journal to Essay" on the facing page.)

## Questions on Meaning

1. Where does Anderson fully state his THESIS? Restate it in your own words.
2. What is Anderson's point in paragraphs 11–20? How does the causal chain he describes here relate to his thesis?
3. What does Anderson mean by the "water-cooler effect" (par. 19)? And what does he mean by "These days our water coolers are increasingly virtual" (21)? What has changed?
4. How do you suppose Anderson expected readers to respond to this essay? What do you think he hoped they would take away from their reading? What in the essay supports your answer?

## Questions on Writing Strategy

1. Why does Anderson open by detailing the sales figures for NSync's *No Strings Attached*? How does this introduction lead into his first major point?
2. Anderson analyzes a number of cause-and-effect relationships. What are they, specifically? How does he tie them together?
3. In his two concluding paragraphs, Anderson uses the pronouns *we/us* and *you*. What does this suggest about his view of his AUDIENCE?
4. **OTHER METHODS** Where in the essay does Anderson use EXAMPLES? What do these examples contribute to his explanation of the "rise and fall of the hit"?

## Questions on Language

1. ANALYZE the language Anderson uses to describe the mass marketing of popular culture. What do his words suggest about his attitude toward such mass marketing?
2. Why does Anderson italicize the word *free* in paragraph 17?
3. Notice Anderson's uses of *culture*, *cultural*, and words suggesting *culture* throughout paragraphs 11–20. How do these repetitions and restatements help to clarify the changes Anderson describes?
4. Consult a dictionary if you are unsure of the meanings of any of the following words: throngs (par. 7); à la carte (8); fragmented, incumbents (9); anomaly, agrarian, propagation (11); synchronizing (15); gregarious (16); homogenized, adulation (17); symmetrical, niches, tyranny, affinity (21); monopoly (22).

## Suggestions for Writing

1. **FROM JOURNAL TO ESSAY** Write an essay in which you explain your own relationship with the media of popular culture—Internet, TV, books, radio, and so on. Which media do you prefer, and why? Have your preferences changed in the past year or two? Give specific examples to support your explanation.
2. Anderson writes of popular music, "There has never been a better time to be an artist or a fan, and there has never been more music made or listened to" (par. 5). Do you agree? Write an essay in which you analyze the state of popular music in the United States today. Base your analysis on your own and others' experiences

with popular music, on your reading about it, and, if possible, on the experiences of musicians.

3. Contemporary culture seems obsessed with celebrities, as evidenced by the popularity of magazines, tabloids, television programs, and Internet sites that track the slightest comings and goings of actors, musicians, models, and even those who are famous simply for being famous. Write an essay in which you speculate about the causes of this obsession with celebrities. What is it about the lives of ordinary people that makes them so interested in the lives of famous people?

4. **CRITICAL WRITING**   Some observers believe that the "niche nation" Anderson promotes (par. 21) may have a downside because the more we congregate with people like ourselves, the less we learn about the world outside. What is your view of this issue in the context of Anderson's essay? Could traditional mass marketing of popular culture have an advantage in introducing us to works we might not select ourselves? Or is such a consideration outweighed by the freedom to make our own culture?

5. **CONNECTIONS**   In "Orange Crush" (p. 164), Yiyun Li describes how she and other Chinese were influenced by TV advertising to desire a packaged orange drink. How do you think advertising affects people's desires to consume popular culture such as a music album, a movie, or a TV show? How if at all has it influenced *you*? Is its influence waning, as Anderson suggests? What if anything takes its place to inform us about what's available to hear or see?

---

## *Chris Anderson on Writing*

In an interview in *Reason Magazine*, Nick Gillespie asked Chris Anderson whether the Internet fosters individual talent as well as it does consumer choice. Anderson's response should encourage anyone who has dreamed of being heard but despaired at the obstacles to reaching an audience.

What we're realizing is that talent and expertise and knowledge and writing ability are much more broadly distributed than our previous forms of identifying it revealed. The old model was if you want to make a movie, you have to get your foot in the door in Hollywood. If you want an audience for your music, you've got to get signed by a label. If you want to write a book, you've got to have a publisher.

The old model said: We control the factory, and you have to go through us. Now everyone's got a factory, and we find that there are more people who have talent and, more important, they're making things that our filters haven't previously recognized as having appeal. They're making stuff because they want to make stuff and because they can. Most of it's crap, but a surprising amount of it is not crap, and you're getting these grassroots, bottoms-up hits that are resonating with subcultures that we traditional gatekeepers would never have bothered with.

## For Discussion

1. Who are the "gatekeepers" Anderson refers to? Why does he include himself in that group?
2. If the old "filters" are no longer useful, how can Internet users sift the good work from the bad?
3. Have you written on a blog, posted music or video on *YouTube*, or otherwise contributed to the Internet culture Anderson describes? What was the response?

# DON DeLILLO

Don DeLillo, one of America's preeminent fiction writers, produces dark and often comic works exploring celebrity, consumerism, and other facets of American culture. The son of Italian immigrants, DeLillo was born in 1936 in New York City and grew up in the Bronx. He graduated from Fordham University in 1958 with a degree in communications and worked in advertising for five years before quitting to work on his first novel, *Americana* (1971). Halfway through the four years it took to write the book, DeLillo says, "it occurred to me almost in a flash that I was a writer. Whatever tentativeness I'd felt about the book dropped away." Since then, DeLillo has published thirteen more novels, including *The Names* (1982), *White Noise* (1985), *Libra* (1988), *Mao II* (1991), *Underworld* (1997), *The Body Artist* (2001), *Cosmopolis* (2003), and, most recently, *Falling Man* (2007), about a survivor of the 2001 World Trade Center attacks. DeLillo received the National Book award for *White Noise*, a PEN/Faulkner award for *Mao II*, and the William Dean Howells Medal from the American Academy of Arts and Letters for *Underworld*.

# *Videotape*

As compelling as fictional TV and movies can be, showing heart-rending tragedy or sickening violence, they can't compare with documentary evidence of the real thing. In this excerpt from the novel *Underworld*, first published as a story in *Antaeus* magazine, DeLillo's narrator explores the reasons for his compulsive fascination with a video slice of life and death. The crime at the center of the story is the work of a serial killer whose presence overshadows the novel.

It shows a man driving a car. It is the simplest sort of family video. You see a man at the wheel of a medium Dodge. 1

It is just a kid aiming her camera through the rear window of the family car at the windshield of the car behind her. 2

You know about families and their video cameras. You know how kids get involved, how the camera shows them that every subject is potentially charged, a million things they never see with the unaided eye. They investigate the meaning of inert objects and dumb pets and they poke at family privacy. They learn to see things twice. 3

It is the kid's own privacy that is being protected here. She is twelve years old and her name is being withheld even though she is neither the victim nor the perpetrator of the crime but only the means of recording it. 4

It shows a man in a sport shirt at the wheel of his car. There is nothing else    5
to see. The car approaches briefly, then falls back.

You know how children with cameras learn to work the exposed moments    6
that define the family cluster. They break every trust, spy out the undefended
space, catching Mom coming out of the bathroom in her cumbrous robe and
turbaned towel, looking bloodless and plucked. It is not a joke. They will
shoot you sitting on the pot if they can manage a suitable vantage.

The tape has the jostled sort of noneventness that marks the family    7
product. Of course the man in this case is not a member of the family but a
stranger in a car, a random figure, someone who has happened along in the
slow lane.

It shows a man in his forties wearing a pale shirt open at the throat, the    8
image washed by reflections and sunglint, with many jostled moments.

It is not just another video homicide. It is a homicide recorded by a child    9
who thought she was doing something simple and maybe halfway clever,
shooting some tape of a man in a car.

He sees the girl and waves briefly, wagging a hand without taking it off the    10
wheel — an underplayed reaction that makes you like him.

It is unrelenting footage that rolls on and on. It has an aimless determina-    11
tion, a persistence that lives outside the subject matter. You are looking into
the mind of home video. It is innocent, it is aimless, it is determined, it is real.

He is bald up the middle of his head, a nice guy in his forties whose whole    12
life seems open to the hand-held camera.

But there is also an element of suspense. You keep on looking not because    13
you know something is going to happen — of course you do know something
is going to happen and you do look for that reason but you might also keep on
looking if you came across this footage for the first time without knowing the
outcome. There is a crude power operating here. You keep on looking because
things combine to hold you fast — a sense of the random, the amateurish, the
accidental, the impending. You don't think of the tape as boring or interesting. It is crude, it is blunt, it is relentless. It is the jostled part of your mind, the
film that runs through your hotel brain under all the thoughts you know you're
thinking.

The world is lurking in the camera, already framed, waiting for the boy or    14
girl who will come along and take up the device, learn the instrument, shooting old Granddad at breakfast, all stroked out so his nostrils gape, the cereal
spoon baby-gripped in his pale fist.

It shows a man alone in a medium Dodge. It seems to go on forever.    15

There's something about the nature of the tape, the grain of the image,    16
the sputtering black-and-white tones, the starkness — you think this is more
real, truer-to-life, than anything around you. The things around you have a

rehearsed and layered and cosmetic look. The tape is superreal, or maybe underreal is the way you want to put it. It is what lies at the scraped bottom of all the layers you have added. And this is another reason why you keep on looking. The tape has a searing realness.

It shows him giving an abbreviated wave, stiff-palmed, like a signal flag at a siding. 17

You know how families make up games. This is just another game in which the child invents the rules as she goes along. She likes the idea of videotaping a man in his car. She has probably never done it before and she sees no reason to vary the format or terminate early or pan to another car. This is her game and she is learning it and playing it at the same time. She feels halfway clever and inventive and maybe slightly intrusive as well, a little bit of brazenness that spices any game. 18

And you keep on looking. You look because this is the nature of the footage, to make a channeled path through time, to give things a shape and a destiny. 19

Of course if she had panned to another car, the right car at the precise time, she would have caught the gunman as he fired. 20

The chance quality of the encounter. The victim, the killer, and the child with a camera. Random energies that approach a common point. There's something here that speaks to you directly, saying terrible things about forces beyond your control, lines of intersection that cut through history and logic and every reasonable layer of human expectation. 21

She wandered into it. The girl got lost and wandered clear-eyed into horror. This is a children's story about straying too far from home. But it isn't the family car that serves as the instrument of the child's curiosity, her inclination to explore. It is the camera that puts her in the tale. 22

You know about holidays and family celebrations and how somebody shows up with a camcorder and the relatives stand around and barely react because they're numbingly accustomed to the process of being taped and decked and shown on the VCR with the coffee and cake. 23

He is hit soon after. If you've seen the tape many times you know from the handwave exactly when he will be hit. It is something, naturally, that you wait for. You say to your wife, if you're at home and she is there, Now here is where he gets it. You say, Janet, hurry up, this is where it happens. 24

Now here is where he gets it. You see him jolted, sort of wire-shocked— then he seizes up and falls toward the door or maybe leans or slides into the door is the proper way to put it. It is awful and unremarkable at the same time. The car stays in the slow lane. It approaches briefly, then falls back. 25

You don't usually call your wife over to the TV set. She has her programs, you have yours. But there's a certain urgency here. You want her to see how it 26 looks. The tape has been running forever and now the thing is finally going to happen and you want her to be here when he's shot.

Here it comes, all right. He is shot, head-shot, and the camera reacts, the child reacts—there is a jolting movement but she keeps on taping, there is a sympathetic response, a nerve response, her heart is beating faster but she keeps the camera trained on the subject as he slides into the door and even as you see him die you're thinking of the girl. At some level the girl has to be present here, watching what you're watching, unprepared—the girl is seeing this cold and you have to marvel at the fact that she keeps the tape rolling.

It shows something awful and unaccompanied. You want your wife to see it because it is real this time, not fancy movie violence—the realness beneath the layers of cosmetic perception. Hurry up, Janet, here it comes. He dies so fast. There is no accompaniment of any kind. It is very stripped. You want to tell her it is realer than real but then she will ask what that means.

The way the camera reacts to the gunshot—a startled reaction that brings pity and terror into the frame, the girl's own shock, the girl's identification with the victim.

You don't see the blood, which is probably trickling behind his ear and down the back of his neck. The way his head is twisted away from the door, the twist of the head gives you only a partial profile and it's the wrong side, it's not the side where he was hit.

And maybe you're being a little aggressive here, practically forcing your wife to watch. Why? What are you telling her? Are you making a little statement? Like I'm going to ruin your day out of ordinary spite. Or a big statement? Like this is the risk of existing. Either way you're rubbing her face in this tape and you don't know why.

It shows the car drifting toward the guardrail and then there's a jostling sense of two other lanes and part of another car, a split-second blur, and the tape ends here, either because the girl stopped shooting or because some central authority, the police or the district attorney or the TV station, decided there was nothing else you had to see.

This is either the tenth or eleventh homicide committed by the Texas Highway Killer. The number is uncertain because the police believe that one of the shootings may have been a copycat crime.

And there is something about videotape, isn't there, and this particular kind of serial crime? This is a crime designed for random taping and immediate playing. You sit there and wonder if this kind of crime became more possible when the means of taping and playing an event—playing it immediately after the taping—became part of the culture. The principal doesn't necessarily commit the sequence of crimes in order to see them taped and played. He commits the crimes as if they were a form of taped-and-played event. The

crimes are inseparable from the idea of taping and playing. You sit there thinking that this is a crime that has found its medium, or vice versa—cheap mass
production, the sequence of repeated images and victims, stark and glary and
more or less unremarkable.

It shows very little in the end. It is a famous murder because it is on tape      35
and because the murderer has done it many times and because the crime was
recorded by a child. So the child is involved, the Video Kid as she is sometimes called because they have to call her something. The tape is famous and
so is she. She is famous in the modern manner of people whose names are
strategically withheld. They are famous without names or faces, spirits living
apart from their bodies, the victims and witnesses, the underage criminals, out
there somewhere at the edges of perception.

Seeing someone at the moment he dies, dying unexpectedly. This is rea-       36
son alone to stay fixed to the screen. It is instructional, watching a man shot
dead as he drives along on a sunny day. It demonstrates an elemental truth,
that every breath you take has two possible endings. And that's another thing.
There's a joke locked away here, a note of cruel slapstick that you are completely willing to appreciate. Maybe the victim's a chump, a dope, classically
unlucky. He had it coming, in a way, like an innocent fool in a silent movie.

You don't want Janet to give you any crap about it's on all the time, they      37
show it a thousand times a day. They show it because it exists, because they
have to show it, because this is why they're out there. The horror freezes your
soul but this doesn't mean that you want them to stop.

*For a reading quiz, sources on Don DeLillo, and annotated links to further readings
on the effects of seeing real-life violence, visit **bedfordstmartins.com
/thebedfordreader**.*

## Journal Writing

Do you identify with the NARRATOR's obsession with the videotape of the man being
shot? When have you seen documentary footage of a crime or disaster, either once or
repeatedly? In your journal, reflect on how the footage affected you. (To take your
journal writing further, see "From Journal to Essay" on the facing page.)

## Questions on Meaning

1. How does the fact that a twelve-year-old girl accidentally recorded the murder affect the narrator's response?
2. Why does the narrator want his wife to watch the death of the man on the tape?
3. In paragraph 34 the narrator makes a causal connection between certain kinds of serial crimes and the fact that videotaping and instant replay have become "part of the culture." What is this connection? Does it seem reasonable to you?

## Questions on Writing Strategy

1. What reasons does the narrator give for his fascination with the replaying videotape?
2. Note how DeLillo's narrator doles out crucial pieces of information. When is it first clear that the video involves a victim? that it records a murder? that a gunshot caused the murder? that the driver was shot? that the video is being run on television? that the crime was committed by a serial killer? What EFFECT does this slow release of details have on your reading of the story?
3. The narrator consistently uses the pronoun *you* rather than *I*. Why do you suppose DeLillo chose this approach? (To see its effect, try rewriting pars. 23–26 with *I* or *me* instead of *you*.)
4. The narrator uses verbs in the present tense—for instance, "It shows" or "Now here is where he gets it." Why is this tense appropriate for the story DeLillo is telling?
5. **OTHER METHODS**   In what way is DESCRIPTION an important part of DeLillo's story?

## Questions on Language

1. In paragraph 7 the narrator refers to the victim as "a random figure." Find other references to randomness and words with similar meanings. What do these contribute to the narrator's vision of the event's greater significance?
2. The narrator says the tape has a "sort of noneventness" (par. 7) and that the crime is, in the end, "more or less unremarkable" (34). What do you think he means?
3. The narrator describes the tape as "superreal, or maybe underreal" and having "a searing realness" (par. 16) and being "realer than real" (28). How do you interpret this language?
4. Consult a dictionary if you are unsure of the meanings of any of the following words: inert (par. 3); perpetrator (4); cumbrous, vantage (6); starkness, searing (16); brazenness (18); principal (34); strategically (35); elemental, slapstick (36).

## Suggestions for Writing

1. **FROM JOURNAL TO ESSAY**   Expand your journal entry into an essay in which you identify and reflect on your responses to documentary footage of a crime or disaster. Were your responses anything like those of the narrator in DeLillo's story, or

were they different? Were your responses affected by how often you saw the footage, whether once, twice, or more often? Why do you think you responded as you did?

2. Think of some important experience you have had—either positive, such as winning an award or having a child, or negative, such as being robbed or being in a car wreck. Write a story about the episode, either true-to-life or fictionalized. Follow DeLillo's example in using the second-person *you* and the present tense of verbs.

3. **CRITICAL WRITING**   ANALYZE DeLillo's use of repetition in "Videotape." What effects does it achieve? In what ways does such repetition echo his theme?

4. **CONNECTIONS**   COMPARE AND CONTRAST the narrator of "Videotape" with the narrator of Alice Walker's "Everyday Use" (p. 267) or Daniel Orozco's "Orientation" (p. 319). How is the narrative voice in each case suitable for the story being told?

---

## *Don DeLillo on Writing*

In a 1993 interview published in *The Paris Review*, DeLillo defined writing as "a concentrated form of thinking." He explained, "I don't know what I think about certain subjects, even today, until I sit down and try to write about them."

When he sits down to work, his discarded draft pages sit nearby. "I want those pages nearby because there's always a chance I'll have to refer to something that's scrawled at the bottom of a sheet of paper somewhere. Discarded pages mark the physical dimensions of a writer's labor—you know, how many shots it took to get a certain paragraph right. . . . I find I'm more ready to discard pages than I used to be. I used to look for things to keep. I used to find ways to save a paragraph or sentence, maybe by relocating it. Now I look for ways to discard things. If I discard a sentence I like, it's almost as satisfying as keeping a sentence I like. I don't think I've become ruthless or perverse—just a bit more willing to believe that nature will restore itself. The instinct to discard is finally a kind of faith. It tells me there's a better way to do this page even though the evidence is not accessible at the present time."

While drafting, DeLillo types each paragraph on a separate page. When he finishes a paragraph, "even a three-line paragraph," he automatically starts the next one on a fresh page. When he first tried this technique, he said, "[it] enabled me to see a given set of sentences more clearly. It made rewriting easier and more effective. The white space on the page helped me concentrate more deeply on what I'd written."

Uncrowded pages help DeLillo concentrate on sentences. "The words . . . have a sculptural quality. They form odd correspondences. They match up not just through meaning but through sound and look. The rhythm of a sentence will accommodate a certain number of syllables. One syllable too many, I look for another word. There's always another word that means nearly the same thing, and if it doesn't then I'll consider altering the meaning of a sentence to keep the rhythm, the syllable beat. I'm completely willing to let language press meaning upon me. Watching the way in which words match up, keeping the balance in a sentence—these are sensuous pleasures. I might want *very* and *only* in the same sentence, spaced in a particular way, exactly so far apart. I might want *rapture* matched with *danger*—I like to match word endings. I type rather than write longhand because I like the way words and letters look . . .—finished, printed, beautifully formed."

## For Discussion

1. Explain DeLillo's definition of *writing* in your own words.
2. Why does DeLillo find satisfaction in his "instinct to discard" parts of his writing that he likes?
3. What does DeLillo mean when he says that writing is filled with "sensuous pleasures"?

# ADDITIONAL WRITING TOPICS

## *Cause and Effect*

1. In a short essay, explain *either* the causes *or* the effects of a situation that concerns you. Narrow your topic enough to treat it in some detail, and provide more than a mere list of causes or effects. If seeking causes, you will have to decide carefully how far back to go in your search for remote causes. If stating effects, fill your essay with examples. Here are some topics to consider:

   Labor strikes in professional sports
   Minors encountering pornography on the Internet
   State laws mandating the use of seat belts in cars (or the wearing of helmets on motorcycles)
   Friction between two roommates, or two friends
   The pressure on students to get good grades
   Some quirk in your personality, or a friend's
   The increasing need for more than one breadwinner per family
   The temptation to do something dishonest to get ahead
   The popularity of a particular television program, comic strip, rock group, or pop singer
   The steady increase in college costs
   The scarcity of people in training for employment as skilled workers: plumbers, tool and die makers, electricians, masons, carpenters, to name a few
   A decision to enter the ministry or a religious order
   The fact that cigarette advertising is banned from television
   The absence of a military draft
   The fact that more couples are choosing to have only one child, or none
   The growing popularity of private elementary and high schools
   Being "born again"
   The fact that women increasingly get jobs formerly regarded as being for men only
   The pressure on young people to conform to the standards of their peers
   The emphasis on competitive sports in high school and college

2. In *Blue Highways* (1982), an account of his rambles around America, William Least Heat Moon explains why Americans, and not the British, settled the vast tract of northern land that lies between the Mississippi and the Rockies. He traces what he believes to be the major cause in this paragraph:

   > Were it not for a web-footed rodent and a haberdashery fad in eighteenth-century Europe, Minnesota might be a Canadian province today. The beaver, almost as much as the horse, helped shape the course of early American history. Some *Mayflower* colonists paid their passage with beaver pelts; and a good fur could bring an Indian three steel knives or a five-foot stack could bring a musket. But even more influential were the trappers and fur traders penetrating the great Northern wilderness between the Mississippi River and the Rocky Mountains, since it was

their presence that helped hold the Near West against British expansion from the north; and it was their explorations that opened the heart of the nation to white settlement. These men, by making pelts the currency of the wilds, laid the base for a new economy that quickly overwhelmed the old. And all because European men of mode simply had to wear a beaver hat.

In a Least Heat Moon–like paragraph of your own, explain how a small cause produced a large effect. You might generate ideas by browsing in a history book — where you might find, for instance, that a cow belonging to Mrs. Patrick O'Leary is believed to have started the Great Chicago Fire of 1871 by kicking over a lighted lantern — or in a collection of *Ripley's Believe It or Not*. If some small event in your life has had large consequences, you might care to write instead from personal experience.

NEED IS A VERY SUBJECTIVE WORD.

THE NEW H2. **HUMMER** LIKE NOTHING ELSE.™                    HUMMER.COM

# 12

# DEFINITION

## *Tracing a Boundary*

◀ **Definition in an advertisement**

This ad for the HUMMER H2 doesn't exactly define *need*.
Instead, it invites viewers to work the HUMMER into their
own personal definitions of *need*. The ad appeared in National
Geographic's outdoors magazine *Adventure*, where its colors
were predominantly blue (the background) and yellow (the
HUMMER). What needs in that magazine's readers might the
ad appeal to? Why is the ad image so stark, and what does each
of its few elements contribute to the appeal? What does the text
contribute? At the same time, what needs in viewers does the
ad ignore or even reject?

## THE METHOD

As a rule, when we hear the word DEFINITION, we immediately think of a dictionary. In that helpful storehouse—a writer's best friend—we find the literal and specific meaning (or meanings) of a word. The dictionary supplies this information concisely: in a sentence, in a phrase, or even in a *synonym*—a single word that means the same thing ("**narrative** [năr-e-tĭv] *n*. **1:** story . . .").

Stating such a definition is often a good way to begin an essay when basic terms may be in doubt. A short definition can clarify your subject to your reader, and perhaps help you to limit what you have to say. If, for instance, you are writing a psychology paper about schizophrenia, you might offer a short definition at the outset, your subject and your key term.

In constructing a short definition, the usual procedure is to state the general class to which the subject belongs and then add any particular features that distinguish it. You could say: "Schizophrenia is a brain disease"—the general class—"whose symptoms include hallucinations, disorganized behavior, incoherence, and, often, withdrawal." Short definitions may be useful at *any* moment in an essay, whenever you introduce a technical term that readers may not know.

When a term is really central to your essay and likely to be misunderstood, a *stipulative definition* may be helpful. This fuller explanation stipulates, or specifies, the particular way you are using a term. The paragraph on pages 485–86, defining *TV addiction*, could be a stipulative definition in an essay on the causes and cures of the addiction.

In this chapter, we are mainly concerned with *extended definition*, a kind of expository writing that relies on a variety of other methods. Suppose you wanted to write an essay to make clear what *poetry* means. You would specify its elements—rhythm, IMAGES, and so on—by using DIVISION or ANALYSIS. You'd probably provide EXAMPLES of each element. You might COMPARE AND CONTRAST poetry with prose. You might discuss the EFFECT of poetry on the reader. (Emily Dickinson, a poet included in this chapter, once stated the effect that reading a poem had on her: "I feel as if the top of my head were taken off.") In fact, extended definition, unlike other methods of writing discussed in this book, is perhaps less a method in itself than the application of a variety of methods to clarify a purpose. Like DESCRIPTION, extended definition tries to *show* a reader its subject. It does so by establishing boundaries, for its writer tries to differentiate a subject from anything that might be confused with it.

When Gloria Naylor, in her essay in this chapter, seeks to define the freighted word *nigger*, she recalls her experiences of the word as an African

American, recounting exactly what she heard in varying situations. Extended definition examines the nature of the subject, carefully summing up its chief characteristics and drawing boundaries around it, striving to answer the question "What makes this what it is, not something else?"

An extended definition can define a word (like *nigger*), a thing (a laser beam), a condition (schizophrenia), a concept (TV addiction), or a general phenomenon (the popularity of *YouTube*). Unlike a sentence definition, or any you would find in a standard dictionary, an extended definition takes room: at least a paragraph, often an entire essay. In having many methods of writing at your disposal, you have ample freedom and wide latitude.

Unlike a definition in a dictionary that sets forth the literal meaning of a word in an unimpassioned manner, some definitions imply biases. Samuel Johnson, the eighteenth-century English critic and dictionary maker, had asked the Earl of Chesterfield for financial help and been ignored. When later the earl tried to befriend him, Johnson replied with a scornful definition: "Is not a Patron, my Lord, one who looks with unconcern on a man struggling for life in the water, and, when he has reached the ground, encumbers him with help?" IRONY, a FIGURE OF SPEECH (metaphor), and a short definition have rarely been wielded with such crushing power. (*Encumbers*, by the way, is a wonderfully physical word in its context: It means "to burden with dead weight.")

## THE PROCESS

### Discovery of Meanings

The purpose of almost any extended definition is to explore a topic in its full complexity, to explain its meaning or sometimes to argue for (or against) a particular meaning. To discover this complexity, you may find it useful to ask yourself the following questions. To illustrate how the questions might work, at least in one instance, let's say you plan to write a paper defining *sexism*.[1]

1. *Is this subject unique, or are there others of its kind? If it resembles others, in what ways? How is it different?* As you can see, these last two questions invite you to COMPARE AND CONTRAST. Applied to the concept of sexism, these questions might prompt you to compare sexism with one or

---

[1] The six questions that follow are freely adapted from those first stated by Richard E. Young, Alton L. Becker, and Kenneth L. Pike, who have applied insights from psychology and linguistics to the writing process. To investigate subjects in greater depth, their own six questions may be used in nine possible combinations, as they explain in detail in *Rhetoric: Discovery and Change* (1970).

two other -isms, such as racism or ageism. Or the questions might remind you that sexists can be both women and men, leading you to note the differences.

2. *In what different forms does it occur, while keeping its own identity?* Specific examples might occur to you: a magazine story you read about a woman's experiences in the army and a girlfriend who is nastily suspicious of all men. Each form—the soldier and the girlfriend—might rate a description.

3. *When and where do we find it? Under what circumstances and in what situations?* Well, where have you been lately? At any parties where sexism reared its ugly head? In any classroom discussions? Consider other areas of your experience: Did you encounter any sexists while holding a job?

4. *What is it at the present moment?* Perhaps you might make the point that sexism was once considered an exclusively male preserve but is now an attribute of women as well. Or you could observe that many men have gone underground with their sexism, refraining from expressing it blatantly while still harboring negative attitudes about women. In either case, you might care to draw examples from life.

5. *What does it do? What are its functions and activities?* Sexists stereotype and sometimes act to exclude or oppress people of the opposite sex. These questions might also invite you to reply with a PROCESS ANALYSIS: You might show, for instance, how a sexist man you know, a personnel director who determines pay scales, systematically eliminates women from better-paying jobs.

6. *How is it put together? What parts make it up? What holds these parts together?* You could apply analysis to the various beliefs and assumptions that, all together, make up sexism. This question might work well in writing about an organization: the personnel director's company, for instance, with its unfair hiring and promotion policies.

Not all these questions will fit every subject under the sun, and some may lead nowhere, but you will usually find them well worth asking. They can make you aware of points to notice, remind you of facts you already know. They can also suggest interesting points you need to find out more about.

## Methods of Development

The preceding questions will give you a good start on using whatever method or methods of writing can best answer the overall question "What is the nature of this subject?" You will probably find yourself making use of much that you have learned earlier from this book. A short definition like the one for *schizophrenia* on page 480 may be a good start for your essay, especially if you think your readers need a quick grounding in the subject. (But feel no duty to place a dictionaryish definition in the INTRODUCTION of every essay you write: The device is overused.) In explaining schizophrenia, if your readers already have at least a vague idea of the meaning of the term and need no short, formal definition of it, you could open your extended definition by DESCRIBING the experiences of a person who has the disease:

> On his twenty-fifth birthday, Michael sensed danger everywhere. The voices in this head argued loudly about whether he should step outside. He could see people walking by who he knew meant him harm — the trick would be to wait for a break in the traffic and make a run for it. But the arguing and another noise — a clanging like a streetcar bell — made it difficult to concentrate, and Michael paced restlessly most of the day.

You could proceed from this opening to explain how Michael's experiences illustrate some symptoms of schizophrenia. You could provide other examples of symptoms. You could, through process analysis, explain how the disease generally starts and progresses. You could use CAUSE AND EFFECT to explore the theories of why schizophrenia occurs — from abnormalities in the part of the brain that controls sensation to incompatibilities in the blood types or antibodies of a mother and her infant.

## Thesis

Opening up your subject with questions and developing it with various methods are good ways to see what your subject has to offer, but they can also leave you with a welter of ideas and a blurred focus. As in description, when all your details build to a DOMINANT IMPRESSION, so in definition you want to center all your ideas and evidence about the subject on a single controlling idea, a THESIS. It's not essential to state this idea in a THESIS STATEMENT, although doing so can serve your readers. It is essential that the idea govern.

Here, from the essays in this chapter, are two thesis statements. Notice how each makes an assertion about the subject, and how we can detect the author's bias toward the subject.

> The people in my grandmother's living room took a word [*nigger*] that whites used to signify worthlessness or degradation and rendered it impotent. . . . Meeting the word head-on, they proved it had absolutely nothing to do with the way they were determined to live their lives.
> —Gloria Naylor, "The Meanings of a Word"

> The word *chink* may have been created to harm, ridicule, and humiliate, but for us [Chinese Americans] it may have done the exact opposite.
> —Christine Leong, "Being a Chink"

Definition

## Evidence

Writing an extended definition, you are like a mapmaker charting a territory, taking in some of what lies within the boundaries and ignoring what lies
outside. The boundaries, of course, may be wide; and for this reason, the writing
of an extended definition sometimes tempts a writer to sweep across a continent
airily and to soar off into abstract clouds. Like any other method of expository
writing, though, definition will work only for the writer who remembers the
world of the senses and supports every generalization with concrete evidence.

There may be no finer illustration of the perils of definition than the
scene, in Charles Dickens's novel *Hard Times,* of the grim schoolroom of a
teacher named Gradgrind, who insists on facts but who completely ignores
living realities. When a girl whose father is a horse trainer is unable to define
a horse, Gradgrind blames her for not knowing what a horse is; and he praises
the definition of a horse supplied by a pet pupil: "Quadruped. Graminivorous.
Forty teeth, namely twenty-four grinders, four eye-teeth, and twelve incisive.
Sheds coat in the spring; in marshy countries, sheds hoofs, too. Hoofs hard,
but requiring to be shod with iron. Age known by marks in mouth." To anyone who didn't already know what a horse is, this list of facts would prove of
little help. In writing an extended definition, never lose sight of the reality
you are attempting to bound, even if its frontiers are as inclusive as those of
*psychological burnout* or *human rights.* Give your reader examples, narrate an
illustrative story, bring in specific description — in whatever method you use,
keep coming down to earth. Without your eyes on the world, you will define
no reality. You might define *animal husbandry* till the cows come home and
never make clear what it means.

---

### FOCUS ON PARAGRAPH AND ESSAY UNITY

When drafting a definition, you may find yourself being pulled away from your
subject by the descriptions, examples, comparisons, and other methods you
use to specify meaning. Let yourself explore byways of your subject — doing so
will help you discover what you think. But in revising you'll need to direct all
paragraphs to your thesis and, within paragraphs, to direct all sentences to the
paragraph topic, generally expressed in a TOPIC SENTENCE. In other words, you'll
need to ensure the UNITY of your essay and its paragraphs.

Gloria Naylor's "The Meanings of a Word" (p. 488) opens with several paragraphs of background to the definition of the word *nigger* as it was used in
Naylor's extended African American family. When Naylor focuses on defining,
she proceeds methodically. As shown in the following outline, the paragraphs
begin with topic sentences that state parts of the definition, which Naylor then

illustrates with examples. (Some parts of the definition require more than a single paragraph, but Naylor keeps the groups of paragraphs focused on a single idea.)

PARAGRAPH 6   In the singular, the word was always applied to . . .

PARAGRAPH 9   When used with a possessive adjective by a woman — "my nigger" — it became a term of . . .

PARAGRAPH 10   In the plural, it became a description of . . .

PARAGRAPH 11   A woman could never be a "nigger" in the singular . . .

PARAGRAPH 13   But if the word was used in a third-person reference or shortened . . . , it always involved . . .

---

### CHECKLIST FOR REVISING A DEFINITION

✔ **MEANINGS**   Have you explored your subject fully, turning up both its obvious and its not-so-obvious meanings?

✔ **METHODS OF DEVELOPMENT**   Have you used an appropriate range of other methods to develop your subject?

✔ **THESIS**   Have you focused your definition and kept within that focus, drawing clear boundaries around your subject?

✔ **EVIDENCE**   Is your definition specific? Do examples, anecdotes, and concrete details both pin the subject down and make it vivid for readers?

✔ **UNITY**   Do all paragraphs focus on your thesis, and do individual paragraphs or groups of paragraphs focus on parts of your definition?

---

## DEFINITION IN PARAGRAPHS

### Writing About Television

The paragraph below SUMMARIZES a definition of *TV addiction*. The paragraph was written for *The Bedford Reader* as an example of definition, but its opening question suggests a broader use than just illustration: In a full essay on the causes and cures of the addiction, the paragraph could serve as a stipulative definition of the essay's key term.

Who is addicted to TV? According to Marie Winn, author of *The Plug-in Drug: Television, Children, and Family Life*, TV addicts   Definition of *TV addiction* are similar to drug or alcohol addicts: They seek a more pleasurable experience than they can get from normal life; they depend on the source of this pleasure; and their lives are damaged by their dependency. TV addicts, says Winn, use TV to screen out the real world of feelings, worries, demands. They watch compulsively—four, five, even six hours on a work day. And they reject (usually passively, sometimes actively) interaction with family or friends, diverting or productive work at hobbies or chores, and chances for change and growth.

*Comparison with drug or alcohol addiction*

*Analysis is of TV addicts' characteristics*

## Writing in an Academic Discipline

This paragraph from a biology textbook defines a term, *homology*, that is useful in explaining the evolution of different species from a common ancestor (the topic at this point in the textbook). The paragraph provides a brief definition, a more extensive one, and finally examples of the concept.

When the character traits found in any two species owe their resemblance to a common ancestry, taxonomists say the states are *homologous*, or are *homologues* of each other. *Homology* is defined as correspondence between two structures due to inheritance from a common ancestor. Homologous structures can be identical in appearance and can even be based on identical genes. However, such structures can diverge until they become very different in both appearance and function. Nevertheless, homologous structures usually retain certain basic features that betray a common ancestry. Consider the forelimbs of vertebrates. It is easy to make a detailed, bone-by-bone, muscle-by-muscle comparison of the forearm of a person and a monkey and to conclude that the forearms, as well as the various parts of the forearm, are homologous. The forelimb of a dog, however, shows marked differences from those of primates in both appearance and function. The forelimb is used for locomotion by dogs but for grasping and manipulation by people and monkeys. Even so, all of the bones can still be matched. The wing of a bird and the flipper of a seal are even more different from each other or from the human forearm, yet they too are constructed around bones that can be matched on a nearly perfect one-to-one basis.

*Definition of homology and related words*

*Short definition*

*Refined definition*

*Examples:*
- *Similar appearance, function, and structure*
- *Dissimilar appearance and function, but similar structure*

— William K. Purves and Gordon H. Orians,
*Life: The Science of Biology*

## DEFINITION IN PRACTICE

Susan Iessi was a freshman at the State University of New York at New Paltz when she volunteered to become a member of Hall Government, a dormitory association dedicated to student support. Discovering that many dorm residents, especially other freshmen, were unclear about the work of Hall Government, Iessi wrote the following statement.

Iessi's main goal of specifying Hall Government's purposes and responsibilities drew her into defining the mission of the association. After she drafted the statement, she showed it to other members. When one reader suggested that she explain the connections between Hall Government and other campus organizations, Iessi agreed: The change would clarify the boundaries of Hall Government. Iessi's final draft appears below.

### The Mission of Hall Government

Hall Government consists of students who volunteer to provide the residents of their dormitory with social and emotional support. Hall Government creates opportunities for residents to meet other residents and build a network of friends through structured discussions, social events, and educational programs. It also mediates in situations such as conflicts between students and teachers or between roommates. The members of Hall Government believe that their support will encourage residents to provide support for each other as well, building a community in which students may learn and thrive during their college years.

Each dormitory's Hall Government functions independently. The groups have no formal relationship with the campus-wide elected student government but are sponsored and funded by the Residence Hall Student Association.

# GLORIA NAYLOR

GLORIA NAYLOR describes herself as "just a girl from Queens who can turn a sentence," but she is well known for bringing African American women vividly within the fold of American literature. She was born in 1950 in New York City and served for some years as a missionary for the Jehovah's Witnesses, working "for better world conditions." While in college, she made her living as a telephone operator. She graduated from Brooklyn College in 1981 and received an MA in African American literature from Yale University in 1983. While teaching at several universities and publishing numerous stories and essays, Naylor has written five interconnected novels: *The Women of Brewster Place* (1982), *Linden Hills* (1985), *Mama Day* (1988), *Bailey's Cafe* (1992), and *The Men of Brewster Place* (1998). *The Women of Brewster Place* won the American Book Award for best first novel. In 2005 Naylor published *1996*, a fictionalized memoir. *Conversations with Gloria Naylor*, a collection of interviews with the author, came out in 2004.

# *The Meanings of a Word*

When she was in third grade, Naylor was stung by a word that seemed new. Only later did she realize that she'd been hearing the word all her life, but in an entirely different context. In "The Meanings of a Word," she uses definition to explore the varying meanings that context creates. The essay first appeared in the *New York Times* in 1986.

The essay following this one, Christine Leong's "Being a Chink," responds directly to Naylor and extends her point about context and meaning.

Language is the subject. It is the written form with which I've managed to keep the wolf away from the door and, in diaries, to keep my sanity. In spite of this, I consider the written word inferior to the spoken, and much of the frustration experienced by novelists is the awareness that whatever we manage to capture in even the most transcendent passages falls far short of the richness of life. Dialogue achieves its power in the dynamics of a fleeting moment of sight, sound, smell, and touch.

I'm not going to enter the debate here about whether it is language that shapes reality or vice versa. That battle is doomed to be waged whenever we seek intermittent reprieve from the chicken and egg dispute. I will simply take the position that the spoken word, like the written word, amounts to a nonsensical arrangement of sounds or letters without a consensus that assigns "meaning." And building from the meanings of what we hear, we order reality. Words themselves are innocuous; it is the consensus that gives them true power.

I remember the first time I heard the word *nigger*. In my third-grade class, our math tests were being passed down the rows, and as I handed the papers to a little boy in back of me, I remarked that once again he had received a much lower mark than I did. He snatched his test from me and spit out that word. Had he called me a nymphomaniac or a necrophiliac, I couldn't have been more puzzled. I didn't know what a nigger was, but I knew that whatever it meant, it was something he shouldn't have called me. This was verified when I raised my hand, and in a loud voice repeated what he had said and watched the teacher scold him for using a "bad" word. I was later to go home and ask the inevitable question that every black parent must face—"Mommy, what does *nigger* mean?"

And what exactly did it mean? Thinking back, I realize that this could not have been the first time the word was used in my presence. I was part of a large extended family that had migrated from the rural South after World War II and formed a close-knit network that gravitated around my maternal grandparents. Their ground-floor apartment in one of the buildings they owned in Harlem was a weekend mecca for my immediate family, along with countless aunts, uncles, and cousins who brought along assorted friends. It was a bustling and open house with assorted neighbors and tenants popping in and out to exchange bits of gossip, pick up an old quarrel, or referee the ongoing checkers game in which my grandmother cheated shamelessly. They were all there to let down their hair and put up their feet after a week of labor in the factories, laundries, and shipyards of New York.

Amid the clamor, which could reach deafening proportions—two or three conversations going on simultaneously, punctuated by the sound of a baby's crying somewhere in the back rooms or out on the street—there was still a rigid set of rules about what was said and how. Older children were sent out of the living room when it was time to get into the juicy details about "you-know-who" up on the third floor who had gone and gotten herself "p-r-e-g-n-a-n-t!" But my parents, knowing that I could spell well beyond my years, always demanded that I follow the others out to play. Beyond sexual misconduct and death, everything else was considered harmless for our young ears. And so among the anecdotes of the triumphs and disappointments in the various workings of their lives, the word *nigger* was used in my presence, but it was set within contexts and inflections that caused it to register in my mind as something else.

In the singular, the word was always applied to a man who had distin-    6
guished himself in some situation that brought their approval for his strength,
intelligence, or drive:

"Did Johnny *really* do that?"    7

"I'm telling you, that nigger pulled in $6,000 of overtime last year. Said he    8
got enough for a down payment on a house."

When used with a possessive adjective by a woman—"my nigger"—it    9
became a term of endearment for her husband or boyfriend. But it could be
more than just a term applied to a man. In their mouths it became the pure
essence of manhood—a disembodied force that channeled their past history
of struggle and present survival against the odds into a victorious statement of
being: "Yeah, that old foreman found out quick enough—you don't mess with
a nigger."

In the plural, it became a description of some group within the commu-    10
nity that had overstepped the bounds of decency as my family defined it. Parents who neglected their children, a drunken couple who fought in public,
people who simply refused to look for work, those with excessively dirty
mouths or unkempt households were all "trifling niggers." This particular circle
could forgive hard times, unemployment, the occasional bout of depression—
they had gone through all of that themselves—but the unforgivable sin was a
lack of self-respect.

A woman could never be a "nigger" in the singular, with its connotation    11
of confirming worth. The noun *girl* was its closest equivalent in that sense, but
only when used in direct address and regardless of the gender doing the
addressing. *Girl* was a token of respect for a woman. The one-syllable word was
drawn out to sound like three in recognition of the extra ounce of wit, nerve,
or daring that the woman had shown in the situation under discussion.

"G-i-r-l, stop. You mean you said that to his face?"    12

But if the word was used in a third-person reference or shortened so that    13
it almost snapped out of the mouth, it always involved some element of communal disapproval. And age became an important factor in these exchanges.
It was only between individuals of the same generation, or from any older person to a younger (but never the other way around), that *girl* would be considered a compliment.

I don't agree with the argument that use of the word *nigger* at this social    14
stratum of the black community was an internalization of racism. The dynamics were the exact opposite: The people in my grandmother's living room took
a word that whites used to signify worthlessness or degradation and rendered
it impotent. Gathering there together, they transformed *nigger* to signify the
varied and complex human beings they knew themselves to be. If the word

was to disappear totally from the mouths of even the most liberal of white society, no one in that room was naive enough to believe it would disappear from white minds. Meeting the word head-on, they proved it had absolutely nothing to do with the way they were determined to live their lives.

So there must have been dozens of times that *nigger* was spoken in front of   15
me before I reached the third grade. But I didn't "hear" it until it was said by a small pair of lips that had already learned it could be a way to humiliate me. That was the word I went home and asked my mother about. And since she knew that I had to grow up in America, she took me in her lap and explained.

*For a reading quiz, sources on Gloria Naylor, and annotated links to further readings on the language of stereotypes, visit **bedfordstmartins.com/thebedfordreader**.*

## Journal Writing

As Naylor shows, the language of stereotypes can be powerful and painful to encounter. In your journal, recall when you have experienced or witnessed this kind of labeling. What were your reactions? Keep in mind that race is but one object of stereotypes. Consider income, education, body type or other physical attributes, sexual preference, activities, or neighborhood, for just a few other characteristics. (To take your journal writing further, see "From Journal to Essay" on the next page.)

## Questions on Meaning

1. Why does Naylor think that written language is inferior to spoken language (par. 1)?
2. In paragraph 15, Naylor says that although the word *nigger* had been used in her presence many times, she didn't really "hear" the word until a mean little boy said it. How do you explain this contradiction?
3. Naylor says that "[t]he people in my grandmother's living room . . . transformed *nigger*" (par. 14). How?
4. What is Naylor's primary PURPOSE in this essay?

## Questions on Writing Strategy

1. In her first two paragraphs, Naylor discusses language in the ABSTRACT. How are these paragraphs connected to her stories about the word *nigger*? Why do you think she begins the essay this way? Is this INTRODUCTION effective or not? Why?

2. Go through Naylor's essay and note which paragraphs discuss the racist uses of *nigger* and which discuss the nonracist uses. How do Naylor's organization and the space she devotes to each use help Naylor make her point? How does Naylor integrate the two definitions to achieve UNITY?
3. Look back at the last two sentences of Naylor's essay. What is the EFFECT of ending on this idea?
4. **OTHER METHODS**  After each definition of the words *nigger* and *girl*, Naylor gives an EXAMPLE in the form of a quotation. These examples are in paragraphs 7–10 (for instance, "Yeah, that old foreman found out quick enough — you don't mess with a nigger" [9]) and paragraph 12 ("G-i-r-l, stop. You mean you said that to his face?"). What do such examples add to Naylor's definitions?

## Questions on Language

1. What is "the chicken and egg dispute" (par. 2)? What does this dispute say about the relationship between language and reality?
2. What do the words *nymphomaniac* and *necrophiliac* CONNOTE in paragraph 3?
3. If you don't know the meanings of the following words, look them up in a dictionary: transcendent, dynamics (par. 1); intermittent, reprieve, consensus, innocuous (2); verified (3); gravitated, mecca (4); clamor, inflections (5); endearment, disembodied (9); unkempt, trifling (10); communal (13); stratum, internalization, degradation, rendered, impotent, naive (14).

## Suggestions for Writing

1. **FROM JOURNAL TO ESSAY**  Using as examples the experiences you wrote about in your journal entry, write an essay modeled on Naylor's in which you define "the meanings of a word" (or words). Do you find, too, that meaning varies with context? If so, make the variations clear.
2. Can you think of other labels that may be defined in more than one way? (These might include *smart, childish, old-fashioned, artistic, proud, attractive, heroic,* and so on.) Choose one such label, and write one paragraph for each possible definition. Be sure to explain the contexts for each definition and to give enough examples so that the meanings are clear.
3. Americans continually debate the use of the word *nigger*. Some have proposed banning the word entirely, while others argue that eliminating the word would erase its role in US history and its painful legacy. Two recent books explore the theoretical and practical issues of the word: Randall Kennedy, *Nigger: The Strange Career of a Troublesome Word* (2002), and Jabari Asim, *The N-Word: Who Can Say It, Who Shouldn't, and Why* (2007). Consult one or both of these books, and form your own opinion about how the word should be treated. Explain your position in an essay.
4. **CRITICAL WRITING**  Naylor claims that words are "nonsensical . . . without a consensus that assigns 'meaning'" (par. 2). If so, how do we understand the meaning of a word like *nigger*, when Naylor has shown us that there is more than one consensus about its meaning? Does Naylor contradict herself? Write an essay that

either supports or refutes Naylor's claim about meaning and context. You will need to consider how she and you define *consensus*.

5. **CONNECTIONS**    The next essay, Christine Leong's "Being a Chink," identifies a moment when Leong was first struck by the negative power of racist language. Write an essay that COMPARES AND CONTRASTS Naylor's and Leong's reactions to a derogatory label. How did the context help shape their reactions?

---

## *Gloria Naylor on Writing*

Studying literature in college was somewhat disappointing for Gloria Naylor. "What I wanted to see," she told William Goldstein of *Publishers Weekly*, "were reflections of me and my existence and experience." Then, reading African American literature in graduate school, she discovered that "blacks have been writing in this country since this country has been writing and have a literary heritage of their own. Unfortunately, they haven't had encouragement or recognition for their efforts. . . . What had happened was that when black people wrote, it wasn't quite [considered] serious work—it was race work or protest work."

For Naylor this discovery was a turning point. "I wanted to become a writer because I felt that my presence as a black woman and my perspective as a woman in general had been underrepresented." Her work tries to "articulate experiences that want articulating—for those readers who reflect the subject matter, black readers, and for those who don't, basically white middle-class readers."

### For Discussion

1. What does Naylor mean when she says that she tries to "articulate experiences that want articulating"?
2. Naylor is motivated to write by a consciousness of herself as an African American and a woman. How do you see this motivation driving her essay "The Meanings of a Word"?

## CHRISTINE LEONG

CHRISTINE LEONG was born in New York City in 1976 and attended Stuyvesant High School there, graduating in 1994. At the Stern School of Business at New York University, she majored in finance and information systems and interned at an investment firm. She graduated with a BS in 1998 and currently works in financial services. In her free time, Leong enjoys a good doughnut and cheering on the New York Yankees. "The one thing I couldn't live without," she says, "is music."

# *Being a Chink*

Leong wrote this essay for her freshman composition class at NYU, and it was published in *Mercer Street, 1995–96*, a collection of NYU students' essays. As you'll see, Leong was inspired by Gloria Naylor's "The Meanings of a Word" (p. 488) to report her own experiences and to define a word that can be either hurtful or warm, depending on the speaker.

The power of language is something that people often underestimate. It is the one thing that allows people to communicate with each other, to be understood, to be heard. It gives us identity, personality, social status, and it also creates communities, defining both insiders and outsiders. Language has the ability to heal or to harm, to praise or belittle, to promote peace or even to glorify hate. But perhaps most important, language is the tool used to define us and differentiate us from the next person. Names and labels are what separate us from each other. Sometimes these things are innocuous, depending on the particular word and the context in which it is used. Often they serve to ridicule and humiliate.

I remember the first time I saw the word *chink*. I used to work over the summers at my father's Chinese restaurant, the Oriental, to earn a few extra dollars of spending money. It was a warm, sunny Friday morning, and I was busy performing my weekly task of cleaning out the storage area under the cash register at the front of the store. Armed with a large can of Pledge furniture polish and an old cloth, I started attacking the old oak shelves, sorting through junk mail that had accumulated over the last week, separating the bills and other important things that had to be set aside for later, before wiping each wooden panel clean. It was a pretty uneventful chore, that is, until I

494

got to the bottom shelf, the last of three. I always hated cleaning this particular shelf because it required me to get down on my hands and knees behind the counter and reach all the way back into the compartment to dig out all the stuff that managed to get wedged against the wall.

After bending to scoop all the papers out of that third cubicle, I began to   3
sort through them haphazardly. A few old menus, a gum wrapper (I always wondered how little things like that got stuffed in there), some promotional flyers, two capless pens, a dusty scratch pad, and something that appeared to be a little white envelope. Nothing seemed unusual until I examined that last item more closely. It was an old MidLantic envelope from the bank across the street. I was just about to crumple it up and throw it into the trash can when I decided to check if there was any money left in it. Too lazy to deal with the actual "chore" of opening the envelope, I held it up to the light.

As the faint yellow glow from the antique light fixture above me shone   4
through the envelope, turning it transparent, my suspicion that it was empty was confirmed. However, what I found was more shocking than anything I could have imagined. There, outlined by the light, was the word *chink* written backwards. I quickly lowered my arm onto the cool, smooth surface of the counter and flipped the envelope onto its other side, refusing to believe what I had just read. On the back, in dark blue ink with a large circle drawn around it, was the word *CHINK* written in my father's handwriting.

Up until that moment, I hadn't known that my father knew such words,   5
and thinking again, perhaps he didn't know this one either. After all, it was a habit of his to write down English words he did not know when he heard them and look them up in the dictionary later that day, learning them and adding them to his vocabulary. My mind began spinning with all the possible reasons he had written this particular word down. I wondered if an angry patron who had come in earlier had called him that.

I was shocked at that possibility, but I was not surprised. Being one of only   6
two Asian families living and running a business in a small suburban town predominately inhabited by old Caucasian people was bound to breed some kind of discrimination, if not hatred. I know that my father might not have known exactly what the word *chink* meant, but he must have had a good idea, because he never came to ask me about it as he did with all the other slang words that couldn't be found in the dictionary. It's funny, though, I do not remember the first time I was called a *chink*. I only remember the pain and outrage I felt the first time I saw it in writing, perhaps the first time I discovered that someone had used that hateful word to degrade my father.

In her essay "The Meanings of a Word," Gloria Naylor examines the var   7
ious meanings of the word *nigger,* definitions that have consensual meanings throughout society and others that vary according to how and when the word

is used. In this piece, Naylor uses personal examples to describe how "[t]he people in [her] grandmother's living room took a word that whites used to signify worthlessness or degradation and rendered it impotent," by transforming *nigger* into a word signifying "the varied and complex human beings that they knew themselves to be." Naylor goes on to add that although none of these people were foolish enough to believe that the word *nigger* would magically be erased from the minds of all humankind, they were convinced that their "head-on" approach of dealing with the label that society had put on them "proved [that] it had absolutely nothing to do with the way they were determined to live their lives."

It has been nearly eight years since that day I stumbled across the bank    8
envelope. Since then we have moved from that suburb in New Jersey to New York City, where the Asian population is much larger, and the word *chink*, although still heard, is either heard less frequently or in a rather "harmless" manner between myself and fellow Chinese (Asian) teenage friends. I do not remember how it happened exactly. I just know that we have been calling each other *chink* for quite a long while now. The word has never been used to belittle or degrade, but rather as a term of endearment, a loving insult between friends, almost but not quite exactly the way *nigger* is sometimes used among black people. It is a practice that we still engage in today, and although we know that there are times when the use of the word *chink* is very inappropriate, it is an accepted term within our circle.

Do not misunderstand us, we are all intelligent Asian youths, all graduat-    9
ing from New York City's top high school, all college students, and we know what the word *chink* truly means. We know, because over the years we have heard it countless times, from strangers on the streets and in stores, from fellow students and peers, and in some instances even from teachers, although it might not have been meant for us to hear.

So you see, even though we may use the term *chink* rather casually, it is    10
only used that way amongst ourselves because we know that when we say it to each other it is truly without malice or harmful intent. I do not think that any of us knows exactly why we do it, but perhaps it is our own way, like the characters in Naylor's piece, of dealing with a label that can never be removed. It is not determined by who we are on the inside, or what we are capable of accomplishing, but instead by what we look like—the shape of our eyes, the color of our skin, the texture of our hair, and our delicate features. Perhaps we intentionally misuse the word as a symbol of our overcoming the stereotypes that American society has imposed upon us, a way of showing that although others have tried to make us feel small, weak, and insignificant, we are the opposite. We are strong, we are determined, we are the voices of the future, and we refuse to let a simple word paralyze us, belittle us, or control us.

The word *chink* may have been created to harm, ridicule, and humiliate,    11
but for us it may have done the exact opposite. In some ways it has helped us
find a certain comfort in each other, each of us knowing what the other has
gone through, a common thread of racism binding us all together, a strange
union born from the word *chink* that was used against us, and a shared goal of
perseverance.

> For a reading quiz and annotated links to further readings on the language of
> stereotypes, visit ***bedfordstmartins.com/thebedfordreader***.

---

## Journal Writing

Although children often assume they will be protected by their parents, Leong presents a situation in which she felt the need to protect her father. Can you identify
with Leong's feelings? Have you ever felt particularly angry or defensive on behalf of
a parent? In your journal, explore why and what happened as a result. (To take your
journal writing further, see "From Journal to Essay" on the next page.)

## Questions on Meaning

1. In paragraph 9 Leong says that she and her friends "know what the word *chink*
   truly means." Where in her essay does she explain this "true" meaning?
2. What has the word *chink* come to mean when Leong and her friends use it?
   Where in the essay does Leong explain this?
3. One might argue that the THESIS of Leong's essay is that language is not absolute.
   Is her PURPOSE, then, to propose a new DEFINITION for a word, to teach the reader
   something about how labels work, or to explain how adapting a racist term can be
   a form of gaining power? How do you know?

## Questions on Writing Strategy

1. Look carefully at Gloria Naylor's essay "The Meanings of a Word" (p. 488). What
   structural similarities do you notice between it and Leong's? Why do you think
   Leong adapts these features of Naylor's essay?
2. In paragraph 3 Leong details all the forgotten items she finds under the counter.
   What is the EFFECT of ending with the "old MidLantic envelope from the bank
   across the street"?
3. What is the main purpose of the extended example from Naylor's essay in paragraph 7?

4. Why is Leong so careful to explain that she and her friends are all intelligent and educated (par. 9)?

5. **OTHER METHODS**   Leong suggests CAUSE AND EFFECT when she expresses shock and disbelief at seeing the word *chink* in writing (par. 4). Why does Leong react so strongly to the writing on the envelope?

## Questions on Language

1. In paragraph 10 Leong explains that she and her friends are "dealing with a label that can never be removed." What other words does she use in this paragraph to suggest the potential helplessness of being permanently labeled?

2. What do the CONNOTATIONS of "term of endearment" (par. 8) indicate about the way Leong and her friends have redefined *chink*?

3. Make sure you know the meanings of the following words: status, belittle, innocuous (par. 1); cubicle, haphazardly (3); Caucasian, degrade (6); consensual (7); malice (10); perseverance (11).

## Suggestions for Writing

1. **FROM JOURNAL TO ESSAY**   Write an essay that explores why and how children might feel compelled to act like parents toward their own parents. Is this a shift that comes with age? with specific circumstances? out of the blue? Make some GENERALIZATIONS about this process, using as EVIDENCE the personal recollections from your journal entry.

2. As Leong explains in her INTRODUCTION, not all labels are intended to be hurtful. Often they are shorthand ways for our families and friends to identify us, perhaps reflecting something about our appearance ("Red," "Slim") or our interests ("Sport," "Chef"). What do your family or friends call you? Write several paragraphs giving a careful definition of this label. Where did it come from? Why is it appropriate (or not)?

3. Research the history of Chinese Americans. When and why did the initial wave of immigration occur? What forces have led to other patterns of immigration over the years? Have Chinese Americans faced different kinds of discrimination than other immigrants have? In an essay, answer these or other questions that occur to you.

4. **CRITICAL WRITING**   In her opening paragraph Leong says that "language is the tool used to define us." But she goes on to explain how she and her friends *refuse* to be defined by racist language. Does this apparent contradiction weaken her essay? Why, or why not? (To answer this question, consider the purpose of Leong's essay; see "Meaning" question 3.)

5. **CONNECTIONS**   Both Leong and Gloria Naylor, in "The Meanings of a Word" (p. 488), show that racist language can be taken over by those against whom it is directed. They also show that for groups or communities to redefine, and thus to own, these racist slurs can be empowering. Do you find their ARGUMENTS convincing, or do these redefinitions reveal what Naylor denies — namely, "an internalization of racism" (par. 14)? In an essay, explain your opinion on this issue, using as evidence passages from Naylor's and Leong's essays as well as insights and EXAMPLES from your own observations and experience.

# *Christine Leong on Writing*

For *The Bedford Reader,* Christine Leong commented on the difficulties of writing and the rewards that can ensue.

Writing is something that comes easily for many people, but unfortunately I am not one of them. For me the writing process is one of the hardest and quite possibly is *the* most nerve-wracking thing that I have ever experienced. I can't even begin to count all the hours I have spent throughout the course of my life staring at a blank computer screen, trying desperately to come up with the right combination of words to express my thoughts and feelings, and although after many hours of frustration I eventually end up with something, I am never happy with it because I am undoubtedly my own worst critic. Perhaps my mentality of "it's not good enough yet" stems from my belief that writing can never really be completed; to me it has no beginning and no end but is rather a small representation of who I am at a given moment in time, and I believe that the more things I experience in life, the more I am able to contribute to my writing. Thus, whatever I write always has the potential of being better; there's always room for improvement via more revisions, greater insight, and about a hundred more drafts.

I used to believe that writing always had to make sense, but since then I have learned that there are many things in this life that do not adhere to this "rule." I now realize that writing doesn't necessarily have to be grammatically correct or even sensible, and the only thing that really matters is that whatever is written is truly inspired. Passion comes through very clearly in a writer's words, and the more emotion that goes into a piece, the more impact it will ultimately have on the reader. In recent years I have learned that there are no real writing guidelines, and that writing is much like any other art form: It can be abstract or it can follow more traditional "themes." However, in order for a piece of writing to be effective, in the sense that it can differentiate itself from any other writing sample and hopefully have some significance to the reader, I believe that it has to come from within.

The majority of what I write about, and that which I feel is worth reading, is inspired by actual experiences that I have had. For example, "Being a Chink" began as an assignment in a freshman writing workshop class in college. When first presented with the task of writing it, I was at a complete loss for words and had absolutely no clue where to start. However, after reading Gloria Naylor's "The Meanings of a Word," I was reminded of one of the most traumatic and memorable events in my life. The piece triggered a very strong memory, and before long I found myself writing down anything that came into my head, letting my thoughts and emotions flow freely in the form of words without thinking about whether or not they made any kind of sense. Many hours later I discovered that I had written the basic structure of what would eventually be my final product. I must honestly say that I can't really recall the actual process of writing "Being a Chink"; it was just an essay that seemed to take on a life and form of its own. Perhaps that, along with its universal theme, is what makes it such a strong piece. It not only is a recollection from my adolescence but is something that defines the very essence of the person that I have become since then.

In retrospect, I now realize that writing "Being a Chink" was not only about completing an essay and fulfilling a writing requirement; it was also about the acknowledgment of my own growth as a person. In many ways, without my initially being aware of it, the piece has helped me come to terms with one of the most controversial issues that I have ever been faced with.

## For Discussion

1. Does Leong's characterization of writing as "nerve-wracking" ring bells with you? How do you overcome writer's block?
2. What do you think about Leong's statement that "writing doesn't necessarily have to be grammatically correct or even sensible, and the only thing that really matters is that whatever is written is truly inspired"? In your experience with writing, what are the roles of correctness, sense, and inspiration? What matters most to you? What matters most to readers?

# THOMAS SOWELL

THOMAS SOWELL has been called "perhaps the leading black scholar among conservatives." His support for free markets and corresponding disdain for government regulations and social programs has endeared him to those on the right of center, while his logic and clarity have earned him respect from those on the left. Born in North Carolina in 1930, Sowell attended a segregated high school and went on to earn three degrees in economics: a BA from Harvard College (1958), an MA from Columbia University (1959), and a PhD from the University of Chicago (1968). He has taught at Harvard, Cornell University, Amherst College, and other schools; served as an economist in government and business; and since 1980 has been affiliated with the Hoover Institution at Stanford University. Sowell writes a syndicated newspaper column and has published over two dozen books on economics, education, and race, including *Affirmative Action Around the World: An Empirical Study* (2004) and *Black Rednecks and White Liberals* (2005). His latest book is *A Man of Letters* (2007), a collection of correspondence to friends, family, and public figures.

## *"Needs"*

What do we really need? In this essay from his collection *Is Reality Optional?* (1993), Sowell says that most of our genuine needs are already met; what we think we need is only what we want. Failing to make this distinction, Sowell believes, hurts us all.

A group of UCLA economists were having lunch together one day at the faculty club. One of them, named Mike, got up to get himself some more coffee. Being a decent sort, he asked: 1

"Does anybody else here need coffee?" 2

"Need?!" another economist cried out in astonishment and outrage. 3

The other economists around the table also pounced on this unfortunate word, while poor Mike retreated to the coffee maker, like someone who felt lucky to escape with his life. 4

Partly this was good clean fun—or what passes for good clean fun among economists. But partly it was a very serious issue. 5

Someone is always talking about what we "need"—more child care centers, more medical research, more housing, more environmental protection. The list goes on and on. All the things we "need" would add up to far more than the gross national product. Obviously we cannot and will not get all the things we "need." 6

Why call them "needs" then? We obviously get along without them, sim-  7
ply because we have no choice. These "needs" are simply things we want—or
that some of us want. Given that we cannot possibly have all the things we
want, we have to make trade-offs. That is what economics is all about.

Words like *needs, rights,* or *entitlements* try to put some things on a  8
pedestal, so that they don't have to face the reality of trade-offs. This is part of
the higher humbug of politics.

Surely some things are really needs, you might say. If that is true, food  9
must be one of those needs, since we would die without it. Huge agricultural
surpluses are one result of this kind of mushy thinking.

There is obviously some amount of food that is urgently required to keep  10
body and soul together. But the average American already takes in far more
food than is necessary to sustain life—and in fact so much food as to make his
lifespan shorter than it would be at a lower weight.

Like virtually everything else, food beyond some point ceases to be as  11
urgently demanded and even ceases to be a benefit. When it reaches the point
of being positively harmful, it can hardly be called a "need." That is why rigid
words like *need* spread so much confusion in our thinking and havoc in our
policies.

Prices force us into trade-offs, which is one of many reasons why the mar-  12
ketplace operates so much more efficiently than political allocation according
to "need," "entitlement," "priorities" or other such rigid notions.

The real issue is almost never whether we should have nothing at all or  13
some unlimited amount, or even some fixed amount of a particular good. The
real issue is what kind of trade-off makes sense. That usually means having
some of many things but not all we want of anything.

Prices tell us what the terms of the trade-offs are. Do we "need" more  14
clothing? At some prices we do and at other prices we can get along with what
we have. I happen to own three suits. But if clothing prices were one-tenth of
what they are, I might have a wardrobe that would knock you dead.

My daughter used to make snide remarks about an old car that I drove  15
for eight years. She stopped only when I told her that I could easily afford to
get a new car, just by not paying her tuition. That's what trade-offs are all
about.

If the government were giving out cars to those who "needed" them, I  16
could have written an application that would have brought tears to your eyes.
I could have gone on talk shows and worked up public sympathy over the ways
my old jalopy was messing up my life—even threatening my life because the
brakes failed completely twice.

If the taxpayers were paying for it, I would have "needed" a new car. But,  17
since it was my money that was being spent, I had a brake job instead.

Politicians take advantage of our mushy thinking by promising to meet our "need" or by giving us a "right" or "entitlement" to this or that. But let's go back to square one. Politicians don't manufacture anything except hot air. Every "need" they meet takes away from some other "need" somewhere else. 18

Every job the government creates is supported by resources taken out of the private sector, where those same resources could have created another job—or maybe two other jobs, given the wastefulness of government. 19

"Needs" are a dangerous concept. Mike the economist suffered only a momentary embarrassment from using the word. Our whole economy and society suffer much more from the mindless policies based on such misconceptions. 20

*For a reading quiz, sources on Thomas Sowell, and annotated links to further readings on the concepts of wants and needs in economics, visit **bedfordstmartins.com /thebedfordreader**.*

---

## Journal Writing

How would you define your own personal needs? In your journal, write about what you require for a comfortable and fulfilled life. (To take your journal writing further, see "From Journal to Essay" on the next page.)

## Questions on Meaning

1. How does Sowell define the customary use of *needs*? What is distinctive about this definition?
2. What would you say is Sowell's underlying PURPOSE in offering his definition?
3. What does Sowell mean when he talks about "trade-offs" (pars. 12–15)?

## Questions on Writing Strategy

1. Why do you think Sowell begins his essay with the story of Mike and the other UCLA economists? How does this story support his point about *needs*?
2. Why does Sowell put quotations marks around *need* in his title and throughout the essay?

3. What is Sowell's reason for writing about food in paragraphs 9–11 and his old car in paragraphs 15–17? Do you think these EXAMPLES help clarify his point?
4. **OTHER METHODS**   How does Sowell use CAUSE AND EFFECT in paragraphs 18–20?

## Questions on Language

1. Check a dictionary for the meanings of *humbug* (par. 8). Why do you think Sowell chose to use this word?
2. If you don't know the meanings of *allocation* and *entitlement* (par. 12), look them up in a dictionary.
3. Sowell refers to *needs* as a "rigid" word (par. 11). What is his point in using this adjective?
4. Point to some examples of informal language in the essay. What is the EFFECT of such language?

## Suggestions for Writing

1. **FROM JOURNAL TO ESSAY**   Based on your journal writing, compose an essay in which you define your own needs. Which needs do you share with most other people, and which are particular to yourself? What trade-offs must you make among your needs?
2. Because government cannot provide everything we think we need, Sowell says, we have to establish priorities for allocating public funds. Write an essay that lays out what you believe should be the priorities in government spending. What must government provide, and what should it not be responsible for? If you wish to do some research into current spending allocations of the federal government, visit *gpoaccess.gov/usbudget*.
3. **CRITICAL WRITING**   Write an essay in which you ANALYZE the UNITY of Sowell's essay. What methods does Sowell use to create unity? Does he digress at all?
4. **CONNECTIONS**   Consider Sowell's essay in COMPARISON with Anna Quindlen's "Homeless" (p. 198), which focuses on the need for a home, and the HUMMER advertisement at the start of this chapter (p. 478), whose theme is need. Using all three works as examples, write your definition of *need*.

# DAGOBERTO GILB

DAGOBERTO GILB was born in Los Angeles in 1950 to a Mexican mother and a German American father. Though he admits to getting into trouble as a teen and says that he "wasn't the best student at all," he enrolled in junior college and went on to earn a BA in philosophy and an MA in religion from the University of California at Santa Barbara. From 1976 to 1991 Gilb pursued a dual career as a carpenter and writer. The stories he wrote then and later, often focusing on working-class Latinos in the Southwest, have been collected in *Winners on the Pass Line* (1985), *The Magic of Blood* (1993), which received a PEN/Hemingway award, and *Woodcuts of Women* (2001). Gilb has also written a novel, *The Last Known Residence of Mickey Acuña* (1994), which was named a *New York Times* Notable Book, and a collection of essays, *Gritos* (2003). Most recently he edited *Hecho en Tejas: An Anthology of Texas Mexican Literature* (2006). Gilb has been a visiting writer at several universities and currently teaches in the creative writing program at Southwest Texas State University.

# *Pride*

*Gritos,* Gilb's essay collection and the source of this piece, takes its title from a Spanish word that translates loosely as "shouts" but more precisely, Gilb explains, as exclamations of "defiance and freedom," "joy and support." All these feelings figure in Gilb's definition of *pride* through the lives of Mexican Americans in El Paso, Texas.

It's almost time to close at the northwest corner of Altura and Copia in El 1 Paso. That means it is so dark that it is as restful as the deepest unremembering sleep, dark as the empty space around this spinning planet, as a black star. Headlights that beam a little cross-eyed from a fatso American car are feeling around the asphalt road up the hill toward the Good Time Store, its yellow plastic smiley face bright like a sugary suck candy. The loose muffler holds only half the misfires, and, dry springs squeaking, the automobile curves slowly into the establishment's lot, swerving to avoid the new self-serve gas pump island. Behind it, across the street, a Texas flag—out too late this and all the nights—pops and slaps in a summer wind that finally is cool.

A good man, gray on the edges, an assistant manager in a brown starched 2 and ironed uniform, is washing the glass windows of the store, lit up by as many watts as Venus, with a roll of paper towels and the blue liquid from a spray bottle. Good night, m'ijo![1] he tells a young boy coming out after playing

[1] Spanish slang, "my son." —EDS.

505

the video game, a Grande Guzzler the size of a wastebasket balanced in one hand, an open bag of Flaming Hot Cheetos, its red dye already smearing his mouth and the hand not carrying the weight of the soda, his white T-shirt, its short sleeves reaching halfway down his wrists, the whole XXL of it billowing and puffing in the outdoor gust.

A plump young woman steps out of that car. She's wearing a party dress, wide scoops out of the top, front, and back, its hemline way above the knees.    3

Did you get a water pump? the assistant manager asks her. Are you going    4
to make it to Horizon City? He's still washing the glass of the storefront, his hand sweeping in small hard circles.

The young woman is patient and calm like a loving mother. I don't know    5
yet, she tells him as she stops close to him, thinking. I guess I should make a call, she says, and her thick-soled shoes, the latest fashion, slap against her heels to one of the pay phones at the front of the store.

Pride is working a job like it's as important as art or war, is the happiness    6
of a new high score on a video arcade game, of a pretty new black dress and shoes. Pride is the deaf and blind confidence of the good people who are too poor but don't notice.

A son is a long time sitting on the front porch where he played all those    7
years with the squirmy dog who still licks his face, both puppies then, even be-fore he played on the winning teams of Little League baseball and City League basketball. They sprint down the sidewalk and across streets, side by side, until they stop to rest on the park grass, where a red ant, or a spider, bites the son's calf. It swells, but he no longer thinks to complain to his mom about it—he's too old now—when he comes home. He gets ready, putting on the shirt and pants his mom would have ironed but he wanted to iron himself. He takes the ride with his best friend since first grade. The hundreds of moms and dads, abuelos y abuelitas, the tios and primos,[2] baby brothers and older married sis-ters, all are at the Special Events Center for the son's high school graduation. His dad is a man bigger than most, and when he walks in his dress eel-skin boots down the cement stairs to get as close to the hardwood basketball-court floor and ceremony to see—m'ijo!—he feels an embarrassing sob bursting from his eyes and mouth. He holds it back, and with his hands, hides the tears that do escape, wipes them with his fingers, because the chavalitos[3] in his aisle are playing and laughing and they are so small and he is so big next to them. And when his son walks to the stage to get his high school diploma and his dad wants to scream his name, he hears how many others, from the floor in caps and gowns and from around the arena, are already screaming it—could

[2] Spanish, "grandfathers and grandmothers," "aunts and uncles," and "cousins."—Eds.
[3] Spanish slang, "little kids."—Eds.

be any name, it could be any son's or daughter's: Alex! Vanessa! Carlos! Veronica! Ricky! Tony! Estella! Isa!—and sees his boy waving back to all of them.

Pride hears gritty dirt blowing against an agave whose stiff fertile stalk, so     8
tall, will not bend—the love of land, rugged like the people who live on it.
Pride sees the sunlight on the Franklin Mountains in the first light of morning
and listens to a neighbor's gallo[4]—the love of culture and history. Pride smells
a sweet, musky drizzle of rain and eats huevos con chile[5] in corn tortillas
heated on a cast-iron pan—the love of heritage.

Pride is the fearless reaction to disrespect and disregard. It is knowing the     9
future will prove that wrong.

Seeing the beauty: Look out there from a height of the mountain and on the     10
north and south of the Rio Grande, to the far away and close, the so many miles
more of fuzz on the wide horizon, knowing how many years the people have
passed and have stayed, the ancestors, the ones who have medaled, limped
back on crutches or died or were heroes from wars in the Pacific or Europe or
Korea or Vietnam or the Persian Gulf, the ones who have raised the fist and
dared to defy, the ones who wash the clothes and cook and serve the meals, who
stitch the factory shoes and the factory slacks, who assemble and sort, the ones
who laugh and the ones who weep, the ones who care, the ones who want more,
the ones who try, the ones who love, those ones with shameless courage and
hardened wisdom, and the old ones still so alive, holding their grandchildren,
and the young ones in their glowing prime, strong and gorgeous, holding each
other, the ones who will be born from them. The desert land is rock-dry and
ungreen. It is brown. Brown like the skin is brown. Beautiful brown.

---

For a reading quiz, sources on Dagoberto Gilb, and annotated links to further readings on Mexican Americans in the United States, visit **bedfordstmartins.com
/thebedfordreader**.

---

## Journal Writing

In your journal, jot down images of pride that occur to you based on your own experiences and observations. Then try briefly to create your own definition—or definitions—of *pride*. (To take your journal writing further, see "From Journal to Essay" on
the next page.)

[4] Spanish, "rooster."—EDS.
[5] Traditional Mexican dish of eggs and peppers.—EDS.

# Questions on Meaning

1. In your own words, SUMMARIZE Gilb's definition of *pride*.
2. How do paragraphs 8–10 contribute to Gilb's definition?
3. What point does Gilb make in his concluding paragraph? How does his final IMAGE serve as a sort of summary?
4. What would you say is Gilb's PURPOSE in this essay?

# Questions on Writing Strategy

1. Why do you think Gilb opens the essay as he does? What impression does he create with the three people in the Good Time Store parking lot?
2. Following paragraphs 1–5, Gilb specifically defines the pride of the people about whom he has just written; however, after paragraph 7 his definition does not apply specifically to the father and son just described. Why do you think he varied his strategy here?
3. ANALYZE Gilb's development of paragraph 7. How would you describe its movement? its ultimate EFFECT?
4. How does Gilb achieve UNITY and COHERENCE in paragraph 8?
5. **OTHER METHODS**   Paragraphs 1–5 rely heavily on DESCRIPTION. Why do you think Gilb describes this scene in such detail?

# Questions on Language

1. In paragraph 1 how does Gilb use specific language to create a distinct impression of the car that pulls into the store's parking lot?
2. What is striking about the verbs Gilb uses in paragraph 8?
3. The first sentence of paragraph 10 is unusually long. How does Gilb manage to maintain its clarity and readability?

# Suggestions for Writing

1. **FROM JOURNAL TO ESSAY**   Using your journal writing as a springboard, write an essay in which you develop your own definition of *pride*. Like Gilb, present specific images and *examples* in addition to statements of your definition.
2. Using Gilb's essay as a model, write an essay of your own that defines another human feeling or characteristic—*happiness*, for example, or *sadness* or *fear* or *courage*. As Gilb does, present a wide range of examples to suggest various aspects of your subject.
3. Research the current situation of Mexican Americans in the United States: population, incomes, living conditions, education levels, occupations, and so forth. Then write an essay in which you present your findings.
4. **CRITICAL WRITING**   Write an essay in which you analyze Gilb's use of language in this essay or in a portion of it. What is the level of his DICTION? What are some especially effective uses of language? What overall impression does Gilb give of himself based on the language he uses?

5. **CONNECTIONS** In "Champion of the World" (p. 93), Maya Angelou writes about the experiences of another minority group in the United States, African Americans. Write an essay in which you COMPARE AND CONTRAST Gilb's presentation of Mexican Americans with Angelou's of African Americans.

---

## *Dagoberto Gilb on Writing*

In the introduction to his essay collection, *Gritos*, Dagoberto Gilb describes the pleasure he gets from writing.

[N]ot only has writing saved my life, . . . it has offered me joy and fun. . . . I assure you, every one of [these essays] has given me such pleasure and satisfaction, the same kind I had when I used to cut wood with my skilsaw and drive nails and build, watch a building rise huge, a fun of the kind that trowels the back of a tile with adhesive and sets it in, a pattern mounting. Each word is a rock I've placed personally into a wall — five go in and I pick through a pile and find another, shift them all around until it's right. I've chipped and nicked at most so they look to me like good sentences, good paragraphs. If I don't think of myself as the smartest, I do feel a strength in my working of the craft, so that every time I finish something, I'm maybe too proud of myself, can hardly believe I did it, that I could. The words are beyond my own physical self or nature, because I was not born to be a writer, I've just done it anyway. Often this work is outright fun, almost as fun as a good construction job where we were all muscles sweating and laughing and building . . . and getting paid at the same time — living and working — except writing work is alone, only an imaginary crew. Sometimes you see that laughter in these essays, but even when it's not haha, when it's like the drudgery of any job, it's still so good when it's finally gone through, completed — that pleasure, that joy.

### For Discussion

1. How is carpentry a metaphor of the writing process for Gilb? (If you need a definition of *metaphor,* see *Figures of speech* in Useful Terms.)
2. What do you think Gilb means by "The words are beyond my own physical self or nature, because I was not born to be a writer"?

# EMILY DICKINSON

For most of her life, EMILY DICKINSON (1830–86) kept to the shadowy privacy of her family mansion in Amherst, Massachusetts, a farming village and the site of Amherst College. Her father, an eminent lawyer, was for a time a United States congressman. One brief trip to Philadelphia and Washington, two semesters at New England Female Seminary, and a few months with nieces in Cambridge, Massachusetts, while having her eyes treated, were all the poet's travels away from home. Her work on her brilliantly original poems intensified in the years 1858–62. In later years, Dickinson withdrew more and more from the life of the town into her private thoughts, correspondence with friends, and the society of only her closest family. During her lifetime, fewer than a dozen of her poems were published, some without her permission. When she died at age fifty-five, more than seventeen hundred poems were discovered in manuscript, stitched into little booklets. A first selection was published in 1890. Since then, her personal legend and the devotion of readers have grown vastly and steadily.

## *"Hope" is the thing with feathers*

This poem resembles most of Dickinson's: It takes a simple shape and uses plain words, yet it is anything but simple or plain. In defining the abstraction *hope* through the image of a bird, Dickinson illuminates the idea while preserving its essential mystery.

> "Hope" is the thing with feathers –
> That perches in the soul –
> And sings the tune without the words–
> And never stops – at all –
>
> And sweetest – in the Gale – is heard –     5
> And sore must be the storm –
> That could abash the little Bird –
> That kept so many warm –
>
> I've heard it in the chillest land –
> And on the strangest Sea –     10
> Yet, never, in Extremity,
> It asked a crumb – of Me.

*For a reading quiz, sources on Emily Dickinson, and annotated links to further readings on the meaning of* hope, *visit* ***bedfordstmartins.com/thebedfordreader***.

---

## Journal Writing

Dickinson's poem describes *hope* as a saving emotion. Has there ever been a point in your life when you relied on hope to get you through a difficult time? In your journal, write a few paragraphs about the problem you faced and how hoping for something better helped (or didn't help) you endure. What did you anticipate? How was your optimism rewarded? (To take your journal writing further, see "From Journal to Essay" on the next page.)

## Questions on Meaning

1. The first line of the poem defines "Hope" as "the thing with feathers." To what is the poet referring? What about that "thing" makes Dickinson's metaphor particularly effective? (If you need a definition of *metaphor*, see *Figures of speech* in Useful Terms.)
2. The second stanza (lines 4–8) seems at first glance to describe the absence of hope. What is the EFFECT of this note of pessimism? Why do you suppose Dickinson included it?
3. To get a better grasp of the poem's overall meaning, PARAPHRASE the third stanza in modern prose, supplying any missing words and your own punctuation as necessary. What does the conclusion reveal about the poet's attitude toward hope?

## Questions on Writing Strategy

1. Explain how Dickinson uses a CONCRETE image to explain an ABSTRACT concept. What makes her ANALOGY effective as a definition? (You may want to look up *analogy* in Useful Terms.)
2. Dickinson uses the bulk of her poem to explain what hope gives, waiting until the final two lines before she mentions what it asks. How does this structure reinforce her main idea?
3. Dickinson was an intensely private writer: Most of her poems went unpublished in her lifetime, and she allowed only a small circle of relatives and friends to read any of her work. What clues in this poem suggest that she wrote it for herself? What clues suggest that she may have had an AUDIENCE in mind?
4. **OTHER METHODS**    In addition to using COMPARISON AND CONTRAST to highlight the similarities between "hope" and "the thing with feathers," Dickinson's definition relies on DESCRIPTION, drawing on sense impressions to give a vivid picture. Which senses does Dickinson invoke? What is the DOMINANT IMPRESSION created by her imagery?

# Questions on Language

1. Dickinson uses just a few words that might be unfamiliar. Make sure you know the definitions of gale (line 5), abash (7), and extremity (11). Because the poem was written long ago, you might want to check historical meanings in the *Oxford English Dictionary*, available in your school's library and probably through the library's Web site.
2. In line 3 Dickinson writes that hope "sings the tune without the words." What does this wordlessness suggest about the emotional nature of hope and the possibility of capturing its meaning in a poem?
3. Like many poets, Dickinson relies heavily on CONNOTATION to pack meaning into few words. Pick two of the following words in the poem (or two others of your own choosing) and explore their connotations: thing (line 1), perches (2), never (4), sore (6), little (7), strangest (10), crumb (12).
4. How does Dickinson use PARALLELISM to emphasize the poem's most important ideas?

# Suggestions for Writing

1. **FROM JOURNAL TO ESSAY**   Expand on your journal entry to write a definition of *hope* based on your own experience. Explain not only what the emotion is but also how it affected you and your circumstances. In your essay, try to reach a conclusion about the value of hope—either as a coping mechanism or as a constructive way of responding to a problem.
2. Dickinson defines *hope* by comparing it to a small songbird. Pick an emotion of your choice—for example, joy, fear, anxiety, or eagerness—and define it by comparing it to an animal or a physical object. You may write your definition in the form of a poem, if you like, or as a prose essay.
3. **CRITICAL WRITING**   "'Hope' is the thing with feathers" was written around 1861—in other words, right when the American Civil War began. Research the political climate in Massachusetts and in Dickinson's own household in the early 1860s, looking in particular for information about New Englanders' reasons for supporting the war and their hopes for what it would accomplish. Apply what you learn to an analysis of the poem as an argument for—or against—supporting the War between the States.
4. **CONNECTIONS**   In "I Have a Dream" (p. 614), Martin Luther King, Jr., uses an IMAGE of hope that is very different from Dickinson's: "With this faith [in racial equality] we will be able to hew out of the mountain of despair a stone of hope" (par. 19). Read King's speech if you haven't already to develop a sense of what hope means to King. Then write a brief essay comparing King's and Dickinson's ideas of hope—their obvious differences but also any similarities, such as what hope can do for the people who hold it.

# Emily Dickinson on Writing

Although Emily Dickinson never spelled out in detail her methods of writing, her practices are clear to us from the work of scholars who have studied her manuscripts. Evidently she liked to rewrite extensively both poetry and prose, with the result that many poems and some letters exist in multiple versions. Usually, a poem proceeded through three stages: a first, worksheet draft; a semifinal draft; and final copy. Occasionally, in later years, she would return to a poem, tinkering, striving for improvements. (In a few cases, she reduced a previously finished poem to a permanent confusion.)

Dickinson admired the work of writer and critic Thomas Wentworth Higginson. In "Letter to a Young Contributor," published in *The Atlantic Monthly* in 1862, he advised novice writers, "Charge your style with life." Echoing Higginson's remark with approval, Dickinson sent him some of her poems and asked, "Are you too deeply occupied to say if my Verse is alive?" Writers might attain liveliness, Higginson had maintained, by choosing plain words, as few of them as possible. We might expect this advice to find favor with Emily Dickinson, who once wrote:

> A word is dead
> When it is said,
> Some say.
>
> I say it just
> Begins to live
> That day.

## For Discussion

1. In what sense might a word begin "to live" when it's said?
2. If *you* had been advised to "charge your style with life," how would you go about it?

# ADDITIONAL WRITING TOPICS

## *Definition*

1. Write an essay in which you define an institution, trend, phenomenon, or abstraction as specifically and concretely as possible. Following are some suggestions designed to stimulate ideas. Before you begin, limit your subject.

| | |
|---|---|
| Responsibility | Leadership |
| Fun | Leisure |
| Sorrow | Originality |
| Unethical behavior | Character |
| The environment | Imagination |
| Education | Democracy |
| Progress | A smile |
| Advertising | A classic (of music, literature, art, |
| Happiness | or film) |
| Fads | Dieting |
| Feminism | Meditation |
| Marriage | Friendship |
| Sportsmanship | |

2. In a brief essay, define one of the following. In each instance, you have a choice of something good or something bad to talk about.

   A good or bad boss
   A good or bad parent
   A good or bad host
   A good or bad TV newscaster
   A good or bad physician
   A good or bad nurse
   A good or bad minister, priest, rabbi, or imam
   A good or bad roommate
   A good or bad driver
   A good or bad disk jockey

3. In a paragraph, define one of the following slang expressions for someone who has never heard the term: *bling, sick, hook up, wack, dis, cred, wicked, poser, wimp, loser, quack, chill, sweet.*

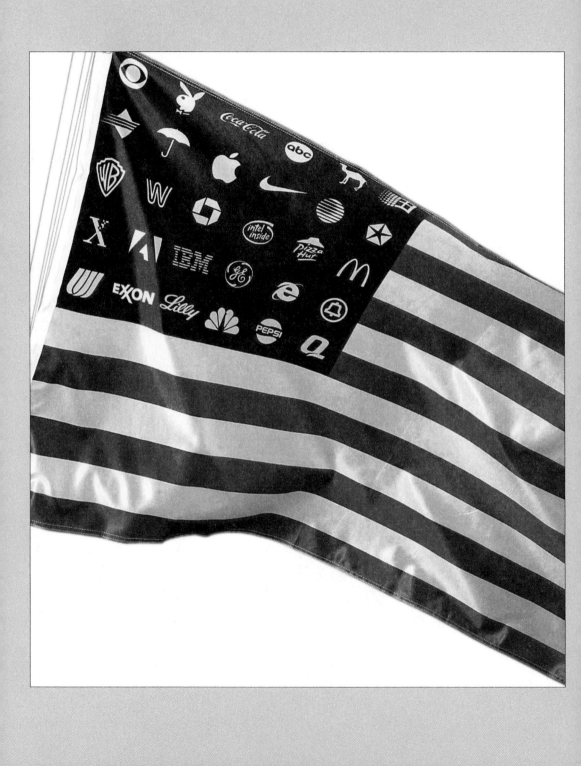

# 13

# ARGUMENT AND PERSUASION

## *Stating Opinions and Proposals*

◄ **Argument and persuasion in an image**

Adbusters Media Foundation, an activist group "concerned about the erosion of our physical and cultural environments by commercial forces," launched its Corporate America flag in 1999. This version appeared in a full-page advertisement in the *New York Times* in 2004. Replacing the American flag's stars with well-known corporate logos, the image adapts a symbol that many Americans revere to make a strong argument about the United States. What is the argument? How do you respond to the image: Are you offended? persuaded? amused? Why? Whatever your view, do you understand why others might think differently?

## THE METHOD

Practically every day, we try to persuade ourselves or someone else. We usually attempt such persuasion without being aware that we follow any special method at all. Often, we'll state an *opinion:* We'll tell someone our own way of viewing things. We say to a friend, "I'm starting to like Senator Clark. Look at all she's done to help people with disabilities. Look at her voting record on toxic waste." And, having stated these opinions, we might go on to make a *proposal,* to recommend that some action be taken. Addressing our friend, we might suggest, "Hey, Senator Clark is talking on campus at four-thirty. Want to come with me and listen to her?"

Sometimes you try to convince yourself that a certain way of interpreting things is right. You even set forth an opinion in writing—as in a letter to a friend who has asked, "Now that you're at New Age College, how do you like the place?" You may write a letter of protest to a landlord who wants to raise your rent, pointing out that the bathroom hot water faucet doesn't work. As a concerned citizen, you may wish to speak your mind in an occasional letter to a newspaper or to your elected representatives.

In many professions, one is expected to persuade people in writing. Before arguing a case in court, a lawyer prepares briefs setting forth all the points in favor of his or her side. Businesspeople regularly put in writing their ideas for new products and ventures, for improvements in cost control and job efficiency. Researchers write proposals for grants to obtain money to support their work. Scientists write and publish papers to persuade the scientific community that their findings are valid, often stating hypotheses, or tentative opinions.

Even if you never produce a single persuasive work (which is very unlikely), you will certainly encounter such works directed at you. In truth, we live our lives under a steady rain of opinions and proposals. Organizations that work for causes campaign with posters and direct mail, all hoping that we will see things their way. Moreover, we are bombarded with proposals from people who wish us to act. Religious leaders urge us to lead more virtuous lives. Advertisers urge us to rush right out and buy the large economy size.

Small wonder, then, that argument and persuasion—and CRITICAL THINK-ING about argument and persuasion—may be among the most useful skills a college student can acquire. Time and again, your instructors will ask you to criticize or to state opinions, either in class or in writing. You may be asked to state your view of anything from the electoral college to animal rights. You may be asked to judge the desirability or undesirability of compulsory testing for drugs or the revision of existing immigration laws. On an examination in, say, sociology, you may be asked, "Suggest three practical approaches to the most pressing needs of disadvantaged people in urban areas." Critically reading other people's arguments and composing your own, you will find, helps you discover what you think, refine it, and share what you believe.

Is there a difference between argument and persuasion? It is, admittedly, not always clear. Strictly speaking, PERSUASION aims to influence readers' actions, or their support for an action, by engaging their beliefs and feelings, while ARGUMENT aims to win readers' agreement with an assertion or claim by engaging their powers of reasoning. But most effective persuasion or argument contains elements of both methods; hence the confusion. In this book we tend to use the terms interchangeably.

One other point: We tend to talk here about *writing* argument and persuasion, but most of what we say has to do with *reading* them as well. When we discuss your need, as a writer, to support your claims, we are also discussing your need, as a reader, to question the support other authors provide for their claims. In reading arguments critically, you apply the critical-thinking skills we discussed in Chapter 1 — ANALYSIS, INFERENCE, SYNTHESIS, EVALUATION — to a particular kind of writing.

## Transaction Between Writer and Reader

Unlike some television advertisers, responsible writers of argument and persuasion do not try to storm people's minds. In writing a paper for a course, you persuade by gentler means: by sharing your view with readers willing to consider it. You'll want to learn how to express your view clearly and vigorously. But to be fair and persuasive, it is important to understand your readers' views as well.

In stating your opinion, you present the truth as you see it: "The immigration laws discourage employers from hiring nonnative workers" or "The immigration laws protect legal aliens." To persuade your readers that your view makes sense, you need not begin by proclaiming that, by Heaven, your view is absolutely right and should prevail. Instead, you might begin by trying to state what your readers probably think, as best you can infer it. You don't consider views that differ from your own merely to flatter your readers. You do so to correct your own view and make it more accurate. Regarded in this light, argument and persuasion aren't cynical ways to pull other people's strings. Writer and reader become two sensible people trying to find a common ground. This view will relieve you, whenever you have to state your opinions in writing, of the terrible obligation to be 100 percent right at all times.

## Elements of Argument

The British philosopher Stephen Toulmin has proposed a useful division of argument into three parts. Adapted to the terminology of this book, they are *claims*, *evidence*, and *assumptions*.

### Claims and Thesis Statements

A CLAIM is an assertion that requires support. It is what an argument tries to convince readers to accept. The central claim—the main point—is almost always stated explicitly in a THESIS STATEMENT like one of the following:

A CLAIM ABOUT REALITY   The war on drugs is not winnable because it cannot eradicate demand or the supply to meet it.

A CLAIM OF VALUE   Drug abuse is a personal matter that should not be subject to law.

A CLAIM FOR A COURSE OF ACTION   The United States must intensify its efforts to reduce production of heroin in Afghanistan.

Usually, but not always, you'll state your thesis at the beginning of your essay, making a play for readers' attention and clueing them in to your purpose. But if you think readers may have difficulty accepting your thesis until they've heard some or all of your argument, then you might save the thesis statement for the middle or end.

The essays in this chapter provide a variety of thesis statements as models. Here are three examples:

Today there is more pressure placed on students to do well [in school]. . . . This new pressure is what is causing the increase in cheating.
—Colleen Wenke, "Too Much Pressure"

Racial profiling is an ugly business. . . . But I'm not opposed to allowing—no, requiring—airlines to pay closer attention to passengers who fit a terrorist profile, which includes national origin.
—Linda Chavez, "Everything Isn't Racial Profiling"

[T]hose of us who are refugees and exiles must live with the double menace of being both possible victims and suspects, sometimes with fatal consequences. Will America ever learn again how to protect itself without sacrificing a great many innocent lives? So that my uncle did not die in vain, I truly hope so.
—Edwidge Danticat, "Not Your Homeland"

### Evidence

A claim is nothing without the EVIDENCE to make it believable and convincing. Toulmin calls evidence *data* or *grounds*, using terms that convey how specific and fundamental it is. Depending on your subject, your evidence may include facts, statistics (facts expressed in numbers), expert opinions, examples, and reported experience. These kinds of evidence should meet certain criteria:

- *Accuracy:* Facts, examples, and opinions are taken from reliable sources and presented without error or distortion.

- *Representation:* Evidence reflects reality, neither slanting nor exaggerating it.
- *Relevance:* Evidence is directly applicable to the claims, reflecting current thinking by recognized experts.
- *Adequacy:* Evidence is sufficient to support the claims entirely, not just in part.

To strengthen the support for your claims, you can also make appeals to readers either directly or indirectly, in the way you present your argument.

- Make a RATIONAL APPEAL by relying on sound reasoning and marshaling evidence that meets the criteria above. See pages 522–26 for more on reasoning.
- Make an ETHICAL APPEAL by showing readers that you are a well-informed person of goodwill, good sense, and good moral character—and, therefore, to be believed. Strengthen the appeal by collecting ample evidence, reasoning carefully, demonstrating respect for opposing views, using an appropriate emotional appeal (see below), and minding your TONE (see pp. 528–29).
- Make an EMOTIONAL APPEAL by acknowledging what you know of readers' sympathies and beliefs and by showing how your argument relates to them. An example in this chapter appears in Colleen Wenke's "Too Much Pressure," when Wenke appeals to readers' sense of fairness (or unfairness) by pointing out that many future leaders may gain their positions by cheating in school. Carefully used, an emotional appeal can stir readers to constructive belief and action by engaging their feelings as well as their minds. Be careful, though, that your emotional appeal is appropriate for your argument. "Do you really want to deprive your children of what's best for them?" asks a pitch for a certain learn-to-read program, appealing to pride or shame while neglecting to provide evidence that the program works.

### Assumptions

The third element of argument, the ASSUMPTION, is in Toulmin's conception the connective tissue between grounds, or evidence, and claims: An assumption explains why the evidence leads to and justifies the claim. Called a *warrant* by Toulmin, an assumption is usually a belief, a principle, or an inference whose truth the writer takes for granted. Here is how an assumption might figure in an argument for one of the claims given earlier:

CLAIM  The United States must intensify its efforts to reduce the production of heroin in Afghanistan.

EVIDENCE   Afghanistan is the world's largest heroin producer and the dominant supplier to the United States.

ASSUMPTION   The United States can and should reduce the production of heroin in other countries when its own citizens are affected.

As important as they are, the assumptions underlying an argument are not always stated. As we will see in the discussion of deductive reasoning (opposite), unstated assumptions can sometimes pitch an argument into trouble.

## Reasoning

When we argue rationally, we reason — that is, we make statements that lead to a conclusion. Two reliable methods of reasoning date back to the Greek philosopher Aristotle, who identified the complementary process of INDUCTIVE REASONING (induction) and DEDUCTIVE REASONING (deduction). In *Zen and the Art of Motorcycle Maintenance*, Robert M. Pirsig gives examples of both processes:

> If the cycle goes over a bump and the engine misfires, and then goes over another bump and the engine misfires, and then goes over another bump and the engine misfires, and then goes over a long smooth stretch of road and there is no misfiring, and then goes over a fourth bump and the engine misfires again, one can logically conclude that the misfiring is caused by the bumps. That is induction: reasoning from particular experiences to general truths.
>
> Deductive inferences do the reverse. They start with general knowledge and predict a specific observation. For example if, from reading the hierarchy of facts about the machine, the mechanic knows the horn of the cycle is powered exclusively by electricity from the battery, then he can logically infer that if the battery is dead the horn will not work. That is deduction.

### Inductive Reasoning

In inductive reasoning, the method of the sciences, we collect bits of evidence on which to base a GENERALIZATION, the claim of the argument. The assumption linking evidence and claim is that what is true for some circumstances is true for others as well. For instance, you might interview a hundred representative students about their attitudes toward changing the school's honor code. You find that 65 percent of your interviewees believe that the code should remain as it is, 15 percent believe that the code should be toughened, 10 percent believe that it should be loosened, and 10 percent have no opinion. You then assume that these statistics can be applied to the student body as a whole and make a claim against changing the code because 65 percent of students don't want change.

The more evidence you have, the more trustworthy your claim will be, but it would never be airtight unless you interviewed every student on campus. Since such thoroughness is almost always impractical if not impossible, you assume in an *inductive leap* that the results can be generalized. The smaller the leap—the more evidence you have—the better.

### Deductive Reasoning

Deductive reasoning works the opposite of inductive reasoning: It moves from a general statement to particular cases. The basis of deduction is the SYL-LOGISM, a three-step form of reasoning practiced by Aristotle:

All men are mortal.

Socrates is a man.

Therefore, Socrates is mortal.

The first statement, called a *major premise*, is an assumption: a fact, principle, or inference that you believe to be true. The second statement, or *minor premise*, is the evidence—the new information about a particular member of the larger group named in the major premise. The third statement, or *conclusion*, is the claim that follows inevitably from the premises. If the premises are true, then the conclusion must be true. Following is another example of a syllogism. You may recognize it from the discussion of assumptions on pages 521–22, only here the statements are simplified and arranged differently:

MAJOR PREMISE (ASSUMPTION)   The United States can and should reduce heroin production when its own citizens are affected.

MINOR PREMISE (EVIDENCE)   The dominant producer of heroin for the US market is Afghanistan.

CONCLUSION (THESIS)   The United States can and should reduce heroin production in Afghanistan.

Problems with deductive reasoning start in the premises. In 1633, Scipio Chiaramonti, professor of philosophy at the University of Pisa, came up with this untrustworthy syllogism: "Animals, which move, have limbs and muscles. The earth has no limbs and muscles. Hence, the earth does not move." This is bad deductive reasoning, and its flaw is to assume that all things need limbs and muscles to move—ignoring raindrops, rivers, and many other moving things.

When they're spelled out like Chiaramonti's, bad syllogisms are pretty easy to spot. But many deductive arguments are not spelled out. Instead, one of the premises goes unstated, as in this statement: "Mayor Perkins was humiliated in his recent bid for reelection, winning only 2,000 out of 5,000 votes."

Argument and Persuasion

The unstated assumption here, the major premise, is "Winning only two-fifths of the votes humiliates a candidate." (The rest of the syllogism: "Mayor Perkins received only two-fifths of the votes. Thus, Mayor Perkins was humiliated.")

The unstated premise isn't necessarily a problem in argument—in fact, it's quite common. But it *is* a problem when it's wrong or unfounded. For instance, in the statement "She shouldn't be elected mayor because her husband has bad ideas on how to run the city," the unstated assumption is that the candidate cannot form ideas independently of her husband. This is a possibility, perhaps, but it requires its own discussion and proof, not concealment behind other assertions.

Here's another argument with an unstated assumption, this one adapted from a magazine advertisement: "Scientists have no proof, just statistical correlations, linking smoking and heart disease, so you needn't worry about the connection." Now, the fact that this ad was placed by a cigarette manufacturer would tip off any reasonably alert reader to beware of bias in the claim. To discover the slant, we need to examine the unstated assumption, which runs something like this: "Since they are not proof, statistical correlations are worthless as guides to behavior." It is true that statistical correlations are not scientific proof, by which we generally mean repeated results obtained under controlled laboratory conditions—the kind of conditions to which human beings cannot ethically be subjected. But statistical correlations *can* establish connections and in fact inform much of our healthful behavior, such as getting physical exercise, avoiding fatty foods, brushing our teeth, and not driving while intoxicated. The advertiser's unstated premise isn't valid, so neither is the argument.

### Logical Fallacies

In arguments we read and hear, we often meet logical FALLACIES: errors in reasoning that lead to wrong conclusions. From the time when you start thinking about your proposition or claim and planning your paper, you'll need to watch out for them. To help you recognize logical fallacies when you see them or hear them, and so guard against them when you write, here is a list of the most common.

- *Non sequitur* (from the Latin, "it does not follow"): stating a conclusion that doesn't follow from one or both premises.

    I've lived in this town a long time—why, my grandfather was the first mayor—so I'm against putting fluoride in the drinking water.

- *Oversimplification:* supplying neat and easy explanations for large and complicated phenomena.

No wonder drug abuse is out of control. Look at how the courts have hobbled police officers.

Oversimplified solutions are also popular:

All these teenage kids that get in trouble with the law—why, they ought to put them in work camps. That would straighten them out!

(See also p. 435.)

- *Hasty generalization:* leaping to a generalization from inadequate or faulty evidence. The most familiar hasty generalization is the stereotype:

    Men aren't sensitive enough to be day-care providers.

    Women are too emotional to fight in combat.

- *Either/or reasoning:* assuming that a reality may be divided into only two parts or extremes; assuming that a given problem has only one of two possible solutions.

    What's to be done about the trade imbalance with Asia? Either we ban all Asian imports, or American industry will collapse.

    Obviously, either/or reasoning is a kind of extreme oversimplification.
- *Argument from doubtful or unidentified authority:*

    Uncle Oswald says that we ought to imprison all sex offenders for life.

    According to reliable sources, my opponent is lying.

- *Argument ad hominem* (from the Latin, "to the man"): attacking a person's views by attacking his or her character.

    Mayor Burns is divorced and estranged from his family. How can we listen to his pleas for a city nursing home?

- *Begging the question:* taking for granted from the start what you set out to demonstrate. When you reason in a *logical* way, you state that because something is true, then, as a result, some other truth follows. When you beg the question, however, you repeat that what is true is true. For instance:

    Dogs are a menace to people because they are dangerous.

    This statement proves nothing, because the idea that dogs are dangerous is already assumed in the statement that they are a menace. Beggars of questions often just repeat what they already believe, only in different words. This fallacy sometimes takes the form of arguing in a circle, or demonstrating a premise by a conclusion and a conclusion by a premise:

    I am in college because that is the right thing to do. Going to college is the right thing to do because it is expected of me.

- *Post hoc, ergo propter hoc* (from the Latin, "after this, therefore because of this"), or *post hoc* for short: assuming that because B follows A, B was caused by A.

  > Ever since the city suspended height restrictions on skyscrapers, the city budget has been balanced.

  (See also p. 435.)

- *False analogy:* the claim of persuasive likeness when no significant likeness exists. An ANALOGY asserts that because two things are comparable in some respects, they are comparable in other respects as well. Analogies cannot serve as evidence in a rational argument because the differences always outweigh the similarities; but analogies can reinforce such arguments *if* the subjects are indeed similar in some ways. If they aren't, the analogy is false. Many observers see the "war on drugs" as a false and damaging analogy because warfare aims for clear victory over a specific, organized enemy, whereas the complete eradication of illegal drugs is probably unrealistic and, in any event, the "enemy" isn't well defined: the drugs themselves? users? sellers? producers? the producing nations? (These critics urge approaching drugs as a social problem to be skillfully managed and reduced.)

## THE PROCESS

### Finding a Subject

Your way into a subject will probably vary depending on whether you're writing an argument that supports an opinion or one that proposes. In stating an opinion, you set forth and support a claim—a truth you believe. You may find such a truth by thinking and feeling, by reading, by talking to your instructors or fellow students, by listening to a discussion of some problem or controversy. Before you run with a subject, take a minute to weigh it: Is this something about which reasonable people disagree? Arguments go nowhere when they start with ideas that are generally accepted (pets should not have to endure physical abuse from their owners) or are beyond the pale (pet owners should be able to hurt their animals if they want).

In stating a proposal, you already have an opinion in mind, and from there, you go on to urge an action or a solution to a problem. Usually, these two statements will take place within the same piece of writing: You will first set forth a view ("The campus honor code is unfair to first offenders"), provide the evidence to support it, and then make your proposal as a remedy ("The campus honor code should be revised to give more latitude to first offenders").

Whatever your subject, resist the temptation to make it big. If you have two weeks to prepare, an argument about the litter problem in your town is probably manageable: In that time you could conduct your own visual research and talk to town officials. But an argument about the litter problem in your town compared with that in similar-sized towns across the state would surely demand more time than you have.

## Organizing

There's no one right way to organize an argument because so much depends on how your readers will greet your claim and your evidence. Below we give some ideas for different situations.

### Introduction

In your opening paragraph or two, draw readers in by connecting them to your subject if possible, showing its significance, and providing any needed background. End the introduction with your thesis statement if you think readers will entertain it before they've seen the evidence. Put the thesis statement later, in the middle or even at the end of the essay, if you think readers need to see some or all of the evidence in order to be open to the idea.

### Body

The body of the essay develops and defends the points that support your thesis. Generally, start with your least important point and build in a crescendo to your strongest point. However, if you think readers may resist your ideas, consider starting strong and then offering the more minor points as reinforcement.

For every point you make, give the evidence that supports it. The methods of development can help here, providing many options for injecting evidence. Say you were arguing for or against further reductions in welfare funding. You might give EXAMPLES of wasteful spending, or of neighborhoods where welfare funds are still needed. You might spell out the CAUSES of social problems that call for welfare funds, or foresee the likely EFFECTS of cutting welfare programs or of keeping them. You could use NARRATION to tell a pointed story; you could use DESCRIPTION to portray certain welfare recipients and their neighborhoods.

### Response to Objections

Part of the body of the essay, but separated here for emphasis, a response to probable objections is crucial to effective argument. If you are arguing fairly, you should be able to face potential criticisms fairly and give your critics due

Argument and Persuasion

credit, reasoning with them, not dismissing them. This is the strategy Linda Chavez uses later in this chapter in "Everything Isn't Racial Profiling" by maintaining, more than once, that racial profiling based on prejudice is wrong and by sympathizing with an Arab American who was not allowed to board a plane because of his ethnicity. As Chavez does, you can tackle possible objections throughout your essay, as they pertain to your points. You can also field objections near the end of the essay, an approach that allows you to draw on all of your evidence. But if you think that readers' own opposing views may stiffen their resistance to your argument, you may want to address those views very early, before developing your own points.

### Conclusion

The conclusion gives you a chance to gather your points, restate your thesis in a fresh way, and leave readers with a compelling final idea. In an essay with a strong emotional component, you may want to end with an appeal to readers' feelings. But even in a mostly rational argument, try to involve readers in some way, showing why they should care or what they can do.

---

**FOCUS ON TONE**

Readers are most likely to be persuaded by an argument when they sense a writer who is reasonable, trustworthy, and sincere. Sound reasoning, strong evidence, and acknowledgment of opposing views do much to convey these attributes, but so does TONE, the attitude implied by choice of words and sentence structures.

Generally, you should try for a tone of moderation in your view of your subject and a tone of respectfulness and goodwill toward readers and opponents.

- State opinions and facts calmly:

   OVEREXCITED   One clueless administrator was quoted in the newspaper as saying she thought many students who claim learning disabilities are faking their difficulties to obtain special treatment! Has she never heard of dyslexia, attention-deficit disorders, and other well-established disabilities?

   CALM   Particularly worrisome was one administrator's statement, quoted in the newspaper, that many students who claim learning disabilities may be "faking" their difficulties to obtain special treatment.

- Replace arrogance with deference and sarcasm with plain speaking:

   ARROGANT   I happen to know that many students would rather party or just bury their heads in the sand than get involved in a serious, worthy campaign against the school's unjust learning-disabled policies.

DEFERENTIAL   Time pressures and lack of information about the issues may be what prevents students from joining the campaign against the school's unjust learning-disabled policies.

SARCASTIC   Of course, the administration knows even without meeting students what is best for every one of them.

PLAIN   The administration should agree to meet with each learning-disabled student to learn about his or her needs.

- Choose words whose CONNOTATIONS convey reasonableness rather than anger, hostility, or another negative emotion:

HOSTILE   The administration coerced some students into dropping their lawsuits. [*Coerced* implies the use of threats or even violence.]

REASONABLE   The administration convinced some students to drop their lawsuits. [*Convinced* implies the use of reason.]

**For exercises on language, visit Exercise Central at *bedfordstmartins.com /thebedfordreader.***

---

## CHECKLIST FOR REVISING ARGUMENT OR PERSUASION

✔ **AUDIENCE**   Have you taken account of your readers' probable views? Have you reasoned with readers, not attacked them? Are your emotional appeals appropriate to readers' likely feelings? Do you acknowledge opposing views?

✔ **THESIS**   Does your argument have a thesis, a claim about how your subject is or should be? Is the thesis narrow enough to argue convincingly in the space and time available? Is it stated clearly? Is it reasonable?

✔ **EVIDENCE**   Is your thesis well supported with facts, statistics, expert opinions, and examples? Is your evidence accurate, representative, relevant, and ample?

✔ **ASSUMPTIONS**   Have you made sound connections between your evidence and your thesis and other claims?

✔ **LOGICAL FALLACIES**   Have you avoided common errors in reasoning, such as oversimplifying or begging the question? (See pp. 524–26 for a list of fallacies.)

✔ **STRUCTURE**   Does your organization lead readers through your argument step by step, building to your strongest ideas and frequently connecting your evidence to your central claim?

✔ **TONE**   Is the tone of your argument reasonable and respectful?

# ARGUMENT AND PERSUASION IN PARAGRAPHS

## Writing About Television

This self-contained paragraph, written for *The Bedford Reader*, argues that TV news aims for entertainment at the expense of serious coverage of events and issues. The argument here could serve a number of different purposes in full essays: For instance, in a paper claiming that television is our least reliable source of news, the paragraph would give one cause of unreliability; or in an essay analyzing television news, the paragraph would examine one element.

Television news has a serious failing: It's show business. Unlike a newspaper, its every image has to entertain the average beer drinker. To score high ratings and win advertisers, the visual medium favors the spectacular: riots, tornados, air crashes. Now that satellite transmission invites live coverage, newscasters go for the fast-breaking story at the expense of thoughtful analysis. "The more you can get data out instantly," says media critic Jeff Greenfield, "the more you rely on instant data to define the news." TV zooms in on people who make news, but, to avoid boredom, won't let them argue or explain. (How can they, in speeches limited to fifteen seconds?) In 2007, as the United States increased its forces in Iraq, President Bush addressed Congress to explain the action. His lengthy remarks were clipped to twenty seconds on one news broadcast, and then an anchorwoman digested the opposition to a single line: "Democrats tonight were critical of the president's actions." During the last two presidential elections, the candidates sometimes deliberately packaged bad news so that it could not be distilled to a sound bite on the evening news—and thus would not make the evening news at all. Americans who rely on television for their news (two-thirds, according to recent polls) exist on a starvation diet.

*Topic sentence: the claim*

*Evidence:*
- *Expert opinion*

- *Facts and examples*

- *Statistic*

## Writing in an Academic Discipline

Taken from a textbook on public relations, the following paragraph argues that lobbyists (who work to persuade public officials in behalf of a cause) are not slick manipulators but something else. The paragraph falls in the textbook's section on lobbying as a form of public relations, and its purpose is to correct a mistaken definition.

Although the public stereotypes a lobbyist as a fast-talking person twisting an elected official's arm to get special concessions, the reality is quite different. Today's lobbyist, who may be fully employed by one industry or represent a variety of clients, is often a quiet-spoken, well-educated man or woman armed with statistics and

*Topic sentence: the claim*

research reports. Robert Gray, former head of Hill and Knowlton's
Washington office and a public affairs expert for thirty years, adds,    • Expert opinion
"Lobbying is no longer a booze and buddies business. It's presenting
honest facts and convincing Congress that your side has more merit
than the other." He rejects lobbying as being simply "influence ped-
dling and button-holing" top administration officials. Although the
public has the perception that lobbying is done only by big business,
Gray correctly points out that a variety of special interests also do it.
These may include such groups as the Sierra Club, Mothers Against    • Facts and examples
Drunk Driving, the National Association of Social Workers, the
American Civil Liberties Union, and the American Federation of
Labor. Even the American Society of Plastic and Reconstructive
Surgeons hired a Washington public relations firm in their battle
against restrictions on breast implants. Lobbying, quite literally, is
an activity in which widely diverse groups and organizations engage
as an exercise of free speech and representation in the marketplace
of ideas. Lobbyists often balance each other and work toward legislative compromises that benefit not only their self-interests but
society as a whole.
　　　—Dennis L. Wilcox, Phillip H. Ault, and Warren K. Agee,
　　　　　　　　　　*Public Relations: Strategies and Tactics*

## ARGUMENT AND PERSUASION IN PRACTICE

As a college freshman, Kristen Corcoran commuted to school at night. In
the letter on the next page, she appealed to her college's president to have a
parking ticket canceled because legal parking was unavailable.

Corcoran's letter is a model of argument for a specific purpose, but it
didn't start out that way. In her much longer first draft, she let her anger push
her into detailing every one of her five previous parking difficulties and criticizing the president personally for not solving the problem. She did not get to
her request to have the ticket canceled until the very end.

Reviewing her draft, Corcoran realized that she was trying to negotiate
with the president, not tell her off, and for that a more direct, conciliatory approach was needed. In the revision that follows, Corcoran focuses immediately on her purpose for writing, summarizes her problems with parking, and
takes the tack of informing, rather than criticizing, the president.

1073 Dogwood Terrace
North Andover, MA 01845
May 2, 2007

President Delores Reed
North State College
755 Little Road
Danvers, MA 01923

Dear President Reed:

I write to ask you to rescind a ten-dollar citation I received on April 4 for parking in North State's Lot E. I know that this lot is reserved for faculty use, but flooding in three of the four commuter lots left me with no reasonable parking alternatives. The campus police have not been able to help me, so I turn to you.

As you know, flooding is a recurring problem at North State, but perhaps you don't know how it affects commuting students. April 4 was one of six evenings this semester when I arrived to find Lots A, C, and D overrun by nearby marshes. On the other nights, Lot B filled quickly with cars and I was forced on two occasions to hunt for parking in the crowded residential areas off-campus. On April 4, I chose not to spend a half-hour finding a space and parked in Lot E. Many of its spaces are vacant at night when there are fewer classes and most campus offices are closed.

I understand from the campus police that North State has no plan for solving this seasonal problem. I, like hundreds of other commuter students, paid fifty dollars for a parking permit in the beginning of the semester and should be able to expect convenient parking like that described in North State's brochures. The parking problem is a serious one that affects not only commuters, who make up more than half of the student body, but also North State's neighbors, who are inconvenienced by crowds of cars monopolizing their streets each spring.

Please rescind my ticket and try to create some solutions to this problem. As a first step, may I suggest amending the school's parking policy to allow commuter use of Lot E in emergencies?

Sincerely,

*Kristen Corcoran*

Kristen Corcoran

# COLLEEN WENke

COLLEEN WENke was born in 1979 and grew up in Queens, New York. After graduating from Boston College in 2001 with a degree in psychology, she moved back to New York City and took a job at a real estate investment and development firm, where she is now a vice president. She received an MA in real estate from New York University and is active in professional organizations such as the New York Building Congress and Young Real Estate Professional Women in Construction. An avid traveler, Wenke spent a semester at the University of New South Wales in Sydney, Australia, and she has taken trips to Europe and Southeast Asia. She is also an enthusiast of extreme sports, such as skydiving, rappelling, white-water rafting, and scuba diving.

## Too Much Pressure

Why do students cheat in school? In this essay written when she was a college freshman, Wenke explores several answers to the question, finding one especially compelling. "Too Much Pressure" was published in the 1998 edition of *Fresh Ink*, a collection of work by students in Boston College's first-year writing course.

Except for using italic type in place of underlining, Wenke's essay follows MLA style for documenting sources, as discussed on pages 62–63. The text does not have the parenthetical citations normally found in MLA style because Wenke names source authors in her sentences and the sources— two Web documents and a television program—did not have numbered pages she could cite.

You hear the clock ticking in your head, and your teacher keeps erasing, in ten-minute decrements, the time you have left to complete the test. You do not remember anything from the last month of class. You probably should have studied more, watched less television, and spent less time on the phone. All the "should haves" are not important now. You need to finish the test and get out of here. The thought of a big fat F and a "See me" on the top of your midterm scares you. You remember the small piece of paper you have hidden in your pocket just in case. For a fleeting moment you think about what will happen if you are caught; then you slip the paper from your pocket onto the desktop. You transfer all the required information onto the test in time. You smile in anticipation of the A you are going to get. You think of how easy it was to cheat. All that matters is getting the grade.

Cheating is taking work done by somebody else, be it a friend or someone you do not know, and writing your name on it and saying it is your work. Any time I walked through my high school cafeteria or the hallways, I saw people cheating. It came in many forms, from copying homework to giving out copies of the exam. Students even wrote the answers to a Scantron exam down the sides of number-2 pencils and gave the pencils to their friends. My history teacher freshman year had a name for these students: "cafeteria scholars." These were the students who pulled 90s by knowing what the test questions were before they got to the classroom. Their friends who had taken the exam earlier in the day would tell them the questions and answers during lunch. The teachers knew that these things went on, yet nobody seemed to do anything about them. I thought this was the way school went. The people who were cheating were doing the best in all of my classes. I would study for hours and still pull Bs. They would pull As.

I remember conversations over the dinner table with my parents on the    3
subject of cheating. My parents were disgusted at the apathetic views my brothers and I held. We really didn't think it was a big deal to copy homework. I thought everyone cheated, probably even my parents and teachers when they were my age. But my parents swore that they had never cheated. Did I believe them? Not really. I thought that they were giving us the "it was so much better when we were growing up" speech.

I soon learned differently. In the article "When the Ends Justify the    4
Means," written by Robin Stansbury, a reporter for the Connecticut newspaper *The Courant*, I found that my parents were telling the truth. Stansbury reports that "cheating in school has probably been around since the first exam was given." But he goes on to say, "State and national statistics show cheating among high-school students has risen dramatically during the past fifty years." Reading this upset me and made me think about what had caused this increase. I hoped this was not a reflection of moral decline in the people who would soon be running my country. I blamed our school system for not instilling the proper values in its students. I figured that the dramatic change in the role of the family over the past generation, from two-parent homes with a working father and a mother who stayed at home and watched her children to families which have only a single parent or in which both parents work outside the home, meant schools needed to include moral standards in the curriculum. I believed schools were not fulfilling their role and therefore were producing students who do not know the difference between right and wrong.

An article written by Robert L. Maginnis, a policy analyst in the Cultural    5
Studies Project at the Family Research Council, indicates my hypothesis had some truth to it. Maginnis states that "the erosion of values is traceable largely to changes in institutions which have traditionally been responsible for imparting them to our youth." He defines "these key institutions [to] include family, school, church, media and government." I agree with Maginnis, but I

can't accept these factors as the only sources in the increase of cheating in the classroom. The facts seem contradictory. If my parents' generation had such high morals and wouldn't cheat, wouldn't they teach their children the same? My parents had taught me that cheating was wrong, yet I seemed to accept it.

There is a new "class" of cheaters today. In the past, as one would expect, the students who cheated were the ones who could not pass or did not do the work. They were the lazy students. But today the majority of the students who admit to cheating are college-bound overachievers. The students who are trying to juggle too many activities are resorting to compromising their integrity for a good grade. There is too much competition between students, which leads to increased pressure to do well. Cheating becomes a way to get the edge over the other students in the class. In addition, penalties for getting caught are mild. If you were caught cheating at my high school, you received a zero for the test. Your parents were not called, and you were not suspended. True, a zero would hurt your grade severely if all grades for each quarter counted. But there was a loophole in the system: Each quarter the lowest grade was dropped. If the zero grade was dropped, it made no difference; the average was not affected. Students who cheated on all the tests but only got caught once still received good grades.

A main difference between school today and school when my parents were enrolled is that we are now very goal-oriented and will compromise our values to achieve these goals. Stansbury sees this compromise of values and reports in his article that "cheating is a daily occurrence in high school. . . . What this says is that many of our students today do not have much internal integrity." Stansbury argues that students "want a goal, and how to get the goal is somewhat irrelevant." Today there is more pressure placed on students to do well. They are expected to receive good grades, play a sport, and volunteer if they are to be looked at by a good college. With a B tainting your transcript, a college might not look at you. This new pressure is what is causing the increase in cheating. Maginnis agrees with Stansbury and goes further, reporting, "A national survey found a shift in motivation away from altruism and toward concern with making money and getting power and status." Like Stansbury, Maginnis says that "students are finding it easier to rationalize lying or cheating in pursuit of their goals." And what goals are these students pursuing? They want the best grades so that they can get into the best schools and get the highest-paying jobs. Starting in the classroom, we are sending the message that it is acceptable to cheat as long as you do not get caught and you do the best.

Dean Morton, a broadcaster for *Good Morning America*, reported that according to a national survey conducted in 1997 by *Who's Who in American High School Students*, as many as 98 percent of students who participated in the survey admitted to cheating. The segment of the show was even entitled "Guess What? Cheaters Do Prosper." Like Stansbury and Maginnis, this survey also concluded that it is now the common belief among students that cheaters are getting ahead in life. Stansbury interviewed several high-school students in his article and discovered that many of them feel cheaters do get ahead in the classroom: "In high school, the cheaters always win. They don't get caught and they are the ones getting 100 on the exams when the noncheaters are getting 80s and 90s. Cheaters do win." We are sending a message to our youth that it is acceptable to cheat as long as you don't get caught and you are getting As. In this kind of society, morals take a back seat to how much you earn and how prosperous you are.

Students who would not usually cheat get sucked into believing it is the 9 only way to get ahead in school: If the cheaters are doing better than they are and not getting caught, then they had better try it. Stansbury proposes that there is such an enormous increase in cheating because more students are joining in: "They see others cheating and they think they are being unfairly disadvantaged." He adds that the "only way many of them feel they can keep in the game, to get into the right schools, is to cheat." In high school I always felt at a disadvantage, because everybody else was cheating and doing better than I was, even if only by a few points. My friends felt the same way, that copying work or cheating was the only way to keep up with the rest of the class. It frustrated me, because the cheaters were not earning their grades. But there were plenty of times when I was in a jam and copied homework from friends. Thinking about this now, I wonder what allowed me to push aside my conviction that cheating was wrong. I wasn't bringing in cheat sheets and didn't know the questions to tests before I got there, but I was cheating nonetheless.

How should we respond to the huge increase in cheating over the past 10 generation? We need to step back and look at the broader picture. We are creating a society in which people feel it is acceptable to cheat. This attitude will not stop in the classroom, but will carry on into the business world. Those who are cheating are the ones getting the grades and getting into the best schools. They are the "smart" ones. They in turn are the ones who will be running our country. They will become the heads of businesses and presidents of big corporations. Are these the people we want to have the power? In all likelihood they will not stop cheating once they get to the top. They become the people we idolize and aspire to be like. Because they are powerful, we consider them clever, highly respectable people. I do not hold any respect for a dishonest cheater. The phrase "honest businessman" will truly be an oxymoron. I am scared to think of the consequences of having cheaters rule our country. Is our society teaching that this is the only way to get ahead in life? Does obtaining status and power make you good? Schools are drifting away from emphasizing learning and are emphasizing the grade instead. When the thirst for knowledge is replenished in a student's mind, the desire for the grade without the work will dissolve. Only then will cheating decline.

## Works Cited

Maginnis, Robert L. "Cheating Scandal Points to Moral Decline." *Family Research Council.* 1994. 3 May 1997 <http://www.frc.org/perspeceivelpv94dled.html>.

Morton, Dean. "Guess What? Cheaters Do Prosper." *Good Morning America.* ABC. WCVB, Boston. 16 Apr. 1997.

Stansbury, Robin. "Cheating in Connecticut's Classrooms: When the Ends Justify the Means." *Hartford Courant* 2 Mar. 1997. 2 May 1997 <http://www.ctnow.com/news/hc-specialUcheating/daY1.html>.

*For a reading quiz and annotated links to further readings on cheating in school, visit **bedfordstmartins.com/thebedfordreader**.*

## Journal Writing

Do you agree with Wenke that most students think cheating is acceptable? In your journal, write down your views of how common cheating is in your school and what students' attitudes are toward it. (To take your journal writing further, see "From Journal to Essay" on the following page.)

## Questions on Meaning

1. What reasons does Wenke suggest for the increase in cheating among students?
2. What does Wenke see as a possible negative consequence of cheating among students today?
3. What solution does Wenke offer for the problem of student cheating?

## Questions on Writing Strategy

1. How effective do you find Wenke's opening paragraph? What does it suggest to you about her intended AUDIENCE?

2. Wenke cites several outside sources in the course of her essay. What do these sources contribute to her argument?
3. What is the EFFECT of Wenke's admission that she herself copied homework from friends in high school (par. 9)? Does this admission add to or detract from Wenke's ethical appeal? Why?
4. **OTHER METHODS** Wenke's argument is based largely on CAUSE AND EFFECT ANALYSIS. Does her analysis seem sound to you? Do you think she overemphasizes some causes or overlooks others? Explain.

## Questions on Language

1. Find examples of COLLOQUIAL EXPRESSIONS in Wenke's essay. What is the effect of such language? Does it strike you as appropriate for her argument?
2. What does Wenke mean when she says, "The phrase 'honest businessman' will truly be an oxymoron" (par. 10)? What is an *oxymoron*?
3. Use a dictionary if necessary to help you define any of the following words: decrements (par. 1); apathetic (3); hypothesis (5); integrity (6); altruism, rationalize (7); replenished (10).

## Suggestions for Writing

1. **FROM JOURNAL TO ESSAY** Based on your journal entry, write an essay in which you analyze the problem of student cheating at your school. Who does it? Why? What do others think about it? What does the school do about it? If cheating is uncommon at your school, analyze why.
2. Wenke refers to the intense pressure students are under today to get good grades as well as to participate in sports and other extracurricular activities. Besides cheating, what are some other consequences of the pressure faced by contemporary students—including positive consequences, if you think there are any? Drawing on your own experiences as well as the experiences of people you know, write an essay about what happens to students when they feel they are under pressure to excel.
3. Wenke wrote her essay in 1998. Has the problem of student cheating improved or worsened since then? Research the problem in several studies published since 1998—the more recent the better. Then write an essay in which you explain the current trend in cheating and what you think causes it.
4. **CRITICAL WRITING** In an essay, EVALUATE Wenke's argument. How well does she convince you of the extent of the problem of student cheating and of its causes? How well do you think she develops her proposed solutions?
5. **CONNECTIONS** In "The Ways We Lie" (p. 408), Stephanie Ericsson categorizes the kinds of lies people tell in everyday life. In what sense is cheating a form of lying? Which of Ericsson's categories might it belong to? On the scale of lying, how bad is cheating? Are cheaters likely to lie in other ways as well?

# BRIAN WILLIAMS

BRIAN WILLIAMS is the anchor and managing editor of *NBC Nightly News*. Born in 1959, he attended both George Washington University and the Catholic University of America before taking an internship with the administration of President Jimmy Carter. He then spent seven years with CBS News and joined NBC's rival news team in 1993, eventually becoming the network's top anchor. He has received five Emmy Awards, four Edward R. Murrow Awards, and in 2005 the Peabody Award for his coverage of Hurricane Katrina and its aftermath. Williams's writing has appeared in the *Los Angeles Times*, the *New York Times*, and *Time* magazine, which honored him in 2007 as one of the "100 Most Influential People." Williams also writes frequently on his blog *The Daily Nightly*, discussing the work that goes into producing *NBC Nightly News*. He and his wife have two children.

## *But Enough About You . . .*

As a nightly news anchor, Williams is in a good position to see how traditional television shows like his are losing viewers to other TV options, the Internet, and personal electronic gear. The media are more democratic, Williams concedes in this essay, but with all that choice we risk tuning out what we need to know.

In the essay following this one — "Won't You Be My Friendster?" — Andie Wurster looks at the new media from a different angle and comes to a different conclusion.

While the mainstream media were having lunch, members of the audience made other plans. They scattered and are still on the move, part of a massive migration. The dynamic driving it? It's all about you. Me. And all the various forms of the first-person singular. 1

Americans have decided the most important person in their lives is . . . them, and our culture is now built upon that idea. It's the User-Generated Generation. 2

For those times when the nine hundred digital options awaiting us in our set-top cable box can seem limiting and claustrophobic, there's the Web. Once inside, the doors swing open to a treasure trove of video: adults juggling kittens, ill-fated dance moves at wedding receptions, political rants delivered to camera with venom and volume. All of it exists to fill a perceived need. 3

Media executives—some still not sure what it is—know only that they want it. And they're willing to pay for it.

The larger dynamic at work is the celebration of self. The implied message     4
is that if it has to do with you, or your life, it's important enough to tell someone. Publish it, record it . . . but for goodness' sake, share it—get it out there
so that others can enjoy it. Or not. The assumption is that an audience of
strangers will be somehow interested, or at the very worst not offended. Intimacies that were once whispered into the phone are now announced
unabashedly into cell phones as loud running conversations in public places.
Diaries once sealed under lock and key are now called "blogs" and posted daily
for all those who care to make the emotional investment.

We've raised a generation of Americans on a mantra of love and the     5
importance of self as taught by brightly colored authority figures with names
like Barney and Elmo. On the theory that celebrating only the winners means
excluding those who place, show or simply show up, parents-turned-coaches
started awarding trophies—entire bedrooms full—to all those who compete.
Today everyone gets celebrated, in part to put an end to the common cruelties
of life that so many of us grew up with.

Now the obligatory confession: In an irony of life that I've not yet fully     6
reconciled myself to, I write a daily blog full of intimate details about one of
the oldest broadcasts on television. While the media landscape of my youth,
with its three television networks, now seems like forced national viewing by
comparison, and while I anchor a broadcast that is routinely viewed by an
audience of ten million or more, it's nothing like it used to be. We work every
bit as hard as our television-news forebears did at gathering, writing and presenting the day's news but to a smaller audience, from which many have been
lured away by a dazzling array of choices and the chance to make their own
news.

It is not possible—even common—to go about your day in America and     7
consume only what you wish to see and hear. There are television networks
that already agree with your views, iPods that play only music you already
know you like, Internet programs ready to filter out all but the news you want
to hear.

The problem is that there's a lot of information out there that citizens in     8
an informed democracy *need* to know in our complicated world with US
troops on the ground along two major fronts. Millions of Americans have
come to regard the act of reading a daily newspaper—on *paper*—as something akin to being dragged by their parents to Colonial Williamsburg. It's a
tactile visit to another time . . . flat, one-dimensional, unexciting, emitting a
slight whiff of decay. It doesn't refresh. It offers no choice. Hell, it doesn't even
move. Worse yet: Nowhere does it greet us by name. It's for everyone.

Does it endanger what passes for the national conversation if we're all     9
talking at once? What if "talking" means typing on a laptop, but the audience
is too distracted to pay attention? The whole notion of "media" is now much
more democratic, but what will the effect be on democracy?

The danger just might be that we miss the next great book or the next great     10
idea, or that we fail to meet the next great challenge, because we are too busy
celebrating ourselves and listening to the same tune we already know by heart.

*For a reading quiz, sources on Brian Williams, and annotated links to further read-ings on the media and the self, visit* **bedfordstmartins.com/thebedfordreader.**

---

## Journal Writing

What kind of news do you follow, and how do you gain access to it? Why do you
choose to follow the stories you do on the outlets you do? (To take your journal writing further, see "From Journal to Essay" on the following page.)

## Questions on Meaning

1. In his opening paragraph, Williams refers to "a massive migration." What is he
   talking about, and what examples of this migration does he give?
2. What is Williams's point in paragraphs 4–5, and how does this point fit into his
   larger argument?
3. What does Williams see as the major problem with the new-media landscape he
   describes?
4. What is Williams's THESIS, and where does he state it?

## Questions on Writing Strategy

1. What EFFECT do you suppose Williams intended to have on readers? What makes
   you think as you do?
2. What is Williams's purpose in paragraph 6? Why does he make this "confession,"
   and how does he deal with its implications?
3. In paragraph 9 Williams asks a series of questions. What is the purpose of these
   questions, and what is their effect?
4. Consider the placement and wording of Williams's thesis. Why do you think
   Williams might have chosen this placement and wording?
5. **OTHER METHODS**   How does Williams's essay use CAUSE AND EFFECT?

## Questions on Language

1. In paragraph 1, Williams refers to the mainstream media as "having lunch." What does this phrase suggest?
2. What does Williams mean by the phrase "User-Generated Generation" (par. 2)?
3. In paragraph 8 Williams says, "Millions of Americans have come to regard the act of reading a daily newspaper — on *paper* — as something akin to being dragged by their parents to Colonial Williamsburg." What is Colonial Williamsburg? What are the implications of this reference?
4. Be sure you are familiar with the following words, checking a dictionary if necessary: claustrophobic (par. 3); intimacies, unabashedly (4); mantra (5); obligatory (6); tactile, emitting, whiff (8).

## Suggestions for Writing

1. **FROM JOURNAL TO ESSAY**   Beginning with an analysis of your own preferences in news reporting and sources, write an essay in which you consider how important you think it is for people to stay informed about what's happening in the world around them. In your essay, also consider the kinds of news you believe people should follow and what you see as the best sources for gaining access to such news.
2. Williams suggests that, for a variety of reasons, Americans have become increasingly self-absorbed. Write an essay in which you offer your own viewpoint on this idea. If you generally agree, offer specific EXAMPLES and speculate about the causes of this change. If you generally disagree, challenge Williams's assumptions with examples that counter his claim.
3. Williams observes that matters most people once considered highly personal now are broadcast publicly and unabashedly through cell phone conversations, blogs, and social-networking sites like *MySpace*. The point can be widened to include TV: the sharing of personal lives with Dr. Phil and Oprah Winfrey, the personal exposure on reality shows such as *The Real World*. Write an essay in which you examine this phenomenon from your own perspective, speculating about its causes and considering its effects on society as a whole.
4. **CRITICAL WRITING**   In an essay, ANALYZE the image that Williams presents of himself, his ethical appeal. Consider specific examples of his language and his TONE, along with what he says about himself and his work. How do you respond to this appeal?
5. **CONNECTIONS**   In the next essay, "Won't You Be My Friendster?" by Andie Wurster, the author initially refers to social-networking Web sites as "time-wasting mirror gazing," a sentiment that Williams would likely share. But Wurster goes on to explain how her experience with such sites changed her opinion. In an essay, consider the extent to which Wurster's essay challenges Williams's and how Williams might respond to Wurster.

# ANDIE WURSTER

ANDIE WURSTER was born in 1982 on an Air Force base in Albuquerque, New Mexico. She studied at Emerson College, earning a BA in writing, literature, and publishing, with an emphasis on children's literature. Her children's book reviews have been published in the *Horn Book Guide* (2003), and she has also written for *Lollapalooza Zine* and *Gauge* magazine. Wurster owns and runs a design and custom invitation company, Run Grady Run. She lives in Seattle, Washington, and in her spare time enjoys reading, sewing, and printmaking.

# *Wont You Be My Friendster?*

Social-networking Web sites such as *Friendster*, *MySpace*, and *Facebook* have become a cultural phenomenon, but just how social are they? For some users, at least, the sites clearly encourage the kind of self-celebration that Brian Williams, in the previous essay, deplores for shutting out the unknown and uncomfortable. But Andie Wurster argues that the sites can do more than that as well: By expanding knowledge and outlooks, they can lower barriers of space and culture that would otherwise divide users. Wurster wrote this essay for *The Bedford Reader*.

First there was *Friendster*. After its early success, other social-networking 1
sites, mainly *Facebook* and *MySpace*, inevitably cropped up. When these sites hit the Internet, I had no plans to take part in them. My friends were joining—posting their pictures, personal information, and lists of favorite everything—but to me it all seemed like time-wasting mirror gazing. Users now had Internet square footage to call their own, and they exploited it to admire themselves and shout their presence from the international rooftop. I preferred to keep my identity where it belonged, in the real world with my real friends and real life.

Finally, though, I gave in to curiosity. My friends were excited about new 2
online acquaintances, discussing music they first heard on the networks, taking me along to parties they'd been invited to online. When I joined, I learned that I and the many other critics of the networks had been both right and wrong about them. They do, in fact, catch users by appealing to the look-at-me attitude of millions of young people around the globe. However, those

millions turn the sites into truly vibrant social networks that not only connect people but also expand their horizons.

Even among people who already know one another, the social networks   3
have a worthy function. In face-to-face interactions with our friends, how often do we try to define ourselves or respond to how they define themselves? As it turns out, those byte-sized lists of likes and dislikes can add up to say something significant, not just to strangers but to the people that we thought we knew. For just-acquaintances who would like to be more, the networks can be icebreakers. For friends who are distant, the networks can provide a daily link to keep the relationship thriving.

Of course, it's in introducing us to people we *don't* know already that the   4
social networks do their most revolutionary work. Instead of being confined to the people in our schools, workplaces, and physical communities, we can meet potential pals all over the world. Unlike our knowns, these unknowns often end up being quite different from ourselves. As someone with a long-term, insular group of friends in her daily life, I have met people I otherwise would never have encountered—people with different cultural backgrounds than my own, people with different interests and different goals. Our friendships started with shared tastes in music but have expanded to take in the very different circumstances of our lives. Such exposure doesn't happen for every participant, but when it does it lowers the barriers of distance, culture, and physical appearance that cause so many problems in the world.

The networks foster connection and action within our physical communi-   5
ties, too. Online invitations for nonvirtual music shows and art openings result in events that bring together diverse people who would normally pass each other on the street without a glance. At the invitation of a friend I'd met online, I attended a private listening party for a band's soon-to-be-released album. By the end of the night, I had met a handful of possible new pals and had joined a volunteer group in my city that runs an after-school program for disadvantaged children. Many of my friends report similar experiences of having their outlooks, and their activities, broadened beyond the previous limits of space and acquaintanceship.

All this is not to say that there aren't problems with the networks. For all   6
the friends I have whose knowledge and interests have grown, at least as many seem to spend half their waking hours refining their own pages and improving their skills as voyeurs as they visit others' pages. For many of the sites' participants, the openness and remoteness of the Internet weaken healthy inhibitions, so that they post pictures of themselves scantily clad or conduct vicious verbal attacks on other users. Mass e-vites have led to out-of-control parties at which property and even attendees have been harmed. The networks themselves have been targeted for allowing too much advertising and maintaining

links to commercial interests. Repeated security breaches put users at risk for spamming and identity theft. And, perhaps most disturbing, the networks' efforts to protect the safety of the youngest users have not always been successful.

These criticisms are all valid, but they are only part of the story. The on-line social networks have given us a new medium that for many users means more communication, expanded sights and knowledge, and, paradoxically, increased experience of the real world. The networks are a place to exhibit oneself, yes, but they are also a place for connecting.    7

*For a reading quiz and annotated links to further readings on the media and the self, visit **bedfordstmartins.com/thebedfordreader**.*

---

## Journal Writing

What is your experience with the social-networking sites that Wurster writes about? Do you use *MySpace*, *Facebook*, or another such site? If so, what do you use it for? What do you see as its benefits and drawbacks? If not, why have you chosen not to participate on these sites? How do you view them and the people who use them? (To take your journal writing further, see "From Journal to Essay" on the following page.)

## Questions on Meaning

1. What is Wurster's THESIS, and where does she state it? What does the thesis suggest may be Wurster's ASSUMPTIONS about her readers' attitudes toward social-networking sites?
2. What does Wurster see as the primary benefits of social-networking sites? Do you agree or disagree with any of them? Why?
3. In paragraph 6 Wurster lays out half a dozen drawbacks of the networking sites. What are they? Do you agree or disagree with any of them? Why?

## Questions on Writing Strategy

1. Wurster's first paragraph is devoted to her initial skepticism of social-networking sites. What is the EFFECT of this opening?
2. Why do you think Wurster presents the networks' benefits in the order she does (pars. 3–5)? Do you think this arrangement is effective, or would you prefer another? Why?

3. Identify Wurster's use of a specific EXAMPLE in paragraph 5. What does it contribute to her argument?
4. **OTHER METHODS**   Where in the essay does Wurster use CAUSE AND EFFECT, and how does it help further her argument?

## Questions on Language

1. What does Wurster mean in paragraph 1 by "time-wasting mirror gazing"?
2. Identify two FIGURES OF SPEECH in paragraph 1. What is the effect of this language?
3. In paragraph 3 Wurster calls the networking sites potential "icebreakers" for acquaintances who want to get to know each other better. What does she mean by "icebreakers"?
4. What are "nonvirtual" events (par. 5)? How are they distinct from "virtual" events?
5. Check a dictionary if you are unfamiliar with the meanings of any of the following words: inevitably (par. 1); vibrant (2); byte (3); insular (4); foster (5); voyeurs, scantily, clad, breaches (6); paradoxically (7).

## Suggestions for Writing

1. **FROM JOURNAL TO ESSAY**   Use your journal writing as a starting point to compose your own argument about the pros or cons, or both, of social-networking sites. As you plan and draft, you may want to respond specifically to points raised by Wurster and, like Wurster, draw on your own experiences of the sites. If you are unfamiliar with the sites, visit one or two of them online to get a feel for the ways people use them.
2. In paragraph 6 Wurster writes, "For many of the sites' participants, the openness and remoteness of the Internet weaken healthy inhibitions, so that they post pictures of themselves scantily clad or conduct vicious verbal attacks on other users." How do you think "the openness and remoteness of the Internet" affect the way people present themselves online? Give plenty of examples from your own observations of Internet behavior.
3. **CRITICAL WRITING**   Much of Wurster's argument relies on EVIDENCE from her personal experience. Write an essay in which you discuss how effective, or not, you find this evidence to be and explore what else, if anything, Wurster might have brought in to support her claims.
4. **CONNECTIONS**   Both Andie Wurster and Brian Williams, in "But Enough About You . . ." (p. 539), use conversational language and a light TONE to write about their subjects—for instance, "Hell, it doesn't even move" (Williams, par. 8) and "time-wasting mirror gazing" (Wurster, 1). Write an essay in which you COMPARE AND CONTRAST the writers' tones. Whose do you prefer, and why?

---

# *Andie Wurster on Writing*

As a young writer who grew up with computers, Andie Wurster is in a good position to answer our question, What effect is technology having on writing, or should it have? She provided the following response for *The Bedford Reader*.

We often hear the lament that technology has quickened our pace so much that the art of writing is disappearing. It's true that technological advancements have created a culture in which writing is often banged out, distributed, gobbled up, and then soon forgotten. Emerging bloggers are as admired as seasoned reporters, and an online literary magazine can be up and running in a matter of hours. With immediate gratification, we risk losing the lasting satisfaction of words thoughtfully wrought and thoughtfully read.

But even in this fast-paced, far-reaching, and wonderfully democratic age, the new generation of writers *can* create art. Embracing the present does not have to mean abandoning the standards of thinking critically and writing carefully and honestly. The world is new, but the writer's responsibilities are not.

## For Discussion

1. What does Wurster see as the negative effects of technology on "the art of writing"?
2. How do you use technology in writing? What are its advantages and disadvantages in various writing situations? How does it affect your view of and ability to fulfill "the writer's responsibilities" mentioned by Wurster?

# KATHA POLLITT

KATHA POLLITT is a poet and an essayist. Her poetry has been praised for its "serious charm" and "spare delicacy" in capturing thought and feeling. Her essays have contained strong and convincing commentary on such topics as surrogate motherhood and women in the media. Pollitt was born in New York City in 1949 and earned a BA from Radcliffe College in 1972. Her verse began appearing in the 1970s in such magazines as *The New Yorker* and *The Atlantic Monthly*; it was collected in the book *Antarctic Traveler* (1982), which won the National Book Critics Circle award in 1983. Pollitt has received several other awards as well, including a grant from the National Endowment for the Arts and a Guggenheim fellowship. Her essays and criticism have appeared in *Mother Jones*, the *New York Times*, *The New Yorker*, and *The Nation*, where she currently writes a regular column. Her books include *Reasonable Creatures: Essays on Women and Feminism* (1994), *Subject to Debate: Sense and Dissent on Women, Politics, and Culture* (2001), and *Learning to Drive and Other Life Stories* (2007). Pollitt lives in New York City.

# *What's Wrong with Gay Marriage?*

In her *Nation* column Pollitt regularly takes on controversial topics from a fresh, unabashedly liberal perspective. In this 2003 essay she counters arguments against marriage between homosexuals, including those posed by Charles Colson in the next essay, "Gay 'Marriage': Societal Suicide" (p. 554).

Both Pollitt and Colson refer to the 2003 decision of the Massachusetts Supreme Judicial Court that gays and lesbians cannot be denied the right to marry under the state constitution. The decision still stands, despite considerable political and judicial wrangling over it. In 2007 a constitutional amendment to ban gay marriage failed in the Massachusetts legislature, deferring change for at least another four years. Partly in response to the Massachusetts decision and to other efforts to legitimate gay marriage, opponents have pressed for an amendment to the US Constitution that would define *marriage* as strictly between a man and a woman, and in November 2004 eleven states passed constitutional amendments either defining marriage as heterosexual or banning same-sex marriage.

Will someone please explain to me how permitting gays and lesbians to 1 marry threatens the institution of marriage? Now that the Massachusetts Supreme Court has declared gay marriage a constitutional right, opponents really have to get their arguments in line. The most popular theory, advanced by David Blankenhorn, Jean Bethke Elshtain and other social conservatives, is that under the tulle and orange blossom, marriage is all about procreation. There's some truth to this as a practical matter—couples often live together and tie the knot only when baby's on the way. But whether or not marriage is the best framework for child rearing, having children isn't a marital requirement. As many have pointed out, the law permits marriage to the infertile, the elderly, the impotent and those with no wish to procreate; it allows married couples to use birth control, to get sterilized, to be celibate. There's something creepily authoritarian and insulting about reducing marriage to procreation, as if intimacy mattered less than biological fitness. It's not a view that anyone outside a right-wing think tank, a Catholic marriage tribunal or an ultra-Orthodox rabbi's court is likely to find persuasive.

So scratch procreation. How about: Marriage is the way women domesticate men. This theory, a favorite of right-wing writer George Gilder, has some statistical support—married men are much less likely than singles to kill people, crash the car, take drugs, commit suicide—although it overlooks such husbandly failings as domestic violence, child abuse, infidelity and abandonment. If a man rapes his wife instead of his date, it probably won't show up on a police blotter, but has civilization moved forward? Of course, this view of marriage as a barbarian-adoption program doesn't explain why women should undertake it—as is obvious from the state of the world, they haven't been too successful at it anyway. Nor does it explain why marriage should be restricted to heterosexual couples. The gay men and lesbians who want to marry don't impinge on the male-improvement project one way or the other. Surely not even Gilder believes that a heterosexual pothead with plans for murder and suicide would be reformed by marrying a lesbian?

What about the argument from history? According to this, marriage has been around forever and has stood the test of time. Actually, though, marriage as we understand it—voluntary, monogamous, legally egalitarian, based on love, involving adults only—is a pretty recent phenomenon. For much of human history, polygyny was the rule—read your Old Testament—and in much of Africa and the Muslim world, it still is. Arranged marriages, forced marriages, child marriages, marriages predicated on the subjugation of women—gay marriage is like a fairy-tale romance compared with most chapters of the history of wedlock.

The trouble with these and other arguments against gay marriage is that they overlook how loose, flexible, individualized and easily dissolved the bonds of marriage already are. Virtually any man and woman can marry, no matter how ill assorted or little acquainted. An eighty-year-old can marry an eighteen-year-old; a john can marry a prostitute; two terminally ill patients can marry each other from their hospital beds. You can get married by proxy, like medieval royalty, and not see each other in the flesh for years. Whatever may have been the case in the past, what undergirds marriage in most people's minds today is not some sociobiological theory about reproduction or male socialization. Nor is it the enormous bundle of privileges society awards to married people. It's love, commitment, stability.

Speaking just for myself, I don't like marriage. I prefer the old-fashioned       5
ideal of monogamous free love, not that it worked out particularly well in my case. As a social mechanism, moreover, marriage seems to me a deeply unfair way of distributing social goods like health insurance and retirement checks, things everyone needs. Why should one's marital status determine how much you pay the doctor, or whether you eat cat food in old age, or whether a child gets a government check if a parent dies? It's outrageous that, for example, a working wife who pays Social Security all her life gets no more back from the system than if she had married a male worker earning the same amount and stayed home. Still, as long as marriage is here, how can it be right to deny it to those who want it? In fact, you would think that, given how many heterosexuals are happy to live in sin, social conservatives would welcome maritally minded gays with open arms. Gays already have the baby — they can adopt in many states, and lesbians can give birth in all of them — so why deprive them of the marital bathwater?

At bottom, the objections to gay marriage are based on religious prej-       6
udice: The marriage of man and woman is "sacred," and opening it to same-sexers violates its sacral nature. That is why so many people can live with civil unions but draw the line at marriage — spiritual union. In fact, polls show a striking correlation of religiosity, especially evangelical Protestantism, with opposition to gay marriage and with belief in homosexuality as a choice, the famous "gay lifestyle." For these people gay marriage is wrong because it lets gays and lesbians avoid turning themselves into the straights God wants them to be. As a matter of law, however, marriage is not about Adam and Eve versus Adam and Steve. It's not about what God blesses; it's about what the government permits. People may think *marriage* is a word wholly owned by religion, but actually it's wholly owned by the state. No matter how big your church wedding, you still have to get a marriage license from city hall. And just as divorced people can marry even if the Catholic Church considers it bigamy, and Muslim and Mormon men can marry only one woman even if their holy books tell them they can wed all the girls in Apartment 3G, two men or two women should be able to marry, even if religions oppose it and it makes some heterosexuals, raised in those religions, uncomfortable.

Gay marriage — it's not about sex, it's about separation of church and       7
state.

*For a reading quiz, sources on Katha Pollitt, and annotated links to further readings on same-sex marriage, visit **bedfordstmartins.com/thebedfordreader**.*

## Journal Writing

Write in your journal about your thoughts on marriage — not necessarily who should be allowed to marry or what you see as the ideal marriage, but rather why you think people marry. What do they hope to gain? What do they give up? How is being married different from simply living together as a couple? Base your entry on your observations and experiences. (To take your journal writing further, see "From Journal to Essay" on the next page.)

## Questions on Meaning

1. What three arguments against same-sex marriage does Pollitt summarize in her first three paragraphs, and how does she refute each argument?
2. What, according to Pollitt, is the common understanding of what marriage is? What is Pollitt's own attitude toward marriage?
3. What does Pollitt believe to be the most basic reason why people object to same-sex marriage?
4. What is Pollitt's THESIS, and where does she state it directly?

## Questions on Writing Strategy

1. What is the EFFECT of Pollitt's opening her essay with the question that she does? of her asking several questions in paragraphs 2 and 5?
2. Why, in paragraphs 1 and 2, does Pollitt admit "some truth" to the point that "marriage is all about procreation" and admit "some statistical support" for the point that "[m]arriage is the way women domesticate men"? How do these concessions affect her argument?
3. ANALYZE Pollitt's TRANSITIONS between paragraphs 1 and 2, 2 and 3, 3 and 4, and 5 and 6. How do they work?
4. Why do you think Pollitt spends a paragraph on her own negative views of marriage? Does this paragraph strengthen or weaken Pollitt's argument?
5. **OTHER METHODS**   How does Pollitt use DIVISION or ANALYSIS to structure her argument?

## Questions on Language

1. Some of the language in paragraph 2 is deliberately humorous. Point to EXAMPLES of humor in the paragraph. Why do you think Pollitt chose to use such language at this point in the essay?

2. In the second-to-last sentence of paragraph 5, why does Pollitt use the phrase "live in sin" rather than, say, "live together without being married"? Does she believe such living situations are sinful?
3. What is Pollitt's point in putting some words in paragraph 6 in quotation marks?
4. Notice the PARALLELISM and repetition in the passage beginning "As a matter of law" in the middle of paragraph 6. What is the effect of the writing here?
5. Consult a dictionary if you are unsure of the meaning of any of the following: tulle, procreation, celibate, authoritarian (par. 1); impinge (2); monogamous, egalitarian, polygyny, subjugation (3); proxy, undergirds (4).

## Suggestions for Writing

1. **FROM JOURNAL TO ESSAY**   Using your journal writing as a starting point, write an essay that presents a detailed view of the function of marriage in contemporary society. Refer to specific examples from your experience as appropriate. If you wish, use your observations and reflections to make a point about same-sex marriage.
2. Pollitt writes in paragraph 3 that "marriage as we understand it . . . is a pretty recent phenomenon." Research the history of marriage, beginning with its earliest forms and including marriage in non-Western cultures. Use your research in an essay to amplify or dispute Pollitt's CLAIM.
3. **CRITICAL WRITING**   Write an essay in which you analyze Pollitt's TONE in the essay. How does she present herself and her attitudes toward others (gays, women, men, opponents of gay marriage)? How do you respond to her tone?
4. **CONNECTIONS**   The next essay, by Charles Colson, argues against same-sex marriage. Write an essay in which you evaluate both Pollitt's and Colson's arguments for their EVIDENCE, reasonableness, fairness, response to opposing views, tone, and overall success. Be as OBJECTIVE as possible: Imagine yourself (if you aren't in fact) undecided on the issue of same-sex marriage.

## *Katha Pollitt on Writing*

Katha Pollitt began writing early. "I started writing poetry when I was in about sixth grade," she told Ruth Coniff of *The Progressive* magazine in 1994. "I used to come home from school and go up to my room and sit on my bed and write my poems. And I was writing angry letters to the newspaper. . . . I recently came across a letter I had written when I was twelve years old to the *New York Times*. It was about some complicated legal case involving someone who was accused of being a spy, but I have absolutely no memory of writing this letter or of what this case was. It was actually like something I would write today. I thought, . . . have I been doing this for that long?"

Coniff observed that Pollitt's poetry is not political and asked why. "Well," Pollitt replied, "I was always a two-track writer. I always wrote poetry and prose. . . . I have to say that I see poetry and political writing as different endeavors. What I want in a poem is not an argument, it's not a statement, it has to do with language. I'm looking for a kind of energized, fresh, alive perception. . . . To me it's much more interesting to read that than to read a poem with whose politics I would agree, but that doesn't have a lot of depth of language and imagination in it. . . . What I like about poetry is the verbal concentration and levels of meaning. A poem with only one level of meaning is not a very interesting poem."

## For Discussion

1. What are your earliest memories of writing? When have you written on your own (that is, not for a school assignment)? What moves you to write?
2. Explore Pollitt's ideas about poetry by looking back at Emily Dickinson's "'Hope' is the thing with feathers" (p. 510). How does the poem illustrate "verbal concentration and levels of meaning"?

## CHARLES COLSON

Born in Boston in 1931, CHARLES COLSON graduated from Brown University in 1953 and earned a law degree from George Washington University. He served in the US Marine Corps and was a partner in a law firm before rising to national prominence—and notoriety—as special counsel to President Richard Nixon during the Watergate scandal that caused Nixon to resign. Colson ended up serving seven months in prison for his involvement in the scandal. After his release in 1974, he founded Prison Fellowship Ministries, an outreach group that provides support both for prisoners and for victims of crime. Colson's many books include the autobiographies *Born Again* (1976) and *Life Sentence* (1979) as well as *Kingdoms in Conflict: An Insider's Challenging View of Politics, Power, and the Pulpit* (1987), *Why America Doesn't Work* (1991), *Justice That Restores* (2001), and *God and Government: An Insider's View on the Boundaries Between Faith and Politics* (2007). Colson is a contributing editor of *Christianity Today* magazine and a commentator on the radio program *BreakPoint*, which takes a Christian perspective on current issues. In 1991 he received the Templeton Prize for Progress in Religion and donated the $1 million prize money to Prison Fellowship Ministries.

## *Gay "Marriage": Societal Suicide*

Written with Anne Morse for *Christianity Today* in 2004, this essay presents a case against same-sex marriage and thus counters the preceding essay, Katha Pollitt's "What's Wrong with Gay Marriage?" For a summary of the legal status of gay marriage as of this writing, see the headnote to Pollitt's essay on page 548.

Is America witnessing the end of marriage? The Supreme Judicial Court        1
of Massachusetts has ordered that the state issue marriage licenses to same-sex couples. (By late March, the Massachusetts legislature voted to recognize same-sex civil unions instead.) An unprecedented period of municipal lawlessness has followed, with officials in California, New York, Oregon, and New Mexico gleefully mocking their state constitutions and laws. The result: Thousands of gays rushed to these municipalities to "marry," while much of the news media egged them on.

In the midst of the chaos, President Bush announced his support for a Fed-    2
eral Marriage Amendment, which assures that this contentious issue will be

debated in every quarter of American life. It should be, because the consequences of having "gay marriage" forced on us by judicial (or mayoral) fiat will
fall on all Americans—not just those who embrace it.

As a supporter of the amendment, I'm well aware of the critical argu-          3
ments. As the president noted, "After more than two centuries of American
jurisprudence, and millennia of human experience, a few judges and local
authorities are presuming to change the most fundamental institution of civilization. Their action has created confusion on an issue that requires clarity."

He's right. Here's the clarity: Marriage is the traditional building block          4
of human society, intended both to unite couples and bring children into
the world. Tragically, the sexual revolution led to the decoupling of marriage
and procreation; same-sex "marriage" would pull them completely apart, leading to an explosive increase in family collapse, out-of-wedlock births—and
crime.

How do we know this? In nearly thirty years of prison ministry, I've wit-          5
nessed the disastrous consequences of family breakdown—in the lives of
thousands of delinquents. Dozens of studies now confirm the evidence I've
seen with my own eyes. Boys who grow up without fathers are at least twice as
likely as other boys to end up in prison. Sixty percent of rapists and 72 percent
of adolescent murderers never knew or lived with their fathers. Even in the
toughest inner-city neighborhoods, just 10 percent of kids from intact families
get into trouble, but 90 percent of those from broken families do. Girls raised
without a father in the home are five times more likely to become mothers
while still adolescents. Children from broken homes have more academic and
behavioral problems at school and are nearly twice as likely to drop out of
high school.

Critics agree with this but claim gay "marriage" will not weaken hetero-          6
sexual marriage. The evidence says they're wrong. Stanley Kurtz of the
Hoover Institution writes: "It follows that once marriage is redefined to
accommodate same-sex couples, that change cannot help but lock in and
reinforce the very cultural separation between marriage and parenthood that
makes gay marriage conceivable to begin with." He cites Norway, where
courts imposed same-sex "marriage" in 1993—a time when Norwegians
enjoyed a low out-of-wedlock birth rate. After the imposition of same-sex
"marriage," Norway's out-of-wedlock birth rate shot up as the link between
marriage and childbearing was broken and cohabitation became the norm.

Gay "marriage" supporters argue that most family tragedies occur because          7
of broken *heterosexual* marriages—including those of many Christians. They
are right. We ought to accept our share of the blame, repent, and clean up our
own house. But the fact that we have badly served the institution of marriage
is not a reflection on the institution itself; it is a reflection on us.

As we debate the wisdom of legalizing gay "marriage," we must remember    8
that, like it or not, there is a natural moral order for the family. History and
tradition—and the teachings of Jews, Muslims, and Christians—support the
overwhelming empirical evidence: The family, led by a married mother and
father, is the best available structure for both child rearing and cultural health.
This is why, although some people will always pair off in unorthodox ways,
society as a whole must never legitimize any form of marriage other than that
of one man and one woman, united with the intention of permanency and the
nurturing of children.

Marriage is not a private institution designed solely for the individual    9
gratification of its participants. If we fail to enact a Federal Marriage Amendment, we can expect, not just more family breakdown, but also more criminals
behind bars and more chaos in our streets.

For a reading quiz, sources on Charles Colson, and annotated links to further readings on same-sex marriage, visit **bedfordstmartins.com/thebedfordreader**.

## Journal Writing

In paragraph 5 Colson makes a number of claims about the effect on children of being
raised by single parents, particularly single mothers. Write in your journal about
friends and family members—or the children of friends and family members—who
have been raised by a single parent. (If you were raised by a single parent, consider
yourself as well.) What have been the effects? (To take your journal writing further,
see "From Journal to Essay" on the facing page.)

## Questions on Meaning

1. What is Colson's THESIS? Where does he state it directly?
2. What evidence does Colson present to link same-sex marriage to an increase in
   out-of-wedlock births? to link single-parent households to increases in crime,
   early parenthood, and other problems of young people? How effective do you find
   this evidence?
3. What other argument does Colson make against same-sex marriage?

## Questions on Writing Strategy

1. ANALYZE the reasoning in Colson's argument. What are its CLAIM and ASSUMP-
   TION? What is the DEDUCTIVE SYLLOGISM?

2. Why does Colson use quotation marks around *marriage* when referring to same-sex unions?
3. What is the EFFECT of the question with which Colson opens his essay?
4. What is the purpose of paragraph 7? Why do you think Colson includes it?
5. **OTHER METHODS**   What role does CAUSE AND EFFECT play in the essay?

## Questions on Language

1. How do the words Colson uses in paragraphs 1 and 2 reinforce his opinion of recent moves to legitimate same-sex marriage?
2. Why do you think Colson uses the words *imposed* and *imposition* in the last two sentences of paragraph 6?
3. Consult a dictionary if you are unsure of the meaning of any of the following: unprecedented, gleefully (par. 1); millennia (3); decoupling, procreation (4); intact (5); unorthodox (8).

## Suggestions for Writing

1. **FROM JOURNAL TO ESSAY**   Using your journal entry as a starting point, write an essay in which you explain what you think are the effects on children of being raised in single-parent households. From what you have seen, do such children fit the patterns described by Colson? If your observations do not coincide with Colson's, how do you account for the differences? (You may want to expand your thinking by reading Brenda DePaulo's "The Myth of Doomed Kids," which also addresses the effects on children of being raised in single-parent households. See p. 350.)
2. Research the current status of same-sex marriage in the United States, including both state laws and constitutional amendments and the proposed amendment to the US Constitution. Then write an essay in which you discuss your findings and predict what you believe will be the future of legally recognized unions between same-sex couples.
3. **CRITICAL WRITING**   Write an essay in which you examine the TONE of Colson's essay. How does the author present himself, his issue, and his opponents? How reasonable do you find his language?
4. **CONNECTIONS**   In the previous essay, Katha Pollitt addresses many of the arguments raised by opponents of same-sex marriage, including those of Colson. Draw on Pollitt's and Colson's essays as you see fit to argue your own views on same-sex marriage.

## ADNAN R. KHAN

ADNAN R. KHAN is a writer and photojournalist based in Toronto, Canada. He is a contributing editor of *Maclean's*, a Canadian magazine of business, politics, and world news, and travels extensively on assignment for the magazine. Khan has reported from Turkey, Pakistan, Afghanistan, and Iraq, where he covered the abuses in Abu Ghraib prison and the search for Saddam Hussein.

# *Close Encounters with US Immigration*

As a journalist, Khan frequently crosses national borders. As a Pakistani Canadian and a Muslim, he receives an especially close look from the guards at US borders. In this essay from *Maclean's* in 2002, Khan uses personal experience as evidence in arguing against racial and ethnic profiling—that is, singling out people as suspicious solely because of religious affiliation or physical characteristics such as skin color.

The fairness and necessity of profiling have been widely debated, especially since the terrorist attacks of September 11, 2001. The issue is one of the many that center on the trade-offs between making the United States more secure from terrorism, on the one hand, and preserving the liberties guaranteed by the US Constitution, on the other. For a different view of profiling, see the next essay, "Everything Isn't Racial Profiling," by Linda Chavez (p. 563). The two essays after that, by Mark Krikorian and Edwidge Danticat, address a related facet of security versus liberty: the laws and policies governing who may be admitted to live in the United States.

I'm getting accustomed to people asking me where I was born. Since 9/11, 1 my brown skin's been a sort of blinking light to many curiosity seekers, my sleepy left eye a source of worry for the growing list of morphological profilers roaming the streets of North America. I usually respond offhandedly. "Pakistan," I say, and turn my attention elsewhere as if that should be enough. It never is. So when an American border official posed the same question to me on a recent trip to the United States, I tried to sound as casual as if it were just another inebriated yokel slurring out a barely comprehensible "Where you from?" It didn't work.

I know America has a right to defend its border, but Muslims are increas- 2 ingly under suspicion these days, even comfortably hyphenated Canadian ones like myself. We should resign ourselves, I suppose, to the cold sterility of waiting rooms at American border crossings where towering models of the Statue of Liberty singe the ceilings and the depressingly happy faces of missing children stare out from dingy bulletin boards. It's our lot, I fatalistically think, to be subjected to overzealous immigration officials, grilling us to the point of near panic, ignoring language barriers, goading and prodding until we stumble over our words. That's more than enough to make us look suspicious, besides our place of birth, of course.

For the group of Muslims milling about for hours in the waiting room with me at the Lewiston-Queenston Bridge near Niagara Falls, the experience was enough to make them pull a Rohinton Mistry[1] and refuse, as did the author, to enter the United States. "I'm never going back," one Pakistani father of four fumed after being fingerprinted and photographed. Another Middle Eastern man, after having his wallet unceremoniously emptied onto a counter before he was whisked away and locked in a back room, only to be released an hour later and told to go back to Canada, refused to discuss his ordeal with me. Both men were Canadian citizens and neither could understand why they were singled out. A few other visible minorities came in and left within an hour, but for Muslims, it would not be so simple.

By the time my interrogation began, I'd lost all hope of making it into the States before nightfall. The stock questions were asked by a droopy-eyed, uniformed immigration official who finally reached the inevitable one: "What were you doing in Afghanistan?" I explained that I'm a freelance photojournalist and I was working for *Maclean's* at the time. I pointed out the "journalist" credentials clearly marked on the Afghan visa in my passport, which elicited an ambiguous "Hmmm" from my interlocutor. Every answer was recorded on a sheet of foolscap. I asked why and he responded cryptically, "What's real is unreal and what's unreal is real."

That could be the slogan for contemporary America—a fraying of reality in the post–9/11 world. And when my car was searched by two white-gloved officials, I felt as if I'd slipped into a David Lynch[2] movie. They dissected my defenseless little Honda and its contents with a zeal that seemed utterly over the top. My notebook and personal organizer were confiscated, and I worried whether I had any cheesy love poetry scribbled into my notes (how embarrassing!) or if my friends' phone numbers would be copied and filed away for future reference.

[1] Fiction writer born in India (1952) and living in Canada. — EDS.
[2] American filmmaker (born 1946), known for creating vivid characters and surreal situations. — EDS.

When the immigration official ushered me into a back room, drably fur-     6
nished with a rectangular table and four chairs, my anxiety level skyrocketed.
Two casually dressed men entered the room and introduced themselves as
members of the Joint Terrorism Task Force.

Now I was scared.     7

They pulled the chairs close together, crowding one corner of the table     8
and asked me to sit down between them. The border patrol agent and his New
York State trooper counterpart rifled through a set of prepared questions.
Their knowledge of Pakistani culture and geography seemed minimal, but I
thought this might be a ploy. (Was I becoming paranoid?) At one point, the
border patrol agent casually asked if I spoke Pakistani, and I was tempted to
respond that while my Pakistani was a bit rough, I could speak Canadian flaw-
lessly. But I refrained. Why tempt fate, I thought, especially when fate's
accomplices had me cornered in a back office of a foreign country.

During the three-hour ordeal, I'd been made to feel like an unwanted out-     9
sider, as if I were guilty of some heinous crime and now it was my responsibility to prove my innocence. The alienation I felt was relatively minor for
someone with few ties to America, but for the thousands of Canadian Muslims
who have loved ones living south of the border, America's rejection of their
kind wounds deeply.

When it was all over, I couldn't help but laugh as I drove back over the     10
bridge, picturing my personal profile wasting kilobytes in an FBI database. I'd
been grilled by three levels of American security and for what? Had America's
national interest really been served?

Back at the Canadian border, a uniformed official inquired about how     11
long I'd stayed in the United States. Just a few hours, I responded, too
ashamed to go into the details.

"And the value of goods you're bringing over?" he asked.     12

"Zero," I replied.     13

"Okay, go home."     14

Gladly.     15

---

*For a reading quiz and annotated links to further readings on the use of profiling to*
*guard against terrorism, visit **bedfordstmartins.com/thebedfordreader**.*

## Journal Writing

Write about a time when you were regarded suspiciously or made to feel unwelcome for reasons you felt were unjustified. How did you respond? How did you feel afterward? (To take your journal writing further, see "From Journal to Essay" below.)

## Questions on Meaning

1. What does Khan say results from the actions of "overzealous immigration officials" (par. 2) who single out people like himself for interrogation? Why does he see this practice as problematic?
2. What does Khan think made him especially suspicious to the immigration officials? Why weren't these suspicions justified?
3. What is Khan's point in paragraph 9? in paragraph 10?
4. What is Khan's THESIS? What seems to be his PURPOSE?

## Questions on Writing Strategy

1. What is the EFFECT of the opening of paragraph 2?
2. What does Khan accomplish in paragraph 3? What does this paragraph contribute to his central point?
3. Why do you think Khan mentions the contents of his notebook and personal organizer (par. 5)?
4. What is the effect of the single sentence in paragraph 7? How would the effect change if Khan had attached this sentence to the preceding paragraph?
5. **OTHER METHODS** This argument is unusual in that it is developed almost entirely by NARRATION. How does Khan's story serve his argumentative purpose?

## Questions on Language

1. ANALYZE the language Khan uses to describe the "waiting rooms at American border crossings" (par. 2).
2. How would you characterize Khan's TONE in this essay? Is it appropriate for his argument? Why, or why not?
3. Consult a dictionary if you are unsure of the meaning of any of the following: morphological, inebriated (par. 1); singe, fatalistically (2); unceremoniously (3); credentials, elicited, ambiguous, foolscap (4); heinous (9).

## Suggestions for Writing

1. **FROM JOURNAL TO ESSAY** Based on your journal entry, write an essay in which you relate your experience of being regarded suspiciously or made to feel unwelcome. Follow Khan's model in telling your story as evidence in an argument against such treatment.

2. Draft an essay in which you respond directly to Khan, explaining what you think about his and other Canadian Muslims' experiences at the US border. If you wish, write your essay in the form of a letter to Khan.

3. How common is Khan's experience, not just at Canadian borders but at other points of entry to the United States, including airports? Are people with an ethnic and/or physical resemblance to the September 11 terrorists generally stopped? Are many such people turned away? What is current US policy on racial or ethnic profiling? Research the answers to these questions, and write an argument based on your findings.

4. **CRITICAL WRITING**   Write an essay in which you analyze Khan's ETHICAL APPEAL — the sense of himself presented in his essay. Base your analysis on the language Khan uses as well as the way he tells his story.

5. **CONNECTIONS**   In the following essay Linda Chavez takes a different view of profiling. Write an essay in which you COMPARE AND CONTRAST Khan's and Chavez's arguments. Where do they agree? Where do they disagree? In your view, whose case is stronger? Why?

# LINDA CHAVEZ

An outspoken voice on issues of civil rights and affirmative action, LINDA CHAVEZ was born in 1947 in Albuquerque, New Mexico, to a Spanish American family long established in the Southwest. She graduated from the University of Colorado (BA, 1970) and did graduate work at the University of California, Los Angeles, and at the University of Maryland. She has held a number of government positions, including director of the White House Office of Public Liaison under President Ronald Reagan and chair of the National Commission on Migrant Education under the first President George Bush. She has published three books: *Out of the Barrio: Toward a New Politics of Hispanic Assimilation* (1991), which argues against affirmative action and bilingual education; *An Unlikely Conservative: The Transformation of a Renegade Democrat (Or How I Became the Most Hated Hispanic in America)* (2002); and *Betrayal: How Union Bosses Shake Down Their Members and Corrupt American Politics* (with Daniel Gray, 2004). Chavez currently chairs the Center for Equal Opportunity, a public-policy research organization. She also writes a syndicated newspaper column, hosts a syndicated radio show, and is a political analyst for Fox News.

# *Everything Isn't Racial Profiling*

In this piece written in 2002 for *townhall.com,* a conservative news and information Web site, Chavez draws in part on her own experiences as a Latina to condemn racial and ethnic profiling in general but to condone its use as a tool against terrorism. For Chavez, the need for security in this case outweighs the need for liberty, a view that opposes her to Adnan R. Khan in the previous essay, "Close Encounters with US Immigration." A related issue of security versus liberty, restrictions on immigrants who seek to live in the United States, is the subject of the next two essays, by Mark Krikorian and Edwidge Danticat.

Racial profiling is an ugly business—and I have been on record opposing it   1
for years. But I'm not opposed to allowing—no, requiring—airlines to pay closer attention to passengers who fit a terrorist profile, which includes national origin. The problem is distinguishing between what is permissible, indeed prudent, behavior and what is merely bigotry. As the Christmas day incident involving an Arab American Secret Service agent who was denied passage on American Airlines makes clear, it's not always easy to tell the difference.

Racial profiling entails picking someone out for special scrutiny simply be-    2
cause of his race. It happens when highway patrolmen pull over blacks who've
committed no traffic violations for spot checks but ignore other drivers who
share similar characteristics, say, out-of-state plates or expensive cars. It happens when security guards at a mall tail black customers in stores or insist on
inspecting only their bags, ignoring whites. The underlying presumption in
these cases is that blacks are more likely to be involved in criminal acts
because of the color of their skin.

This kind of racial profiling is both morally wrong and ineffective. But    3
there are times when it makes sense to include race or national origin in a
larger criminal profile, particularly if you're dealing with a crime that has
already been committed or is ongoing and the participants all come from a
single ethnic or racial group.

It would make no sense if witnesses identified a six-foot-tall, blond male    4
fleeing a homicide but police stopped females, short men, or blacks or Latinos
for questioning. Likewise, if you stopped every tall, blond man, a lot of innocent people would be inconvenienced, if only temporarily. Which brings us to
the case of the Arab American Secret Service agent.

Walid Shater was allowed initially to board an American Airlines plane    5
in Baltimore headed for Texas, carrying a loaded gun, but then was pulled off
the plane, along with a handful of other passengers, for questioning. In the
intervening ninety minutes, Shater's lawyers allege that he was mistreated and
denied the right to fly because he was an Arab American, while the pilot
claims that the agent became loud and abusive, leading him to keep Shater off
the flight.

I can fully sympathize with the agent's anger—but I don't think the air-    6
line acted improperly. I've had encounters similar to Shater's, largely because
of my appearance. When I used to travel frequently in Europe from the mid-
'80s to the mid-'90s, I was routinely questioned more than other passengers, I
suspect because I look vaguely Middle Eastern—or as one airline agent put it,
"Your passport's American, but you don't look American."

On a trip from Israel in 1985, where I was an official government guest of    7
the Israelis, security agents at Tel Aviv Airport questioned me for almost an
hour. "But you can't keep me from leaving Israel," I protested. "No, but we can
keep you from doing so on an airplane," the guard responded. They finally let
me go when another passenger, who recognized me from the newspapers,
vouched for me.

On another flight, this time from Switzerland, I was asked to deboard the    8
plane after the passengers were in their seats and was questioned about items
in my checked luggage. It was humiliating to be called off the plane and to

have the passengers told the flight would be delayed because of concerns about one of the passenger's bags.

But I didn't rush to file a discrimination complaint. I didn't like being singled out, but I understood why I was being subjected to more scrutiny. At the time I was hassled, Middle Eastern terrorism was very prevalent in Europe, and female terrorists were operating as well as men, usually on stolen or phony passports. It wasn't unreasonable for airlines to look at me a little more closely than other passengers given these facts.     9

In Shater's case, nineteen Arab terrorists killed more than three thousand Americans on September 11, and several of the hijackers possessed stolen identification cards and pilots' uniforms. It wasn't unreasonable for the American Airlines pilot to be extra cautious with Shater under the circumstances, despite his official ID. As a law enforcement officer himself, Shater might have cut these guys a little more slack.     10

Sure it's unpleasant to be a suspect when you're innocent. But it's worse to overlook terrorists because we ignored their pertinent characteristics. I sometimes felt annoyed when I was singled out, but I also felt safer because the airlines were doing their job.     11

*For a reading quiz, sources on Linda Chavez, and annotated links to further readings on the use of profiling to guard against terrorism, visit **bedfordstmartins.com /thebedfordreader**.*

---

## Journal Writing

How likely are you to be suspicious of another person based on his or her appearance? Can you think of instances when people's looks (skin color, manner of dress, body type, or whatever) led you to feel you had something to fear from them — or might lead you to feel that way? In your journal, explore your thoughts about such "profiling." (To take your journal writing further, see "From Journal to Essay" on the next page.)

## Questions on Meaning

1. What incident apparently prompted Chavez's essay?
2. How does Chavez distinguish between racial profiling that is "morally wrong and ineffective" and profiling that "include[s] race or national origin in a larger criminal profile" (par. 3)?

3. Why does Chavez say that denying air passage to Walid Shater was reasonable?
4. What is Chavez's THESIS?

## Questions on Writing Strategy

1. What is Chavez's point in describing the search for the hypothetical "six-foot-tall, blond male" in paragraph 4?
2. Why does Chavez relate ANECDOTES about herself in paragraphs 7 and 8?
3. What is the EFFECT of Chavez's final sentence?
4. **OTHER METHODS**   Where does Chavez make prominent use of COMPARISON AND CONTRAST and DEFINITION? Why does she rely on these methods?

## Questions on Language

1. What modifiers does Chavez use to describe the kinds of racial profiling that she finds unacceptable and acceptable? How do these modifiers further her argument?
2. How would you describe Chavez's TONE in the essay?
3. Consult a dictionary if you are unsure of the meaning of any of the following: prudent (par. 1); scrutiny, presumption (2); prevalent (9).

## Suggestions for Writing

1. **FROM JOURNAL TO ESSAY**   Based on your journal entry, write an essay exploring the features of other people's appearance that do or might arouse your suspicions. What justifies your suspicions? What might be prejudice on your part?
2. How can airlines make their planes secure without infringing on the liberty of passengers who fit a terrorist profile? Or should all such passengers be singled out for scrutiny? Write an essay answering these questions, addressing an AUDIENCE that includes both people who might be profiled as potential terrorists and people who advocate broad profiling.
3. Research the case of Walid Shater and several other cases since September 11, 2001, in which Arab Americans have been removed from airplanes, detained, or otherwise profiled as terrorists and then have been cleared of suspicion. Write an essay in which you use these examples to argue for or against the right of those profiled to sue the authorities who targeted them.
4. **CRITICAL WRITING**   Write an essay examining the organization of Chavez's essay. What does Chavez accomplish in each paragraph? How effectively does she use TRANSITIONS to move from paragraph to paragraph?
5. **CONNECTIONS**   In paragraph 6 Chavez reports once being told by an airline agent, "Your passport's American, but you don't look American." Adnan R. Khan may not have heard "you don't look American" at the US border, but the experience he reports in "Close Encounters with US Immigration" (p. 558) conveyed that message. What does it mean to "look American" in a country as diverse as the United States? In an essay, define or dispute this phrase. Should an American look be used to determine who enters the United States without difficulty and who doesn't? Why, or why not?

# MARK KRIKORIAN

MARK KRIKORIAN is executive director of the Center for Immigration Studies, a research organization that advocates stricter US immigration policy and enforcement. He was born in 1961 in New Haven, Connecticut, received a BA in 1982 from Georgetown University, and received an MA in 1984 from the Fletcher School of Law and Diplomacy at Tufts University. He has served as an editor at the *Winchester* (Virginia) *Star* and the monthly newsletter of the Federation for Immigration Reform. In addition to his work at the Center for Immigration Studies, Krikorian also writes for the *National Review Online*.

## *Safety Through Immigration Control*

In this essay first published in the *Providence Journal* in 2004, Krikorian argues that the relatively open borders of the United States are an invitation to terrorists for whom "the brass ring . . . is mass killings of civilians on American soil." The only way to stop them, Krikorian insists, is to restrict immigration tightly and to enforce the rules.

    For another view of the effects of strict immigration policies, see the next essay, Edwidge Danticat's "Not Your Homeland."

Supporters of high immigration have tried to de-link immigration control from security. A week after the September 11, 2001, hijackings, the head of the American Immigration Lawyers Association said, "I don't think [9/11] can be attributed to the failure of our immigration laws." Even the 9/11 Commission[1]—which in January held hearings on the immigration failures that had contributed to the attacks—is devoting inordinate attention, as we saw the other week, to peripheral issues, such as who sent what memo to whom.

While ordinary people don't need hearings to know there's a link between immigration and security, a fuller understanding of the issue is necessary if we are to fix what needs to be fixed and reduce the likelihood of future attacks.

---

[1] The National Commission on Terrorist Attacks upon the United States was created in 2002 by Congress and the President to investigate the circumstances of the attacks on September 11, 2001.—EDS.

Deputy Defense Secretary Paul Wolfowitz said in October 2002:          3

> Sixty years ago, when we said, "home front," we were referring to citizens
> back home, doing their part to support the war front.[2] Since last September,
> however, the home front has become a battlefront, every bit as real as any
> we've known before.

The reality of the home front isn't confined to the threat posed by Islamic terrorism. No enemy, whatever his ideology, has any hope of defeating America's
armies in the field, and must therefore resort to what scholars call "asymmetric" or "fourth-generation" warfare: terrorism and related tactics, which we
saw before 9/11 in the Mideast and East Africa, and which we are now seeing
in Iraq. But the brass ring of such a strategy is mass killings of civilians on
American soil.

Our objective on the home front is different from that faced by the mili-      4
tary, because the goal is defensive: to block and disrupt the enemy's ability to
carry out attacks on our territory. This will then allow offensive forces, if
needed, to find, pin down and kill the enemy overseas. So the burden of
homeland defense is not borne by our armed forces but by agencies seen as
civilian entities—mainly, the Department of Homeland Security. And of the
DHS's many responsibilities, immigration control is central. The reason is elementary: No matter the weapon or delivery system—hijacked airliners, ship-
ping containers, suitcase nukes, anthrax spores—terrorists are needed to carry
out the attacks. And those terrorists have to enter and operate in the United
States. In a very real sense, the primary weapons of our enemies are not the
inanimate objects at all but, rather, the terrorists themselves, especially in the
case of suicide attackers.

Thus, keeping the terrorists out, or apprehending them after they get in,      5
is indispensable to victory. In the words of the administration's July 2002
"National Strategy for Homeland Security":

> Our great power leaves these enemies with few conventional options for
> doing us harm. One such option is to take advantage of our freedom and
> openness by secretly inserting terrorists into our country to attack our home-
> land. Homeland security seeks to deny this avenue of attack to our enemies
> and thus to provide a secure foundation for America's global engagement.

Our enemies have repeatedly exercised this option of inserting terrorists      6
by exploiting weaknesses in our immigration system. A Center for Immigration Studies analysis found that nearly every element of the immigration sys-

---

[2] Wolfowitz refers to World War II.—EDS.

tem has been penetrated by the enemy. Of the forty-eight al-Qaida[3] operatives who have committed terrorist acts here since 1993 (including the 9/11 hijackers), a third were here on various temporary visas, another third were legal residents or naturalized citizens, a fourth were illegal aliens, and the rest had pending asylum applications. Nearly half of the total had, at some point or another, violated immigration laws.

An immigration system designed for homeland security, therefore, needs    7
to apply to all stages in the process: issuing visas overseas, screening people at the borders and airports, and enforcing the rules inside the country. Nor can we focus all our efforts on Mideasterners and ignore people from elsewhere; that may make sense in the short term — as triage, if you will — but in the longer term we need comprehensive improvements, because al-Qaida is adapting. The FBI has warned local law enforcement that al-Qaida is already exploring the use of Chechen terrorists,[4] people with Russian passports who won't draw our attention if we're focusing mainly on Saudis and Egyptians.

None of this is to say that there are no other weapons against domestic    8
terrorist attacks. We certainly need more effective international coordination, improved intelligence gathering and distribution, and special military operations. But in the end, the lack of effective immigration control leaves us naked in the face of the enemy.

---

*For a reading quiz, sources on Mark Krikorian, and annotated links to further readings on immigration policies and their effects, visit **bedfordstmartins.com /thebedfordreader**.*

---

## Journal Writing

Throughout this essay, Krikorian refers to "our enemies" and "the enemy." What does the word *enemy* mean to you? In your journal, write about whom you consider to be your personal enemies and the enemies of the United States or another country with

---

[3] Al-Qaida (also spelled al-Qaeda or al-Qa'ida) is the international terrorist organization responsible for the 9/11 attacks as well as many other acts of violence around the world. — EDS.
[4] Chechnya is a republic of Russia. Its battles for independence from Russia have included acts of terrorism. — EDS.

which you identify. (To take your journal writing further, see "From Journal to Essay" below.)

## Questions on Meaning

1. How would you summarize Krikorian's THESIS? Where does he state it?
2. In what ways is Krikorian critical of the 9/11 Commission?
3. What is Krikorian's point in paragraph 4? What are the objectives of homeland defense?
4. How does Krikorian say the immigration system should protect homeland security?

## Questions on Writing Strategy

1. Why might Krikorian have chosen to open his essay as he does? What is the EFFECT of his first two paragraphs?
2. Identify the primary APPEALS Krikorian makes in the essay. Do you find them effective?
3. What kinds of EVIDENCE does Krikorian offer to support his claim? Is his evidence convincing? Why, or why not?
4. What is notable about Krikorian's concluding paragraph?

## Questions on Language

1. In paragraph 3 Krikorian writes that "the brass ring of [terrorism] is mass killings of civilians on American soil." What does he mean by "brass ring"? What is the source of this term?
2. In paragraph 6 Krikorian uses the term *triage* to refer to immigration control efforts that may be useful in the short term. What is the meaning of *triage*, and how is he using the word here?
3. Do some research about "asymmetric" and "fourth-generation" warfare (par. 3). To what do these terms refer specifically?
4. If you are unfamiliar with the following words, check a dictionary for their meanings: peripheral (par. 1); ideology (3); anthrax, inanimate (4); visas, naturalized citizens, pending, asylum (6).

## Suggestions for Writing

1. **FROM JOURNAL TO ESSAY**   Using your journal entry as a starting point, write an essay in which you offer a multifaceted DEFINITION of the word *enemy*. How do you use the term? How do you regard other people's use of it? What are some of the benefits and drawbacks of defining others as enemies? Have your thoughts about the concept of "the enemy" evolved over time?
2. Write an essay in which you present your view on an aspect of US immigration policy or practice that you have strong opinions about—for example, amnesty for illegal immigrants, treatment of asylum seekers, or restrictions on immigration since 9/11. Before beginning your draft, do some research to support

your position and also to explore opposing views so that you answer them squarely and fairly.

3. **CRITICAL WRITING**    How does Krikorian develop the subject of immigration control? What specific examples does he give? Based on his essay, how well do you understand the policies and laws of immigration control of the Department of Homeland Security? What questions would you like to ask Krikorian, if any, and why?

4. **CONNECTIONS**    In the next essay Edwidge Danticat writes about what she sees as the unwarranted detention and mistreatment of Haitians seeking asylum in the United States. Write an essay in which you COMPARE AND CONTRAST the ways Krikorian and Danticat present their cases. Which argument do you find more effective? Why?

# EDWIDGE DANTICAT

EDWIDGE DANTICAT was born in Port-au-Prince, Haiti, in 1969. When she was a child, her parents emigrated to New York to find work, leaving her to be raised by an aunt and uncle until she too emigrated at the age of twelve. She went to school in Brooklyn, New York, and then enrolled in Barnard College, intending to study nursing. However, a love of reading and writing inspired her to change her major to French literature. After graduation in 1990, Danticat pursued an MFA at Brown University (1993). Her first novel, which she wrote as her thesis at Brown, was *Breath, Eyes, Memory* (1994). *Krik Krak* (1995), a collection of short stories, was a finalist for the National Book Award. Danticat's third novel, *The Dew Breaker* (2004), follows the story of a former Haitian prison guard whose job involved haunting acts of torture.

# *Not Your Homeland*

Danticat's birth country, Haiti, is a Caribbean island nation of about 6.5 million people. The poorest country in the Americas, Haiti has experienced social and political upheaval since the 1980s. In 2004 violent conflicts between government forces and rebel groups prompted intervention by the United States and the United Nations, but the violence continues and thousands of civilians have been killed. Fearing for their lives, many Haitians have sought asylum in the United States, some entering legally, many not. In this 2005 essay from *The Nation*, Danticat reports on the conditions she observed in US detention centers, where thousands of would-be immigrants have been held as possible security threats. Surely, she argues, US security does not demand the treatment suffered by the detainees.

From the outside, it looks like any other South Florida hotel. There is a 1 pool, green grass and tall palms bordering the parking lot. An ordinary guest may not even be aware that his or her stopover for the night is indeed a prison, a holding facility for women and children who have fled their countries, in haste, in desperation, hoping for a better life.

A year and four months after September 11, 2001, I visited, along with 2 some friends, a Comfort Suites hotel in Miami where several Haitian women and children were jailed. One of the people we met there was a three-year-old girl who had been asking for a single thing for weeks. The little girl wanted to sit under one of those tall palm trees in the hotel courtyard, feel the sunshine on her face and touch the green grass with her feet. Tearfully, her mother said she could not grant her that. Nor could she even dream of it for herself.

We also met a little boy who was wearing one of the gray adult-size 3 T-shirts all the detainees in the hotel wore. There was no uniform small enough for him, so the little boy didn't have pants. We met a pretty young woman who told us that she'd lost a lot of weight, not only because of the sorrow that plagued her constrained life—a life in which she was forbidden even to stand in the hotel hallway—but also because she couldn't bring herself to eat. The food she was fed would neither "stay up nor down," she said. Either she vomited it or it gave her diarrhea.

The women in that hotel also told us how six of them must live together 4 in one room, how some of them were forced to sleep on the floor when there wasn't enough space on the beds or couches. They told us how they missed their own clothes and seeing their children play in the sun, how they had perhaps been wrong about America. Maybe it no longer had any room for them. Maybe it had mistaken them for criminals or terrorists.

Once we were quickly ushered out of the hotel, my mind returned to the 5 Krome Detention Center in Miami, which we had visited earlier that day. Even before setting foot on its premises, Krome had always seemed like a strange myth to me, a cross between Alcatraz and hell. I'd imagined it as something like the Brooklyn Navy Yard detention center, where my parents had taken me on Sunday afternoons in the early 1980s, when I was a teenager in New York, to visit with Haitian asylum seekers we did not know but feared we might, people who, as my father used to say, "could have very well been us."

Krome's silent despair became tangible when a group of Haitian men in 6 identical dark-blue uniforms walked into a barbed wire courtyard to address our delegation that morning. "My name is . . . ," they began. "I came on the July boat." Or, "I came on the December boat." Or the most famous one of all, the October 29, 2002, boat, the landing of which was broadcast live on CNN and other national television outlets.

As if suddenly empowered by this brief opportunity to break their silence, 7 the men spoke in clear, loud voices, some inventing parables to explain their circumstances. One man told the story of a mad dog that forced a person to seek shelter at a neighbor's house. "If mad dogs are chasing you, shouldn't your neighbor shelter you?" he asked.

One man asked us to tell the world that the detainees were sometimes 8 beaten. He told us of a friend who had his back broken by a guard and was deported before he could get medical attention. They said that the rooms they slept in were so cold that they shivered all night long. They spoke of arbitrary curfews, how they were woken up at 6 AM and forced to go back to those cold rooms by 6 PM.

One man said, "If I had a bullet, I'd have shot myself already. I'm not a    9
criminal. I'm not used to prison."

I met an older man who came from Bel Air, the same area in Port-au-    10
Prince where I spent the first twelve years of my life. His eyes were red. He
couldn't stop crying. His mother had died the week before, he said, and he was
heartbroken that he couldn't attend her funeral.

Two months after that visit, then Attorney General John Ashcroft vetoed    11
an immigration judge's decision to release an eighteen-year-old Haitian boy
named David Joseph, whom we'd met at Krome that day. Ashcroft argued that
Joseph had to remain in custody because he posed a threat to national security. He further stated that Haiti harbors Pakistani and Palestinian terrorists,
but the government could offer no proof for this charge in response to a Freedom of Information Act request from the Florida Immigration Advocacy
Center. The truth was that, like many of the other refugees we had seen that
day, David Joseph had fled his home not because he wanted to harm the
United States but because it was impossible for him to live in his own country. Scorned by their neighbors for their parents' political views, he and his
brother had been stoned and burned, their father severely beaten. Had he not
fled, he would have been killed.

In November 2004 David Joseph was deported after two years in deten-    12
tion, even though the area in Haiti where he was from had recently been dev-
astated by a season of tropical storms that resulted in three thousand deaths
and left a quarter-million people homeless. He also had no family to return to,
since no one knew, least of all him, whether any of his relatives were alive
or dead.

In the fall of 2004 I too suffered a devastating loss in a way I had never    13
expected or imagined.

On Sunday, October 24, 2004, United Nations troops and Haitian police    14
forces launched an antigang operation in Bel Air, where my eighty-one-year-
old uncle, Joseph Danticat, had been living for fifty years. During the operation the UN "peacekeepers," accompanied by the Haitian police, used the
roof of my uncle's three-story house, school and church compound to fire at
the gangs. When the forces left Bel Air the gang members came to my uncle's
home, told him that fifteen of their friends had been killed and said he had to
pay for the burials or die. Knowing he'd never be able to produce the kind of
money they were seeking, my uncle asked for a few minutes to make a phone
call, grabbed some important papers and fled to a nearby house.

My uncle hid under a neighbor's bed for three days as the gang members    15
searched for him. When they were not able to find him, they ransacked his
home and church and set his office on fire. A few days later a family member
helped him escape the neighborhood, and on October 29, 2004, he took a

plane to Miami, just as he had done many times for more than thirty years. He had a valid multiple-entry visa. But when immigration officials at Miami International Airport asked how long he would be staying in the United States, he explained that he would be killed if he returned to Haiti and that he wanted "temporary" asylum. He was immediately arrested and taken to Krome, where medicine he had brought with him from Haiti for an inflamed prostate and high blood pressure was taken away from him. On November 3, 2004, while still in the custody of the Krome Detention Center, and thus the Department of Homeland Security, he died at a nearby hospital.

As my uncle lay dying in a hospital bed in a ward reserved for hardened    16 criminals, my repeated requests to visit him were denied by Department of Homeland Security and Krome officials for what I was told were "security reasons." In other words, my uncle was treated like a criminal when his only offense was thinking that he could find shelter in the United States.

Before this tragedy struck our family, I had not quite heeded my father's    17 warning and never truly believed that the asylum seekers we visited so often could really include one so close to us. However, nothing proves more than what happened to my uncle, an elderly man of the cloth, that we all live with a certain level of risk in post–9/11 America. Still, those of us who are refugees and exiles must live with the double menace of being both possible victims and suspects, sometimes with fatal consequences. Will America ever learn again how to protect itself without sacrificing a great many innocent lives? So that my uncle did not die in vain, I truly hope so.

---

*For a reading quiz, sources on Edwidge Danticat, and annotated links to further readings on immigration policies and their effects, visit **bedfordstmartins.com /thebedfordreader**.*

---

## Journal Writing

Write about a time when you were punished unjustifiably, when you were innocent of what you were punished for. What were the circumstances, and what was the punishment? How did the situation make you feel about whoever punished you? about yourself? about others involved, such as anyone who may have gotten you into trouble to begin with? (To take your journal writing further, see "From Journal to Essay" on the following page.)

# Questions on Meaning

1. What does Danticat point to as the US government's justification for detaining and deporting Haitian asylum seekers? What does she think of this justification? How do you know?
2. What, according to Danticat, leads most Haitians who seek asylum in the United States to do so?
3. Where in the essay does Danticat state her THESIS? How would you restate it?
4. How do you suppose Danticat hoped readers would respond to this essay? What is her PURPOSE? What is your response, and why?

# Questions on Writing Strategy

1. How is Danticat's essay organized? What is the effect of this organization?
2. What assumptions does Danticat make about her AUDIENCE's familiarity with the situation in Haiti and the plight of Haitian refugees in the United States?
3. How does Danticat try to elicit sympathy for the people she writes about? What kinds of details does she offer about them? How would you describe the primary APPEAL of her argument?
4. Where in the essay does Danticat write about herself? What is the point of her doing so?
5. **OTHER METHODS**   Danticat uses NARRATION in paragraphs 14–15, framing the story with two dates. Why is the story important? What does the date frame contribute to it?

# Questions on Language

1. In paragraph 7 Danticat quotes a detainee's parable for his situation. What is a *parable*? What does this parable mean?
2. Danticat says that she imagined the Krome Detention Center as "a cross between Alcatraz and hell" (par. 5). What does she mean?
3. In paragraph 14 Danticat puts the word *peacekeepers* in quotation marks. Why?
4. If you are unfamiliar with any of the following words, check a dictionary for their meanings: constrained (par. 3); asylum (5); tangible (6); arbitrary (8); devastating (13); ransacked (15).

# Suggestions for Writing

1. **FROM JOURNAL TO ESSAY**   Based on your journal entry, write an essay in which you narrate your experience (or, perhaps, experiences) with being punished unjustifiably. As you plan and draft your essay, try to draw a larger point about the results of unjustifiable punishment in general.
2. In her final paragraph Danticat writes that "we all live with a certain level of risk in post–9/11 America." How has the continued threat of terrorist attacks affected your life and the lives of others you know? How has this threat affected the country more generally? Do you and other people feel safer now than in the months

immediately following 9/11? Why, or why not? Write an essay in which you detail your view of the aftereffects of 9/11.

3. Research how US immigration officials determine which would-be immigrants to the United States will be denied entrance, based on country of origin and other factors. In an essay, explain these policies and evaluate their fairness as you see it.

4. **CRITICAL WRITING**   Evaluate Danticat's TONE in this essay. What contributes to this tone, and to what extent does it serve her purpose in writing? How might a different tone have changed your response to the essay?

5. **CONNECTIONS**   In the preceding essay, Mark Krikorian defends the immigration policies of the Department of Homeland Security, writing that "the lack of effective immigration control leaves us naked in the face of the enemy." Write an essay in which you consider how Danticat might respond to Krikorian and how Krikorian might respond to Danticat. Could they come to any common ground, or are their viewpoints too far opposed to reach any sort of agreement?

---

## *Edwidge Danticat on Writing*

In an interview upon the publication of her novel *Breath, Eyes, Memory,* Edwidge Danticat explained why she chose to write in English when she first arrived in the United States from Haiti.

I came to the United States at an interesting time in my life, at twelve years old, on the cusp of adolescence. I think if we had moved to Spain, I probably would have written in Spanish. My primary language was Haitian Creole, which at the time that I was in school in Haiti was not taught in a consistent written form. My instruction was done in French, which I only spoke in school and not at home. When I came here I was completely between languages. It's not unusual for me to run into young people, for example, who have been here for a year and stutter through both their primary language and English because the new language is settling into them in a very obvious way. I came to English at a time when I was not adept enough at French to write creatively in French and did not know how to write in Creole because it had not been taught to me in school, so my writing in English was as much an act of personal translation as it was an act of creative collaboration with the new place I was in. My writing in English is a consequence of my migration, in the same way that immigrant children speaking to each other in English is a consequence of their migration.

## For Discussion

1. How would using the language of her new country be "an act of creative collaboration" for a recent immigrant?
2. If you have immigrated to the United States, to what extent does Danticat's
   experience ring true to you? Did you also speak English to other immigrants as a
   way of adapting to your new culture?

# ADDITIONAL WRITING TOPICS

## *Argument and Persuasion*

1. Write a persuasive essay in which you express a deeply felt opinion. In it, address a particular person or audience. For instance, you might direct your essay

   To a friend unwilling to attend a ballet performance (or a wrestling match) with you on the grounds that such an event is a waste of time
   To a teacher who asserts that more term papers, and longer ones, are necessary for students to master academic writing
   To a developer who plans to tear down a historic house
   To someone who sees no purpose in studying a foreign language
   To a high-school class whose members don't want to go to college
   To an older generation skeptical of the value of current popular music
   To an atheist who asserts that religion just distracts us from the here and now
   To the members of a library board who want to ban a book you love

2. Write a letter to your campus newspaper or a city newspaper in which you argue for or against a certain cause or view. You may wish to object to a particular feature or editorial in the paper. Send your letter and see if it is published.

3. Write a short letter to your congressional or state representative, arguing in favor of (or against) the passage of some pending legislation. See a news magazine or a newspaper for a worthwhile bill to write about. Or else write in favor of some continuing cause: for instance, requiring (or not requiring) cars to reduce exhaust emissions, reducing (or increasing) military spending, providing (or reducing) aid to the arts, expanding (or reducing) government loans to college students.

4. Write an essay arguing that something you believe strongly about should be changed, removed, abolished, enforced, repeated, revised, reinstated, or reconsidered. Be sure to propose some plan for carrying out whatever suggestions you make. Possible topics, listed to start you thinking, are these:

   Gun laws
   Graduation requirements
   ROTC programs in schools and colleges
   Movie ratings (G, PG, PG-13, R, NC-17, X)
   School prayer
   Fraternities and sororities
   Dress codes in primary and secondary schools

# PART THREE

# MIXING THE METHODS

**E**verywhere in this book, we have tried to prove how flexible the methods of development are. All the preceding essays offer superb examples of DESCRIPTION or CLASSIFICATION or DEFINITION or ARGUMENT, but every one also illustrates other methods, too — description in PROCESS ANALYSIS, ANALYSIS and NARRATION in COMPARISON, EXAMPLES and CAUSE AND EFFECT in argument.

In this part of the book, we take this point even further by abandoning the individual methods. Instead, we offer a collection of twelve essays, many of them considered classics, all of them by well-known writers. The selections range widely in their subjects and approaches, but they share a significant feature: All the authors draw on whatever methods of development, at whatever length, will help them achieve their PURPOSES with readers. (To show how the writers combine methods, we have highlighted the most significant ones in the note preceding each essay.)

You have already begun to command the methods by focusing on them individually, making each a part of your kit of writing tools. Now, when you face a writing assignment, you can consider whether and how each method may help you sharpen your focus, develop your ideas, and achieve your aim. Indeed, as we noted in Chapter 2, one way to approach a subject is to apply each method to it, one by one. The following list distills the discussion on pages 36–37 to a set of questions that you can ask about any subject:

1. *Narration:* Can you tell a story about the subject?
2. *Description:* Can you use your senses to illuminate the subject?
3. *Example:* Can you point to instances that will make the subject concrete and specific?
4. *Comparison and contrast:* Will setting the subject alongside another generate useful information?
5. *Process analysis:* Will a step-by-step explanation of how the subject works add to the reader's understanding?
6. *Division or analysis:* Can slicing the subject into its parts produce a clearer vision of it?
7. *Classification:* Is it worthwhile to sort the subject into kinds or groups?
8. *Cause and effect:* Does it add to the subject to ask why it happened or what its results are?
9. *Definition:* Can you trace a boundary that will clarify the meaning of the subject?
10. *Argument and persuasion:* Can you back up an opinion or make a proposal about the subject?

Rarely will every one of these questions produce fruit for a given essay, but inevitably two or three or four will. Try the whole list when you're stuck at the beginning of an assignment or when you're snagged in the middle of a draft. You'll find the questions are as good at removing obstacles as they are at generating ideas.

# SANDRA CISNEROS

Born in 1954 in Chicago, SANDRA CISNEROS attended Loyola University, where she received a BA in 1976. Two years later, she earned an MFA from the University of Iowa Writers' Workshop. While at Iowa, she embraced her Chicano heritage in her writing, turning to her childhood for inspiration. Most of her published work deals explicitly with issues of ethnic heritage, poverty, and personal identity. She is the author of two novels, *The House on Mango Street* (1984), for which she won the American Book Award, and *Caramelo* (2003); a collection of short stories, *Woman Hollering Creek* (1991); and four books of poetry, including *My Wicked, Wicked Ways* (1987) and *Loose Woman* (1994). Cisneros has received numerous awards, including two from the National Endowment for the Arts, a Lannan Foundation Literary Award, the Texas Medal of the Arts, and a MacArthur Fellowship.

# *Only Daughter*

Growing up, Cisneros faced expectations placed on girls by both American society and her Mexican American culture. Her father had little interest in reading, and his only ambition for his daughter was marriage, yet he proved to be the main reason that she became a writer. In this essay from a 1990 *Glamour* magazine, Cisneros explains why.

"Only Daughter" mixes several methods of development to show the difficult yet fruitful bond between daughter and father:

Narration (Chap. 4): paragraphs 9–12, 15–22
Description (Chap. 5): paragraphs 7, 13, 16–21
Cause and effect (Chap. 11): paragraphs 3, 5, 7, 8
Definition (Chap. 12): paragraphs 1–2

Once, several years ago, when I was just starting out my writing career, I was asked to write my own contributor's note for an anthology I was part of. I wrote: "I am the only daughter in a family of six sons. *That* explains everything."

Well, I've thought about that ever since, and yes, it explains a lot to me, but for the reader's sake I should have written: "I am the only daughter in a *Mexican* family of six sons." Or even: "I am the only daughter of a Mexican father and a Mexican-American mother." Or: "I am the only daughter of a working-class family of nine." All of these had everything to do with who I am today.

I was/am the only daughter and *only* a daughter. Being an only daughter in a family of six sons forced me by circumstance to spend a lot of time by myself because my brothers felt it beneath them to play with a *girl* in public. But that aloneness, that loneliness, was good for a would-be writer—it allowed me time to think and think, to imagine, to read and prepare myself.

Being only a daughter for my father meant my destiny would lead me to become someone's wife. That's what he believed. But when I was in fifth grade and shared my plans for college with him, I was sure he understood. I remember my father saying, *"Que bueno, mi'ja,* that's good." That meant a lot to me, especially since my brothers thought the idea hilarious. What I didn't realize was that my father thought college was good for girls—for finding a husband. After four years in college and two more in graduate school, and still no husband, my father shakes his head even now and says I wasted all that education.

In retrospect, I'm lucky my father believed daughters were meant for husbands. It meant it didn't matter if I majored in something silly like English. After all, I'd find a nice professional eventually, right? This allowed me the liberty to putter about embroidering my little poems and stories without my father interrupting with so much as a "What's that you're writing?"

But the truth is, I wanted him to interrupt. I wanted my father to understand what it was I was scribbling, to introduce me as "My only daughter, the writer." Not as "This is my only daughter. She teaches." *El maestra*—teacher. Not even *profesora.*

In a sense, everything I have ever written has been for him, to win his approval even though I know my father can't read English words, even though my father's only reading includes the brown-ink *Esto* sports magazines from Mexico City and the bloody *¡Alarma!* magazines that feature yet another sighting of *La Virgen de Guadalupe* on a tortilla or a wife's revenge on her philandering husband by bashing his skull in with a *molcajete* (a kitchen mortar made of volcanic rock). Or the *fotonovelas,* the little picture paperbacks with tragedy and trauma erupting from the characters' mouths in bubbles.

My father represents, then, the public majority. A public who is uninterested in reading, and yet one whom I am writing about and for, and privately trying to woo.

When we were growing up in Chicago, we moved a lot because of my father. He suffered periodic bouts of nostalgia. Then we'd have to let go our flat, store the furniture with mother's relatives, load the station wagon with baggage and bologna sandwiches, and head south. To Mexico City.

We came back, of course. To yet another Chicago flat, another Chicago neighborhood, another Catholic school. Each time, my father would seek out the parish priest in order to get a tuition break, and complain or boast: "I have seven sons."

He meant *siete hijos,* seven children, but he translated it as "sons." "I have seven sons." To anyone who would listen. The Sears Roebuck employee who sold us the washing machine. The short-order cook where my father ate his ham-and-eggs breakfasts. "I have seven sons." As if he deserved a medal from the state.

My papa. He didn't mean anything by that mistranslation, I'm sure. But somehow I could feel myself being erased. I'd tug my father's sleeve and whisper: "Not seven sons. Six! and *one daughter.*" 12

When my oldest brother graduated from medical school, he fulfilled my father's dream that we study hard and use this—our heads, instead of this—our hands. Even now my father's hands are thick and yellow, stubbed by a history of hammer and nails and twine and coils and springs. "Use this," my father said, tapping his head, "and not this," showing us those hands. He always looked tired when he said it. 13

Wasn't college an investment? And hadn't I spent all those years in college? And if I didn't marry, what was it all for? Why would anyone go to college and then choose to be poor? Especially someone who had always been poor. 14

Last year, after ten years of writing professionally, the financial rewards started to trickle in. My second National Endowment for the Arts Fellowship. A guest professorship at the University of California, Berkeley. My book, which sold to a major New York publishing house. 15

At Christmas, I flew home to Chicago. The house was throbbing, same as always; hot *tamales* and sweet *tamales* hissing in my mother's pressure cooker, and everybody—mother, six brothers, wives, babies, aunts, cousins—talking too loud and at the same time, like in a Fellini[1] film, because that's just how we are. 16

I went upstairs to my father's room. One of my stories had just been translated into Spanish and published in an anthology of Chicano writing, and I wanted to show it to him. Ever since he recovered from a stroke two years ago, my father likes to spend his leisure hours horizontally. And that's how I found him, watching a Pedro Infante movie on Galavision and eating rice pudding. 17

There was a glass filmed with milk on the bedside table. There were several vials of pills and balled Kleenex. And on the floor, one black sock and a plastic urinal that I didn't want to look at but looked at anyway. Pedro Infante was about to burst into song, and my father was laughing. 18

I'm not sure if it was because my story was translated into Spanish, or because it was published in Mexico, or perhaps because the story dealt with Tepeyac, the *colonia* my father was raised in, but at any rate, my father punched the mute button on his remote control and read my story. 19

I sat on the bed next to my father and waited. He read it very slowly. As if he were reading each line over and over. He laughed at all the right places and 20

---

[1] Federico Fellini (1920–93), an Italian, directed *La Strada*, *La Dolce Vita*, *Satyricon*, and other movies. — EDS.

read lines he liked out loud. He pointed and asked questions: "Is this So-and-so?" "Yes," I said. He kept reading.

When he was finally finished, after what seemed like hours, my father    21
looked up and asked: "Where can we get more copies of this for the relatives?"

Of all the wonderful things that happened to me last year, that was the    22
most wonderful.

*For a reading quiz, sources on Sandra Cisneros, and annotated links to further readings on parent-child relationships, visit **bedfordstmartins.com/thebedfordreader**.*

## Journal Writing

Cisneros's father thinks of success primarily in terms of financial rewards. Do you agree? In your journal, consider the meaning of *success*, focusing on these questions: Whom in your own life do you consider to be successful, and why? Where do your ideas of success come from — your parents? your friends? your schooling? the media? (To take your journal writing further, see "From Journal to Essay" on the next page.)

## Questions on Meaning

1. What do you take to be Cisneros's main PURPOSE in this essay?
2. Cisneros writes, "I am the only daughter in a family of six sons. *That* explains everything" (par. 1). What does it explain in this essay?
3. What are some of the parallels Cisneros draws between her father and "the public majority" (par. 8)?
4. Why do you think her father's appreciation of her story was, for Cisneros, "the most wonderful" thing that happened to her in a year that was already good?

## Questions on Writing Strategy

1. Does Cisneros seem to be writing mainly for other Mexican Americans or for a wider AUDIENCE? Cite passages from the essay to support your answer.
2. What can you INFER about Cisneros's stories and poems from the information about her education (par. 4), the details about her father's reading (7–8), and the list of her successes (15)?
3. **MIXED METHODS** Cisneros's INTRODUCTION (pars. 1–2) gives a DEFINITION of the author. How effective is this introduction for setting up the essay that follows?

4. **MIXED METHODS**   Perhaps a third of Cisneros's essay is devoted to a NARRATIVE and DESCRIPTION of a Christmas visit home (pars. 16–22). Why do you think Cisneros relates this incident in so much detail? What do we gain from knowing what was cooking, what her father was watching on TV, or what questions he asked as he read Cisneros's story?

## Questions on Language

1. What are the contrasting ideas in Cisneros's paired phrases "the only daughter and *only* a daughter" (par. 3)?
2. How do Cisneros's words convey her feeling about her father's translation of *siete hijos* as "seven sons" (pars. 11–12)?
3. Consult a dictionary if you need help in defining the following: retrospect, putter (par. 5); philandering, mortar (7); woo (8).

## Suggestions for Writing

1. **FROM JOURNAL TO ESSAY**   Write an extended definition of *success* that also examines the sources of your definition, as you explored them in your journal. (The sources could be negative as well as positive—that is, your own ideas may have formed in reaction *against* others' ideas as well as in agreement *with* them.) Be sure your essay has a clear THESIS and plenty of EXAMPLES to make your definition precise.
2. Cisneros writes of differences from her father that frustrated her but that also motivated her to achieve. In a narrative and descriptive essay, relate some aspect of a relationship with a parent or other figure of authority that you found troubling or even maddening at the time but that now seems to have shaped you in positive ways. Did a parent (or someone else) push you to study when you wanted to play sports or hang out with your friends? make you attend religious services when they seemed unimportant? refuse to acknowledge accomplishments you were proud of? try to direct you onto a path you didn't care to take?
3. **CRITICAL WRITING**   Cisneros attributes many of her father's attitudes to his Mexican heritage. As an extension of the previous assignment, consider whether Cisneros's experiences are particular to Mexican American families or are common in all families, whatever their ethnicity. Are conflicts between children and their parents inevitable, do you think? Why, or why not?
4. **CONNECTIONS**   Cisneros's essay is one of several in this book that explore the experience of growing away from one's parents; other essays include Amy Tan's "Fish Cheeks" (p. 99), Brad Manning's "Arm Wrestling with My Father" (p. 146), Sarah Vowell's "Shooting Dad" (p. 154), Yiyun Li's "Orange Crush" (p. 164), Maxine Hong Kingston's "No Name Woman" (p. 620), and Richard Rodriguez's "Aria" (p. 651). Looking at one or two of these essays along with Cisneros's, compare and contrast the authors' relations with their parents. How are the parents themselves and the authors' feelings similar or different? Use quotations or paraphrases from the essays as evidence for your ideas.
5. **CONNECTIONS**   The authors highlighted in the previous question all use dialog to make the interactions with their parents vivid. Try your hand at using dialog

in a brief narrative that recalls a significant incident between yourself and a parent. Then write briefly about your experience using dialog: How easy or difficult was it to remember who said what? How easy or difficult was it to make the speakers sound like themselves?

---

## Sandra Cisneros on Writing

A bilingual author, Sandra Cisneros writes primarily in English. Yet Spanish influences her English sentences, and she frequently uses Spanish words in her prose. She spoke with Feroza Jussawalla and Reed Way Dasenbrock about how Spanish affects her writing:

"What it does is change the rhythm of my writing. I think that incorporating the Spanish, for me, allows me to create new expressions in English — to say things that have never been said before. And I get to do that by translating literally. I love calling stories by Spanish expressions. I have this story called 'Salvador, Late or Early.' It's a nice title. It means 'sooner or later,' *tarde o temprano*, which literally translates as 'late or early.' All of a sudden something happens to the English, something really new is happening, a new spice is added to the English language."

In some of her work, Cisneros uses Spanish and then offers a translation for English readers. At other times, she thinks complete translation is unnecessary: "See, sometimes, you don't have to say the whole thing. Now I'm learning how you can say something in English so that you know the person is saying it in Spanish. I like that. You can say a phrase in Spanish, and you can choose not to translate it, but you can make it understood through the context. 'And then my *abuelita* called me a *sin verguenza* and cried because I am without shame,' you see? Just in the sentence you can weave it in. To me it's really fun to be doing that; to me it's like I've uncovered this whole mother lode that I haven't tapped into. All the *expresiones* in Spanish when translated make English wonderful."

That said, Cisneros believes that "[t]he readers who are going to like my stories the best and catch all the subtexts and all the subtleties, that even my editor can't catch, are Chicanas. When there are Chicanas in the audience, and they laugh, they are laughing at stuff that we talk about among ourselves. And there's no way that my editor at Random House is ever going to get those jokes." This seems particularly true, she finds, when she's making use of Mexican and Southwestern myths and legends about which the general public might not be aware. "That's why I say the real ones who are going to get it are the Latinos, the Chicanos. They're going to get it in that they're going to understand the myth and how I've revised it. When I talked to someone at *Interview* magazine, I had to explain to him what I was doing with *la llorona,* *La Malinche,* and the Virgin of Guadalupe in the story ['Woman Hollering Creek']. But he said, 'Hey, I didn't know that, but I still got the story.' You can get it at some other level. He reminded me, 'Sandra, if you're from Ireland, you're going to get a lot more out of Joyce than if you're not, but just because you're not Irish doesn't mean you're not going to get it at another level.'"

## For Discussion

1. In the passages quoted here, Sandra Cisneros is talking about her fiction writing. Do her thoughts about Spanish apply to the kind of English she uses when she writes a nonfiction piece like "Only Daughter"?
2. In "Only Daughter," Sandra Cisneros writes of her father: "In a sense, everything I have ever written has been for him, to win his approval, even though I know my father can't read English words. . . ." How does this square with her claim that Chicana readers are her best readers?
3. Who is the reader who would best understand your essays?

# JOAN DIDION

A writer whose fame is fourfold — as novelist, essayist, journalist, and screen-writer — JOAN DIDION was born in 1934 in California, where her family had lived for five generations. After graduation from the University of California, Berkeley, she spent a few years in New York, working as a feature editor for the fashion magazine *Vogue*. She gained wide notice in the 1960s and 1970s with the publication of the essay collections *Slouching Towards Bethlehem* (1968) and *The White Album* (1979) and the novels *River Run* (1963), *Play It as It Lays* (1971), and *A Book of Common Prayer* (1977). *Salvador* (1983), her book-length essay based on a visit to war-torn El Salvador, and *Miami* (1987), a study of Cuban exiles in Florida, also received close attention. With her late husband, John Gregory Dunne, Didion coauthored a number of screenplays, notably for *A Star Is Born* (1976), *True Confessions* (1981), and *Up Close and Personal* (1996). Her latest books are *The Last Thing He Wanted* (1996), a novel; *Political Fictions* (2001) and *Fixed Ideas: America Since 9.11* (2003), both critiques of US politics; *Where I Was From* (2003), a memoir and an assessment of Didion's native California; and *The Year of Magical Thinking* (2005), a memoir of life after Dunne's sudden death.

# *In Bed*

In this essay from *The White Album*, Didion explains migraine headaches in general and her own in particular. Any migraine sufferer will recognize the pain and debility she describes. Even nonsufferers are likely to wince under the spell of Didion's vivid, sensuous prose.

Didion draws on half a dozen methods of development to give a full picture of migraine:

Narration (Chap. 4): paragraphs 1–2, 7–8
Description (Chap. 5): paragraphs 1–2, 7–8
Example (Chap. 6): paragraphs 2–3, 5, 7
Process analysis (Chap. 8): paragraphs 3–5, 7–8
Cause and effect (Chap. 11): paragraph 6
Definition (Chap. 12): paragraph 3

Three, four, sometimes five times a month, I spend the day in bed with a    1
migraine headache, insensible to the world around me. Almost every day of every month, between these attacks, I feel the sudden irrational irritation and flush of blood into the cerebral arteries which tell me that migraine is on its way, and I take certain drugs to avert its arrival. If I did not take the drugs, I would be able to function perhaps one day in four. The physiological error called migraine is, in brief, central to the given of my life. When I was fifteen,

sixteen, even twenty-five, I used to think that I could rid myself of this error by simply denying it, character over chemistry. "Do you have headaches *sometimes? frequently? never?*" the application forms would demand. "Check one." Wary of the trap, wanting whatever it was that the successful circumnavigation of that particular form could bring (a job, a scholarship, the respect of mankind and the grace of God), I would check one. "*Sometimes*," I would lie. That in fact I spent one or two days a week almost unconscious with pain seemed a shameful secret, evidence not merely of some chemical inferiority but of all my bad attitudes, unpleasant tempers, wrongthink.

For I had no brain tumor, no eyestrain, no high blood pressure, nothing     2
wrong with me at all: I simply had migraine headaches, and migraine headaches were, as everyone who did not have them knew, imaginary. I fought migraine then, ignored the warnings sent, went to school and later to work in spite of it, sat through lectures in Middle English and presentations to advertisers with involuntary tears running down the right side of my face, threw up in washrooms, stumbled home by instinct, emptied ice trays onto my bed and tried to freeze the pain in my right temple, wished only for a neurosurgeon who would do a lobotomy on house call, and cursed my imagination.

It was a long time before I began thinking mechanistically enough to     3
accept migraine for what it was: something with which I would be living, the way some people live with diabetes. Migraine is something more than the fancy of a neurotic imagination. It is an essentially hereditary complex of symptoms, the most frequently noted but by no means the most unpleasant of which is a vascular headache of blinding severity, suffered by a surprising number of women, a fair number of men (Thomas Jefferson had migraine, and so did Ulysses S. Grant, the day he accepted Lee's surrender), and by some unfortunate children as young as two years old. (I had my first when I was eight. It came on during a fire drill at the Columbia School in Colorado Springs, Colorado. I was taken first home and then to the infirmary at Peterson Field, where my father was stationed. The Air Corps doctor prescribed an enema.) Almost anything can trigger a specific attack of migraine: stress, allergy, fatigue, an abrupt change in barometric pressure, a contretemps over a parking ticket. A flashing light. A fire drill. One inherits, of course, only the predisposition. In other words I spent yesterday in bed with a headache not merely because of my bad attitudes, unpleasant tempers and wrongthink, but because both my grandmothers had migraine, my father has migraine and my mother has migraine.

No one knows precisely what it is that is inherited. The chemistry of     4
migraine, however, seems to have some connection with the nerve hormone named serotonin, which is naturally present in the brain. The amount of serotonin in the blood falls sharply at the onset of migraine, and one migraine

drug, Methysergide, or Sansert, seems to have some effect on serotonin. Methy-sergide is a derivative of lysergic acid (in fact Sandoz Pharmaceuticals first synthesized LSD-25 while looking for a migraine cure), and its use is hemmed about with so many contraindications and side effects that most doctors pre-scribe it only in the most incapacitating cases. Methysergide, when it is pre-scribed, is taken daily, as a preventive; another preventive which works for some people is old-fashioned ergotamine tartrate, which helps to constrict the swelling blood vessels during the "aura," the period which in most cases pre-cedes the actual headache.

Once an attack is under way, however, no drug touches it. Migraine gives     5
some people mild hallucinations, temporarily blinds others, shows up not only as a headache but as a gastrointestinal disturbance, a painful sensitivity to all sensory stimuli, an abrupt overpowering fatigue, a strokelike aphasia, and a crippling inability to make even the most routine connections. When I am in a migraine aura (for some people the aura lasts fifteen minutes, for others sev-eral hours), I will drive through red lights, lose the house keys, spill whatever I am holding, lose the ability to focus my eyes or frame coherent sentences, and generally give the appearance of being on drugs, or drunk. The actual headache, when it comes, brings with it chills, sweating, nausea, a debility that seems to stretch the very limits of endurance. That no one dies of mi-graine seems, to someone deep into an attack, an ambiguous blessing.

My husband also has migraine, which is unfortunate for him but fortunate     6
for me: Perhaps nothing so tends to prolong an attack as the accusing eye of someone who has never had a headache. "Why not take a couple of aspirin," the unafflicted will say from the doorway, or "I'd have a headache, too, spend-ing a beautiful day like this inside with all the shades drawn." All of us who have migraine suffer not only from the attacks themselves but from this com-mon conviction that we are perversely refusing to cure ourselves by taking a couple of aspirin, that we are making ourselves sick, that we "bring it on our-selves." And in the most immediate sense, the sense of why we have a headache this Tuesday and not last Thursday, of course we often do. There certainly is what doctors call a "migraine personality," and that personality tends to be ambitious, inward, intolerant of error, rather rigidly organized, per-fectionist. "You don't look like a migraine personality," a doctor once said to me. "Your hair's messy. But I suppose you're a compulsive housekeeper." Actu-ally my house is kept even more negligently than my hair, but the doctor was right nonetheless: Perfectionism can also take the form of spending most of a week writing and rewriting and not writing a single paragraph.

But not all perfectionists have migraine, and not all migrainous people     7
have migraine personalities. We do not escape heredity. I have tried in most of the available ways to escape my own migrainous heredity (at one point I

learned to give myself two daily injections of histamine with a hypodermic needle, even though the needle so frightened me that I had to close my eyes when I did it), but I still have migraine. And I have learned now to live with it, learned when to expect it, how to outwit it, even how to regard it, when it does come, as more friend than lodger. We have reached a certain understanding, my migraine and I. It never comes when I am in real trouble. Tell me that my house is burned down, my husband has left me, that there is gunfighting in the streets and panic in the banks, and I will not respond by getting a headache. It comes instead when I am fighting not an open but a guerrilla war with my own life, during weeks of small household confusions, lost laundry, unhappy help, canceled appointments, on days when the telephone rings too much and I get no work done and the wind is coming up. On days like that my friend comes uninvited.

And once it comes, now that I am wise in its ways, I no longer fight it. I   8
lie down and let it happen. At first every small apprehension is magnified, every anxiety a pounding terror. Then the pain comes, and I concentrate only on that. Right there is the usefulness of migraine, there in that imposed yoga, the concentration on the pain. For when the pain recedes, ten or twelve hours later, everything goes with it, all the hidden resentments, all the vain anxieties. The migraine has acted as a circuit breaker, and the fuses have emerged intact. There is a pleasant convalescent euphoria. I open the windows and feel the air, eat gratefully, sleep well. I notice the particular nature of a flower in a glass on the stair landing. I count my blessings.

*For a reading quiz, sources on Joan Didion, and annotated links to further readings on migraine headaches and their sufferers, visit **bedfordstmartins.com /thebedfordreader**.*

## Journal Writing

Write a passage of OBJECTIVE DESCRIPTION about an illness you know intimately, even a cold. Or, if you prefer, pick an unwelcome mood you know: the blues, for instance, or an irresistible desire to giggle during a solemn ceremony. Then, on the same subject, write a second passage — this time, a SUBJECTIVE DESCRIPTION of the same malady or mood. (To take your journal writing further, see "From Journal to Essay" on the next page.)

## Questions on Meaning

1. According to the author, how do migraines differ from ordinary headaches? What are their distinctive traits?
2. What once made Didion ashamed to admit that she suffered from migraines? How does her former sense of shame help to explain her reason for writing?
3. While imparting facts about migraine, what does Didion simultaneously reveal about her own personality?
4. Sum up in your own words the tremendous experience that Didion describes in the final paragraph.

## Questions on Writing Strategy

1. Didion's essay mixes subjective description based on personal experience with objective information based on medical knowledge. How does she signal her transitions from subjective to objective and from objective back to subjective?
2. Point to a few examples of sensuous detail in Didion's writing. What do such IMAGES contribute to her essay's EFFECT?
3. In paragraph 2 Didion declares that she "wished only for a neurosurgeon who would do a lobotomy on house call"; later (par. 5) she remarks, "That no one dies of migraine seems, to someone deep into an attack, an ambiguous blessing." Does she mean for readers to take her literally? How do you know? (See *hyperbole* under *Figures of speech* in Useful Terms.)
4. **MIXED METHODS**    In paragraph 5 the author uses strings of EXAMPLES. What is the effect of these examples? What GENERALIZATION do they support?
5. **MIXED METHODS**    What do Didion's two uses of PROCESS ANALYSIS (pars. 3–5 and 7–8) contribute to her essay?

## Questions on Language

1. How would you characterize Didion's word choice: colorful, utilitarian, flowery, careless, or lyrical? Support your answer with examples.
2. In the title of Didion's essay, what arrests you? Is this title a teaser, having little to do with the essay, or does it fit?
3. Speaking in paragraph 1 of the "circumnavigation" of an application form, Didion employs a metaphor. In paragraph 7 she introduces another — "a guerrilla war." In paragraph 8 she uses a simile — "The migraine has acted as a circuit breaker." Comment on the aptness of these FIGURES OF SPEECH.
4. Consult a dictionary if you need help in defining the following: vascular, contretemps, predisposition (par. 3); synthesized, contraindications, aura (4); aphasia (5).

## Suggestions for Writing

1. **FROM JOURNAL TO ESSAY**    Expand your journal entry into a full descriptive essay, blending objective and subjective description as you see fit to explain your illness or mood, to convey the way it makes you feel, and to show how it affects your life.

2. Didion mentions "the accusing eye" (par. 6) she endures from those who don't suffer migraine. Write an essay in which you express and defend something about yourself that other people don't seem to understand. It could be a disability, a need for solitude, a habit, a hobby or interest that others find odd or dull. Explain the reactions you receive and how you respond to and cope with them.

3. **CRITICAL WRITING**　Write an essay examining Didion's TONE. Are there passages in which she seems self-pitying? courageous? determined? resigned? triumphant? What is the overall tone of the essay? Is it effective? Why?

4. **CONNECTIONS**　COMPARE Didion's essay to Nancy Mairs's "Disability" (p. 13). Mairs and Didion describe how multiple sclerosis and migraine, respectively, affect their lives. What is the PURPOSE of each essay? What do Mairs and Didion want us to understand about them and their lives? How does each want us to respond?

5. **CONNECTIONS**　Both Joan Didion's "In Bed" and Ian Frazier's "How to Operate the Shower Curtain" (p. 302) offer close, detailed studies of particular inconveniences. Write a description of something small that annoys you — not breakfast, but burnt toast; not going to bed, but being kept awake by a cricket. Focus on minute details to convey the object or experience to readers.

---

# *Joan Didion on Writing*

In "Why I Write," an essay published by the *New York Times Book Review*, adapted from her Regents' Lecture at the University of California at Berkeley, Joan Didion writes, "I stole the title for this talk, from George Orwell [see p. 634]. One reason I stole it was that I like the sound of the words: Why I Write. There you have three short unambiguous words that share a sound, and the sound they share is this:

*I*

*I*

*I*

In many ways writing is the act of saying *I*, of imposing oneself upon other people, of saying *listen to me, see it my way, change your mind. . . .*"

Didion's "way," though, comes not from notions of how the world works or should work but from its observable details. She writes, "I am not in the least an intellectual, which is not to say that when I hear the word 'intellectual' I reach for my gun, but only to say that I do not think in abstracts. During the years when I was an undergraduate at Berkeley I tried, with a kind of hopeless late-adolescent energy, to buy some temporary visa into the world of ideas, to forge for myself a mind that could deal with the abstract. . . . In short, I tried to think. I failed. My attention veered inexorably back to the specific, to the tangible, to what was generally considered, by everyone I knew then and for that matter have known since, the peripheral. I would try to contemplate the Hegelian dialectic and would find myself concentrating instead on the flowering pear tree outside my window and the particular way the petals fell on my floor."

Later in the essay, Didion writes, "During those years I was traveling on what I knew to be a very shaky passport, forged papers: I knew that I was no legitimate resident in any world of ideas. I knew I couldn't think. All I knew then was what I wasn't, and it took me some years to discover what I was.

"Which was a writer.

"By which I mean not a 'good' writer or a 'bad' writer but simply a writer, a person whose most absorbed and passionate hours are spent arranging words on pieces of paper. Had my credentials been in order I would never have become a writer. Had I been blessed with even limited access to my own mind there would have been no reason to write. I write entirely to find out what I'm thinking, what I'm looking at, what I see, and what it means. What I want and what I fear. . . . *What is going on in these pictures in my mind?*"

In the essay, Didion emphasizes that these mental pictures have a grammar. "Grammar is a piano I play by ear, since I seem to have been out of school the year the rules were mentioned. All I know about grammar is its infinite power. To shift the structure of a sentence alters the meaning of that sentence, as definitely and inflexibly as the position of a camera alters the meaning of the object photographed. Many people know about camera angles now, but not so many know about sentences. The arrangement of the words matters, and the arrangement you want can be found in the picture in your mind. The picture dictates the arrangement. The picture dictates whether this will be a sentence with or without clauses, a sentence that ends hard or a dying-fall sentence, long or short, active or passive. The picture tells you how to arrange the words and the arrangement of the words tells you, or tells me, what's going on in the picture."

## For Discussion

1. What is Didion's definition of thinking? Do you agree with it?
2. To what extent does Didion's writing support her remarks about how and why she writes?
3. What does Didion mean when she says that grammar has "infinite power"? Power to do what?

# BARBARA EHRENREICH

Born in 1941 in Butte, Montana, BARBARA EHRENREICH is an essayist and investigative journalist known for sharp political and social criticism. After graduating from Reed College, she received a PhD in biology from Rockefeller University and taught briefly while becoming an activist and writer. She has contributed to dozens of periodicals, among them *The New Republic*, *Mother Jones*, *Time*, and *The Atlantic Monthly*. She currently writes a column for *The Progressive*. Her many books include *Poverty in the American Dream: Women and Children First* (1983), *Fear of Falling: The Inner Life of the Middle Class* (1989), *Blood Rites: Origins and History of the Passions of War* (1997), *Nickel and Dimed: On (Not) Getting By in America* (2001), and, most recently, *Dancing in the Streets: A History of Collective Joy* (2006). The recipient of numerous grants and awards, Ehrenreich is also a fellow at the New York Institute for the Humanities and a scholar at the Institute for Policy Studies.

# *The Roots of War*

Why do human beings make war? In this essay written for *The Progressive* in April 2003, Ehrenreich challenges conventional explanations of war — that it is inherently male, for instance, or innately human. With typical clarity and force, she argues instead that war is "a parasite on human societies."

"The Roots of War" mainly analyzes causes and effects to argue for a particular explanation of human warfare and a particular approach to warfare. But Ehrenreich draws on several other methods as well to develop the essay:

Example (Chap. 6): paragraphs 3, 4, 6, 7
Comparison and contrast (Chap. 7): paragraphs 4, 6, 8–9
Process analysis (Chap. 8): paragraphs 4, 6
Division or analysis (Chap. 9): paragraphs 2–4
Cause and effect (Chap. 11): throughout
Definition (Chap. 12): paragraph 4
Argument and persuasion (Chap. 13): paragraphs 9–10

Only three types of creatures engage in warfare — humans, chimpanzees, and ants. Among humans, warfare is so ubiquitous and historically commonplace that we are often tempted to attribute it to some innate predisposition for slaughter — a gene, perhaps, manifested as a murderous hormone. The earliest archeological evidence of war is from 12,000 years ago, well before such innovations as capitalism and cities and at the very beginning of settled, agricultural life. Sweeping through recorded history, you can find a predilection for warfare among hunter-gatherers, herding and farming peoples, industrial and even postindustrial societies, democracies, and dictatorships. The good

1

old pop-feminist explanation—testosterone—would seem, at first sight, to fit the facts.

But war is too complex and collective an activity to be accounted for by   2
any warlike instinct lurking within the individual psyche. Battles, in which the violence occurs, are only one part of war, most of which consists of preparation for battle—training, the manufacture of weapons, the organization of supply lines, etc. There is no plausible instinct, for example, that could impel a man to leave home, cut his hair short, and drill for hours in tight formation.

Contrary to the biological theories of war, it is not easy to get men to fight.   3
In recent centuries, men have often gone to great lengths to avoid war—fleeing their homelands, shooting off their index fingers, feigning insanity. So unreliable was the rank and file of the famed eighteenth-century Prussian army that military rules forbade camping near wooded areas: The troops would simply melt away into the trees. Even when men are duly assembled for battle, killing is not something that seems to come naturally to them. As Lieutenant Colonel Dave Grossman argued in his book *On Killing: The Psychological Cost of Learning to Kill in War and Society*, one of the great challenges of military training is to get soldiers to shoot directly at individual enemies.

What is it, then, that has made war such an inescapable part of the human   4
experience? Each war, of course, appears to the participants to have an immediate purpose—to crush the "Hun," preserve democracy, disarm Saddam, or whatever—that makes it noble and necessary. But those who study war dispassionately, as a recurrent event with no moral content, have observed a certain mathematical pattern: that of "epidemicity," or the tendency of war to spread in the manner of an infectious disease. Obviously, war is not a symptom of disease or the work of microbes, but it does spread geographically in a diseaselike manner, usually as groups take up warfare in response to warlike neighbors. It also spreads through time, as the losses suffered in one war call forth new wars of retaliation. Think of World War I, which breaks out for no good reason at all, draws in most of Europe as well as the United States, and then "reproduces" itself, after a couple of decades, as World War II.

In other words, as the Dutch social scientist Henk Houweling puts it, "one   5
of the causes of war is war itself." Wars produce warlike societies, which, in turn, make the world more dangerous for other societies, which are thus recruited into being war-prone themselves. Just as there is no gene for war, neither is there a single type or feature of society—patriarchy or hierarchy—that generates it. War begets war and shapes human societies as it does so.

In general, war shapes human societies by requiring that they possess two   6
things: one, some group or class of men (and, in some historical settings, women) who are trained to fight; and, two, the resources to arm and feed them. These requirements have often been compatible with patriarchal cul-

tures dominated by a warrior elite—knights or samurai—as in medieval Europe or Japan. But not always: Different ways of fighting seem to lead to different forms of social and political organization. Historian Victor Hansen has argued that the phalanx formation adopted by the ancient Greeks, with its stress on equality and interdependence, was a factor favoring the emergence of democracy among nonslave Greek males. And there is no question but that the mass, gun-wielding armies that appeared in Europe in the seventeenth century contributed to the development of the modern nation-state—if only as a bureaucratic apparatus to collect the taxes required to support these armies.

Marx[1] was wrong, then: It is not only the "means of production" that shape societies, but the means of destruction. In our own time, the costs of war, or war readiness, are probably larger than at any time in history, in relation to other human needs, due to the pressure on nations not only to maintain a mass standing army—the United States supports about a million men and women at arms—but to keep up with an extremely expensive, ever-changing technology of killing. The cost squeeze has led to a new type of society, perhaps best termed a "depleted" state, in which the military has drained resources from all other social functions. North Korea is a particularly ghoulish example, where starvation coexists with nuclear-weapons development. But the USSR also crumbled under the weight of militarism, and the United States brandishes its military might around the world while, at this moment, cutting school lunches and health care for the poor.                            7

"Addiction" provides only a pallid and imprecise analogy for the human relationship to war; parasitism—or even predation—is more to the point. However and whenever war began, it has persisted and propagated itself with the terrifying tenacity of a beast attached to the neck of living prey, feeding on human effort and blood.                            8

If this is what we are up against, it won't do much good to try to uproot whatever warlike inclinations may dwell within our minds. Abjuring violent speech and imagery, critiquing masculinist culture, and promoting respect for human diversity—all of these are worthy projects, but they will make little contribution to the abolition of war. It would be far better to think of war as something external to ourselves, something which has to be uprooted, everywhere, down to the last weapon and bellicose pageant.                            9

The "epidemicity" of war has one other clear implication: War cannot be used as a means to prevent or abolish war. True, for some time to come, urgent                            10

---

[1] Karl Marx (1818–93), German political philosopher and founder of modern socialism, maintained that a society's mode of economic production—how goods are produced, who produces them, and who profits from their production—determines the society's politics, culture, and stability.—EDS.

threats from other heavily armed states will require at least the threat of armed force in response. But these must be very urgent threats and extremely restrained responses. To indulge, one more time, in the metaphor of war as a kind of living thing, a parasite on human societies: The idea of a war to end war is one of its oldest, and cruelest, tricks.

---

For a reading quiz, sources on Barbara Ehrenreich, and annotated links to further readings on human warfare, visit **bedfordstmartins.com/thebedfordreader**.

---

## Journal Writing

Ehrenreich dismisses the idea of "some innate predisposition for slaughter" in human beings (par. 1). Take this point about biology down to the level of the individual: To what extent were you born with a predisposition toward your characteristics—kindness, aggressiveness, athleticism, intelligence, shyness, musical talent, and so on? (To take your journal writing further, see "From Journal to Essay" on the following page.)

## Questions on Meaning

1. In paragraph 3 Ehrenreich refers to "biological theories of war." What are these theories, and why does she dismiss them?
2. Ehrenreich's THESIS develops over the course of the essay. What is it?
3. According to Ehrenreich, why are the costs of war higher today than in the past?
4. What point does Ehrenreich make with the examples of North Korea and the former Soviet Union in paragraph 7?

## Questions on Writing Strategy

1. Ehrenreich published this essay about a month after the United States and its allies invaded Iraq in 2003. How might the timing relate to her PURPOSE in writing the essay? What do you think her purpose is?
2. What ANALOGY does Ehrenreich use to explain the root cause of war (par. 4)? What is her purpose in using it?
3. Where in the essay does Ehrenreich cite the opinions of experts? What does this strategy contribute to the essay?
4. **MIXED METHODS**   What does Ehrenreich COMPARE AND CONTRAST in paragraph 6? What purpose does the comparison serve?
5. **MIXED METHODS**   Explain how Ehrenreich uses CAUSE AND EFFECT to build to the ARGUMENT in paragraphs 9–10.

## Questions on Language

1. Why do you think Ehrenreich prefers the words *parasitism* and *predation* over *addiction* to describe our relationship to war (par. 8)? What do the CONNOTATIONS of these words suggest about her viewpoint?
2. How does Ehrenreich's TONE shift between paragraphs 1–6 and paragraphs 7–10? What is the EFFECT of this shift?
3. If any of the following words are unfamiliar, be sure to look them up in a dictionary: ubiquitous, predilection, testosterone (par. 1); feigning, duly (3); microbes (4); patriarchy, hierarchy, begets (5); phalanx (6); brandishes (7); pallid, propagated, tenacity (8); abjuring, bellicose (9).

## Suggestions for Writing

1. **FROM JOURNAL TO ESSAY**   Working from your journal entry, write an essay that explores the debate about heredity versus environment, nature versus nurture, as it applies to you. Using specific EXAMPLES, discuss the extent to which you think genes or your surroundings have shaped who you are.
2. Ehrenreich writes about the causes of warfare in general. In the library or on the Web, research the causes proposed for a particular war that interests you. How, if at all, do the various explanations jibe with Ehrenreich's explanation? Which explanations do you find most compelling, and why? Write an essay that explores and takes a position on the various causal explanations.
3. **CRITICAL WRITING**   Respond to Ehrenreich's conclusion that "[w]ar cannot be used as a means to prevent or abolish war" (par. 10). How well does Ehrenreich support this claim? In an essay, ANALYZE and EVALUATE Ehrenreich's argument, looking in particular at her EVIDENCE, her reasoning, and whether and how she considers possible opposing arguments.
4. **CONNECTIONS**   In paragraph 7 Ehrenreich implies that governments should spend less money on their military and more on social programs. In an essay, discuss how Ehrenreich's point about the trade-off between military and social spending corresponds to the ideas in Thomas Sowell's "'Needs'" (p. 501).
5. **CONNECTIONS**   Four essays in this book deal with how the United States does or should respond to the threat of terrorism: Adnan R. Khan's "Close Encounters with US Immigration" (p. 558), Linda Chavez's "Everything Isn't Racial Profiling" (p. 563), Mark Krikorian's "Safety Through Immigration Control" (p. 567), and Edwidge Danticat's "Not Your Homeland" (p. 572). Ehrenreich doesn't address terrorism or war in response to it. How might terrorism fit into her argument, or why would it not fit? In an essay, explain your answer.

---

# *Barbara Ehrenreich on Writing*

The printed word, in the view of Barbara Ehrenreich, should be a powerful instrument for reform. In an article in *Mother Jones*, though, she complains about a tacit censorship in American magazines that has sometimes prevented her from fulfilling her purpose as a writer. Ehrenreich recalls the difficulties she had in trying to persuade the editor of a national magazine to assign her a story on the plight of Third World women refugees. "Sorry," said the editor, "Third World women have never done anything for me."

Ehrenreich infers that writers who write for such magazines must follow a rule: "You must learn not to stray from your assigned sociodemographic stereotype." She observes, "As a woman, I am generally asked to write on 'women's topics,' such as cooking, divorce, how to succeed in business, diet fads, and the return of the bustle. These are all fine topics and give great scope to my talents, but when I ask, in faltering tones, for an assignment . . . on the trade deficit, I am likely to be told that *anyone* (Bill, Gerry, Bob) could cover that, whereas my 'voice' is *essential* for the aerobic toothbrushing story. This is not, strictly speaking, 'censorship'—just a division of labor in which white men cover politics, foreign policy, and the economy, and the rest of us cover what's left over, such as the bustle."

Over the years Ehrenreich has had many manuscripts rejected by editors who comment, "too angry," "too depressing," and "Where's the bright side?" She agrees with writer Herbert Gold, who once deduced that the American media want only "happy stories about happy people with happy problems." She concludes, "You can write about anything—death squads, AIDS . . . — so long as you make it 'upbeat.'" Despite such discouragements, Ehrenreich continues her battle to "disturb the stupor induced by six straight pages of Calvin Klein ads."

## For Discussion

1. Is Ehrenreich right about "a tacit censorship in American magazines"? Check a recent issue of a magazine that prints signed articles. How many of the articles *not* on "women's topics" are written by women? How many are written by men?
2. To what extent do you agree with Ehrenreich—and with Herbert Gold—that the American media are interested only in "upbeat" stories?

# STEPHEN JAY GOULD

A paleontologist and collector of snails, STEPHEN JAY GOULD was born in New York City in 1941, went to Antioch College, and took a doctorate from Columbia University. From the age of twenty-five, Gould taught biology, geology, and the history of science at Harvard, where his courses were among the most popular. Although he often wrote for specialists (*Ontogeny and Phylogeny*, 1977), Gould is best known for essays that explore science in prose a layperson can enjoy. For twenty-seven years, until 2000, he wrote a monthly column for *Natural History* magazine. These and other essays have been collected in many books, including *Hens' Teeth and Horses' Toes* (1983), *Eight Little Piggies* (1993), *Dinosaur in a Haystack* (1995), and *Leonardo's Mountain of Clams and the Diet of Worms* (1998). His most recent books are *Rocks of Ages* (1999), which attempts to heal the rift between science and religion; *The Structure of Evolutionary Theory* (2002), in which he proposes a new framework for thinking about Darwinism; and *I Have Landed: Splashes and Reflections from a Life in Natural History* (2002), a collection of essays. In 1981 Gould received a grant from the MacArthur Foundation. In 1999 he became president of the American Association for the Advancement of Science. He died in 2002 at the age of sixty.

# *A Biological Homage to Mickey Mouse*

In this selection from *The Panda's Thumb*, a 1980 collection of *Natural History* essays, Gould takes the fiftieth birthday of Mickey Mouse as the occasion for witty yet serious observations about human evolution. The original Mickey changed greatly over the years, growing not older and wiser but younger and better behaved. How, you might ask, does the evolution of Mickey apply to us humans? Gould tells all.

Gould draws on a number of methods to trace Mickey's evolution, and our own:

Narration (Chap. 4): paragraphs 3, 7
Description (Chap. 5): paragraphs 1, 2, 6, 8, 13
Comparison and contrast (Chap. 7): paragraphs 11, 13, 16–18, 20
Process analysis (Chap. 8): paragraphs 5–6, 10, 17–18
Division or analysis (Chap. 9): paragraphs 4, 7–8, 10, 15
Cause and effect (Chap. 11): paragraphs 3–4, 7–8, 12–15, 18–19
Definition (Chap. 12): paragraphs 16–17

Age often turns fire to placidity. Lytton Strachey, in his incisive portrait of   1
Florence Nightingale,[1] writes of her declining years:

[1] Strachey (1880–1932) was an English historian. Nightingale (1820–1910) was an English nurse who founded the modern practice of nursing. —EDS.

Destiny, having waited very patiently, played a queer trick on Miss Nightingale. The benevolence and public spirit of that long life had only been equalled by its acerbity. Her virtue had dwelt in hardness. . . . And now the sarcastic years brought the proud woman her punishment. She was not to die as she had lived. The sting was to be taken out of her; she was to be made soft; she was to be reduced to compliance and complacency.

I was therefore not surprised—although the analogy may strike some
people as sacrilegious—to discover that the creature who gave his name as a synonym for insipidity had a gutsier youth. Mickey Mouse turned a respectable fifty last year. To mark the occasion, many theaters replayed his debut performance in *Steamboat Willie* (1928). The original Mickey was a rambunctious, even slightly sadistic fellow. In a remarkable sequence, exploiting the exciting new development of sound, Mickey and Minnie pummel, squeeze, and twist the animals on board to produce a rousing chorus of "Turkey in the Straw." They honk a duck with a tight embrace, crank a goat's tail, tweak a pig's nipples, bang a cow's teeth as a stand-in xylophone, and play bagpipe on her udder.

Christopher Finch, in his semiofficial pictorial history of Disney's work,
comments: "The Mickey Mouse who hit the movie houses in the late twenties was not quite the well-behaved character most of us are familiar with today. He was mischievous, to say the least, and even displayed a streak of cruelty." But Mickey soon cleaned up his act, leaving to gossip and speculation only his unresolved relationship with Minnie and the status of Morty and Ferdie. Finch continues: "Mickey . . . had become virtually a national symbol, and as such he was expected to behave properly at all times. If he occasionally stepped out of line, any number of letters would arrive at the studio from citizens and organizations who felt that the nation's moral well-being was in their hands. . . . Eventually he would be pressured into the role of straight man."[2]

As Mickey's personality softened, his appearance changed. Many Disney
fans are aware of this transformation through time, but few (I suspect) have recognized the coordinating theme behind all the alterations—in fact, I am not sure that the Disney artists themselves explicitly realized what they were doing, since the changes appeared in such a halting and piecemeal fashion. In short, the blander and inoffensive Mickey became progressively more juvenile in appearance. (Since Mickey's chronological age never altered—like most cartoon characters he stands impervious to the ravages of time—this change in appearance at a constant age is a true evolutionary transformation.

[2] Finch's book is *The Art of Walt Disney: From Mickey Mouse to the Magic Kingdom* (1975, rev. 2004). —EDS.

Progressive juvenilization as an evolutionary phenomenon is called *neoteny*. More on this later.)

The characteristic changes of form during human growth have inspired   5 a substantial biological literature. Since the head-end of an embryo differentiates first and grows more rapidly in utero than the foot-end (an antero-posterior gradient, in technical language), a newborn child possesses a relatively large head attached to a medium-sized body with diminutive legs and feet. This gradient is reversed through growth as legs and feet overtake the front end. Heads continue to grow but so much more slowly than the rest of the body that relative head size decreases.

In addition, a suite of changes pervades the head itself during human   6 growth. The brain grows very slowly after age three, and the bulbous cranium of a young child gives way to the more slanted, lower-browed configuration of adulthood. The eyes scarcely grow at all and relative eye size declines precipitously. But the jaw gets bigger and bigger. Children, compared with adults, have larger heads and eyes, smaller jaws, a more prominent, bulging cranium, and smaller, pudgier legs and feet. Adult heads are altogether more apish, I'm sorry to say.

Mickey, however, has traveled this ontogenetic pathway in reverse during   7 his fifty years among us. He has assumed an ever more childlike appearance as the ratty character of *Steamboat Willie* became the cute and inoffensive host to a magic kingdom. By 1940, the former tweaker of a pig's nipples gets a kick in

**Mickey's Evolution During Fifty Years (left to right)**    As Mickey became increasingly well behaved over the years, his appearance became more youthful. Measurements of three stages in his development revealed a larger relative head size, larger eyes, and an enlarged cranium—all traits of juvenility. © Disney Enterprises, Inc.

the ass for insubordination (as the *Sorcerer's Apprentice* in *Fantasia*). By 1953, his last cartoon, he has gone fishing and cannot even subdue a squirting clam.

The Disney artists transformed Mickey in clever silence, often using sug-   8
gestive devices that mimic nature's own changes by different routes. To give him the shorter and pudgier legs of youth, they lowered his pants line and cov-ered his spindly legs with a baggy outfit. (His arms and legs also thickened sub-stantially — and acquired joints for a floppier appearance.) His head grew relatively larger and its features more youthful. The length of Mickey's snout has not altered, but decreasing protrusion is more subtly suggested by a pro-nounced thickening. Mickey's eye has grown in two modes: first, by a major, discontinuous evolutionary shift as the entire eye of ancestral Mickey became the pupil of his descendants, and second, by gradual increase thereafter.

Mickey's improvement in cranial bulging followed an interesting path   9
since his evolution has always been constrained by the unaltered convention of representing his head as a circle with appended ears and an oblong snout. The circle's form could not be altered to provide a bulging cranium directly. Instead, Mickey's ears moved back, increasing the distance between nose and ears, and giving him a rounded, rather than a sloping, forehead.

To give these observations the cachet of quantitative science, I applied   10
my best pair of dial calipers to three stages of the official phylogeny — the thin-nosed, ears-forward figure of the early 1930s (stage 1), the latter-day Jack

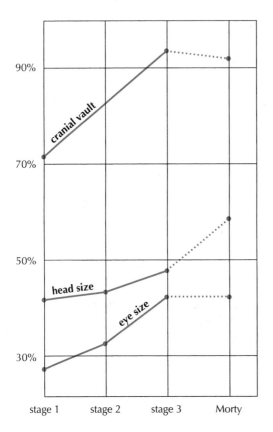

**The "Evolution" of Mickey Mouse**   At an early stage in his evolution, Mickey had a smaller head, cranial vault, and eyes. He evolved toward the characteristics of his young nephew Morty (connected to Mickey by a dotted line).

of *Mickey and the Beanstalk* (1947, stage 2), and the modern mouse (stage 3). I measured three signs of Mickey's creeping juvenility: increasing eye size (maximum height) as a percentage of head length (base of the nose to top of rear ear); increasing head length as a percentage of body length; and increasing cranial vault size measured by rearward displacement of the front ear (base of the nose to top of front ear as a percentage of base of the nose to top of rear ear).

All three percentages increased steadily—eye size from 27 to 42 percent [11] of head length; head length from 42.7 to 48.1 percent of body length; and nose to front ear from 71.7 to a whopping 95.6 percent of nose to rear ear. For comparison, I measured Mickey's young "nephew" Morty Mouse. In each case, Mickey has clearly been evolving toward youthful stages of his stock, although he still has a way to go for head length.

You may, indeed, now ask what an at least marginally respectable scientist [12] has been doing with a mouse like that. In part, fiddling around and having fun, of course. (I still prefer *Pinocchio* to *Citizen Kane*.) But I do have a serious

Humans feel affection for animals with juvenile features: large eyes, bulging craniums, retreating chins (left column). Small-eyed, long-snouted animals (right column) do not elicit the same response.

From *Studies in Animal and Human Behavior*, vol. 2, by Konrad Lorenz (London: Methuen, 1971).

point—two, in fact—to make. We must first ask why Disney chose to change his most famous character so gradually and persistently in the same direction? National symbols are not altered capriciously and market researchers (for the doll industry in particular) have spent a good deal of time and practical effort learning what features appeal to people as cute and friendly. Biologists also have spent a great deal of time studying a similar subject in a wide range of animals.

In one of his most famous articles, Konrad Lorenz[3] argues that humans use 13 the characteristic differences in form between babies and adults as important behavioral cues. He believes that features of juvenility trigger "innate releasing mechanisms" for affection and nurturing in adult humans. When we see a living creature with babyish features, we feel an automatic surge of disarming tenderness. The adaptive value of this response can scarcely be questioned, for we must nurture our babies. Lorenz, by the way, lists among his releasers the very features of babyhood that Disney affixed progressively to Mickey: "a relatively large head, predominance of the brain capsule, large and low-lying eyes, bulging cheek region, short and thick extremities, a springy elastic consistency, and clumsy movements." . . .

Lorenz emphasizes the power that juvenile features hold over us, and the 14 abstract quality of their influence, by pointing out that we judge other animals

[3] Lorenz (1903–89) was an Austrian psychologist, winner of a Nobel Prize.—EDS.

by the same criteria—although the judgment may be utterly inappropriate in an evolutionary context. We are, in short, fooled by an evolved response to our own babies, and we transfer our reaction to the same set of features in other animals. . . .

I submit that Mickey Mouse's evolutionary road down the course of his    15
own growth in reverse reflects the unconscious discovery of this biological principle by Disney and his artists. In fact, the emotional status of most Disney characters rests on the same set of distinctions. To this extent, the Magic Kingdom trades on a biological illusion—our ability to abstract and our propensity to transfer inappropriately to other animals the fitting responses we make to changing form in the growth of our own bodies. . . .

As a second, serious biological comment on Mickey's odyssey in form, I    16
note that his path to eternal youth repeats, in epitome, our own evolutionary story. For humans are neotenic. We have evolved by retaining to adulthood the originally juvenile features of our ancestors. Our australopithecine forebears,[4] like Mickey in *Steamboat Willie*, had projecting jaws and low vaulted craniums.

Our embryonic skulls scarcely differ from those of chimpanzees. And we follow the same path of changing form through growth: relative decrease of the cranial vault since brains grow so much more slowly than bodies after birth, and continuous relative increase of the jaw. But while chimps accentuate these changes, producing an adult strikingly different in form from a baby, we proceed much more slowly down the same path and never get nearly so far. Thus, as adults, we retain juvenile features. To be sure, we change enough to produce a notable difference between baby and adult, but our alteration is far smaller than that experienced by chimps and other primates.

A marked slowdown of developmental rates has triggered our neoteny.    17
Primates are slow developers among mammals, but we have accentuated the trend to a degree matched by no other mammal. We have very long periods of gestation, markedly extended childhoods, and the longest life span of any mammal. The morphological features of eternal youth have served us well. Our enlarged brain is, at least in part, a result of extending rapid prenatal growth rates to later ages. (In all mammals, the brain grows rapidly in utero but often very little after birth. We have extended this fetal phase into postnatal life.)

But the changes in timing themselves have been just as important. We are    18
preeminently learning animals, and our extended childhood permits the transference of culture by education. Many animals display flexibility and

---

[4] *Australopithecus*, an extinct ancestor of humans, lived about 4 million to 1.5 million years ago. —EDS.

play in childhood but follow rigidly programmed patterns as adults. Lorenz writes . . . : "The characteristic which is so vital for the human peculiarity of the true man — that of always remaining in a state of development — is quite certainly a gift which we owe to the neotenous nature of mankind."

In short, we, like Mickey, never grow up although we, alas, do grow old.   20 Best wishes to you, Mickey, for your next half-century. May we stay as young as you, but grow a bit wiser.

For a reading quiz, sources on Stephen Jay Gould, and annotated links to further readings on Mickey Mouse and on evolution, visit **bedfordstmartins.com /thebedfordreader**.

## Journal Writing

Gould writes, paraphrasing Konrad Lorenz, that innately "[w]hen we see a living creature with babyish features, we feel an automatic surge of disarming tenderness" (par. 13). How do you respond to this statement? In your experience is it true of people generally, or are some people more predisposed to such feelings than others? What is your own reaction to babies and young animals? Write a journal entry in which you consider these questions. (To take your journal writing further, see "From Journal to Essay" on the following page.)

## Questions on Meaning

1. How, according to Gould, did Mickey Mouse change in terms of behavior over the years? To what does Gould attribute this change?
2. What basic point does Gould make about changes to Mickey Mouse's appearance over the years? How are these changes related to the concept of neoteny (pars. 4, 16)?
3. How exactly did Mickey Mouse's appearance change? In addition to Gould's statements about the changes, what do you observe yourself in the illustration on pages 606–07?
4. What are Gould's two "serious" comments (pars. 12 and 16)? State his points in your own words.

## Questions on Writing Strategy

1. What is the PURPOSE of each visual image included by Gould? Does each seem necessary?

2. What is the point of paragraphs 10–11? Is Gould serious? How do you respond to these paragraphs?
3. **MIXED METHODS**   How does PROCESS ANALYSIS serve Gould in paragraphs 5–6? Why does he explain human physical development in such detail?
4. **MIXED METHODS**   How is Gould's third illustration (p. 610) a model of COMPARISON AND CONTRAST? What subjects does Gould compare and contrast in paragraphs 17–18?

## Questions on Language

1. In what sense is Mickey Mouse, as Gould claims, "a synonym for insipidity" (par. 2)? What do *synonym* and *insipidity* mean? In everyday speech, what does *Mickey Mouse* mean when used as an adjective?
2. Gould uses vivid verbs in the last two sentences of paragraph 2. What is their EFFECT?
3. How would you characterize Gould's DICTION in this essay? What does his diction suggest about his intended AUDIENCE? Does he assume that readers are scientists like himself?
4. Consult a dictionary if you are uncertain of the meaning of any of the following: homage (title); sacrilegious, rambunctious, sadistic, pummel (par. 2); mischievous (3); explicitly, piecemeal, impervious (4); in utero, gradient (5); suite, pervades, bulbous, cranium (6); ontogenetic (7); protrusion (8); oblong (9); cachet, quantitative, calipers, phylogeny (10); innate (13); odyssey, epitome (16); accentuate (17); morphological (18); preeminently (19).

## Suggestions for Writing

1. **FROM JOURNAL TO ESSAY**   Based on your journal entry, write an essay that examines people's responses to animals (including humans) with babyish features. Does everyone respond the same way, in your experience? If you see variation, what do you think accounts for it: upbringing? gender? heredity? personality? distraction? Use EXAMPLES from your experience to illustrate and support your ideas.
2. At a library or video store, locate a sampling of Mickey Mouse cartoons from the original *Steamboat Willie* (1928) through the last of the series in the 1950s. Write an essay that traces the evolution of Mickey's personality and behavior over the years. You might also consider his stature today as a symbol for the Walt Disney Company. For more information on Mickey Mouse, visit the "ultimate unofficial" site, maintained by Chris Gibson, at *mickey-mouse.com*.
3. Research the work of Stephen Jay Gould, looking for reviews of his books as well as interviews with him. In an essay, consider Gould's achievements as a scientist and a writer.
4. **CONNECTIONS**   "The Roots of War," by Barbara Ehrenreich (p. 598), is another scientific essay written by a biology PhD for a nonspecialist audience. In an essay compare and contrast Gould's essay with Ehrenreich's. Do both writers succeed equally well in presenting complex concepts in ways that most readers can understand? Use quotations and PARAPHRASES from both essays to support your ideas.

5. **CONNECTIONS**  In "The Capricious Camera" (p. 358), Laila Ayad describes a photograph of a young girl and attempts to interpret its historical meanings. Using Gould's and Ayad's essays for examples, write an essay of your own in which you discuss how writers can create meaning through DESCRIPTION and ANALYSIS of visual images.

---

# Stephen Jay Gould on Writing

In his prologue to *The Flamingo's Smile*, Stephen Jay Gould positions himself in a long and respectable tradition of writers who communicate scientific ideas to a general audience. To popularize, he says, does not mean to trivialize, cheapen, or adulterate. "I follow one cardinal rule in writing these essays," he insists. "No compromises. I will make language accessible by defining or eliminating jargon; I will not simplify concepts. I can state all sorts of highfalutin, moral justifications for this approach (and I do believe in them), but the basic reason is simple and personal. I write these essays primarily to aid my own quest to learn and understand as much as possible about nature in the short time allotted."

In his own view, Gould was lucky: He was a writer carried along by a single, fascinating theme. "If my volumes work at all, they owe their reputation to coherence supplied by the common theme of evolutionary theory. I have a wonderful advantage among essayists because no other theme so beautifully encompasses both the particulars that fascinate and the generalities that instruct. . . . Each essay is both a single long argument and a welding together of particulars."

## For Discussion

1. What differences would occur naturally between the work of a scientist writing for other scientists and the work of Gould, who wrote about science for a general AUDIENCE?
2. How does the author defend himself against the possible charge that, as a popularizer of science, he trivializes his subject?

# MARTIN LUTHER KING, JR.

MARTIN LUTHER KING, JR. (1929–68), was born in Atlanta, the son of a Baptist minister, and was himself ordained in the same denomination. Stepping to the forefront of the civil rights movement in 1955, King led African Americans in a boycott of segregated city buses in Montgomery, Alabama; became the first president of the Southern Christian Leadership Conference; and staged sit-ins and mass marches that helped bring about the Civil Rights Act passed by Congress in 1964 and the Voting Rights Act of 1965. He received the Nobel Peace Prize in 1964. While King preached "nonviolent resistance," he was himself the target of violence. He was stabbed in New York, pelted with stones in Chicago; his home in Montgomery was bombed; and ultimately he was assassinated in Memphis by a sniper. On his tombstone near Atlanta's Ebenezer Baptist Church are these words from the spiritual he quotes at the conclusion of "I Have a Dream": "Free at last, free at last, thank God almighty, I'm free at last." Martin Luther King's birthday, January 15, is now a national holiday.

## *I Have a Dream*

In Washington, DC, on August 28, 1963, King's campaign of nonviolent resistance reached its historic climax. On that date, commemorating the centennial of Lincoln's Emancipation Proclamation freeing the slaves, King led a march of 200,000 persons, black and white, from the Washington Monument to the Lincoln Memorial. Before this throng, and to millions who watched on television, he delivered this unforgettable speech.

Intended to inspire and motivate its audience, King's speech is a model of a certain kind of persuasion. To make his point, King draws on a number of methods:

Narration (Chap. 4): paragraphs 1–2
Description (Chap. 5): paragraphs 2, 4
Example (Chap. 6): paragraphs 6–9, 12–16, 21–22
Comparison and contrast (Chap. 7): paragraphs 3–4, 6
Cause and effect (Chap. 11): paragraphs 5, 7, 19
Argument and persuasion (Chap. 13): throughout

Five score years ago, a great American, in whose symbolic shadow we 1 stand, signed the Emancipation Proclamation. This momentous decree came as a great beacon light of hope to millions of Negro slaves who had been seared in the flames of withering injustice. It came as a joyous daybreak to end the long night of captivity.

But one hundred years later, we must face the tragic fact that the Negro 2 is still not free. One hundred years later, the life of the Negro is still sadly crippled by the manacles of segregation and the chains of discrimination. One hundred years later, the Negro lives on a lonely island of poverty in the midst of a vast ocean of material prosperity. One hundred years later, the Negro is still languishing in the corners of American society and finds himself in exile in his own land. So we have come here today to dramatize an appalling condition.

In a sense we have come to our nation's capital to cash a check. When the architects of our republic wrote the magnificent words of the Constitution and the Declaration of Independence, they were signing a promissory note to which every American was to fall heir. This note was a promise that all men would be guaranteed the unalienable rights of life, liberty, and the pursuit of happiness.

It is obvious today that America has defaulted on this promissory note insofar as her citizens of color are concerned. Instead of honoring this sacred obligation, America has given the Negro people a bad check; a check which has come back marked "insufficient funds." But we refuse to believe that the bank of justice is bankrupt. We refuse to believe that there are insufficient funds in the great vaults of opportunity of this nation. So we have come to cash this check—a check that will give us upon demand the riches of freedom and the security of justice. We have also come to this hallowed spot to remind America of the fierce urgency of *now*. This is no time to engage in the luxury of cooling off or to take the tranquilizing drugs of gradualism. *Now* is the time to make real the promises of Democracy. *Now* is the time to rise from the dark and desolate valley of segregation to the sunlit path of racial justice. *Now* is the time to open the doors of opportunity to all of God's children. *Now* is the time to lift our nation from the quicksands of racial injustice to the solid rock of brotherhood.

It would be fatal for the nation to overlook the urgency of the moment and to underestimate the determination of the Negro. This sweltering summer of the Negro's legitimate discontent will not pass until there is an invigorating autumn of freedom and equality; 1963 is not an end, but a beginning. Those who hope that the Negro needed to blow off steam and will now be content will have a rude awakening if the nation returns to business as usual. There will be neither rest nor tranquillity in America until the Negro is granted his citizenship rights. The whirlwinds of revolt will continue to shake the foundations of our nation until the bright day of justice emerges.

But there is something that I must say to my people who stand on the warm threshold which leads into the palace of justice. In the process of gaining our rightful place we must not be guilty of wrongful deeds. Let us not seek to satisfy our thirst for freedom by drinking from the cup of bitterness and hatred. We must forever conduct our struggle on the high plane of dig-

nity and discipline. We must not allow our creative protest to degenerate
into physical violence. Again and again we must rise to the majestic heights
of meeting physical force with soul force. The marvelous new militancy
which has engulfed the Negro community must not lead us to a distrust of all
white people, for many of our white brothers, as evidenced by their presence
here today, have come to realize that their destiny is tied up with our destiny
and their freedom is inextricably bound to our freedom. We cannot walk
alone.

And as we walk, we must make the pledge that we shall march ahead. We      7
cannot turn back. There are those who are asking the devotees of civil rights,
"When will you be satisfied?" We can never be satisfied as long as the Negro is
the victim of the unspeakable horrors of police brutality. We can never be satisfied as long as our bodies, heavy with the fatigue of travel, cannot gain lodg-
ing in the motels of the highways and the hotels of the cities. We cannot be
satisfied as long as the Negro's basic mobility is from a smaller ghetto to a
larger one. We can never be satisfied as long as a Negro in Mississippi cannot
vote and a Negro in New York believes he has nothing for which to vote. No,
no, we are not satisfied, and we will not be satisfied until justice rolls down like
waters and righteousness like a mighty stream.

I am not unmindful that some of you have come here out of great trials      8
and tribulations. Some of you have come fresh from narrow jail cells. Some of
you have come from areas where your quest for freedom left you battered by
the storms of persecution and staggered by the winds of police brutality. You
have been the veterans of creative suffering. Continue to work with the faith
that unearned suffering is redemptive.

Go back to Mississippi, go back to Alabama, go back to South Carolina,      9
go back to Georgia, go back to Louisiana, go back to the slums and ghettos of
our northern cities, knowing that somehow this situation can and will be
changed. Let us not wallow in the valley of despair.

I say to you today, my friends, that in spite of the difficulties and frustra-   10
tions of the moment I still have a dream. It is a dream deeply rooted in the
American dream.

I have a dream that one day this nation will rise up and live out the true    11
meaning of its creed: "We hold these truths to be self-evident; that all men are
created equal."

I have a dream that one day on the red hills of Georgia the sons of former   12
slaves and the sons of former slaveowners will be able to sit down together at
the table of brotherhood.

I have a dream that one day even the state of Mississippi, a desert state     13
sweltering with the heat of injustice and oppression, will be transformed into
an oasis of freedom and justice.

I have a dream that my four little children will one day live in a nation    14
where they will not be judged by the color of their skin but by the content of
their character.

I have a dream today.    15

I have a dream that one day the state of Alabama, whose governor's lips    16
are presently dripping with the words of interposition and nullification, will
be transformed into a situation where little black boys and black girls will be
able to join hands with little white boys and white girls and walk together as
sisters and brothers.

I have a dream today.    17

I have a dream that one day every valley shall be exalted, every hill and    18
mountain shall be made low, the rough places will be made plain, and the
crooked places will be made straight, and the glory of the Lord shall be
revealed, and all flesh shall see it together.

This is our hope. This is the faith with which I return to the South. With    19
this faith we will be able to hew out of the mountain of despair a stone of
hope. With this faith we will be able to transform the jangling discords of
our nation into a beautiful symphony of brotherhood. With this faith we
will be able to work together, to pray together, to struggle together, to go to
jail together, to stand up for freedom together, knowing that we will be free
one day.

This will be the day when all of God's children will be able to sing with    20
new meaning

> My country, 'tis of thee,
> Sweet land of liberty,
>   Of thee I sing:
> Land where my fathers died,
> Land of the pilgrims' pride,
> From every mountainside
>   Let freedom ring.

And if America is to be a great nation this must become true. So let free-    21
dom ring from the prodigious hilltops of New Hampshire. Let freedom ring
from the mighty mountains of New York. Let freedom ring from the height-
ening Alleghenies of Pennsylvania!

Let freedom ring from the snowcapped Rockies of Colorado!    22

Let freedom ring from the curvaceous peaks of California!    23

But not only that; let freedom ring from Stone Mountain of Georgia!    24

Let freedom ring from Lookout Mountain of Tennessee!    25

Let freedom ring from every hill and molehill of Mississippi. From every    26
mountainside, let freedom ring.

When we let freedom ring, when we let it ring from every village and     27
every hamlet, from every state and every city, we will be able to speed up that
day when all of God's children, black men and white men, Jews and Gentiles,
Protestants and Catholics, will be able to join hands and sing in the words of
the old Negro spiritual, "Free at last! free at last! thank God almighty, we are
free at last!"

*For a reading quiz, sources on Martin Luther King, Jr., and annotated links to further
readings on the civil rights movement in the United States, visit **bedfordstmartins
.com/thebedfordreader**.*

## Journal Writing

Do you think we have moved closer to fulfilling King's dream in the decades since he
gave this famous speech? In your journal, explore why or why not. (To take your journal writing further, see "From Journal to Essay" on the next page.)

## Questions on Meaning

1. What is the apparent PURPOSE of this speech?
2. What THESIS does King develop in his first four paragraphs?
3. What does King mean by the "marvelous new militancy which has engulfed the
   Negro community" (par. 6)? Does this contradict King's nonviolent philosophy?
4. In what passages of his speech does King notice events of history? Where does he
   acknowledge the historic occasion on which he is speaking?

## Questions on Writing Strategy

1. What indicates that King's words were meant primarily for an AUDIENCE of listeners, and only secondarily for a reading audience? To hear these indications, try
   reading the speech aloud. What uses of PARALLELISM do you notice?
2. Where in the speech does King acknowledge that not all of his listeners are
   African American?
3. How much EMPHASIS does King place on the past? How much does he place on
   the future?
4. **MIXED METHODS**     Analyze the ETHICAL APPEAL of King's ARGUMENT (see p. 521).
   Where in the speech, for instance, does he present himself as reasonable despite
   his passion? To what extent does his personal authority lend power to his words?

5. **MIXED METHODS**   The DESCRIPTION in paragraphs 2 and 4 depends on metaphor, a FIGURE OF SPEECH in which one thing is said to be another thing. How do the metaphors in these paragraphs work for King's purpose?

## Questions on Language

1. In general, is the language of King's speech ABSTRACT or CONCRETE? How is this level appropriate to his message and to the span of history with which he deals?
2. Point to memorable figures of speech besides those examined in the "Mixed Methods" question on the preceding page.
3. Define momentous (par. 1); manacles, languishing (2); promissory note, unalienable (3); defaulted, hallowed, gradualism (4); inextricably (6); mobility, ghetto (7); tribulations, redemptive (8); interposition, nullification (16); prodigious (21); curvaceous (23); hamlet (27).

## Suggestions for Writing

1. **FROM JOURNAL TO ESSAY**   Use your journal entry to write an essay that explains your sense of how well the United States has progressed toward realizing King's dream. You may choose to focus on America as a whole or on your particular community, but you should use specific EVIDENCE to support your opinion.
2. Propose some course of action in a situation that you consider an injustice. Racial injustice is one possible area, or unfairness to any minority, or to women, children, the elderly, ex-convicts, the disabled, the poor. If possible, narrow your subject to a particular incident or a local situation on which you can write knowledgeably.
3. **CRITICAL WRITING**   What can you INFER from this speech about King's own attitudes toward oppression and injustice? Does he follow his own injunction not "to satisfy our thirst for freedom by drinking from the cup of bitterness and hatred" (par. 6)? Explain your answer, using evidence from the speech.
4. **CONNECTIONS**   King's "I Have a Dream" and Edward Said's "Clashing Civilizations?" (p. 665) both seek to influence readers, either to cause them to act or to change their views. Yet the two authors take very different approaches to achieve their purposes. COMPARE AND CONTRAST the authors' persuasive strategies, considering especially their effectiveness for the situation each writes about and the audience each addresses.
5. **CONNECTIONS**   King's speech was delivered in 1963. Brent Staples's essay "Black Men and Public Space" (p. 208) was first published in 1986. In an essay, explore the changes, if any, that are evident in the ASSUMPTIONS the authors make about their audiences' attitudes, about race in general, and about racism.

# MAXINE HONG KINGSTON

MAXINE HONG KINGSTON grew up caught between two complex and very different cultures: the China of her parents and the America of her surroundings. In her first two books, *The Woman Warrior: Memoirs of a Girlhood Among Ghosts* (1976) and *China Men* (1980), Kingston combines Chinese myth and history with family tales to create a dreamlike world that shifts between reality and fantasy. Born in 1940 in Stockton, California, Kingston was the first American-born child of a scholar and a medical practitioner who became laundry workers in this country. After graduating from the University of California at Berkeley (BA, 1962), Kingston taught English at California and Hawaii high schools, at the University of Hawaii, and for many years at UC Berkeley. She has contributed essays, poems, and stories to *The New Yorker*, the *New York Times Magazine*, *Ms.*, and other periodicals. Other books by Kingston include a collection of essays, *Hawai'i One Summer* (1987); a novel, *Tripmaster Monkey: His Fake Book* (1989); a collection of lectures and verse, *To Be a Poet* (2002); and a blend of fiction and nonfiction, *The Fifth Book of Peace* (2003). Most recently, Kingston edited *Veterans of War, Veterans of Peace* (2006), a collection of essays written in workshops she holds for military veterans.

## No Name Woman

"No Name Woman" is part of *The Woman Warrior*. Like much of Kingston's writing, it blends the "talk-stories" of Kingston's elders, her own vivid imaginings, and the reality of her experience—this time to discover why her Chinese aunt drowned herself in the family well.

Kingston develops "No Name Woman" with four main methods, all intertwined: In the context of narrating her own experiences, she seeks the causes of her aunt's suicide by comparing various narratives of it, and she employs description to make the narratives concrete and vivid. The main uses of these methods appear below:

Narration (Chap. 4): paragraphs 1–8, 14, 16–20, 23, 28–30, 34–35, 37–46
Description (Chap. 5): paragraphs 4–8, 21, 23–27, 31, 37, 40–46
Comparison and contrast (Chap. 7): paragraphs 15–18, 20–24, 27–28, 31
Cause and effect (Chap. 11): paragraphs 10–11, 15–18, 21–25, 29–31,
     33–39, 44–48

"You must not tell anyone," my mother said, "what I am about to tell you.  1
In China your father had a sister who killed herself. She jumped into the family well. We say that your father has all brothers because it is as if she had never been born.

"In 1924 just a few days after our village celebrated seventeen hurry-up  2
weddings—to make sure that every young man who went 'out on the road'

would responsibly come home—your father and his brothers and your grandfather and his brothers and your aunt's new husband sailed for America, the Gold Mountain. It was your grandfather's last trip. Those lucky enough to get contracts waved good-bye from the decks. They fed and guarded the stowaways and helped them off in Cuba, New York, Bali, Hawaii. 'We'll meet in California next year,' they said. All of them sent money home.

"I remember looking at your aunt one day when she and I were dressing; 3 I had not noticed before that she had such a protruding melon of a stomach. But I did not think, 'She's pregnant,' until she began to look like other pregnant women, her shirt pulling and the white tops of her black pants showing. She could not have been pregnant, you see, because her husband had been gone for years. No one said anything. We did not discuss it. In early summer she was ready to have the child, long after the time when it could have been possible.

"The village had also been counting. On the night the baby was to be 4 born the villagers raided our house. Some were crying. Like a great saw, teeth strung with lights, files of people walked zigzag across our land, tearing the rice. Their lanterns doubled in the disturbed black water, which drained away through the broken bunds. As the villagers closed in, we could see that some of them, probably men and women we knew well, wore white masks. The people with long hair hung it over their faces. Women with short hair made it stand up on end. Some had tied white bands around their foreheads, arms, and legs.

"At first they threw mud and rocks at the house. Then they threw eggs 5 and began slaughtering our stock. We could hear the animals scream their deaths—the roosters, the pigs, a last great roar from the ox. Familiar wild heads flared in our night windows; the villagers encircled us. Some of the faces stopped to peer at us, their eyes rushing like searchlights. The hands flattened against the panes, framed heads, and left red prints.

"The villagers broke in the front and the back doors at the same time, 6 even though we had not locked the doors against them. Their knives dripped with the blood of our animals. They smeared blood on the doors and walls. One woman swung a chicken, whose throat she had slit, splattering blood in red arcs about her. We stood together in the middle of our house, in the family hall with the pictures and tables of the ancestors around us, and looked straight ahead.

"At that time the house had only two wings. When the men came back, 7 we would build two more to enclose our courtyard and a third one to begin a second courtyard. The villagers pushed through both wings, even your grandparents' rooms, to find your aunt's, which was also mine until the men returned. From this room a new wing for one of the younger families would grow. They ripped up her clothes and shoes and broke her combs, grinding them underfoot. They tore her work from the loom. They scattered the cooking fire and rolled the new weaving in it. We could hear them in the kitchen breaking our bowls and banging the pots. They overturned the great waist-high earthenware jugs; duck eggs, pickled fruits, vegetables burst out and mixed in acrid torrents. The old woman from the next field swept a broom through the air and loosed the spirits-of-the-broom over our heads. 'Pig.' 'Ghost.' 'Pig,' they sobbed and scolded while they ruined our house.

"When they left, they took sugar and oranges to bless themselves. They  8
cut pieces from the dead animals. Some of them took bowls that were not broken and clothes that were not torn. Afterward we swept up the rice and sewed it back up into sacks. But the smells from the spilled preserves lasted. Your aunt gave birth in the pigsty that night. The next morning when I went up for the water, I found her and the baby plugging up the family well.

"Don't let your father know that I told you. He denies her. Now that you  9
have started to menstruate, what happened to her could happen to you. Don't humiliate us. You wouldn't like to be forgotten as if you had never been born. The villagers are watchful."

Whenever she had to warn us about life, my mother told stories that ran  10
like this one, a story to grow up on. She tested our strength to establish realities. Those in the emigrant generations who could not reassert brute survival died young and far from home. Those of us in the first American generations have had to figure out how the invisible world the emigrants built around our childhoods fit in solid America.

The emigrants confused the gods by diverting their curses, misleading  11
them with crooked streets and false names. They must try to confuse their offspring as well, who, I suppose, threaten them in similar ways—always trying to get things straight, always trying to name the unspeakable. The Chinese I know hide their names; sojourners take new names when their lives change and guard their real names with silence.

Chinese-Americans, when you try to understand what things in you are  12
Chinese, how do you separate what is peculiar to childhood, to poverty, insanities, one family, your mother who marked your growing with stories, from what is Chinese? What is Chinese tradition and what is the movies?

If I want to learn what clothes my aunt wore, whether flashy or ordinary,  13
I would have to begin, "Remember Father's drowned-in-the-well sister?" I cannot ask that. My mother has told me once and for all the useful parts. She will add nothing unless powered by Necessity, a riverbank that guides her life. She plants vegetable gardens rather than lawns; she carries the odd-shaped tomatoes home from the fields and eats food left for the gods.

Whenever we did frivolous things, we used up energy; we flew high kites.    14
We children came up off the ground over the melting cones our parents
brought home from work and the American movie on New Year's Day—*Oh,
You Beautiful Doll* with Betty Grable one year, and *She Wore a Yellow Ribbon*
with John Wayne another year. After the one carnival ride each, we paid in
guilt; our tired father counted his change on the dark walk home.

Adultery is extravagance. Could people who hatch their own chicks and    15
eat the embryos and the heads for delicacies and boil the feet in vinegar for
party food, leaving only the gravel, eating even the gizzard lining—could
such people engender a prodigal aunt? To be a woman, to have a daughter in
starvation time was a waste enough. My aunt could not have been the lone
romantic who gave up everything for sex. Women in the old China did not
choose. Some man had commanded her to lie with him and be his secret evil.
I wonder whether he masked himself when he joined the raid on her family.

Perhaps she encountered him in the fields or on the mountain where the    16
daughters-in-law collected fuel. Or perhaps he first noticed her in the marketplace. He was not a stranger because the village housed no strangers. She had
to have dealings with him other than sex. Perhaps he worked an adjoining
field, or he sold her the cloth for the dress she sewed and wore. His demand
must have surprised, then terrified her. She obeyed him; she always did as she
was told.

When the family found a young man in the next village to be her husband,    17
she stood tractably beside the best rooster, his proxy, and promised before they
met that she would be his forever. She was lucky that he was her age and she
would be the first wife, an advantage secure now. The night she first saw him,
he had sex with her. Then he left for America. She had almost forgotten what
he looked like. When she tried to envision him, she only saw the black and
white face in the group photograph the men had had taken before leaving.

The other man was not, after all, much different from her husband. They    18
both gave orders: she followed. "If you tell your family, I'll beat you. I'll kill
you. Be here again next week." No one talked sex, ever. And she might have
separated the rapes from the rest of living if only she did not have to buy her
oil from him or gather wood in the same forest. I want her fear to have lasted
just as long as rape lasted so that the fear could have been contained. No
drawn-out fear. But women at sex hazarded birth and hence lifetimes. The fear
did not stop but permeated everywhere. She told the man, "I think I'm pregnant." He organized the raid against her.

On nights when my mother and father talked about their life back home,    19
sometimes they mentioned an "outcast table" whose business they still seemed
to be settling, their voices tight. In a commensal tradition, where food is precious, the powerful older people made wrongdoers eat alone. Instead of letting

them start separate new lives like the Japanese, who could become samurais and geishas, the Chinese family, faces averted but eyes glowering sideways, hung on to the offenders and fed them leftovers. My aunt must have lived in the same house as my parents and eaten at an outcast table. My mother spoke about the raid as if she had seen it, when she and my aunt, a daughter-in-law to a different household, should not have been living together at all. Daughters-in-law lived with their husbands' parents, not their own; a synonym for marriage in Chinese is "taking a daughter-in-law." Her husband's parents could have sold her, mortgaged her, stoned her. But they had sent her back to her own mother and father, a mysterious act hinting at disgraces not told me. Perhaps they had thrown her out to deflect the avengers.

She was the only daughter; her four brothers went with her father, husband, and uncles "out on the road" and for some years became western men. When the goods were divided among the family, three of the brothers took land, and the youngest, my father, chose an education. After my grandparents gave their daughter away to her husband's family, they had dispensed all the adventure and all the property. They expected her alone to keep the traditional ways, which her brothers, now among the barbarians, could fumble without detection. The heavy, deep-rooted women were to maintain the past against the flood, safe for returning. But the rare urge west had fixed upon our family, and so my aunt crossed boundaries not delineated in space.

The work of preservation demands that the feelings playing about in one's guts not be turned into action. Just watch their passing like cherry blossoms. But perhaps my aunt, my forerunner, caught in a slow life, let dreams grow and fade and after some months or years went toward what persisted. Fear at the enormities of the forbidden kept her desires delicate, wire and bone. She looked at a man because she liked the way the hair was tucked behind his ears, or she liked the question-mark line of a long torso curving at the shoulder and straight at the hip. For warm eyes or a soft voice or a slow walk—that's all—a few hairs, a line, a brightness, a sound, a pace, she gave up family. She offered us up for a charm that vanished with tiredness, a pigtail that didn't toss when the wind died. Why, the wrong lighting could erase the dearest thing about him.

It could very well have been, however, that my aunt did not take subtle enjoyment of her friend, but, a wild woman, kept rollicking company. Imagining her free with sex doesn't fit, though. I don't know any women like that, or men either. Unless I see her life branching into mine, she gives me no ancestral help.

To sustain her being in love, she often worked at herself in the mirror, guessing at the colors and shapes that would interest him, changing them frequently in order to hit on the right combination. She wanted him to look back.

On a farm near the sea, a woman who tended her appearance reaped a    24
reputation for eccentricity. All the married women blunt-cut their hair in
flaps about their ears or pulled it back in tight buns. No nonsense. Neither
style blew easily into heart-catching tangles. And at their weddings they displayed themselves in their long hair for the last time. "It brushed the backs of
my knees," my mother tells me. "It was braided, and even so, it brushed the
backs of my knees."

At the mirror my aunt combed individuality into her bob. A bun could    25
have been contrived to escape into black streamers blowing in the wind or in
quiet wisps about her face, but only the older women in our picture album wear
buns. She brushed her hair back from her forehead, tucking the flaps behind her
ears. She looped a piece of thread, knotted into a circle between her index fingers and thumbs, and ran the double strand across her forehead. When she
closed her fingers as if she were making a pair of shadow geese bite, the string
twisted together catching the little hairs. Then she pulled the thread away from
her skin, ripping the hairs out neatly, her eyes watering from the needles of pain.
Opening her fingers, she cleaned the thread, then rolled it along her hairline
and the tops of her eyebrows. My mother did the same to me and my sisters and
herself. I used to believe that the expression "caught by the short hairs" meant a
captive held with a depilatory string. It especially hurt at the temples, but my
mother said we were lucky we didn't have to have our feet bound when we were
seven. Sisters used to sit on their beds and cry together, she said, as their mothers or their slave removed the bandages for a few minutes each night and let the
blood gush back into their veins. I hope that the man my aunt loved appreciated
a smooth brow, that he wasn't just a tits-and-ass man.

Once my aunt found a freckle on her chin, at a spot that the almanac said    26
predestined her for unhappiness. She dug it out with a hot needle and washed
the wound with peroxide.

More attention to her looks than these pullings of hairs and pickings at    27
spots would have caused gossip among the villagers. They owned work clothes
and good clothes, and they wore good clothes for feasting the new seasons.
But since a woman combing her hair hexes beginnings, my aunt rarely found
an occasion to look her best. Women looked like great sea snails — the corded
wood, babies, and laundry they carried were the whorls on their backs. The
Chinese did not admire a bent back; goddesses and warriors stood straight.
Still there must have been a marvelous freeing of beauty when a worker laid
down her burden and stretched and arched.

Such commonplace loveliness, however, was not enough for my aunt. She    28
dreamed of a lover for the fifteen days of New Year's, the time for families to
exchange visits, money, and food. She plied her secret comb. And sure
enough she cursed the year, the family, the village, and herself.

Even as her hair lured her imminent lover, many other men looked at her. 29
Uncles, cousins, nephews, brothers would have looked, too, had they been
home between journeys. Perhaps they had already been restraining their
curiosity, and they left, fearful that their glances, like a field of nesting birds,
might be startled and caught. Poverty hurt, and that was their first reason for
leaving. But another, final reason for leaving the crowded house was the
never-said.

She may have been unusually beloved, the precious only daughter, spoiled 30
and mirror gazing because of the affection the family lavished on her. When
her husband left, they welcomed the chance to take her back from the in-laws;
she could live like the little daughter for just a while longer. There are stories
that my grandfather was different from other people, "crazy ever since the little
Jap bayoneted him in the head." He used to put his naked penis on the dinner
table, laughing. And one day he brought home a baby girl, wrapped up inside
his brown western-style greatcoat. He had traded one of his sons, probably my
father, the youngest, for her. My grandmother made him trade back. When he
finally got a daughter of his own, he doted on her. They must have all loved
her, except perhaps my father, the only brother who never went back to
China, having once been traded for a girl.

Brothers and sisters, newly men and women, had to efface their sexual 31
color and present plain miens. Disturbing hair and eyes, a smile like no other,
threatened the ideal of five generations living under one roof. To focus blurs,
people shouted face to face and yelled from room to room. The immigrants I
know have loud voices, unmodulated to American tones even after years away
from the village where they called their friendships out across the fields. I have
not been able to stop my mother's screams in public libraries or over tele-
phones. Walking erect (knees straight, toes pointed forward, not pigeon-toed,
which is Chinese-feminine) and speaking in an inaudible voice, I have tried
to turn myself American-feminine. Chinese communication was loud, public.
Only sick people had to whisper. But at the dinner table, where the family
members came nearest one another, no one could talk, not the outcasts nor
any eaters. Every word that falls from the mouth is a coin lost. Silently they
gave and accepted food with both hands. A preoccupied child who took his
bowl with one hand got a sideways glare. A complete moment of total attention is due everyone alike. Children and lovers have no singularity here, but
my aunt used a secret voice, a separate attentiveness.

She kept the man's name to herself throughout her labor and dying; she 32
did not accuse him that he be punished with her. To save her inseminator's
name she gave silent birth.

He may have been somebody in her own household, but intercourse with 33
a man outside the family would have been no less abhorrent. All the village

were kinsmen, and the titles shouted in loud country voices never let kinship be forgotten. Any man within visiting distance would have been neutralized as a lover — "brother," "younger brother," "older brother" — one hundred and fifteen relationship titles. Parents researched birth charts probably not so much to assure good fortune as to circumvent incest in a population that has but one hundred surnames. Everybody has eight million relatives. How useless then sexual mannerisms, how dangerous.

As if it came from an atavism deeper than fear, I used to add "brother"   34 silently to boys' names. It hexed the boys, who would or would not ask me to dance, and made them less scary and as familiar and deserving of benevolence as girls.

But, of course, I hexed myself also — no dates. I should have stood up,   35 both arms waving, and shouted out across libraries, "Hey, you! Love me back." I had no idea, though, how to make attraction selective, how to control its direction and magnitude. If I made myself American-pretty so that the five or six Chinese boys in the class fell in love with me, everyone else — the Caucasian, Negro, and Japanese boys — would too. Sisterliness, dignified and honorable, made much more sense.

Attraction eludes control so stubbornly that whole societies designed to   36 organize relationships among people cannot keep order, not even when they bind people to one another from childhood and raise them together. Among the very poor and the wealthy, brothers married their adopted sisters, like doves. Our family allowed some romance, paying adult brides' prices and providing dowries so that their sons and daughters could marry strangers. Marriage promises to turn strangers into friendly relatives — a nation of siblings.

In the village structure, spirits shimmered among the live creatures, bal-   37 anced and held in equilibrium by time and land. But one human being flaring up into violence could open up a black hole, a maelstrom that pulled in the sky. The frightened villagers, who depended on one another to maintain the real, went to my aunt to show her a personal, physical representation of the break she made in the "roundness." Misallying couples snapped off the future, which was to be embodied in true offspring. The villagers punished her for acting as if she could have a private life, secret and apart from them.

If my aunt had betrayed the family at a time of large grain yields and   38 peace, when many boys were born, and wings were being built on many houses, perhaps she might have escaped such severe punishment. But the men — hungry, greedy, tired of planting in dry soil, cuckolded — had been forced to leave the village in order to send food-money home. There were ghost plagues, bandit plagues, wars with the Japanese, floods. My Chinese brother and sister had died of an unknown sickness. Adultery, perhaps only a mistake during good times, became a crime when the village needed food.

The round moon cakes and round doorways, the round tables of graduated    39
size that fit one roundness inside another, round windows and rice bowls—
these talismans had lost their power to warn this family of the law: A family
must be whole, faithfully keeping the descent line by having sons to feed the
old and the dead who in turn look after the family. The villagers came to show
my aunt and lover-in-hiding a broken house. The villagers were speeding up
the circling of events because she was too shortsighted to see that her infidelity had already harmed the village, that waves of consequences would
return unpredictably, sometimes in disguise, as now, to hurt her. This roundness had to be made coin-sized so that she would see its circumference: punish
her at the birth of her baby. Awaken her to the inexorable. People who refused
fatalism because they could invent small resources insisted on culpability.
Deny accidents and wrest fault from the stars.

After the villagers left, their lanterns now scattering in various directions    40
toward home, the family broke their silence and cursed her. "Aiaa, we're going
to die. Death is coming. Death is coming. Look what you've done. You've
killed us. Ghost! Dead Ghost! Ghost! You've never been born." She ran out
into the fields, far enough from the house so that she could no longer hear
their voices, and pressed herself against the earth, her own land no more.
When she felt the birth coming, she thought that she had been hurt. Her body
seized together. "They've hurt me too much," she thought. "This is gall, and it
will kill me." With forehead and knees against the earth, her body convulsed
and then relaxed. She turned on her back, lay on the ground. The black well
of sky and stars went out and out and out forever; her body and her complexity seemed to disappear. She was one of the stars, a bright dot in blackness,
without home, without a companion, in eternal cold and silence. An agoraphobia rose in her, speeding higher and higher, bigger and bigger; she would
not be able to contain it; there would be no end to fear.

Flayed, unprotected against space, she felt pain return, focusing her body.    41
This pain chilled her—a cold, steady kind of surface pain. Inside, spasmodically, the other pain, the pain of the child, heated her. For hours she lay
on the ground, alternately body and space. Sometimes a vision of normal
comfort obliterated reality: She saw the family in the evening gambling at
the dinner table, the young people massaging their elders' backs. She saw
them congratulating one another, high joy on the mornings the rice shoots
came up. When these pictures burst, the stars drew out further apart. Black
space opened.

She got to her feet to fight better and remembered that old-fashioned    42
women gave birth in their pigsties to fool the jealous, pain-dealing gods, who
do not snatch piglets. Before the next spasms could stop her, she ran to the
pigsty, each step a rushing out into emptiness. She climbed over the fence and

knelt in the dirt. It was good to have a fence enclosing her, a tribal person alone.

Laboring, this woman who had carried her child as a foreign growth that 43 sickened her every day, expelled it at last. She reached down to touch the hot, wet, moving mass, surely smaller than anything human, and could feel that it was human after all—fingers, toes, nails, nose. She pulled it up on to her belly, and it lay curled there, butt in the air, feet precisely tucked one under the other. She opened her loose shirt and buttoned the child inside. After resting, it squirmed and thrashed and she pushed it up to her breast. It turned its head this way and that until it found her nipple. There, it made little snuffling noises. She clenched her teeth at its preciousness, lovely as a young calf, a piglet, a little dog.

She may have gone to the pigsty as a last act of responsibility: She would 44 protect this child as she had protected its father. It would look after her soul, leaving supplies on her grave. But how would this tiny child without family find her grave when there would be no marker for her anywhere, neither in the earth nor the family hall? No one would give her a family hall name. She had taken the child with her into the wastes. At its birth the two of them had felt the same raw pain of separation, a wound that only the family pressing tight could close. A child with no descent line would not soften her life but only trail after her, ghostlike, begging her to give it purpose. At dawn the villagers on their way to the fields would stand around the fence and look.

Full of milk, the little ghost slept. When it awoke, she hardened her 45 breasts against the milk that crying loosens. Toward morning she picked up the baby and walked to the well.

Carrying the baby to the well shows loving. Otherwise abandon it. Turn 46 its face into the mud. Mothers who love their children take them along. It was probably a girl; there is some hope of forgiveness for boys.

"Don't tell anyone you had an aunt. Your father does not want to hear her 47 name. She has never been born." I have believed that sex was unspeakable and words so strong and fathers so frail that "aunt" would do my father mysterious harm. I have thought that my family, having settled among immigrants who had also been their neighbors in the ancestral land, needed to clean their name, and a wrong word would incite the kinspeople even here. But there is more to this silence: They want me to participate in her punishment. And I have.

In the twenty years since I heard this story I have not asked for details nor 48 said my aunt's name; I do not know it. People who comfort the dead can also chase after them to hurt them further—a reverse ancestor worship. The real punishment was not the raid swiftly inflicted by the villagers, but the family's deliberately forgetting her. Her betrayal so maddened them, they saw to it that she would suffer forever, even after death. Always hungry, always needing, she would have to beg food from other ghosts, snatch and steal it from those whose living descendants give them gifts. She would have to fight the ghosts massed at crossroads for the buns a few thoughtful citizens leave to decoy her away from village and home so that the ancestral spirits could feast unharassed. At peace, they could act like gods, not ghosts, their descent lines providing them with paper suits and dresses, spirit money, paper houses, paper automobiles, chicken, meat, and rice into eternity—essences delivered up in smoke and flames, steam and incense rising from each rice bowl. In an attempt to make the Chinese care for people outside the family, Chairman Mao encourages us now to give our paper replicas to the spirits of outstanding soldiers and workers, no matter whose ancestors they may be. My aunt remains forever hungry. Goods are not distributed evenly among the dead.

My aunt haunts me—her ghost drawn to me because now, after fifty years    49 of neglect, I alone devote pages of paper to her, though not origamied into houses and clothes. I do not think she always means me well. I am telling on her, and she was a spite suicide, drowning herself in the drinking water. The Chinese are always very frightened of the drowned one, whose weeping ghost, wet hair hanging and skin bloated, waits silently by the water to pull down a substitute.

> *For a reading quiz, sources on Maxine Hong Kingston, and annotated links to further readings on Chinese culture and on Chinese American culture, visit* **bedfordstmartins.com/thebedfordreader**.

---

## Journal Writing

Most of us have heard family stories that left lasting impressions—ghost stories like Kingston's, biographies of ancestors, explanations for traditions, family superstitions, and so on. Write in your journal about a family story you remember vividly from your childhood. (To take your journal writing further, see "From Journal to Essay" on the next page.)

## Questions on Meaning

1. What PURPOSE does Kingston have in telling her aunt's story? How does this differ from her mother's purpose in relating the tale?

2. According to Kingston, who could have been the father of her aunt's child? Who could not?
3. Kingston says that her mother told stories "to warn us about life." What warning does this story provide?
4. Why is Kingston so fascinated by her aunt's life and death?

## Questions on Writing Strategy

1. Whom does Kingston seem to include in her AUDIENCE: her family and other older Chinese? second-generation Chinese Americans like herself? other Americans? How might she expect each of these groups to respond to her essay?
2. Why is Kingston's opening line—her mother's "You must not tell anyone"—especially fitting for this essay? What secrets are being told? Why does Kingston divulge them?
3. As Kingston tells her tale of her aunt, some events are based on her mother's story or her knowledge of Chinese customs, and some are wholly imaginary. What is the EFFECT of blending these several threads of reality, perception, and imagination?
4. **MIXED METHODS**  Examine the details in the two contrasting NARRATIVES of how Kingston's aunt became pregnant: one in paragraphs 15–18 and the other in paragraphs 21–28. How do the details create different realities? Which version does Kingston seem more committed to? Why?
5. **MIXED METHODS**  Kingston COMPARES AND CONTRASTS various versions of her aunt's story, trying to find the CAUSES that led her aunt to drown in the well. In the end, what causes does Kingston seem to accept?

## Questions on Language

1. How does Kingston's language—lyrical, poetic, full of FIGURES OF SPEECH and other IMAGES—reveal her relationship to her Chinese heritage? Find phrases that are especially striking.
2. Look up any of these words you do not know: bunds (par. 4); acrid (7); frivolous (14); tractably, proxy (17); hazarded (18); commensal (19); delineated (20); depilatory (25); plied (28); miens (31); abhorrent, circumvent (33); atavism (34); maelstrom (37); talismans, inexorable, fatalism, culpability (39); gall, agoraphobia (40); spasmodically (41).
3. Sometimes Kingston indicates that she is reconstructing or imagining events through verbs like "would have" and words like "maybe" and "perhaps" ("Perhaps she encountered him in the fields," par. 16). Other times she presents obviously imaginary events as if they actually happened ("Once my aunt found a freckle on her chin," 26). What effect does Kingston achieve with these apparent inconsistencies?

## Suggestions for Writing

1. **FROM JOURNAL TO ESSAY**  Develop the family story from your journal into a narrative essay. Build in the context of the story as well: Who told it to you? What

purpose did he or she have in telling it to you? How does it illustrate your family's beliefs and values?

2. Write an essay explaining the role of ancestors in Chinese family and religious life, supplementing what Kingston says with research in the library or on the Web or (if you are Chinese American) drawing on your own experiences.

3. **CRITICAL WRITING**   ANALYZE the ideas about gender roles revealed in "No Name Woman," both in China and in the Chinese American culture Kingston grew up in. How have these ideas affected Kingston? Do you perceive any semblance of them in contemporary American culture?

4. **CONNECTIONS**   Both Kingston and Gloria Naylor, in "The Meanings of a Word" (p. 488), examine communication within their families. Relate an incident or incidents from your own childhood that portray something about the communication within your family. You might want to focus on the language of communication, such as the words used to discuss (or not discuss) a taboo topic, the special family meanings for familiar words, a misunderstanding between you and an adult about something the adult said. Use dialog and as much CONCRETE detail as you can to clarify your experience and its significance.

5. **CONNECTIONS**   Amy Tan in "Fish Cheeks" (p. 99) and Christine Leong in "Being a Chink" (p. 494) also write about relationships between parents and children in Chinese American families. In an essay, analyze what these two essays along with Kingston's suggest about the experiences of the children of Chinese immigrants to the United States.

---

# *Maxine Hong Kingston on Writing*

In an interview with Jean W. Ross published in *Contemporary Authors* in 1984, Maxine Hong Kingston discusses the writing and revising of *The Woman Warrior*. Ross asks Kingston to clarify an earlier statement that she had "no idea how people who don't write endure their lives." Kingston replies: "When I said that, I was thinking about how words and stories create order. Some of the things that happen to us in life seem to have no meaning, but when you write them down you find the meanings for them; or, as you translate life into words, you force a meaning. Meaning is intrinsic in words and stories."

Ross then asks if Kingston used an outline and planned to blend fact with legend in *The Woman Warrior*. "Oh no, no," Kingston answers. "What I have at the beginning of a book is not an outline. I have no idea of how stories will end or where the beginning will lead. Sometimes I draw pictures. I draw a blob and then I have a little arrow and it goes to this other blob, if you want to call that an outline. It's hardly even words; it's like a doodle. Then when it turns into words, I find the words lead me to various scenes and stories which I don't know about until I get there. I don't see the order until very late in the writing and sometimes the ending just comes. I just run up against it. All of a sudden the book's over and I didn't know it would be over."

A question from Ross about whether her emotions enter her writing leads Kingston to talk about revision. "Well, when I first set something down I feel the emotions I write about. But when I do a second draft, third draft, ninth draft, then I don't feel very emotional. The rewriting is very intellectual; all my education and reading and intellect are involved. The mechanics of sentences, how one phrase or word goes with another one — all that happens in later drafts. There's a very emotional first draft and a very technical last draft."

## For Discussion

1. Do you agree with Kingston that when you write things down you find their meaning? Give examples of when the writing process has or hasn't clarified an experience for you.
2. Kingston doodles as a way to discover her material. How do you discover what you have to say?
3. What does Kingston mean by "[t]he mechanics of sentences"? Do you consider this element as you revise?

# GEORGE ORWELL

GEORGE ORWELL was the pen name of Eric Blair (1903–50), born in Bengal, India, the son of an English civil servant. After attending Eton on a scholarship, he joined the British police in Burma, where he acquired a distrust for the methods of the empire. Then followed years of tramping, odd jobs, and near-starvation—recalled in *Down and Out in Paris and London* (1933). From living on the fringe of society and from reporting on English miners and factory workers, Orwell deepened his sympathy with underdogs. Severely wounded while fighting in the Spanish civil war, he wrote a memoir, *Homage to Catalonia* (1938), voicing disillusionment with Loyalists who, he claimed, sought not to free Spain but to exterminate their political enemies. A socialist by conviction, Orwell kept pointing to the dangers of a collective state run by totalitarians. In *Animal Farm* (1945), he satirized Soviet bureaucracy; and in his famous novel *Nineteen Eighty-Four* (1949), he foresaw a regimented England whose government perverts truth and spies on citizens by two-way television. (The motto of the state and its leader: Big Brother Is Watching You.)

# *Shooting an Elephant*

Orwell wrote compellingly of his five years as a police officer in Burma, a southeast Asian country (now known as Myanmar) that the British began colonizing in the early 1800s and ruled until 1947. In this selection from *Shooting an Elephant and Other Essays* (1950), Orwell combines personal experience and piercing insight to expose both an oppressive government and himself as the government's hireling.

"Shooting an Elephant" is foremost a narrative, but Orwell uses description, example, and cause and effect as well to develop and give significance to his tale.

Narration (Chap. 4): throughout
Description (Chap. 5): paragraphs 2, 4–12
Example (Chap. 6): paragraphs 1–2, 4, 14
Cause and effect (Chap. 11): paragraphs 1–2, 6–7

In Moulmein, in Lower Burma, I was hated by large numbers of people— 1
the only time in my life that I have been important enough for this to happen to me. I was subdivisional police officer of the town, and in an aimless, petty kind of way anti-European feeling was very bitter. No one had the guts to raise a riot, but if a European woman went through the bazaars alone somebody would probably spit betel juice over her dress. As a police officer I was an obvious target and was baited whenever it seemed safe to do so. When a nimble Burman tripped me up on the football field and the referee (another Burman) looked the other way, the crowd yelled with hideous laughter. This happened

more than once. In the end the sneering yellow faces of young men that met me everywhere, the insults hooted after me when I was at a safe distance, got badly on my nerves. The young Buddhist priests were the worst of all. There were several thousands of them in the town and none of them seemed to have anything to do except stand on street corners and jeer at Europeans.

All this was perplexing and upsetting. For at that time I had already made up my mind that imperialism was an evil thing and the sooner I chucked up my job and got out of it the better. Theoretically — and secretly, of course — I was all for the Burmese and all against the oppressors, the British. As for the job I was doing, I hated it more bitterly than I can perhaps make clear. In a job like that you see the dirty work of Empire at close quarters. The wretched prisoners huddling in the stinking cages of the lockups, the grey, cowed faces of the long-term convicts, the scarred buttocks of the men who had been flogged with bamboos — all these oppressed me with an intolerable sense of guilt. But I could get nothing into perspective. I was young and ill-educated and I had had to think out my problems in the utter silence that is imposed on every Englishman in the East. I did not even know that the British Empire is dying, still less did I know that it is a great deal better than the younger empires that are going to supplant it. All I knew was that I was stuck between my hatred of the empire I served and my rage against the evil-spirited little beasts who tried to make my job impossible. With one part of my mind I thought of the British Raj[1] as an unbreakable tyranny, as something clamped down, in *saecula saeculorum*,[2] upon the will of prostrate peoples; with another part I thought that the greatest joy in the world would be to drive a bayonet into a Buddhist priest's guts. Feelings like these are the normal by-products of imperialism; ask any Anglo-Indian official, if you can catch him off duty.

One day something happened which in a roundabout way was enlightening. It was a tiny incident in itself, but it gave me a better glimpse than I had had before of the real nature of imperialism — the real motives for which despotic governments act. Early one morning the subinspector at a police station the other end of town rang me up on the phone and said that an elephant was ravaging the bazaar. Would I please come and do something about it? I did not know what I could do, but I wanted to see what was happening and I got on to a pony and started out. I took my rifle, an old .44 Winchester and much too small to kill an elephant, but I thought the noise might be useful *in terrorem*.[3] Various Burmans stopped me on the way and told me about the elephant's doings. It was not, of course, a wild elephant, but a tame one which

2

3

---

[1] British imperial government. *Raj* in Hindi means "reign," a word similar to *rajah*, "ruler." — EDS.

[2] Latin, "world without end." — EDS.

[3] Latin, "to give warning." — EDS.

had gone "must." It had been chained up, as tame elephants always are when their attack of "must" is due, but on the previous night it had broken its chain and escaped. Its mahout,[4] the only person who could manage it when it was in that state, had set out in pursuit, but had taken the wrong direction and was now twelve hours' journey away, and in the morning the elephant had suddenly reappeared in the town. The Burmese population had no weapons and were quite helpless against it. It had already destroyed somebody's bamboo hut, killed a cow and raided some fruit stalls and devoured the stock; also it had met the municipal rubbish van and, when the driver jumped out and took to his heels, had turned the van over and inflicted violences upon it.

The Burmese subinspector and some Indian constables were waiting for me in the quarter where the elephant had been seen. It was a very poor quarter, a labyrinth of squalid bamboo huts, thatched with palmleaf, winding all over a steep hillside. I remember that it was a cloudy, stuffy morning at the beginning of the rains. We began questioning the people as to where the elephant had gone and, as usual, failed to get any definite information. That is invariably the case in the East; a story always sounds clear enough at a distance, but the nearer you get to the scene of events the vaguer it becomes. Some of the people said that the elephant had gone in one direction, some said that he had gone in another, some professed not even to have heard of any elephant. I had almost made up my mind that the whole story was a pack of lies, when we heard yells a little distance away. There was a loud, scandalized cry of "Go away, child! Go away this instant!" and an old woman with a switch in her hand came round the corner of a hut, violently shooing away a crowd of naked children. Some more women followed, clicking their tongues and exclaiming; evidently there was something that the children ought not to have seen. I rounded the hut and saw a man's dead body sprawling in the mud. He was an Indian, a black Dravidian coolie, almost naked, and he could not have been dead many minutes. The people said that the elephant had come suddenly upon him round the corner of the hut, caught him with its trunk, put its foot on his back and ground him into the earth. This was the rainy season and the ground was soft, and his face had scored a trench a foot deep and a couple of yards long. He was lying on his belly with arms crucified and head sharply twisted to one side. His face was coated with mud, the eyes wide open, the teeth bared and grinning with an expression of unendurable agony. (Never tell me, by the way, that the dead look peaceful. Most of the corpses I have seen looked devilish.) The friction of the great beast's foot had stripped the skin from his back as neatly as one skins a rabbit. As soon as I saw the dead man I sent an orderly to a friend's house nearby to borrow an elephant rifle. I

[4] Keeper or groom, a servant of the elephant's owner. —EDS.

had already sent back the pony, not wanting it to go mad with fright and throw me if it smelled the elephant.

The orderly came back in a few minutes with a rifle and five cartridges, and meanwhile some Burmans had arrived and told us that the elephant was in the paddy fields below, only a few hundred yards away. As I started forward practically the whole population of the quarter flocked out of the houses and followed me. They had seen the rifle and were all shouting excitedly that I was going to shoot the elephant. They had not shown much interest in the elephant when he was merely ravaging their homes, but it was different now that he was going to be shot. It was a bit of fun to them, as it would be to an English crowd; besides they wanted the meat. It made me vaguely uneasy. I had no intention of shooting the elephant—I had merely sent for the rifle to defend myself if necessary—and it is always unnerving to have a crowd following you. I marched down the hill, looking and feeling a fool, with the rifle over my shoulder and an ever-growing army of people jostling at my heels. At the bottom, when you got away from the huts, there was a metalled road and beyond that a miry waste of paddy fields a thousand yards across, not yet ploughed but soggy from the first rains and dotted with coarse grass. The elephant was standing eight yards from the road, his left side towards us. He took not the slightest notice of the crowd's approach. He was tearing up bunches of grass, beating them against his knees to clean them and stuffing them into his mouth.

I had halted on the road. As soon as I saw the elephant I knew with perfect certainty that I ought not to shoot him. It is a serious matter to shoot a working elephant—it is comparable to destroying a huge and costly piece of machinery—and obviously one ought not to do it if it can possibly be avoided. And at that distance, peacefully eating, the elephant looked no more dangerous than a cow. I thought then and I think now that his attack of "must" was already passing off; in which case he would merely wander harmlessly about until the mahout came back and caught him. Moreover, I did not in the least want to shoot him. I decided that I would watch him for a little while to make sure that he did not turn savage again, and then go home.

But at that moment, I glanced round at the crowd that had followed me. It was an immense crowd, two thousand at the least and growing every minute. It blocked the road for a long distance on either side. I looked at the sea of yellow faces above the garish clothes—faces all happy and excited over this bit of fun, all certain that the elephant was going to be shot. They were watching me as they would watch a conjuror about to perform a trick. They did not like me, but with the magical rifle in my hands I was momentarily worth watching. And suddenly I realized that I should have to shoot the elephant after all. The people expected it of me and I had got to do it; I could feel their two thousand wills pressing me forward, irresistibly. And it was at this moment, as I stood there with the rifle in my hands, that I first grasped the hollowness, the futility of the white man's dominion in the East. Here was I, the white man with his gun, standing in front of the unarmed native crowd— seemingly the leading actor of the piece; but in reality I was only an absurd puppet pushed to and fro by the will of those yellow faces behind. I perceived in this moment that when the white man turns tyrant it is his own freedom that he destroys. He becomes a sort of hollow, posing dummy, the conventionalized figure of a sahib. For it is the condition of his rule that he shall spend his life in trying to impress the "natives," and so in every crisis he has got to do what the "natives" expect of him. He wears a mask, and his face grows to fit it. I had got to shoot the elephant. I had committed myself to doing it when I sent for the rifle. A sahib has got to act like a sahib; he has got to appear resolute, to know his own mind and do definite things. To come all that way, rifle in hand, with two thousand people marching at my heels, and then to trail feebly away, having done nothing—no, that was impossible. The crowd would laugh at me. And my whole life, every white man's life in the East, was one long struggle not to be laughed at.

But I did not want to shoot the elephant. I watched him beating his    8 bunch of grass against his knees, with that preoccupied grandmotherly air that elephants have. It seemed to me that it would be murder to shoot him. At that age I was not squeamish about killing animals, but I had never shot an elephant and never wanted to. (Somehow it always seems worse to kill a *large* animal.) Besides, there was the beast's owner to be considered. Alive, the elephant was worth at least a hundred pounds; dead, he would only be worth the value of his tusks, five pounds, possibly. But I had got to act quickly. I turned to some experienced-looking Burmans who had been there when we arrived, and asked them how the elephant had been behaving. They all said the same thing: He took no notice of you if you left him alone, but he might charge if you went too close to him.

It was perfectly clear to me what I ought to do. I ought to walk up to    9 within, say, twenty-five yards of the elephant and test his behavior. If he charged, I could shoot; if he took no notice of me, it would be safe to leave him until the mahout came back. But also I knew that I was going to do no such thing. I was a poor shot with a rifle and the ground was soft mud into which one would sink at every step. If the elephant charged and I missed him, I should have about as much chance as a toad under a steamroller. But even then I was not thinking particularly of my own skin, only of the watchful yellow faces behind. For at that moment, with the crowd watching me, I was not afraid in the ordinary sense, as I would have been if I had been alone. A white man mustn't be frightened in front of "natives"; and so, in general, he isn't frightened. The sole thought in my mind was that if anything went wrong those two thousand Burmans would see me pursued, caught, trampled on, and reduced to a grinning corpse like that Indian up the hill. And if that happened it was quite probable that some of them would laugh. That would never do. There was only one alternative. I shoved the cartridges into the magazine and lay down on the road to get a better aim.

The crowd grew very still, and a deep, low, happy sigh, as of people who                    10
see the theater curtain go up at last, breathed from innumerable throats. They were going to have their bit of fun after all. The rifle was a beautiful German thing with cross-hair sights. I did not then know that in shooting an elephant one would shoot to cut an imaginary bar running from ear-hole to ear-hole. I ought, therefore, as the elephant was sideways on, to have aimed straight at his ear-hole; actually I aimed several inches in front of this, thinking the brain would be further forward.

When I pulled the trigger I did not hear the bang or feel the kick—one                    11
never does when a shot goes home—but I heard the devilish roar of glee that went up from the crowd. In that instant, in too short a time, one would have thought, even for the bullet to get there, a mysterious, terrible change had come over the elephant. He neither stirred nor fell, but every line of his body had altered. He looked suddenly stricken, shrunken, immensely old, as though the frightful impact of the bullet had paralyzed him without knocking him down. At last, after what seemed a long time—it might have been five seconds, I dare say—he sagged flabbily to his knees. His mouth slobbered. An enormous senility seemed to have settled upon him. One could have imagined him thousands of years old. I fired again into the same spot. At the second shot he did not collapse but climbed with desperate slowness to his feet and stood weakly upright, with legs sagging and head drooping. I fired a third time. That was the shot that did for him. You could see the agony of it jolt his whole body and knock the last remnant of strength from his legs. But in falling he seemed for a moment to rise, for as his hind legs collapsed beneath him he seemed to tower upward like a huge rock toppling, his trunk reaching skywards like a tree. He trumpeted, for the first and only time. And then down he came, his belly towards me, with a crash that seemed to shake the ground even where I lay.

I got up. The Burmans were already racing past me across the mud. It was                    12
obvious that the elephant would never rise again, but he was not dead. He was breathing very rhythmically with long rattling gasps, his great mound of a side painfully rising and falling. His mouth was wide open. I could see far down into caverns of pale pink throat. I waited a long time for him to die, but his breathing did not weaken. Finally I fired my two remaining shots into the spot where I thought his heart must be. The thick blood welled out of him like red

velvet, but still he did not die. His body did not even jerk when the shots hit him, the tortured breathing continued without a pause. He was dying, very slowly and in great agony, but in some world remote from me where not even a bullet could damage him further. I felt I had got to put an end to that dreadful noise. It seemed dreadful to see the great beast lying there, powerless to move and yet powerless to die, and not even to be able to finish him. I sent back for my small rifle and poured shot after shot into his heart and down his throat. They seemed to make no impression. The tortured gasps continued as steadily as the ticking of a clock.

In the end I could not stand it any longer and went away. I heard later that    13
it took him half an hour to die. Burmans were bringing dahs and baskets even before I left, and I was told they had stripped his body almost to the bones by the afternoon.

Afterwards, of course, there were endless discussions about the shooting of    14
the elephant. The owner was furious, but he was only an Indian and could do nothing. Besides, legally I had done the right thing, for a mad elephant has to be killed, like a mad dog, if its owner fails to control it. Among the Europeans opinion was divided. The older men said I was right, the younger men said it was a damn shame to shoot an elephant for killing a coolie, because the elephant was worth more than any damn Coringhee coolie. And afterwards I was very glad that the coolie had been killed; it put me legally in the right and it gave me sufficient pretext for shooting the elephant. I often wondered whether any of the others grasped that I had done it solely to avoid looking a fool.

> For a reading quiz, sources on George Orwell, and annotated links to further
> readings on British imperial rule in Burma, visit **bedfordstmartins.com**
> **/thebedfordreader**.

## Journal Writing

How do you respond to Orwell's decision to shoot the elephant even though he believed it unnecessary to do so? Do you have any sympathy for his action? Recall a time when you acted against your better judgment in order to save face in front of others. Write as honestly as you can about what motivated you and what mistakes you made. (To take your journal writing further, see "From Journal to Essay" on the next page.)

## Questions on Meaning

1. How would you answer the exasperated student who, after reading this essay, exploded, "Why didn't Orwell just leave his gun at home?"
2. Why did Orwell shoot the elephant?
3. Describe the epiphany that Orwell experiences in the course of the event he writes about. (An *epiphany* is a sudden realization of a truth.)
4. In the last paragraph of his essay, Orwell says he was "glad that the coolie had been killed." How do you account for this remark?
5. What is the PURPOSE of this essay?

## Questions on Writing Strategy

1. In addition to serving as an INTRODUCTION to Orwell's essay, what function is performed by paragraphs 1 and 2?
2. From what circumstances does the IRONY of Orwell's essay spring?
3. What does "Shooting an Elephant" gain from having been written years after the events it recounts?
4. **MIXED METHODS**   What does the blend of NARRATION and DESCRIPTION in paragraphs 11–12 contribute to the story? How does it further Orwell's purpose?
5. **MIXED METHODS**   How do the EXAMPLES in paragraphs 1 and 2 illustrate Orwell's conflict about his work as a police officer in Burma?

## Questions on Language

1. What do you understand by Orwell's statement that the elephant had "gone 'must'" (par. 3)? Look up *must* or its variant *musth* in your dictionary.
2. What examples of English (as opposed to American) usage do you find in Orwell's essay?
3. Define, if necessary, bazaars, betel (par. 1); intolerable, supplant, prostrate (2); despotic (3); labyrinth, squalid, invariably (4); dominion, sahib (7); magazine (9); innumerable (10); senility (11).

## Suggestions for Writing

1. **FROM JOURNAL TO ESSAY**   Write a narrative essay from your journal entry. Tell the story of your action, and consider what the results were, what you might have done differently, and what you learned from the experience.
2. With what examples of governmental face-saving are you familiar? If none leaps to mind, read a newspaper or watch the news on television to catch public officials in the act of covering themselves. (Not only national government but also local or student government may provide examples.) In an essay, ANALYZE two or three examples: What do you think was really going on that needed covering? Did the officials succeed in saving face, or did their efforts fail? Were the efforts harmful in any way?
3. **CRITICAL WRITING**   Orwell is honest with himself and his readers in acknowledging his mistakes as a government official. Write an essay that examines the degree to which confession may, or may not, erase blameworthiness for misdeeds. Does

Orwell remain just as guilty as he would have been if he had not taken responsibility for his actions? Why, or why not? Feel free to supplement your analysis of Orwell's case with examples from your own life or from the news.

4. **CONNECTIONS**    Read William Lutz's "The World of Doublespeak" (p. 418), which CLASSIFIES language that deliberately conceals or misleads. In an essay, examine which of Lutz's categories of doublespeak seem to arise from the motives Orwell describes in paragraph 7: the need "to impress," to do what is expected of one, "to appear resolute," "not to be laughed at." Use specific examples from Lutz's essay — or from your own experience — to support your ideas.

5. **CONNECTIONS**    Like "Shooting an Elephant," Maya Angelou's "Champion of the World" (p. 93) also blends narration and description. COMPARE AND CONTRAST the two essays, not on their purposes, which are vastly different, but on this blending. What senses do the authors rely on? How do they keep their narratives moving? How much of themselves do they inject into their essays?

---

## *George Orwell on Writing*

George Orwell explains the motives for his own writing in the essay "Why I Write" (1946), from which we reprint the following excerpts.

What I have most wanted to do throughout the past ten years is to make political writing into an art. My starting point is always a feeling of partisanship, a sense of injustice. When I sit down to write a book, I do not say to myself, "I am going to produce a work of art." I write it because there is some lie that I want to expose, some fact to which I want to draw attention, and my initial concern is to get a hearing. But I could not do the work of writing a book, or even a long magazine article, if it were not also an esthetic experience. Anyone who cares to examine my work will see that even when it is downright propaganda it contains much that a full-time politician would consider irrelevant. I am not able, and I do not want, completely to abandon the worldview that I acquired in childhood. So long as I remain alive and well I shall continue to feel strongly about prose style, to love the surface of the earth, and to take a pleasure in solid objects and scraps of useless information. It is no use trying to suppress that side of myself. The job is to reconcile my ingrained likes and dislikes with the essentially public, nonindividual activities that this age forces on all of us.

It is not easy. It raises problems of construction and of language, and it raises in a new way the problem of truthfulness. Let me give just one example of the cruder kind of difficulty that arises. My book about the Spanish civil war, *Homage to Catalonia*, is, of course, a frankly political book, but in the main it is written with a certain detachment and regard for form. I did try very hard in it to tell the whole truth without violating my literary instincts. But among other things it contains a long chapter, full of newspaper quotations and the like, defending the Trotskyists who were accused of plotting with Franco. Clearly such a chapter, which after a year or two would lose its interest for any ordinary reader, must ruin the book. A critic whom I respect read me a lecture about it. "Why did you put in all that stuff?" he said. "You've turned what might have been a good book into journalism." What he said was true, but I could not have done otherwise. I happened to know, what very few people in England had been allowed to know, that innocent men were being falsely accused. If I had not been angry about that I should never have written the book.

In one form or another this problem comes up again. The problem of language is subtler and would take too long to discuss. I will only say that of late years I have tried to write less picturesquely and more exactly. In any case I find that by the time you have perfected any style of writing, you have always outgrown it. *Animal Farm* was the first book in which I tried, with full consciousness of what I was doing, to fuse political purpose and artistic purpose into the whole. . . .

Looking back through the last page or two, I see that I have made it appear as though my motives in writing were wholly public-spirited. I don't want to leave that as the final impression. All writers are vain, selfish, and lazy, and at the very bottom of their motives there lies a mystery. Writing a book is a horrible, exhausting struggle, like a long bout of some painful illness. One would never undertake such a thing if one were not driven on by some demon whom one can neither resist nor understand. For all one knows that demon is simply the same instinct that makes a baby squall for attention. And yet it is also true that one can write nothing readable unless one constantly struggles to efface one's own personality. Good prose is like a windowpane. I cannot say with certainty which of my motives are the strongest, but I know which of them deserve to be followed. And looking back through my work, I see that it is invariably where I lacked a *political* purpose that I wrote lifeless books and was betrayed into purple passages, sentences without meaning, decorative adjectives, and humbug generally.

## For Discussion

1. What does Orwell mean by his "political purpose" in writing? by his "artistic purpose"? How did he sometimes find it hard to fulfill both purposes?
2. Think about Orwell's remark that "one can write nothing readable unless one constantly struggles to efface one's own personality." From your own experience, have you found any truth in this observation, or any reason to think otherwise?

# FRANCINE PROSE

FRANCINE PROSE is the author of more than twelve novels as well as a children's book, several short-story collections, and works of nonfiction, such as *Gluttony* (2003) and *Caravaggio: Painter of Miracles* (2005). She was born in Brooklyn, New York, and graduated from Radcliffe College in 1968. She has received Guggenheim and Fulbright fellowships and has served as a judge for literary prizes. In 2001 she was elected president of the PEN American Center, the US branch of an international literary organization. Prose's novel *Blue Angel* (2001), a satire set on a college campus, was nominated for the National Book Award. Her most recent novel, *A Changed Man* (2005), about a reformed neo-Nazi, won the Dayton Literary Peace Award. Prose lives in New York and teaches writing at Bard College.

# *What Words Can Tell*

"What Words Can Tell" (editors' title) comes from Prose's book *Reading like a Writer: A Guide for People Who Love Books and for Those Who Want to Write Them* (2006). In this excerpt, Prose gives a detailed reading of the opening paragraph of "A Good Man Is Hard to Find," a short story by the southern American writer Flannery O'Connor (1925–64). In the story a family on vacation intersects the path of an escaped convict, known only as The Misfit. Prose's analysis of O'Connor's words is a model of close attention illuminating a written work.

The primary methods of development Prose uses are example and division or analysis, but she also draws on several other methods:

Description (Chap. 5): paragraphs 7–11
Example (Chap. 6): paragraphs 4–12
Comparison and contrast (Chap. 7): paragraphs 2, 6–7, 11
Process analysis (Chap. 8): paragraphs 3–4
Division or analysis (Chap. 9): paragraphs 5–12
Cause and effect (Chap. 11): paragraphs 7, 12
Argument and persuasion (Chap. 13): paragraphs 2, 12–13

1   Part of a reader's job is to find out why certain writers endure. This may require some rewiring, unhooking the connection that makes you think you have to have an *opinion* about the book and reconnecting that wire to whatever terminal lets you see reading as something that might move or delight you. . . .

2   With so much reading ahead of you, the temptation might be to speed up. But in fact it's essential to slow down and read every word. Because one important thing that can be learned by reading slowly is the seemingly obvious but oddly underappreciated fact that language is the medium we use in much the

same way a composer uses notes, the way a painter uses paint. I realize it may seem obvious, but it's surprising how easily we lose sight of the fact that words are the raw material out of which literature is crafted.

Every page was once a blank page, just as every word that appears on it    3 now was not always there, but instead reflects the final result of countless large and small deliberations. All the elements of good writing depend on the writer's skill in choosing one word instead of another. And what grabs and keeps our interest has everything to do with those choices.

One way to compel yourself to slow down and stop at every word is to ask    4 yourself what sort of information each word — each word choice — is convey- ing. Reading with that question in mind, let's consider the wealth of informa- tion provided by the first paragraph of Flannery O'Connor's "A Good Man Is Hard to Find":

> The grandmother didn't want to go to Florida. She wanted to visit some of her connections in east Tennessee and she was seizing at every chance to change Bailey's mind. Bailey was the son she lived with, her only boy. He was sitting on the edge of his chair at the table, bent over the orange sports sec- tion of the *Journal*. "Now look here, Bailey," she said, "see here, read this," and she stood with one hand on her thin hip and the other rattling the news- paper at his bald head. "Here this fellow that calls himself The Misfit is aloose from the Federal Pen and headed toward Florida and you read here what it says he did to these people. Just you read it. I wouldn't take my chil- dren in any direction with a criminal like that aloose in it. I couldn't answer to my conscience if I did."

The first simple declarative sentence could hardly be more plain: subject,    5 verb, infinitive, preposition. There is not one adjective or adverb to distract us from the central fact. But how much is contained in these eight little words!

Here, as in the openings of many stories and novels, we are confronted by    6 one important choice that a writer of fiction needs to make: the question of what to call her characters. Joe, Joe Smith, Mr. Smith? Not, in this case, Grandma or Grandma Smith (no one in this story has a last name) or, let's say, Ethel or Ethel Smith or Mrs. Smith, or any of the myriad terms of address that might have established different degrees of psychic distance and sympathy between the reader and the old woman.

Calling her "the grandmother" at once reduces her to her role in the    7 family, as does the fact that her daughter-in-law is never called anything but "the children's mother." At the same time, the title gives her (like The Misfit) an archetypal, mythic role that elevates her and keeps us from getting too chummy with this woman whose name we never learn, even as the writer is preparing our hearts to break at the critical moment to which the grand- mother's whole life and the events of the story have led her.

*The grandmother didn't want to go to Florida.* The first sentence is a refusal, which, in its very simplicity, emphasizes the force with which the old woman is digging in her heels. It's a concentrated act of negative will, which we will come to understand in all its tragic folly—that is, the foolishness of attempting to exert one's will when fate or destiny (or as O'Connor would argue, God) has other plans for us. And finally, the no-nonsense austerity of the sentence's construction gives it a kind of authority that—like *Moby-Dick*'s[1] first sentence, "Call me Ishmael"—makes us feel that the author is in control, an authority that draws us farther into the story.

The first part of the second sentence—"She wanted to visit some of her connections in east Tennessee"—locates us in geography, that is, in the South. And that one word, *connections* (as opposed to *relatives* or *family* or *people*), reveals the grandmother's sense of her own faded gentility, of having come down in the world, a semi-deluded self-image that, like the illusions of many other O'Connor characters, will contribute to the character's downfall.

The sentence's second half—"she was seizing at every chance to change Bailey's mind"—seizes our own attention more strongly than it would have had O'Connor written, say, "*taking* every chance." The verb quietly but succinctly telegraphs both the grandmother's fierceness and the passivity of Bailey, "the son she lived with, her only boy," two phrases that convey their domestic situation as well as the infantilizing dominance and the simultaneous tenderness that the grandmother feels toward her son. That word *boy* will take on tragic resonance later. "Bailey Boy!" the old woman will cry after her son is killed by The Misfit, who is already about to make his appearance in the newspaper that the grandmother is "rattling" at her boy's bald head. Meanwhile, the paradox of a bald, presumably middle-aged boy leads us to make certain accurate conclusions about the family constellation.

The Misfit is "aloose"—here we find one of those words by which O'Connor conveys the rhythm and flavor of a local dialect without subjecting us to the annoying apostrophes, dropped g's, the shootin' and talkin' and cussin', and the bad grammar with which other authors attempt to transcribe regional speech. The final sentences of the paragraph—"I wouldn't take my children in any direction with a criminal like that aloose in it. I couldn't answer to my conscience if I did"—encapsulate the hilarious and maddening quality of the grandmother's manipulativeness. She'll use *anything*, even an imagined encounter with an escaped criminal, to divert the family vacation from Florida to east Tennessee. And her apparently unlikely fantasy of encountering The Misfit may cause us to reflect on the peculiar egocentrism and narcissism of those people who are constantly convinced that, however minuscule the

8

9

10

11

---

[1] A novel by the American writer Herman Melville (1819–91). —EDS.

odds, the stray bullet will somehow find *them*. Meanwhile, again because of word choice, the final sentence is already alluding to those questions of conscience, morality, the spirit and soul that will reveal themselves as being at the heart of O'Connor's story.

Given the size of the country, we think, they can't *possibly* run into the   12 criminal about whom the grandmother has warned them. And yet we may recall Chekhov's[2] remark that the gun we see onstage in an early scene should probably go off by the play's end. So what *is* going to happen? This short passage has already ushered us into a world that is realistic but at the same time beyond the reach of ordinary logic, and into a narrative that we will follow from this introduction as inexorably as the grandmother is destined to meet a fate that (we *do* suspect) will involve The Misfit. Pared and edited down, highly concentrated, a model of compression from which it would be hard to excise one word, this single passage achieves all this, or more, since there will be additional subtleties and complexities obvious only to each individual reader.

Skimming just won't suffice if we hope to extract one fraction, such as the   13 fraction above, of what a writer's words can teach us about how to use the language.

*For a reading quiz, sources on Francine Prose, and annotated links to further readings on the skill of close reading, visit **bedfordstmartins.com /thebedfordreader**.*

---

## Journal Writing

Prose's book *Reading like a Writer* holds that careful reading like that she demonstrates in this excerpt can teach the skills of effective writing. How convinced are you of this connection between reading and writing? Is it reasonable to expect student writers to follow the example set by professionals? In your journal, consider what you've learned about writing from your reading. How, if at all, have you tried to adopt another writer's techniques, and how successful was the effort? (To take your journal writing further, see "From Journal to Essay" on the next page.)

---

[2] Anton Chekhov (1860–1904), Russian writer of plays and stories. — EDS.

## Questions on Meaning

1. To what end does Prose examine the first paragraph of Flannery O'Connor's short story? What is her PURPOSE?
2. What is Prose's THESIS?
3. Why is Prose so impressed by the introductory paragraph of "A Good Man Is Hard to Find"?

## Questions on Writing Strategy

1. For whom is Prose writing? What clues in the text reveal how she imagines her AUDIENCE?
2. To what extent does Prose ASSUME that her readers are familiar with Flannery O'Connor's "A Good Man Is Hard to Find"? How does she ensure that readers can follow her ANALYSIS even if they haven't read the story?
3. **MIXED METHODS**   How does Prose use a single extended EXAMPLE to make a point about reading and writing?
4. **MIXED METHODS**   Prose relies on DIVISION or ANALYSIS to illuminate O'Connor's writing. How does she reassemble the parts to reach a conclusion about a broader subject?

## Questions on Language

1. Identify two FIGURES OF SPEECH in Prose's first three paragraphs and explain what they contribute to her essay.
2. Why do you suppose the author switches from the second person (*you*) in her introduction to the first-person plural (*we*) in her examination of O'Connor's paragraph? What is the EFFECT of this shift?
3. What are the implications of Prose's ALLUSIONS to Herman Melville's *Moby-Dick* (par. 8) and Anton Chekhov's axiom about guns appearing on stage (12)?
4. Check a dictionary if any of the following words are unfamiliar to you: deliberations (par. 3); conveying (4); declarative (5); myriad, psychic (6); archetypal (7); austerity (8); gentility (9); succinctly, telegraphs, infantilizing, resonance, constellation (10); transcribe, encapsulate, egocentrism, narcissism, minuscule (11); inexorably, excise (12).

## Suggestions for Writing

1. **FROM JOURNAL TO ESSAY**   Building on the comments you made in your journal, write an essay for an audience of novice writers that explains what, if anything, they can learn about writing from reading.
2. Read any one of the following short stories in this book: Shirley Jackson's "The Lottery" (p. 123), James Joyce's "Araby" (p. 175), Jamaica Kincaid's "Girl" (p. 367), Daniel Orozco's "Orientation" (p. 319), or Don DeLillo's "Videotape" (p. 468). Following Prose's analysis as a model, do a close reading of a short passage from the story. (You may choose the first paragraph, as Prose does, or any

brief passage that conveys a lot of meaning, but be sure to select an excerpt that has enough substance to support an analysis.) Explain your interpretation in a brief essay.

3. **CRITICAL WRITING**   Locate a copy of Flannery O'Connor's short story "A Good Man Is Hard to Find" and read it for yourself. Then write an essay that responds to Prose's analysis of the first paragraph. Do you agree with her analysis, or do you read the paragraph differently? Why?

4. **CONNECTIONS**   While Prose examines a paragraph from Flannery O'Connor's story to discover the author's strategies, Armin A. Brott, in his essay "Not All Men Are Sly Foxes" (p. 345), takes a close look at several children's books to raise a concern about the subtle messages they convey. Both writers, in other words, assume that works of fiction carry meanings beyond mere entertainment. What do you think of this approach to literature? Using Prose and Brott as examples, write an essay that considers both what is gained by analyzing works of fiction and what, if anything, may be lost.

5. **CONNECTIONS**   In her essay "But What Do You Mean?" (p. 391), Deborah Tannen looks at some of the ways in which men and women communicate. In a brief essay, consider how Tannen's discussion of gender differences might add another layer of meaning to the grandmother's words in the passage from "A Good Man Is Hard to Find."

## *Francine Prose on Writing*

On the Web site *Barnes & Noble Book Clubs* ("Where Readers and Writers Meet"), Francine Prose was asked by a reader about an apparent contradiction in her book *Reading like a Writer:* She stresses the importance of correct grammar in writing, and yet she admiringly quotes an ungrammatical passage by the noted American fiction writer Philip Roth. "The problem with so many grammatical mistakes," Prose responds, "is that they call attention to themselves. You know that something is wrong with the sentence even if you don't know precisely what it is. And it's distracting. The whole point of grammar is clarity—to help us to write, and to understand, as clearly and comprehensively as possible." As for Philip Roth's errors, Prose explains, "Never—not for a moment—are we confused about what Roth means, nor do we feel he's making a mistake or that he's not in control of the language."

### For Discussion

1. Why does Prose accept Roth's grammatical errors but disapprove of those made by others?

2. In what way does grammar "help us to write, and to understand, as clearly and comprehensively as possible"? Have you had the experience of reading someone else's writing and not being able to understand it at first—finding it "distracting"—because of grammatical errors? Or has your writing been misunderstood because of such errors?

# RICHARD RODRIGUEZ

The son of Spanish-speaking Mexican Americans, RICHARD RODRIGUEZ was born in 1944 in San Francisco. After graduation from Stanford in 1967, he earned an MA from Columbia, studied at the Warburg Institute in London, and received a PhD in English literature from the University of California at Berkeley. He once taught but now devotes himself to writing and lecturing. Rodriguez's essays have appeared in *The American Scholar, Change*, and many other magazines. He is an editor at Pacific News Service and a contributing editor for *US News & World Report, Harper's*, and the *Los Angeles Times*. His on-air essays for PBS's *NewsHour with Jim Lehrer* won him the George Foster Peabody Award in 1997. In 1982 he published *Hunger of Memory*, a widely discussed book of autobiographical essays. *Mexico's Children* (1991) is a study of Mexicans in America, and *Days of Obligation: An Argument with My Mexican Father* (1992) is also a memoir. Rodriguez's latest book is *Brown* (2002), in which he explores color and race in American society.

# *Aria: A Memoir of a Bilingual Childhood*

"Aria: A Memoir of a Bilingual Childhood" is taken from *Hunger of Memory*. First published in *The American Scholar* in 1981, this poignant memoir sets forth the author's views of bilingual education. To the child Rodriguez, Spanish was a private language, English a public one. The boy would not have learned faster and better if his teachers had allowed him the use of his native language in school. Since Rodriguez wrote this essay, bilingual education has remained controversial, and in recent years it has lost ground. The No Child Left Behind Act of 2001 eliminated requirements that schools give English-language learners access to their first languages and emphasized students' accountability for learning and testing in English.

Rodriguez uses four main methods of development to serve a fifth, argument. The argument is pervasive but most explicit in the paragraphs listed below.

Narration (Chap. 4): paragraphs 1–3, 5–9, 13, 16–18, 21, 23–37
Description (Chap. 5): paragraphs 7–11, 13, 16–18, 21, 23–29
Comparison and contrast (Chap. 7): paragraphs 10–11, 14, 22, 29–30, 33–35, 38–40
Cause and effect (Chap. 11): paragraphs 12, 15, 18–20, 28–32, 36, 38–40
Argument and persuasion (Chap. 13): paragraphs 4, 19–20, 38–39

I remember, to start with, that day in Sacramento, in a California now 1 nearly thirty years past, when I first entered a classroom—able to understand about fifty stray English words. The third of four children, I had been preceded by my older brother and sister to a neighborhood Roman Catholic school. But neither of them had revealed very much about their classroom experiences.

They left each morning and returned each afternoon, always together, speaking Spanish as they climbed the five steps to the porch. And their mysterious books, wrapped in brown shopping-bag paper, remained on the table next to the door, closed firmly behind them.

An accident of geography sent me to a school where all my classmates     2
were white and many were the children of doctors and lawyers and business executives. On that first day of school, my classmates must certainly have been uneasy to find themselves apart from their families, in the first institution of their lives. But I was astonished. I was fated to be the "problem student" in class.

The nun said, in a friendly but oddly impersonal voice: "Boys and girls,     3
this is Richard Rodriguez." (I heard her sound it out: *Rich-heard Road-ree-guess*.) It was the first time I had heard anyone say my name in English. "Richard," the nun repeated more slowly, writing my name down in her book. Quickly I turned to see my mother's face dissolve in a watery blur behind the pebbled-glass door.

Now, many years later, I hear of something called "bilingual education" —     4
a scheme proposed in the late 1960s by Hispanic-American social activists, later endorsed by a congressional vote. It is a program that seeks to permit non–English-speaking children (many from lower-class homes) to use their "family language" as the language of school. Such, at least, is the aim its supporters announce. I hear them, and am forced to say no: It is not possible for a child, any child, ever to use his family's language in school. Not to understand this is to misunderstand the public uses of schooling and to trivialize the nature of intimate life.

Memory teaches me what I know of these matters. The boy reminds the     5
adult. I was a bilingual child, but of a certain kind: "socially disadvantaged," the son of working-class parents, both Mexican immigrants.

In the early years of my boyhood, my parents coped very well in America.     6
My father had steady work. My mother managed at home. They were nobody's victims. When we moved to a house many blocks from the Mexican-American section of town, they were not intimidated by those two or three neighbors who initially tried to make us unwelcome. ("Keep your brats away from my sidewalk!") But despite all they achieved, or perhaps because they had so much to achieve, they lacked any deep feeling of ease, of belonging in public. They regarded the people at work or in crowds as being very distant from us. Those were the others, *los gringos*. That term was interchangeable in their speech with another, even more telling: *los americanos*.

I grew up in a house where the only regular guests were my relations. On     7
a certain day, enormous families of relatives would visit us, and there would be so many people that the noise and the bodies would spill out to the backyard

and onto the front porch. Then for weeks no one would come. (If the doorbell rang, it was usually a salesman.) Our house stood apart—gaudy yellow in a row of white bungalows. We were the people with the noisy dog, the people who raised chickens. We were the foreigners on the block. A few neighbors would smile and wave at us. We waved back. But until I was seven years old, I did not know the name of the old couple living next door or the names of the kids living across the street.

In public, my father and mother spoke a hesitant, accented, and not always grammatical English. And then they would have to strain, their bodies tense, to catch the sense of what was rapidly said by *los gringos*. At home, they returned to Spanish. The language of their Mexican past sounded in counterpoint to the English spoken in public. The words would come quickly, with ease. Conveyed through those sounds was the pleasing, soothing, consoling reminder that one was at home. 8

During those years when I was first learning to speak, my mother and father addressed me only in Spanish; in Spanish I learned to reply. By contrast, English *(inglés)* was the language I came to associate with gringos, rarely heard in the house. I learned my first words of English overhearing my parents speaking to strangers. At six years of age, I knew just enough words for my mother to trust me on errands to stores one block away—but no more. 9

I was then a listening child, careful to hear the very different sounds of Spanish and English. Wide-eyed with hearing, I'd listen to sounds more than to words. First, there were English (gringo) sounds. So many words still were unknown to me that when the butcher or the lady at the drugstore said something, exotic polysyllabic sounds would bloom in the midst of their sentences. Often the speech of people in public seemed to me very loud, booming with confidence. The man behind the counter would literally ask, "What can I do for you?" But by being so firm and clear, the sound of his voice said that he was a gringo; he belonged in public society. There were also the high, nasal notes of middle-class American speech—which I rarely am conscious of hearing today because I hear them so often, but could not stop hearing when I was a boy. Crowds at Safeway or at bus stops were noisy with the birdlike sounds of *los gringos*. I'd move away from them all—all the chirping chatter above me. 10

My own sounds I was unable to hear, but I knew that I spoke English poorly. My words could not extend to form complete thoughts. And the words I did speak I didn't know well enough to make distinct sounds. (Listeners would usually lower their heads to hear better what I was trying to say.) But it was one thing for *me* to speak English with difficulty; it was more troubling to hear my parents speaking in public: their high-whining vowels and guttural consonants; their sentences that got stuck with "eh" and "ah" sounds; the confused syntax; the hesitant rhythm of sounds so different from the way gringos 11 spoke. I'd notice, moreover, that my parents' voices were softer than those of gringos we would meet.

I am tempted to say now that none of this mattered. (In adulthood I am 12 embarrassed by childhood fears.) And, in a way, it didn't matter very much that my parents could not speak English with ease. Their linguistic difficulties had no serious consequences. My mother and father made themselves understood at the county hospital clinic and at government offices. And yet, in another way, it mattered very much. It was unsettling to hear my parents struggle with English. Hearing them, I'd grow nervous, and my clutching trust in their protection and power would be weakened.

There were many times like the night at a brightly lit gasoline station (a 13 blaring white memory) when I stood uneasily hearing my father talk to a teenage attendant. I do not recall what they were saying, but I cannot forget the sounds my father made as he spoke. At one point his words slid together to form one long word—sounds as confused as the threads of blue and green oil in the puddle next to my shoes. His voice rushed through what he had left to say. Toward the end, he reached falsetto notes, appealing to his listener's understanding. I looked away at the lights of passing automobiles. I tried not to hear any more. But I heard only too well the attendant's reply, his calm, easy tones. Shortly afterward, headed for home, I shivered when my father put his hand on my shoulder. The very first chance that I got, I evaded his grasp and ran on ahead into the dark, skipping with feigned boyish exuberance.

But then there was Spanish: *español*, the language rarely heard away from 14 the house; *español*, the language which seemed to me therefore a private language, my family's language. To hear its sounds was to feel myself specially recognized as one of the family, apart from *los otros*. A simple remark, an inconsequential comment could convey that assurance. My parents would say something to me and I would feel embraced by the sounds of their words. Those sounds said: *I am speaking with ease in Spanish. I am addressing you in words I never use with los gringos. I recognize you as someone special, close, like no one outside. You belong with us. In the family. Ricardo.*

At the age of six, well past the time when most middle-class children no 15 longer notice the difference between sounds uttered at home and words spoken in public, I had a different experience. I lived in a world compounded of sounds. I was a child longer than most. I lived in a magical world, surrounded by sounds both pleasing and fearful. I shared with my family a language enchantingly private—different from that used in the city around us.

Just opening or closing the screen door behind me was an important experience. I'd rarely leave home all alone or without feeling reluctance. Walking down the sidewalk, under the canopy of tall trees, I'd warily notice the (suddenly) silent neighborhood kids who stood warily watching me. Nervously, 16

I'd arrive at the grocery store to hear there the sounds of the gringo, reminding me that in this so-big world I was a foreigner. But if leaving home was never routine, neither was coming back. Walking toward our house, climbing the steps from the sidewalk, in summer when the front door was open, I'd hear voices beyond the screen door talking in Spanish. For a second or two I'd stay, linger there listening. Smiling, I'd hear my mother call out, saying in Spanish, "Is that you, Richard?" Those were her words, but all the while her sounds would assure me: *You are home now. Come close inside. With us.* "*Sí*," I'd reply.

Once more inside the house, I would resume my place in the family. The  17
sounds would grow harder to hear. Once more at home, I would grow less conscious of them. It required, however, no more than the blurt of the doorbell to alert me all over again to listen to sounds. The house would turn instantly quiet while my mother went to the door. I'd hear her hard English sounds. I'd wait to hear her voice turn to soft-sounding Spanish, which assured me, as surely as did the clicking tongue of the lock on the door, that the stranger was gone.

Plainly it is not healthy to hear such sounds so often. It is not healthy to  18
distinguish public from private sounds so easily. I remained cloistered by sounds, timid and shy in public, too dependent on the voices at home. I remember many nights when my father would come back from work, and I'd hear him call out to my mother in Spanish, sounding relieved. In Spanish, his voice would sound the light and free notes that he never could manage in English. Some nights I'd jump up just hearing his voice. My brother and I would come running into the room where he was with our mother. Our laughing (so deep was the pleasure!) became screaming. Like others who feel the pain of public alienation, we transformed the knowledge of our public separateness into a consoling reminder of our intimacy. Excited, our voices joined in a celebration of sounds. *We are speaking now the way we never speak out in public—we are together*, the sounds told me. Some nights no one seemed willing to loosen the hold that sounds had on us. At dinner we invented new words that sounded Spanish, but made sense only to us. We pieced together new words by taking, say, an English verb and giving it Spanish endings. My mother's instructions at bedtime would be lacquered with mock-urgent tones. Or a word like *sí*, sounded in several notes, would convey added measures of feeling. Tongues lingered around the edges of words, especially fat vowels, and we happily sounded that military drum roll, the twirling roar of the Spanish *r*. Family language, my family's sounds: the voices of my parents and sisters and brother. Their voices insisting: *You belong here. We are family members. Related. Special to one another. Listen!* Voices singing and sighing, rising and straining, then surging, teeming with pleasure which burst syllables into fragments of laughter. At times it seemed there was steady quiet only

when, from another room, the rustling whispers of my parents faded and I edged closer to sleep.

Supporters of bilingual education imply today that students like me miss a great deal by not being taught in their family's language. What they seem not to recognize is that, as a socially disadvantaged child, I regarded Spanish as a private language. It was a ghetto language that deepened and strengthened my feeling of separateness. What I needed to learn in school was that I had the right, and the obligation, to speak the public language. The odd truth is that my first-grade classmates could have become bilingual, in the conventional sense of the word, more easily than I. Had they been taught early (as upper-middle-class children often are taught) a "second language" like Spanish or French, they could have regarded it simply as another public language. In my case, such bilingualism could not have been so quickly achieved. What I did not believe was that I could speak a single public language.   19

Without question, it would have pleased me to have heard my teachers address me in Spanish when I entered the classroom. I would have felt much less afraid. I would have imagined that my instructors were somehow "related" to me; I would indeed have heard their Spanish as my family's language. I would have trusted them and responded with ease. But I would have delayed—postponed for how long?—having to learn the language of public society. I would have evaded—and for how long?—learning the great lesson of school: that I had a public identity.   20

Fortunately, my teachers were unsentimental about their responsibility. What they understood was that I needed to speak public English. So their voices would search me out, asking me questions. Each time I heard them I'd look up in surprise to see a nun's face frowning at me. I'd mumble, not really meaning to answer. The nun would persist. "Richard, stand up. Don't look at the floor. Speak up. Speak to the entire class, not just to me!" But I couldn't believe English could be my language to use. (In part, I did not want to believe it.) I continued to mumble. I resisted the teacher's demands. (Did I somehow suspect that once I learned this public language my family life would be changed?) Silent, waiting for the bell to sound, I remained dazed, diffident, afraid.   21

Because I wrongly imagined that English was intrinsically a public language and Spanish was intrinsically private, I easily noted the difference between classroom language and the language at home. At school, words were directed to a general audience of listeners. ("Boys and girls . . .") Words were meaningfully ordered. And the point was not self-expression alone, but to make oneself understood by many others. The teacher quizzed: "Boys and girls, why do we use that word in this sentence? Could we think of a better word to use there? Would the sentence change its meaning if the words were   22 differently arranged? Isn't there a better way of saying much the same thing?" (I couldn't say. I wouldn't try to say.)

Three months passed. Five. A half year. Unsmiling, ever watchful, my       23 teachers noted my silence. They began to connect my behavior with the slow progress my brother and sisters were making. Until, one Saturday morning, three nuns arrived at the house to talk to our parents. Stiffly they sat on the blue living-room sofa. From the doorway of another room, spying on the visitors, I noted the incongruity, the clash of two worlds, the faces and voices of school intruding upon the familiar setting of home. I overheard one voice gently wondering, "Do your children speak only Spanish at home, Mrs. Rodriguez?" While another voice added, "That Richard especially seems so timid and shy."

*That Rich-heard!*       24

With great tact, the visitors continued, "Is it possible for you and your       25 husband to encourage your children to practice their English when they are home?" Of course my parents complied. What would they not do for their children's well-being? And how could they question the Church's authority which those women represented? In an instant they agreed to give up the language (the sounds) which had revealed and accentuated our family's closeness. The moment after the visitors left, the change was observed. "*Ahora,* speak to us only *en inglés,*" my father and mother told us.

At first, it seemed a kind of game. After dinner each night, the family       26 gathered together to practice "our" English. It was still then *inglés,* a language foreign to us, so we felt drawn to it as strangers. Laughing, we would try to define words we could not pronounce. We played with strange English sounds, often overanglicizing our pronunciations. And we filled the smiling gaps of our sentences with familiar Spanish sounds. But that was cheating, somebody shouted, and everyone laughed.

In school, meanwhile, like my brother and sisters, I was required to attend       27 a daily tutoring session. I needed a full year of this special work. I also needed my teachers to keep my attention from straying in class by calling out, "*Rich-heard*"—their English voices slowly loosening the ties to my other name, with its three notes, *Ri-car-do.* Most of all, I needed to hear my mother and father speak to me in a moment of seriousness in "broken"—suddenly heartbreaking—English. This scene was inevitable. One Saturday morning I entered the kitchen where my parents were talking, but I did not realize that they were talking in Spanish until, the moment they saw me, their voices changed and they began speaking English. The gringo sounds they uttered startled me. Pushed me away. In that moment of trivial misunderstanding and profound insight, I felt my throat twisted by unsounded grief. I simply turned and left the room. But I had no place to escape to where I could grieve in Spanish. My brother and sisters were speaking English in another part of the house.

Again and again in the days following, as I grew increasingly angry, I was obliged to hear my mother and father encouraging me: "Speak to us *en inglés*." Only then did I determine to learn classroom English. Thus, sometime afterward it happened: One day in school, I raised my hand to volunteer an answer to a question. I spoke out in a loud voice and I did not think it remarkable when the entire class understood. That day I moved very far from being the disadvantaged child I had been only days earlier. Taken hold at last was the belief, the calming assurance, that I *belonged* in public. 28

Shortly after, I stopped hearing the high, troubling sounds of *los gringos*. A more and more confident speaker of English, I didn't listen to how strangers sounded when they talked to me. With so many English-speaking people around me, I no longer heard American accents. Conversations quickened. Listening to persons whose voices sounded eccentrically pitched, I might note their sounds for a few seconds, but then I'd concentrate on what they were saying. Now when I heard someone's tone of voice — angry or questioning or sarcastic or happy or sad — I didn't distinguish it from the words it expressed. Sound and word were thus tightly wedded. At the end of each day I was often bemused, and always relieved, to realize how "soundless," though crowded with words, my day in public had been. An eight-year-old boy, I finally came to accept what had been technically true since my birth: I was an American citizen. 29

But diminished by then was the special feeling of closeness at home. Gone was the desperate, urgent, intense feeling of being at home among those with whom I felt intimate. Our family remained a loving family, but one greatly changed. We were no longer so close, no longer bound tightly together by the knowledge of our separateness from *los gringos*. Neither my older brother nor my sisters rushed home after school anymore. Nor did I. When I arrived home, often there would be neighborhood kids in the house. Or the house would be empty of sounds. 30

Following the dramatic Americanization of their children, even my parents grew more publicly confident — especially my mother. First she learned the names of all the people on the block. Then she decided we needed to have a telephone in our house. My father, for his part, continued to use the word *gringo*, but it was no longer charged with bitterness or distrust. Stripped of any emotional content, the word simply became a name for those Americans not of Hispanic descent. Hearing him, sometimes, I wasn't sure if he was pronouncing the Spanish word *gringo*, or saying gringo in English. 31

There was a new silence at home. As we children learned more and more English, we shared fewer and fewer words with our parents. Sentences needed to be spoken slowly when one of us addressed our mother or father. Often the 32 parent wouldn't understand. The child would need to repeat himself. Still the parent misunderstood. The young voice, frustrated, would end up saying, "Never mind"—the subject was closed. Dinners would be noisy with the clinking of knives and forks against dishes. My mother would smile softly between her remarks; my father, at the other end of the table, would chew and chew his food while he stared over the heads of his children.

My mother! My father! After English became my primary language, I no  33 longer knew what words to use in addressing my parents. The old Spanish words (those tender accents of sound) I had earlier used—*mamá* and *papá*— I couldn't use anymore. They would have been all-too-painful reminders of how much had changed in my life. On the other hand, the words I heard neighborhood kids call their parents seemed equally unsatisfactory. "Mother" and "father," "ma," "pa," "dad," "pop" (how I hated the all-American sound of that last word)—all these I felt were unsuitable terms of address for *my* parents. As a result, I never used them at home. Whenever I'd speak to my parents, I would try to get their attention by looking at them. In public conversations, I'd refer to them as my "parents" or my "mother" and "father."

My mother and father, for their part, responded differently, as their children  34 spoke to them less. My mother grew restless, seemed troubled and anxious at the scarceness of words exchanged in the house. She would question me about my day when I came home from school. She smiled at my small talk. She pried at the edges of my sentences to get me to say something more. ("What . . . ?") She'd join conversations she overheard, but her intrusions often stopped her children's talking. By contrast, my father seemed to grow reconciled to the new quiet. Though his English somewhat improved, he tended more and more to retire into silence. At dinner he spoke very little. One night his children and even his wife helplessly giggled at his garbled English pronunciation of the Catholic "Grace Before Meals." Thereafter he made his wife recite the prayer at the start of each meal, even on formal occasions when there were guests in the house.

Hers became the public voice of the family. On official business it was she,  35 not my father, who would usually talk to strangers on the phone or in stores. We children grew so accustomed to his silence that years later we would routinely refer to his "shyness." (My mother often tried to explain: Both of his parents died when he was eight. He was raised by an uncle who treated him as little more than a menial servant. He was never encouraged to speak. He grew up alone—a man of few words.) But I realized my father was not shy whenever I'd watch him speaking Spanish with relatives. Using Spanish, he was quickly effusive. Especially when talking with other men, his voice would spark, flicker, flare alive with varied sounds. In Spanish he expressed ideas and feelings he rarely revealed when speaking English. With firm Spanish sounds he conveyed a confidence and authority that English would never allow him.

The silence at home, however, was not simply the result of fewer words ₃₆ passing between parents and children. More profound for me was the silence created by my inattention to sounds. At about the time I no longer bothered to listen with care to the sounds of English in public, I grew careless about listening to the sounds made by the family when they spoke. Most of the time I would hear someone speaking at home and didn't distinguish his sounds from the words people uttered in public. I didn't even pay much attention to my parents' accented and ungrammatical speech — at least not at home. Only when I was with them in public would I become alert to their accents. But even then their sounds caused me less and less concern. For I was growing increasingly confident of my own public identity.

I would have been happier about my public success had I not recalled, ₃₇ sometimes, what it had been like earlier, when my family conveyed its intimacy through a set of conveniently private sounds. Sometimes in public, hearing a stranger, I'd hark back to my lost past. A Mexican farm worker approached me one day downtown. He wanted directions to some place. "*Hijito*, . . ." he said. And his voice stirred old longings. Another time I was standing beside my mother in the visiting room of a Carmelite convent, before the dense screen which rendered the nuns shadowy figures. I heard several of them speaking Spanish in their busy, singsong, overlapping voices, assuring my mother that, yes, yes, we were remembered, all our family was remembered, in their prayers. Those voices echoed faraway family sounds. Another day a dark-faced old woman touched my shoulder lightly to steady herself as she boarded a bus. She murmured something to me I couldn't quite comprehend. Her Spanish voice came near, like the face of a never-before-seen relative in the instant before I was kissed. That voice, like so many of the Spanish voices I'd hear in public, recalled the golden age of my childhood.

Bilingual educators say today that children lose a degree of "individuality" ₃₈ by becoming assimilated into public society. (Bilingual schooling is a program popularized in the seventies, that decade when middle-class "ethnics" began to resist the process of assimilation — the "American melting pot.") But the bilingualists oversimplify when they scorn the value and necessity of assimilation. They do not seem to realize that a person is individualized in two ways. So they do not realize that, while one suffers a diminished sense of *private* individuality by being assimilated into public society, such assimilation makes possible the achievement of *public* individuality.

Simplistically again, the bilingualists insist that a student should be ₃₉ reminded of his difference from others in mass society, of his "heritage." But they equate mere separateness with individuality. The fact is that only in private — with intimates — is separateness from the crowd a prerequisite for individuality; an intimate "tells" me that I am unique, unlike all others, apart from the crowd. In public, by contrast, full individuality is achieved, paradoxically, by those who are able to consider themselves members of the crowd. Thus it happened for me. Only when I was able to think of myself as an American, no longer an alien in gringo society, could I seek the rights and opportunities necessary for full public individuality. The social and political advantages I enjoy as a man began on the day I came to believe that my name is indeed *Rich-heard Road-ree-guess*. It is true that my public society today is often impersonal; in fact, my public society is usually mass society. But despite the anonymity of the crowd, and despite the fact that the individuality I achieve in public is often tenuous—because it depends on my being one in a crowd—I celebrate the day I acquired my new name. Those middle-class ethnics who scorn assimilation seem to me filled with decadent self-pity, obsessed by the burden of public life. Dangerously, they romanticize public separateness and trivialize the dilemma of those who are truly socially disadvantaged.

If I rehearse here the changes in my private life after my Americanization,    40 it is finally to emphasize a public gain. The loss implies the gain. The house I returned to each afternoon was quiet. Intimate sounds no longer greeted me at the door. Inside there were other noises. The telephone rang. Neighborhood kids ran past the door of the bedroom where I was reading my schoolbooks— covered with brown shopping-bag paper. Once I learned the public language, it would never again be easy for me to hear intimate family voices. More and more of my day was spent hearing words, not sounds. But that may only be a way of saying that on the day I raised my hand in class and spoke loudly to an entire roomful of faces, my childhood started to end.

*For a reading quiz, sources on Richard Rodriguez, and annotated links to further readings on bilingual education, visit* **bedfordstmartins.com/thebedfordreader**.

## Journal Writing

Rodriguez remembers thinking as a child, "We are speaking now the way we never speak out in public—we are together" (par. 18). In your journal, write about any aspect of language spoken by you and your family when you were a child—language different from what you heard in public. Perhaps, like Rodriguez's family, your family spoke a language other than the dominant one in the larger culture. Or perhaps your private language consisted of a special vocabulary, inside jokes, ALLUSIONS, particular tones of voice, or other differences. (To take your journal writing further, see "From Journal to Essay" on the next page.)

## Questions on Meaning

1. Rodriguez's essay is both memoir and ARGUMENT. What is the thrust of the author's argument?
2. How did the child Rodriguez react when, in his presence, his parents had to struggle to make themselves understood by *"los gringos"*?
3. What does the author mean when he says, "I was a child longer than most" (par. 15)?
4. According to the author, what impact did the Rodriguez children's use of English have on relationships within the family?
5. Contrast the child Rodriguez's view of the nuns who insisted he speak English with his adult view.

## Questions on Writing Strategy

1. How effective an INTRODUCTION is Rodriguez's first paragraph?
2. Several times in his essay Rodriguez shifts from memoir to argument and back again. What is the overall EFFECT of these shifts? Do they strengthen or weaken the author's stance against bilingual education?
3. Twice in his essay (in pars. 1 and 40) the author mentions schoolbooks wrapped in shopping-bag paper. How does the use of this detail enhance his argument?
4. What AUDIENCE probably would not like this essay? Why would they not like it?
5. **MIXED METHODS**   Examine how Rodriguez uses DESCRIPTION to COMPARE AND CONTRAST the sounds of Spanish and English (pars. 10, 11, 13, 14, 18, 33, 37). What sounds does he evoke? What are the differences among them?
6. **MIXED METHODS**   Rodriguez's essay is an argument supported mainly by personal NARRATIVE—Rodriguez's own experience. What kind of ETHICAL APPEAL (p. 521) does the narrative make? What can we INFER about Rodriguez's personality, intellect, fairness, and trustworthiness?

## Questions on Language

1. Consult the dictionary if you need help defining these words: counterpoint (par. 8); polysyllabic (10); guttural, syntax (11); falsetto, exuberance (13); inconsequential (14); cloistered, lacquered (18); diffident (21); intrinsically (22); incongruity (23); bemused (29); effusive (35); assimilated (38); paradoxically, tenuous, decadent (39).
2. In Rodriguez's essay, how do the words *public* and *private* relate to the issue of bilingual education? What important distinction does the author make between *individuality* and *separateness* (par. 39)?
3. What exactly does the author mean when he says, "More and more of my day was spent hearing words, not sounds" (par. 40)?

## Suggestions for Writing

1. **FROM JOURNAL TO ESSAY**   Expanding on your journal entry, write an essay DEFINING the distinctive quality of the language spoken in your home when you were a child. What effect, if any, did this language have on you when you went out into

public? Does it influence your memories of childhood? Do you revert to this private language when you are with your family?

2. Bilingual education is a controversial issue with EVIDENCE and strong feelings on both sides. In a page or so of preliminary writing, respond to Rodriguez's essay with your own gut feelings on the issue. Then do some library research to extend, support, or refute your views. In a well-reasoned and well-supported essay, give your opinion on whether or not public schools should teach children in their "family language."

3. **CRITICAL WRITING**   In his argument against bilingual education, Rodriguez offers no data from studies, no testimony from education experts, indeed no evidence at all except his personal experience. In an essay, ANALYZE and EVALUATE this evidence: How convincing do you find it? Is it adequate to support the argument? (In your essay consider Rodriguez's ethical appeal, the topic of the sixth question on writing strategy.)

4. **CONNECTIONS**   Rodriguez's mother and father seem to have had a definite idea of their parental obligations to their children. Look at Jamaica Kincaid's story "Girl" (p. 367) and write a COMPARISON between that mother's sense of parental obligations and the Rodriguezes'. What, for example, is the connection between good parenting and teaching one's child to conform? In both cases, you will have to infer the parents' values from their actions and words. Use evidence from both works to support your inferences.

5. **CONNECTIONS**   In "No Name Woman" (p. 620), Maxine Hong Kingston also writes about the effect of her family's silences on her growth into adulthood. In an essay, compare and contrast the experiences of Rodriguez and Kingston, focusing on the two writers' views of how communication fuels both intimacy and distance within families.

---

## *Richard Rodriguez on Writing*

For *The Bedford Reader*, Richard Rodriguez described the writing of "Aria."

From grammar school to college, my teachers offered perennial encouragement: "Write about what you know." Every year I would respond with the student's complaint: "I have nothing to write about . . . I haven't done anything." (Writers, real writers, I thought, lived in New York or Paris; they smoked on the back jackets of library books, their chores done.)

Stories die for not being told. My story got told because I had received an education; my teachers had given me the skill of stringing words together in a coherent line. But it was not until I was a man that I felt any need to write my story. A few years ago I left graduate school, quit teaching for political reasons (to protest affirmative action). But after leaving the classroom, as the months passed, I grew desperate to talk to serious people about serious things. In the great journals of the world, I noticed, there was conversation of a sort, glamorous company of a sort, and I determined to join it. I began writing to stay alive—not as a job, but to stay alive.

Even as you see my essay now, in cool printer's type, I look at some pages and cannot remember having written them. Or else I can remember earlier versions—unused incident, character, description (rooms, faces)—crumbled and discarded. Flung from possibility. They hit the wastebasket, those pages, and yet, defying gravity with a scratchy, starchy resilience, tried to reopen themselves. Then they fell silent. I read certain other sentences now and they recall the very day they were composed—the afternoon of rain or the telephone call that was to come a few moments after, the house, the room where these sentences were composed, the pattern of the rug, the wastebasket. (In all there were about thirty or forty versions that preceded this final "Aria.") I tried to describe my experiences exactly, at once to discover myself and to reveal myself. Always I had to write against the fear I felt that no one would be able to understand what I was saying.

As a reader, I have been struck by the way those novels and essays that are most particular, most particularly about one other life and time (Hannibal, Missouri; one summer; a slave; the loveliness of a muddy river) most fully achieve universality and call to be cherished. It is a paradox apparently: The more a writer unearths the detail that makes a life singular, the more a reader is led to feel a kind of sharing. Perhaps the reason we are able to respond to the life that is so different is because we all, each of us, think privately that we are different from one another. And the more closely we examine another life in its misery or wisdom or foolishness, the more it seems we take some version of ourselves.

It is, in any case, finally you that I end up having to trust not to laugh, not to snicker. Even as you regard me in these lines, I try to imagine your face as you read. You who read "Aria," especially those of you with your theme-divining yellow felt pen poised in your hand, you for whom this essay is yet another assignment, please do not forget that it is my life I am handing you in these pages—memories that are as personal for me as family photographs in an old cigar box.

## For Discussion

1. What seems to be Rodriguez's attitude toward his AUDIENCE when he writes? Do you think he writes chiefly for his readers, or for himself? Defend your answer.
2. Rodriguez tells us what he said when, as a student, he was told, "Write about what you know." What do you think he would say now?

# EDWARD SAID

EDWARD SAID was born in Jerusalem in 1935 and educated at Victoria College in Cairo, Egypt. As a boy he attended boarding school in Massachusetts, and then he went to Princeton and Harvard universities, taking a PhD from Harvard in 1964. Until his death in 2003, Said was professor of English and comparative literature at Columbia University. He wrote much literary criticism during his life, but his fame and notoriety came from his political writing. His book *Orientalism* (1978) was nominated for the National Book Critics Circle Award, translated into thirty-six languages, and acclaimed for its unblinkered view of the ideology and racism behind Western attitudes toward Islam. But that work and others also brought Said virulent attacks in print, occasional death threats, and, for his support of the Palestinian cause, the label "professor of terror." In his lifetime Said received many awards, including the Picasso Medal (1994), the Spinoza Prize (1999), and the Lannan Foundation Lifetime Achievement Award (2001). His memoir, *Out of Place* (1999), received *The New Yorker*'s award for nonfiction. An accomplished pianist, Said also wrote frequently on music and was music critic for *The Nation*.

# *Clashing Civilizations?*

Just after the terrorist attacks of September 11, 2001, Said published an essay, "We All Swim Together," in *New Statesman*. This excerpt from the essay takes strong issue with the view that the West and Islam are definable, inevitably opposed "civilizations." To Said, such concepts are not only misleading but also dangerous.

Said's essay is overall an argument against a certain comparison, classification, and definition, developed by other methods as well:

Narration (Chap. 4): paragraphs 1, 6
Example (Chap. 6): paragraphs 3, 4, 6
Comparison and contrast (Chap. 7): paragraphs 2–4, 6–7
Division or analysis (Chap. 9): paragraphs 2–7
Classification (Chap. 10): paragraphs 1–3, 6–7
Cause and effect (Chap. 11): paragraphs 1, 3–7
Definition (Chap. 12): paragraphs 5–7
Argument and persuasion (Chap. 13): throughout

Samuel Huntington's article "The Clash of Civilizations?" appeared in    1
the summer 1993 issue of *Foreign Affairs*, where it immediately attracted a surprising amount of attention and reaction. Because the article was intended to supply Americans with an original thesis about "a new phase" in world politics after the end of the Cold War, Huntington's terms of argument

seemed compellingly large, bold, even visionary. "It is my hypothesis," he wrote,

> that . . . the great divisions among humankind and the dominating source of conflict will be cultural. Nation-states will remain the most powerful actors in world affairs, but the principal conflicts of global politics will occur between nations and groups of different civilizations. The clash of civilizations will dominate global politics. The fault lines between civilizations will be the battle lines of the future.

Most of the argument in the pages that followed relied on a vague notion    2
of something Huntington called "civilization identity" and "the interactions among seven or eight [sic] major civilizations," of which the conflict between two of them, Islam and the West, gets the lion's share of his attention. In this belligerent kind of thought, he relies heavily on a 1990 article by the veteran orientalist Bernard Lewis, whose ideological colors are manifest in its title, "The Roots of Muslim Rage." In both articles, the personification of enormous entities called "the West" and "Islam" is recklessly affirmed, as if hugely complicated matters such as identity and culture existed in a cartoonlike world where Popeye and Bluto bash each other mercilessly, with one always more virtuous pugilist getting the upper hand over his adversary. Certainly neither Huntington nor Lewis has much time to spare for the internal dynamics and plurality of every civilization; or for considering that the major contest in most modern cultures concerns the definition or interpretation of each culture; or for the unattractive possibility that a great deal of demagogy and downright ignorance is involved in presuming to speak for a whole religion or civilization. No, the West is the West, and Islam is Islam.

The basic model of west versus the rest (the Cold War opposition refor-    3
mulated) is what has persisted, often insidiously and implicitly, in discussion since the terrible events of September 11. The carefully planned and horrendous, pathologically motivated suicide attack and mass slaughter by a small group of deranged militants has been turned into proof of Huntington's thesis. Instead of seeing it for what it is—the capture of big ideas (I use the word loosely) by a tiny band of crazed fanatics for criminal purposes—international luminaries from the former Pakistani prime minister Benazir Bhutto to the Italian prime minister, Silvio Berlusconi, have pontificated about Islam's troubles and, in the latter's case, have used Huntington's ideas to rant on about the West's superiority, how "we" have Mozart and Michelangelo and they don't.

But why not instead see parallels, admittedly less spectacular in their    4
destructiveness, to Osama Bin Laden and his followers in such cults as the Branch Davidians, or the disciples of the Reverend Jim Jones in Guyana, or the Japanese Aum Shinrikyo? Even *The Economist*, in its issue of September

22–28, 2001, couldn't resist reaching for the vast generalization, praising Huntington extravagantly for his "cruel and sweeping, but nonetheless acute" observations about Islam. "Today," the journal says, Huntington writes that "the world's billion or so Muslims are 'convinced of the superiority of their culture, and obsessed with the inferiority of their power.'" Did he canvass one hundred Indonesians, two hundred Moroccans, five hundred Egyptians and fifty Bosnians? Even if he did, what sort of sample is that?

Uncountable are the editorials in every American and European news-         5
paper and magazine of note adding to this vocabulary of gigantism and apoc-
alypse, each use of which is plainly designed to inflame the reader's indignant passion as a member of the "West," and what we need to do. Churchillian rhetoric[1] is used inappropriately by self-appointed combatants in the West's, and especially America's, war against its haters, despoilers, destroyers, with scant attention to complex histories that defy such reductiveness and have seeped from one territory into another, overriding the boundaries that are sup-posed to separate us all into divided armed camps.

This is the problem with unedifying labels such as *Islam* and *the West*:         6
They mislead and confuse the mind, which is trying to make sense of a disor-derly reality that won't be pigeonholed. I remember interrupting a man who, after a lecture I had given at a West Bank[2] university in 1994, rose from the audience and started to attack my ideas as "Western," as opposed to the strict Islamic ones he espoused. "Why are you wearing a suit and tie?" was the first retort that came to mind. "They're Western, too." He sat down with an embarrassed smile on his face, but I recalled the incident when information on the September 11 terrorists started to come in: how they had mastered all the technical details required to inflict their homicidal evil on the World Trade Center, the Pentagon and the aircraft they had commandeered. Where does one draw the line between "Western" technology and, as Berlusconi declared, "Islam's" inability to be a part of "modernity"?

One cannot easily do so. How finally inadequate are the labels, general-         7
izations and cultural assertions. At some level, for instance, primitive passions and sophisticated know-how converge in ways that give the lie to a fortified boundary not only between "West" and "Islam," but also between past and present, us and them, to say nothing of the very concepts of identity and nation-ality about which there is unending debate. A unilateral decision made to undertake crusades, to oppose their evil with our good, to extirpate terrorism

---

[1] A statesman and gifted orator, Winston Churchill (1874–1965) was British prime minis-ter during World War II, when his stirring speeches fortified his embattled nation's resolve to fight the Germans. — EDS.

[2] Disputed territory adjacent to Israel, controlled partly by Israel and partly by the Pales-tinian Authority. — EDS.

and, in Paul Wolfowitz's[3] nihilistic vocabulary, to end nations entirely, doesn't make the supposed entities any easier to see; rather, it speaks to how much simpler it is to make bellicose statements for the purpose of mobilizing collective passions than to reflect, examine, sort out what it is we are dealing with in reality, the interconnectedness of innumerable lives, "ours" as well as "theirs."

*For a reading quiz, sources on Edward Said, and annotated links to further readings on Western views of Islam, visit **bedfordstmartins.com/thebedfordreader**.*

## Journal Writing

Write in your journal about the images of Islam that you see in the US media. Based on news reports and other media presentations, what view would an average American have of Islam? (To take your journal writing further, see "From Journal to Essay" on the next page.)

## Questions on Meaning

1. SUMMARIZE the views to which Said responds. How were these views affected by the events of September 11, 2001?
2. Summarize Said's ARGUMENT in response to Huntington's and others' views on the West and Islam.
3. What is Said's point in paragraph 6?
4. What is Said's THESIS? Where does he state it?

## Questions on Writing Strategy

1. What is Said's point in referring to Popeye and Bluto in paragraph 2?
2. Why does Said compare Osama Bin Laden and his followers to "such cults as the Branch Davidians, or the disciples of the Reverend Jim Jones in Guyana, or the Japanese Aum Shinrikyo" (par. 4)?
3. Look for places where Said puts words in quotation marks though not actually quoting anyone in particular. What do the quotation marks signify?
4. **MIXED METHODS**   What does Said use DIVISION or ANALYSIS for in paragraph 2? What PURPOSE does this paragraph serve in Said's argument?
5. **MIXED METHODS**   How does Said's EXAMPLE and NARRATION about the West Bank man who challenged him contribute to his point in paragraph 6?

[3] Deputy secretary of defense (2001–05) under President George W. Bush. —EDS.

## Questions on Language

1. What words does Said use to characterize the attitude of those he is criticizing? What is the EFFECT of his language? How do you respond to it?
2. In quoting Huntington in paragraph 2, what does Said intend by the use of *sic* in brackets?
3. In paragraph 3 Said refers to the September 11 terrorist attack as "the capture of big ideas (I use the word loosely) by a tiny band of crazed fanatics for criminal purposes." What does he mean by the sentence in parentheses?
4. Consult a dictionary if you are unsure of the meaning of any of the following: visionary (par. 1); belligerent, personification, pugilist, plurality, demagogy (2); insidiously, luminaries, pontificated (3); gigantism, apocalypse, reductiveness (5); unedifying (6); unilateral, extirpate, nihilistic, bellicose, mobilizing (7).

## Suggestions for Writing

1. **FROM JOURNAL TO ESSAY**  Based on your journal entry, write an essay in which you analyze images of Islam presented by the US media. (You may want to supplement your current knowledge with research among news magazines and television and radio news and talk shows.) EVALUATE the accuracy of these images.
2. Do you think that there is an inevitable "clash of civilizations" between Islam and the West? Write an essay in which you respond to the view of Samuel P. Huntington, Bernard Lewis, and others quoted by Said.
3. **CRITICAL WRITING**  Write an essay in which you analyze the TONE of Said's essay. Does the tone reinforce Said's argument? Is it effective? Why, or why not?
4. **CONNECTIONS**  Throughout his essay Said suggests that Western culture is not necessarily superior to Islamic culture, asking why we are reluctant to examine the less flattering parallels between the two. Write an essay in which you examine Fatema Mernissi's "Size 6: The Western Women's Harem" (p. 252) as a response to Said's implied challenge.
5. **CONNECTIONS**  Adnan R. Khan, in "Close Encounters with US Immigration" (p. 558), and Linda Chavez, in "Everything Isn't Racial Profiling" (p. 563), both address attitudes toward Muslims since September 11, 2001. In an essay bring these two authors face to face with Said. Where might the three writers agree? Where might they disagree?

# JONATHAN SWIFT

JONATHAN SWIFT (1667–1745), the son of English parents who had settled in Ireland, divided his energies among literature, politics, and the Church of England. Dissatisfied with the quiet life of an Anglican parish priest, Swift spent much of his time in London hobnobbing with writers and producing pamphlets in support of the Tory Party. In 1713 Queen Anne rewarded his political services with an assignment the London-loving Swift didn't want: to supervise St. Patrick's Cathedral in Dublin. There, as Dean Swift, he ended his days—beloved by the Irish, whose interests he defended against the English government. Although Swift's chief works include the remarkable satires *The Battle of the Books* and *A Tale of a Tub* (both 1704) and scores of fine poems, he is best remembered for *Gulliver's Travels* (1726), an account of four imaginary voyages. This classic is always abridged when it is given to children because of its frank descriptions of human filth and viciousness. In *Gulliver's Travels*, Swift pays tribute to the reasoning portion of "that animal called man," and delivers a stinging rebuke to the rest of him.

# *A Modest Proposal*

Three consecutive years of drought and sparse crops had worked hardship upon the Irish when Swift wrote this ferocious essay in the summer of 1729. At the time, there were said to be thirty-five thousand wandering beggars in the country: Whole families had quit their farms and had taken to the roads. Large landowners, of English ancestry, preferred to ignore their tenants' sufferings and lived abroad to dodge taxes and payment of church duties. Swift had no special fondness for the Irish, but he hated the inhumanity he witnessed.

Although printed as a pamphlet in Dublin, Swift's essay is clearly meant for English readers as well as Irish ones. When circulated, the pamphlet caused a sensation in both Ireland and England and had to be reprinted seven times in the same year. Swift is an expert with plain, vigorous English prose, and "A Modest Proposal" is a masterpiece of SATIRE and IRONY. (If you are uncertain what Swift argues for, see the discussion of these devices in Useful Terms.)

"A Modest Proposal" is an argument developed chiefly by process analysis and cause and effect. These two methods mix with notable uses of description, example, and comparison and contrast.

Description (Chap. 5): paragraphs 1–2, 19
Example (Chap. 6): paragraphs 1–2, 6, 10, 14, 18, 32
Comparison and contrast (Chap. 7): paragraph 17
Process analysis (Chap. 8): paragraphs 4, 6–7, 10–17
Cause and effect (Chap. 11): paragraphs 4–5, 13, 21–29, 31, 33
Argument and persuasion (Chap. 13): throughout

*For Preventing the Children of Poor People in Ireland
from Being a Burden to Their Parents or Country,
and for Making Them Beneficial to the Public*

It is a melancholy object to those who walk through this great town[1] or
travel in the country, when they see the streets, the roads, and cabin doors,
crowded with beggars of the female sex, followed by three, four, or six children, all in rags and importuning every passenger for an alms. These mothers,
instead of being able to work for their honest livelihood, are forced to employ
all their time in strolling to beg sustenance for their helpless infants, who, as
they grow up, either turn thieves for want of work, or leave their dear native
country to fight for the Pretender in Spain, or sell themselves to the Barbados.[2]

I think it is agreed by all parties that this prodigious number of children in
the arms, or on the backs, or at the heels of their mothers, and frequently of
their fathers, is in the present deplorable state of the kingdom a very great
additional grievance; and therefore whoever could find out a fair, cheap, and
easy method of making these children sound, useful members of the commonwealth would deserve so well of the public as to have his statue set up for a pre-
server of the nation.

But my intention is very far from being confined to provide only for the
children of professed beggars; it is of a much greater extent, and shall take
in the whole number of infants at a certain age who are born of parents in effect as little able to support them as those who demand our charity in the
streets.

As to my own part, having turned my thoughts for many years upon this
important subject, and maturely weighed the several schemes of other projectors,[3] I have always found them grossly mistaken in their computation. It is
true, a child just dropped from its dam may be supported by her milk for a solar
year, with little other nourishment; at most not above the value of two
shillings, which the mother may certainly get, or the value in scraps, by her
lawful occupation of begging; and it is exactly at one year that I propose to
provide for them in such a manner as instead of being a charge upon their parents or the parish, or wanting food and raiment for the rest of their lives, they
shall on the contrary contribute to the feeding, and partly to the clothing, of
many thousands.

1

2

3

4

[1] Dublin.—EDS.
[2] The Pretender was James Stuart, exiled in Spain; in 1718 many Irishmen had joined an
army seeking to restore him to the English throne. Others wishing to emigrate had signed
papers as indentured servants, agreeing to work for a number of years in the Barbados or other
British colonies in exchange for their ocean passage.—EDS.
[3] Planners.—EDS.

There is likewise another great advantage in my scheme, that it will pre-      5
vent those voluntary abortions, and that horrid practice of women murdering
their bastard children, alas, too frequent among us, sacrificing the poor innocent babes, I doubt, more to avoid the expense than the shame, which would
move tears and pity in the most savage and inhuman breast.

The number of souls in this kingdom being usually reckoned one million      6
and a half, of these I calculate there may be about two hundred thousand
couples whose wives are breeders; from which number I subtract thirty thousand couples who are able to maintain their own children, although I apprehend there cannot be so many under the present distress of the kingdom; but
this being granted, there will remain an hundred and seventy thousand breeders. I again subtract fifty thousand for those women who miscarry, or whose
children die by accident or disease within the year. There only remain an hundred and twenty thousand children of poor parents annually born. The question therefore is, how this number shall be reared and provided for, which, as
I have already said, under the present situation of affairs, is utterly impossible
by all the methods hitherto proposed. For we can neither employ them in
handicraft or agriculture; we neither build houses (I mean in the country) nor
cultivate land. They can very seldom pick up a livelihood stealing till they
arrive at six years old, except where they are of towardly parts;[4] although I
confess they learn the rudiments much earlier, during which time they can
however be looked upon only as probationers, as I have been informed by a
principal gentleman in the country of Cavan, who protested to me that he
never knew above one or two instances under the age of six, even in a part of
the kingdom so renowned for the quickest proficiency in that art.

I am assured by our merchants that a boy or a girl before twelve years old      7
is no salable commodity; and even when they come to this age they will not
yield above three pounds, or three pounds and half a crown at most on the
Exchange; which cannot turn to account either to the parents or the kingdom, the charge of nutriment and rags having been at least four times that
value.

I shall now therefore humbly propose my own thoughts, which I hope will      8
not be liable to the least objection.

I have been assured by a very knowing American of my acquaintance in      9
London, that a young healthy child well nursed is at a year old a most delicious, nourishing, and wholesome food, whether stewed, roasted, baked, or
boiled; and I make no doubt that it will equally serve in a fricassee or a ragout.[5]

I do therefore humbly offer it to public consideration that of the hundred      10

---

[4] Teachable wits, innate abilities. —EDS.
[5] Stew. —EDS.

and twenty thousand children, already computed, twenty thousand may be reserved for breed, whereof only one fourth part to be males, which is more than we allow to sheep, black cattle, or swine; and my reason is that these children are seldom the fruits of marriage, a circumstance not much regarded by our savages, therefore one male will be sufficient to serve four females. That the remaining hundred thousand may at a year old be offered in sale to the persons of quality and fortune through the kingdom, always advising the mother to let them suck plentifully in the last month, so as to render them plump and fat for a good table. A child will make two dishes at an entertainment for friends; and when the family dines alone, the fore or hind quarter will make a reasonable dish, and seasoned with a little pepper or salt will be very good boiled on the fourth day, especially in winter.

I have reckoned upon a medium that a child just born will weigh twelve pounds, and in a solar year if tolerably nursed increaseth to twenty-eight pounds.

I grant this food will be somewhat dear, and therefore very proper for landlords, who, as they have already devoured most of the parents, seem to have the best title to the children.

Infant's flesh will be in season throughout the year, but more plentiful in March, and a little before and after. For we are told by a grave author, an eminent French physician,[6] that fish being a prolific diet, there are more children born in Roman Catholic countries about nine months after Lent than at any other season; therefore, reckoning a year after Lent, the markets will be more glutted than usual, because the number of popish infants is at least three to one in this kingdom; and therefore it will have one other collateral advantage, by lessening the number of Papists among us.

I have already computed the charge of nursing a beggar's child (in which list I reckon all cottagers, laborers, and four-fifths of the farmers) to be about two shillings per annum, rags included; and I believe no gentleman would repine to give ten shillings for the carcass of a good fat child, which, as I have said, will make four dishes of excellent nutritive meat, when he hath only some particular friend or his own family to dine with him. Thus the squire will learn to be a good landlord, and grow people among the tenants; the mother will have eight shillings net profit, and be fit for work till she produces another child.

Those who are more thrifty (as I must confess the times require) may flay the carcass; the skin of which artificially[7] dressed will make admirable gloves for ladies, and summer boots for fine gentlemen.

---

[6] Swift's favorite French writer, François Rabelais, sixteenth-century author; not "grave" at all, but a broad humorist. — EDS.

[7] With art or craft. — EDS.

As to our city of Dublin, shambles[8] may be appointed for this purpose in      16
the most convenient parts of it, and butchers we may be assured will not be
wanting; although I rather recommend buying the children alive, and dressing
them hot from the knife as we do roasting pigs.

A very worthy person, a true lover of his country, and whose virtues I      17
highly esteem, was lately pleased in discoursing on this matter to offer a refinement upon my scheme. He said that many gentlemen of his kingdom, having
of late destroyed their deer, he conceived that the want of venison might be
well supplied by the bodies of young lads and maidens, not exceeding fourteen
years of age nor under twelve, so great a number of both sexes in every county
being now ready to starve for want of work and service; and these to be dis-
posed of by their parents, if alive, or otherwise by their nearest relations. But
with due deference to so excellent a friend and so deserving a patriot, I cannot be altogether in his sentiments; for as to the males, my American acquaintance assured me from frequent experience that their flesh was generally tough
and lean, like that of our schoolboys, by continual exercise, and their taste dis-
agreeable; and to fatten them would not answer the charge. Then as to the
females, it would, I think with humble submission, be a loss to the public,
because they soon would become breeders themselves; and besides, it is not
improbable that some scrupulous people might be apt to censure such a practice (although indeed very unjustly) as a little bordering upon cruelty; which,
I confess, hath always been with me the strongest objection against any project, how well soever intended.

But in order to justify my friend, he confessed that this expedient was put      18
into his head by the famous Psalmanazar,[9] a native of the island Formosa, who
came from thence to London above twenty years ago, and in conversation
told my friend that in his country when any young person happened to be put
to death, the executioner sold the carcass to persons of quality as a prime
dainty; and that in his time the body of a plump girl of fifteen, who was crucified for an attempt to poison the emperor, was sold to his Imperial Majesty's
prime minister of state, and other great mandarins of the court, in joints from
the gibbet, at four hundred crowns. Neither indeed can I deny that if the same
use were made of several plump young girls in this town, who without one
single groat to their fortunes cannot stir abroad without a chair, and appear at
the playhouse and assemblies in foreign fineries which they never will pay for,
the kingdom would not be the worse.

---

[8] Butcher shops or slaughterhouses. —EDS.
[9] Georges Psalmanazar—a Frenchman who pretended to be Japanese, the author of a completely imaginary *Description of the Isle Formosa* (1705)—had become a well-known figure in
gullible London society. —EDS.

Some persons of a desponding spirit are in great concern about that vast number of poor people who are aged, diseased, or maimed, and I have been desired to employ my thoughts what course may be taken to ease the nation of so grievous an encumbrance. But I am not in the least pain upon that matter, because it is very well known that they are every day dying and rotting by cold and famine, and filth and vermin, as fast as can be reasonably expected. And as to the younger laborers, they are now in almost as hopeful a condition. They cannot get work, and consequently pine away for want of nourishment to a degree that if any time they are accidentally hired to common labor, they have not strength to perform it; and thus the country and themselves are happily delivered from the evils to come. 19

I have too long digressed, and therefore shall return to my subject. I think the advantages by the proposal which I have made are obvious and many, as well as of the highest importance. 20

For first, as I have already observed, it would greatly lessen the number of Papists, with whom we are yearly overrun, being the principal breeders of the nation as well as our most dangerous enemies; and who stay at home on purpose to deliver the kingdom to the Pretender, hoping to take their advantage by the absence of so many good Protestants, who have chosen rather to leave their country than to stay at home and pay tithes against their conscience to an Episcopal curate. 21

Secondly, the poorer tenants will have something valuable of their own, which by law may be made liable to distress,[10] and help to pay their landlord's rent, their corn and cattle being already seized and money a thing unknown. 22

Thirdly, whereas the maintenance of an hundred thousand children, from two years old and upwards, cannot be computed at less than ten shillings a piece per annum, the nation's stock will be thereby increased fifty thousand pounds per annum, besides the profit of a new dish introduced to the tables of all gentlemen of fortune in the kingdom who have any refinement in taste. And the money will circulate among ourselves, the goods being entirely of our own growth and manufacture. 23

Fourthly, the constant breeders, besides the gain of eight shillings sterling per annum by the sale of their children, will be rid of the charge of maintaining them after the first year. 24

Fifthly, this food would likewise bring great custom to taverns, where the vintners will certainly be so prudent as to procure the best receipts for dressing it to perfection, and consequently have their houses frequented by all the fine gentlemen, who justly value themselves upon their knowledge in good 25

---

[10] Subject to seizure by creditors. —EDS.

eating; and a skillful cook, who understands how to oblige his guests, will contrive to make it as expensive as they please.

Sixthly, this would be a great inducement to marriage, which all wise 26 nations have either encouraged by rewards or enforced by laws and penalties. It would increase the care and tenderness of mothers toward their children, when they were sure of a settlement for life to the poor babes, provided in some sort by the public, to their annual profit instead of expense. We should see an honest emulation among the married women, which of them could bring the fattest child to the market. Men would become as fond of their wives during the time of their pregnancy as they are now of their mares in foal, their cows in calf, or sows when they are ready to farrow; nor offer to beat or kick them (as is too frequent a practice) for fear of a miscarriage.

Many other advantages might be enumerated. For instance, the addition 27 of some thousand carcasses in our exportation of barreled beef, the propagation of swine's flesh, and improvements in the art of making good bacon, so much wanted among us by the great destruction of pigs, too frequent at our tables, which are no way comparable in taste or magnificence to a well-grown, fat, yearling child, which roasted whole will make a considerable figure at a lord mayor's feast or any other public entertainment. But this and many others I omit, being studious of brevity.

Supposing that one thousand families in this city would be constant cus- 28 tomers for infants' flesh, besides others who might have it at merry meetings, particularly weddings and christenings, I compute that Dublin would take off annually about twenty thousand carcasses, and the rest of the kingdom (where probably they will be sold somewhat cheaper) the remaining eighty thousand.

I can think of no one objection that will possibly be raised against this 29 proposal, unless it should be urged that the number of people will be thereby much lessened in the kingdom. This I freely own, and it was indeed one principal design in offering it to the world. I desire the reader will observe, that I calculate my remedy for this one individual kingdom of Ireland and for no other that ever was, is, or I think ever can be upon earth. Therefore let no man talk to me of other expedients: of taxing our absentees at five shillings a pound: of using neither clothes nor household furniture except what is of our own growth and manufacture: of utterly rejecting the materials and instruments that promote foreign luxury: of curing the expensiveness of pride, vanity, idleness, and gaming in our women: of introducing a vein of parsimony, prudence, and temperance: of learning to love our country, in the want of which we differ even from Laplanders and the inhabitants of Topinamboo:[11]

---

[11] A district of Brazil. —EDS.

of quitting our animosities and factions, nor acting any longer like the Jews, who were murdering one another at the very moment their city was taken:[12] of being a little cautious not to sell our country and conscience for nothing: of teaching landlords to have at least one degree of mercy toward their tenants: lastly, of putting a spirit of honesty, industry, and skill into our shopkeepers; who, if a resolution could now be taken to buy only our native goods, would immediately unite to cheat and exact upon us in the price, the measure, and the goodness, nor could ever yet be brought to make one fair proposal of just dealing, though often and earnestly invited to it.

Therefore I repeat, let no man talk to me of these and the like expedients, till he hath at least some glimpse of hope that there will ever be some hearty and sincere attempt to put them in practice.       30

But as to myself, having been wearied out for many years with offering vain, idle, visionary thoughts, and at length utterly despairing of success, I fortunately fell upon this proposal, which, as it is wholly new, so it hath something solid and real, of no expense and little trouble, full in our own power, and whereby we can incur no danger in disobliging England. For this kind of commodity will not bear exportation, the flesh being of too tender a consistence to admit a long continuance in salt, although perhaps I could name a country which would be glad to eat up our whole nation without it.       31

After all, I am not so violently bent upon my own opinion as to reject any offer proposed by wise men, which shall be found equally innocent, cheap, easy, and effectual. But before something of that kind shall be advanced in contradiction to my scheme, and offering a better, I desire the author or authors will be pleased maturely to consider two points. First, as things now stand, how they will be able to find food and raiment for an hundred thousand useless mouths and backs. And secondly, there being a round million of creatures in human figure throughout this kingdom, whose sole subsistence put into a common stock would leave them in debt two millions of pounds sterling, adding those who are beggars by profession to the bulk of farmers, cottagers, and laborers, with their wives and children who are beggars in effect; I desire those politicians who dislike my overture, and may perhaps be so bold to attempt an answer, that they will first ask the parents of these mortals whether they would not at this day think it a great happiness to have been sold for food at a year old in this manner I prescribe, and thereby have avoided such a perpetual scene of misfortunes as they have since gone through by the oppression of landlords, the impossibility of paying rent without money or trade, the want of common sustenance, with neither house nor clothes to       32

---

[12] During the Roman siege of Jerusalem (AD 70), prominent Jews were executed on the charge of being in league with the enemy. —EDS.

cover them from the inclemencies of the weather, and the most inevitable prospect of entailing the like or greater miseries upon their breed forever.

I profess, in the sincerity of my heart, that I have not the least personal interest in endeavoring to promote this necessary work, having no other motive than the public good of my country, by advancing our trade, providing for infants, relieving the poor, and giving some pleasure to the rich. I have no children by which I can propose to get a single penny; the youngest being nine years old, and my wife past childbearing.   33

For a reading quiz, sources on Jonathan Swift, and annotated links to further readings on eighteenth-century Ireland, visit **bedfordstmartins.com/thebedfordreader**.

## Journal Writing

Swift's proposal is aimed at a serious social problem of his day. In your journal, consider a contemporary problem that—like the poverty and starvation Swift describes—seems to require drastic action. For instance, do you believe that a particular group of people is neglected, mistreated, or victimized? Turn to the news media for ideas if no problem comes immediately to mind. (To take your journal writing further, see "From Journal to Essay" on the next page.)

## Questions on Meaning

1. On the surface, what is Swift proposing?
2. Beneath his IRONY, what is Swift's argument?
3. What do you take to be the PURPOSE of Swift's essay?
4. How does the introductory paragraph serve Swift's purpose?
5. Comment on the statement "I can think of no one objection that will possibly be raised against this proposal" (par. 29). What objections can you think of?

## Questions on Writing Strategy

1. Describe the mask of the personage through whom Swift writes.
2. By what means does the writer attest to his reasonableness?
3. At what point in the essay did it become clear to you that the proposal isn't modest but horrible?
4. **MIXED METHODS**   As an ARGUMENT, does "A Modest Proposal" appeal primarily to reason or to emotion? (See p. 521 for a discussion of the distinction.)

5. **MIXED METHODS**   What does Swift's argument gain by his careful attention to PROCESS ANALYSIS and to CAUSE AND EFFECT?

## Questions on Language

1. How does Swift's choice of words enforce the monstrousness of his proposal? Note especially words from the vocabulary of breeding and butchery.
2. Consult your dictionary for the meanings of any of the following words not yet in your vocabulary: importuning, sustenance (par. 1); prodigious, commonwealth (2); computation, raiment (4); apprehend, rudiments, probationers (6); nutriment (7); fricassee (9); repine (14); flay (15); scrupulous, censure (17); mandarins (18); desponding, encumbrance (19); per annum (23); vintners (25); emulation, foal, farrow (26); expedients, parsimony, animosities (29); disobliging, consistence (31); overture, inclemencies (32).

## Suggestions for Writing

1. **FROM JOURNAL TO ESSAY**   Write an essay in which you propose a solution to the problem raised in your journal. Your essay may be either of the following:
   a. A straight argument, giving EVIDENCE, in which you set forth possible solutions to the problem.
   b. An ironic proposal in the manner of Swift. If you do this one, find a device other than cannibalism to eliminate the victims or their problems. You don't want to imitate Swift too closely; he is probably inimitable.
2. In an encyclopedia, look into what has happened in Ireland since Swift wrote. Choose a specific contemporary aspect of Irish-English relations, research it in books and periodicals, and write a report on it.
3. **CRITICAL WRITING**   Choose several examples of irony in "A Modest Proposal" that you find particularly effective. In a brief essay, ANALYZE Swift's use of irony. Do your examples of irony depend on understating, overstating, or saying the opposite of what is meant? How do they improve on literal statements? What is the value of irony in argument?
4. **CONNECTIONS**   Read Jessica Mitford's "Behind the Formaldehyde Curtain" (p. 308) alongside "A Modest Proposal," and analyze the use of irony and humor in these two essays. How heavily does each author depend on irony and humor to make his or her argument? Do these elements strengthen both authors' arguments? What evidence does each offer that would also work in a more straightforward argument?
5. **CONNECTIONS**   Analyze the ways Swift and Martin Luther King, Jr., in "I Have a Dream" (p. 614), create sympathy for the oppressed groups they are concerned about. Concentrate not only on what they say but on the words they use and their TONE. Then write a process analysis explaining techniques for portraying oppression so as to win the reader's sympathy. Use quotations or PARAPHRASES from Swift's and King's essays as EXAMPLES. If you can think of other techniques that neither author uses, by all means include and illustrate them as well.

## *Jonathan Swift on Writing*

Although surely one of the most inventive writers in English literature, Swift voiced his contempt for writers of his day who bragged of their newness and originality. In *The Battle of the Books,* he compares such a self-professed original to a spider who "spins and spits wholly from himself, and scorns to own any obligation or assistance from without." Swift has the fable-writer Aesop praise that writer who, like a bee gathering nectar, draws from many sources.

> Erect your schemes with as much method and skill as you please; yet if the materials be nothing but dirt, spun out of your own entrails (the guts of modern brains), the edifice will conclude at last in a cobweb. . . . As for us Ancients, we are content, with the bee, to pretend to nothing of our own beyond our wings and our voice, that is to say, our flights and our language. For the rest, whatever we have got has been by infinite labor and search and ranging through every corner of nature; the difference is, that, instead of dirt and poison, we have rather chosen to fill our hives with honey and wax, thus furnishing mankind with the two noblest of things, which are sweetness and light.

Swift's advice for a writer would seem to be: Don't just invent things out of thin air; read the best writers of the past. Observe and converse. Do legwork.

Interestingly, when in *Gulliver's Travels* Swift portrays his ideal beings, the Houyhnhnms, a race of noble and intelligent horses, he includes no writers at all in their society. "The Houyhnhnms have no letters," Gulliver observes, "and consequently their knowledge is all traditional." Still, "in poetry they must be allowed to excel all other mortals; wherein the justness of their description are indeed inimitable." (Those very traits—striking comparisons and detailed descriptions—make much of Swift's own writing memorable.)

In his great book, in "A Modest Proposal," and in virtually all he wrote, Swift's purpose was forthright and evident. He declared in "Verses on the Death of Dr. Swift,"

> As with a moral view designed
> To cure the vices of mankind:
> Yet malice never was his aim;
> He lashed the vice but spared the name.
> No individual could resent,
> Where thousands equally were meant.
> His satire points at no defect
> But what all mortals may correct.

## For Discussion

1. Try applying Swift's parable of the spider and the bee to our own day. How much truth is left in it?
2. Reread thoughtfully the quotation from Swift's poem. According to the poet, what faults or abuses can a satiric writer fall into? How may these be avoided?
3. What do you take to be Swift's main PURPOSE as a writer? In your own words, SUMMARIZE it.

# E. B. WHITE

ELWYN BROOKS WHITE (1899–1985) for half a century was a regular contributor to *The New Yorker*, and his essays, editorials, anonymous features for "The Talk of the Town," and fillers helped build the magazine a reputation for wit and good writing. If as a child you read *Charlotte's Web* (1952), you have met E. B. White before. The book reflects some of his own life on a farm in North Brooklin, Maine. His *Letters* were collected in 1976, his *Essays* in 1977, and his *Poems and Sketches* in 1981. On July 4, 1963, President Kennedy named White in the first group of Americans to receive the Presidential Medal of Freedom, with a citation that called him "an essayist whose concise comment . . . has revealed to yet another age the vigor of the English sentence."

## *Once More to the Lake*

"Once More to the Lake" first appeared in *Harper's* magazine in 1941. Perhaps if a duller writer had written the essay, or an essay with the same title, we wouldn't much care about it, for at first its subject seems as personal and ordinary as a letter home. White's loving and exact portrayal, however, brings this lakeside camp to life for us. In the end, the writer arrives at an awareness that shocks him—shocks us, too, with a familiar sensory detail.

"Once More to the Lake" is a stunning mixture of description and narration, but it is also more. To make his observations and emotions clear and immediate, White relies extensively on several other methods of development as well.

Narration (Chap. 4): throughout
Description (Chap. 5): throughout
Example (Chap. 6): paragraphs 2, 7–8, 11, 12
Comparison and contrast (Chap. 7): paragraphs 4–7, 9–10, 11–12
Process analysis (Chap. 8): paragraphs 9, 10, 12

### *August 1941*

One summer, along about 1904, my father rented a camp on a lake in Maine and took us all there for the month of August. We all got ringworm from some kittens and had to rub Pond's Extract on our arms and legs night and morning, and my father rolled over in a canoe with all his clothes on; but outside of that the vacation was a success and from then on none of us ever thought there was any place in the world like that lake in Maine. We returned summer after summer—always on August 1 for one month. I have since become a salt-water man, but sometimes in summer there are days when the restlessness of the tides and the fearful cold of the sea water and the incessant wind that blows across the afternoon and into the evening make me wish for the placidity of a lake in the woods. A few weeks ago this feeling got so strong I bought myself a couple of bass hooks and a spinner and returned to the lake where we used to go, for a week's fishing and to revisit old haunts.

I took along my son, who had never had any fresh water up his nose and who had seen lily pads only from train windows. On the journey over to the lake I began to wonder what it would be like. I wondered how time would have marred this unique, this holy spot—the coves and streams, the hills that the sun set behind, the camps and the paths behind the camps. I was sure that the tarred road would have found it out, and I wondered in what other ways it would be desolated. It is strange how much you can remember about places like that once you allow your mind to return into the grooves that lead back. You remember one thing, and that suddenly reminds you of another thing. I guess I remembered clearest of all the early mornings, when the lake was cool and motionless, remembered how the bedroom smelled of the lumber it was made of and of the wet woods whose scent entered through the screen. The partitions in the camp were thin and did not extend clear to the top of the rooms, and as I was always the first up I would dress softly so as not to wake the others, and sneak out into the sweet outdoors and start out in the canoe, keeping close along the shore in the long shadows of the pines. I remembered being very careful never to rub my paddle against the gunwale for fear of disturbing the stillness of the cathedral.

The lake had never been what you would call a wild lake. There were cottages sprinkled around the shores, and it was in farming country although the shores of the lake were quite heavily wooded. Some of the cottages were owned by nearby farmers, and you would live at the shore and eat your meals at the farmhouse. That's what our family did. But although it wasn't wild, it was a fairly large and undisturbed lake and there were places in it that, to a child at least, seemed infinitely remote and primeval.

I was right about the tar: It led to within half a mile of the shore. But when I got back there, with my boy, and we settled into a camp near a farmhouse and into the kind of summertime I had known, I could tell that it was going to be pretty much the same as it had been before—I knew it, lying in bed the first morning smelling the bedroom and hearing the boy sneak quietly out and go off along the shore in a boat. I began to sustain the illusion that he was I, and therefore, by simple transposition, that I was my father. This sensation persisted, kept cropping up all the time we were there. It was not an entirely new feeling, but in this setting it grew much stronger. I seemed to be living a dual existence. I would be in the middle of some simple act, I would be picking up a bait box or laying down a table fork, or I would be saying something and suddenly it would be not I but my father who was saying the words or making the gesture. It gave me a creepy sensation.

We went fishing the first morning. I felt the same damp moss covering the worms in the bait can, and saw the dragonfly alight on the tip of my rod as it hovered a few inches from the surface of the water. It was the arrival of this fly that convinced me beyond any doubt that everything was as it always had been, that the years were a mirage and that there had been no years. The small waves were the same, chucking the rowboat under the chin as we fished at anchor, and the boat was the same boat, the same color green and the ribs broken in the same places, and under the floorboards the same fresh water leavings and debris — the dead hellgrammite, the wisps of moss, the rusty discarded fishhook, the dried blood from yesterday's catch. We stared silently at the tips of our rods, at the dragonflies that came and went. I lowered the tip of mine into the water, tentatively, pensively dislodging the fly, which darted two feet away, poised, darted two feet back, and came to rest again a little farther up the rod. There had been no years between the ducking of this dragonfly and the other one — the one that was part of memory. I looked at the boy, who was silently watching his fly, and it was my hands that held his rod, my eyes watching. I felt dizzy and didn't know which rod I was at the end of. 5

We caught two bass, hauling them in briskly as though they were mackerel, pulling them over the side of the boat in a businesslike manner without any landing net, and stunning them with a blow on the back of the head. When we got back for a swim before lunch, the lake was exactly where we had left it, the same number of inches from the dock, and there was only the merest suggestion of a breeze. This seemed an utterly enchanted sea, this lake you could leave to its own devices for a few hours and come back to, and find that it had not stirred, this constant and trustworthy body of water. In the shallows, the dark, water-soaked sticks and twigs, smooth and old, were undulating in clusters on the bottom against the clean ribbed sand, and the track of the mussel was plain. A school of minnows swam by, each minnow with its small individual shadow, doubling the attendance, so clear and sharp in the sunlight. Some of the other campers were in swimming, along the shore, one of them with a cake of soap, and the water felt thin and clear and unsubstantial. Over the years there had been this person with the cake of soap, this cultist, and here he was. There had been no years. 6

Up to the farmhouse to dinner through the teeming dusty field, the road under our sneakers was only a two-track road. The middle track was missing, the one with the marks of the hooves and the splotches of dried, flaky manure. There had always been three tracks to choose from in choosing which track to walk in; now the choice was narrowed down to two. For a moment I missed terribly the middle alternative. But the way led past the tennis court, and 7 something about the way it lay there in the sun reassured me; the tape had loosened along the backline, the alleys were green with plantains and other weeds, and the net (installed in June and removed in September) sagged in the dry noon, and the whole place steamed with midday heat and hunger and emptiness. There was a choice of pie for dessert, and one was blueberry and one was apple, and the waitresses were the same country girls, there having been no passage of time, only the illusion of it as in a dropped curtain — the waitresses were still fifteen; their hair had been washed, that was the only difference — they had been to the movies and seen the pretty girls with the clean hair.

Summertime, oh, summertime, pattern of life indelible, the fade-proof lake, the woods unshatterable, the pasture with the sweetfern and the juniper forever and ever, summer without end; this was the background, and the life along the shore was the design, the cottages with their innocent and tranquil design, their tiny docks with the flagpole and the American flag floating against the white clouds in the blue sky, the little paths over the roots of the trees leading from camp to camp and the paths leading back to the outhouses and the can of lime for sprinkling, and at the souvenir counters at the store the miniature birchbark canoes and the postcards that showed things looking a little better than they looked. This was the American family at play, escaping the city heat, wondering whether the newcomers in the camp at the head of the cove were "common" or "nice," wondering whether it was true that the people who drove up for Sunday dinner at the farmhouse were turned away because there wasn't enough chicken.

It seemed to me, as I kept remembering all this, that those times and those summers had been infinitely precious and worth saving. There had been jollity and peace and goodness. The arriving (at the beginning of August) had been so big a business in itself, at the railway station the farm wagon drawn up, the first smell of the pine-laden air, the first glimpse of the smiling farmer, and the great importance of the trunks and your father's enormous authority in such matters, and the feel of the wagon under you for the long ten-mile haul, and at the top of the last long hill catching the first view of the lake after eleven months of not seeing this cherished body of water. The shouts and cries of the other campers when they saw you, and the trunks to be unpacked, to give up their rich burden. (Arriving was less exciting nowadays, when you sneaked up in your car and parked it under a tree near the camp and took out the bags and in five minutes it was all over, no fuss, no loud wonderful fuss about trunks.)

Peace and goodness and jollity. The only thing that was wrong now, really, was the sound of the place, an unfamiliar nervous sound of the outboard motors. This was the note that jarred, the one thing that would sometimes break the illusion and set the years moving. In those other summertimes all motors were inboard; and when they were at a little distance, the noise they made was a sedative, an ingredient of summer sleep. They were one-cylinder and two-cylinder engines, and some were make-and-break and some were jump-spark, but they all made a sleepy sound across the lake. The one-lungers throbbed and fluttered, and the twin-cylinder ones purred and purred, and that was a quiet sound, too. But now the campers all had outboards. In the daytime, in the hot mornings, these motors made a petulant irritable sound; at night in the still evening when the afterglow lit the water, they whined about one's ears like mosquitoes. My boy loved our rented outboard, and his great desire was to achieve single-handed mastery over it, and authority, and he soon learned the trick of choking it a little (but not too much), and the adjustment of the needle valve. Watching him I would remember the things you could do with the old one-cylinder engine with the heavy flywheel, how you could have it eating out of your hand if you got really close to it spiritually. Motorboats in those days didn't have clutches, and you would make a landing by shutting off the motor at the proper time and coasting in with a dead rudder. But there was a way of reversing them, if you learned the trick, by cutting the switch and putting it on again exactly on the final dying revolution of the flywheel, so that it would kick back against compression and begin reversing. Approaching a dock in a strong following breeze, it was difficult to slow up sufficiently by the ordinary coasting method, and if a boy felt he had complete mastery over his motor, he was tempted to keep it running beyond its time and then reverse it a few feet from the dock. It took a cool nerve, because if you threw the switch a twentieth of a second too soon you would catch the flywheel when it still had speed enough to go up past center, and the boat would leap ahead, charging bull-fashion at the dock.

We had a good week at the camp. The bass were biting well and the sun 11 shone endlessly, day after day. We would be tired at night and lie down in the accumulated heat of the little bedrooms after the long hot day and the breeze would stir almost imperceptibly outside and the smell of the swamp drift in through the rusty screens. Sleep would come easily and in the morning the red squirrel would be on the roof, tapping out his gay routine. I kept remembering everything, lying in bed in the mornings—the small steamboat that had a long rounded stern like the lip of a Ubangi, and how quietly she ran on the moonlight sails, when the older boys played their mandolins and the girls sang and we ate doughnuts dipped in sugar, and how sweet the music was on the water in the shining night, and what it had felt like to think about girls then. After breakfast we would go up to the store and the things were in the same place—the minnows in a bottle, the plugs and spinners disarranged and pawed over by the youngsters from the boys' camp, the Fig Newtons and the

Beeman's gum. Outside, the road was tarred and cars stood in front of the store. Inside, all was just as it had always been, except there was more Coca-Cola and not so much Moxie and root beer and birch beer and sarsaparilla. We would walk out with a bottle of pop apiece and sometimes the pop would backfire up our noses and hurt. We explored the streams, quietly, where the turtles slid off the sunny logs and dug their way into the soft bottom; and we lay on the town wharf and fed worms to the tame bass. Everywhere we went I had trouble making out which was I, the one walking at my side, the one walking in my pants.

One afternoon while we were at the lake a thunderstorm came up. It was    12
like the revival of an old melodrama that I had seen long ago with childish awe. The second-act climax of the drama of the electrical disturbance over a lake in America had not changed in any important respect. This was the big scene, still the big scene. The whole thing was so familiar, the first feeling of oppression and heat and a general air around camp of not wanting to go very far away. In midafternoon (it was all the same) a curious darkening of the sky, and a lull in everything that had made life tick; and then the way the boats suddenly swung the other way at their moorings with the coming of a breeze out of the new quarter, and the premonitory rumble. Then the kettle drum, then the snare, then the bass drum and cymbals, then crackling light against the dark, and the gods grinning and licking their chops in the hills. Afterward the calm, the rain steadily rustling in the calm lake, the return of light and hope and spirits, and the campers running out in joy and relief to go swimming in the rain, their bright cries perpetuating the deathless joke about how they were getting simply drenched, and the children screaming with delight at the new sensation of bathing in the rain, and the joke about getting drenched linking the generations in a strong indestructible chain. And the comedian who waded in carrying an umbrella.

When the others went swimming my son said he was going in, too. He    13
pulled his dripping trunks from the line where they had hung all through the shower and wrung them out. Languidly, and with no thought of going in, I watched him, his hard little body, skinny and bare, saw him wince slightly as he pulled up around his vitals the small, soggy, icy garment. As he buckled the swollen belt, suddenly my groin felt the chill of death.

*For a reading quiz, sources on E. B. White, and annotated links to further readings on vacation memories and on fatherhood, visit **bedfordstmartins.com /thebedfordreader**.*

## Journal Writing

White strongly evokes the lake camp as a place that was important to him as a child. What place or places were most important to you as a child? In your journal, jot down some memories. (To take your journal writing further, see "From Journal to Essay" on the next page.)

## Questions on Meaning

1. How do you account for the distortions that creep into the author's sense of time?
2. What does the discussion of inboard and outboard motors (par. 10) have to do with the author's divided sense of time?
3. To what degree does White make us aware of his son's impression of this trip to the lake?
4. What do you take to be White's main PURPOSE in the essay? At what point do you become aware of it?

## Questions on Writing Strategy

1. In paragraph 4 the author first introduces his confused feeling that he has gone back in time to his own childhood, an idea that he repeats and expands throughout his account. What is the function of these repetitions?
2. Try to describe the impact of the essay's final paragraph. By what means is it achieved?
3. To what extent is this essay written to appeal to any but middle-aged readers? Is it comprehensible to anyone whose vacations were never spent at a Maine summer cottage?
4. What is the TONE of White's essay?
5. **MIXED METHODS**   White's DESCRIPTION depends on many IMAGES that are not FIGURES OF SPEECH but literal translations of sensory impressions. Locate four such images.
6. **MIXED METHODS**   Within White's description and NARRATION of his visit to the lake, what purpose is served by the COMPARISON AND CONTRAST between the lake now and when he was a boy?

## Questions on Language

1. Be sure you know the meanings of the following words: incessant, placidity (par. 1); gunwale (2); primeval (3); transposition (4); hellgrammite (5); undulating, cultist (6); indelible, tranquil (8); petulant (10); imperceptibly (11); premonitory (12); languidly (13).
2. Comment on White's DICTION in his reference to the lake as "this unique, this holy spot" (par. 2).
3. Explain what White is describing in the sentence that begins, "Then the kettle drum" (par. 12). Where else does the author use figures of speech?

## Suggestions for Writing

1. **FROM JOURNAL TO ESSAY**  Choose one of the places suggested by your journal entry, and write an essay describing the place now, revisiting it as an adult. (If you haven't visited the place since childhood, you can imagine what seeing it now would be like.) Your description should draw on your childhood memories, making them as vivid as possible for the reader, but you should also consider how your POINT OF VIEW toward the place differs now.
2. In a descriptive paragraph about a real or imagined place, try to appeal to each of your reader's five senses.
3. **CRITICAL WRITING**  While on the vacation he describes, White wrote to his wife, Katharine, "This place is as American as a drink of Coca Cola. The white collar family having its annual liberty." Obviously, not everyone has a chance at the lakeside summers White enjoyed. To what extent, if at all, does White's privileged point of view deprive his essay of universal meaning and significance? Write an essay answering this question. Back up your ideas with EVIDENCE from White's essay.
4. **CONNECTIONS**  In White's "Once More to the Lake" and Brad Manning's "Arm Wrestling with My Father" (p. 146), the writers reveal a changing sense of what it means to be a father. Write an essay that examines the similarities and differences in their definitions of fatherhood. How does a changing idea of what it means to be a son connect with this redefinition of fatherhood?
5. **CONNECTIONS**  White's essay is full of images that place his audience in a setting important to him in childhood. Yiyun Li, in "Orange Crush" (p. 164), also uses vivid images to evoke childhood and to explore how her interpretation of those images changed as she grew older. After reading these two essays, write an essay of your own describing four or five significant images from your childhood, perhaps involving people, places, objects, or moments in time. Like White and Li, try to make your readers understand how those images take on new meaning from an adult perspective.

---

# *E. B. White on Writing*

"You asked me about writing—how I did it," E. B. White replied to a seventeen-year-old who had written to him, wanting to become a professional writer but feeling discouraged. "There is no trick to it. If you like to write and want to write, you write, no matter where you are or what else you are doing or whether anyone pays any heed. I must have written half a million words (mostly in my journal) before I had anything published, save for a couple of short items in *St. Nicholas*.[1] If you want to write about feelings, about the end of the summer, about growing, write about it. A great deal of writing is not

[1] A magazine for children, popular early in the twentieth century. —EDS.

'plotted'—most of my essays have no plot structure, they are a ramble in the woods, or a ramble in the basement of my mind. You ask, 'Who cares?' Everybody cares. You say, 'It's been written before.' Everything has been written before. . . . Henry Thoreau, who wrote *Walden*, said, 'I learned this at least by my experiment: that if one advances confidently in the direction of his dreams and endeavors to live the life which he has imagined, he will meet with a success unexpected in common hours.' The sentence, after more than a hundred years, is still alive. So, advance confidently."

In trying to characterize his own writing, White was modest in his claims. To his brother Stanley Hart White, he once remarked, "I discovered a long time ago that writing of the small things of the day, the trivial matters of the heart, the inconsequential but near things of this living, was the only kind of creative work which I could accomplish with any sincerity or grace. As a reporter, I was a flop, because I always came back laden not with facts about the case, but with a mind full of the little difficulties and amusements I had encountered in my travels. Not till *The New Yorker* came along did I ever find any means of expressing those impertinences and irrelevancies. Thus yesterday, setting out to get a story on how police horses are trained, I ended by writing a story entitled 'How Police Horses Are Trained' which never even mentions a police horse, but has to do entirely with my own absurd adventures at police headquarters. The rewards of such endeavor are not that I have acquired an audience or a following, as you suggest (fame of any kind being a Pyrrhic victory[2]), but that sometimes in writing of myself—which is the only subject anyone knows intimately—I have occasionally had the exquisite thrill of putting my finger on a little capsule of truth, and heard it give the faint squeak of mortality under my pressure, an antic sound."

## For Discussion

1. Sometimes young writers are counseled to study the market and then try to write something that will sell. How would you expect E. B. White to have reacted to such advice?
2. What, exactly, does White mean when he says, "Everything has been written before"? How might an aspiring writer take this remark as encouragement?
3. What interesting distinction does White make between reporting and essay writing?

---

[2] A victory won at great cost. The Greek king Pyrrhus defeated the Romans in 279 BC but exclaimed afterward, "One more such victory and I am lost."—EDS.

# USEFUL TERMS

**Abstract and concrete**   Two kinds of language. *Abstract* words refer to ideas, conditions, and qualities we cannot directly perceive: *truth, love, courage, evil, poverty, progressive*. *Concrete* words indicate things we can know with our senses: *tree, chair, bird, pen, motorcycle, perfume, thunderclap*. Concrete words lend vigor and clarity to writing, for they help a reader to picture things. See IMAGE.

    Writers of expository and argumentative essays tend to shift back and forth from one kind of language to the other. They often begin a paragraph with a general statement full of abstract words ("There is *hope* for the *future* of *motoring*"). Then they usually go on to give examples and present evidence in sentences full of concrete words ("Inventor *Jones* claims his *car* will go from *Fresno* to *Los Angeles* on a *gallon* of *peanut oil*"). Inexperienced writers often use too many abstract words and not enough concrete ones. (See also pp. 42–43.)

**Active voice**   The form of the verb when the sentence subject is the actor: *Trees* [subject] *shed* [active verb] *their leaves in autumn*. Contrast PASSIVE VOICE.

**Allude, allusion**   To refer to a person, place, or thing believed to be common knowledge (*allude*), or the act or result of doing so (*allusion*). An allusion may point to a famous event, a familiar saying, a noted personality, a well-known story or song. Usually brief, an allusion is a space-saving way to convey much meaning. For example, the statement "The game was Coach Johnson's Waterloo" informs the reader that, like Napoleon meeting defeat in a celebrated battle, the coach led a confrontation resulting in his downfall and that of his team. If the writer is also showing Johnson's character, the allusion might further tell us that the coach is a man of Napoleonic ambition and pride. To make an effective allusion, you have to ensure that it will be clear to your audience. Not every reader, for example, would understand an allusion to a neighbor, to a seventeenth-century Russian harpsichordist, or to a little-known stock-car driver.

**Analogy**   An extended comparison based on the like features of two unlike things: one familiar or easily understood, the other unfamiliar, abstract, or complicated. For instance, most people know at least vaguely how the human eye works: The pupil adjusts to admit light, which registers as an image on the retina at the back of the eye. You might use this familiar information to explain something less familiar to many people, such as how a camera works: The aperture (like the pupil) adjusts to admit light, which registers as an image on the film (like the retina) at the back of the camera. Analogies are especially helpful for explaining technical information in a way that is nontechnical, more easily grasped. For example, the spacecraft *Voyager 2* transmitted spectacular pictures of Saturn to Earth. To explain the difficulty of their achievement, NASA scientists compared their feat to a golfer sinking a putt from five hundred miles away. Because it can make abstract ideas vivid and memorable, analogy is also a favorite device of philosophers, politicians, and preachers. In his celebrated speech "I Have a Dream" (p. 614), Martin Luther King, Jr., draws a remarkable analogy to express the anger and disappointment of African Americans that, one hundred years after Lincoln's Emancipation Proclamation, their full freedom has yet to be achieved. "It is obvious today," declares King, "that America has defaulted on this promissory note"; and he compares the Founding Fathers' written guarantee—of the rights of life, liberty, and the pursuit of happiness—to a bad check returned for insufficient funds.

Analogy is similar to the method of COMPARISON AND CONTRAST. Both identify the distinctive features of two things and then set the features side by side. But a comparison explains two obviously similar things—two Civil War generals, two responses to a mess—and considers both their differences and their similarities. An analogy yokes two apparently unlike things (eye and camera, spaceflight and golf, guaranteed human rights and bad checks) and focuses only on their major similarities. Analogy is thus an extended *metaphor*, the FIGURE OF SPEECH that declares one thing to be another—even though it isn't, in a strictly literal sense—for the purpose of making us aware of similarity: "Hope," writes Emily Dickinson in the poem on page 510, "is the thing with feathers / That perches in the soul."

In an ARGUMENT, analogy can make readers more receptive to a point or inspire them, but it can't prove anything because in the end the subjects are dissimilar. A false analogy is a logical FALLACY that claims a fundamental likeness when none exists. See page 526.

**Analyze, analysis**   To separate a subject into its parts (*analyze*), or the act or result of doing so (*analysis*, also called *division*). Analysis is a key skill in CRITICAL THINKING, READING, AND WRITING; see page 18. It is also considered a method of development; see Chapter 9.

**Anecdote**   A brief NARRATIVE, or retelling of a story or event. Anecdotes have many uses: as essay openers or closers, as examples, as sheer entertainment. See Chapter 4.

**Appeals**   Resources writers draw on to connect with and persuade readers:

- A **rational appeal** asks readers to use their intellects and their powers of reasoning. It relies on established conventions of logic and evidence.
- An **emotional appeal** asks readers to respond out of their beliefs, values, or feelings. It inspires, affirms, frightens, angers.
- An **ethical appeal** asks readers to look favorably on the writer. It stresses the writer's intelligence, competence, fairness, morality, and other qualities desirable in a trustworthy debater or teacher.

See also page 521.

**Argument**   A mode of writing intended to win readers' agreement with an assertion by engaging their powers of reasoning. Argument often overlaps PERSUASION. See Chapter 13.

**Assume, assumption**   To take something for granted (*assume*), or a belief or opinion taken for granted (*assumption*). Whether stated or unstated, assumptions influence a writer's choices of subject, viewpoint, EVIDENCE, and even language. See also pages 19 and 521–22.

**Audience**   A writer's readers. Having in mind a particular audience helps the writer in choosing strategies. Imagine, for instance, that you are writing two reviews of a new movie, one for the students who read the campus newspaper, the other for amateur and professional filmmakers who read *Millimeter*. For the first audience, you might write about the actors, the plot, and especially dramatic scenes. You might judge the picture and urge your readers to see it—or to avoid it. Writing for *Millimeter*, you might discuss special effects, shooting techniques, problems in editing and in mixing picture and sound. In this review, you might use more specialized and technical terms. Obviously, an awareness of the interests and knowledge of your readers, in each case, would help you decide how to write. If you told readers of the campus paper too much about filming techniques, you would lose most of them. If you told *Millimeter*'s readers the film's plot in detail, probably you would put them to sleep.

You can increase your awareness of your audience by asking yourself a few questions before you begin to write. Who are to be your readers? What is their age level? background? education? Where do they live? What are their beliefs and attitudes? What interests them? What, if anything, sets them apart from most people? How familiar are they with your subject? Knowing your audience can help you write so that your readers will not only understand you better but care more deeply about what you say.

**Cause and effect**   A method of development in which a writer ANALYZES reasons for an action, event, or decision, or analyzes its consequences. See Chapter 11. See also EFFECT.

**Chronological order**   The arrangement of events as they occurred or occur in time, first to last. Most NARRATION and PROCESS ANALYSIS use chronological order.

**Claim**   The proposition that an ARGUMENT demonstrates, generally expressed in a THESIS STATEMENT. See page 520.

**Classification**   A method of development in which a writer sorts out plural things (contact sports, college students, kinds of music) into categories. See Chapter 10.

**Cliché**   A worn-out, trite expression that a writer employs thoughtlessly. Although at one time the expression may have been colorful, from heavy use it has lost its luster. It is now "old as the hills." In conversation, most of us sometimes use clichés, but in writing they "stick out like sore thumbs." Alert writers, when they revise, replace a cliché with a fresh, concrete expression. Writers who have trouble recognizing clichés should be suspicious of any phrase they've heard before and should try to read more widely. Their problem is that, so many expressions being new to them, they do not know which ones are full of moths.

**Coherence**   The clear connection of the parts in effective writing so that the reader can easily follow the flow of ideas between sentences, paragraphs, and larger divisions, and can see how they relate successively to one another.

In making your essay coherent, you may find certain devices useful. TRANSITIONS, for instance, can bridge ideas. Reminders of points you have stated earlier are helpful to a reader who may have forgotten them — as readers tend to do sometimes, particularly if your essay is long. However, a coherent essay is not one merely pasted together with transitions and reminders. It derives its coherence from the clear relationship between its THESIS (or central idea) and all its parts. (See also pp. 228–29.)

**Colloquial expressions**   Words and phrases occurring primarily in speech and in informal writing that seeks a relaxed, conversational tone. "My favorite chow is a burger and a shake" or "This math exam has me wired" may be acceptable in talking to a roommate, in corresponding with a friend, or in writing a humorous essay for general readers. Such choices of words, however, would be out of place in formal writing — in, say, a laboratory report or a letter to your senator. Contractions (*let's, don't, we'll*) and abbreviated words (*photo, sales rep, ad*) are the shorthand of spoken language. Good writers use such expressions with an awareness that they produce an effect of casualness.

**Comparison and contrast**   Two methods of development usually found together. Using them, a writer examines the similarities and differences between two things to reveal their natures. See Chapter 7.

**Conclusion**   The sentences or paragraphs that bring an essay to a satisfying and logical end. A conclusion is purposefully crafted to give a sense of unity and completeness to the whole essay. The best conclusions evolve naturally out of what has gone before and convince the reader that the essay is indeed at an end, not that the writer has run out of steam.

Conclusions vary in type and length depending on the nature and scope of the essay. A long research paper may require several paragraphs of summary to review and emphasize the main points. A short essay, however, may benefit from a few brief closing sentences.

In concluding an essay, beware of diminishing the impact of your writing by finishing on a weak note. Don't apologize for what you have or have not written, or cram in a final detail that would have been better placed elsewhere.

Although there are no set formulas for closing, the following list presents several options:

- Restate the thesis of your essay, and perhaps your main points.
- Mention the broader implications or significance of your topic.
- Give a final example that pulls all the parts of your discussion together.

- Offer a prediction.
- End with the most important point as the culmination of your essay's development.
- Suggest how the reader can apply the information you have just imparted.
- End with a bit of drama or flourish. Tell an ANECDOTE, offer an appropriate quotation, ask a question, make a final insightful remark. Keep in mind, however, that an ending shouldn't sound false and gimmicky. It truly has to conclude.

**Concrete**   See ABSTRACT AND CONCRETE.

**Connotation and denotation**   Two types of meanings most words have. *Denotation* is the explicit, literal, dictionary definition of a word. *Connotation* refers to a word's implied meaning, resonant with associations. The denotation of *blood* is "the fluid that circulates in the vascular system." The connotations of *blood* range from *life force* to *gore* to *family bond*. A doctor might use the word *blood* for its denotation, and a mystery writer might rely on the word's connotations to heighten a scene.

Because people have different experiences, they bring to the same word different associations. A conservative's emotional response to the word *welfare* is not likely to be the same as a liberal's. And referring to your senator as a *diplomat* evokes a different response, from the senator and from others, than would *baby-kisser, political hack,* or even *politician.* The effective use of words involves knowing both what they mean literally and what they are likely to suggest.

**Critical thinking, reading, and writing**   A group of interlocking skills that are essential for college work and beyond. Each seeks the meaning beneath the surface of a statement, poem, editorial, picture, advertisement, Web site, or other "text." Using ANALYSIS, INFERENCE, SYNTHESIS, and often EVALUATION, the critical thinker, reader, and writer separates this text into its elements in order to see and judge meanings, relations, and ASSUMPTIONS that might otherwise remain buried. See also pages 17–20, 25–30, 51–60, 333–34.

**Data**   A name for EVIDENCE favored by philosopher Stephen Toulmin in his conception of ARGUMENT. See page 520.

**Deductive reasoning, deduction**   The method of reasoning from the general to the particular: From information about what we already know, we deduce what we need or want to know. See Chapter 13, pages 523–24.

**Definition**   A statement of the literal and specific meaning or meanings of a word or a method of developing an essay. In the latter, the writer usually explains the nature of a word, a thing, a concept, or a phenomenon. Such a definition may employ NARRATION, DESCRIPTION, or any other method. See Chapter 12.

**Denotation**   See CONNOTATION AND DENOTATION.

**Description**   A mode of writing that conveys the evidence of the senses: sight, hearing, touch, taste, smell. See Chapter 5.

**Diction**   The choice of words. Every written or spoken statement contains diction of some kind. To describe certain aspects of diction, the following terms may be useful:

- **Standard English:** the common American language, words and grammatical forms that are used and expected in school, business, and other sites.
- **Nonstandard English:** words and grammatical forms such as *theirselves* and *ain't* that are used mainly by people who speak a dialect other than standard English.

- **Dialect:** a variety of English based on differences in geography, education, or social background. Dialect is usually spoken but may be written. Maya Angelou's essay in Chapter 4 transcribes the words of dialect speakers ("'He gone whip him till that white boy call him Momma'").
- **Slang:** certain words in highly informal speech or writing, or in the speech of a particular group—for example, *blow off, dis, dweeb*.
- **Colloquial expressions:** words and phrases from conversation. See COLLO-QUIAL EXPRESSIONS for examples.
- **Regional terms:** words heard in a certain locality, such as *spritzing* for "raining" in Pennsylvania Dutch country.
- **Technical terms:** words and phrases that form the vocabulary of a particular discipline (*monocotyledon* from botany), occupation (*drawplate* from die-making), or avocation (*interval training* from running). See also JARGON.
- **Archaisms:** old-fashioned expressions, once common but now used to suggest an earlier style, such as *ere* and *forsooth*.
- **Obsolete diction:** words that have passed out of use (such as the verb *werien*, "to protect or defend," and the noun *isetnesses*, "agreements"). *Obsolete* may also refer to certain meanings of words no longer current (*fond* for foolish, *clipping* for hugging or embracing).
- **Pretentious diction:** use of words more numerous and elaborate than necessary, such as *institution of higher learning* for college, and *partake of solid nourishment* for eat.

Archaic, obsolete, and pretentious diction usually have no place in good writing unless for ironic or humorous effect: the journalist and critic H. L. Mencken delighted in the hifalutin use of *tonsorial studio* instead of barber shop. Still, any diction may be the right diction for a certain occasion: The choice of words depends on a writer's PURPOSE and AUDIENCE.

**Discovery**   The stage of the writing process before the first draft. It may include deciding on a topic, narrowing the topic, creating or finding ideas, doing reading and other research, defining PURPOSE and AUDIENCE, planning and arranging material. Discovery may follow from daydreaming or meditation, reading, or perhaps carefully ransacking memory. In practice, though, it usually involves considerable writing and is aided by the act of writing. The operations of discovery—reading, research, further idea creation, and refinement of subject, purpose, and audience—may all continue well into drafting as well. See also pages 34–37.

**Division**   See ANALYZE, ANALYSIS.

**Dominant impression**   The main idea a writer conveys about a subject through DESCRIPTION—that an elephant is gigantic, for example, or an experience scary. See also Chapter 5.

**Drafting**   The stage of the writing process during which a writer expresses ideas in complete sentences, links them, and arranges them in a sequence. See also pages 38, 40–43.

**Effect**   The result of an event or action, usually considered together with CAUSE as a method of development. See the discussion of cause and effect in Chapter 11. In discussing writing, the term *effect* also refers to the impression a word, sentence, paragraph, or entire work makes on the reader: how convincing it is, whether it elicits an emotional response, what associations it conjures up, and so on.

**Emotional appeal**   See APPEALS.

**Emphasis**   The stress or special importance given to a certain point or element to make it stand out. A skillful writer draws attention to what is most important in a sentence, a paragraph, or an essay by controlling emphasis in any of the following ways:

- **Proportion:** Important ideas are given greater coverage than minor points.
- **Position:** The beginnings and ends of sentences, paragraphs, and larger divisions are the strongest positions. Placing key ideas in these spots helps draw attention to their importance. The end is the stronger position, for what stands last stands out. A sentence in which less important details precede the main point is called a **periodic sentence:** "Having disguised himself as a guard and walked through the courtyard to the side gate, the prisoner made his escape." A sentence in which the main point precedes less important details is a **loose sentence:** "Autumn is orange: gourds in baskets at roadside stands, the harvest moon hanging like a pumpkin, and oak leaves flashing like goldfish."
- **Repetition:** Careful repetition of key words or phrases can give them greater importance. (Careless repetition, however, can cause boredom.)
- **Mechanical devices:** Italics (underlining), capital letters, and exclamation points can make words or sentences stand out. Writers sometimes fall back on these devices, however, after failing to show significance by other means. Italics and exclamation points can be useful in reporting speech, but excessive use sounds exaggerated or bombastic.

**Essay**   A short nonfiction composition on one central theme or subject in which the writer may offer personal views. Essays are sometimes classified as either formal or informal. In general, a **formal essay** is one whose DICTION is that of the written language (not colloquial speech), serious in TONE, and usually focused on a subject the writer believes is important. (For example, see Bruce Catton's "Grant and Lee.") An **informal essay,** in contrast, is more likely to admit COLLOQUIAL EXPRESSIONS; the writer's tone tends to be lighter, perhaps humorous, and the subject is likely to be personal, sometimes even trivial. (See Dave Barry's "Batting Clean-Up and Striking Out.") These distinctions, however, are rough ones: An essay such as Judy Brady's "I Want a Wife" uses colloquial language and speaks of personal experience, but its tone is serious and its subject important.

**Ethical appeal**   See APPEALS.

**Euphemism**   The use of inoffensive language in place of language that readers or listeners may find hurtful, distasteful, frightening, or otherwise objectionable — for instance, a police officer's announcing that someone *passed on* rather than *died*, or a politician's calling for *revenue enhancement* rather than *taxation*. Writers sometimes use euphemism out of consideration for readers' feelings, but just as often they use it to deceive readers or shirk responsibility. (For more on euphemism, see William Lutz's "The World of Doublespeak" in Chap. 10.)

**Evaluate, evaluation**   To judge the merits of something (*evaluate*) or the act or result of doing so (*evaluation*). Evaluation is often part of CRITICAL THINKING, READING, AND WRITING. In evaluating a work of writing, you base your judgment on your ANALYSIS of it and your sense of its quality or value. See also pages 19–20, 29–30, 57–59.

**Evidence**   The details that support an argument or an explanation, including facts, examples, and expert opinions. A writer's opinions and GENERALIZATIONS must rest upon evidence. See pages 520–21.

**Example**   Also called **exemplification** or **illustration**, a method of development in which the writer provides instances of a general idea. See Chapter 6. An *example* is a verbal illustration.

**Exposition**   The mode of prose writing that explains (or exposes) its subject. Its function is to inform, to instruct, or to set forth ideas: the major trade routes in the Middle East, how to make a dulcimer, why the United States consumes more energy than it needs. Exposition may call various methods to its service: EXAMPLE, COMPARISON AND CONTRAST, PROCESS ANALYSIS, and so on. Most college writing is at least partly exposition, and so are most of the essays in this book.

**Fallacies**   Errors in reasoning. See pages 524–26 for a list and examples.

**Figures of speech**   Expressions that depart from the literal meanings of words for the sake of emphasis or vividness. To say "She's a jewel" doesn't mean that the subject of praise is literally a kind of shining stone; the statement makes sense because its CONNOTATIONS come to mind: rare, priceless, worth cherishing. Some figures of speech involve comparisons of two objects apparently unlike:

- A **simile** (from the Latin, "likeness") states the comparison directly, usually connecting the two things using *like, as,* or *than:* "The moon is like a snowball," "He's as lazy as a cat full of cream," "My feet are flatter than flyswatters."
- A **metaphor** (from the Greek, "transfer") declares one thing to *be* another: "A mighty fortress is our God," "The sheep were bolls of cotton on the hill." (A **dead metaphor** is a word or phrase that, originally a figure of speech, has come to be literal through common usage: "the *hands* of a clock.")
- **Personification** is a simile or metaphor that assigns human traits to inanimate objects or abstractions: "A stoop-shouldered refrigerator hummed quietly to itself," "The solution to the math problem sat there winking at me."

Other figures of speech consist of deliberate misrepresentations:

- **Hyperbole** (from the Greek, "throwing beyond") is a conscious exaggeration: "I'm so hungry I could eat a saddle," "I'd wait for you a thousand years."
- The opposite of hyperbole, **understatement**, creates an ironic or humorous effect: "I accepted the ride. At the moment, I didn't feel like walking across the Mojave Desert."
- A **paradox** (from the Greek, "conflicting with expectation") is a seemingly self-contradictory statement that, on reflection, makes sense: "Children are the poor person's wealth" (wealth can be monetary, or it can be spiritual). *Paradox* may also refer to a situation that is inexplicable or contradictory, such as the restriction of one group's rights in order to secure the rights of another group.

**Flashback**   A technique of NARRATION in which the sequence of events is interrupted to recall an earlier period.

**Focus**   The narrowing of a subject to make it manageable. Beginning with a general subject, you concentrate on a certain aspect of it. For instance, you may select crafts as a general subject, then decide your main interest lies in weaving. You could focus your essay still further by narrowing it to operating a hand loom. You also focus your writing according to who will read it (AUDIENCE) or what you want it to achieve (PURPOSE).

**General and specific**    Terms that describe the relative number of instances or objects included in the group signified by a word. *General* words name a group or class (*flowers*); *specific* words limit the class by naming its individual members (*rose, violet, dahlia, marigold*). Words may be arranged in a series from more general to more specific: *clothes, pants, jeans, Levis*. The word *cat* is more specific than *animal*, but less specific than *tiger cat*, or *Garfield*. See also ABSTRACT AND CONCRETE and pages 142–43.

**Generalization**    A statement about a class based on an examination of some of its members: "Lions are fierce." The more members examined and the more representative they are of the class, the sturdier the generalization. The statement "Solar heat saves home owners money" would be challenged by home owners who have yet to recover their installation costs. "Solar heat can save home owners money in the long run" would be a sounder generalization. Insufficient or nonrepresentative EVIDENCE often leads to a hasty generalization, such as "All freshmen hate their roommates" or "Men never express their feelings." Words such as *all, every, only, never,* and *always* have to be used with care: "Some men don't express their feelings" is more credible. Making a trustworthy generalization involves the use of INDUCTIVE REASONING (discussed on pp. 522–23).

**Grounds**    A name for EVIDENCE favored by philosopher Stephen Toulmin in his conception of ARGUMENT. See page 520.

**Hyperbole**    See FIGURES OF SPEECH.

**Illustration**    Another name for EXAMPLE. See Chapter 6.

**Image**    A word or word sequence that evokes a sensory experience. Whether literal ("We picked two red apples") or figurative ("His cheeks looked like two red apples, buffed and shining"), an image appeals to the reader's memory of seeing, hearing, smelling, touching, or tasting. Images add concreteness to fiction — "The farm looked as tiny and still as a seashell, with the little knob of a house surrounded by its curved furrows of tomato plants" (Eudora Welty in a short story, "The Whistle") — and are an important element in poetry. But writers of essays, too, use images to bring ideas down to earth. See also FIGURES OF SPEECH.

**Inductive reasoning, induction**    The process of reasoning to a conclusion about an entire class by examining some of its members. See pages 522–23.

**Infer, inference**    To draw a conclusion (*infer*), or the act or result of doing so (*inference*). In CRITICAL THINKING, READING, AND WRITING, inference is the means to understanding a writer's meaning, ASSUMPTIONS, PURPOSE, fairness, and other attributes. See also pages 19 and 28–29.

**Introduction**    The opening of a written work. Often it states the writer's subject, narrows it, and communicates the writer's main idea (THESIS). Introductions vary in length, depending on their purposes. A research paper may need several paragraphs to set forth its central idea and its plan of organization; a brief, informal essay may need only a sentence or two for an introduction. Whether long or short, good introductions tell readers no more than they need to know when they begin reading. Here are a few possible ways to open an essay effectively:

- State your central idea, or thesis, perhaps showing why you care about it.
- Present startling facts about your subject.
- Tell an illustrative ANECDOTE.

- Give background information that will help your reader understand your subject, or see why it is important.
- Begin with an arresting quotation.
- Ask a challenging question. (In your essay, you'll go on to answer it.)

**Irony**   A manner of speaking or writing that does not directly state a discrepancy, but implies one. **Verbal irony** is the intentional use of words to suggest a meaning other than literal: "What a mansion!" (said of a shack); "There's nothing like sunshine" (said on a foggy morning). (For more examples, see the essays by Jessica Mitford, Linnea Saukko, and Judy Brady.) If irony is delivered contemptuously with an intent to hurt, we call it **sarcasm:** "Oh, you're a real friend!" (said to someone who refuses to lend the speaker the coins to make a phone call). With **situational irony,** the circumstances themselves are incongruous, run contrary to expectations, or twist fate: Juliet regains consciousness only to find that Romeo, believing her dead, has stabbed himself. See also SATIRE.

**Jargon**   Strictly speaking, the special vocabulary of a trade or profession. The term has also come to mean inflated, vague, meaningless language of any kind. It is characterized by wordiness, ABSTRACTIONS galore, pretentious DICTION, and needlessly complicated word order. Whenever you meet a sentence that obviously could express its idea in fewer words and shorter ones, chances are that it is jargon. For instance: "The motivating force compelling her to opt continually for the most labor-intensive mode of operation in performing her functions was consistently observed to be the single constant and regular factor in her behavior patterns." Translation: "She did everything the hard way." (For more on such jargon, see William Lutz's "The World of Doublespeak" in Chap. 10.)

**Journal**   A record of one's thoughts, kept daily or at least regularly. Keeping a journal faithfully can help a writer gain confidence and develop ideas. See also page 35.

**Metaphor**   See FIGURES OF SPEECH.

**Narration**   The mode of writing that tells a story. See Chapter 4.

**Narrator**   The teller of a story, usually either in the first PERSON (*I*) or in the third (*he, she, it, they*). See pages 84–85.

**Nonstandard English**   See DICTION.

**Objective and subjective**   Kinds of writing that differ in emphasis. In *objective* writing, the emphasis falls on the topic; in *subjective* writing, it falls on the writer's view of the topic. Objective writing occurs in factual journalism, science reports, certain PROCESS ANALYSES (such as recipes, directions, and instructions), and logical arguments in which the writer attempts to downplay personal feelings and opinions. Subjective writing sets forth the writer's feelings, opinions, and interpretations. It occurs in friendly letters, journals, bylined feature stories and columns in newspapers, personal essays, and ARGUMENTS that appeal to emotion. Few essays, however, contain one kind of writing exclusive of the other.

**Paradox**   See FIGURES OF SPEECH.

**Paragraph**   A group of closely related sentences that develop a central idea. In an essay, a paragraph is the most important unit of thought because it is both self-contained and part of the larger whole. Paragraphs separate long and involved ideas into smaller parts that are more manageable for the writer and easier for the reader to take in. Good paragraphs, like good essays, possess UNITY and COHERENCE. The central idea is usually stated in a TOPIC SENTENCE, often found at the beginning of the paragraph that relates directly to the essay's THESIS. All other sentences in the paragraph relate to this topic sentence, defining it, explaining it, illustrating it, providing it with evidence and support. If you meet a unified and coherent paragraph that has no topic sentence, it will contain a central idea that no sentence in it explicitly states, but that every sentence in it clearly implies. See also pages 228–29 (paragraph coherence), 379–80 (paragraph development), and 484–85 (paragraph unity).

**Parallelism, parallel structure**   A habit of good writers: keeping ideas of equal importance in similar grammatical form. A writer may place nouns side by side ("*Trees* and *streams* are my weekend tonic") or in a series ("Give me *wind, sea,* and *stars*"). Phrases, too, may be arranged in parallel structure ("*Out of my bed, into my shoes, up to my classroom* — that's my life"); or clauses ("Ask not what your country can do for you; ask what you can do for your country").

Parallelism may be found not only in single sentences, but in larger units as well. A paragraph might read: "Rhythm is everywhere. It throbs in the rain forests of Brazil. It vibrates ballroom floors in Vienna. It snaps its fingers on street corners in Chicago." In a whole essay, parallelism may be the principle used to arrange ideas in a balanced or harmonious structure. See the famous speech given by Martin Luther King, Jr. (p. 614), in which paragraphs 11–18 all begin with the words "I have a dream" and describe an imagined future. Not only does such a parallel structure organize ideas, but it also lends them force.

**Paraphrase**   Putting another writer's thoughts into your own words. In writing a research paper or an essay containing EVIDENCE gathered from your reading, you will find it necessary to paraphrase — unless you are using another writer's very words with quotation marks around them — and to acknowledge your sources. Contrast SUMMARY. And see pages 54–55.

**Passive voice**   The form of the verb when the sentence subject is acted upon: *The report* [subject] *was published* [passive verb] *anonymously.* Contrast ACTIVE VOICE.

**Person**   A grammatical distinction made between the speaker, the one spoken to, and the one spoken about. In the first person (*I, we*), the subject is speaking. In the second person (*you*), the subject is being spoken to. In the third person (*he, she, it*), the subject is being spoken about. The point of view of an essay or work of fiction is often specified according to person: "This short story is told from a first-person point of view." See POINT OF VIEW.

**Personification**   See FIGURES OF SPEECH.

**Persuasion**   A mode of writing intended to influence people's actions by engaging their beliefs and feelings. Persuasion often overlaps ARGUMENT. See Chapter 13.

**Plagiarism**   The use of someone else's ideas or words as if they were your own, without acknowledging the original author. See pages 60–62.

**Point of view**   In an essay, the physical position or the mental angle from which a writer beholds a subject. On the subject of starlings, the following three writers would likely have different points of view: An ornithologist might write OBJECTIVELY about the introduction of these birds into North America, a farmer might advise other farmers how to prevent the birds from eating seed, and a bird-watcher might SUBJECTIVELY describe a first glad sighting of an unusual species. Furthermore, the PERSON of each essay would probably differ: The scientist might present a scholarly paper in the third person, the farmer might offer advice in the second, and the bird-watcher might recount the experience in the first.

**Premise**   A proposition or ASSUMPTION that leads to a conclusion. See pages 523–24 for examples.

**Process analysis**   A method of development that most often explains step by step how something is done or how to do something. See Chapter 8.

**Purpose**   A writer's reason for trying to convey a particular idea (THESIS) about a particular subject to a particular AUDIENCE of readers. Though it may emerge gradually during the writing process, in the end purpose should govern every element of a piece of writing.

In trying to define the purpose of an essay you read, ask yourself, "Why did the writer write this?" or "What was this writer trying to achieve?" Even though you cannot know the writer's intentions with absolute certainty, an effective essay will make some purpose clear.

**Rational appeal**   See APPEALS.

**Revision**   The stage of the writing process during which a writer "re-sees" a draft from the viewpoint of a reader. Revision usually involves two steps, first considering fundamental matters such as PURPOSE and organization, and then editing for surface matters such as smooth TRANSITIONS and error-free sentences. See pages 38–39, 43–47.

**Rhetoric**   The study (and the art) of using language effectively. *Rhetoric* also has a negative CONNOTATION of empty or pretentious language meant to waffle, stall, or even deceive. This is the meaning in "The president had nothing substantial to say about taxes, just the usual rhetoric."

**Rhetorical question**   A question posed for effect, one that requires no answer. Instead, it often provokes thought, lends emphasis to a point, asserts or denies something without making a direct statement, launches further discussion, introduces an opinion, or leads the reader where the writer intends. Sometimes a writer throws one in to introduce variety in a paragraph full of declarative sentences. The following questions are rhetorical: "When will the United States learn that sending people into space does not feed them on the earth?" "Shall I compare thee to a summer's day?" "What is the point of making money if you've no one but yourself to spend it on?" Both reader and writer know what the answers are supposed to be. (1) Someday, if the United States ever wises up. (2) Yes. (3) None.

**Sarcasm**   See IRONY.

**Satire**   A form of writing that employs wit to attack folly. Unlike most comedy, the purpose of satire is not merely to entertain, but to bring about enlightenment— even reform. Usually, satire employs irony—as in Linnea Saukko's "How to Poison the Earth" and Jonathan Swift's "A Modest Proposal." See also IRONY.

**Scene**   In a NARRATION, an event retold in detail to re-create an experience. See Chapter 4.

**Sentimentality**   A quality sometimes found in writing that fails to communicate. Such writing calls for an extreme emotional response on the part of an AUDIENCE, although its writer fails to supply adequate reason for any such reaction. A sentimental writer delights in waxing teary over certain objects: great-grandmother's portrait, the first stick of chewing gum baby chewed (now a shapeless wad), an empty popcorn box saved from the World Series of 1996. Sentimental writing usually results when writers shut their eyes to the actual world, preferring to snuffle the sweet scents of remembrance.

**Signal phrase**   Words used to introduce a quotation, PARAPHRASE, or SUMMARY, often including the source author's name and generally telling readers how the source material should be interpreted: "Nelson argues that the legislation will backfire." See also page 56.

**Simile**   See FIGURES OF SPEECH.

**Slang**   See DICTION.

**Specific**   See GENERAL AND SPECIFIC.

**Standard English**   See DICTION.

**Strategy**   Whatever means a writer employs to write effectively. The methods set forth in this book are strategies; but so are narrowing a subject, organizing ideas clearly, using TRANSITIONS, writing with an awareness of your reader, and other effective writing practices.

**Style**   The distinctive manner in which a writer writes. Style may be seen especially in the writer's choice of words and sentence structures. Two writers may write on the same subject, even express similar ideas, but it is style that gives each writer's work a personality.

**Subjective**   See OBJECTIVE AND SUBJECTIVE.

**Summarize, summary**   To condense a work (essay, movie, news story) to its essence (*summarize*), or the act or result of doing so (*summary*). Summarizing a piece of writing in one's own words is an effective way to understand it. (See p. 17.) Summarizing (and acknowledging) others' writing in your own text is a good way to support your ideas. (See p. 54.) Contrast PARAPHRASE.

**Suspense**   Often an element in NARRATION: the pleasurable expectation or anxiety we feel that keeps us reading a story. In an exciting mystery story, suspense is constant: How will it all turn out? Will the detective get to the scene in time to prevent another murder? But there can be suspense in less melodramatic accounts as well.

**Syllogism**   A three-step form of reasoning that employs DEDUCTION. See page 523 for an illustration.

**Symbol**   A visible object or action that suggests further meaning. The flag suggests country, the crown suggests royalty — these are conventional symbols familiar to us. Life abounds in such clear-cut symbols. Football teams use dolphins and rams for easy identification; married couples symbolize their union with a ring.

In writing, symbols usually do not have such a one-to-one correspondence, but evoke a whole constellation of associations. In Herman Melville's *Moby-Dick*, the whale suggests more than the large mammal it is. It hints at evil, obsession, and the untamable forces of nature. Such a symbol carries meanings too complex or elusive to be neatly defined.

Although more common in fiction and poetry, symbols can be used to good purpose in nonfiction because they often communicate an idea in a compact and concrete way.

**Synthesize, synthesis**   To link elements into a whole (*synthesize*), or the act or result of doing so (*synthesis*). In CRITICAL THINKING, READING, AND WRITING, synthesis is the key step during which you use your own perspective to reassemble a work you have ANALYZED or to connect the work with others. (See pp. 19 and 29.) Synthesis is a hallmark of academic writing in which you respond to others' work or use multiple sources to support your ideas. (See pp. 53–54, 59–60.)

**Thesis**   The central idea in a work of writing, to which everything else in the work refers. In some way, each sentence and PARAGRAPH in an effective essay serves to support the thesis and to make it clear and explicit to readers. Good writers, while writing, often set down a **thesis statement** or **thesis sentence** to help them define their purpose. They also often include this statement in their essay as a promise and a guide to readers. See also pages 20, 37–38, and 336.

**Tone**   The way a writer expresses his or her regard for subject, AUDIENCE, or self. Through word choice, sentence structures, and what is actually said, the writer conveys an attitude and sets a prevailing spirit. Tone in writing varies as greatly as tone of voice varies in conversation. It can be serious, distant, flippant, angry, enthusiastic, sincere, sympathetic. Whatever tone a writer chooses, usually it informs an entire essay and helps a reader decide how to respond. For works of strong tone, see the essays by Maya Angelou, Jessica Mitford, Judy Brady, Russell Baker, Edwidge Danticat, and Martin Luther King, Jr. See also pages 528–29.

**Topic sentence**   The statement of the central idea in a PARAGRAPH, usually asserting one aspect of an essay's THESIS. Often the topic sentence will appear at (or near) the beginning of the paragraph, announcing the idea and beginning its development. Because all other sentences in the paragraph explain and support this central idea, the topic sentence is a way to create UNITY.

**Transitions**   Words, phrases, sentences, or even paragraphs that relate ideas. In moving from one topic to the next, a writer has to bring the reader along by showing how the ideas are developing, what bearing a new thought or detail has on an earlier discussion, or why a new topic is being introduced. A clear purpose, strong ideas, and logical development certainly aid COHERENCE, but to ensure that the reader is following along, good writers provide signals, or transitions.

To bridge sentences or paragraphs and to point out relationships within them, you can use some of the following devices of transition:

- Repeat or restate words or phrases to produce an echo in the reader's mind.
- Use PARALLEL STRUCTURES to produce a rhythm that moves the reader forward.
- Use pronouns to refer back to nouns in earlier passages.
- Use transitional words and phrases. These may indicate a relationship of time (*right away, later, soon, meanwhile, in a few minutes, that night*), proximity (*beside, close to, distant from, nearby, facing*), effect (*therefore, for this reason, as a result, consequently*), comparison (*similarly, in the same way, likewise*), or contrast (*yet, but, nevertheless, however, despite*). Some words and phrases of transition simply add on: *besides, too, also, moreover, in addition to, second, last, in the end.*

**Understatement**   See FIGURES OF SPEECH.

**Unity**   The quality of good writing in which all parts relate to the THESIS. In a unified essay, all words, sentences, and PARAGRAPHS support the single central idea. Your first step in achieving unity is to state your thesis; your next step is to organize your thoughts so that they make your thesis clear. See also pages 484–85.

**Voice**   In writing, the sense of the author's character, personality, and attitude that comes through the words. See TONE.

**Warrant**   The name for ASSUMPTION favored by philosopher Stephen Toulmin in his conception of ARGUMENT. See pages 521–22.

## Acknowledgments

Sarah Adams. "Be Cool to the Pizza Dude," copyright © 2005 by Sarah Adams. From the book *This I Believe*, edited by Jay Allison and Dan Gediman, copyright © 2006 by This I Believe, Inc. Reprinted by arrangement with Henry Holt and Company, LLC.

Chris Anderson. "The Rise and Fall of the Hit" from *The Long Tail: Why the Future of Business Is Selling Less of More* by Chris Anderson. Copyright © 2006 by Chris Anderson. Reprinted by permission of Hyperion. All rights reserved.

Maya Angelou. "Champion of the World" from *I Know Why the Caged Bird Sings*. Copyright © 1969 and renewed 1997 by Maya Angelou. Used by permission of Random House, Inc. "Maya Angelou on Writing" excerpted from Sheila Weller, "Work in Progress/Maya Angelou," from *Intellectual Digest*, June 1973. Reprinted with the permission of Sheila Weller.

Barbara Lazear Ascher. "On Compassion" from *The Habit of Loving*. Copyright © 1986, 1987, 1989 by Barbara Lazear Ascher. Used by permission of Random House, Inc. "Barbara Lazear Ascher on Writing" excerpted from Barbara Lazear Ascher selection in *Contemporary Authors* by Gale Group. Copyright © 1989. Reprinted with permission from Gale, a division of Thomson Learning: http://www.thomsonrights.com, fax: 800-730-2215.

Russell Baker. "The Plot Against People," *New York Times,* June 18, 1968; p. 46. Copyright © 1968 by The New York Times Company. Reprinted with permission. "Russell Baker on Writing," previously appeared as "Computer Fallout" in *New York Times Magazine,* October 11, 1987. Copyright © 1987 by The New York Times Company. Reprinted with permission.

Dave Barry. "Batting Clean-Up and Striking Out" from *Dave Barry's Greatest Hits* by Dave Barry. Copyright © 1988 by Dave Barry. Reprinted with the permission of Crown Publishers, Inc. "Dave Barry on Writing" excerpted from Dave Barry selection in *Contemporary Authors* by Gale Group. Copyright © 1992. Reprinted with permission from Gale, a division of Thomson Learning: http://www.thomsonrights.com, fax: 800-730-2215.

Robert Benchley. "My Face" from *After 1903—What?* by Robert Benchley and with drawings by Gluyas Williams. Copyright © 1938 by Robert C. Benchley, renewed © 1966 by Gertrude Benchley. Reprinted by permission of HarperCollins Publishers.

Judy Brady. "I Want a Wife." Copyright © 1970 by Judy Brady. Reprinted with the permission of the author.

Suzanne Britt. "Neat People vs. Sloppy People" from *Show and Tell*. Copyright © 1982 by Suzanne Britt. Reprinted with the permission of the author.

Armin A. Brott. "Not All Men Are Sly Foxes" from *Newsweek* (1992). Reprinted with the permission of the author.

Bruce Catton. "Grant and Lee: A Study in Contrasts," copyright © 1956 by United States Capitol Historical Society. All rights reserved. Reprinted with permission. "Bruce Catton on Writing" excerpted from Oliver Jensen's introduction to *Bruce Catton's America*. Copyright © 1979.

George Chauncey. "The Legacy of Antigay Discrimination" from *Why Marriage? The History Shaping Today's Debate over Gay Equality* by George Chauncey. Copyright © 2004 by George Chauncey. Reprinted by permission of Basic Books, a member of Perseus Books Group.

Linda Chavez. "Everything Isn't Racial Profiling" from Townhall.com (January 9, 2002). Copyright © 2002 by Linda Chavez. By permission of Linda Chavez and Creators Syndicate, Inc.

Sandra Cisneros. "Only Daughter." Copyright © 1990 by Sandra Cisneros. First published in *Glamour*, November 1990. Reprinted by permission of Susan Bergholz Literary Services, New York, NY, and Lamy, NM. All rights reserved. "Sandra Cisneros on Writing" excerpted from *Interviews with Writers of the Post-Colonial World*, edited by Feroza Jussawalla and Reed Way Dasenbrock. Copyright © 1992 by the University Press of Mississippi. Reprinted with permission.

Jessica Cohen. "Grade A: The Market for a Yale Woman's Eggs" from *The Atlantic Monthly* (December 2002). Copyright © 2002 by Jessica Cohen. Reprinted with the permission of the author.

Charles Colson with Anne Morse. "Gay 'Marriage': Societal Suicide" from *Christianity Today*, June 2004, as found at http://www.christianitytoday.com/ct/2004/006/8.72.html. Reprinted with the permission of Dr. Charles Colson.

Edwidge Danticat. "Not Your Homeland." Reprinted with permission from September 26, 2005, issue of *The Nation*. For subscription information, call 1-800-333-8536. Portions of each week's *Nation* magazine can be accessed at http://www.thenation.com. "Edwidge Danticat on Writing" excerpted from an "Author Q&A" with Edwidge Danticat, copyright © 1998. Reprinted by permission of Edwidge Danticat and Aragi Inc.

Don DeLillo. "Videotape" from *Underworld* by Don DeLillo. Copyright © 1997 by Don DeLillo. Reprinted with the permission of Scribner, an imprint of Simon & Schuster Adult Publishing Group. Originally appeared in *Antaeus* (Fall 1994). All rights reserved. "Don DeLillo on Writing" excerpted from *The Paris Review*, no. 128 (Fall 1993).

Bella DePaulo. "The Myth of Doomed Kids" from *Singled Out: How Singles Are Stereotyped, Stigmatized, and Ignored, and Still Live Happily Ever After* by Bella DePaulo. Copyright © 2006 by Bella DePaulo. Reprinted by permission of St. Martin's Press, LLC, and Bella DePaulo. "Bella DePaulo on Writing" excerpted from "Q&A with Bella DePaulo, Ph.D." posted on belladepaulo.com. Reprinted by permission of Bella DePaulo.

Emily Dickinson. "'Hope' is the thing with feathers." Reprinted by permission of the publishers and the Trustees of Amherst College from *The Poems of Emily Dickinson*, Thomas H. Johnson, ed., Cambridge, Mass.: The Belknap Press of Harvard University Press. Copyright © 1951, 1955, 1979, 1983 by the President and Fellows of Harvard College.

Joan Didion. "In Bed" from *The White Album* by Joan Didion. Copyright © 1979 by Joan Didion. Reprinted by permission of Farrar, Straus & Giroux, LLC. "Joan Didion on Writing" excerpted from "Why I Write" by Joan Didion. First appeared in the *New York Times Book Review*, December 5, 1976. Copyright © 1976 by The New York Times Company. Reprinted by permission.

Annie Dillard. "The Chase" (our editors' title) excerpted from pages 45–49 of *An American Childhood* by Annie Dillard. Copyright © 1987 by Annie Dillard. Reprinted by permission of HarperCollins Publishers.

Chitra Divakaruni. "Live Free and Starve." This article first appeared in Salon.com, at http://www.salon.com. An online version remains in the *Salon* archives. Reprinted with permission. "Chitra Divakaruni on Writing" excerpted from "Women's Places" interview by Katie Bolick, *Atlantic Unbound* (April 8, 1998), http://www.theatlantic.com/unbound/factfict/ff9804.html.

Barbara Ehrenreich. "The Roots of War," *The Progressive*, April 10, 2003. Reprinted with the permission of *The Progressive*, 409 East Main Street, Madison, WI 53703.

Gretel Ehrlich. "Chronicles of Ice" from *The Future of Ice: A Journey into Cold* by Gretel Ehrlich. Copyright © 2004 by Gretel Ehrlich. Used by permission of Pantheon Books, a division of Random House, Inc. "Gretel Ehrlich on Writing" excerpted from "A Call from One Kingdom to Another" in *Talking on the Water* by Jonathan White (San Francisco: Sierra Club Books, 1994). Copyright © 1994. Used by permission.

Stephanie Ericsson. "The Ways We Lie." Originally published in the November/December 1992 issue of *The Utne Reader*. Copyright © 1992 by Stephanie Ericsson. Reprinted by the permission of Dunham Literary Inc. as agent for the author. "Stephanie Ericsson on Writing" excerpted from "Amazon.com Talks to Stephanie Ericsson," http://www.amazon.com/exec/obidos/show-interview/e-s-ricssontephanie.

Ian Frazier. "How to Use a Shower Curtain," *The New Yorker*, January 8, 2007. Copyright © 2007 by Ian Frazier. Used by permission of the author.

Dagoberto Gilb. "Pride" from *Gritos: Essays by Dagoberto Gilb*. Copyright © 2003 by Dagoberto Gilb. "Dagoberto Gilb on Writing" excerpted from *Gritos: Essays by Dagoberto Gilb*. Copyright © 2003 by Dagoberto Gilb. Reprinted by permission of Dagoberto Gilb.

Stephen Jay Gould. "A Biological Homage to Mickey Mouse" from *The Panda's Thumb: More Reflections in Natural History*. Copyright © 1980 by Stephen Jay Gould. Used by permission of

Naylor on Writing" excerpted from William Goldstein, "A Talk with Gloria Naylor," from *Publishers Weekly* (September 9, 1983). Copyright © 1983 by Publishers Weekly.

Daniel Orozco. "Orientation" from *Seattle Review* (1994). Copyright © 1994 by Daniel Orozco. Reprinted with the permission of the author. "Daniel Orozco on Writing" excerpted from an interview with Will Allison in *Novel and Short Story Writer's Market*.

George Orwell. "Shooting an Elephant" from *Shooting an Elephant and Other Essays* by George Orwell. Copyright 1950 by Sonia Brownell Orwell and renewed © 1978 by Sonia Pitt-Rivers. Reprinted by permission of Harcourt, Inc. "George Orwell on Writing" excerpted from *Such, Such Were the Joys*. Copyright 1952 and renewed 1980 by Sonia Brownell Orwell. Reprinted by permission of Harcourt Brace & Company.

Katha Pollitt. "What's Wrong with Gay Marriage?" (editors' title; originally titled "Adam and Steve — Together at Last"), *The Nation*, December 15, 2003. Copyright © 2003 by Katha Pollitt. Reprinted with the permission of the author. "Katha Pollitt on Writing" excerpted from Ruth Conniff, "An Interview with Katha Pollitt," *The Progressive* 58:12 (December 1994). Copyright © 1994. Reprinted by permission from *The Progressive*, 409 E. Main St., Madison, WI 53703, http://www.progressive.org.

Francine Prose. "What Words Can Tell" (editors' title) excerpted from pages 15–19 of *Reading Like a Writer* by Francine Prose. Copyright © 2006 by Francine Prose. Reprinted by permission of HarperCollins Publishers.

Anna Quindlen. "Homeless" from *Living Out Loud*. Copyright © 1987 by Anna Quindlen. "Anna Quindlen on Writing" excerpted from "In the Beginning" in *Living Out Loud*. Copyright © 1987 by Anna Quindlen. Used by permission of Random House, Inc.

Richard Rodriguez. "Aria: A Memoir of a Bilingual Childhood." Copyright © 1980 by Richard Rodriguez. Originally appeared in *The American Scholar*. Reprinted by permission of Georges Borchardt, Inc., on behalf of the author.

Roger Rosenblatt. "We Are Free to Be You, Me, Stupid, and Dead" from *Where We Stand* by Roger Rosenblatt. Copyright © 2002 by Roger Rosenblatt. Reprinted by permission of Harcourt, Inc.

Edward Said. "Clashing Civilizations?" excerpted from "We All Swim Together" in *The New Statesman* 14, no. 678 (October 15, 2001). Copyright © 2001 by New Statesman Ltd. All rights reserved. Reprinted with permission.

Luc Sante. "What Secrets Tell," *New York Times Magazine*, December 3, 2000. Copyright © 2000 by The New York Times Company. Reprinted with permission.

Thomas Sowell. "Needs" from *Is Reality Optional? and Other Essays* (Stanford, Calif.: Hoover Institution Press, 1993). Copyright © 1993 by Thomas Sowell. Reprinted with the permission of the author.

Brent Staples. "Black Men and Public Space," *Harper's*, December 1986. Reprinted with the permission of the author. "Brent Staples on Writing," copyright © 1991 by St. Martin's Press. Reprinted with permission.

Amy Tan. "Fish Cheeks." Copyright © 1987 by Amy Tan. First appeared in *Seventeen Magazine*. Reprinted by permission of the author and the Sandra Dijkstra Literary Agency. "Amy Tan on Writing" excerpted from "Mother Tongue." Copyright © 1990 by Amy Tan. First appeared in *The Threepenny Review*. Reprinted by permission of the author and the Sandra Dijkstra Literary Agency.

Deborah Tannen. "But What Do You Mean?" from *Talking from 9 to 5* by Deborah Tannen. Copyright © 1994 by Deborah Tannen. Reprinted by permission of HarperCollins Publishers. "Deborah Tannen on Writing" excerpted from "The Place of the Personal in Scholarship" in *PMLA* 111.5 (October 1996).

Harold Taw. "Finding Prosperity by Feeding Monkeys," copyright © 2005 by Harold Taw. From the book *This I Believe*, edited by Jay Allison and Dan Gediman, copyright © 2006 by This I Believe, Inc. Reprinted by arrangement with Henry Holt and Company, LLC.

Sarah Vowell. "Shooting Dad" from *Take the Cannoli* by Sarah Vowell. Copyright © 2000 by Sarah

# INDEX

**Page numbers in bold type refer to definitions in the glossary, Useful Terms.**

Abstract and concrete, **691**
Abstract language
  Benchley on, 174
  Didion on, 596–97
Academic writing, 51–78
  analysis and, 52
  assumptions and, 52
  audience and, 57
  author and, 58–59
  comparison and contrast with, 52
  effect in, 52
  evaluating sources and, 57
  evidence and, 51, 57–58
  forming a response and, 53
  integrating source material and, 54–56
  introducing source material and, 55–56
  MLA documentation in, 54, 62–73
  online sources and, 58–59
  paraphrase and, 54–55
  plagiarism and, 60–62
  primary and secondary sources in, 57–58
  purpose and, 57
  quotation and, 54–55
  responding to a text and, 52–54
  summary and, 52, 54
  synthesis and, 52–54, 59–60
  thesis and, 51
  writing from research and, 56–60
Active voice, **691**

Adams, Sarah, 455
  "Be Cool to the Pizza Dude," 455–56
Adbusters Media Foundation
  *Corporate America Flag* (advertisement), 516
Allude, allusion, **691–92**
*American Gothic* (painting by Grant Wood), 222
Analogy, **692**
  argument and persuasion and, 526, 692
  comparison and contrast and, 225
  process analysis and, 285
Analyze, analysis, **692**. *See also* Division or analysis; Process analysis.
  argument and persuasion and, 519
  academic writing and, 52
  critical reading and, 18, 20–25
  critical thinking with, 18, 20–22, 695, 697, 703
  mixing other methods with, 582
  of visual images, 25–30
  writing situation and, 32–34
Anaya, Rosie, 2, 5, 16, 32, 35, 40, 51, 53, 59–60, 74
  "Mental Illness on Television," 40–43; 43–46; 46–47; 47–49, 53
  "The Best Kept Secret on Campus," 51, 74–78
Anderson, Chris, 459, 466–67
  Chris Anderson on Writing, 466–67
  "The Rise and Fall of the Hit," 459–64
Angelou, Maya, 2, 93, 97–98, 696, 704
  "Champion of the World," 2, 93–96
  Maya Angelou on Writing, 97–98

Anecdote, **692**
   argument and persuasion and, 82–83
   example and, 188
   Krull on, 206–207
   narration and, 82–83
   Rosenblatt on, 219–20
   Staples on, 212–214
Appeals, **693**
   emotional, 521, 693, **697**
   ethical, 521, 693, **697**
   rational, 521, 693, **702**
"Araby" (Joyce), 175–80
Argument and persuasion, 516–79, **693**
   additional writing topics for, 579
   analogy in, 526, 692
   analysis in, 519
   anecdotes and, 82–83
   assumptions and, 521
   audience and, 529
   authority and, 525
   cause and effect and, 23, 527
   checklist for revising, 529
   circular, 525
   claims, evidence, and assumptions in,
      519–24, 529
   comparison and contrast in, 23, 224
   conclusion and, 523
   critical thinking and, 518
   data or grounds in, 520
   deductive reasoning in, 522–24
   description and, 23, 139, 527
   emotional appeal in, 521
   ethical appeal in, 521
   evaluation in, 519
   evidence and, 520–21, 529
   example and, 23, 527
   generalization in, 522–23
   illustrations of, in practice, 531
   inductive reasoning in, 522–23
   inference in, 519
   logical fallacies and, 524–26, 529
   major premise and, 523
   method of, 37, 518–26
   minor premise and, 523
   mixing other methods with, 582–83,
      598–601, 614–18, 644–47, 651–61,
      665–68, 670–78
   narration and, 82, 527
   opinion and, 518
   paragraph illustrations of, 530–31
   persuasion and, 519
   process analysis and, 519
   process of, 526–29
   proposal and, 518
   rational appeal in, 521
   structure and, 527–28, 529

   syllogism in, 523
   synthesis in, 519
   thesis and, 520, 529
   tone and, 528–29
   Toulmin, Stephen and, 519–22
   warrant and, 521, 529
   writing process and, 37
"Aria: A Memoir of a Bilingual Childhood"
   (Rodriguez), 651–61
"Arm Wrestling with My Father" (Manning),
   146–50
Ascher, Barbara Lazear, 54–56, 60–62, 67, 193,
   197
   Barbara Lazear Ascher on Writing, 197
   "On Compassion," 54, 56, 60, 62, 67, 193–95
Assume, assumption, **693**
   academic writing and, 52
   argument and persuasion and, 521, 529
   critical reading and, 19, 26
   division or analysis and, 333
   example and, 188
Attitude
   Benchley on, 174
   DePaulo on, 356–57
   Ehrlich on, 300–01
   Frazier on, 306–07
   Gilb on, 509
   Javdani on, 453–54
   Krull on, 206–07
   Pollitt on, 552–53
   Vowell on, 162–63
   Wurster on, 547
Audience, **693**
   academic writing and, 57
   Anderson on, 466–67
   argument and persuasion and, 529
   Barry on, 243–44
   Benchley on, 174
   Cisneros on, 589–90
   critical reading and, 11, 22
   DePaulo on, 356–57
   description and, 139–40
   Ehrlich on, 300–01
   Javdani on, 453–54
   narration and, 86, 89
   Rosenblatt on, 219–20
   Tan on, 102–03
   Vowell on, 162–63
   writing process and, 33–34
Author
   academic writing and, 58–59
   critical reading and, 10–11
Authority, 525
Ayad, Laila, 2, 51, 358
   "The Capricious Camera," 51, 358–64
Awareness, Britt on, 237–38

Baker, Russell, 37, 384, 388–90, 704
  Russell Baker on Writing, 388–90
  "The Plot Against People," 10, 37, 384–86
Barry, Dave, 239, 243–44, 697
  "Batting Clean-Up and Striking Out,"
    239–41, 697
  Dave Barry on Writing, 243–44
"Batting Clean-Up and Striking Out" (Barry),
  239–41, 697
"Be Cool to the Pizza Dude" (Adams), 455–56
"Behind the Formaldehyde Curtain" (Mit-
  ford), 308–15
"Being a Chink" (Leong), 494–97
Benchley, Robert, 170, 174
  "My Face," 170–72
  Robert Benchley on Writing, 174
"Best Kept Secret on Campus, The" (Anaya),
  51, 74–78
Binary classification, 377
Bilingualism
  Cisneros on, 589–90
  Danticat on, 577–78
  Li on, 168–69
  Rodriguez on, 663–64
  Tan on, 102–03
"Biological Homage to Mickey Mouse, A"
  (Gould), 604–11
"Black Men and Public Space" (Staples), 208–10
Brady, Judy, 240, 697, 700, 704
  "I Want a Wife," 10, 340–42, 697
Britt, Suzanne, 10, 233, 237–38
  "Neat People vs. Sloppy People," 10, 233–35
  Suzanne Britt on Writing, 237–38
Brott, Armin A., 345
  "Not All Men Are Sly Foxes," 345–47
"But Enough about You . . ." (Williams),
  539–41
"But What Do You Mean?" (Tannen), 391–97

"Capricious Camera, The" (Ayad), 51, 358
Categories in classification, 378–79
Catton, Bruce, 2, 37, 245, 250–51, 697
  Bruce Catton on Writing, 250–51
  "Grant and Lee: A Study in Contrasts," 2,
    10, 37, 245–48, 697
Causal chain, 434–35, 438
Cause and effect, 3, 430–77, **693**
  additional writing topics for, 476–77
  argument and persuasion and, 23, 527
  chain in, 434–35, 438
  checklist for revising, 437–38
  clarity and conciseness in, 437, 438
  completeness of, 437
  critical reading and, 23
  division or analysis and, 432
  definition and, 483

evidence in, 434
illustration of, in practice, 439–41
immediate cause in, 432
logical fallacies and, 435, 438
major or minor cause in, 435
method of, 36, 432–433
mixing other methods with, 582–83,
  584–87, 591–94, 598–601, 604–11,
  614–18, 620–30, 634–40, 644–47,
  651–61, 665–68, 670–78
paragraph illustrations of, 438–39
pentad, Burke's and, 436
process of, 433–38
purpose of, 433–34
remote cause in, 432
subject and, 433–34, 437
thesis and, 433–34, 437
writing process and, 36
"Celebrating the Pity of Brotherly Love"
  (Krull), 203–04
Censorship
  Ehrenreich on, 603
  Li on, 168–69
"Champion of the World" (Angelou), 2, 93–96
Charles Atlas
  How Joe's Body Brought Him Fame Instead of
    Shame (advertisement), 80
"Chase, The" (Dillard), 104–07
Chast, Roz
  Deconstructing Lunch (cartoon), 330
Chauncey, George, 51, 260
  "The Legacy of Antigay Discrimination,"
    51, 260–64
Chavez, Linda, 563
  "Everything Isn't Racial Profiling," 563–65
"Chronicles of Ice" (Ehrlich), 295
Chronological order, **693**
  narration and, 87–88, 89
Cisneros, Sandra, 584, 589–90
  "Only Daughter," 584–87
  Sandra Cisneros on Writing, 589–90
"Clashing Civilizations" (Said), 665–68
Claim, **693**
  argument and persuasion and, 519–24, 529
Clarity and conciseness
  Ascher on, 197
  Benchley on, 174
  cause and effect and, 437, 438
  Prose on, 649–50
Classification, 374–79, **693**
  additional writing topics for, 429
  binary, 377
  categories in, 378–79
  checklist for revising, 380
  completeness of, 380
  complex, 377

consistency in, 380
definition and, 429
description and, 377
division or analysis and, 376, 380
evaluation and, 377
examples and, 429
illustration of, in practice, 381–83
method of, 4, 36, 376–77
mixing other methods with, 582–83, 665–68
paragraph development in, 380
paragraph development, focus on, 379–80
paragraph illustrations of, 380–81
principle of, 380
process analysis and, 284, 376
process of, 377–80
purpose of, 376, 377–78, 380, 429
thesis in, 377–78
writing process and, 36
Cliché, **694**
"Close Encounters with US Immigration"
    (Khan), 558–60
Cohen, Jessica, 2, 114, 121–22
    "Grade A: The Market for a Yale Woman's
    Eggs," 114–19
    Jessica Cohen on Writing, 121–22
Coherence, **694**
    comparison and contrast and, 228–29
    critical reading and, 23
    Vowell on, 162–63
Colloquial expressions, **694**
Collaboration, 40, 43
Colson, Charles, 554
    "Gay 'Marriage': Societal Suicide," 554–56
Comic writing. *See* Humor.
Community
    Anderson on, 466–67
    Divakaruni on, 446–47
Comparison and contrast, 222–78, **694**
    academic writing and, 52
    additional writing topics for, 278
    analogy and, 225
    argument and persuasion and, 23, 224
    checklist for revising, 229
    coherence and, 229
    conclusion and, 227
    critical reading and, 23
    definition and, 480, 481–82
    description and, 139
    division or analysis and, 224
    evaluation of, 225
    flexibility and, 228, 229
    illustration of, in practice, 231–32
    method of, 3, 23, 36, 224–25
    mixing other methods with, 582–83,
        598–01, 604–11, 614–18, 620–30,
        644–47, 651–61, 665–68, 670–78, 682–87

organization of, 226–27, 229
paragraph coherence, focus on, 228–29
paragraph illustrations of, 229–31
parallel wording and, 231
process of, 225–29
purposes of, 224–25, 229
subjects of, 229
summary and, 227
thesis statement and, 226, 229
transitions and, 228
writing process and, 36
Completeness
    cause and effect and, 437
    classification and, 380
    division or analysis and, 336
    process analysis and, 287
Complex classification, 377
Computers, Baker on, 388–90
Conclusion, **694–95**
    argument and persuasion and, 523
    comparison and contrast and, 227
    narration and, 84
Concrete language, **695**
    description and, 142–43
Connotation, **695**
    critical reading and, 24–25
Consistency
    classification and, 380
    division or analysis and, 336
    process analysis and, 285, 287
Contrast. *See* Comparison and contrast.
*Corporate America Flag* (Adbusters advertise-
    ment), 516
Craft
    Baker on, 388–90
    Benchley on, 174
    DeLillo on, 474–75
    Dickinson on, 513
    Ehrlich on, 300–01
    Frazier on, 306–07
    Gilb on, 509
    Javdani on, 453–54
    Prose on, 649–50
    Sante on, 407
    Wurster on, 547
Creative process
    Angelou on, 97–98
    Danticat on, 577–78
    DeLillo on, 474–75
    Dickinson on, 513
    Ehrlich on, 300–01
    Javdani on, 453–54
    Krull on, 206–07
    Wurster on, 547
Critical reading, 9–12, 16–26. *See also* Critical
    thinking, reading, and writing, **695**.

Critical reading *(continued)*
 analysis and, 18, 20–25
 assumptions and, 19
 audience and, 11, 22
 author and, 10–11
 cause and effect and, 23
 coherence in, 23
 comparison and contrast and, 23
 connotations and, 24–25
 description and, 23
 evaluation and, 19–20
 evidence in, 22–23
 example and, 23
 figures of speech in, 25
 first reading and, 12
 inference and, 19
 irony in, 24
 journal writing and, 16
 language and, 24–25
 meaning and, 20
 metaphor and, 25
 mixing other methods with, 582–83
 narration and, 23
 publication information and, 11
 purpose and, 20–22
 simile and, 25
 strategy and, 22–24
 structure and, 23–24
 summarizing during, 17
 synthesis and, 19
 thesis and, 10, 20
 thinking critically during, 17–18
 title and, 10
 tone and, 10
 understatement and, 25
 unity in, 23
 visual images and, 25–30
Critical thinking. *See also* Critical thinking,
  reading, and writing, **695**.
 analysis during, 18, 20–22, 695, 697, 703
 argument and persuasion and, 518
 division or analysis and, 333–334
 writing process and, 31
 Wurster on, 547
Cultural/racial differences and writing
 Cisneros on, 589–90
 Danticat on, 577–78
 Li on, 168–69
 Naylor on, 493
 Tan on, 102–03

Danticat, Edwidge, 572, 577, 704
 Edwidge Danticat on Writing, 577
 "Not Your Homeland," 572–75
Data, **695**
 argument and persuasion and, 520

*Deconstructing Lunch* (Chast cartoon), 330
Deductive reasoning, deduction, **695**
 argument and persuasion and, 522–24
Definition, 3, 478–514, **695**
 additional writing topics for, 514
 cause and effect and, 483
 checklist for revising, 485
 classification and, 429
 comparison and contrast and, 480, 481–82
 description and, 480, 483
 division or analysis and, 480
 dominant impression and, 483
 effect and, 480
 evidence and, 484, 485
 examples and, 480
 extended, 480
 figure of speech and, 481
 illustration of, in practice, 486–87
 images and, 480
 introduction and, 483
 irony and, 481
 meanings and, 485
 method of, 37, 480–81, 485
 mixing other methods with, 582–83,
   584–87, 591–94, 598–601, 604–11,
   665–68
 paragraph and essay unity, focus on,
   484–85
 paragraph illustrations of, 485–86
 process analysis and, 287, 482
 process of, 481–85
 stipulative, 480
 summary and, 485
 thesis in, 483, 485
 unity and, 485
 writing process and, 37
DeLillo, Don, 468, 474–75
 Don DeLillo on Writing, 474–75
 "Videotape," 468–72
Denotation, **695**
DePaulo, Bella, 51, 350, 356–57
 Bella DePaulo on Writing, 356–57
 "The Myth of Doomed Kids," 51, 350–54
Description, 3, 136–83, **695**
 additional writing topics for, 183
 argument and persuasion and, 23, 139, 527
 audience and, 139–40
 checklist for revising, 143
 classification and, 377
 comparison and contrast and, 139
 critical reading and, 23
 definition and, 480, 483
 details and, 143
 dominant impression and, 140–41, 143
 effect and, 139
 example and, 188

figures of speech and, 142
illustration of, in practice, 145
images in, 142
method of, 4, 36, 138–39
mixing other methods with, 582–83,
    584–87, 591–94, 604–11, 614–18,
    620–30, 634–40, 644–47, 651–61,
    670–78, 682–87
narration and, 86–87, 139, 183
objectivity and, 138–39, 143, 183
organization and, 143
paragraph illustrations of, 143–44
point of view and, 141, 143
process analysis and, 327
purpose and, 138, 139–40
specific and concrete language and, 142–43
subjectivity and, 138–39, 143, 183
thesis and, 140–41
writing process and, 36
Details
    description and, 143
    Ehrlich on, 300–01
    narration and, 85
    Staples on, 213–14
Dialog, in narration, 89
Dickinson, Emily, 510, 513, 692
    Emily Dickinson on Writing, 513
    "'Hope' is the thing with feathers," 510, 692
Diction, **695–96**
Didion, Joan, 591, 596–97
    "In Bed," 591–94
    Joan Didion on Writing, 596–97
Dillard, Annie, 104, 109
    Annie Dillard on Writing, 109
    "The Chase," 104–07
Directive process analysis, 282, 327–28
"Disability" (Mairs), 5, 10–12, 13–15, 17,
    20–21, 24, 32, 35–36, 40–49, 51, 74
Discovery, 31, 34–37, **696**
    Gould on, 613
Divakaruni, Chitra, 37, 442, 446–47
    Chitra Divakaruni on Writing, 446–47
    "Live Free and Starve," 10, 37, 442–44
Division or analysis, 330–72, **696**
    additional writing topics for, 372
    assumptions and, 333
    cause and effect and, 432
    checklist for revising, 336–37
    classification and, 376, 380
    comparison and contrast and, 224
    completeness and, 336
    consistency and, 336
    critical reading and, 18
    critical thinking and, 333–34
    definition and, 480
    evidence in, 335–36, 337

illustration of, in practice, 338–39
inference and, 333
method of, 36, 332–34
mixing other methods with, 582–83,
    598–601, 604–11, 644–47, 665–68
paragraph illustrations of, 337–38
process analysis and, 282
process of, 334–37
purpose in, 334
significance and, 337
synthesis and, 333
thesis statement and, 335, 336
truth to subject in, 337
writing process and, 36
Dominant impression, **696**
    definition and, 483
    description and, 140–41, 143
*Doug and Mizan's House, East River, 1993*
    (Morton photograph), 136
Drafts and drafting, **696**
    DeLillo on, 474–75
    Dillard on, 109
    Javdani on, 453–54
    Kingston on, 632–33
    Krull on, 206–07
    Manning on, 152–53
    writing process and, 38, 40–49

Editing, 38–39
    Baker on, 388–90
    Barry on, 243–44
    DeLillo on, 474–75
    Didion on, 596–97
    Dillard on, 109
    example of (Anaya), 40–49
    Javdani on, 453–54
    Manning on, 152–53
    Saukko on, 294
Effect, **696**. *See also* Cause and effect.
    academic writing and, 52
    Anderson on, 466–67
    definition and, 480
    description and, 139
    Gilb on, 509
    Jackson on, 132–33
    Javdani on, 453–54
    Rosenblatt on, 219–20
    Vowell on, 162–63
Ehrenreich, Barbara, 598, 602–03
    Barbara Ehrenreich on Writing, 602–03
    *The Roots of War*, 598–601
Ehrlich, Gretel, 295, 300–01
    "Chronicles of Ice," 295–98
    Gretel Ehrlich on Writing, 300–01
Emotional appeal, 521, **697**
Emphasis, 39, **697**

Ericsson, Stephanie, 10, 408, 417
  Stephanie Ericsson on Writing, 417
  "The Ways We Lie," 10, 408–15
Essay, **697**
  Ascher on, 197
  Gould on, 613
  Staples on, 212–14
  White on, 689–90
Ethical appeal, 521, **697**
Euphemism, **697**
  Mitford on, 318
Evaluate, evaluation, **697**
  academic writing and, 57
  argument and persuasion and, 519
  classification and, 377
  comparison and contrast and, 225
  critical reading and, 19–20
  Krull on, 206–07
"Everyday Use" (Walker), 267
"Everything Isn't Racial Profiling" (Chavez), 563–65
Evidence, **698**
  academic writing and, 51, 57–58
  argument and persuasion and, 520–21, 529
  cause and effect and, 434
  critical reading and, 22–23
  definition and, 484, 485
  division or analysis and, 335–36, 337
  Staples on, 213–14
  writing process and, 33–34
Example, 3, 184–221, **698**
  additional writing topics for, 221
  anecdote and, 188
  argument and persuasion and, 23, 527
  assumption and, 188
  checklist for revising, 189–90
  classification and, 429
  critical reading and, 23
  definition and, 480
  description and, 188
  exposition and, 188
  generalization and, 186–87, 189, 221
  illustration of, in practice, 191–92
  method of, 36, 186
  mixing other methods with, 582–83, 591–94, 598–601, 614–18, 634–40, 644–47, 665–68, 670–78, 682–87
  narration and, 188
  paragraph illustrations of, 190–91
  process of, 187–90
  purpose and, 187
  relevance and, 190
  sentence variety and, 189–90
  support and, 189
  specifics and, 189

topic sentence and, 186
  thesis and, 187, 221
  writing process and, 36
Experience
  Cohen on, 121–22
  Danticat on, 577–78
  DePaulo on, 356–57
  Divakaruni on, 446–47
  Ehrlich on, 300–01
  Krull on, 206–07
  Leong on, 499–500
  Rosenblatt on, 219–20
Exposition, **698**
  example and, 188
Extended definition, 480

Fallacies, **698**. *See* Logical fallacies.
Figures of speech, **698**
  critical reading and, 25
  definition and, 481
  description and, 142
Flexibility, 228, 229
Frazier, Ian, 302, 306
  "How to Operate the Shower Curtain," 302–04
  Ian Frazier on Writing, 306
Freewriting, 35
"Finding Prosperity by Feeding Monkeys" (Taw), 110–11
"Fish Cheeks" (Tan), 99–100
First drafts
  Javdani on, 453–54
  Krull on, 206–07
  Manning on, 152–53
First person, Tannen on, 399–400
First reading, 12
Flashback, 87, 89, **698**
Focus, **698–99**
Form
  Anderson on, 466–67
  Angelou on, 97–98
  Vowell on, 162–63
  White on, 689–90
Forming a response, 53

*Garbage In . . .*, (Thompson cartoon), 430
"Gay 'Marriage': Societal Suicide" (Colson), 554–56
General and specific, **699**
Generalization, **699**
  argument and persuasion and, 522–23
  example and, 186–87, 189, 221
Gilb, Dagoberto, 505, 509
  Dagoberto Gilb on Writing, 509
  "Pride," 505–07
"Girl" (Kincaid), 367–68

Gould, Stephen Jay, 604, 613
   "A Biological Homage to Mickey Mouse,"
     604–11
   Stephen Jay Gould on Writing, 613
"Grade A: The Market for a Yale Woman's
   Eggs" (Cohen), 114
Grammar
   Didion on, 596–97
   Javdani on, 453–54
   Prose on, 649–50
"Grant and Lee: A Study in Contrasts" (Cat-
   ton), 2, 10, 37, 245–48, 697
Grounds, **699**

"Homeless" (Quindlen), 67, 198–200
"'Hope' is the thing with feathers" (Dickin-
   son), 510, 692
*How Joe's Body Brought Him Fame Instead of
   Shame* (Charles Atlas advertisement),
   80
"How to Operate the Shower Curtain" (Fra-
   zier), 302–04
"How to Poison the Earth" (Saukko), 290–92,
   702
HUMMER H2
   *Need Is a Very Subjective Word* (advertise-
     ment), 478
Humor
   Barry on, 243–44
   Benchley and, 174
   Mitford and, 318
Hyperbole, **699**

"I Have a Dream" (King), 614–18, 692
"I Want a Wife" (Brady), 10, 340–42, 697
Illustration, **699**. *See also* Example.
Image, **699**
   definition and, 480
   description and, 142
Immediate cause, 432
"In Bed" (Didion), 591–94
Indifference
   Britt on, 237–38
   Rosenblatt on, 219–20
Inductive reasoning, induction, **699**
   argument and persuasion and, 522–23
Infer, inference, **699**
   argument and persuasion and, 519
   critical reading and, 19
   division or analysis and, 333
Informative process analysis, 282, 327–28
*In medias res*, 87
"In practice" illustrations
   using argument and persuasion, 531–32
   using cause and effect, 439–41
   using classification, 381–83

   using comparison and contrast, 231–32
   using definition, 486–87
   using description, 145
   using division or analysis, 338–39
   using example, 191–92
   using narration, 91–92
   using process analysis, 288–89
Inspiration
   Barry on, 243–44
   Ehrlich on, 300–01
   Javdani on, 453–54
   Krull on, 206–07
   Leong on, 499–500
   Naylor on, 493
   Walker on, 276–77
Integrating source material, 54–56
Internet. *See* Online sources.
Introducing source material, 55–56
Introduction, **699–700**
   definition and, 483
   Javdani on, 453–54
Irony, **700**
   critical reading and, 24
   definition and, 481

Jackson, Shirley, 123, 132–33
   Shirley Jackson on Writing, 132–33
   "The Lottery," 123–130
Jargon, **700**
   Gould on, 613
   Mitford on, 318
Javdani, Marie, 2, 51, 448, 453–54
   Marie Javdani on Writing, 453–54
   *Plata o Plomo: Silver or Lead*," 51, 448–51
Jokes. *See* Anecdote; Humor.
Journalism
   Ehrenreich on, 603
   Orwell on, 642–43
   Quindlen on, 201–02
   Rosenblatt on, 219–20
   Staples on, 212–14
Journal, **700**
   critical reading and, 16
   White on, 689–90
   writing process and, 32–33, 35, 40–41, 43
Joyce, James, 175
   "Araby," 175–80

Khan, Adnan R., 558
   "Close Encounters with US Immigration,"
     558–60
Kincaid, Jamaica, 367, 370–71
   "Girl," 367–68
   Jamaica Kincaid on Writing, 370–71
King Jr., Martin Luther, 614, 692, 701, 704
   "I Have a Dream," 614–18, 692

Kingston, Maxine Hong, 620, 632–33
  Maxine Hong Kingston on Writing, 632–33
  "No Name Woman," 620–30
Krikorian, Mark, 567
  "Safety Through Immigration Control,"
    567–69
Krull, Andrew Koritz, 2, 203, 206–07
  Andrew Koritz Krull on Writing, 206–07
  "Celebrating the Pity of Brotherly Love,"
    203–04

Language
  critical reading and, 24–25
  Benchley on, 174
  Danticat on, 577–78
  DeLillo on, 474–75
  Dickinson on, 513
  Didion on, 596–97
  Gould on, 613
  Li on, 168–69
  Mairs and, 24–25
  Naylor on, 493
  Orwell on, 642–43
  Prose on, 649–50
  Sante on, 407
  Tan on, 102–03
"Legacy of Antigay Discrimination, The"
    (Chauncey), 51, 260–64
Le Lievre, Glen
  Low-Energy Drinks (cartoon), 184
Leong, Christine, 494, 499–500
  "Being a Chink," 494–97
  Christine Leong on Writing, 499–500
Lesser, Erik S., 26, 28, 29, 30
  Nicole Waugh, 6, with her father, Chief War-
    rant Officer Joel Waugh, departing from Fort
    Benning, GA (photograph), 26, 27
Li, Yiyun, 4, 164, 168–69
  Yiyun Li on Writing, 168–69
  "Orange Crush," 4, 164–66
Literature, Naylor on, 493
"Live Free and Starve" (Divakaruni), 10,
    442–44
Logical fallacies. See also fallacies.
  argument and persuasion and, 524–26, 529
  cause and effect and, 435, 438
"Lottery, The" (Jackson), 123–30
Low-Energy Drinks (Le Lievre cartoon), 184
Lutz, William, 418, 426–27, 697, 700
  "The World of Doublespeak," 418–24, 697,
    700
  William Lutz on Writing, 426–27

Magazines, Ehrenreich on writing for, 603
Mairs, Nancy, 5, 10–13, 16–17, 20–25, 32,
    35–36, 40–49, 51, 53, 74

"Disability," 5, 10–12, 13–15, 17, 20–21, 24,
    32, 35–36, 40–49, 51, 74
Major cause, 435
Major premise, 523
Manning, Brad, 2, 146, 152–53
  "Arm Wrestling with My Father," 146–50
  Brad Manning on Writing, 152–53
McNamee, Wally
  Workers Making Dolls (photograph), 280
Meaning
  critical reading and, 20
  definition and, 485
  Kingston on, 632–33
  Pollitt on, 552–53
  Prose on, 649–50
  Rosenblatt on, 219–20
"Meanings of a Word, The" (Naylor), 488–91
"Mental Illness on Television" (Anaya),
    40–43, 43–46, 46–47, 47–49
Mernissi, Fatema, 252
  "Size 6: The Western Women's Harem,"
    252–57
Metaphor, **700**
  critical reading and, 25
Methods. See also entries to individual methods.
  Baker on, 388–90
  DeLillo on, 474–75
  Javdani on, 453–54
  Sante on, 407
Minor cause, 435
Minor premise
  in argument and persuasion, 523
Mitford, Jessica, 308, 318, 700, 704
  "Behind the Formaldehyde Curtain,"
    308–15
  Jessica Mitford on Writing, 318
MLA (Modern Language Association) style,
    54, 62–73
"Modest Proposal, A" (Swift), 670–78, 702
"More They Learn, the More They Earn, The"
    (State Farm Insurance graph), 374
Morton, Margaret
  Doug and Mizan's House, East River, 1993
    (photograph), 136
Motives for writing
  Anderson on, 466–67
  Catton on, 251
  Cohen on, 121–22
  Didion on, 596–97
  Ericsson on, 417
  Gould on, 613
  Javdani on, 453–54
  Kincaid on, 370–71
  Naylor on, 493
  Orwell on, 642–43
  Pollitt on, 552–53

Quindlen on, 201–02
Rodriguez on, 663–64
Rosenblatt on, 219–20
Staples on, 212–14
*Mounted Nazi Troops on the Lookout for Likely Polish Children* (photograph), 359
"My Face" (Benchley), 170–72
"Myth of Doomed Kids, The" (DePaulo), 51, 350–54

Narration, 3, 80–135, **700**
   additional writing topics for, 135
   anecdote and, 82–83
   argument and persuasion and, 82, 527
   audience and, 86, 89
   checklist for revising, 89
   chronological order and, 87–88, 89
   conclusion and, 84
   critical reading and, 23
   description and, 86–87, 139, 183
   details and, 85
   dialog and, 89
   example and, 188
   flashback and, 87, 89
   illustration of, in practice, 91–92
   *in medias res* and, 87
   Krull on, 206–07
   method of, 36, 82–83
   mixing other methods with, 582–83, 584–87, 591–94, 604–11, 614–18, 620–30, 634–40, 651–61, 665–68, 682–87
   paragraph illustrations of, 90–91
   person and, 84
   point of view and, 84, 89
   process analysis and, 285
   process of, 83–89
   purpose and, 83, 86, 89
   Rosenblatt on, 220
   scene and, 86–87
   subjectivity in, 84
   summary and, 86–87
   thesis and, 83–84, 89
   transitions and, 88, 89, **704**
   verbs and, 88–89
   writing process and, 36
Narrator, 84, **700**
Naylor, Gloria, 488, 493
   Gloria Naylor on Writing, 493
   "The Meanings of a Word," 488–91
"Neat People vs. Sloppy People" (Britt), 10, 233–35
*Need Is a Very Subjective Word* (advertisement for the HUMMER H2), 478
"Needs" (Sowell), 501–03
News stories. *See* Journalism.

*Nicole Waugh, 6, with her father, Chief Warrant Officer Joel Waugh, departing from Fort Benning, GA* (Lesser photograph), 26, 27
"No Name Woman" (Kingston), 620–30
Nonstandard English, **700**
"Not All Men Are Sly Foxes" (Brott), 345–47
"Not Your Homeland" (Danticat), 572–75

Objective and subjective, **700**
Objectivity, 138–39, 143, 183
Observation
   Britt on, 237–38
   DePaulo on, 356–57
   Ehrlich on, 300–01
   Rosenblatt on, 219–20
"On Compassion" (Ascher), 54, 56, 60, 62, 67, 193–95
Online sources
   academic writing and, 58–59
   authorship or sponsorship of, 58–59
   currency of, 59
   links or references to, 59
"Only Daughter" (Cisneros), 584–87
Opinion, 518
"Orange Crush" (Li), 4, 164–66
Organization
   comparison and contrast and, 226–27, 229
   description and, 143
   Javdani on, 453–54
   process analysis and, 287
"Orientation" (Orozco), 319–24
Originality
   Anderson on, 466–67
   Benchley on, 174
   Dickinson on, 513
   Swift on, 680–81
Orozco, Daniel, 319, 325–26
   Daniel Orozco on Writing, 325–26
   "Orientation," 319–24
Orwell, George, 634, 642–43
   George Orwell on Writing, 642–43
   "Shooting an Elephant," 634–40
Outline, Kingston on, 632–33

Paradox, **700**
Paragraph, **700–01**
   classification and, 379–80
   comparison and contrast and, 228–29
   definition and, 484–85
   DeLillo on, 474–75
   writing process and, 39
Parallelism, parallel structure, **701**
   writing process and, 39
Parallel wording, 231
Paraphrase, 54–55, **701**
Passive voice, **701**

Pentad, Burke's, 436
Person, **701**
  Tannen on, 399–400
  narration and, 84
Personification, **701**
Persuasion, **701**. *See also* Argument and persuasion.
Place for writing, Kincaid on, 371
Plagiarism, **701**
  academic writing and, 60–62
"*Plata o Plomo:* Silver or Lead" (Javdani), 448–51
Pleasures of writing, Gilb on, 509
"Plot Against People, The" (Baker), 10, 384–86
Poetry
  Dickinson on, 513
  Pollitt on, 552–53
Point of view, **701**
  DePaulo on, 356–57
  description and, 141, 143
  narration and, 84, 89
Political writing
  Ehrenreich on, 603
  Orwell on, 642–43
  Pollitt on, 552–53
  Rosenblatt on, 219–20
Pollitt, Katha, 548, 552–53
  Katha Pollitt on Writing, 552–53
  "What's Wrong with Gay Marriage?," 548–50
Premise, **702**
Preparation for writing
  Angelou on, 97–98
  Catton on, 251
  Frazier on, 306–07
  Javdani on, 453–54
"Pride" (Gilb), 505–07
Primary and secondary sources, 57–58
Process analysis, 280–328, **702**
  additional writing topics for, 327–28
  analogy and, 285
  checklist for revising, 286–87
  classification and, 284, 376
  completeness and, 287
  consistency and, 287
  consistency, focus on, 285
  definition and, 287, 482
  description and, 327
  directive process analysis, 282, 327–28
  division or analysis and, 282
  informative process analysis, 282, 327–28
  illustration of, in practice, 288–89
  method of, 36, 282–83
  mixing other methods with, 582–83, 591–94, 598–601, 604–11, 644–47, 670–78, 682–87

narration and, 285
organization of, 287
paragraph illustrations of, 287–88
purposes of, 282
process of, 283–87
thesis and, 283, 286
tone in, 328
transitions in, 284, 287, 327
writing process and, 36
Process
  Ascher on, 197
  Baker on, 388–90
  Britt on, 237–38
  Cohen on, 121–22
  DeLillo on, 474–75
  example of (Anaya), 40–49
  Gilb on, 509
  Jackson on, 132–33
  Javdani on, 453–54
  Kingston on, 632–33
  Krull on, 206–07
  Lutz on, 426–27
  Orozco on, 325–26
  Rodriguez on, 663–64
  Wurster on, 547
Principle, 380
Procrastination
  Lutz on, 426–27
  Manning on, 152–53
Proposal, 518
Prose, Francine, 644, 649
  Francine Prose on Writing, 649
  "What Words Can Tell," 644–47
Publication information, as aid in critical reading, 11
Purpose, **702**
  academic writing and, 57
  classification and, 376, 377–78, 380, 429
  comparison and contrast and, 224–25, 229
  critical reading and, 20–22
  description and, 138, 139–40
  division or analysis and, 334
  example and, 187
  Javdani on, 453–54
  narration and, 83, 86, 89
  Orwell on, 642–43
  process analysis and, 282
  Saukko on, 294
  Swift on, 680–81
  writing process and, 33–34

Quindlen, Anna, 67, 198, 201–02
  Anna Quindlen on Writing, 201–02
  "Homeless," 67, 198–200
Quotation, 54–55

Rational appeal, **702**
   argument and persuasion and, 521
Reactions to work
   Anderson on, 466–67
   Jackson on, 132–33
   Krull on, 206–07
Readers. *See* Audience.
Reading and writing. *See* Critical thinking,
   reading, and writing.
Relevance, 190
Remote cause, 432
Reporting. *See* Journalism.
Research
   Mitford on, 318
Responding to a text, 52–54
Revision, **702**
   Baker on, 388–90
   Barry on, 243–44
   Catton on, 251
   DeLillo on, 474–75
   Didion on, 596–97
   Dillard on, 109
   Javdani on, 453–54
   Kingston on, 632–33
   Krull on, 206–07
   Lutz on, 426–27
   Manning on, 152–53
   Orozco on, 325–26
   Rodriguez on, 663–64
   Saukko on, 294
   writing process and, 38–39, 44–49
Rhetoric, **702**
Rhetorical question, **702**
Rhythm, Angelou on, 97–98
"Rise and Fall of the Hit, The" (Anderson),
   459–64
Rodriguez, Richard, 651, 663–64
   "Aria: A Memoir of a Bilingual Childhood,"
   651–61
   Richard Rodriguez on Writing, 663–64
"Roots of War, The" (Ehrenreich), 598–601
Rosenblatt, Roger, 215, 219–20
   Roger Rosenblatt on Writing, 219–20
   "We Are Free to Be You, Me, Stupid, and
   Dead," 215–17
*Rural Rehabilitation Client* (Shahn photograph),
   222

"Safety Through Immigration Control"
   (Krikorian), 567–69
Said, Edward, 665
   "Clashing Civilizations," 665–68
Sante, Luc, 401, 407
   Luc Sante on Writing, 407
   "What Secrets Tell," 401–05
Sarcasm, **702**

Satire, **702**
Saukko, Linnea, 2, 290, 294, 700, 702
   "How to Poison the Earth," 290–92, 702
   Linnea Saukko on Writing, 294
Scene, **702**
   narration and, 86–87
Scholarly writing
   DePaulo on, 356–57
   Tannen on, 399–400
Scientific writing, Gould on, 613
Self-discovery
   Britt on, 237–38
   DePaulo on, 356–57
   Didion on, 596–97
   Ehrlich on, 300–01
   Ericsson on, 417
   Kincaid on, 370–71
   Li on, 168–69
   Pollitt on, 552–53
   Quindlen on, 201–02
   Rodriguez on, 663–64
   Staples on, 212–14
Sensory experience
   Didion on, 596–97
   Ehrlich on, 300–01
Sentence
   Angelou on, 97–98
   Baker on, 388–90
   DeLillo on, 474–75
   Didion on, 596–97
   Dillard on, 109
   Kingston on, 632–33
   Staples on, 212–14
   Tan on, 102–03
   Vowell on, 162–63
Sentence variety, 189, 190
Sentimentality, **702**
Shahn, Ben
   *Rural Rehabilitation Client* (photograph),
   222
"Shooting an Elephant" (Orwell), 634–40
"Shooting Dad" (Vowell), 154–60
Signal phrase, **703**
Significance, 337
Simile, **703**
   critical reading and, 25
Situation, Pollitt on, 552–53
Slang, **703**
Society. *See* Writer and society.
Sources. *See also* MLA (Modern Language
   Association).
   documentation of, 54, 62–73
   evaluation of, 57–60
   integration of, 54–56
   paraphrasing, 54–55
   primary versus secondary, 57

Sources (*continued*)
 quotation, 55
 summary, 54
Sowell, Thomas, 501
 "Needs," 501–03
Specific, **703**
Specific language
 description and, 142–43
 example and, 189
Stages in writing
 Krull on, 206–07
 Javdani on, 453–54
 Orozco on, 325–26
 Staples on, 212–14
Standard English, **703**
Staples, Brent, 208, 213–14
 "Black Men and Public Space," 208–10
 Brent Staples on Writing, 212–14
State Farm Insurance
 "The More They Learn, the More They
  Earn" (graph), 374
Stipulative, 480
Storytelling. *See* Narration.
Strategy, **703**
 critical reading and, 22–24
Structure
 Angelou on, 97–98
 argument and persuasion and, 527–28, 529
 critical reading and, 23–24
 Javdani on, 453–54
 White on, 689–90
Style, **703**
 Benchley on, 174
 Dickinson on, 513
 Prose on, 649–50
 Tan on, 102–03
Subject, 32–33
 Angelou on, 97–98
 cause and effect and, 433–34, 437
 comparison and contrast and, 229
 DePaulo on, 356–57
 Ehrlich on, 300–01
 Frazier on, 306–07
 Javdani on, 453–54
 Mitford on, 318
 Rosenblatt on, 220
 Saukko on, 294
 White on, 689–90
 writing process and, 32
Subjective, objective and, **703**
Subjectivity
 Britt on, 237–38
 description and, 138–39, 143, 183
 narration and, 84
 Saukko on, 294
 Tannen on, 399–400

Summarize, summary, **703**
 academic writing and, 52, 54
 comparison and contrast and, 227
 critical reading and, 17
 definition and, 485
 narration and, 86–87
Support, 189
Suspense, **703**
Swift, Jonathan, 670, 680, 702
 "A Modest Proposal," 670–78, 702
 Jonathan Swift on Writing, 680
Syllogism, **703**
 argument and persuasion and, 523
Symbol, **703**
Syntax
 Didion on, 596–97
Synthesize, synthesis, **703**
 academic writing and, 52–54, 59–60
 argument and persuasion and, 519
 critical reading and, 19
 division or analysis and, 333

Tan, Amy, 99, 102–03
 Amy Tan on Writing, 102–03
 "Fish Cheeks," 99–100
Tannen, Deborah, 391, 399–400
 "But What Do You Mean?," 391–97
 Deborah Tannen on Writing,
  399–400
Taw, Harold, 110
 "Finding Prosperity by Feeding
  Monkeys," 110–11
Technology
 Anderson on, 466–67
 Baker on, 388–90
 Wurster on, 547
Theme, Gould on, 613
Thesis, **704**
 academic writing and, 51
 argument and persuasion and, 520, 529
 cause and effect and, 433–34, 437
 classification and, 377–78
 comparison and contrast and, 226, 229
 critical reading and, 10, 20
 definition and, 483, 485
 description and, 140–41
 division or analysis and, 335, 336
 example and, 187, 221
 narration and, 83–84
 process analysis and, 283, 286
 writing process and, 37–38
Thinking, critical. *See* Critical thinking,
  reading, and writing.
Thompson, Mike
 *Garbage In . . .*, (cartoon), 430
Title, 10

Tone, **704**
  argument and persuasion and, 529
  critical reading and, 10, 24
  process analysis and, 328
"Too Much Pressure" (Wenke), 51,
  533–37
Topic sentence, **704**
  example and, 186
Toulmin, Stephen, 519–22
Training, Ascher on, 197
Transitions, **704**
  comparison and contrast and, 228
  narration and, 88, 89
  process analysis and, 284, 287, 327
  writing process and, 39
Translation
  Cisneros on, 589–90
  Danticat on, 577–78
  Li on, 168–69
  Tan on, 102–03
Truth
  Ehrlich on, 300–01
  Orwell on, 642–43
  White on, 689–90
Truth to subject
  division or analysis and, 337

Understatement, **704**
  critical reading and, 25
Unity, **704**
  critical reading and, 23
  definition and, 484–85

Verbs, 88–89
*Videotape* (DeLillo), 468
Viewpoint. *See* Point of view.
Visual images, 25–30
  analysis of, 26, 28
  critical reading of, 25–30
  evaluation of, 26, 29–30
  inference and, 26, 28–29
  in process analysis, 25–30
  synthesis with, 26, 29
  thinking critically about, 25–30
Voice, **704**
Vowell, Sarah, 154, 162–63
  Sarah Vowell on Writing, 162–63
  "Shooting Dad," 154–60

Walker, Alice, 267, 276–77
  Alice Walker on Writing, 276–77
  "Everyday Use," 267–74
Warrant, **704**
  argument and persuasion and, 521
"Ways We Lie, The" (Ericsson), 10, 408

"We Are Free to Be You, Me, Stupid, and
  Dead" (Rosenblatt), 215
Wenke, Colleen, 2, 51, 533
  "Too Much Pressure," 51, 533–37
"What Secrets Tell" (Sante), 401–05
"What Words Can Tell" (Prose), 644–47
"What's Wrong with Gay Marriage?" (Pollitt),
  548–50
White, E. B., 2, 682, 689–90
  E. B. White on Writing, 689–90
  "Once More to the Lake," 682–87
Williams, Brian, 539
  "But Enough about You . . .," 539–41
"Won't You Be My Friendster?" (Wurster),
  543
Wood, Grant
  *American Gothic* (painting), 222
Word processors. *See* Computers.
Words. *See* Language.
*Workers Making Dolls* (McNamee photograph),
  280
Work habits
  DeLillo on, 474–75
  Gilb on, 509
  Javdani on, 453–54
  Lutz on, 426–27
  Pollitt on, 552–53
  Wurster on, 547
"World of Doublespeak, The" (Lutz), 418–24,
  697, 700
Writer and society
  Anderson on, 466–67
  DePaulo on, 356–57
  Divakaruni on, 446–47
  Ehrenreich on, 602–03
  Orwell on, 642–43
  Rodriguez on, 663–64
  Rosenblatt on, 219–20
  Saukko on, 294
  Swift on, 680–81
  Walker on, 276–77
Writing
  abstract language in
    Benchley on, 174
    Didion on, 596–97
  anecdote in
    Krull on, 206–07
    Rosenblatt on, 219–20
    Staples on, 212–14
  attitude toward
    Benchley on, 174
    DePaulo on, 356–57
    Ehrlich on, 300–01
    Frazier on, 306–07
    Gilb on, 509
    Javdani on, 453–54

Writing, attitude toward (*continued*)
  Krull on, 206–07
  Pollitt on, 552–53
  Vowell on, 162–63
  Wurster on, 547
 audience for
  Anderson on, 466–67
  Barry on, 243–44
  Benchley on, 174
  Cisneros on, 589–90
  DePaulo on, 356–57
  Ehrlich on, 300–01
  Javdani on, 453–54
  Rosenblatt on, 219–20
  Tan on, 102–03
  Vowell on, 162–63
 awareness during, Britt on, 237–38
 bilingualism and
  Cisneros on, 589–90
  Danticat on, 577–78
  Li on, 168–69
  Rodriguez on, 663–64
  Tan on, 102–03
 censorship of
  Ehrenreich on, 602–03
  Li on, 168–69
 clarity and conciseness in
  Ascher on, 197
  Benchley on, 174
  Prose on, 649–50
 coherence of, Vowell on, 162–63
 community and
  Anderson on, 466–67
  Divakaruni on, 446–47
 craft of
  Baker on, 388–90
  Benchley on, 174
  DeLillo on, 474–75
  Dickinson on, 513
  Ehrlich on, 300–01
  Frazier on, 306–07
  Gilb on, 509
  Javdani on, 453–54
  Prose on, 649–50
  Sante on, 407
  Wurster on, 547
 creative process and
  Angelou on, 97–98
  Danticat on, 577–78
  DeLillo on, 474–75
  Dickinson on, 513
  Ehrlich on, 300–01
  Javdani on, 453–54
  Krull on, 206–07
  Wurster on, 547
 critical thinking during, Wurster on, 547

 cultural/racial differences and
  Cisneros on, 589–90
  Danticat on, 577–78
  Li on, 168–69
  Naylor on, 493
  Tan on, 102–03
 details in
  Ehrlich on, 300–01
  Staples on, 212–14
 discovery, Gould on, 613
 drafts and drafting during
  DeLillo on, 474–75
  Dillard on, 109
  Javdani on, 453–54
  Kingston on, 632–33
  Krull on, 206–07
  Manning on, 152–53
 editing during
  Baker on, 388–90
  Barry on, 243–44
  DeLillo on, 474–75
  Didion on, 596–97
  Dillard on, 109
  example of (Anaya), 40–49
  Javdani on, 453–54
  Manning on, 152–53
  Saukko on, 294
 effect of
  Anderson on, 466–67
  Gilb on, 509
  Jackson on, 132–33
  Javdani on, 453–54
  Rosenblatt on, 219–20
  Vowell on, 162–63
 essay and
  Ascher on, 197
  Gould on, 613
  Staples on, 212–14
  White on, 689–90
 euphemism and, Mitford on, 318
 evaluation of, Krull on, 206–07
 evidence in, Staples on, 212–14
 experience and
  Cohen on, 121–22
  Danticat on, 577–78
  DePaulo on, 356–57
  Divakaruni on, 446–47
  Ehrlich on, 300–01
  Krull on, 206–07
  Leong on, 499–500
  Rosenblatt on, 219–20
 first drafts of
  Javdani on, 453–54
  Krull on, 206–07
  Manning on, 152–53
 first person in, Tannen on, 399–400

form and
  Anderson on, 466–67
  Angelou on, 97–98
  Vowell on, 162–63
  White on, 689–90
from research, 56–60
grammar and
  Didion on, 596–97
  Javdani on, 453–54
  Prose on, 649–50
humor and
  Barry on, 243–44
  Benchley on, 174
  Mitford on, 318
indifference and
  Britt on, 237–38
  Rosenblatt on, 219–20
inspiration for
  Barry on, 243–44
  Ehrlich on, 300–01
  Javdani on, 453–54
  Krull on, 206–07
  Leong on, 499–500
  Naylor on, 493
  Walker on, 276–77
introduction and, Javdani on,
  453–54
jargon in
  Gould on, 613
  Mitford on, 318
journalism and
  Ehrenreich on, 602–03
  Orwell on, 642–43
  Quindlen on, 201–02
  Rosenblatt on, 219–20
  Staples on, 212–14
journal and, White on, 689–90
language and
  Benchley on, 174
  Danticat on, 577–78
  DeLillo on, 474–75
  Dickinson on, 513
  Didion on, 596–97
  Gould on, 613
  Li on, 168–69
  Mairs and, 24–25
  Naylor on, 493
  Orwell on, 642–43
  Prose on, 649–50
  Sante on, 407
  Tan on, 102–03
literature and, Naylor on, 493
magazines, Ehrenreich on, 603
meaning and
  Kingston on, 632–33
  Pollitt on, 552–53

Prose on, 649–50
  Rosenblatt on, 219–20
methods of. *See also* entries to individual
  methods.
  Baker on, 388–90
  DeLillo on, 474–75
  Javdani on, 453–54
  Sante on, 407
motives for
  Anderson on, 466–67
  Catton on, 250–51
  Cohen on, 121–22
  Didion on, 596–97
  Ericsson on, 417
  Gould on, 613
  Javdani on, 453–54
  Kincaid on, 370–71
  Naylor on, 493
  Orwell on, 642–43
  Pollitt on, 552–53
  Quindlen on, 202
  Rodriguez on, 663–64
  Rosenblatt on, 219–20
  Staples on, 212–14
narration and
  Krull on, 206–07
  Rosenblatt on, 219–20
observation
  Britt on, 237–38
  DePaulo on, 356–57
  Ehrlich on, 300–01
  Rosenblatt on, 219–20
organization of, Javdani on, 453–54
originality of
  Anderson on, 466–67
  Benchley on, 174
  Dickinson on, 513
  Swift on, 680–81
paragraph and, DeLillo on, 474–75
person and, Tannen on, 399–400
place for, Kincaid on, 370–71
pleasures of, Gilb on, 509
poetry and
  Dickinson on, 513
  Pollitt on, 552–53
point of view in, DePaulo on, 356–57
politics and
  Ehrenreich on, 602–03
  Orwell on, 642–43
  Pollitt on, 552–53
  Rosenblatt on, 219–20
preparation for
  Angelou on, 97–98
  Catton on, 250–51
  Frazier on, 306–07
  Javdani on, 453–54

Writing (*continued*)
  process of
    Ascher on, 197
    Baker on, 388–90
    Britt on, 237–38
    Cohen on, 121–22
    DeLillo on, 474–75
    example of (Anaya), 40–49
    Gilb on, 509
    Jackson on, 132–33
    Javdani on, 453–54
    Kingston on, 632–33
    Krull on, 206–07
    Lutz on, 426–27
    Orozco on, 325–26
    Rodriguez on, 663–64
    Wurster on, 547
  procrastination during
    Lutz on, 427–28
    Manning on, 152–53
  purpose of
    Javdani on, 453–54
    Orwell on, 642–43
    Saukko on, 294
    Swift on, 680–81
  reactions to work
    Anderson on, 466–67
    Jackson on, 132–33
    Krull on, 206–07
  research and, Mitford on, 318
  revision during
    Baker on, 388–90
    Barry on, 243–44
    Catton on, 250–51
    DeLillo on, 474–75
    Didion on, 596–97
    Dillard on, 109
    Javdani on, 453–54
    Kingston on, 632–33
    Krull on, 206–07
    Lutz on, 426–27
    Manning on, 152–53
    Orozco on, 326
    Rodriguez on, 663–64
    Saukko on, 294
  rhythm of, Angelou on, 97–98
  scholarly and
    DePaulo on, 356–57
    Tannen on, 399–400
  science and, Gould on, 613
  self-discovery
    Britt on, 237–38
    DePaulo on, 356–57
    Didion on, 596–97
    Ehrlich on, 300–01
    Ericsson on, 417
    Kincaid on, 370–71

    Li on, 168–69
    Pollitt on, 552–53
    Quindlen on, 201–02
    Rodriguez on, 663–64
    Staples on, 212–14
  sensory experience and
    Didion on, 596–97
    Ehrlich on, 300–01
  sentence and
    Angelou on, 97–98
    Baker on, 388–90
    DeLillo on, 474–75
    Didion on, 596–97
    Dillard on, 109
    Kingston on, 632–33
    Staples on, 212–14
    Tan on, 102–03
    Vowell on, 162–63
  situation, Pollitt on, 552–53
  society and
    Anderson on, 466–67
    DePaulo on, 356–57
    Divakaruni on, 446–47
    Ehrenreich on, 602–03
    Orwell on, 642–43
    Rodriguez on, 663–64
    Rosenblatt on, 219–20
    Saukko on, 294
    Swift on, 680–81
    Walker on, 276–77
  stages in
    Javdani on, 453–54
    Krull on, 206–07
    Orozco on, 325–26
    Staples on, 212–14
  structure of
    Angelou on, 97–98
    Javdani on, 453–54
    White on, 689–90
  style and
    Benchley on, 174
    Dickinson on, 513
    Prose on, 649–50
    Tan on, 102–03
  subject of
    Angelou on, 97–98
    DePaulo on, 356–57
    Ehrlich on, 300–01
    Frazier on, 306–07
    Javdani on, 453–54
    Mitford on, 318
    Rosenblatt on, 219–20
    Saukko on, 294
    White on, 689–90
  subjectivity in
    Britt on, 237–38
    Saukko on, 294

Tannen on, 399–400
syntax and, Didion on, 596–97
technology and
    Anderson on, 466–67
    Baker on, 388–90
    Wurster on, 547
theme and, Gould on, 613
training, Ascher on, 197
translation and
    Cisneros on, 589–90
    Danticat on, 577–78
    Li on, 168–69
    Tan on, 102–03
truth and
    Ehrlich on, 300–01
    Orwell on, 642–43
    White on, 689–90
work habits in
    DeLillo on, 474–75
    Gilb on, 509
    Javdani on, 453–54
    Lutz on, 426–27
    Pollitt on, 552–53
    Wurster on, 547
Writing process, the, 31–49
    analysis of the writing situation in, 32–34
    argument and persuasion and, 37
    audience and, 33–34
    cause and effect and, 36
    classification and, 36
    collaborating during, 40, 43
    comparison and contrast and, 36
    critical thinking in, 31
    definition and, 37
    description and, 36
    discovery during, 34–37
    division or analysis and, 36
    drafting during, 38, 40–49
    emphasis and, 39
    evidence and, 33–34
    example and, 36
    freewriting and, 35
    journal writing and, 32–33, 35, 40–41, 43
    methods of, 36–37
    narration and, 36
    paragraph and, 39
    parallelism and, 39
    process analysis and, 36
    purpose and, 33–34
    questions for editing and, 39
    questions for revision and, 39
    revising and editing during, 38–39, 44–49
    subject and, 32
    thesis and, 37–38
    transitions and, 39

Writers on,
    Anderson on, 466–67
    Angelou on, 97–98
    Ascher on, 197
    Baker on, 388–90
    Barry on, 243–44
    Benchley on, 174
    Britt on, 237–38
    Catton on, 250–51
    Cisneros on, 589–90
    Cohen on, 121–22
    Danticat on, 577–78
    DeLillo on, 474–75
    DePaulo on, 356–57
    Dickinson on, 513
    Didion on, 596–97
    Dillard on, 109
    Divakaruni on, 446–47
    Ehrenreich on, 602–03
    Ehrlich on, 300–01
    Ericsson on, 417
    Frazier on, 306–07
    Gilb on, 509
    Gould on, 613
    Jackson on, 132–33
    Javdani on, 453–54
    Kincaid on, 370–71
    Kingston on, 632–33
    Krull on, 206–07
    Leong on, 499–500
    Li on, 168–69
    Lutz on, 426–27
    Manning on, 152–53
    Mitford on, 318
    Naylor on, 493
    Orozco on, 325–26
    Orwell on, 642–43
    Pollitt on, 552–53
    Prose on, 649–50
    Quindlen on, 201–02
    Rodriguez on, 663–64
    Rosenblatt on, 219–20
    Sante on, 407
    Saukko on, 294
    Staples on, 212–14
    Swift on, 680–81
    Tan on, 102–03
    Tannen on, 399–400
    Vowell on, 162–63
    Walker on, 276–77
    White on, 689–90
    Wurster on, 547
Wurster, Andie, 543, 547
    Andie Wurster on Writing, 547
    "Won't You Be My Friendster?," 543–45

# Need more help with writing and research? Visit our Web sites.

## Re:Writing

### bedfordstmartins.com/rewriting

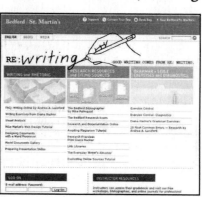

Good writing comes from *Re:Writing*, a collection of our most widely used online resources on a free, easy-to-access Web site. High-quality plagiarism tutorials, model documents, style and grammar exercises, visual analysis activities, research guides, bibliography tools, and much more are available now — no access code required!

## Exercise Central

### bedfordstmartins.com/exercisecentral

Still completely free, and still offering the largest database of editing exercises on the Internet, *Exercise Central* is now a comprehensive resource for skill development as well as skill assessment. In addition to more than 8,000 exercises with immediate feedback and reporting, *Exercise Central* can help identify your strengths and weaknesses, recommend personalized study plans, and provide tutorials for common problems.